Best Books for Children

Recent Titles in the
Children's and Young Adult Literature Reference Series
Catherine Barr, Series Editor

Popular Series Fiction for Middle School and Teen Readers:
A Reading and Selection Guide
Rebecca L. Thomas and Catherine Barr

Fantasy Literature for Children and Young Adults: A Comprehensive Guide.
Fifth Edition
Ruth Nadelman Lynn

The Children's and Young Adult Literature Handbook:
A Research and Reference Guide
John T. Gillespie

A to Zoo: Subject Access to Children's Picture Books. Seventh Edition
Carolyn W. Lima and John A. Lima

Best Books for Children: Preschool through Grade 6. Eighth Edition
Catherine Barr and John T. Gillespie

The Newbery/Printz Companion:
Booktalks and Related Materials for Award Winners and Honor Books
John T. Gillespie and Corinne J. Naden

Books Kids Will Sit Still For 3: A Read-Aloud Guide
Judy Freeman

Classic Teenplots: A Booktalk Guide to Use with Readers Ages 12–18
John T. Gillespie and Corinne J. Naden

Best Books for Middle School and Junior High Readers: Grades 6–9.
Supplement to the First Edition
John T. Gillespie and Catherine Barr

Best Books for High School Readers: Grades 9–12. Supplement to the First Edition
John T. Gillespie and Catherine Barr

War and Peace: A Guide to Literature and New Media, Grades 4–8
Virginia A. Walter

Across Cultures: A Guide to Multicultural Literature for Children
Kathy East and Rebecca L. Thomas

Best Books for Children

Preschool through Grade 6

Supplement to the Eighth Edition

Catherine Barr

John T. Gillespie

Children's and Young Adult Literature Reference Series
Catherine Barr, Series Editor

LIBRARIES UNLIMITED

U N I M I T E D

A Member of the Greenwood Publishing Group

Westport, Connecticut • London

Library of Congress Cataloging-in-Publication Data

Barr, Catherine, 1951-
  Best books for children : preschool through grade 6.—Supplement to the 8th ed. / by Catherine Barr and John
T. Gillespie.
      p. cm.— (Children's and young adult literature reference series)
  Rev. ed. of: Best books for children / John T. Gillespie. 7th ed. 2002.
  Includes bibliographical references and index.
  ISBN-13 978-1-59158-574-9 (alk. paper)
  1. Children— Books and reading—United States. 2. Children's literature—Bibliography. 3. Best books—
United States. I. Gillespie, John Thomas, 1928- Best books for children. II. Title. III. Series.
Z1037.G48 2007
011.62—dc22   2005030882

British Library Cataloguing in Publication Data is available.

Library of Congress Catalog Card Number: 2005030882
ISBN-13: 978-1-59158-574-9

First published in 2007

Libraries Unlimited, 88 Post Road West, Westport, CT 06881
A Member of the Greenwood Publishing Group, Inc.
www.lu.com

Printed in the United States of America

The paper used in this book complies with the
Permanent Paper Standard issued by the National
Information Standards Organization (Z39.48–1984).

10   9   8   7   6   5   4   3   2   1

Contents

Biography

Social Institutions and Issues

Personal Development

Physical and Applied Sciences

Contents

Recreation

Major Subjects Arranged Alphabetically

Preface

This supplement to the eighth edition of *Best Books for Children* (2006) covers reviewing journals over a two-year period through March 2007. There are 4,529 titles listed in this supplement; of these, 4,234 are individually numbered entries and 295 are cited within the annotations.

Those familiar with the eighth (and previous) editions of *Best Books for Children* will notice that an identical topical arrangement has been used in the main body of the supplement and that the same subject headings appear in the subject/grade level index. Similarly, the same criteria for selecting entries and the same methods of presentation have been used.

A number of sources were used to compile this bibliography, but reviews in five journals were used most extensively. They were: *Booklist* (BL), *Bulletin of the Center for Children's Books* (BCCB), *Horn Book* (HB), *Horn Book Guide* (HBG), and *School Library Journal* (SLJ). Usually at least two recommendations were required from these or other sources for a title to be considered for listing. However, there were exceptions to this rule, particularly with series books where only a single review could be located. If that review was positive, then the book became a candidate for inclusion. To ensure that quality standards were being upheld, particularly with series books, many of the titles were examined and evaluated by the editors using copies supplied by the publisher.

A note or two about the placement of books under various topical headings. The "Imaginative Stories" section in the Books for Younger Readers area is divided into two categories: "Fantasies" and "Imaginary Animals." The first contains both books that depict humans, usually children, in fanciful, unrealistic situations and books that include mythological beasts. The "Imaginary Animals" category includes stories about anthropomorphized beasts in which animals engage in human activities (such as pigs going to school).

The Books for Younger Readers section ends with a listing of "Books for Beginning Readers." This area contains books of fiction easy enough to be read by beginning readers. Nonfiction beginning readers are integrated into the appropriate subject area with mention in the annotation that the work is suitable for beginning readers. Interactive books, like pop-ups, are integrated into appropriate sections with a mention of their format in the annotation. Beginning chapter books are found in the Fiction for Older Readers area with an indication in their annotations that they are easily read. In the fiction section labeled "Ethnic Groups," only those novels in which ethnicity is the central theme are included. Similarly in the nonfiction Biography section, under "African Americans" for example, only those individuals who have been associated primarily with race-related activities are included. Martin Luther King, Jr., is listed there, but a life story of Magic Johnson would be in sports biographies.

Some types of books have been omitted from this bibliography. These include reference books such as dictionaries and encyclopedias and professional books such as other bibliographies or selection aids. A feature retained from the eighth edition is an introductory listing of "Major Subjects Arranged Alphabetically." This special list provides both the range of entry numbers and page numbers for the largest subject areas covered in the volume.

As in previous editions, titles in the main section of the book are assigned an entry number. The entry contains the following information where applicable: (1) author or editor; (2) title; (3) suitable grade levels; (4) adapter or translator; (5) indication of illustrations or illustrator's name; (6) series title; (7) date of publication; (8) publisher and price of hardbound edition (LB=library binding); (9) ISBN of hardbound edition; (10) paperback publisher (if no publisher is listed, it is the same as the hardbound edition) and price; (11) ISBN of paperback edition; (12) annotation; (13) review citations; (14) Dewey Decimal number.

This supplement contains three indexes: author/illustrator, book title, and subject/grade level. The subject/grade level index includes hundreds of subject headings. Within each subject, entries are listed according to grade-level suitability. The following codes are used to give approximate grade levels:

(P) (Primary) preschool through grade 3
(PI) (Primary-Intermediate) grades 2 through 4
(I) (Intermediate) grades 4 through 6
(IJ) (Intermediate-Junior High) grades 5 through 8 or higher

More exact grade-level suitabilities are given in parenthesis for each book in the main entry.

To facilitate quick reference, all listings in the indexes refer the user to an entry number, not a page number.

It is hoped that this bibliography will be used with the parent volume in four different ways: (1) as a tool to evaluate collections; (2) as a book selection tool; (3) as an aid to giving reading guidance to children; and (4) as a base for the preparation of bibliographies and reading lists.

Many thanks to my coauthor John Gillespie for his continuing contributions, to Barbara Ittner of Libraries Unlimited for her encouragement and support, and to Christine McNaull and Julie Miller, who make production of this book possible.

Catherine Barr

Literature

Books for Younger Readers

Alphabet, Concept, and Counting Books

Alphabet Books

1 Allen, Susan, and Jane Lindaman. *Written Anything Good Lately?* (1–4). Illus. by Vicky Enright. 2006, Millbrook LB $15.95 (0-7613-2426-7). 32pp. This attractive alphabet book introduces different types of writing — an autobiography, a brilliant book report, detailed directions, Valentine's verses, and so forth. (Rev: HBG 10/06; LMC 11–12/06; SLJ 4/06) [808]

2 Bar-El, Dan. *Alphabetter* (PS–1). Illus. by Graham Ross. 2006, Orca $17.95 (1-55143-439-3). The alphabet and the 26 children taking part in an activity are out of synch; the child holding A needs an item held by B and so forth; a humorous and interesting approach. (Rev: SLJ 12/06)

3 Beccia, Carlyn. *Who Put the B in Ballyhoo?* (2–4). Illus. 2007, Houghton $16.00 (978-0-618-71718-7). 32pp. From A for awesome to Z for zippy, this is an alphabetical of circus acts of the past. (Rev: BL 4/1/07)

4 Blackstone, Stella. *Alligator Alphabet* (PS). Illus. by Stephanie Bauer. 2005, Barefoot Bks. $16.99 (1-84148-494-6). A bright A to Z of animal parent-and-baby pairs. (Rev: SLJ 1/06)

5 Bruel, Nick. *Bad Kitty* (K–2). 2005, Roaring Brook $15.95 (1-59643-069-9). 40pp. In this cleverly conceived alphabet book, a cat misbehaves wildly when she discovers that the only foods in the house are unappealing vegetables ranging from asparagus to zucchini. (Rev: BL 12/15/05; SLJ 10/05)

6 *C Is for Caboose: Riding the Rails from A to Z* (PS–1). Illus. 2007, Chronicle $14.95 (0-8118-

5643-7). 32pp. A simple alphabet book that offers lots of railroad lore and an attractive vintage look. (Rev: BL 4/15/07) [385]

7 Castella, Krystina, and Brian Boyl. *Discovering Nature's Alphabet* (2–10). Photos by authors. 2006, Heyday $15.95 (1-59714-021-X). Photographs of letters of the alphabet formed by nature will fascinate children and adults. (Rev: SLJ 5/06)

8 Compestine, Ying Chang. *D Is for Dragon Dance* (K–1). Illus. by YongSheng Xuan. 2006, Holiday $16.95 (0-8234-1887-1). 32pp. Bright illustrations are the highlight of this alphabet book about the Chinese New Year. (Rev: BL 2/1/06; SLJ 3/06) [394.261]

9 Cronin, Doreen. *Click, Clack, Quackity-Quack: An Alphabetical Adventure* (PS). Illus. by Betsy Lewin. 2005, Simon & Schuster $12.95 (0-689-87715-3). 24pp. Set in a barnyard and featuring the cows that type (from *Click, Clack, Moo*), this appealing alphabet book follows preparations for a picnic. (Rev: BL 9/15/05; SLJ 11/05*)

10 Delessert, Etienne. *A Was an Apple Pie: An English Nursery Rhyme* (PS–2). Illus. 2005, Creative Editions $18.95 (1-56846-196-8). 32pp. Colorful modern art graces this alphabet book based on a 17th-century nursery rhyme. (Rev: BL 1/1–15/06; SLJ 1/06) [428.1]

11 DiTerlizzi, Tony. *G Is for One Gzonk! An Alpha-Number-Bet Book* (K–3). Illus. by author. 2006, Simon & Schuster $16.95 (0-689-85290-8). This clever tribute to Dr. Seuss and Edward Lear takes readers on a chaotic romp through a poetic alphabet full of fantastic beings and unruly numbers. (Rev: SLJ 10/06)

12 Doran, Ella, and others. *A Is for Artist: An Alphabet* (PS–2). Illus. 2005, Abrams $19.95 (1-85437-

556-3). 56pp. This striking alphabet book introduces young readers to art in a wide array of forms, ranging from a simple black-and-white photograph to the multicolored paint spatters of an abstract painting. (Rev: BL 11/1/05)

13 Downie, Mary Alice. *A Pioneer ABC* (K–2). Illus. by Mary Jane Gerber. 2005, Tundra $15.95 (0-88776-688-9). This attractive alphabet book shows young readers what life was like for Loyalists who migrated to Canada after the American Revolution. (Rev: SLJ 11/05)

14 Doyle, Charlotte. *The Bouncing, Dancing, Galloping ABC* (PS). Illus. by Julia Gorton. 2006, Putnam $10.99 (0-399-23778-X). 32pp. In this lively alphabet book, two young brothers and their friend explore various forms of locomotion. (Rev: BL 4/1/06)

15 Elya, Susan Middleton. *F Is for Fiesta* (K–2). Illus. by G. Brian Karas. 2006, Putnam $11.99 (0-399-24225-2). 32pp. This small, bright alphabet book presents Spanish words relating to celebrations within a mainly English text. (Rev: BL 2/1/06; SLJ 2/06)

16 Grobler, Piet. *Little Bird's ABC* (PS). Illus. 2005, Front St. $8.95 (1-932425-52-7). 32pp. A small, square beautifully illustrated alphabet of birds making often humorous sounds. (Rev: BL 11/15/05; SLJ 12/05) [411]

17 Hanson, Anders. *Nan and Nick* (PS–1). Series: First Sounds. 2005, ABDO LB $13.94 (1-59679-176-4). 23pp. An alphabet book, part of a series, featuring photographs of items that begin with the letter N, followed by simple rebus sentences using the words. (Rev: SLJ 7/05) [428.1]

18 Janovitz, Marilyn. *A, B, See!* (PS–2). Illus. by author. 2005, Chronicle $10.95 (0-8118-4673-3). Each letter of the alphabet morphs to become an animal (A becomes an alligator) in this lift-the-flap book. (Rev: SLJ 7/05)

19 Jocelyn, Marthe. *ABC x 3: English, Español, Français* (PS–K). Illus. by Tom Slaughter. 2005, Tundra $12.95 (0-88776-707-9). 32pp. This multilingual alphabet book gives words in English, French, and Spanish, often underlining their similarity. (Rev: BL 12/15/05; SLJ 10/05) [411]

20 Kontis, Alethea. *Alpha Oops! The Day Z Went First* (K–2). Illus. by Bob Kolar. 2006, Candlewick $15.99 (0-7636-2728-3). 56pp. Z is tired of being last in the alphabet, and other letters also decide they want better. (Rev: BL 9/1/06; SLJ 9/06)

21 Layne, Steven L., and Deborah Dover Layne. *T Is for Teachers: A School Alphabet* (K–4). Illus. by Doris Ettlinger. 2005, Sleeping Bear $16.95 (1-58536-159-3). An informative, rhyming alphabet book celebrating the joys of school. (Rev: SLJ 8/05)

22 Lear, Edward, and Suse MacDonald. *A Was Once an Apple Pie* (PS–K). Illus. 2005, Scholastic $12.99 (0-439-66056-4). 32pp. Lear's nonsense alphabet is only slightly altered in this version with bright, folksy artwork. (Rev: BL 8/05; SLJ 8/05*) [821]

23 Lobel, Anita. *Animal Antics: A to Z* (PS). Illus. , Greenwillow $15.99 (0-06-051814-6). 32pp. Striking circus-themed illustrations spotlight animals from "adoring alligators" to "zany zebras." (Rev: BL 11/1/05; SLJ 9/05) [791.3]

24 McLeod, Bob. *Superhero ABC* (K–3). Illus. 2006, HarperCollins $15.99 (0-06-074514-2). 40pp. From Astro-Man ("Astro-Man is Always Alert for An Alien Attack") to the Zinger, this alphabet book leaps off the pages. (Rev: BCCB 2/06; BL 1/1–15/06*; HB 3–4/06; HBG 10/06; SLJ 2/06*)

25 McLimans, David. *Gone Wild: An Endangered Animal Alphabet* (3–6). Illus. by author. 2006, Walker $16.95 (0-8027-9563-3). This strikingly illustrated alphabet book introduces a different endangered animal for each letter from A to Z. (Rev: SLJ 11/06)

26 Marino, Gianna. *Zoopa: An Animal Alphabet* (PS–2). Illus. by author. 2005, Chronicle $14.95 (0-8118-4789-6). This clever, colorful title introduces a menagerie of animals, from ant to zebra. (Rev: SLJ 10/05)

27 Mora, Pat. *¡Marimba! Animales from A to Z* (PS–1). Illus. by Doug Cushman. 2006, Clarion $16.00 (0-618-19453-3). 32pp. A happy A to Z of animals frolic down the street in English and Spanish. (Rev: SLJ 11/06)

28 Murphy, Liz. *ABC Doctor* (PS–K). Illus. 2007, Blue Apple $15.95 (978-1-59354-593-2). 36pp. Introduces the ABCs of a visit to the doctor's office, with reassuring explanations. (Rev: BL 4/1/07)

29 Nickle, John. *Alphabet Explosion! Search and Count from Alien to Zebra* (PS–2). Illus. by author. 2006, Random $16.95 (0-375-83598-9). 40pp. A hunt-and-seek game in which young readers search for animals and objects whose names begin with each letter of the alphabet. (Rev: BL 10/1/06; SLJ 9/06) [428.1]

30 Pallotta, Jerry. *The Construction Alphabet Book* (PS–2). Illus. by Rob Bolster. 2006, Charlesbridge $16.95 (1-57091-437-0); paper $7.95 (1-57091-438-9). 32pp. From aerial lift to zipper, this volume offers arresting illustrations plus pertinent facts. (Rev: BL 7/06; SLJ 8/06) [624]

31 Plant, Andrew. *Could a Tyrannosaurus Play Table Tennis?* (K–4). Illus. by author. 2006, Kane/Miller paper $8.95 (1-929132-97-2). Combines the merits of an alphabet book and a guide to dinosaurs, introducing a prehistoric reptile for every letter from A to Z and profiling each featured dinosaur by era, size, diet, and habitat, along with a lighthearted illustration. (Rev: SLJ 8/06)

BOOKS FOR YOUNGER READERS: *Alphabet, Concept, and Counting Books*

32 Raczka, Bob. *3-D ABC: A Sculptural Alphabet* (PS–2). Illus. Series: Bob Raczka's Art Adventures. 2006, Lerner LB $23.93 (0-7613-9456-7). 32pp. This cleverly crafted alphabet book introduces a wide array of 20th-century sculptures. (Rev: BL 11/1/06; SLJ 11/06*) [730]

33 Salzmann, Mary Elizabeth. *Ann and Alan* (PS–1). Series: First Sounds. 2005, ABDO LB $13.94 (1-59679-126-8). 23pp. An alphabet book, part of a series, featuring photographs of items that begin with the letter A, followed by simple rebus sentences using the words. Also use *Deb and Dan* (2005). (Rev: SLJ 7/05)

34 Seeger, Laura Vaccaro. *Walter Was Worried* (PS–2). 2005, Roaring Brook $15.95 (1-59643-066-8). The weather provokes different reactions in children whose names start with each letter of the alphabet. (Rev: SLJ 8/05)

35 Shulman, Mark. *A Is for Zebra* (1–3). Illus. by Tamara Petrosino. 2006, Sterling $14.95 (1-4027-3494-8). 32pp. With colorful cartoons, this funny variation on the traditional alphabet book turns the spotlight on the final letter of each word, as in the title example. (Rev: BL 3/15/06) [428.1]

36 Shulman, Mark. *AA Is for Aardvark: Double the Letters, Double the Fun* (PS–3). Illus. by Tamara Petrosino. 2005, Sterling LB $14.95 (1-4027-2871-9). Letters appearing twice in a row are the focus of this inventive and effective alphabet book. (Rev: SLJ 2/06)

37 Smith, Marie, and Roland Smith. *Z Is for Zookeeper: A Zoo Alphabet* (K–4). Illus. by Henry Cole. 2005, Sleeping Bear $16.95 (1-58536-158-5). "Animals," "brooms," and "quarantine" are only three of the letters in this text that also includes additional information for the curious reader. (Rev: SLJ 9/05)

38 Sobel, June. *Shiver Me Letters: A Pirate ABC* (PS–2). Illus. by Henry Cole. 2006, Harcourt $16.00 (0-15-216732-3). 32pp. Animal buccaneers may have to walk the plank if they don't manage to track down every letter from A to Z. (Rev: BL 6/1–15/06; SLJ 6/06)

39 Spirin, Gennady. *A Apple Pie* (PS–2). Illus. 2005, Philomel $16.99 (0-399-23981-2). 32pp. This whimsical alphabet book full of lovely, detailed watercolor paintings revives a 17th-century nursery rhyme and introduces verbs for the letters from A to Z. (Rev: BL 11/1/05; SLJ 9/05)

40 Vidrine, Beverly Barras. *Thanksgiving Day Alphabet* (1–3). Illus. by Alison Davis Lyne. 2006, Pelican paper $7.95 (1-58980-338-8). This colorful Thanksgiving alphabet book introduces people, places, and things related to the holiday's history. (Rev: SLJ 11/06) [394.2649]

41 Wallace, Nancy Elizabeth. *Alphabet House* (PS–2). Illus. 2005, Marshall Cavendish $16.95 (0-7614-5192-7). 32pp. Inside Alphabet House, which is home to a rabbit family, young readers will find multiple examples of words that begin with each letter of the alphabet. (Rev: BL 11/1/05; SLJ 10/05)

42 Wells, Rosemary. *Max's ABC* (PS–K). 2006, Viking $15.99 (0-670-06074-7). 32pp. Brief episodes featuring rabbit siblings Max and Ruby introduce every letter from A to Z. (Rev: BL 6/1–15/06; SLJ 5/06)

43 Wood, Audrey. *Alphabet Rescue* (PS–2). Illus. by Bruce Wood. 2006, Scholastic $15.99 (0-439-85316-8). 40pp. Readers join the lowercase letters of the alphabet as they repair an old fire truck and come to the rescue of other letters that need help. (Rev: BL 11/15/06; SLJ 10/06)

Concept Books

GENERAL

44 Abramson, Beverley. *Off We Go!* (PS). Photos by author. 2006, Tundra $15.95 (0-88776-728-1). Multicultural children enjoy a multitude of energetic activities in this book of few words. (Rev: HBG 10/06; SLJ 6/06)

45 Asim, Jabari. *Whose Knees Are These?* (PS). Illus. by LeUyen Pham. 2006, Little, Brown $6.99 (0-316-73576-0). A happy brown-skinned baby rejoices in bending knees in this simple board book with simple rhymes and lively illustrations. Also use *Whose Toes Are Those?* (2006). (Rev: SLJ 6/06)

46 Barraclough, Sue. *Fast and Slow* (PS–K). Illus. Series: How Do Things Move? 2006, Raintree LB $14.95 (1-4109-2261-8). 24pp. The concept of speed is illustrated in spreads depicting two objects moving at different paces. (Rev: BL 4/1/06) [531]

47 Behrens, Janice. *Let's Find Rain Forest Animals: Up, Down, Around* (PS–1). Illus. Series: Let's Find Out. 2007, Scholastic LB $18.00 (0-531-14874-2). 32pp. Readers guess which rain forest animals are shown in cropped photographs and in the process learn "position" words; factual information is appended. (Rev: BL 4/1/07) [591.734]

48 Blackstone, Stella. *I Wish I Were a Pilot* (PS–1). Illus. by Max Grover. 2005, Barefoot Bks. $15.99 (1-84148-341-9). A colorful introduction to different modes of transportation. (Rev: SLJ 3/06)

49 Brown, Lisa. *How to Be* (PS–2). 2006, HarperCollins $15.99 (0-06-054635-2). 32pp. A little brother and sister have lots of fun imitating different animals. (Rev: BL 7/06; SLJ 6/06)

50 Brown, Margaret Wise. *Bumble Bugs and Elephants: A Big and Little Book* (PS). Illus. by Clement Hurd. 2006, HarperCollins $14.99 (0-06-074512-6). With its appealing blend of colorful artwork and rhythmic text, this picture book originally published in 1938 provides simple examples of opposite sizes in the animal world. (Rev: SLJ 3/06)

51 Bullard, Lisa. *Long and Short: An Animal Opposite Book* (K–2). Series: A+ Books: Animal Opposites. 2005, Capstone LB $22.60 (0-7368-4275-6). 32pp. Animal pairings — a python and a bat, for example — introduce the concept of opposites. (Rev: SLJ 1/06) [590]

52 Bullard, Lisa. *Loud and Quiet: An Animal Opposites Book* (K–2). Series: A+ Books: Animal Opposites. 2005, Capstone LB $22.60 (0-7368-4276-4). 32pp. Animals that make quite different sounds — a whale and a bat, for example — introduce the concept of opposites. Also use *Wet and Dry: An Animal Opposites Book* (2005). (Rev: SLJ 1/06) [591.59]

53 Crowther, Robert. *Opposites* (PS–1). Illus. 2005, Candlewick $12.99 (0-7636-2783-6). 16pp. Bright collage artwork and clever, sturdy pull-tab and lift-the-flap features illustrate opposites — happy and sad, full and empty, and so forth. (Rev: BL 9/1/05; SLJ 9/05) [428.1]

54 Gravett, Emily. *Orange Pear Apple Bear* (PS–1). Illus. by author. 2007, Simon & Schuster $12.99 (978-1-4169-3999-3). A brown bear stars in this book about shapes, colors, and sequence. (Rev: SLJ 4/07*)

55 Harper, Charise Mericle. *Amy and Ivan* (PS). Illus. by author. 2006, Tricycle $12.95 (1-58246-134-1). 24pp. Amy is planning a surprise party for her friend Ivan in this bright, square, lift-the-flap book with numbers and colors for children to name. (Rev: BL 5/15/06; SLJ 9/06)

56 Hicks, Barbara Jean. *I Like Black and White* (PS). Illus. by Lila Prap. 2006, ME Media $9.95 (1-58925-057-5). 24pp. Simple black-and-white art (with color accents) and brief, rhyming text depict animals, patterns, and shapes. (Rev: BL 5/15/06)

57 Hutchins, Hazel. *A Second Is a Hiccup: A Child's Book of Time* (PS–2). Illus. by Kady MacDonald Denton. 2007, Scholastic $16.99 (978-0-439-83106-2). Children will recognize the many examples given here for seconds, minutes, and hours and what can be accomplished within their parameters. (Rev: BL 1/1–15/07; SLJ 3/07*)

58 Jenkins, Emily. *Hug, Hug, Hug! A Bea and HaHa Book* (PS). Illus. by Tomek Bogacki. Series: Bea and HaHa. 2006, Farrar $5.95 (0-374-30581-1). A cute hippo and a friendly ferret share a blanket in this sweet board book for little ones. Also use *Num, Num, Num! A Bea and HaHa Book* (2006). (Rev: SLJ 6/06)

59 Jolivet, Joëlle. *Almost Everything* (PS–2). Illus. 2005, Roaring Brook $19.95 (1-59643-090-7). 40pp. This large-format collection of images, a follow-up to *Zoo-ology* (2003), is organized into 13 categories, including tools, the human body, histori-cal costumes, and trees and flowers. (Rev: BL 11/1/05; SLJ 11/05) [423]

60 Katz, Karen. *A Potty for Me! A Lift-the-Flap Instruction Manual* (PS). Illus. by author. 2005, Simon & Schuster $7.99 (0-689-87423-5). A child learns to use the potty in this encouraging book with entertaining flaps to lift. (Rev: SLJ 8/05)

61 Katz, Karen. *Ten Tiny Tickles* (PS). Illus. 2005, Simon & Schuster $14.95 (0-689-85976-7). 32pp. A simple book that celebrates the various parts of a baby and offers counting opportunities as well. (Rev: BL 7/05; SLJ 7/05)

62 Lewison, Wendy Cheyette. *Two Is for Twins* (PS). Illus. by Hiroe Nakata. 2006, Viking $16.99 (0-670-06128-X). 40pp. This bright picture book celebrates things that come in pairs, especially twins. (Rev: BL 5/15/06; SLJ 4/06)

63 Marks, Jennifer L. *Sorting by Size* (K–3). Series: Sorting. 2006, Capstone LB $23.93 (978-0-7368-6740-5). 32pp. Simple text and everyday examples show how to sort by size; also use *Sorting Money* and *Sorting Toys* (both 2006). (Rev: SLJ 4/07)

64 Miura, Taro. *Tools* (PS–K). Illus. 2006, Chronicle $15.95 (0-8118-5519-8). 40pp. This attractive introduction to a wide array of tools offers children the chance to guess which occupations they are used in. (Rev: BL 11/1/06; SLJ 10/06) [621.9]

65 Pearson, Susan. *Hooray for Feet!* (PS–1). Illus. by Roxanna Baer-Block. 2005, Blue Apple $12.95 (1-59354-093-0). In rhyming text, this appealing picture book celebrates feet and the many wonders they can perform. (Rev: SLJ 11/05)

66 Petelinsek, Kathleen, and E. Russell Primm. *Opposites / Los contrarios* (K–2). Illus. by Nichole Day Diggins. Series: Talking Hands. 2006, The Child's World LB $21.36 (1-59296-454-0). 24pp. Students demonstrate simple words using American Sign Language; the text is in both English and Spanish. (Rev: SLJ 6/06) [419]

67 Raschka, Chris. *Five for a Little One* (PS–K). Illus. by author. 2006, Simon & Schuster $16.95 (0-689-84599-5). 48pp. A thoughtful young bunny shares the glories of the five senses in this picture book with unusual, eye-catching illustrations. (Rev: BL 6/1–15/06; SLJ 7/06)

68 Redding, Sue. *Up Above and Down Below* (PS). Illus. by author. 2006, Chronicle $14.95 (0-8118-4876-0). 32pp. Worlds above and below — hikers and cavers, golfers and gophers, cruise passengers and crew, for example — are contrasted in this imaginative book for preschoolers. (Rev: BL 5/15/06; SLJ 7/06)

69 Seeger, Laura Vaccaro. *Black? White! Day? Night!* (PS–2). Illus. 2006, Roaring Brook $16.95 (1-59643-185-7). 24pp. A creative introduction to opposites using full-page flaps, cutouts, and bright colors. (Rev: BCCB 11/06; BL 11/1/06; HBG 4/07; SLJ 11/06*) [428.1]

70 Silvano, Wendi. *What Does the Wind Say?* (PS–K). Illus. by Joan M. Delehanty. 2006, North-Word $15.95 (1-55971-954-0). A gentle book with watercolor illustrations and rhyming text that poses questions about various parts of nature — "What do the stars do?" "What does the moon play?" (Rev: SLJ 11/06)

71 Small, Mary. *Being Respectful: A Book About Respectfulness* (K–2). Illus. by Stacey Previn. Series: Way to Be! 2005, Picture Window LB $16.95 (1-4048-1053-6). 24pp. Examples of respectful behavior are presented in a series of vignettes. (Rev: BL 10/15/05) [179]

72 Sper, Emily. *The Kids' Fun Book of Jewish Time* (1–4). Illus. by author. 2006, Jewish Lights $16.99 (1-58023-311-2). Lift-the-flap and pull-the-tab features add interest to this introduction to the Jewish calendar. (Rev: SLJ 11/06) [296.4]

73 Timmers, Leo. *Who Is Driving?* (PS–K). Illus. 2007, Bloomsbury $12.95 (978-1-59990-021-6). 32pp. Readers must guess which animal is driving each of seven vehicles in this interesting picture puzzle with clue-laden illustrations. (Rev: BL 12/15/06)

COLORS

74 Fontes, Justine. *Black Meets White* (PS–2). Illus. by Geoff Waring. 2005, Candlewick $12.99 (0-7636-1933-7). Cutouts and lift-the-flap features highlight this tale of two colors, which cleverly introduces various patterns. (Rev: SLJ 11/05)

75 Mockford, Caroline. *Cleo's Color Book* (PS). Illus. by author. 2006, Barefoot Bks. $15.99 (1-905236-30-1). 32pp. The orange cat featured in *Cleo's Alphabet Book* and *Cleo's Counting Book* (both 2003) observes the colors around her in this beginning concept book. (Rev: BL 5/15/06; SLJ 4/06)

76 Wood, Audrey. *The Deep Blue Sea: A Book of Colors* (PS). Illus. by Bruce Wood. 2005, Scholastic $15.99 (0-439-75382-1). 40pp. Bright tropical artwork introduces basic colors. (Rev: BL 7/05; SLJ 8/05)

PERCEPTION

77 Carter, David A. *One Red Dot* (K–2). Illus. by author. 2005, Simon & Schuster $19.95 (0-689-87769-2). This attractive pop-up book challenges readers to find the single red dot that is hidden somewhere in each of its ten paper sculptures. (Rev: SLJ 11/05)

78 Ciboul, Adele. *The Five Senses* (PS–K). Trans. by Anthea Bell. Illus. by Clementine Colliner. Series: Explore Your World. 2006, Firefly $15.95 (1-55407-007-4). 28pp. An appealing, interactive introduction to the senses, with lots of pullouts, flaps, pictures, and photos. (Rev: BL 10/15/06) [612.8]

79 Kuskin, Karla. *Green as a Bean* (PS–2). Illus. by Melissa Iwai. 2007, HarperCollins $16.99 (978-0-06-075332-0). Thought-provoking "what if" questions challenge young readers to consider what they might be if they were different colors, textures, shapes, sounds, or sizes; previously published as *Square as a House*. (Rev: BL 11/1/06; SLJ 2/07)

SIZE AND SHAPE

80 Blackstone, Stella. *Ship Shapes* (PS). Illus. by Siobhan Bell. 2006, Barefoot Bks. $15.99 (1-905236-34-4). Two children and a dog set sail on a raft and encounter a variety of different shapes. (Rev: SLJ 8/06)

81 *Museum Shapes* (PS–2). Illus. 2005, Little, Brown $16.99 (0-316-05698-7). 48pp. Using artifacts from the collections of New York's Metropolitan Museum of Art, this concept book introduces readers to ten geometric forms, including the square, circle, rectangle, triangle, crescent, heart, star, and diamond. (Rev: BL 10/1/05; SLJ 12/05) [516]

82 Rau, Dana Meachen. *Rectangles* (PS–2). Illus. Series: Bookworms: The Shape of the World. 2006, Marshall Cavendish $15.95 (0-7614-2282-X). 23pp. A bright, small-format introduction to rectangles with minimal text. (Rev: BL 10/15/06; SLJ 1/07) [516]

83 Wilson, Zachary. *A Circle in the Sky* (K–2). Illus. by JoAnn Aldinolfi. 2006, Children's Pr. LB $19.50 (0-531-12570-X). 32pp. A small girl's imaginative ideas serve as a framework for introducing four basic shapes. (Rev: BL 11/15/06)

Counting and Number Books

84 Bates, Ivan. *Five Little Ducks* (PS). Illus. 2006, Scholastic $12.99 (0-439-74693-0). 24pp. Based on the classic children's song, this counting book follows a mother duck as she tries to round up her wandering ducklings. (Rev: BL 1/1–15/06; SLJ 2/06)

85 Berry, Lynne. *Duck Skates* (PS–K). Illus. by Hiroe Nakata. 2005, Holt $15.95 (0-8050-7219-5). 32pp. Simple math concepts and numbers from 1 to 10 are integrated into this appealing picture-book story of five ducks enjoying a snowy day. (Rev: BL 10/1/05; SLJ 11/05)

86 Blackstone, Stella. *Counting Cockatoos* (PS–K). Illus. by Stephanie Bauer. 2006, Barefoot Bks. $16.99 (1-905236-31-X). Beautifully painted birds and other animals frolic on the pages of this book that counts from 1 to 12. (Rev: SLJ 5/06)

87 Boueri, Marijean. *Lebanon 1-2-3* (PS–2). Illus. by MonaTrad Dabaji. 2005, Publishing Works $16.95 (1-933002-03-4). 32pp. Set in Lebanon, this brightly illustrated, trilingual (Arabic, English, and French) counting book introduces the numbers from 1 to 10. (Rev: BL 11/1/05; SLJ 11/05) [513.2]

88 Butler, John. *Ten in the Den* (PS–1). Illus. by author. 2005, Peachtree $15.95 (1-56145-344-7). Taking a cue from the rhyme "Ten in the Bed," ten cuddly animals roll one by one down a hill and settle in for a nap. (Rev: SLJ 9/05)

89 Byrd, Lee Merrill. *Lover Boy / Juanito el cariñoso: A Bilingual Counting Book* (PS–2). Trans. by David Dorado Romo. Illus. by Francisco Delgado. 2006, Cinco Puntos $15.95 (0-938317-38-5). A little boy enjoys giving kisses to everyone he sees (whether they enjoy it or not) in this book that counts kisses in English and Spanish. (Rev: SLJ 6/06)

90 Chae, In Seon. *How Do You Count a Dozen Ducklings?* (PS–1). Illus. by Seung Ha Rew. 2006, Albert Whitman $16.95 (0-8075-1718-6). 32pp. A mother duck uses various math strategies to keep track of her newly hatched ducklings. (Rev: BL 9/15/06; SLJ 9/06)

91 Clements, Andrew. *A Million Dots*. 48th ed. (K–3). Illus. by Mike Reed. 2006, Simon & Schuster $16.95 (0-689-85824-8). 48pp. The million dots on these pages will give young readers a feeling for the magnitude of the number, enhanced by the numerical facts/trivia scattered through the book. (Rev: BL 6/1–15/06; SLJ 7/06) [513.2]

92 Cronin, Doreen. *Click, Clack, Splish, Splash: A Counting Adventure* (PS). Illus. by Betsy Lewin. 2006, Simon & Schuster $12.95 (0-689-87716-1). 24pp. A cumulative counting book about farm animals sneaking off for a secret fishing trip. (Rev: BL 1/1–15/06; SLJ 1/06)

93 *Curious George Learns to Count from 1 to 100* (PS–2). Illus. by Anna Grossnickle Hines. 2005, Houghton $16.00 (0-618-47602-4). 64pp. As part of his town's centennial celebration, the inquisitive little monkey learns how to count to 100. (Rev: BL 9/15/05; SLJ 10/05)

94 Delessert, Etienne. *Hungry for Numbers* (PS–2). Illus. by author. 2006, Creative Editions $18.95 (1-56846-198-4). 32pp. Ten hungry creatures eat delicious fruit — from one banana to ten blueberries. (Rev: SLJ 11/06)

95 Donaldson, Julia. *One Ted Falls Out of Bed* (PS–2). Illus. by Anna Currey. 2006, Holt $15.95 (0-8050-7787-1). 32pp. An impressive assortment of toys and three mice come to the aid of a teddy bear that's fallen out of his owner's bed, giving the reader the opportunity to count up to 10 and down again. (Rev: BL 6/1–15/06; SLJ 6/06)

96 Durango, Julia. *Cha-Cha-Chimps* (PS–K). Illus. by Eleanor Taylor. 2006, Simon & Schuster $15.95 (0-689-86456-6). 32pp. Ten little chimps go to Mambo Jamba's for a lively dance session in this rhythmic counting book. (Rev: BL 1/1–15/06; SLJ 2/06)

97 Ehrhardt, Karen. *This Jazz Man* (PS–2). Illus. by R. G. Roth. 2006, Harcourt $16.00 (0-15-205307-7). 32pp. The well-known song "This Old Man" is presented here with a lively jazz theme, featuring different jazz musicians as children rhyme and count to nine. (Rev: BL 11/15/06; SLJ 12/06)

98 Ewing, Susan. *Ten Rowdy Ravens* (PS–6). Illus. by Evon Zerbetz. 2005, Alaska Northwest $15.95 (0-88240-606-X); paper $8.95 (0-88240-610-8). The mischievous nature of ravens is highlighted in this entertaining counting book. (Rev: SLJ 1/06)

99 Fisher, Aileen. *Know What I Saw?* (PS). Illus. by Deborah Durland DeSaix. 2005, Roaring Brook $16.95 (1-59643-055-9). 32pp. From 10 collies and 9 baby chicks through a basket of kittens and a single puppy, this counting book explores the natural world. (Rev: BL 9/15/05; SLJ 9/05)

100 Franco, Betsy. *Birdsongs* (PS–2). Illus. by Steve Jenkins. 2007, Simon & Schuster $16.99 (0-689-87777-3). 32pp. Nature lesson and counting book are combined in this beautifully illustrated collection of avian collages. (Rev: BL 1/1–15/07; SLJ 1/07)

101 Fromental, Jean-Luc, and Joëlle Jolivet. *365 Penguins* (PS–2). Illus. 2006, Abrams $17.95 (0-8109-4460-X). 32pp. A family's problems — and mathematical calculations — multiply when an additional penguin arrives every day for a year; a lively, oversize picture book. (Rev: BL 1/1–15/07; SLJ 12/06)

102 Gayzagian, Doris K. *One White Wishing Stone: A Beach Day Counting Book* (PS). Illus. by Kristina Swarner. 2006, National Geographic $16.95 (0-7922-5110-5). In this gentle counting book, a little girl spending a day at the beach with her mother counts off the wondrous treasures she discovers for her sandcastle. (Rev: SLJ 11/06)

103 Giganti, Paul. *How Many Blue Birds Flew Away? A Counting Book with a Difference* (PS–K). Illus. by Donald Crews. 2005, Greenwillow $15.99 (0-06-000762-1). 32pp. Attractive colorful illustrations pose addition and subtraction puzzles. (Rev: BL 10/15/05; SLJ 9/05)

104 Gillham, Bill. *How Many Sharks in the Bath?* (PS). Illus. by Christyan Fox. 2005, Frances Lincoln $14.95 (1-84507-288-X). The zany animal antics in this colorful counting book give readers an opportunity to practice numbers from 0 to 10. (Rev: SLJ 1/06)

105 Ginkel, Anne. *I've Got an Elephant* (PS–2). Illus. by Janie Bynum. 2006, Peachtree $16.95 (1-56145-373-0). 32pp. A little girl's elephant gets lonely when she goes to school and invites an elephant friend over, and then another, and then another — until this rhyming counting book reaches 10. (Rev: BL 9/15/06; SLJ 9/06)

106 Gosline, Andrea Alban. *Ten Little Wishes: A Baby Animal Counting Book* (PS). 2007, HarperCollins $12.99 (0-06-053410-9). 40pp. A gentle rhyming counting book that combines a baby sister and baby animals. (Rev: BL 2/1/07)

107 Katz, Karen. *Mommy Hugs* (PS). Illus. 2006, Simon & Schuster $12.95 (0-689-87772-2). 32pp. This appealing counting book deals in the hugs that a baby gets throughout the day. (Rev: BL 2/15/06; SLJ 4/06)

108 Keller, Laurie. *Grandpa Gazillion's Number Yard* (PS–K). Illus. 2005, Holt $16.95 (0-8050-6282-3). 32pp. Junkyard owner Grandpa Gazillion sees numbers in very different ways, introducing his concepts for using 1 through 20. (Rev: BL 11/15/05; SLJ 11/05)

109 Kelly, Mij. *One More Sheep* (PS–2). Illus. by Russell Ayto. 2006, Peachtree $16.95 (1-56145-378-1). 30pp. Sam always falls asleep when he tries to count his herd of 10 sheep, and one night when a wolf (dressed in sheep's clothing) tries to sneak in, the sheep must work hard to keep Sam awake so he can count to 11. (Rev: BL 11/15/06; SLJ 10/06)

110 Kimmelman, Leslie. *How Do I Love You?* (PS–1). Illus. by Lisa McCue. 2005, HarperCollins $14.99 (0-06-001200-5). In this counting-book celebration of parental love, an adult crocodile lists 20 reasons why it loves its child. (Rev: SLJ 2/06)

111 Koller, Jackie French. *Seven Spunky Monkeys* (K–2). Illus. by Lynn Munsinger. 2005, Harcourt $16.00 (0-15-202519-7). Over a week, a group of seven monkeys dwindles down to none as each in turn falls in love and runs off to get married; an entertaining companion to *One Monkey Too Many* (1999). (Rev: SLJ 9/05)

112 Koontz, Robin. *Up All Night Counting: A Pop-up Book* (PS–K). Illus. by author. 2006, Simon & Schuster $10.95 (1-4169-0706-8). This colorful 1-to-10 counting book with pop-ups and flaps features nighttime creatures such as bats, owls, flying squirrels, raccoons, crickets, and foxes. (Rev: SLJ 8/06)

113 Kroll, Virginia. *Equal Shmequal* (K–3). Illus. by Philomena O'Neill. 2005, Charlesbridge paper $6.95 (1-57091-892-9). 32pp. The animals want to play tug-of-war like the children in the playground but have trouble working out how to divide into equal teams. (Rev: SLJ 9/05)

114 Law, Diane. *Come Out and Play* (PS). 2006, North-South $9.95 (0-7358-2060-0). 24pp. A counting book that incorporates multiculturalism through language (each number is shown in English, Spanish, German, French, and Chinese) and through the characters (the children are of different ethnicities and live in different settings). (Rev: BL 5/1/06; SLJ 7/06)

115 Ljungkvist, Laura. *Follow the Line* (K–2). Illus. by author. 2006, Viking $16.99 (0-670-06049-6). The line leads through all sorts of settings, encouraging children to count objects ranging from fire hydrants to babies sleeping in a village. (Rev: SLJ 5/06)

116 Murphy, Stuart J. *Jack the Builder* (PS). Illus. by Michael Rex. Series: MathStart. 2006, HarperCollins $15.99 (0-06-055774-5); paper $4.99 (0-06-055775-3). 40pp. As Jack keeps adding more blocks, he can make more and more sophisticated constructions. (Rev: BL 1/1–15/06) [513.2]

117 Murphy, Stuart J. *Leaping Lizards* (PS–K). Illus. by JoAnn Adinolfi. Series: Math Start. 2005, HarperCollins $15.99 (0-06-000130-5); paper $4.99 (0-06-000132-1). 40pp. An ever-growing cast of lizards aboard many kinds of transport teaches young readers to count by multiples of five and ten. (Rev: BL 9/15/05; SLJ 3/06) [513.2]

118 Parenteau, Shirley. *One Frog Sang* (K–2). Illus. by Cynthia Jabar. 2006, Candlewick $15.99 (978-0-7636-2394-4). From 1 to 10, and down again, groups of frogs enjoy a spring evening. (Rev: SLJ 4/07)

119 Perl, Erica S. *Ninety-Three in My Family* (K–3). Illus. by Mike Lester. 2006, Abrams $15.95 (0-8109-5760-4). In a funny story full of counting opportunities, a young boy identifies the members of his extended family that includes his parents, two sisters, and a mind-boggling assortment of pets and other creatures, including a pygmy hippo. (Rev: SLJ 10/06)

120 Reiser, Lynn. *Hardworking Puppies* (PS–2). 2006, Harcourt $16.00 (0-15-205404-9). 40pp. In this attractive countdown tale, ten bored puppies — one by one — are assigned professional tasks such as guide dog, sled dog, therapy dog. (Rev: BL 6/1–15/06; SLJ 4/06)

121 Rose, Deborah Lee. *The Twelve Days of Winter: A School Counting Book* (K–3). Illus. by Carey Armstrong-Ellis. 2006, Abrams $14.95 (0-8109-5472-9). The melody of "The Twelve Days of Christmas" provides the framework for this cumulative counting verse that celebrates the joys of winter. (Rev: SLJ 10/06)

122 Schulman, Janet. *10 Trick-or-Treaters: A Halloween Counting Book* (PS–K). Illus. by Linda Davick. 2005, Knopf $9.95 (0-375-83225-4). Ten little trick-or-treaters head out into the night, but one by one are scared off by various Halloween creatures. (Rev: SLJ 8/05)

123 Shahan, Sherry. *Cool Cats Counting* (K–3). Illus. by Paula Barragán. 2005, August House $16.95 (0-87483-757-X). Lively illustrations and rhythmic text introduce numbers from 1 to 10, with a translation of the key words into Spanish. (Rev: SLJ 10/05)

124 Smith, Maggie. *One Naked Baby: Counting to Ten and Back Again* (PS). Illus. by author. 2007, Knopf $15.99 (0-375-83329-3). A simple, colorful counting book in which a harried mother tries to cope with her lively toddler at bath time. (Rev: SLJ 1/07)

125 Ziefert, Harriet. *Knick-Knack Paddywhack* (PS–K). Illus. by Emily Bolam. 2005, Sterling $5.95 (1-4027-2292-3). A boy, a dog, some bones, and an old man figure in this appealing counting-oriented version of the familiar song. (Rev: SLJ 10/05)

Bedtime Books and Nursery Rhymes

Bedtime Books

126 Alborough, Jez. *Yes* (PS). Illus. 2006, Candlewick $15.99 (0-7636-3183-3). 40pp. Bobo, the chimp seen in *Hug* (2000) is back and this time he's excited about having a bath but definitely not ready to go to bed. (Rev: BL 11/15/06; SLJ 10/06)

127 Anderson, Christine. *Bedtime!* (PS). Illus. by Steven Salerno. 2005, Philomel $14.99 (0-399-24004-7). 32pp. Melanie puts off going to bed, so her mother lavishes the usual bedtime routine on the family dog. (Rev: BL 9/15/05; SLJ 9/05)

128 Ashman, Linda. *Starry Safari* (PS–K). Illus. by Jeff Mack. 2005, Harcourt $16.00 (0-15-204766-2). 40pp. A little girl with a vivid imagination turns bedtime into an exciting safari. (Rev: BL 8/05; SLJ 7/05)

129 Brunelle, Nicholas. *Snow Moon* (K–2). Illus. by author. 2005, Viking $15.99 (0-670-06024-0). On a moonlit night, a young boy follows an owl to a magic place where snowy white owls congregate by the hundreds. (Rev: SLJ 12/05)

130 Cabrera, Jane. *Ten in the Bed* (PS). Illus. 2006, Holiday $16.95 (0-8234-2027-2). 32pp. In a goodnight countdown, ten stuffed animals with different occupations strut their stuff. (Rev: BL 10/1/06; SLJ 9/06)

131 Cooper, Elisha. *Bear Dreams* (PS). 2006, Greenwillow $16.99 (0-06-087428-7). 40pp. It's almost time to hibernate, but Bear, a cub, has places to go and things to do, until finally he tires himself out. (Rev: BL 10/1/06; SLJ 9/06)

132 Davies, Jacqueline. *The Night Is Singing* (PS–K). Illus. by Krysten Brooker. 2006, Dial $16.99 (0-8037-3004-7). 40pp. The sounds of the night lull a

little girl to sleep in this rhyming, soothing picture book. (Rev: BL 5/15/06; SLJ 6/06)

133 Deacon, Alex. *While You Are Sleeping* (PS). 2006, Farrar $16.50 (0-374-38330-8). 36pp. This whimsical bedtime book shows how a young girl's stuffed animals stand guard over her as she sleeps. (Rev: BL 8/06; SLJ 9/06)

134 Deniers, Dominique. *Every Single Night* (PS–K). Trans. by Sarah Quinn. Illus. by Nicolas Debon. 2006, Groundwood $17.95 (0-88899-699-3). 32pp. Little Simon simply can't fall asleep until his father completes their nighttime ritual full of images of a wonderful world full of nature. (Rev: BL 3/15/06; SLJ 5/06)

135 Ehrlich, Fred. *Does a Baboon Sleep in a Bed?* (PS). Illus. by Emily Bolam. Series: Early Experiences. 2006, Blue Apple $13.50 (1-59354-142-2); paper $5.95 (1-59354-143-0). 32pp. Where do animals sleep? Not in beds, as people do, informs this bedtime book, which offers factual information about the sleeping habits of six different kinds of animals. (Rev: BL 5/15/06) [649]

136 Fancher, Lou. *Star Climbing* (PS–K). Illus. by Steve Johnson. 2006, HarperCollins $15.99 (0-06-073901-0). 32pp. An angel-like child conducts a tour of the constellations before finally falling asleep. (Rev: BL 2/15/06; SLJ 4/06)

137 Ferrkri, Della Ross. *How Will I Ever Sleep in This Bed?* (PS). Illus. by Capucine Mazille. 2005, Sterling LB $12.95 (1-4027-1492-0). Unable to adjust to his new, larger bed, a young boy fills it up with his stuffed toys, leaving no room for himself. (Rev: SLJ 1/06)

138 Fore, S. J. *Tiger Can't Sleep* (PS–1). Illus. by R. W. Alley. 2006, Viking $15.99 (0-670-06078-X). 32pp. An imaginative little boy tries to get the noisy tiger in his closet to quiet down so he can get some sleep. (Rev: BL 12/15/05; SLJ 2/06)

139 Freedman, Claire. *Snuggle Up, Sleepy Ones* (PS–1). Illus. by Tina Macnaughton. 2005, Good Bks. $16.00 (1-56148-475-X). A sleepytime book with cuddly animals settling in for the night. (Rev: SLJ 7/05)

140 Glass, Beth Raisner, and Susan Lubner. *Noises at Night* (PS–1). Illus. by Bruce Whatley. 2005, Abrams $15.95 (0-8109-5750-7). In this unusual bedtime story told in rhyming couplets, the mysterious sounds of nighttime inspire a young boy to dream of grand adventures with his teddy bear. (Rev: SLJ 10/05)

141 Guy, Ginger Foglesong. *Go Back to Bed!* (K–2). Illus. by James Bernardin. 2006, Carolrhoda LB $15.95 (1-57505-750-6). Edwin comes up with lots of excuses not to go to sleep and imagines exciting things happening downstairs. (Rev: SLJ 6/06)

142 Harris, Peter. *The Night Pirates* (PS–K). Illus. by Deborah Allwright. 2006, Scholastic $16.99 (0-439-79959-7). 32pp. A boy named Tom joins a band of tough girl pirates in this rhyming bedtime story full of humor. (Rev: BL 2/1/06; SLJ 3/06)

143 Hindley, Judy. *Sleepy Places* (PS–K). Illus. by Tor Freeman. 2006, Candlewick $15.99 (0-7636-2983-9). 32pp. This colorful bedtime book examines the various places where animals sleep. (Rev: BL 4/15/06; SLJ 5/06)

144 Inches, Alison. *The Stuffed Animals Get Ready for Bed* (PS–K). Illus. by Bryan Langdo. 2006, Harcourt $16.00 (0-15-216466-9). 32pp. It's bedtime, but the stuffed animals aren't sleepy yet and it's up to their young owner to get them settled down. (Rev: BL 8/06; SLJ 9/06)

145 Ives, Penny. *Rabbit Pie* (PS). Illus. 2006, Viking $15.99 (0-670-05951-X). 32pp. A mother rabbit follows nightly rituals as she readies her six little bunnies for sleep. (Rev: BL 1/1–15/06; SLJ 5/06)

146 Kanevsky, Polly. *Sleepy Boy* (K–2). Illus. by Stephanie Anderson. 2006, Simon & Schuster $15.95 (0-689-86735-2). 32pp. A small boy remembers the lion cub he saw at the zoo as he cuddles with his daddy in this charming bedtime book. (Rev: BL 4/15/06; SLJ 5/06)

147 Lareau, Kara. *Snowbaby Could Not Sleep* (PS). Illus. by Jim Ishikawa. 2005, Little, Brown $14.99 (0-316-60703-7). 32pp. In this appealing bedtime book, Snowmama and Snowpapa come up with a clever solution when Snowbaby is unable to fall asleep. (Rev: BL 1/1–15/06; SLJ 1/06)

148 Lloyd-Jones, Sally. *Time to Say Goodnight* (PS). Illus. by Jane Chapman. 2006, HarperCollins $15.99 (0-06-054328-0). 32pp. While most animal mothers are urging their young ones to sleep, the mother owl is waking her brood up. (Rev: BL 2/1/06; SLJ 3/06)

149 MacDonald, Margaret Read. *The Squeaky Door* (PS–2). Illus. by Mary Newell Depalma. 2006, HarperCollins $12.99 (0-06-028373-4). 40pp. A funny retelling of the story of a boy who can't sleep because he's scared of his squeaking door, with eye-catching typography and bright cartoon illustrations. (Rev: BL 12/1/05; SLJ 1/06)

150 Melling, David. *Good Knight Sleep Tight* (PS–2). Illus. 2006, Barron's $14.99 (0-7641-5878-3). 32pp. The baby princess cannot sleep because the cat has destroyed her pillow, so an intrepid young knight is sent in search of suitably fluffy material. (Rev: BL 2/1/06; SLJ 3/06)

151 Morales, Yuyi. *Little Night* (PS–2). Illus. 2007, Roaring Brook $16.95 (978-1-59643-088-4). 32pp. Although she doesn't want to go to bed, Little Night has a bath in falling stars and a nightdress crocheted from clouds. (Rev: BL 2/1/07)

152 Myers, Tim. *Dark Sparkle Tea: And Other Bedtime Poems* (2–4). Illus. by Kelley Cunningham. 2006, Boyds Mills $16.95 (1-59078-288-7). 32pp. Rhythmic poems featuring funny, lively wordplay describe bouncy bedtimes. (Rev: BL 3/15/06; SLJ 6/06) [811]

153 Neubecker, Robert. *Beasty Bath* (PS–1). Illus. by author. 2005, Scholastic $14.99 (0-439-64000-8). As she has a bath and gets ready for bed, a little girl imagines herself as many beasts and monsters. (Rev: SLJ 1/06)

154 Noda, Takayo. *Song of the Flowers* (PS). Illus. 2006, Dial $16.99 (0-8037-2934-0). 32pp. A poetic refrain of questions and answers featuring flora and fauna leads to requests for lullabies. (Rev: BL 2/15/06; SLJ 3/06) [811]

155 Numeroff, Laura. *When Sheep Sleep* (PS–K). Illus. by David McPhail. 2006, Abrams $15.95 (0-8109-5469-9). 32pp. A little girl, struggling to fall asleep, decides to try counting sheep but is disheartened to find that all the sheep are already asleep. (Rev: BL 9/1/06; SLJ 10/06)

156 Oppenheim, Joanne. *The Prince's Bedtime* (PS–1). Illus. by Miriam Latimer. 2006, Barefoot Bks. $16.99 (1-84148-597-7). The prince refuses to sleep despite many inducements until a wise woman arrives with bedtime stories. (Rev: SLJ 12/06)

157 Owens, Mary Beth. *Panda Whispers* (PS–2). Illus. by author. 2007, Dutton $16.99 (978-0-525-47171-4). After a succession of animals wish their babies happy dreams, a father does the same to his human child. (Rev: SLJ 4/07)

158 Peck, Jan. *Way Up High in a Tall Green Tree* (PS–1). Illus. by Valeria Petrone. 2005, Simon & Schuster $15.95 (1-4169-0071-3). A girl says goodnight to all sorts of jungle animals, then settles down to sleep in her bed full of similar rainforest toys. (Rev: SLJ 9/05)

159 Peters, Lisa Westberg. *Sleepyhead Bear* (PS). Illus. by Ian Schoenherr. 2006, Greenwillow $16.99 (0-06-059675-9). 32pp. Little Bear, glad to find some friendly butterflies after being bothered by pesky bugs, settles down for a good night's sleep in this simple bedtime book. (Rev: BL 5/15/06; SLJ 5/06)

160 Puttock, Simon. *Earth to Stella!* (PS–2). Illus. by Philip Hopman. 2006, Clarion $16.00 (0-618-58535-4). 32pp. As she brushes her teeth and gets ready for bed, young Stella alternates between her fantasy of outer space and the reality of her attentive father. (Rev: SLJ 3/06)

161 Rex, Michael. *You Can Do Anything, Daddy!* (PS–K). Illus. 2007, Putnam $14.99 (978-0-399-24298-4). 32pp. When a little boy at bedtime asks his tie-wearing dad if he'd save him if pirates took him, the action morphs into an adventurous rescue full of pirates, snakes, robots, and more, with the son proffering apple juice and bandages at its end; detail-filled illustrations emulate comics. (Rev: BL 1/1–15/07)

162 Rockhill, Dennis. *Ocean Whisper / Susurro del oceano* (PS–2). Trans. by Eida de la Vega. Illus. by author. 2005, Raven Tree $16.95 (0-9741992-4-9). 32pp. A bilingual poem introduces a wordless picture book in which a boy's whale poster and goldfish morph into a dreamlike undersea world. (Rev: SLJ 2/06)

163 Rockwell, Anne. *Here Comes the Night* (PS–K). Illus. by author. 2006, Holt $16.95 (0-8050-7663-8). A little boy's mommy helps him get ready for bed and drift off to dreamland. (Rev: SLJ 6/06)

164 Russo, Marisabina. *The Bunnies Are Not in Their Beds* (K–2). Illus. by author. 2006, Random $15.99 (978-0-375-83961-0). Three bunny siblings are too full of energy to go to sleep despite their parents' frequent admonitions. (Rev: BL 2/1/07; SLJ 12/06)

165 Sayles, Elizabeth. *The Goldfish Yawned* (PS–1). Illus. by author. 2005, Holt $16.95 (0-8050-7624-7). A sleepy young child sets sail on a magical boat trip. (Rev: SLJ 1/06)

166 Schroeder, Lisa. *Baby Can't Sleep* (PS). Illus. by Viviana Garofoli. 2005, Sterling LB $12.95 (1-4027-2171-4). Counting sheep doesn't always put babies to sleep! (Rev: SLJ 1/06)

167 Shulevitz, Uri. *So Sleepy Story* (PS). Illus. by author. 2006, Farrar $16.00 (0-374-37031-1). 32pp. A magical dance in the middle of the night enlivens a small boy's room. (Rev: BCCB 10/06; BL 7/06; HB 1–2/07; HBG 4/07; SLJ 8/06*)

168 Smee, Nicola. *No Bed Without Ted* (PS–1). Illus. by author. 2005, Bloomsbury $14.95 (1-58234-963-0). A girl heading for bed can't find her favorite teddy bear without her mother's help in this lift-the-flap book. (Rev: SLJ 7/05)

169 Sobel, June. *The Goodnight Train* (PS–K). Illus. by Laura Huliska-Beith. 2006, Harcourt $16.00 (0-15-205436-7). The Goodnight Train picks up a cast of colorful characters as it counts down the time until lights-out. (Rev: SLJ 10/06)

170 Vestergaard, Hope. *Hillside Lullaby* (PS). Illus. by Maggie Moore. 2006, Dutton $15.99 (0-525-47215-0). 32pp. The sounds of nature lull an infant to sleep in this appealing bedtime book. (Rev: BL 2/15/06; SLJ 2/06)

171 Weeks, Sarah. *Counting Ovejas* (2–4). Illus. by David Diaz. 2006, Simon & Schuster $16.95 (0-689-86750-6). 40pp. A young insomniac learns to count sheep in English and Spanish. (Rev: BL 6/1–15/06; SLJ 6/06)

172 Wilson, Karma. *Sleepyhead* (PS). Illus. by John Segal. 2006, Simon & Schuster $15.95 (1-4169-

1241-X). 32pp. A kitten tries to get her teddy bear ready to go to bed but he keeps putting it off with pleas for more hugs, kisses, books, drinks, and so forth. (Rev: BL 11/15/06; SLJ 10/06)

173 Yolen, Jane. *Sleep, Black Bear, Sleep* (K–2). Illus. by Brooke Dyer. 2007, HarperCollins $15.99 (0-06-081560-4). 32pp. A lulling rhyme and snuggly illustrations of animals in their various beds grace this bedtime book. (Rev: BL 11/15/06; SLJ 2/07)

174 Ziefert, Harriet. *Mommy, I Want to Sleep in Your Bed!* (PS). Illus. by Elliot Kreloff. 2005, Blue Apple $15.95 (1-59354-103-1). 40pp. Charlie the puppy begs to sleep with his parents but finally is happily tucked in after a story. (Rev: BL 12/15/05; SLJ 11/05)

Nursery Rhymes

175 Engelbreit, Mary. *Mary Engelbreit's Mother Goose: One Hundred Best-Loved Verses* (PS–1). 2005, HarperCollins $19.99 (0-06-008171-6). 128pp. Popular illustrator Engelbreit offers her artistic interpretation of 100 well-known and less-familiar nursery rhymes. (Rev: SLJ 3/06) [398.8]

176 French, Vivian. *The Daddy Goose Treasury* (PS–K). Illus. by AnnaLaura Cantone, et al. 2006, Scholastic $18.99 (0-439-79608-3). 93pp. Daddy Goose, a relative of Mother Goose, provides the back stories for nursery rhymes such as "Little Miss Muffet" and "Old King Cole." (Rev: SLJ 9/06) [398.8]

177 Grey, Mini. *The Adventures of the Dish and the Spoon* (K–3). 2006, Knopf $16.95 (0-375-83691-8). 32pp. This tale fleshes out the adventures of the Dish that ran away with the Spoon, a romance that goes bad when the two rob a bank to continue financing their high life. (Rev: BL 6/1–15/06; SLJ 4/06)

178 *Hickory, Dickory, Dock: And Other Favorite Nursery Rhymes* (PS). Illus. by Sanja Rescek. 2006, Tiger Tales $7.95 (1-58925-786-3). A gentle board-book collection of classic nursery rhymes illustrated with cartoon art. Also use *Twinkle, Twinkle, Little Star: And Other Favorite Bedtime Rhymes* (2006). (Rev: SLJ 4/06) [398.8]

179 Hoberman, Mary Ann. *You Read to Me, I'll Read to You: Very Short Mother Goose Tales to Read Together* (1–4). Illus. by Michael Emberley. 2005, Little, Brown $16.99 (0-316-14431-2). 32pp. Variations on familiar Mother Goose rhymes, meant to be read aloud by two readers. (Rev: SLJ 9/05) [398.2]

180 Martin, Bill. *"Fire! Fire!" Said Mrs. McGuire* (PS–1). Illus. by Vladimir Radunsky. 2006, Harcourt $16.00 (0-15-205725-0). 32pp. A group of mice sound the alarm when they think they see a fire through a keyhole in this rhyming picture book; a final cutout reveals candles on the cat's birthday cake. (Rev: BL 5/1/06; SLJ 6/06) [811]

181 Pearson, Tracey Campbell. *Little Miss Muffet* (PS). Illus. by author. 2005, Farrar $5.95 (0-374-30862-4). This adaptation of the popular nursery rhyme shows a young girl acting out the story line, spider and all. (Rev: SLJ 10/05) [398.8]

182 Pierce, Terry, ed. *Counting Your Way: Number Nursery Rhymes* (PS–K). Illus. by Andrea Petrlik Huseinovic. 2007, Picture Window $18.95 (978-1-4048-2346-4). 32pp. Twenty familiar rhymes featuring numbers are highlighted on attractively illustrated pages. (Rev: BL 4/1/07) [398.8]

183 Sierra, Judy. *Schoolyard Rhymes* (K–3). Illus. by Melissa Sweet. 2005, Knopf $15.95 (0-375-82516-9). 40pp. This collection of schoolyard rhymes includes such favorites as "Liar, Liar, Pants on Fire" and "Lady with the Alligator Purse." (Rev: BL 8/05; SLJ 10/05) [398.8]

184 *Teddy Bear, Teddy Bear: A Traditional Rhyme* (PS). Illus. by Timothy Bush. 2005, HarperCollins $14.99 (0-06-057835-1). A new take on the familiar rhyme, with hand motions for children to perform along with the chant. (Rev: SLJ 7/05) [398.8]

185 Trapani, Iza. *Here We Go 'Round the Mulberry Bush* (PS–1). Illus. by author. 2006, Charlesbridge paper $6.95 (1-58091-699-3). Animals feast on a vegetable garden in this take on the familiar nursery rhyme. (Rev: SLJ 7/06) [398.8]

186 Yolen, Jane, ed. *This Little Piggy* (PS). Illus. by Will Hillenbrand. 2006, Candlewick $19.99 (0-7636-1348-7). 80pp. A large-format anthology of rhymes, songs, lap games, and finger plays of various kinds, with annotations, pig-filled illustrations, musical notations, and an accompanying CD. (Rev: BL 1/1–15/06*; SLJ 2/06*) [398.8]

Stories Without Words

187 Faller, Regis. *Polo: The Runaway Book* (PS–2). Illus. by author. 2006, Roaring Brook $16.95 (1-59643-189-X). 80pp. In this almost-wordless picture-book adventure, Polo the dog chases an alien that has run off with his new book. (Rev: BL 12/1/06; SLJ 1/07*)

188 Kamm, Katja. *Invisible / Visible* (PS–2). Illus. by author. 2006, North-South $12.95 (0-7358-2052-X). A wordless picture book in which elements appear and disappear depending on colors and other visual tricks. (Rev: SLJ 7/06)

189 Lehman, Barbara. *Museum Trip* (PS–2). Illus. 2006, Houghton $15.00 (0-618-58125-1). 40pp. A boy on a visit to an art museum suddenly finds himself inside a series of artistic mazes; a wordless book with clever illustrations. (Rev: BL 4/15/06*; HB 5–6/06; HBG 10/06; LMC 2/07; SLJ 5/06)

190 Rogers, Gregory. *Midsummer Knight* (K–2). 2007, Roaring Brook $16.95 (978-1-59643-183-6). 32pp. A wordless story in which an Elizabethan bear enters a world reminiscent of Shakespeare's *A Midsummer Night's Dream* and finds himself embroiled in royal intrigue. (Rev: BL 4/1/07)

191 Schories, Pat. *Jack and the Night Visitors* (PS–K). Illus. 2006, Front St. $13.95 (1-932425-33-0). 32pp. Jack the dog and his young master entertain aliens in this wordless but very expressive picture book, the third in a series. (Rev: BL 4/15/06; SLJ 6/06)

192 Varon, Sara. *Chicken and Cat* (PS–2). Illus. 2006, Scholastic $16.99 (0-439-63406-7). 20pp. Cat comes to visit Chicken in New York City but is not impressed with urban life, and the two decide to plant a garden; a wordless story that manages to cover a number of themes. (Rev: BL 2/1/06; SLJ 5/06*)

Picture Books

Imaginative Stories

FANTASIES

193 Almond, David. *Kate, the Cat and the Moon* (PS–2). Illus. by Steve Lambert. 2005, Doubleday $15.95 (0-385-74691-1). 32pp. On a night with a full moon, Kate is transformed into a cat and joins her own pet on a journey through magical scenes under the stars; includes a fold-out. (Rev: BCCB 10/05; BL 7/05; HBG 4/06; LMC 1/06; SLJ 9/05)

194 Amico, Tom, and James Proimos. *Raisin and Grape* (PS). Illus. by Andy Snair. 2006, Dial $12.99 (0-8037-3091-8). 32pp. A young green grape and his wrinkly purple Grandpa go for a walk and exchange some stories and ideas. (Rev: BCCB 3/06; BL 5/1/06; HBG 10/06; SLJ 3/06)

195 Andreae, Giles. *Captain Flinn and the Pirate Dinosaurs* (1–3). Illus. by Russell Ayto. 2005, Simon & Schuster $15.95 (1-4169-0713-0). 32pp. A schoolboy finds a pirate crying in his classroom's supply closet and volunteers to help the hapless buccaneer regain control of his ship, which has been stolen by dinosaurs. (Rev: BCCB 12/05; BL 12/1/05; HBG 4/06; SLJ 12/05)

196 Arnold, Caroline. *The Terrible Hodag and the Animal Catchers* (1–3). Illus. by John Sandford. 2006, Front St. $15.95 (1-59078-166-X). 32pp. Olee Swenson and his lumberjack friends help to protect the Hodag, a blueberry-eating monster, from capture. (Rev: BL 4/1/06; HBG 10/06; LMC 1/07; SLJ 3/06)

197 Ashman, Linda. *What Could Be Better Than This?* (PS–2). Illus. by Linda S. Wingerter. 2006, Dutton $16.99 (0-525-46954-0). A mother and father tell their child about their previous lives (as a king and a daring seagoing queen) and their happiness in adopting a simple forest life in which to bring up their baby. (Rev: SLJ 4/07)

198 Balouch, Kristen. *Mystery Bottle* (K–3). Illus. 2006, Hyperion $15.99 (0-7868-0999-X). 32pp. A mysterious bottle whisks a 7-year-old boy on a fantastical journey to Iran and a meeting with his grandfather. (Rev: BL 2/1/06)

199 Bateman, Teresa. *Fiona's Luck* (K–5). Illus. by Kelly Murphy. 2007, Charlesbridge $15.95 (978-1-57091-651-9). A leprechaun king gets upset with humans' profligate use of luck and steals the luck away, leaving an unhappy population and a girl called Fiona who is determined to get it back; set against the backdrop of the potato famine. (Rev: SLJ 4/07)

200 Bateman, Teresa. *Keeper of Soles* (K–2). Illus. by Yayo. 2006, Holiday $16.95 (0-8234-1734-4). 32pp. Colin the cobbler outsmarts the Grim Reaper, persuading him he needs "soles" not "souls" and offering him progressively more impressive footwear. (Rev: BL 3/1/06; SLJ 4/06)

201 Baynton, Martin. *Jane and the Dragon* (K–3). Illus. by author. 2007, Candlewick paper $4.99 (978-0-7636-3570-1). In her zeal to become a knight despite those who say all knights are men, Jane sets out to rescue the prince from a dragon, becomes a great friend of the dragon, and goes on to become a real knight; a tie-in to an animated TV series. (Rev: SLJ 4/07)

202 Beaty, Andrea. *When Giants Come To Play* (PS–2). Illus. by Kevin Hawkes. 2006, Abrams $16.95 (0-8109-5759-0). 32pp. Young Anna whiles away an idyllic summer afternoon in the company of two very large playmates. (Rev: BL 9/15/06; SLJ 10/06)

203 Bell, Cece. *Sock Monkey Rides Again* (PS–2). Illus. by author. 2007, Candlewick $13.99 (0-7636-3089-6). Cast in a starring role as a singing cowboy, Sock Monkey seems poised to make it big, but his future begins to look a little shaky when he can't bring himself to kiss the leading lady. (Rev: SLJ 1/07)

204 Berkeley, Jon. *Chopsticks* (2–4). Illus. 2005, Random $16.95 (0-375-83309-9). 32pp. When the moon is full over Hong Kong, Chopsticks the mouse and a wooden dragon he helped to free take off on wonderful adventures. (Rev: BL 12/1/05; SLJ 12/05)

205 Bernasconi, Pablo. *The Wizard, the Ugly, and the Book of Shame* (1–4). Illus. by author. 2005, Bloomsbury $16.95 (0-7475-8399-4). While the wizard is away, his assistant sets off a disastrous

chain of events when he tries to cast a spell on his own. (Rev: SLJ 1/06)

206 Blaikie, Lynn. *Beyond the Northern Lights* (PS–2). Illus. 2006, Fitzhenry & Whiteside $16.95 (1-55005-123-7). 32pp. A young girl imagines wonderful flights with a raven to the seas and skies of the north of the world. (Rev: BL 1/1–15/07; SLJ 3/07)

207 Bolliger, Max. *The Happy Troll* (K–3). Trans. from German by Nina Ignatowicz. Illus. by Peter Sís. 2005, Holt $16.95 (0-8050-6982-8). A singing troll is happy until he trades his talent for wealth. (Rev: SLJ 7/05)

208 Briant, Ed. *Seven Stories* (PS–2). Illus. 2005, Roaring Brook $16.95 (1-59643-056-7). 32pp. A young girl's sleep is disrupted by rowdy neighbors, who seem to be characters from such popular fairy tales as "Goldilocks and the Three Bears," "Jack and the Beanstalk," and "Cinderella"; the vertical format of the book and evocative illustrations add atmosphere. (Rev: BL 1/1–15/06; SLJ 1/06)

209 Briggs, Raymond. *The Puddleman* (K–2). Illus. 2006, Trafalgar paper $7.99 (0-09-945642-7). 32pp. Out for a walk with his grandfather, a young boy is disappointed by the lack of puddles until he runs into the Puddleman, who has some on his back. (Rev: BL 11/1/06)

210 Brown, Jeff. *Flat Stanley* (K–3). Illus. by Scott Nash. 2006, HarperCollins $16.99 (0-06-112904-6). Flattened to a thickness of half an inch, Stanley Lambchop discovers that his new shape has some decided advantages in this new version sporting full-page cartoon illustrations. (Rev: SLJ 12/06)

211 Brownlow, Mike. *Mickey Moonbeam* (PS–2). Illus. by author. 2006, Bloomsbury $16.95 (1-58234-704-2). Mickey Moonbeam receives a distress call from his pen pal Quiggle and rushes in his spaceship to the rescue, only to discover that Quiggle is gigantic! (Rev: SLJ 11/06)

212 Bunting, Eve. *My Robot* (K–2). Illus. by Dagmar Fehlau. Series: Green Light Reader. 2006, Harcourt $12.95 (0-15-205593-2). 24pp. In this beginning reader with brief sentences and a repetitive refrain, a young African American boy describes the attributes of Cecil, the robot who is his best friend. (Rev: BL 3/15/06; SLJ 6/06)

213 Bunting, Eve. *That's What Leprechauns Do* (PS–2). Illus. by Emily Arnold McCully. 2006, Clarion $16.00 (0-618-35410-7). 32pp. The job of three leprechauns is to place the pot of gold at the end of rainbows, but mischief often diverts them, and nobody ever finds the gold anyway. (Rev: BL 1/1–15/06; SLJ 2/06)

214 Cepeda, Joe. *The Swing* (PS–3). Illus. by author. 2006, Scholastic $15.99 (0-439-14260-1). Embarrassed by her family, which is constantly losing things, Josey retreats to her swing and discovers that the old oak tree magically contains all the lost items. (Rev: SLJ 10/06)

215 Cowen-Fletcher, Jane. *Nell's Elf* (K–2). Illus. by author. 2006, Candlewick $14.99 (0-7636-2391-1). A little girl bored on a rainy day cheers up when the elf she draws comes alive and shows her how to enjoy life. (Rev: SLJ 4/06)

216 Czernecki, Stefan. *Lilliput 5357* (PS–2). Illus. by author. 2006, Simply Read $16.95 (1-894965-32-9). Driven from his playground by a bunch of bullies, Lilliput 5357, a diminutive robot, searches desperately for somewhere new to play. (Rev: SLJ 4/06)

217 Day, Jan. *Kissimmee Pete, Cracker Cow Hunter: A Tall Tale* (2–4). Illus. by Janeen Mason. 2005, Pelican $15.95 (1-58980-325-6). Kissimmee Pete, a cowboy on Florida's frontier, is involved in a ever-escalating series of adventures that add to the string of adjectives describing his prowess. (Rev: SLJ 12/05)

218 Day, Lucille Lang. *Chain Letter* (1–3). Illus. by Doug Dworkin. 2005, Heyday $14.95 (1-59714-011-2). An outrageous chain letter makes its way around the globe in this tongue-in-cheek tale. (Rev: SLJ 9/05)

219 DeFelice, Cynthia. *One Potato, Two Potato* (1–3). 2006, Farrar $16.00 (0-374-35640-8). 32pp. A poor elderly Irish couple used to sharing their one chair, their one coat, are down to their last potato when they discover a magic pot in this appealing adaptation of a Chinese folk tale. (Rev: BL 9/1/06; SLJ 8/06)

220 dePaola, Tomie. *Angels, Angels Everywhere* (PS). Illus. by author. 2005, Putnam $14.99 (0-399-24370-4). DePaola presents angels who provide guidance for children in almost every aspect of daily life — including "the wake up angel," "the popcorn angel," and "the babysitting angel." (Rev: SLJ 10/05)

221 Ditchfield, Christin. *Cowlick!* (PS–K). Illus. by Rosalind Beardshaw. 2007, Random $14.99 (0-375-83540-7). 40pp. Interpreting its title literally, this rhyming romp depicts a cow depositing drooly kisses upon slumbering children's heads, with predictable results next morning. (Rev: BL 1/1–15/07; SLJ 1/07)

222 Doherty, Berlie. *Jinnie Ghost* (2–4). Illus. by Jane Ray. 2005, Frances Lincoln $16.95 (1-84507-292-8). 44pp. Jinnie Ghost visits sleeping children throughout the night, leaving each one with a different dream. (Rev: BL 10/15/05; SLJ 2/06)

223 Donaldson, Julia. *Charlie Cook's Favorite Book* (PS–2). Illus. by Axel Scheffler. 2006, Dial $16.99 (0-8037-3142-6). 32pp. Charlie is led through ten different fairy tales by the books' characters themselves in this amusing circular take on some familiar stories. (Rev: BL 5/1/06; SLJ 7/06)

224 Donohue, Moira Rose. *Alfie the Apostrophe* (1–3). Illus. by JoAnn Adinolfi. 2006, Albert Whitman $16.95 (0-8075-0255-3). 32pp. A lively tale about a little apostrophe who makes his mark trying out for a school talent show directed by Mr. Asterisk. (Rev: BL 8/06; SLJ 8/06)

225 Doyle, Malachy. *The Dancing Tiger* (K–2). Illus. by Steve Johnson and Lou Fancher. 2005, Viking $15.99 (0-670-06020-8). A girl and a tiger dance together by the full moon in this nicely illustrated story with poetic text. (Rev: SLJ 7/05)

226 Ellery, Amanda. *If I Had a Dragon* (PS–2). Illus. by Tom Ellery. 2006, Simon & Schuster $14.95 (1-4169-0924-9). 40pp. A boy imagines what would happen if his baby brother were a dragon, and decides he likes having a human sibling better. (Rev: BL 7/06; SLJ 7/06)

227 Federspiel, Jürg. *Alligator Mike* (1–3). Illus. by Petra Rappo. 2007, North-South $15.95 (978-0-7358-2124-8). Mike discovers that New York City is full of unhappy alligators that want to go home to Florida and decides to do what he can to help. (Rev: SLJ 4/07)

228 Floyd, Madeleine. *Cold Paws, Warm Heart* (PS). Illus. 2005, Candlewick $15.99 (0-7636-2761-5). 32pp. A little girl named Hannah seeks to warm up a lonely polar bear named Cold Paws. (Rev: BL 12/1/05; SLJ 7/06)

229 Fowles, Shelley. *Climbing Rosa* (PS–2). Illus. 2006, Frances Lincoln $15.95 (1-84507-079-8). 32pp. Brightly colored artwork enlivens this tale of Rosa, a poor young woman who climbs a towering tree to win the hand of a prince. (Rev: BL 4/1/06; SLJ 5/06)

230 Franson, Scott E. *Un-Brella* (PS–3). Illus. by author. 2007, Roaring Brook $15.95 (978-1-59643-179-9). A little girl enjoys a day at the beach although it's snowing out and conversely a day in the snow during a hot summer, all with the help of her "un-brella." (Rev: SLJ 4/07)

231 Frazier, Craig. *Stanley Goes Fishing* (PS–1). Illus. by author. Series: Stanley. 2006, Chronicle $15.95 (0-8118-5244-X). Stanley, having no luck fishing in a stream, tries in the sky instead and there they are! (Rev: SLJ 6/06)

232 Gall, Chris. *Dear Fish* (1–4). Illus. by author. 2006, Little, Brown $16.99 (0-316-05847-5). All sorts of fish venture onto land to visit Peter after he sends them an invitation in the form of a message in a bottle. (Rev: SLJ 5/06)

233 Garland, Michael. *Miss Smith Reads Again!* (K–3). Illus. by author. Series: Miss Smith. 2006, Dutton $16.99 (0-525-47722-5). This follow-up to *Miss Smith's Incredible Storybook* finds Miss Smith's class transported to the age of the dinosaurs when she reads from Arthur Conan Doyle's *The Lost World*. (Rev: SLJ 7/06)

234 Grambling, Lois G. *Can I Bring My Pterodactyl to School, Ms. Johnson?* (PS–K). Illus. by Judy Love. 2006, Charlesbridge $16.95 (1-58089-044-X); paper $6.95 (1-58089-141-1). 32pp. A boy tries to convince his teacher to let him bring a pterodactyl to school. (Rev: BL 12/15/05; SLJ 3/06)

235 Gutiérrez, Elisa. *Picturescape* (PS–2). Illus. by author. 2005, Simply Read $16.95 (1-894965-24-8). A boy's trip to an art museum turns into a magical excursion as each colorful painting transports him to a thrilling new location; a beautifully illustrated wordless book. (Rev: SLJ 2/06)

236 Haas, Irene. *Bess and Bella* (PS–K). Illus. 2006, Simon & Schuster $14.95 (1-4169-0013-6). 32pp. A bird called Bella drops in with a suitcase of goodies cheers Bess's lonely winter. (Rev: BL 12/15/05*; HBG 10/06; SLJ 2/06)

237 Hächler, Bruno. *What Does My Teddy Bear Do All Night?* (PS–K). Trans. from German by Charise Myngher. Illus. by Birte Müller. 2005, Minedition $14.99 (0-698-40029-1). A young girl and her teddy bear play together long after the child's bedtime, and even after the child finally falls asleep her faithful stuffed animal keeps watch over her. (Rev: SLJ 12/05)

238 Hale, Nathan. *The Devil You Know* (K–4). Illus. by author. 2005, Walker $16.95 (0-8027-8981-1). The Fells get more than they bargained for when they invite Ms. Phisto into their home to get rid of their resident devil. (Rev: SLJ 8/05)

239 Hao, K. T. *Little Stone Buddha* (PS–2). Illus. by Giuliano Ferri. 2005, Purple Bear $15.95 (1-933327-01-4). 32pp. A little stone statue of Buddha comes to life and wanders the mountains giving aid to travelers and the creatures of the wilderness; excellent illustrations extend the mood. (Rev: BL 10/15/05; SLJ 3/06)

240 Hazen, Barbara Shook. *Who Is Your Favorite Monster, Mama?* (PS–2). Illus. by Maryann Kovalski. 2006, Hyperion $15.99 (0-7868-1810-7). 32pp. Mama Monster reassures little Harry when he feels slighted by the attention she gives to his siblings. (Rev: BL 7/06; SLJ 4/06)

241 Heidbreder, Robert. *A Sea-Wishing Day* (PS–2). Illus. by Kady MacDonald Denton. 2007, Kids Can $15.95 (978-1-55337-707-8). 32pp. A little boy's imagination carries him and his dog, Skipper, on an exciting high-seas adventure. (Rev: BL 3/15/07)

242 Heine, Theresa. *Star Seeker: A Journey to Outer Space* (2–4). Illus. by Victor Tavares. 2006, Barefoot Bks. $16.99 (1-905236-36-0). 32pp. Strong illustrations of the planets and other bodies enhance the rhyming text in this fantasy of travel into space aboard a series of unlikely conveyances — including armchairs, hobby horses, and paper airplanes. (Rev: BL 4/15/06; SLJ 3/07)

243 Hennessy, B. G. *Claire and the Unicorn Happy Ever After* (K–3). Illus. by Susan Mitchell. 2006, Simon & Schuster $12.95 (1-4169-0815-3). Claire and her toy unicorn journey to a land full of literary characters and ask what it takes to make someone happy ever after. (Rev: SLJ 2/06)

244 Hogg, Gary. *Beautiful Buehla and the Zany Zoo Makeover* (PS–1). Illus. by Victoria Chess. 2006, HarperCollins $15.99 (0-06-009420-6). 32pp. It's picture day at the zoo, and Beautiful Buehla gives the reluctant animals quite extreme makeovers. (Rev: BL 5/1/06; SLJ 5/06)

245 Ichikawa, Satomi. *I Am Pangoo the Penguin* (PS–K). Illus. by author. 2006, Philomel $16.99 (0-399-23313-X). A stuffed penguin, worried his young owner is more interested in his new toys, runs away in search of a new home. (Rev: SLJ 10/06)

246 Impey, Rose. *Wanda Witch and the Wobbly Fang* (K–2). Illus. by Katharine McEwen. 2006, Scholastic paper $3.99 (0-439-78450-6). 32pp. When Wanda Witch hears that the Fang Fairy brings rewards for fangs that have fallen out, she casts a spell that causes all her teeth to fall out. (Rev: SLJ 8/06)

247 Issacs, Anne. *Pancakes for Supper!* (PS–2). Illus. by Mark Teague. 2006, Scholastic $15.99 (0-439-64483-6). 40pp. Alone in the wilderness after falling from her parents' wagon, young Toby uses her wits — and most of her clothes — to bargain her way back to civilization in this entertaining tall tale with arresting illustrations. (Rev: BCCB 11/06; BL 10/15/06; HB 11–12/06; HBG 4/07; LMC 3/07; SLJ 10/06*)

248 Jennings, Sharon. *The Happily Ever Afternoon* (PS–K). Illus. by Ron Lightburn. 2006, Annick LB $19.95 (1-55037-945-3); paper $7.95 (1-55037-944-5). 24pp. As his parents prepare for his birthday party, an imaginative little boy battles dragons — the family cat and dog — to get to the treasure, a kitchen full of birthday treats. (Rev: BL 8/06)

249 Kain, Karen. *The Nutcracker* (1–3). Illus. by Rajka Kupesic. 2005, Tundra $18.95 (0-88776-696-X). 32pp. In this handsome adaptation of "The Nutcracker" based on a National Ballet of Canada production, Marie and her brother Misha watch the toys battle and visit the Sugar Plum Fairy's palace. (Rev: BL 11/1/05; SLJ 10/05) [792.8]

250 Kann, Victoria, and Elizabeth Kann. *Pinkalicious* (K–2). 2006, HarperCollins $15.99 (0-06-077639-0). 40pp. Despite warnings from her parents, a little girl gobbles up so many pink cupcakes that she turns pink herself. (Rev: BL 6/1–15/06; SLJ 8/06)

251 Kennedy, Kim. *Pirate Peter's Giant Adventure* (PS–2). Illus. by Doug Kennedy. 2006, Abrams $15.95 (0-8109-5965-8). 32pp. Pirate Pete and his trusty parrot sidekick brave the perils of Thunder Island to rescue the Sea-Fairy Sapphire and return it to the sea; a sequel to *Pirate Pete* (2002). (Rev: BL 6/1–15/06)

252 Kleven, Elisa. *The Paper Princess Flies Again: (With Her Dog!)* (K–2). Illus. 2005, Tricycle $15.95 (1-58246-146-5). 32pp. The Paper Princess (a paper doll) and her faithful canine companion embark on an adventure-filled search for a gift to give to Lucy, their owner. (Rev: BL 12/1/05; SLJ 12/05)

253 Krensky, Stephen. *Too Many Leprechauns: Or How That Pot o' Gold Got to the End of the Rainbow* (K–4). Illus. by Dan Andreasen. 2007, Simon & Schuster $12.99 (978-0-689-85112-4). A horde of leprechauns descends on the quiet Irish town of Dingle, and Finn O'Finnegan decides to find a way to get them to leave. (Rev: BL 2/15/07; SLJ 2/07)

254 Laube, Sigrid. *The Flower Ball* (K–3). Trans. from German by Philip Boehm. Illus. by Silke Leffler. 2006, Pumpkin House $15.95 (0-9646010-2-8). When a carrot and a cauliflower attend the Flower Ball, the flowers realize that vegetables aren't so bad after all. (Rev: SLJ 7/06)

255 Lehman, Barbara. *Rainstorm* (PS–2). Illus. 2007, Houghton $16.00 (978-0-618-75639-1). 32pp. On a rainy, shut-in day, a boy finds a chest and a key that lead him down a ladder, up some stairs and onto a sunny island with playmates at the ready; sophisticated, boldly lined art captures the recurrent adventures in this wordless fantasy. (Rev: BL 1/1–15/07)

256 Le Néouanic, Lionel. *Little Smudge* (PS–1). Illus. by author. 2006, Boxer Bks. LB $14.95 (1-905417-22-5). The artwork stands out in this story of a little black smudge searching for acceptance by other shapes. (Rev: SLJ 1/07)

257 Lewis, Kim. *Hooray for Harry* (PS–2). 2006, Candlewick $15.99 (0-7636-2962-6). 32pp. Accompanied by his friends Lulu the lamb and Ted the teddy bear, Harry the stuffed elephant goes in search of his missing blanket. (Rev: BL 6/1–15/06; SLJ 4/06)

258 López, Brigitta Garcia. *Dreamflight* (K–2). Trans. by Marianne Martens. Illus. 2005, North-South $16.95 (0-7358-2024-4). 40pp. Young Max awakens one night to discover his rather plump guardian angel driving around his bedroom in a racing car. (Rev: BL 12/15/05)

259 Lucas, David. *Nutmeg* (1–3). 2006, Knopf $16.95 (0-375-83519-9). 32pp. Pigtailed Nutmeg is tired of the same old fare for breakfast, lunch, and dinner, but things get a little crazy after she receives a magic spoon. (Rev: BL 8/06; SLJ 8/06)

260 McAllister, Angela. *Mama and Little Joe* (PS). Illus. by Terry Milne. 2007, Simon & Schuster $15.99 (978-1-4169-1631-4). 32pp. Timeworn and tattered, stuffed kangaroos Mama and Little Joe get

the cold shoulder from the newer, brighter stuffed toys at their new home, but when Little Joe is accidentally discarded the newer toys rise to the occasion and offer to help find him. (Rev: BL 4/1/07)

261 McCaughrean, Geraldine. *Blue Moon Mountain* (1–3). Illus. by Nicki Palin. 2007, Simply Read $16.95 (978-1-894965-56-9). 32pp. Joy follows a moonlit path to Blue Mountain, the magical home of the fantastical creatures of myth, legend, and literature. (Rev: BL 3/15/07; SLJ 4/1/07)

262 McDonald, Megan. *When the Library Lights Go Out* (PS–2). Illus. by Katherine Tillotson. 2005, Simon & Schuster $16.95 (0-689-86170-2). 40pp. After the library has closed for the night, storytime puppets Rabbit and Lion launch a search for their friend Hermit Crab. (Rev: BL 11/1/05; SLJ 11/05)

263 MacDonald, Ross. *Bad Baby* (K–2). Illus. 2005, Roaring Brook $16.95 (1-59643-064-8). 32pp. Superhero Jack, first seen in *Another Perfect Day* (2002), begins to rethink his wish for a little sister when the reality turns out to be far different than he had imagined. (Rev: BCCB 11/05; BL 10/1/05*; HB 9–10/05; HBG 4/06; SLJ 9/05)

264 McKissack, Patricia C. *Where Crocodiles Have Wings* (K–2). Illus. by Bob Barner. 2005, Holiday $16.95 (0-8234-1748-4). 32pp. A rhyming fantasy set in a land where "surprises grow on trees" full of happy animals engaging in unusual activities. (Rev: BL 9/15/05; SLJ 10/05)

265 McPhail, David. *Boy on the Brink* (PS–2). Illus. by author. 2006, Holt $15.95 (0-8050-7618-2). 32pp. In his dreams, a boy reviews and expands dramatically on the day's events. (Rev: BL 5/15/06; SLJ 5/06)

266 MacRae, Tom. *The Opposite* (1–3). Illus. by Elena Odriozola. 2006, Peachtree $15.95 (1-56145-371-4). After the Opposite, a strange-looking creature, appears in his bedroom one morning, Nate finds that everything he does turns out the opposite of what he intended. (Rev: SLJ 10/06)

267 Mayhew, James. *The Knight Who Took All Day* (K–2). Illus. by author. 2005, Scholastic $15.99 (0-439-74829-1). Determined to impress a princess by vanquishing a dragon, a self-centered knight has so much trouble finding one that the princess tames the beast herself. (Rev: SLJ 10/05)

268 Meddaugh, Susan. *The Witch's Walking Stick* (PS–2). Illus. 2005, Houghton $16.00 (0-618-52948-9). 32pp. Bullied by her older brother and sister, Margaret runs away and happens upon a magic stick (acquiring a new canine friend in the process); she then uses the stick to cast suitably awful spells on her evil siblings. (Rev: BL 7/05; SLJ 9/05)

269 Milgrim, David. *Another Day in the Milky Way* (PS–1). Illus. by author. 2007, Putnam $15.99 (978-0-399-24548-0). Upset when he wakes up on the wrong planet, young Monty looks desperately for someone who can help him get back to Earth and then remembers he's been in this situation before. (Rev: BL 2/15/07; SLJ 2/07)

270 Montijo, Rhode. *Cloud Boy* (PS–2). Illus. by author. 2006, Simon & Schuster $12.95 (1-4169-0199-X). To while away his lonely days, a cloud boy high in the sky fashions all sorts of fantastical creatures out of clouds and enjoys the attention his creations receive from the children down on earth. (Rev: SLJ 4/06)

271 Morrissey, Dean, and Stephen Krensky. *The Crimson Comet* (PS–2). Illus. by Dean Morrissey. 2006, HarperCollins $16.99 (0-06-008068-X). Nora becomes alarmed when the light of the moon suddenly blinks out, so she and her brother Jack board a rocket and head off to see if they can offer assistance to the Man-in-the-Moon. (Rev: SLJ 12/06)

272 Moser, Lisa. *The Monster in the Backpack* (1–2). Illus. by Noah Z. Jones. 2006, Candlewick $14.99 (0-7636-2390-3). 40pp. Initially startled to discover a monster in her backpack, Annie soon develops a warm spot in her heart for the strange and mischievous yet endearing creature. (Rev: SLJ 8/06)

273 Myers, Tim. *Good Babies* (1–3). Illus. by Kelly Murphy. 2005, Candlewick $15.99 (0-7636-2227-3). A witch looks forward to the mayhem that will follow when she swaps a baby troll for a human infant and is sorely disappointed when her plan backfires. (Rev: SLJ 12/05)

274 Neubecker, Robert. *Courage of the Blue Boy* (PS–K). Illus. 2006, Tricycle $15.95 (1-58246-182-1). 32pp. A blue boy and his blue cow search for lands with other colors and eventually find a multicolor city that has no blue; it's up to the boy to add this. (Rev: BL 11/1/06; SLJ 11/06)

275 Newman, Marlene. *Myron's Magic Cow* (K–3). Illus. by Jago. 2005, Barefoot Bks. $16.99 (1-84148-496-2). Sent to buy some milk at a nearby store, young Myron comes home instead with a magical cow that can talk and grant wishes. (Rev: SLJ 1/06)

276 Nez, John. *One Smart Cookie* (PS–2). 2006, Albert Whitman $15.95 (0-8075-6099-5). 32pp. Cookie the dog comes to school and outshines Duffy and Nash in reading and writing ability. (Rev: BL 9/15/06; SLJ 10/06)

277 Nishimura, Kae. *I Am Dodo: Not a True Story* (PS–3). Illus. by author. 2005, Clarion $15.00 (0-618-33614-1). 32pp. A lone surviving dodo living in New York City is eager to elude capture. (Rev: SLJ 9/05)

278 O'Connor, George. *Sally and the Something* (PS–2). 2006, Roaring Brook $16.95 (1-59643-141-5). 32pp. Bored young Sally sets off for the pond where she befriends a strange-looking creature and

they try to find activities they both enjoy. (Rev: BL 6/1–15/06; SLJ 3/06)

279 Oddino, Licia. *Finn and the Fairies* (K–3). Illus. by Alessandra Toni. 2006, Purple Bear $15.95 (1-933327-17-0). 32pp. Finn the tailor has always doubted the existence of fairies, but he becomes a believer when the tiny creatures ask him to create formal gowns for a party they're planning. (Rev: BL 6/1–15/06; SLJ 10/06)

280 Peck, Jan. *Way Far Away on a Wild Safari* (PS–K). Illus. by Valeria Petrone. 2006, Simon & Schuster $15.95 (1-4169-0072-1). A little boy's safari through the African savannah turns out to be a date with Grandma's animal cookies. (Rev: SLJ 6/06)

281 Perret, Delphine. *The Big Bad Wolf and Me* (1–3). Illus. 2006, Sterling $9.95 (1-4027-3725-4). 64pp. With his confidence almost gone, Big Bad Wolf is not very scary at all, so Boy takes pity and tries to help poor animal to recoup. (Rev: BL 11/1/06)

282 Pinkney, Andrea Davis. *Peggony-Po: A Whale of a Tale* (K–2). Illus. by Brian Pinkney. 2006, Hyperion $16.99 (0-7868-1958-8). 32pp. Peggony-Po, a young boy carved from a piece of driftwood by a peg-legged African American sailor, tries to retrieve the leg of his creator from the whale that ate it in this action-packed tall tale. (Rev: BL 4/1/06; SLJ 6/06*)

283 Polacco, Patricia. *Emma Kate* (PS–2). Illus. 2005, Philomel $16.99 (0-399-24452-2). 32pp. A little girl and her elephant best friend do everything together — even having their tonsils out at the same time — and it may take readers some time to work out that it is the girl who is imaginary, not the elephant. (Rev: BL 9/15/05; SLJ 11/05)

284 Polacco, Patricia. *Something About Hensley's* (PS–4). Illus. by author. 2006, Philomel $16.99 (0-399-24538-3). Newly relocated to the town, a family in dire straits finds its every wish magically fulfilled in Hensley's general store. (Rev: SLJ 8/06)

285 Rasmussen, Halfdan. *The Ladder* (K–3). Trans. by Marilyn Nelson. Illus. by Pierre Pratt. 2006, Candlewick $17.99 (0-7636-2282-6). 62pp. A ladder sets off to view more of the world and encounters many people who wish to climb it. (Rev: BL 6/1–15/06)

286 Rawson, Katherine. *If You Were a Parrot* (K–2). Illus. by Sherry Rogers. 2006, Sylvan Dell $15.95 (0-9764943-9-6). Illustrations of children with parrot features — beaks, feet, voice, and feathers — show the power of imagination and inform about parrots' physical and behavioral characteristics. (Rev: SLJ 12/06)

287 Reed, Neil. *The Midnight Unicorn* (K–2). Illus. by author. 2006, Sterling LB $14.95 (1-4027-3218-X). Millie and her dog Casper go on a wonderful journey when the statue of a unicorn springs to life. (Rev: SLJ 1/07)

288 Reynolds, Peter. *So Few of Me* (K–3). Illus. by author. 2006, Candlewick $14.00 (0-7636-2623-6). Young Leo feels so overburdened that he wishes there were more of him to handle all his tasks, but when his wish is granted — many times over — he soon finds himself longing for the good old days. (Rev: SLJ 12/06)

289 Robertson, M. P. *The Dragon Snatcher* (PS–2). Illus. 2005, Dial $16.99 (0-8037-3103-5). 32pp. George and his dragon sidekick work to foil an evil wizard who's determined to rid the world of dragons; the third installment in a series that began with *The Egg* (2001) and *The Great Dragon Rescue* (2004). (Rev: BL 12/1/05; SLJ 10/05)

290 Rohmann, Eric. *Clara and Asha* (PS–2). Illus. 2005, Roaring Brook $16.95 (1-59643-031-1). 40pp. This story of a little girl's friendship with an imaginary giant fish named Asha features arresting illustrations. (Rev: BL 7/05; SLJ 8/05)

291 Root, Phyllis. *Lucia and the Light* (K–3). Illus. by Mary GrandPré. 2006, Candlewick $16.99 (0-7636-2296-6). 32pp. Brave Lucia battles frightening trolls in order to rescue the sun and bring back the daylight that has disappeared from her northern winter. (Rev: BL 12/1/06*; SLJ 12/06)

292 Santoro, Scott. *Farm-Fresh Cats* (PS–2). Illus. by author. 2006, HarperCollins $15.99 (0-06-078178-5). Life gets confusing for farmer Ray and his wife Norma when green cats mysteriously turn up in the field where they planted cabbages. (Rev: SLJ 8/06)

293 Satrapi, Marjane. *Monsters Are Afraid of the Moon* (PS). Illus. by author. 2006, Bloomsbury $15.95 (1-58234-744-1). Marie cuts the moon out of the sky and puts it in her bedroom to keep monsters at bay, but this causes widespread unrest among the cat population and the cat king must step in to resolve the situation. (Rev: SLJ 10/06)

294 Schneider, Christine. *I'm Bored!* (K–2). Illus. by Hervé Pinel. 2006, Clarion $15.00 (0-618-65760-6). 36pp. Charlie is amazed to find that his toys are just as bored as he is and together they stage an elaborate imaginary battle. (Rev: SLJ 4/06)

295 Schubert, Ingrid, and Dieter Schubert. *There's a Crocodile Under My Bed!* (PS–1). Illus. by authors. 2005, Front St. $15.95 (1-932425-48-9). Little Peggy overcomes her fears and befriends the crocodile beneath her bed. (Rev: SLJ 12/05)

296 Schwartz, Amy, and Leonard Marcus. *Oscar: The Big Adventure of a Little Sock Monkey* (K–3). Illus. by Amy Schwartz. 2006, HarperCollins $16.99 (0-06-072622-9). 32pp. Oscar the sock monkey braves the wilds of New York City to get to his owner, Susie, when she forgets to take an important item to school. (Rev: BL 5/15/06; SLJ 6/06)

297 Seibold, J. Otto. *The Fuchsia Is Now* (PS–K). Illus. by author. 2006, Scholastic $16.99 (0-439-63559-4). A little girl named Fuchsia has her wishes granted by a fairy when she adorns a favorite hat with a flower. (Rev: SLJ 5/06)

298 Selick, Henry. *Moongirl* (K–2). Illus. by Peter Chan. 2006, Candlewick $22.99 (0-7636-3068-3). 48pp. Out for a night of fishing with his squirrel friend, Leon finds himself pulled into a magical adventure on the moon; based on the animated short by the same name, this edition includes a DVD. (Rev: BL 11/1/06; SLJ 12/06)

299 Shea, Pegi Deitz. *The Boy and the Spell* (K–3). Illus. by Serena Riglietti. Series: Musical Stories. 2007, Pumpkin House $16.95 (978-0-964601-04-8). 32pp. When Thomas has a tantrum in his bedroom, his various possessions rebel and set out to teach him a lesson; based on the story line of the opera *L'Enfant et les Sortilèges* with music by Maurice Ravel and libretto by Colette. (Rev: BL 4/1/07)

300 Shields, Gillian. *The Starlight Baby* (PS). Illus. by Elizabeth Harbour. 2006, Simon & Schuster $15.95 (1-4169-1456-0). 32pp. A woman hears the cry of a motherless child and rushes out into the night in this offbeat blend of poetic text and pastel watercolors. (Rev: BL 2/1/06; SLJ 4/06)

301 Slater, Dashka. *Firefighters in the Dark* (PS–1). Illus. by Nicoletta Ceccoli. 2006, Houghton $16.00 (0-618-55459-9). With sirens sounding in the distance, a young girl imagines the rescues that are under way — saving princesses, rescuing boys who have bounced into space . . . (Rev: SLJ 10/06)

302 Sperring, Mark. *Mermaid Dreams* (PS–K). Illus. by the Pope Twins. 2006, Scholastic $16.99 (0-439-79610-5). As her mother gets her ready for bed, young Meriam recounts the undersea adventures of her day. (Rev: SLJ 8/06)

303 Stewart, Joel. *Dexter Bexley and the Big Blue Beastie* (PS–2). Illus. 2007, Holiday $16.95 (978-0-8234-2068-1). 32pp. Dexter Bexley runs into a voracious Big Blue Beastie who threatens to eat the boy, but Dexter resourcefully comes up with one idea after another to keep the creature otherwise occupied. (Rev: BL 4/1/07)

304 Taber, Tory, and Norman Taber. *Rufus at Work* (PS–K). Illus. by authors. 2005, Walker $16.95 (0-8027-8984-6). Rufus the cat is upset when his young mistress calls him lazy and recounts all the duties he handles for her on a daily basis. (Rev: SLJ 11/05)

305 Tauss, Marc. *Superhero* (PS–2). Illus. 2005, Scholastic $16.99 (0-439-62734-6). 40pp. Maleek, an African American boy with a secret identity, springs into action when his city's parks and playgrounds start mysteriously disappearing. (Rev: BL 8/05; SLJ 12/05)

306 Thomas, Shelley Moore. *Take Care, Good Knight* (PS–2). Illus. by Paul Meisel. 2006, Dutton $15.99 (0-525-47695-4). 32pp. When a wizard leaves three little dragons in charge of his cats while he's away, disaster threatens until the Good Knight shows up to set things right; a large-format picture-book featuring the characters from the Easy Readers series. (Rev: BL 9/15/06)

307 Tillman, Nancy. *On the Night You Were Born* (PS). Illus. by author. 2006, Feiwel & Friends $16.95 (978-0-312-34606-5). 32pp. The wind, rain, moon, and a variety of creatures big and small welcome the wondrous arrival of a baby, and celebrate its uniqueness. (Rev: BL 12/1/06)

308 Tripp, Paul. *Tubby the Tuba* (K–3). Illus. by Henry Cole. 2006, Dutton $16.99 (0-525-47717-9). 32pp. With a little help from a friendly frog, Tubby the tuba shows the orchestra that he can play melodies just as well as any other instrument; packaged with a CD, this is a story that first appeared in a film in 1947. (Rev: BL 12/1/06; SLJ 11/06)

309 Willard, Nancy. *Sweep Dreams* (PS–K). Illus. by Mary GrandPré. 2005, Little, Brown $16.99 (0-316-94008-9). 32pp. A lonely man falls in love with a magical broom and has the strength to let her go when she wants to be free. (Rev: BL 7/05; SLJ 7/05)

310 Willems, Mo. *Leonardo, the Terrible Monster* (PS–K). Illus. 2005, Hyperion $15.99 (0-7868-5294-1). 48pp. Leonardo's failure to frighten anyone leads him to formulate a plan to "scare the tuna salad" out of young Sam. (Rev: BL 7/05; SLJ 8/05*)

311 Williams, Arlene. *Tiny Tortilla* (PS). Illus. by G. Brian Karas. 2005, Dutton $15.99 (0-525-47382-3). 32pp. Hungry Juan Carlos discovers that his tiny piece of tortilla has magical properties. (Rev: BL 7/05; SLJ 8/05)

312 Wood, David. *Under the Bed!* (PS–K). Illus. by Richard Fowler. 2006, Barron's $9.99 (0-7641-5926-7). A huge pop-up monster, revealed on the final page of the book, is under Dad's bed. (Rev: SLJ 7/06)

313 Wood, Nancy. *How the Tiny People Grew Tall: An Original Creation Tale* (PS–2). Illus. by Rebecca Walsh. 2005, Candlewick $16.99 (0-7636-1543-9). 32pp. Inspired by Native American creation myths, this original tale tells how the Tiny People emerged from the earth's core and grow steadily taller as they learned more and more from the animals about the world around them. (Rev: BL 11/15/05; SLJ 1/06)

314 Wood, Nancy. *Mr. and Mrs. God in the Creation Kitchen* (K–2). Illus. by Timothy Basil Bring. 2006, Candlewick $16.99 (0-7636-1258-8). 32pp. In this amusing twist on the creation story, Mr. and Mrs. God work feverishly in their heavenly kitchen

to whip up the Earth and the creatures that will populate it. (Rev: BCCB 5/06; BL 4/15/06*; HBG 10/06; LMC 10/06; SLJ 6/06)

315 Wormell, Christopher. *The Sea Monster* (K–3). Illus. by author. 2005, Jonathan Cape $16.99 (0-224-07025-8). When a little boy is pulled out to sea by the strong currents, a kindly sea monster comes to his rescue. (Rev: SLJ 3/06)

316 Yang, James. *Joey and Jet in Space* (PS–2). Illus. by author. Series: Joey and Jet. 2006, Simon & Schuster $15.95 (0-689-86927-4). When Joey's dog Jet disappears, Joey searches everywhere — even outer space. (Rev: SLJ 6/06)

317 Yoo, Taeeun. *The Little Red Fish* (PS–2). 2007, Dial $15.99 (0-8037-3145-0). 40pp. On a trip to a library with his grandfather, young boy falls into a fantasy world when he awakes to find his pet fish is missing; a beautiful and unusual book, much of it wordless. (Rev: BL 4/15/07)

318 Yorinks, Arthur. *Mommy?* (1–3). Illus. by Maurice Sendak. 2006, Scholastic $24.95 (0-439-88050-5). 12pp. In this lively, almost wordless pop-up book, a pajama-clad boy encounters all sorts of monsters as he wanders through creepy surroundings in search of his mother. (Rev: BL 8/06)

IMAGINARY ANIMALS

319 Alborough, Jez. *Hit the Ball Duck* (PS–1). Illus. 2006, Kane/Miller $15.95 (1-929132-96-4). 32pp. Duck's baseball game with Goat, Sheep, and Frog turns into a search and recovery effort when the ball goes astray. (Rev: BL 2/15/06; HBG 10/06)

320 Alborough, Jez. *Tall* (PS). Illus. by author. 2005, Candlewick $15.99 (0-7636-2784-4). The other animals try to help Bobo (the chimpanzee of 2000's *Hug*) to feel tall, but in the end he is glad to be little enough to be cuddled by his mama. (Rev: BL 9/1/05; SLJ 9/05)

321 Allen, Jonathan. *I'm Not Cute!* (PS–K). Illus. 2006, Hyperion $14.99 (0-7868-3720-9). 32pp. Baby Owl rejects all compliments, asserting that he is really "a huge, sleek hunting machine," until his mother agrees that he's not cute and realizes that it's definitely time for bed. (Rev: BCCB 6/06; BL 4/15/06; HBG 10/06; SLJ 3/06)

322 Anderson, Peggy Perry. *Joe on the Go* (PS–1). Illus. 2007, Houghton $16.00 (978-0-618-77331-2). 32pp. Little Joe the frog has a hard time getting anyone to play with him at the family reunion until Grandma arrives. (Rev: BL 3/15/07; HBG 10/07)

323 Anholt, Catherine, and Laurence Anholt. *Happy Birthday Chimp and Zee* (PS). Illus. by authors. 2006, Frances Lincoln $15.95 (1-84507-507-2). For Chimp and Zee, monkey twins, the highlight of their birthday is a party thrown by their friends, a party they almost miss when they become lost in a swamp. (Rev: SLJ 4/06)

324 Arnold, Marsha Diane, and Vernise Elaine Pelzel. *Hugs on the Wind* (PS–K). Illus. by Elisa Warnick. 2006, Abrams $15.95 (0-8109-5968-2). A gentle story of Little Cottontail, who misses his grandfather and decides to send him hugs and kisses via the wind. (Rev: HBG 10/06; SLJ 3/06)

325 Aroner, Miriam. *Clink, Clank, Clunk!* (PS). Illus. by Dominic Catalano. 2006, Boyds Mills $15.95 (1-59078-270-4). Rabbit's car is on its last legs, but he manages to drive his animal friends to town one last time before junking the vehicle and buying a shiny red auto to replace it. (Rev: HBG 10/06; SLJ 4/06)

326 Asher, Sandy. *What a Party!* (PS–1). Illus. by Keith Graves. 2007, Philomel $15.99 (978-0-399-24496-4). Excited about the birthday party for his grandfather, Froggie doesn't want all the fun to end. (Rev: BL 2/1/07; SLJ 2/07)

327 Bailey, Linda. *The Farm Team* (PS–2). Illus. by Bill Slavin. 2006, Kids Can $16.95 (1-55337-850-4). 32pp. The animals from Farmer Stolski's farm compete valiantly in a championship hockey game against their archrivals, the Bush League Bandits, a team made up of creatures from the wild. (Rev: BL 10/1/06; SLJ 11/06)

328 Barber, Tom. *A Tale of Two Goats* (K–4). Illus. by Rosalind Beardshaw. 2005, Barron's $12.95 (0-7641-5847-3). The strong friendship between two goats — Muriel and Myrtle — finally transcends the territoriality of the two farmers who own them. (Rev: SLJ 11/05)

329 Bardhan-Quallen, Sudipta. *Tightrope Poppy the High-Wire Pig* (PS–2). Illus. by Sarah Dillard. 2006, Sterling LB $14.95 (1-4027-2411-X). When the circus holds auditions, Poppy the pig decides to realize her dream of becoming a tightrope walker. (Rev: SLJ 3/06)

330 Barnes, Laura T. *Ernest and Elston* (PS–2). Illus. by Carol A. Camburn. 2005, Barnesyard $15.95 (0-9674681-6-7). Elston the rooster worries that his crowing disturbs the other farm animals, and Ernest, a miniature donkey endowed with sympathy and understanding, tries to reassure him that he's perfect. (Rev: SLJ 10/05)

331 Baum, Louis. *The Mouse Who Braved Bedtime* (PS). Illus. by Sue Hellard. 2006, Bloomsbury $16.95 (1-58234-691-7). Troubled by a persistent nightmare, Milo the mouse seeks advice from family members but in the end must find the courage to confront his fears. (Rev: SLJ 10/06)

332 Beaumont, Karen. *Move Over, Rover!* (PS–K). Illus. by Jane Dyer. 2006, Harcourt $16.00 (0-15-201979-0). 40pp. Rover the dog offers shelter in his doghouse during a rainstorm and it gets very crowded until Skunk arrives. (Rev: BL 9/1/06; SLJ 9/06)

333 Bedford, David. *Little Otter's Big Journey* (K–2). Illus. by Susan Winter. 2006, Good Bks. $16.00 (1-56148-548-9). Left on his own when his mother goes in search of food, Little Otter enjoys himself at first but soon begins to miss her and asks other animals to help him find her. (Rev: SLJ 12/06)

334 Bernstein, Dan. *The Tortoise and the Hare Race Again* (PS–2). Illus. by Andrew Glass. 2006, Holiday House $16.95 (0-8234-1867-7). Neither tortoise nor hare is truly pleased by the outcome of their first race, so they schedule a rematch. (Rev: SLJ 4/06)

335 Blathwayt, Benedict. *Dinosaur Chase!* (PS–1). Illus. by author. 2006, Hutchinson $16.99 (0-09-189293-7). Fin the dinosaur is having a good time with his friends when a group of bullies tries to break up their fun; detailed illustrations enhance the story. (Rev: SLJ 9/06)

336 Blight, Peter. *The Lonely Giraffe* (PS). Illus. by Michael Terry. 2005, Bloomsbury $16.99 (0-7475-6894-4). The story of a previously ignored giraffe who uses his long neck to help others and make new friends. (Rev: SLJ 7/05)

337 Bonnett-Rampersaud, Louise. *Bubble and Squeak* (PS–1). Illus. by Susan Banta. 2006, Marshall Cavendish $14.99 (0-7614-5310-5). Older mouse sister Bubble is definitely not afraid of monsters but asks her mother what she would do if her younger sibling was afraid in the night. (Rev: SLJ 10/06)

338 Bosca, Francesca. *The Three Grasshoppers* (PS–2). Illus. by Giuliano Ferri. 2006, Purple Bear $15.95 (1-933327-13-8). 32pp. Three grasshopper friends who have enjoyed playing music together turn to preparations for winter and find themselves constantly in dispute; the detailed illustrations make the story of their reconciliation compelling. (Rev: BL 5/15/06; SLJ 8/06)

339 Bradley, Kimberly Brubaker. *Ballerino Nate* (PS–K). Illus. by R. W. Alley. 2006, Dial $16.99 (0-8037-2954-5). 32pp. Nate the puppy's desire to become a ballet dancer is diminished when his older brother insists that only girls can be ballerinas. (Rev: BL 2/1/06; SLJ 3/06)

340 Breen, Steve. *Stick* (PS–K). Illus. 2007, Dial $16.99 (0-8037-3124-8). 32pp. Brave little frog Stick is transported off for a great adventure when he tries to catch a dragonfly; the colorful and varied illustrations add to the humor and tension. (Rev: BL 3/15/07)

341 Brennan-Nelson, Denise. *Grady the Goose* (PS–3). Illus. by Michael Glenn Monroe. 2006, Sleeping Bear $16.95 (1-58536-282-4). Young goose Grady, who is prone to wandering, is left behind when her family flies south and faces many dangers before a farmer comes to her aid. (Rev: SLJ 1/07)

342 Brett, Jan. *Hedgie Blasts Off!* (PS–2). 2006, Putnam $16.99 (0-399-24621-5). 32pp. Hedgie's dream of becoming an astronaut comes true when the diminutive hedgehog is dispatched to the planet Mikkop on a mission to repair a malfunctioning volcano. (Rev: BL 8/06; SLJ 9/06)

343 Brett, Jan. *Honey . . . Honey . . . Lion!* (PS–2). Illus. 2005, Putnam $16.99 (0-399-24463-8). 32pp. A honeyguide bird takes revenge on a greedy honey badger and leads him through a variety of obstacles that end at the feet of a lion. (Rev: BL 9/1/05; SLJ 9/05)

344 Brooks, Erik. *Slow Days, Fast Friends* (PS–2). Illus. by author. 2005, Albert Whitman $16.95 (0-8075-7437-6). Forced by injury to move at a very slow pace, Howard the cheetah befriends Quince the sloth and learns to appreciate the joys of nature. (Rev: SLJ 1/06)

345 Brown, Marc. *D.W.'s Guide to Perfect Manners* (PS–2). Illus. by author. 2006, Little, Brown $15.99 (0-316-12106-1). Arthur the aardvark challenges little sister D.W. to be the model of good behavior for a full 24 hours. (Rev: SLJ 8/06)

346 Brunhoff, Laurent de. *Babar's World Tour* (PS–2). Illus. Series: Babar. 2005, Abrams $16.95 (0-8109-5780-9). 48pp. Babar and Celeste take their children on a round-the-world tour in this large-format picture book. (Rev: BL 10/1/05; SLJ 1/06)

347 Buckingham, Matt. *Bright Stanley* (PS–K). Illus. by author. 2006, Tiger Tales $15.95 (1-58925-059-1). Hurrying to catch up with the other fish in his school, Stanley encounters a number of fascinating underwater characters; gold-foil scales adorn Stanley and his school. (Rev: SLJ 1/07)

348 Bunting, Eve. *Hurry! Hurry!* (PS–K). Illus. by Jeff Mack. 2007, Harcourt $16.00 (978-0-15-205410-6). 40pp. All the animals of the farmyard gather to greet a new chick into the world. (Rev: BL 2/1/07)

349 Burg, Sarah Emmanuelle. *One More Egg* (PS–1). Illus. by author. 2006, North-South $15.95 (0-7358-2001-5). In search of an egg, a rabbit and a chicken tour the farm meeting its residents; point readers to the endpapers to get the full story. (Rev: SLJ 2/06)

350 Butler, John. *Ten in the Meadow* (PS). Illus. by author. 2006, Peachtree $15.95 (1-56145-372-2). Bear and nine of his animal friends play a game of hide-and-seek. (Rev: SLJ 9/06)

351 Butler, M. Christina. *One Winter's Day* (PS–1). Illus. by Tina Macnaughton. 2006, Good Bks. $16.00 (1-56148-532-2). After his flimsy hut blows away during a snowstorm, Little Hedgehog travels to shelter in his friend Badger's house and along the way generously gives his warm clothes to other shivering animals. (Rev: SLJ 11/06)

352 Butler, M. Christina. *Snow Friends* (PS). Illus. by Tina Macnaughton. 2005, Good Bks. $16.00 (1-56148-485-7). After Little Bear and his animal friends make a snowman, they decide to make a smaller snowman to keep the first one company; pages have a "sparkling glitter" finish. (Rev: SLJ 11/05)

353 Bynum, Janie. *Nutmeg and Barley* (K–2). 2006, Candlewick $15.99 (0-7636-2382-2). 32pp. Nutmeg the squirrel and Barley the mouse have little in common, but their friendship transcends their differences. (Rev: BL 2/1/06; SLJ 1/06)

354 Callahan, Sean. *The Bear Hug* (PS–K). Illus. by Laura J. Bryant. 2006, Albert Whitman $15.95 (0-8075-0596-X). Cubby's grandfather teaches him bear behavior, including how to hug. (Rev: SLJ 3/06)

355 Carlson, Nancy. *First Grade, Here I Come!* (PS–1). 2006, Viking $15.99 (0-670-06127-1). 32pp. Henry the mouse reviews his experiences on the first day in first grade and realizes he quite enjoyed it after all. (Rev: BL 8/06; SLJ 7/06)

356 Carlson, Nancy. *Think Big!* (PS–2). Illus. by author. 2005, Carolrhoda $15.95 (1-57505-622-4). A very small frog learns to love his size after some encouragement from his mother. (Rev: SLJ 9/05)

357 Chen, Chih-Yuan. *The Featherless Chicken* (K–3). Illus. by author. 2006, Heryin $16.95 (0-9762-0569-6). A featherless young chicken agonizes about his looks and his rejection by his peers. (Rev: SLJ 10/06)

358 Clarke, Jane. *Dippy's Sleepover* (PS–1). Illus. by Mary McQuillan. 2006, Barron's paper $6.99 (0-7641-3425-6). Dippy the dinosaur is delighted to be invited to spend the night at his friend Spike's house, but he worries about wetting the bed, a problem he's been experiencing at home. (Rev: SLJ 8/06)

359 Cooper, Helen. *A Pipkin of Pepper* (PS–2). Illus. 2005, Farrar $16.00 (0-374-35953-9). 32pp. Duck gets lost when he accompanies friends Cat and Squirrel to the city to buy salt for the soup in this companion to *Pumpkin Soup* (1997). (Rev: BL 8/05; SLJ 9/05)

360 Cousins, Lucy. *Maisy, Charley, and the Wobbly Tooth* (PS–1). Series: Maisy. 2006, Candlewick $12.99 (0-7636-2904-9). 32pp. Supportive mouse Maisy accompanies her crocodile friend Charlie to the dentist, where he learns about brushing his teeth. (Rev: BL 5/1/06)

361 Cousins, Lucy. *Maisy Goes to the Library* (PS–K). Illus. 2005, Candlewick $12.99 (0-7636-2669-4). 32pp. In this colorfully illustrated picture book, Maisy the mouse goes to the library in search of a book about fish and a peaceful setting in which to read it. (Rev: BL 8/05; SLJ 8/05)

362 Crimi, Carolyn. *Henry and the Buccaneer Bunnies* (PS–2). Illus. by John Manders. 2005, Candlewick $15.99 (0-7636-2449-7). 40pp. More interested in books than buccaneering, Henry the bunny endures the taunts of his shipmates but saves the day with his book smarts when their pirate ship is wrecked on a desert island. (Rev: BL 12/1/05; SLJ 11/05)

363 Cronin, Doreen. *Dooby Dooby Moo* (PS–3). Illus. by Betsy Lewin. 2006, Simon & Schuster $16.95 (0-689-84507-3). 40pp. In this lively farmyard tale, Farmer Brown's animals compete in a local talent show in hopes of winning the first prize — a trampoline. (Rev: BL 8/06; SLJ 8/06)

364 Crummel, Susan Stevens. *Ten-Gallon Bart* (K–2). Illus. by Dorothy Donohue. 2006, Marshall Cavendish $16.95 (0-7614-5246-X). 32pp. Ten-Gallon Bart, the canine sheriff of Dog City, is convinced to put his retirement plans on hold when he hears that Billy the Kid, an outlaw goat, is headed for town; colorful language and humorous collage illustrations capture the feel of the Old West. (Rev: BL 4/1/06; SLJ 4/06)

365 Cuyler, Margery. *Groundhog Stays Up Late* (PS–2). Illus. by Jean Cassels. 2005, Walker $16.95 (0-8027-8939-0). 32pp. Awake during a cold and lonely winter, Groundhog tricks his sensible, hibernating friends into waking up early only to have them plot an effective revenge. (Rev: BL 12/1/05; SLJ 12/05)

366 Daly, Niki. *Welcome to Zanzibar Road* (PS–3). 2006, Clarion $16.00 (0-618-64926-3). 32pp. A gentle story about the animals living in the busy community of Zanzibar Road, including Mama Jumbo, who adopts chicken Little Chiko. (Rev: BL 5/1/06; SLJ 7/06)

367 D'Amico, Carmela. *Ella Sets the Stage* (PS–1). Illus. by Steve D'Amico. 2006, Scholastic $16.99 (0-439-83152-0). 48pp. Ella the elephant is initially afraid of the forthcoming talent show, but discovers that she has a distinct gift for organization and planning. (Rev: BL 10/15/06; SLJ 10/06)

368 D'Amico, Carmela. *Ella Takes the Cake* (PS–K). Illus. by Steven D'Amico. 2005, Scholastic $16.99 (0-439-62794-X). 48pp. Ella the elephant wants to help out in her mother's bakery and finally proves she can be useful when she successfully delivers a cake to a customer. (Rev: BL 8/05; SLJ 9/05)

369 deGroat, Diane. *Brand-New Pencils, Brand-New Books* (PS–2). Illus. 2005, HarperCollins $15.99 (0-06-072613-X). 32pp. Gilbert's excitement about starting first grade is mixed with fears; but at the end of the day he recognizes that it wasn't all bad. (Rev: BL 8/05; SLJ 9/05)

370 deGroat, Diane. *No More Pencils, No More Books, No More Teacher's Dirty Looks!* (K–2). Series: Gilbert and Friends. 2006, HarperCollins $15.99 (0-06-079114-4). 32pp. As the end-of-school awards ceremony nears, Gilbert the possum worries there will be no prize for him. (Rev: BL 6/1–15/06; SLJ 6/06)

371 Delaney, Michael. *Birdbrain Amos, Mr. Fun* (2–3). Illus. by author. Series: Amos. 2006, Philomel $15.99 (0-399-24278-3). 160pp. Amos the hippo, determined to show Amoeba, the tick bird who lives on his head, that he's fun takes her — and her relatives and, more importantly, her imaginary friend — on a trip to the Serengeti. (Rev: SLJ 7/06)

372 Delessert, Etienne. *Alert!* (1–3). Illus. by author. 2007, Houghton $17.00 (978-0-618-73474-0). 31pp. A solitary mole called Tobias loves his pebble collection and is distraught when he hears from a so-called friend that there are robbers about.. (Rev: SLJ 4/07)

373 dePaola, Tomie. *Little Grunt and the Big Egg: A Prehistoric Fairy Tale* (PS–2). Illus. by author. 2006, Putnam $16.99 (0-399-24529-4). 32pp. A new edition of the story about the prehistoric boy who adopts a dinosaur called George. (Rev: BL 5/15/06)

374 DiCamillo, Kate. *Mercy Watson Goes for a Ride* (PS–2). Illus. by Chris Van Dusen. Series: Mercy Watson. 2006, Candlewick $12.99 (0-7636-2332-6). 80pp. Plump pig Mercy gives Mr. Watson an unexpectedly exciting ride in his pink Cadillac. (Rev: BL 5/1/06; SLJ 6/06)

375 Donnio, Sylviane. *I'd Really Like to Eat a Child* (PS–K). Trans. from French by Leslie Martin. Illus. by Dorothée de Monfreid. 2007, Random $14.99 (978-0-375-83761-6). A small crocodile tired of the food his mother offers says he would prefer to eat a child and sets off to do so. (Rev: SLJ 4/07)

376 Downey, Lynn. *Matilda's Humdinger* (1–3). Illus. by Tim Bowers. 2006, Knopf $15.95 (0-375-82403-0). Matilda the cat is a terrible waitress but a great storyteller. (Rev: SLJ 10/06)

377 Downey, Lynn. *The Tattletale* (PS–K). Illus. by Pam Paparone. 2006, Holt $16.95 (0-8050-7152-0). 32pp. Humorous art adds to the fun in this story about two pig brothers that carries a message about telling tales and bullying. (Rev: BL 11/1/06; SLJ 11/06)

378 Doyle, Malachy. *Big Pig* (PS–2). Illus. by John Bendall-Brunello. 2006, Simon & Schuster $19.95 (0-689-87484-7); paper $9.99 (0-689-87485-5). Pig has grown too big to keep in the house, so John Henry must take the ample porker to the local pig farm, but when John Henry has a mishap on the way home, Pig comes to the rescue. (Rev: SLJ 11/06)

379 Dunbar, Joyce. *Where's My Sock?* (PS–2). Illus. by Sanja Rescek. 2006, Scholastic $15.99 (0-439-74831-3). 32pp. Pippin the mouse can't find his yellow sock and enlists the help of Tog the cat; they find socks all over the house and match them all up (in a very colorful fold-out) only to discover the missing sock where they least expected. (Rev: BL 1/1–15/06; SLJ 2/06)

380 Edvall, Lilian. *The Rabbit Who Couldn't Find His Daddy* (PS–2). Trans. from Swedish by Elisahctli Kallick Dyssegaard. Illus. by Sara Gimbergsson. 2006, Farrar $16.00 (91-29-66429-2). Rabbit wakes up in the middle of the night and can't find Daddy, so he and his little sister set off to find him and get locked out of the house. (Rev: SLJ 4/06)

381 Edwards, Pamela Duncan. *The Mixed-Up Rooster* (PS). Illus. by Megan Lloyd. 2006, HarperCollins $15.99 (0-06-028999-6). 32pp. A rooster who prefers to stay up at night finds a new position on the farm in this entertaining story. (Rev: BL 7/06; SLJ 8/06)

382 Edwards, Pamela Duncan. *Ms. Bitsy Bat's Kindergarten* (PS–K). Illus. by Henry Cole. 2005, Hyperion $15.99 (0-7868-0669-9). 32pp. The second day of kindergarten proves stressful when the students learn that Mr. Fox won't be back. (Rev: BL 8/05; SLJ 8/05)

383 Edwards, Wallace. *The Extinct Files: My Science Project* (K–3). Illus. by author. 2006, Kids Can $17.95 (1-55337-971-3). Wally's science project reveals a great deal about contemporary dinosaurs' physical characteristics, habitat, diet, communication, and defenses — much of it unexpected. (Rev: SLJ 11/06)

384 Egan, Tim. *Roasted Peanuts* (1–3). Illus. 2006, Houghton $16.00 (0-618-33718-0). 32pp. Sam the horse and Jackson the cat are best friends who love baseball but although Jackson is a great pitcher only Sam is talented enough to make the team; Jackson gets a job selling peanuts, however, and his throwing skills have results. (Rev: BL 4/15/06; SLJ 5/06)

385 Elliott, L. M. *Hunter and Stripe and the Soccer Showdown* (PS–2). Illus. by Lynn Munsinger. 2005, HarperCollins $15.99 (0-06-052759-5). 32pp. The friendship between raccoons Hunter and Stripe is tested when they end up on rival soccer teams. (Rev: BL 9/1/05; SLJ 9/05)

386 Elya, Susan Middleton. *Sophie's Trophy* (PS–2). Illus. by Viviana Garofoli. 2006, Putnam $15.99 (0-399-24199-X). 32pp. Jealous of her brother who's won numerous awards for his good looks, Sophie the toad sings a solo at the county fair and wins a prize of her own. (Rev: BL 6/1–15/06; SLJ 8/06)

387 Emmett, Jonathan. *Diamond in the Snow* (PS–2). Illus. by Vanessa Cabban. 2007, Candlewick $15.99 (978-0-7636-3117-8). A young mole emerges from his hole to see his first snow, and decides that an icicle is a diamond. (Rev: SLJ 4/07)

388 Emmett, Jonathan. *I Love You Always and Forever* (PS–K). Illus. by Daniel Howarth. 2007, Scholastic $14.99 (978-0-439-91654-7). Father mouse Longtail and daughter Littletail spend an enjoyable day together that ends with reassurances of love; wonderful illustrations blend with the gentle text. (Rev: SLJ 4/07)

389 Emmett, Jonathan. *This Way, Ruby!* (PS). Illus. by Rebecca Harry. 2007, Scholastic $16.99 (978-0-439-87992-7). Ruby the duckling moves more slowly than her siblings but her powers of observation are keen, which proves a godsend when there is an unexpected storm. (Rev: BL 12/15/06; SLJ 2/07)

390 Erlbruch, Wolf. *The Miracle of the Bears* (K–2). Trans. from German by Michael Reynolds. Illus. by author. 2006, Europa paper $14.95 (1-933372-21-4). A young bear tackles — in an appropriately vague way — the perennial question of where babies come from; funny with a touch of romance. (Rev: SLJ 11/06)

391 Ernst, Lisa Campbell. *Sylvia Jean, Drama Queen* (PS–2). Illus. 2005, Dutton $16.99 (0-525-46962-1). 40pp. When a town-wide costume party is announced, everyone assumes that Sylvia Jean, a fashion-conscious piglet, will take home the grand prize for best costume. (Rev: BL 9/15/05; SLJ 9/05)

392 Evans, Cambria. *Martha Moth Makes Socks* (PS–2). Illus. by author. 2006, Houghton $16.00 (0-618-55745-8). In preparation for her birthday celebration with friends Flit and Flora, Martha Moth samples some of the delectable clothing items she plans to serve at the party, but she overdoes it, leaving little to share with her guests. (Rev: BL 5/1/06; SLJ 4/06)

393 Falconer, Ian. *Olivia Forms a Band* (PS–1). Illus. by author. 2006, Simon & Schuster $17.95 (1-4169-2454-X). 50pp. Disconsolate when she learns that there will be no band performing at the fireworks exhibition, Olivia the energetic pig comes up with a plan to supply the music all by herself. (Rev: BL 6/1–15/06; SLJ 6/06*)

394 Faller, Regis. *The Adventures of Polo* (PS–2). Illus. 2006, Roaring Brook $16.95 (1-59643-160-1). 80pp. In this wordless graphic novel, Polo the dog sets off in a tiny boat on a series of magical adventures. (Rev: BL 3/15/06; SLJ 6/06*)

395 Fleming, Denise. *The Cow Who Clucked* (PS–2). 2006, Holt $16.95 (0-8050-7265-9). 40pp. Cow awakens to find that she is clucking like a chicken and sets out to track down her missing "moo." (Rev: BL 9/1/06; SLJ 8/06*)

396 Foley, Greg. *Thank You Bear* (PS–K). Illus. 2007, Viking $15.99 (978-0-670-06165-5). 32pp. Bear is quite pleased with his latest find — a tiny, empty box — and is disappointed by his friends' reactions until he shows it to Mouse, who promptly curls up in it. (Rev: BL 4/15/07; SLJ 3/07*)

397 Fox, Diane, and Christyan Fox. *Tyson the Terrible* (PS–2). Illus. by authors. 2007, Bloomsbury $12.95 (978-1-58234-734-9). Far less formidable than the reputation that precedes him, Tyson the little Tyrannosaurus rex turns out to be just a lonely dinosaur looking for some friends. (Rev: SLJ 2/07)

398 Fraser, Mary Ann. *I.Q., It's Time* (PS–K). Illus. by author. 2005, Walker $15.95 (0-8027-8978-1). Adorable mouse I.Q. (last seen in 2003's *I.Q. Goes to the Library*) is back in the classroom, helping the children tell time as they get ready for Parents' Night. (Rev: SLJ 8/05)

399 Freeman, Don. *Earl the Squirrel* (PS–K). Illus. 2005, Viking $15.99 (0-670-06019-4). 48pp. Earl the squirrel must learn to find acorns on his own in this funny, action-packed posthumous story by the author of *Corduroy*. (Rev: BL 9/15/05; SLJ 10/05)

400 Friend, Catherine. *The Perfect Nest* (K–2). Illus. by John Manders. 2007, Candlewick $16.99 (978-0-7636-2430-9). Jack the cat has a longing for a lovely omelet and builds a perfect nest, which succeeds in drawing a chicken, a duck, and a goose, but sadly Jack's plan just won't work. (Rev: SLJ 3/07*)

401 Fuge, Charles. *Swim, Little Wombat, Swim!* (PS–K). Illus. by author. 2005, Sterling LB $12.95 (1-4027-2375-X). Little Wombat meets a platypus and learns how to swim as well as not to make snap judgements. (Rev: SLJ 11/05)

402 Galloway, Ruth. *Clumsy Crab* (PS–K). Illus. by author. 2005, Tiger Tales $15.95 (1-58925-050-8). Nipper the crab is not fond of his clumsy claws until he realizes they will allow him to save Octopus when he is entangled in seaweed. (Rev: SLJ 2/06)

403 Gantos, Jack. *Best in Show for Rotten Ralph* (1–3). Illus. by Nicole Rubel. Series: Rotten Ralph Rotten Reader. 2005, Farrar $15.00 (0-374-36358-7). 48pp. Rotten Ralph tries to get in shape so he can beat his horrible cousin Percy in the cat show. (Rev: BL 9/15/05; SLJ 8/05)

404 Gavril, David. *Penelope Nuthatch and the Big Surprise* (PS–2). Illus. 2006, Abrams $14.95 (0-8109-5762-0). 32pp. Penelope Nuthatch thinks her friend Luther is taking her to the ballet and spends time and money preening and primping; so she is very disappointed to find that her "unforgettable surprise" is a trip to a water park, and it takes a while for her to recover and join in. (Rev: BL 1/1–15/06; SLJ 2/06)

405 Gay, Marie-Louise. *Caramba* (K–3). Illus. 2005, Groundwood $16.95 (0-88899-667-5). 40pp. Caramba the cat is sad that he cannot to fly like the other cats, but then he finds out that unlike them he is able to swim! (Rev: BL 10/1/05; SLJ 11/05)

406 Geisert, Arthur. *Lights Out* (K–3). Illus. 2005, Houghton $16.00 (0-618-47892-2). 32pp. In this compelling, nearly wordless picture book, an ingenious little pig who's afraid of the dark figures out an elaborate contraption that will turn off his bedroom light after he's already fallen asleep. (Rev: BCCB 10/05; BL 11/1/05*; HB 11–12/05; HBG 4/06; SLJ 12/05)

407 Geisert, Arthur. *Oops* (K–3). 2006, Houghton $16.00 (0-618-60904-0). 32pp. Just a little spilled milk sets off a chain of events that destroys a pig family's house in this wordless story. (Rev: BL 9/1/06; SLJ 10/06)

408 Geraghty, Paul. *Rotten and Rascal: The Two Terrible Pterosaur Twins* (K–1). Illus. by author. 2006, Barron's $12.99 (0-7641-5918-6). Twin pterosaurs are forever squabbling noisily about which one is better, but the constant bickering takes on a whole new meaning when a T. rex tries to decide which of them is "the fattest, the juiciest, the crunchiest, the tastiest;" this cautionary tale is not for the faint of heart. (Rev: SLJ 8/06)

409 Gerritsen, Paula. *Nuts* (PS–2). Illus. 2006, Front St. $15.95 (1-932425-66-7). 32pp. With an autumn chill in the air, Mouse travels to the nut tree to gather food for the coming winter but discovers that all the nuts have blown away. (Rev: BL 3/1/06; SLJ 3/06)

410 Giffard, Hannah. *Pablo Goes Hunting* (1–3). Illus. 2005, Frances Lincoln $15.95 (1-84507-284-7). 32pp. Pablo the fox kit and his siblings Poppy and Pumpkin encounter numerous obstacles in their search for food; a spin-off from a cartoon series. (Rev: BL 9/1/05)

411 Goppel, Christine. *Anna Aphid* (PS–3). Illus. by author. 2005, North-South $16.95 (0-7358-2007-4). Anna Aphid enjoys an exciting tour of the world, which readers can see is simply a plant sitting on a windowsill. (Rev: SLJ 3/06)

412 Gorbachev, Valeri. *Big Little Elephant* (K–2). Illus. 2005, Harcourt $16.00 (0-15-205195-3). 32pp. Little Elephant finds his size can be a real obstacle when it comes to playing with his newfound friends. (Rev: BL 10/1/05; SLJ 9/05)

413 Gorbachev, Valeri. *Heron and Turtle* (PS–2). Illus. by author. 2006, Philomel $15.99 (0-399-24321-6). Heron and Turtle are close friends despite their difference in size. (Rev: SLJ 11/06)

414 Gravett, Emily. *Wolves* (PS–2). Illus. by author. 2006, Simon & Schuster $15.95 (1-4169-1491-9). 40pp. A rabbit is so engrossed in reading the book about wolves that he borrowed from the library that he doesn't realize he's face to face with a real live wolf. (Rev: BL 12/1/06; SLJ 8/06*)

415 Greene, Stephanie. *Pig Pickin'* (1–3). Illus. by Joe Mathieu. Series: Moose and Hildy. 2006, Marshall Cavendish $14.99 (0-7614-5324-5). 56pp. Hildy the pig asks Moose to join her on a trip down south to a pig pickin', an event she mistakenly believes is a porcine beauty contest. (Rev: SLJ 10/06)

416 Gretz, Susanna. *Riley and Rose in the Picture* (K–3). Illus. 2005, Candlewick $16.99 (0-7636-2681-3). 32pp. Riley the dog and Rose the cat, natural antagonists, try to get along by drawing pictures inside on a rainy day. (Rev: BL 8/05; SLJ 9/05)

417 Gusti. *Half of an Elephant* (K–3). Illus. by author. 2006, Kane/Miller $15.95 (1-933605-09-X). A wacky, inventively illustrated tale of a world split in two, as the front half of an odd-looking elephant desperately tries to find its back half. (Rev: SLJ 9/06)

418 Hager, Sarah. *Dancing Matilda* (PS–2). Illus. by Kelly Murphy. 2005, HarperCollins $15.99 (0-06-051452-3). A little kangaroo named Matilda dances her way through the pages of this book with rhyming text and lovely illustrations. (Rev: SLJ 8/05)

419 Hample, Stoo. *I Will Kiss You: Lots and Lots and Lots!* (PS). 2005, Candlewick $15.99 (0-7636-2787-9). 32pp. A mother bunny enumerates the many opportunities each day offers for planting a kiss on her toddler. (Rev: BL 2/1/06; SLJ 5/06)

420 Harper, Jamie. *Miss Mingo and the First Day of School* (K–3). Illus. by author. 2006, Candlewick $15.99 (0-7636-2410-1). On the first day of school, Miss Mingo the flamingo and her animal students discuss the characteristics that make them special and different. (Rev: SLJ 8/06)

421 Harrison, David L. *Farmer's Dog Goes to the Forest: Rhymes for Two Voices* (K–3). Illus. by Arden Johnson-Petrov. 2005, Boyds Mills $15.95 (1-59078-242-9). 32pp. A farmer's dog exchanges simple rhyming questions and answers with the animals in this sequel to *Farmer's Garden* (2005). (Rev: BL 9/1/05; SLJ 9/05)

422 Hartland, Jessie. *Clementine in the City* (PS–K). Illus. 2005, Viking $15.99 (0-670-05929-3). 40pp. Tired of small town life, Clementine the poodle comes New York to join the circus and finds much to enjoy in the big city. (Rev: BL 8/05; SLJ 8/05)

423 Harvey, Damian. *Just the Thing!* (PS). Illus. by Lynne Chapman. 2005, Gingham Dog $15.95 (0-7696-4300-0). Big Gorilla, irritated by a pesky itch on his back, travels far and wide in search of relief but finally finds a cure back home. (Rev: SLJ 1/06)

424 Hayward, Linda. *The King's Chorus* (PS–2). Illus. by Jennifer P. Goldfinger. 2006, Clarion $16.00 (0-618-51618-2). 32pp. Kadoodle the rooster keeps the whole barnyard awake with his constant crowing until Honketta the goose comes up with a solution. (Rev: BL 2/15/07)

425 Heinz, Brian. *Red Fox at McCloskey's Farm* (K–4). Illus. by Chris Sheban. 2006, Creative Editions $17.95 (1-56846-195-X). 30pp. In this action-packed rhyming tale, Farmer McCloskey and his hound dog foil Fox's plan to raid the hen house. (Rev: SLJ 11/06)

426 Hill, Karen. *I Am Good at Being Me* (K–2). Illus. by Renee Graef. 2005, Simon & Schuster $9.99 (1-4169-0512-X); paper $3.99 (1-4169-0319-

4). 24pp. A tiny bird struggles to find out what God's purpose is for her life in this faith-based easy-reader. (Rev: BL 10/1/05)

427 Hill, Ros. *Shamoo: A Whale of a Cow* (PS–2). Illus. by author. 2005, Milk & Cookies $15.95 (0-689-04634-0). After running away from the farm, a water-loving cow named Shamoo heads for the ocean where he befriends a humpback whale and learns the ways of the sea but finds he's longing for home. (Rev: SLJ 11/05)

428 Hill, Susanna Leonard. *Punxsutawney Phyllis* (K–3). Illus. by Jeffrey Ebbeler. 2005, Holiday $16.95 (0-8234-1872-3). 32pp. Punxsutawney Phyllis, a groundhog, hopes to take over the weather forecasting duties long performed by her Uncle Phil. (Rev: BL 12/1/05; SLJ 10/05)

429 Hillenbrand, Jane. *What a Treasure!* (PS–K). Illus. by Will Hillenbrand. 2006, Holiday House $16.95 (0-8234-1896-0). When Mole gets a new shovel he begins to dig for treasure; he finds lots of things for his friends (twigs, shells, nuts) but the best treasure is his own — a new mole friend. (Rev: SLJ 4/06)

430 Hillenbrand, Will. *My Book Box* (PS–K). Illus. by author. 2006, Harcourt $16.00 (0-15-202029-2). A diminutive elephant finds a cardboard box and considers all the things that he might be able to do with it before finally deciding to make it into a book box. (Rev: SLJ 10/06)

431 Hills, Tad. *Duck, Duck, Goose* (PS–1). Illus. by author. 2006, Random $14.95 (0-375-83611-X). A foolish duck and a goose squabble over a spotted ball they think is an egg, but finally realize their mistake and become friends. (Rev: BL 3/1/07; SLJ 1/06)

432 Himmelman, John. *Tudley Didn't Know* (PS–2). Illus. by author. 2006, Sylvan Dell $15.95 (0-9764943-6-1). 32pp. Because he doesn't know he can't, Tudley the turtle is ready to try anything — flying, singing, hopping, and so forth. (Rev: BL 5/15/06; SLJ 8/06)

433 Hobbie, Holly. *Toot and Puddle: Wish You Were Here* (PS–3). Illus. by author. 2005, Little, Brown $16.99 (0-316-36602-1). Stung by a bee while off on an exotic trip, Toot the pig turns violet and must be nursed back to health by his friends Puddle and Opal. (Rev: SLJ 10/05)

434 Hockinson, Liz. *Marcello the Movie Mouse* (1–3). Illus. by Kathryn Otoshi. 2006, KO Kids $16.95 (0-9723946-2-1). Marcello Mousetriani, a tiny mouse who lives in a movie theater, works feverishly to realize his dream of making a film of his own. (Rev: SLJ 9/06)

435 Holabird, Katharine. *Angelina at the Palace* (K–2). Illus. by Helen Craig. Series: Angelina Ballerina. 2005, Viking $12.99 (0-670-06048-8). When her dance teacher falls ill, Angelina the mouse must teach a special dance to three of Mouseland's princesses. (Rev: SLJ 10/05)

436 Horacek, Petr. *Silly Suzy Goose* (PS–1). Illus. 2006, Candlewick $14.99 (0-7636-3040-3). 32pp. Suzy Goose longs to be different and imagines herself as all kinds of other animals, but a frightening encounter with a lion convinces her that there is safety in numbers; exuberant art enhances the fun. (Rev: BL 2/15/06*; HBG 10/06; SLJ 4/06)

437 Horse, Harry. *Little Rabbit Runaway* (PS–K). Illus. 2005, Peachtree $15.95 (1-56145-343-9). 32pp. Upset when his parents scold him, Little Rabbit runs away from home, but it's not long before he wishes he could return. (Rev: BL 10/1/05; SLJ 9/05)

438 Howe, James. *Rabbit-cadabra!* (2–4). Illus. by Jeff Mack. Series: Bunnicula and Friends. 2006, Simon & Schuster $14.95 (0-689-85727-6). 42pp. An easy chapter book about Chester, Howie, and Harold's plan to outsmart a magician who's bringing his vampire-bunny act to Toby's school. (Rev: SLJ 6/06)

439 Hume, Lachie. *Clancy the Courageous Cow* (PS–2). Illus. 2007, Greenwillow $16.99 (978-0-06-117249-6). 32pp. An outcast among his fellow Belted Galloway cattle because he has no belt, Clancy is in despair until he uses his unique appearance to infiltrate the neighboring Hereford herd, with which the Belted Galloways have long been feuding. (Rev: BL 3/15/07; SLJ 3/07)

440 Hunter, Jana Novotny. *I Can Do It!* (PS). Illus. by Lucy Richards. 2006, Frances Lincoln $15.95 (1-84507-127-1). Little Guinea Pig has a satisfying day at preschool, finding perfect activities to match his moods. (Rev: SLJ 8/06)

441 Jenkins, Emily. *Love You When You Whine* (PS). Illus. by Sergio Ruzzier. 2006, Farrar $15.00 (0-374-34652-6). A mother cat loves her little daughter no matter what mischief she does — from whining and painting the walls to having a terrible tantrum. (Rev: SLJ 10/06)

442 Jenkins, Emily. *Plonk, Plonk, Plonk! A Bea and HaHa Book* (PS). Illus. by Tomek Bogacki. 2006, Farrar $5.95 (0-374-30585-4). HaHa the ferret wants to play, but his friend, Bea the hippo, refuses to be tempted away from her piano practice. (Rev: SLJ 9/06)

443 Johansen, Hanna. *The Duck and the Owl* (1–3). Illus. by Kathi Bhend. 2005, Godine $17.95 (1-56792-285-6). 72pp. A duck and an owl dance around the idea of friendship but find their different behaviors and characteristics difficult to overcome. (Rev: BL 1/1–15/06; SLJ 2/06)

444 Keller, Holly. *Nosy Rosie* (PS). 2006, Greenwillow $16.99 (0-06-078758-9). 32pp. Nosy Rosie's super-sensitive fox nose comes in handy one day when a baby is lost in the woods. (Rev: BL 7/06; SLJ 9/06*)

445 Keller, Holly. *Sophie's Window* (PS–2). Illus. 2005, Greenwillow $15.99 (0-06-056282-X). 32pp. When Caruso, a little pigeon who is afraid to fly, is blown out of his family home, he is rescued by a nice dog called Sophie. (Rev: BL 9/15/05; SLJ 8/05)

446 Kelley, Ellen A. *Buckamoo Girls* (2–4). Illus. by Tom Curry. 2006, Abrams $15.95 (0-8109-5471-0). Cows Susanna and Joanna imagine themselves as the Buckamoo Girls, two adventurous cowgirls having a rollicking good time in the Wild, Wild West. (Rev: SLJ 1/07)

447 Kelley, Ellen A. *My Life as a Chicken* (PS–2). Illus. by Michael Slack. 2007, Harcourt $16.00 (978-0-15-205306-2). 40pp. In this action-packed picture-book story told in rhyming text, chicken Pauline Poulet is constantly on the move, bouncing from one near-tragedy to the next in an adventure that includes pirates, a typhoon, and a balloon ride. (Rev: BL 4/1/07)

448 Kempter, Christa. *Dear Little Lamb* (PS–2). Trans. from German by Michelle Maczka. Illus. by Frauke Weldin. 2006, North-South $16.95 (0-7358-2086-4). A clever wolf strikes up a pen-pal relationship with a young lamb, hoping eventually for a tasty meal, but the lamb's smart mother sees the danger and scuppers the wolf's plot. (Rev: SLJ 10/06)

449 Kim, Byung-Gyu, and K. T. Hao. *The 100th Customer* (PS–2). Illus. by Giuliano Ferri. 2005, Purple Bear $15.95 (1-933327-03-0). 32pp. In this heartwarming tale about the power of generosity, Ben Bear and Chris Croc, co-owners of a pizza restaurant arrange to help a hungry boy and his grandmother. (Rev: BL 11/1/05; SLJ 1/06)

450 Kindermans, Martine. *You and Me* (PS). Trans. by Sasha Quinton. Illus. by author. 2006, Philomel $15.99 (0-399-24471-9). A mother goose expresses her love for her gosling in this gentle book with lovely watercolor art. (Rev: SLJ 1/06)

451 Kitamura, Satoshi. *Igor: The Bird Who Couldn't Sing* (PS–2). Illus. by author. 2005, Farrar $16.00 (0-374-33558-3). Igor is sad that he can't sing as well as the other birds until he finds a Dodo who appreciates his voice. (Rev: SLJ 9/05)

452 Kitamura, Satoshi. *Pablo the Artist* (K–2). Illus. 2006, Farrar $16.00 (0-374-35687-4). 32pp. Pablo the elephant can't find a suitable subject for a painting to exhibit at the art show until a dream leaves him overflowing with inspiration. (Rev: BL 2/15/06; SLJ 2/06)

453 Kleven, Elisa. *The Wishing Ball* (PS–K). Illus. 2006, Farrar $16.00 (0-374-38449-5). 32pp. Convinced that a rubber ball will bring her luck, Nellie, a stray cat, follows the bouncing ball and succeeds in finds a happy new life. (Rev: BL 2/1/06; SLJ 2/06)

454 Klise, Kate. *Why Do You Cry? Not a Sob Story* (PS–2). Illus. by M. Sarah Klise. 2006, Holt $16.95 (0-8050-7319-1). 32pp. Little Rabbit finds out that crying's OK when others reveal what makes them cry. (Rev: BL 5/1/06; SLJ 7/06)

455 Knister. *A Promise Is a Promise* (PS–1). Trans. from German by Kathryn Bishop. Illus. by Eve Tharlet. 2006, Minedition $15.99 (0-698-40040-2). Bruno the marmot befriends a bright yellow dandelion and, when she has gone to seed, honors her wish that he blow her seeds away, although this worries him greatly. (Rev: SLJ 8/06)

456 Knudsen, Michelle. *Library Lion* (PS–2). Illus. by Kevin Hawkes. 2006, Candlewick $15.99 (0-7636-2262-1). 48pp. Miss Merriweather, the head librarian, is very particular about the library's rules, but she's not sure what to do when a lion pays a visit. (Rev: BL 8/06; SLJ 8/06*)

457 Kortepeter, Paul. *Oliver's Red Toboggan* (PS–1). Illus. by Susan Wheeler. 2006, Dutton $15.99 (0-525-47752-7). Oliver is not good about sharing his sled when he and his bunny sister Emily have a snow day, but the two hear their mother's urging and later offer to help other animals harmed by the storm. (Rev: SLJ 12/06)

458 Kressley, Carson. *You're Different and That's Super* (PS–1). Illus. by Jared Lee. 2005, Simon & Schuster $12.95 (1-4169-0070-5). 64pp. Trumpet is different from all the other foals — he has a horn — and he suffers prejudice until his uniqueness comes in handy when fire strikes the farm. (Rev: SLJ 5/06)

459 Krishnaswami, Uma. *Remembering Grandpa* (K–3). Illus. by Layne Johnson. 2007, Boyds Mills $16.95 (978-1-59078-424-2). A little rabbit tries to ease her grandmother's grief over her husband's death. (Rev: SLJ 4/07)

460 Kroll, Steven. *Jungle Bullies* (PS–1). Illus. by Vincent Nguyen. 2006, Marshall Cavendish $16.99 (0-7614-5297-4). Mama Monkey teaches the bullying bigger animals a lesson about sharing. (Rev: SLJ 11/06)

461 Kroll, Virginia. *On the Way to Kindergarten* (PS–2). Illus. by Elisabeth Schlossberg. 2006, Putnam $15.99 (0-399-24168-X). 32pp. As Bear gets ready to go to kindergarten, rhyming couplets celebrate the many milestones in his first five years of development. (Rev: BL 2/15/06; SLJ 3/06)

462 Kroll, Virginia. *Really Rabbits* (PS–2). Illus. by Philomena O'Neill. 2006, Charlesbridge $16.95 (1-57091-897-X); paper $6.95 (1-57091-898-8). 32pp. Pet rabbits Tulip and Snuggle mystify their human owners when they help out around the house during the night in hopes of getting more attention during the day. (Rev: BL 7/06; SLJ 8/06)

463 Kromhout, Rindert. *Little Donkey and the Baby-Sitter* (PS–K). Trans. by Marianne Martens. Illus. by Annemarie van Haeringen. 2006, North-South $15.95 (0-7358-2057-0). A little donkey causes all sorts of trouble for his hen baby-sitter in this gentle and amusing book. (Rev: SLJ 7/06)

464 Krupinski, Loretta. *Pirate Treasure* (PS–2). Illus. 2006, Dutton $15.99 (0-525-47579-6). 40pp. When a storm drives their pirate ship upriver, Captain Oliver and First Mate Rosie, both mice, decide to trade their buccaneering ways for life as farmers. (Rev: BL 2/15/06; SLJ 3/06)

465 Kulka, Joe. *Wolf's Coming!* (PS). Illus. 2007, Carolrhoda $15.95 (978-1-57505-930-3). 32pp. Word spreads among the woodland animals that the wolf is coming and they all scurry inside, but only to give him a pleasant surprise on his birthday. (Rev: BL 4/15/07)

466 Kuper, Peter. *Theo and the Blue Note* (PS–4). Illus. by author. 2006, Viking $15.99 (0-670-06137-9). Theo the saxophone-playing cat has only mastered one blue note, but when he is transported to a jazz festival on the moon he sits in on a session with such greats as Nat King Cobra and Duck Ellington. (Rev: SLJ 10/06)

467 Lamb, Albert. *Sam's Winter Hat* (PS). Illus. by David McPhail. 2006, Scholastic $6.99 (0-439-79304-1). 32pp. Sam Bear is very forgetful and needs the help of his family and friends to find all of his misplaced items, including the blue winter hat his Grandma made. (Rev: BL 12/1/06; SLJ 10/06)

468 Landolf, Diane Wright. *Hog and Dog* (PS–K). Illus. by Jennifer Beck Harris. Series: Step into Reading. 2005, Random LB $11.99 (0-375-93165-1); paper $3.99 (0-375-83165-7). 32pp. Hog and Dog are good friends despite the occasional disagreement in this fast-paced book for beginning readers. (Rev: BL 10/15/05)

469 Landry, Leo. *Fat Bat and Swoop* (1–3). Illus. by author. 2005, Holt $15.95 (0-8050-7003-6). 64pp. Full of mischief, Fat Bat and Swoop the owl scare Emily the cow only to find themselves scared by Emily in return. (Rev: SLJ 12/05)

470 Landstrom, Lena. *Boo and Baa Have Company* (PS–2). Trans. by Joan Sandin. Illus. by Olof Landstrom. 2006, Farrar $15.00 (9-129-66546-9). 40pp. Comical mishaps ensue when sheep Boo and Baa attempt to rescue a cat stuck in a tree and to do some vacuuming. (Rev: BL 8/06; HB 9–10/06; HBG 4/07; SLJ 9/06)

471 Landstrom, Lena. *Four Hens and a Rooster* (PS–2). Trans. by Joan Sandin. Illus. by Olof Landstrom. 2005, Farrar $16.00 (91-29-66336-9). 28pp. Tired of being pushed around by a bullying rooster, four hens take a class in self-esteem. (Rev: BL 10/1/05; SLJ 12/05)

472 Layne, Steven L. *Love the Baby* (PS–K). Illus. by Ard Hoyt. 2007, Pelican $15.95 (978-1-58980-392-3). 32pp. A young rabbit has trouble adjusting to the arrival of his new sibling. (Rev: BL 4/1/07)

473 Lester, Helen. *Batter Up Wombat* (PS–K). Illus. by Lynn Munsinger. 2006, Houghton $16.00 (0-618-73784-7). 32pp. Wordplay abounds in this story of an Australian wombat whose efforts to play ball are unusual, but whose skill at digging tunnels is much appreciated when the National Wildlife League game is interrupted by a tornado. (Rev: BL 9/15/06; SLJ 10/06)

474 Lester, Helen. *Tacky and the Winter Games* (PS–2). Illus. by Lynn Munsinger. 2005, Houghton $16.00 (0-618-55659-1). 32pp. The wacky behavior of Tacky, a very independent-minded penguin, could cost his teammates the chance to win a medal at the Winter Games. (Rev: BL 9/1/05; SLJ 10/05)

475 Lewis, Gill. *The Most Precious Thing* (PS). Illus. by Louise Ho. 2006, Good Bks. $16.00 (1-56148-534-9). Little Bear and her mother stroll through the woods identifying precious things — the daughter being the most precious of all. (Rev: SLJ 12/06)

476 Lewis, Kevin. *Dinosaur Dinosaur* (PS–2). Illus. by Daniel Kirk. 2006, Scholastic $15.99 (0-439-60371-4). 32pp. A dinosaur kid has a typical dinosaur (human) day in rhyming text and humorous art full of details like "The Dinosaur Times" newspaper, Dino Puffs cereal, and a "trilobite farm." (Rev: BL 2/1/06; SLJ 3/06)

477 Lies, Brian. *Bats at the Beach* (K–2). 2006, Houghton $16.00 (0-618-55744-X). 32pp. A family of bats spends a pleasant night at the beach, using "moon-tan lotion" and eating "bug-mallows." (Rev: BL 8/06; SLJ 6/06)

478 Lincoln, Hazel. *Little Elephant's Trunk* (PS–K). Illus. by author. 2006, Albert Whitman $15.95 (0-8075-4591-0). A baby elephant unsure what to do with his trunk watches his elders and experiments. (Rev: SLJ 10/06)

479 Lloyd, Sam. *Mr. Pusskins: A Love Story* (PS–2). Illus. by author. 2006, Simon & Schuster $14.95 (1-4169-2517-1). 32pp. Tired of the smothering love of his young owner, Mr. Pusskins the cat sets off to see what life is like outside his narrowly defined world, but he soon longs for the comforts of home. (Rev: BL 11/1/06; HBG 4/07; SLJ 1/07)

480 Lobel, Gill. *Too Small for Honey Cake* (PS–2). Illus. by Sebastien Braun. 2006, Harcourt $16.00 (0-15-206097-9). 32pp. Little Fox is sad when he thinks the new baby has taken his place in Daddy Fox's heart. (Rev: BL 9/1/06; SLJ 10/06)

481 Lobel, Gillian. *Little Honey Bear and the Smiley Moon* (PS–2). Illus. by Tim Warnes. 2006, Good Bks. $16.00 (1-56148-533-0). Little Honey Bear, Lily Long Ears, and Teeny Tiny Mouse hope to visit the moon but become lost in the dark woods and are eventually rescued by Mommy Bear. (Rev: SLJ 11/06)

482 Loomis, Christine. *Hattie Hippo* (PS). Illus. by Robert Neubecker. 2006, Scholastic $16.99 (0-439-54340-1). 32pp. Four episodes follow Hattie the young hippo through a series of minor mishaps. (Rev: BL 8/06; SLJ 8/06)

483 Lund, Deb. *All Aboard the Dinotrain* (K–2). Illus. by Howard Fine. 2006, Harcourt $16.00 (0-15-205237-2). 40pp. In this spirited sequel to *Dinosailors* (2003), a band of adventurous dinosaurs goes for a memorable ride on a runaway train. (Rev: BL 4/1/06; SLJ 5/06)

484 McAllister, Angela. *Brave Bitsy and the Bear* (PS–3). Illus. by Tiphanie Beeke. 2006, Clarion $16.00 (0-618-63994-2). 29pp. Grateful for the help of a big bear who helped her to get back home when she was lost in the woods, Bitsy the toy bunny finds a way to repay his kindness. (Rev: SLJ 10/06)

485 McAllister, Angela. *Take a Kiss to School* (PS). Illus. by Sue Hellard. 2006, Bloomsbury $15.95 (1-58234-702-6). 32pp. Digby the mole's mother gives him a reassuring collection of kisses to build up his courage for his second day at school. (Rev: BL 8/06; SLJ 7/06)

486 McCully, Emily Arnold. *School* (PS–K). Illus. 2005, HarperCollins $15.99 (0-06-623856-0). 32pp. Bitty the mouse follows her older siblings to school and has a happy time in this new version of the 1987 wordless classic that features brief text and a larger format. (Rev: BL 8/05; SLJ 9/05)

487 MacDonald, Alan. *Wilfred to the Rescue* (PS–K). Illus. by Lizzie Sanders. 2006, Simon & Schuster $15.95 (1-4169-0901-X). 32pp. When Sissy the vole goes missing after a flood in Brambly Hedge, Wilfred the mouse sets off to find her and bring her home; this picture book is "based on the world created by Jill Barklem." (Rev: BL 3/1/06; SLJ 3/06)

488 McDonnell, Patrick. *The Gift of Nothing* (1–4). Illus. by author. 2005, Little, Brown $14.99 (0-316-11488-X). Mooch the cat puzzles over an appropriate gift for Earl, a dog who has everything in this book featuring the characters from the "Mutts" comic strip. (Rev: SLJ 1/06)

489 McDonnell, Patrick. *Just Like Heaven* (K–3). Illus. by author. 2006, Little, Brown $14.99 (0-316-11493-6). In this sequel to *The Gift of Nothing*, Mooch the cat awakens from a nap to find himself surrounded by fog and, hearing children laughing and smelling perfume, assumes he's in heaven. (Rev: SLJ 11/06)

490 McGuinness-Kelly, Tracy-Lee. *Bad Cat Puts on His Top Hat* (PS–2). Illus. 2005, Little, Brown $15.99 (0-316-60547-6). 32pp. Bad Cat, a mischievous but well-meaning feline, has a series of adventures in his hometown, which he calls the Big Stinky. (Rev: BL 7/05; SLJ 8/05)

491 McMillan, Bruce. *The Problem with Chickens* (PS–2). Illus. by Gunnella. 2005, Houghton $16.00

(0-618-58581-8). 32pp. The chickens bought by the women of an Icelandic village begin to act more like their owners than like birds. (Rev: BL 9/15/05; SLJ 9/05*)

492 McPhail, David. *Big Brown Bear Goes to Town* (PS–1). Illus. by author. 2006, Harcourt $16.00 (0-15-205317-4). 40pp. Big Brown Bear has an idea to protect his friend Rat's car from the elements, so together the two go into town to get the necessary materials. (Rev: BL 6/1–15/06; SLJ 5/06)

493 Martin, David. *All for Pie, Pie for All* (PS–2). Illus. by Valeri Gorbachev. 2006, Candlewick $15.99 (0-7636-2393-8). 32pp. After the cat family enjoys an apple pie cooked by Grandma Cat, the remaining piece is carted away by Grandma Mouse, who sees that her whole family is fed, leaving a tiny piece that provides a satisfying meal for a family of ants. (Rev: BL 9/15/06)

494 Mercer, Peggy. *Ten Cows to Texas* (K–2). Illus. by Bill Crews. 2005, Handprint $16.95 (1-59354-116-3). 40pp. With dreams of stardom dancing in their heads, Mimi the cow and nine of her bovine sisters embark on a road trip from Lonesome Cow, Georgia, to an audition in El Paso, Texas. (Rev: BL 12/1/05; SLJ 11/05)

495 Meserve, Adria. *No Room for Napoleon* (K–2). Illus. 2006, Farrar $16.00 (0-374-35536-3). 32pp. A pushy dog named Napoleon is welcomed to an island by its first settlers — Crab, Bunny, and Bear — but the Napoleon's bossy ways soon force the trio to search for a new home. (Rev: BL 3/1/06; SLJ 5/06)

496 Miller, Pat. *Substitute Groundhog* (K–3). Illus. by Kathi Ember. 2006, Albert Whitman $15.95 (0-8075-7643-3). Sidelined by the flu just before his big weather-predicting day, Groundhog auditions other animals to replace him. (Rev: SLJ 12/06)

497 Moncomble, Gérard. *Pippin* (PS–2). Trans. by Alexandra Simon. Illus. by Xavière Devos. 2006, North-South $15.95 (0-7358-2062-7). Pippin the kitten is normal in most respects but he cannot purr. (Rev: SLJ 4/06)

498 Moon, Nicola. *Alligator Tails and Crocodile Cakes* (1–3). Illus. by Andy Ellis. Series: I Am Reading. 2005, Kingfisher paper $3.95 (0-7534-5853-5). 48pp. Two short stories for beginning readers star Alligator and Crocodile, who play a game of hide-and-seek (difficult with those long revealing tails!) and bake a cake. (Rev: BL 12/1/05; SLJ 9/05)

499 Morgan, Michaela. *Dear Bunny* (K–2). Illus. by Caroline Jayne Church. 2006, Scholastic $15.99 (0-439-74833-X). 32pp. Tino and Teeny, two shy but lovestruck bunnies, leave each other love notes that are shredded by a family of mice building a nest; all ends well when the mice realize what they have done and make amends. (Rev: BL 2/1/06; SLJ 1/06)

500 Morton-Shaw, Christine, and Greg Shaw. *Wake Up, Sleepy Bear!* (PS–K). Illus. by John Butler. 2006, Viking $12.99 (0-670-06175-1). In this gentle tale told in rhyming verse, young woodland animals awaken from sleep and are urged to assemble to welcome a newborn fawn. (Rev: SLJ 11/06)

501 Mozelle, Shirley. *The Bear Upstairs* (PS–3). Illus. by Doug Cushman. 2005, Holt $16.95 (0-8050-6820-1). A bear moving into a new apartment makes so much noise that his downstairs neighbor, also a bear, goes to complain, but the two find they have much in common and end up sitting down to breakfast together. (Rev: SLJ 11/05)

502 Muntean, Michaela. *Do Not Open This Book!* (K–3). Illus. by Pascal LeMaitre. 2006, Scholastic $15.99 (0-439-66037-4). 32pp. The action here centers on a cranky pink pig/would-be author who objects to those who are trying to read his work in progress; the simple process of turning the pages draws the reader into the story. (Rev: BL 3/15/06)

503 Murray, Marjorie Dennis. *Hippo Goes Bananas!* (PS–1). Illus. by Kevin O'Malley. 2006, Marshall Cavendish $14.95 (0-7614-5224-9). Hippo has a toothache, and his strange behavior unnerves the other animals in this cumulative tale. (Rev: SLJ 5/06)

504 Napoli, Donna Jo, and Eva Furrow. *Bobby the Bold* (PS–2). Illus. by Ard Hoyt. 2006, Dial $16.99 (0-8037-2990-1). 32pp. Ignored by the chimps with which he's quartered at the zoo, Bobby the bonobo escapes to visit a hair salon for a makeover that he hopes will help him to fit in; cartoon-style art animates this lesson about being different. (Rev: BL 4/1/06; SLJ 6/06)

505 Nitto, Tomio. *The Red Rock: A Graphic Fable* (K–2). 2006, Groundwood $15.95 (0-88899-669-1). 32pp. To save his beloved valley from destruction by developers, Old Beaver and his animal friends mount a campaign to block the project. (Rev: BL 4/15/06; LMC 11–12/06)

506 Noguès, Jean-Come. *House for a Mouse* (PS–2). Trans. by J. Alison James. Illus. by Anne Velghe. 2005, North-South $15.95 (0-7358-2017-1). While searching for a home of her own, Little Mouse encounters an artist and agrees to pose as his model. (Rev: SLJ 11/05)

507 Nolan, Janet. *A Father's Day Thank You* (PS–K). Illus. by Kathi Ember. 2007, Albert Whitman $15.95 (978-0-8075-2291-2). 32pp. For Father's Day, Harvey the bear cub decides to do a drawing of all the things his dad has done for him. (Rev: BL 4/1/07)

508 Numeroff, Laura. *If You Give a Pig a Party* (PS–2). Illus. by Felicia Bond. 2005, HarperCollins $15.99 (0-06-028326-2). 32pp. The enthusiastic protagonist of *If You Give a Pig a Pancake* (1998) is back, this time wanting a better and better party. (Rev: BL 10/15/05)

509 Odanaka, Barbara. *Smash! Mash! Crash! There Goes the Trash!* (PS–2). Illus. by Will Hillenbrand. 2006, Simon & Schuster $15.95 (0-689-85160-X). 32pp. From their bedroom, two little pigs watch a pair of garbage trucks making their early morning rounds, picking up everything from old furniture to stinky diapers; rhyming text and expressive illustrations add to the fun. (Rev: BL 12/1/06; SLJ 11/06)

510 Oh, Jiwon. *Mr. Monkey's Classroom* (K–2). Illus. 2005, HarperCollins $14.99 (0-06-055721-4). 32pp. On his first day at school, Mouse becomes jealous when his friend Cat — one year older — rushes off to join old friends; a sequel to *Cat and Mouse: A Delicious Tale* (2003). (Rev: BL 8/05)

511 Ohi, Ruth. *Clara and the Bossy* (PS–2). Illus. 2006, Firefly LB $19.95 (1-55037-943-7); paper $5.95 (1-55037-942-9). 32pp. Clara the guinea pig learns some important lessons about being true to herself when a bossy new friend's demands become too much. (Rev: BL 8/06)

512 O'Keefe, Susan Heyboer. *Baby Day* (PS). Illus. by Robin Spowart. 2006, Boyds Mills $15.95 (1-59078-981-0). 32pp. A day in the life of a baby bear looked after by loving parents. (Rev: BL 3/1/06)

513 Palatini, Margie. *Bad Boys Get Cookie!* (K–3). Illus. by Henry Cole. 2006, HarperCollins $16.99 (0-06-074436-7). Wolves Willy and Wally — last seen in *Bad Boys* (2003) — pass themselves off as detectives and set go off in pursuit of a cookie that's run away from the bakery. (Rev: SLJ 10/06)

514 Palatini, Margie. *Oink?* (PS–2). Illus. by Henry Cole. 2006, Simon & Schuster $15.95 (0-689-86258-X). 40pp. Two pigs — Thomas and Joseph — successfully resist the other farm animals' pressure to get in shape. (Rev: BL 3/15/06; SLJ 3/06)

515 Palatini, Margie. *Shelly* (PS–2). Illus. by Guy Francis. 2006, Dutton $15.99 (0-525-47565-6). 32pp. Reluctant duckling Shelly remains in his shell while his three slightly older siblings are already developing their own personalities. (Rev: BL 2/1/06; SLJ 2/06)

516 Parr, Todd. *Otto Goes to School* (PS). Illus. 2005, Little, Brown $9.99 (0-316-83533-1). 24pp. Otto, the colorful dog with many human characteristics, heads off for his first day at school. (Rev: BL 8/05; SLJ 9/05)

517 Pearson, Susan. *Slugs in Love* (K–2). Illus. by Kevin O'Malley. 2006, Marshall Cavendish $16.99 (0-7614-5311-3). Marylou, a shy garden slug, writes love poems in slime to a slug named Herbie, but his replies keep going astray and she doesn't know how he feels about her until they finally meet at a tomato. (Rev: SLJ 3/07*)

518 Pedersen, Janet. *Pino and the Signora's Pasta* (PS–1). Illus. 2005, Candlewick $16.99 (0-7636-2396-2). 32pp. Tired of the pasta the Signora serves each night, Pino the cat searches Rome for culinary treats only to realize that good food isn't everything. (Rev: BL 9/1/05; SLJ 9/05)

519 Pennypacker, Sara. *Pierre in Love* (PS–2). Illus. by Petra Mathers. 2007, Scholastic $16.99 (978-0-439-51740-9). 40pp. Pierre the mouse/fisherman is smitten with Catherine the rabbit/ballet teacher but has trouble plucking up courage to declare his love. (Rev: BL 12/15/06; SLJ 3/07)

520 Petz, Moritz. *Wish You Were Here* (PS–2). Illus. by Quentin Greban. 2005, North-South $15.95 (0-7358-2005-8). 32pp. Separated for five long days, friends Hedgehog and Mouse exchange letters and eagerly anticipate their reunion. (Rev: BL 10/1/05; SLJ 12/05)

521 Pfister, Marcus. *Holey Moley* (K–2). Trans. by J. Alison James. 2006, North-South $16.95 (0-7358-2064-3). Two brothers who happen to be moles learn that it's better to work together than to argue. (Rev: SLJ 6/06)

522 Prince, Joshua. *I Saw an Ant in a Parking Lot* (PS–2). Illus. by Macky Pamintuan. 2007, Sterling $19.95 (978-1-4027-3823-4). 24pp. As a parking lot attendant watches in horror, a minivan and a meandering ant seem certain to cross paths with disastrous results; the comical art adds to the general silliness. (Rev: BL 4/1/07)

523 Pritchett, Dylan. *The First Music* (K–3). Illus. by Erin Bennett Banks. 2006, August House $16.95 (0-87483-776-6). 32pp. All the animals of the jungle, each with their own sound, join together to create music in this rhythmic cumulative African tale. (Rev: BL 11/15/06; SLJ 1/07)

524 Rawlinson, Julia. *Fletcher and the Falling Leaves* (PS–2). Illus. by Tiphanie Beeke. 2006, Greenwillow $15.99 (0-06-113401-5). 32pp. When his favorite tree begins to lose its leaves, Fletcher the fox becomes convinced that the tree is sick. (Rev: BL 8/06; SLJ 8/06*)

525 Rayner, Catherine. *Augustus and His Smile* (PS–2). Illus. by author. 2006, Good Bks. $16.00 (1-56148-510-1). Augustus the tiger travels the world looking for his lost smile only to find it while looking into a puddle. (Rev: SLJ 8/06)

526 Reid, Barbara. *The Subway Mouse* (PS–2). Illus. 2005, Scholastic $15.95 (0-439-72827-4). 40pp. Nib the mouse, who has lived his entire life in a busy subway station, sets out to find what lies beyond the confines of his subterranean world; clever 3-D photo-collages bring the story to life. (Rev: BL 9/1/05*; HBG 10/05; LMC 10/05; SLJ 8/05)

527 Reiser, Lynn. *Play Ball with Me!* (PS–1). Illus. by author. 2006, Knopf $9.95 (0-375-83244-0). Readers guess which game — basketball, soccer, baseball, or football — a kitten will play next as they turn the pages of this sturdy book with creative die-cut pages. (Rev: SLJ 8/06)

528 Reynolds, Aaron. *Chicks and Salsa* (K–2). Illus. by Paulette Bogan. 2005, Bloomsbury $15.95 (1-58234-972-X). A rooster with gourmet aspirations inspires Farmer Nuthatcher's other animals to add some zest and imagination to their eating habits. (Rev: SLJ 11/05)

529 Ritchie, Alison. *What Bear Likes Best!* (PS–K). Illus. by Dubravka Kolanovic. 2005, Good Bks. $16.00 (1-56148-473-3). Sometimes, Bear is just too big and gets in everyone's way, but his friends love him anyway. (Rev: SLJ 8/05)

530 Rocco, John. *Wolf! Wolf!* (K–3). Illus. by author. 2007, Hyperion $15.99 (1-4231-0012-3). The Aesop fable about a boy who cries wolf is reconfigured in an Asian setting with humorous twists. (Rev: SLJ 2/07)

531 Roth, Susan L. *Great Big Guinea Pigs* (K–2). Illus. 2006, Bloomsbury $17.95 (1-58234-724-7). 32pp. To help her son fall asleep, a mother guinea pig tells him a tale about their oversized prehistoric ancestors; this is fiction served full of facts. (Rev: BL 10/15/06; HBG 4/07; LMC 3/07; SLJ 11/06)

532 Rowe, John A. *Moondog* (PS–2). Illus. by author. 2005, Minedition $14.99 (0-698-40031-3). When a spaceship from Earth lands on the moon, Moondog conjures up a plot to discourage Earthlings from developing his beloved homeland and in the process encourages them to clean up their act at home. (Rev: SLJ 1/06)

533 Rubel, Nicole. *Ham and Pickles: First Day of School* (K–2). 2006, Harcourt $16.00 (0-15-205039-6). 32pp. Pickles the guinea pig is worried about her first day of school and her older brother Ham is definitely not helping. (Rev: BL 8/06; SLJ 7/06)

534 Ruelle, Karen Gray. *Dear Tooth Fairy* (K–2). Illus. by author. Series: A Harry and Emily Adventure. 2006, Holiday House $14.95 (0-8234-1929-0). 32pp. Emily, a kitten, is thrilled when her loose tooth finally comes out and she receives a visit from the Tooth Fairy. (Rev: BL 3/1/06; SLJ 5/06)

535 Ruzzier, Sergio. *The Room of Wonders* (1–3). Illus. 2006, Farrar $16.00 (0-374-36343-9). 40pp. Visitors marvel at the collection of Pius Pelosi, a pack rat, but can't quite understand why he gives an ordinary pebble the star treatment. (Rev: BL 2/15/06; SLJ 5/06)

536 Ryan, Pam Muñoz. *Nacho and Lolita* (1–3). Illus. by Claudia Rueda. 2005, Scholastic $16.99 (0-439-26968-7). 40pp. This charming story, inspired by a Mexican folk tale, features a rare and beautiful pitacohi bird that falls in love with a swallow and uses his colorful feathers to guide her home to San Juan Capistrano after her annual migration. (Rev: BL 10/1/05; SLJ 10/05)

537 Ryder, Joanne. *Bear of My Heart* (PS). Illus. by Margie Moore. 2006, Simon & Schuster $12.95 (978-0-689-85947-2). A mother bear expresses her love for her cub in tender words and lovely illustrations. (Rev: SLJ 2/07)

538 Ryder, Joanne. *Dance by the Light of the Moon* (PS–2). Illus. by Guy Francis. 2007, Hyperion $15.99 (0-7868-1820-4). 40pp. Weaving in the chorus from the song "Buffalo Gals," this upbeat rhyming tale centers on a moonlit barn dance attended by gussied-up animals. (Rev: BL 1/1–15/07; SLJ 1/07)

539 Rylant, Cynthia. *The Octopus* (2–4). Illus. by Preston McDaniels. 2005, Simon & Schuster $14.95 (0-689-86246-6). 64pp. The Lighthouse Family, consisting of Pandora the mother cat, Sebold the father dog, and two mice children, forges a friendship with Cleo, a shy octopus. (Rev: BL 10/1/05)

540 Sadler, Marilyn. *Money, Money, Honey Bunny!* (PS–K). Illus. by Roger Bollen. Series: Bright and Early Books. 2006, Random $8.99 (0-375-83370-6). 39pp. This appealing beginning reader describes in rhyming text the uncommonly generous ways of Honey Bunny, who shops for gifts for her friends. (Rev: BL 11/15/05; SLJ 2/06)

541 Salley, Coleen. *Epossumondas Saves the Day* (K–3). Illus. by Janet Stevens. 2006, Harcourt $16.00 (0-15-205701-3). It's his birthday and Mama is baking biscuits for Epossumondas the possum when she realizes she needs sody sallyratus; several guests head out to the store but fail to return, so the birthday boy goes to investigate. (Rev: SLJ 12/06*)

542 Saltzberg, Barney. *Star of the Week* (K–2). Illus. 2006, Candlewick $15.99 (0-7636-2914-6). 32pp. Stanley the hamster's turn as Star of the Week at school does not start off well. (Rev: BL 2/1/06; SLJ 2/06)

543 Santore, Charles. *Three Hungry Pigs and the Wolf Who Came to Dinner* (K–2). Illus. 2005, Random $16.95 (0-375-82646-6). 32pp. Banished after she samples the white truffles she's supposed to be hunting, Bianca and her piglets find an unlikely ally in a wolf. (Rev: BL 11/15/05)

544 Schachner, Judy. *Skippyjon Jones in Mummy Trouble* (K–3). Illus. by author. 2006, Dutton $16.99 (0-525-47754-3). Skippyjon, the adventurous Siamese kitten who thinks he is a chihuahua, takes a trip to ancient Egypt. (Rev: SLJ 11/06)

545 Schneider, Howie. *Wilky the White House Cockroach* (PS–2). Illus. 2006, Putnam $16.99 (0-399-24388-7). 32pp. When Wilky the cockroach takes up residence in the White House, the president and his staff move heaven and earth to track down the offending bug. (Rev: BL 10/15/06)

546 Schoenherr, Ian. *Pip and Squeak* (PS–1). Illus. by author. 2007, HarperCollins $16.99 (0-06-087253-5). Pip and Squeak, mice on the way to rabbit Gus's birthday party, realize they have forgotten the present (a lump of cheese) and must find a substitute; the illustrations offer interesting perspectives. (Rev: BL 1/1/07; SLJ 1/07)

547 Schwartz, Corey Rosen, and Tali Klein. *Hop! Plop!* (PS–2). Illus. by Olivier Dunrea. 2006, Walker $15.95 (0-8027-8056-3). 32pp. Elephant and Mouse are friends, but they find it difficult to play together. (Rev: BL 4/15/06; SLJ 5/06)

548 Schwartz, Roslyn. *Tales from Parc la Fontaine* (K–1). Illus. by author. Series: Parc la Fontaine. 2006, Firefly $19.95 (1-55451-044-9); paper $7.95 (1-55451-043-0). 48pp. Three short stories present the lives and aspirations of three thoughtful creatures — a pet bird trying to "act wild," a lonely snail called Fiona, and a bug called Angela who has only one day of life. (Rev: BL 11/1/06; SLJ 1/07)

549 Scotton, Rob. *Russell and the Lost Treasure* (PS–2). 2006, HarperCollins $15.99 (0-06-059851-4). 32pp. Armed with the Super-Duper Treasure Seeker, Russell the sheep sets off to track down the lost treasure of Frogsbottom and at first believes he has only found junk; a sequel to *Russell the Sheep* (2005). (Rev: BL 6/1–15/06; SLJ 5/06)

550 Scotton, Rob. *Russell the Sheep* (PS–1). Illus. 2005, HarperCollins $15.99 (0-06-059848-4). 40pp. Russell the sheep just can't sleep; he tries counting feet — and then stars — and then sheep . . . (Rev: BL 8/05; SLJ 4/05)

551 Segal, John. *Carrot Soup* (PS–2). Illus. 2006, Simon & Schuster $12.95 (0-689-87702-1). 32pp. Rabbit loves carrots and looks after his garden carefully, so he is very upset when all his carrots disappear, but his unhappiness evaporates when he gets home and finds all his friends there with bowls of soup. (Rev: BL 2/15/06; SLJ 5/06)

552 Senderak, Carol Hunt. *Mommy in My Pocket* (PS–1). Illus. by Hiroe Nakata. 2006, Hyperion $12.99 (0-7868-5596-7). A young rabbit nervous about her first day at school wishes she could shrink her mother and take her along. (Rev: SLJ 3/06)

553 Shannon, George. *The Secret Chicken Club* (PS–2). Illus. by Deborah Zemke. 2005, Handprint $15.95 (1-59354-118-X). 40pp. Three humorous episodes set in the farmyard of *Wise Acres* (2004) feature Debbie the cow who wants to be part of the Secret Chicken Club and an ambitious rooster. (Rev: BL 12/15/05; SLJ 1/06)

554 Shea, Bob. *New Socks* (PS–2). Illus. by author. 2007, Little, Brown $12.99 (978-0-316-01357-4). A self-confident little chicken flaunts his spiffy new orange socks, which will give him great prestige — even gaining recognition from the president. (Rev: SLJ 4/07)

555 Shore, Diane Z., and Jessica Alexander. *Look Both Ways: A Cautionary Tale* (PS–2). Illus. by Teri Weidner. 2005, Bloomsbury $15.95 (1-58234-968-

1). Little Filbert the squirrel learns to be careful crossing the street after a close call. (Rev: SLJ 7/05)

556 Sidjanski, Brigitte. *Little Chicken and Little Fox* (PS–2). Illus. by Sarah Emmanuelle Burg. 2006, Minedition $16.99 (0-698-40044-5). Against the advice of others, a little chicken befriends a young fox who's lost, and together they set out to find the fox's parents. (Rev: SLJ 11/06)

557 Simmonds, Posy. *Baker Cat* (PS–2). Illus. 2006, Red Fox paper $8.99 (0-09-945596-X). 32pp. The baker's cat is so overworked that the mice take pity on him, but this entente cordiale may have its limits. (Rev: BL 3/1/06)

558 Smee, Nicola. *Clip-Clop* (PS–K). Illus. by author. 2006, Boxer Bks. $18.95 (1-905417-09-8). Mr. Horse takes his animal friends on a rollicking ride that ends with a fall into a haystack. (Rev: SLJ 6/06*)

559 Sneed, Brad. *Deputy Harvey and the Ant Cow Caper* (K–3). Illus. by author. 2005, Dial $16.99 (0-8037-3023-3). Deputy Harvey of Ant Hill vows to track down the culprits responsible for rustling half of the community's herd of ant cows. (Rev: SLJ 11/05)

560 Stanley, Mandy. *Lettice the Flower Girl* (PS–K). Illus. by author. 2006, Simon & Schuster $9.95 (1-4169-1157-X). Lettice the bunny has the time of her life serving as flower girl at her dance teacher's wedding. (Rev: SLJ 2/06)

561 Stewart, Amber. *Rabbit Ears* (PS–2). Illus. by Laura Rankin. 2006, Bloomsbury $16.95 (1-58234-959-2). 32pp. Hopscotch will do almost anything to avoid having his ears washed and it comes as a revelation when he sees his older cousin Bobtail washing his own. (Rev: BL 2/1/06; SLJ 4/06)

562 Stiegemeyer, Julie. *Cheep! Cheep!* (PS–K). Illus. by Carol Baicker-McKee. 2006, Bloomsbury $9.95 (1-58234-682-8). A simple story for very young children about three chicks who fall asleep while watching over an egg. (Rev: SLJ 3/06)

563 Stock, Catherine. *A Porc in New York* (PS–2). Illus. 2007, Holiday $16.95 (978-0-8234-1994-4). 32pp. Having already been introduced to the delights of Paris in *A Spree in Paree* (2004), French farmer Monmouton's farm animals decide it's time to see New York City and see such wonders as "Blooming Dells." (Rev: BL 3/15/07; HBG 10/07)

564 Sutton, Jane. *The Trouble with Cauliflower* (PS–2). Illus. by Jim Harris. 2006, Dial $16.99 (0-8037-2707-0). 32pp. Mortimer the koala is sure cauliflower brings bad luck, but he eats a bowl or two to please his friend Sadie. (Rev: BL 2/15/06; SLJ 3/06)

565 Swallow, Pamela C. *Groundhog Gets a Say* (K–2). Illus. by Denise Brunkus. 2005, Putnam $15.99 (0-399-23876-X). 40pp. A proud groundhog expound on the attributes of his species in this humorous text with excellent illustrations. (Rev: BL 12/15/05; SLJ 1/06)

566 Tankard, Jeremy. *Grumpy Bird* (PS–K). Illus. by author. 2007, Scholastic $12.99 (978-0-439-85147-3). Too grumpy to fly, Bird decides to take a walk through the forest and is joined by one animal after another until the walk has turned into a game and brightened Bird's mood remarkably. (Rev: SLJ 2/07)

567 Thompson, Lauren. *Little Quack's New Friend* (PS–K). Illus. by Derek Anderson. 2006, Simon & Schuster $14.95 (0-689-86893-6). Little Quack the duck meets Little Ribbit the frog, and together the new friends enjoy a fun-filled day at the pond. (Rev: SLJ 2/06)

568 Thompson, Lauren. *Mouse's First Fall* (PS). Illus. by Buket Erdogan. 2006, Simon & Schuster $12.95 (0-689-85837-X). 32pp. In this picture-book celebration of fall, Mouse and his sister Minka frolic among the brightly colored leaves; a new installment in the series that includes *Mouse's First Spring* (2005). (Rev: BL 9/15/06; SLJ 10/06)

569 Thompson, Lauren. *Mouse's First Snow* (PS–2). Illus. by Buket Erdogan. 2005, Simon & Schuster $12.95 (0-689-85836-1). With his father's help, Mouse learns to sled, skate, and create things with snow. (Rev: BL 11/15/05; SLJ 4/06)

570 Tomlinson, Jill. *The Cat Who Wanted to Go Home* (PS–2). Illus. by Paul Howard. 2006, Egmont $17.99 (1-4052-0600-4). A French cat named Suzy, looking for a comfortable place for a nap, climbs unsuspecting into the basket of a hot-air balloon and awakes to find herself on the way to England. (Rev: SLJ 1/07)

571 Urbanovic, Jackie. *Duck at the Door* (PS–2). 2007, HarperCollins $16.99 (978-0-06-121438-7). 32pp. Max the duck, left behind when his flock flies south, takes refuge in a house already full of pets and makes a bit of a nuisance of himself. (Rev: BL 4/1/07; SLJ 3/07)

572 Usui, Kanako. *The Fantastic Mr. Wani* (PS–1). Illus. by author. 2006, Tiger Tales $15.95 (1-58925-054-0). In a rush to get to a party, Mr. Wani the crocodile gets help from a series of kindly creatures. (Rev: SLJ 4/06)

573 Vischer, Phil. *Sidney and Norman: A Tale of Two Pigs* (K–3). Illus. by Justin Gerard. 2006, Thomas Nelson $15.99 (1-4003-0834-8). 32pp. In this fable-like tale of two very different pigs who are invited to visit God, young readers learn some valuable lessons about the pitfalls of judging others. (Rev: BL 10/1/06)

574 Waddell, Martin. *Sleep Tight, Little Bear* (PS–K). Illus. by Barbara Firth. Series: Little Bear. 2005, Candlewick $15.99 (0-7636-2439-X). 32pp. Little Bear finds a small cave and makes it his own

special place; when he gets permission to spend the night there alone, however, he finds himself thinking of home. (Rev: BL 1/1–15/06; SLJ 12/05)

575 Waechter, Philip. *Me!* (PS–K). Trans. by Christopher Franceschelli. Illus. 2005, Handprint $9.95 (1-59354-087-6). 64pp. Minimal text and simple illustrations tell the story of a bear whose self-confidence is all bravado. (Rev: BL 7/05; SLJ 7/05)

576 Wallace, Nancy Elizabeth. *The Kindness Quilt* (PS–2). 2006, Marshall Cavendish paper $16.99 (0-7614-5313-X). 48pp. After hearing the Aesop's fable about the lion and the mouse, Minna the bunny and her classmates are inspired to show kindness to others and to make a giant kindness quilt. (Rev: BL 10/1/06; SLJ 11/06)

577 Walton, Rick. *Bunny School: A Learning Fun-for-All* (PS–K). Illus. by Paige Miglio. 2005, HarperCollins $15.99 (0-06-057508-5). 32pp. At Cottontail School, the bunnies enjoy their first day; rhyming verses and detailed illustrations depict typical experiences. (Rev: BL 8/05; SLJ 9/05)

578 Walton, Rick. *The Remarkable Friendship of Mr. Cat and Mr. Rat* (K–2). Illus. by Lisa McCue. 2006, Putnam $14.99 (0-399-23899-9). A misunderstanding turns Mr. Cat and Mr. Rat's mutual dislike into genuine friendship. (Rev: SLJ 12/06)

579 Watt, Melanie. *Augustine* (PS–2). 2006, Kids Can $16.95 (1-55337-885-7). 32pp. Augustine the penguin is nervous about the family's move to the North Pole, but her artistic talent means she makes friends quickly; this is an interesting introduction to famous paintings. (Rev: BL 11/15/06; SLJ 11/06)

580 Watt, Melanie. *Scaredy Squirrel* (1–3). 2006, Kids Can $14.95 (1-55337-959-4). 40pp. Imagining all the dangers around him, Scaredy Squirrel doesn't dare venture from his tree — until the day he discovers he can fly. (Rev: BL 5/1/06; SLJ 6/06)

581 Watts, Leslie Elizabeth. *The Baabaasheep Quartet* (PS–2). Illus. 2005, Fitzhenry & Whiteside $16.95 (1-55041-890-4). 32pp. Four sheep have difficulty adjusting to life in the city but are optimistic when they see a singing contest they mistakenly believe is for sheep only. (Rev: BL 12/15/05; SLJ 2/06)

582 Weeks, Sarah. *Overboard!* (PS). Illus. by Sam Williams. 2006, Harcourt $14.00 (0-15-205046-9). 40pp. Rhythmic text and colorful artwork celebrate a toddler's fascination with tossing objects of every kind "overboard." (Rev: BL 2/15/06; SLJ 4/06)

583 Wells, Rosemary. *Carry Me!* (PS). Illus. 2006, Hyperion $15.99 (0-7868-0396-7). 32pp. An alert baby bunny with an attentive mother and father enjoys asking its parents to carry, sing, talk, tell stories . . . (Rev: BCCB 2/06; BL 11/1/05; HBG 10/06; SLJ 1/06)

584 Weninger, Brigitte. *A Ball for All* (PS–1). Trans. from German by Kathryn Bishop. Illus. by Eve Tharlet. 2006, Minedition $16.99 (0-698-40049-6). Max Mouse and his animal friends enjoy playing a game of ball until Rico Raccoon, the local bully, shows up and steals the ball; the following day Max urges his friends to invite Rico to join them and they all have fun together. (Rev: SLJ 11/06)

585 Weninger, Brigitte. *Miko Goes on Vacation* (PS). Illus. by Stephanie Roehe. 2006, Penguin $10.99 (0-698-40017-8). 32pp. Young mice Miko and Mia become good friends after Miko asks Mia to look after his stuffed animal, Mimiki, while he goes swimming. (Rev: BL 2/1/06; SLJ 4/06)

586 Weninger, Brigitte. *Miko Wants a Dog* (PS–K). Trans. from German by Charise Myngheer. Illus. by Stephanie Roehe. 2006, Minedition $10.99 (0-698-40016-X). Miko the mouse desperately wants a dog, but when his mother says he is not yet ready for a pet, he helps out the neighbors with their new puppy. (Rev: SLJ 4/06)

587 Weninger, Brigitte. *One for All — All for One* (PS–1). Trans. from German by Kathryn Bishop. Illus. by Eve Tharlet. 2005, Minedition $14.99 (0-698-40034-8). A small band of creatures, each with a specific shortcoming, join forces to face the world in this predictable story with warm, appealing illustrations. (Rev: SLJ 12/05)

588 Weninger, Brigitte. *Stay in Bed, Davy* (PS–1). Trans. by Marianne Martens. Illus. by Eve Tharlet. 2006, North-South $15.95 (0-7358-2048-1). Davy the rabbit is sick and his mother has told him to stay in bed, but his friend Eddie and cousin Kiki still find ways to have fun. (Rev: SLJ 3/06)

589 Weston, Carrie. *If a Chicken Stayed for Supper* (PS–3). Illus. by Sophie Fatus. 2007, Holiday $16.95 (978-0-8234-2067-4). 32pp. Five little foxes disobediently leave their den while their mother is out hunting for a chicken; when they become lost, a chicken volunteers to guide them home, posing a dilemma for mother. (Rev: BL 3/15/07)

590 Wheeler, Lisa. *Castaway Cats* (K–2). Illus. by Ponder Goembel. 2006, Simon & Schuster $16.95 (0-689-86232-6). 32pp. Stranded on a desert island, 15 independently minded cats decide to build a boat, and although they don't succeed in this they do set aside their differences and eventually decide to stay on the island. (Rev: BL 8/06; SLJ 6/06*)

591 Wheeler, Lisa. *Hokey Pokey: Another Prickly Love Story* (PS–1). Illus. by Janie Bynum. 2006, Little, Brown $15.99 (0-316-00090-6). Eager to please his girlfriend, Barb the hedgehog, Cushion the porcupine tries to learn how to dance, but his attempts all end in failure until Barb offers to provide the lessons; a sequel to *Porcupining: A Prickly Love Story* (2003). (Rev: SLJ 1/06)

592 Willems, Mo. *Don't Let the Pigeon Stay Up Late!* (PS). Illus. 2006, Hyperion $12.99 (0-7868-3746-2). 32pp. The irrepressible pigeon of *Don't Let the Pigeon Drive the Bus!* is not tired and has no intention of going to bed. (Rev: BL 2/15/06; SLJ 4/06*)

593 Willems, Mo. *My Friend Is Sad* (PS–1). Illus. Series: Elephant and Piggie. 2007, Hyperion $8.99 (1-4231-0297-5). 64pp. Gerald the elephant is sad and Piggie, dressing in costumes, does his best to cheer him up but fails because Gerald does not recognize his best friend, and believes Piggie is missing all the fun. (Rev: BCCB 7–8/07; BL 4/1/07; HB 5–6/07)

594 Willems, Mo. *The Pigeon Has Feelings, Too!* (PS). Illus. by author. 2005, Hyperion $6.99 (0-7868-3650-4). The pigeon of *Don't Let the Pigeon Drive the Bus* (2003) is back in this board book, making all sorts of faces to reveal his emotions. (Rev: SLJ 8/05)

595 Willems, Mo. *Today I Will Fly!* (PS–1). Illus. by author. 2007, Hyperion $8.99 (1-4231-0295-9). 64pp. Piggie's announcement that he plans to fly is met with skepticism by his pal, Gerald the elephant. (Rev: BCCB 7–8/07; BL 4/1/07; HB 5–6/07)

596 Williams, Barbara. *Albert's Gift for Grandmother* (K–2). Illus. by Doug Cushman. 2006, Candlewick $15.99 (0-7636-2097-1). 32pp. Downcast because he doesn't have a gift for his grandmother's birthday, Albert the turtle, first seen in *Albert's Impossible Toothache* (2003), finally comes up with an idea that he thinks will please her. (Rev: BL 11/1/06; SLJ 12/06)

597 Willis, Jeanne. *Gorilla! Gorilla!* (PS–2). Illus. by Tony Ross. 2006, Simon & Schuster $15.95 (1-4169-1490-0). A mouse who has lost her baby is chased around the world by a fierce gorilla — who is only trying to help. (Rev: SLJ 7/06)

598 Wilson, Karma. *Animal Strike at the Zoo. It's True* (PS–3). Illus. by Margaret Spengler. 2006, HarperCollins $15.99 (0-06-057502-6). A sad little girl reminds the animals at the zoo that their job really is important. (Rev: SLJ 6/06)

599 Wilson, Karma. *Bear's New Friend* (PS–2). Illus. by Jane Chapman. Series: Bear. 2006, Simon & Schuster $16.95 (0-689-85984-8). Who could Bear's new friend be? Readers will enjoy the clues that lead to the discovery of an owl in a tree. (Rev: SLJ 7/06)

600 Wilson, Karma. *Dinos in the Snow!* (K–2). Illus. by Laura Rader. 2005, Little, Brown $15.99 (0-316-00948-2). In this lively picture book, the playful dinosaurs from *Dinos on the Go!* (2004) frolic in the snow, tossing snowballs, making snowmen, skating, skiing, and sledding. (Rev: SLJ 12/05)

601 Winget, Susan. *Tucker's Four-Carrot School Day* (PS–1). Illus. 2005, HarperCollins $12.99 (0-

06-054642-5). 40pp. A kindly teacher and a photo of his family help Tucker Rabbit to survive his first day at school. (Rev: BL 8/05; SLJ 9/05)

602 Wise, William. *Zany Zoo* (K–2). Illus. by Lynn Munsinger. 2006, Houghton $16.00 (0-618-18891-6). 32pp. Wacky animals and even wackier word-play are presented in this appealing blend of rhyming verse and colorful artwork. (Rev: BL 4/15/06; SLJ 8/06)

603 Wood, Douglas. *What Grandmas Can't Do* (PS–K). Illus. by Doug Cushman. 2005, Simon & Schuster $14.95 (0-689-84647-9). A follow-up to *What Moms Can't Do* (2001) and *What Dads Can't Do* (2000), this loving picture book features a dinosaur grandma who can't hug without a kiss, but is capable of plenty of other things. (Rev: SLJ 7/05)

604 Wu, Liz. *Rosa Farm* (2–4). Illus. by Matt Phelan. 2006, Knopf $15.95 (0-375-83681-0). 134pp. Gallileon, a young rooster, is nervous about filling in for his father, but welcoming the rising sun turns out to be only the beginning of a difficult day. (Rev: SLJ 1/07)

605 Yee, Wong Herbert. *Upstairs Mouse, Downstairs Mole* (1–3). Illus. 2005, Houghton $15.00 (0-618-47313-0). 48pp. Mole and Mouse, who live in the same oak tree, overcome their differences and forge a strong friendship. (Rev: BL 11/1/05; SLJ 10/05)

606 Yolen, Jane. *Baby Bear's Chairs* (PS). Illus. by Melissa Sweet. 2005, Harcourt $16.00 (0-15-205114-7). 40pp. A tiny bear realizes that no chair can match the comfort of sitting in his father's lap. (Rev: BL 12/1/05)

607 Yolen, Jane. *Dimity Duck* (PS). Illus. by Sebastien Braun. 2006, Philomel $15.99 (0-399-24632-0). 32pp. Appealing art and rhyming verse follow Dimity Duck through a satisfying day, including playtime with her friend Frumity Frog then happily climbing into her nest for bedtime. (Rev: BL 6/1–15/06; SLJ 6/06)

608 Ziefert, Harriet. *Buzzy Had a Little Lamb* (PS). Illus. 2005, Blue Apple $9.95 (1-59354-068-X). 32pp. Buzzy the donkey can't bear the thought of being separated from his beloved stuffed lamb, but he must learn to adjust when it's time to begin school. (Rev: BL 7/05; SLJ 8/05)

Realistic Stories

ADVENTURE STORIES

609 Agee, Jon. *Terrific* (K–2). Illus. 2005, Hyperion $15.95 (0-7868-5184-8). 32pp. Stranded on a desert island when his cruise ship sinks, Eugene Mudge — who views life through the lens of his pessimism — begins to change his negative attitude when a talking parrot takes him under his wing. (Rev: BL 10/15/05; HB 11–12/05; LMC 2/06; SLJ 9/05)

610 Becker, Shari. *Maxwell's Mountain* (2–4). Illus. by Nicole Wong. 2006, Charlesbridge $15.95 (1-58089-047-4). 32pp. Maxwell is a serious but adventurous little boy and he prepares carefully for his climb up the mountain in the playground near his new house. (Rev: BL 2/1/06; SLJ 2/06)

611 Cosentino, Ralph. *The Marvelous Misadventures of Fun-Boy* (PS–2). Illus. by author. 2006, Viking $15.99 (0-670-05961-7). Fun-Boy's adventures-gone-wrong are chronicled in a series of 12 brief and funny comic-strip vignettes that are virtually wordless. (Rev: SLJ 2/06)

612 Di Fiori, Larry. *Jackie and the Shadow Snatcher* (K–2). Illus. 2006, Knopf $15.95 (0-375-87515-8). 32pp. With the help of his dog Baxter and elderly friend Mr. Socrates, young Jackie hopes to recover his shadow from the villainous Shadow Snatcher in this picture-book-sized graphic novel set in the first half of the 20th century with detailed black-and-white illustrations. (Rev: BL 4/15/06; SLJ 7/06)

613 Fleming, Candace. *Sunny Boy! The Life and Times of a Tortoise* (K–2). Illus. by Anne Wilsdorf. 2005, Farrar $16.00 (0-374-37297-7). 40pp. In this fact-based picture book, Sunny Boy, a 100-year-old tortoise, tells about the many adventures in his life, including a trip over Niagara Falls in a barrel with his daredevil owner. (Rev: BL 8/05; SLJ 8/05)

614 Huggins, Peter. *Trosclair and the Alligator* (PS–2). Illus. by Lindsey Gardiner. 2006, Star Bright $15.95 (1-932065-98-9). 32pp. Trosclair ignores his father's advice and goes searching for turtle eggs in a Louisiana swamp that's dominated by a rogue alligator known as Gargantua. (Rev: BL 4/15/06; SLJ 3/06)

615 Jardine, Alan. *Sloop John B: A Pirate's Tale* (PS–1). Illus. by Jimmy Pickering. 2005, Milk & Cookies $17.95 (0-689-03596-9). A boy and his grandfather fight off pirates aboard the *John B* in this beautifully illustrated book inspired by the traditional folk song; comes with a music CD. (Rev: SLJ 7/05)

616 McCarthy, Meghan. *Steal Back the Mona Lisa!* (K–2). Illus. by author. 2006, Harcourt $16.00 (0-15-205368-9). Jack sets out to track down the "crooked crooks" who stole da Vinci's painting from the Louvre; full of humor and melodrama, and with a note that describes a time it really was stolen. (Rev: SLJ 10/06)

617 Mauner, Claudia, and Elisa Smalley. *Zoe Sophia in New York: The Mystery of the Pink Phoenix Papers* (1–3). 2006, Chronicle $14.95 (0-8118-4877-9). 32pp. Zoe Sophia's Great-Aunt Dorothy comes to New York for a visit, during which they see many sites and search for a missing diary; a sequel to *Zoe Sophia's Scrapbook* (2003). (Rev: BL 6/1–15/06; SLJ 4/06)

618 Mitton, Tony. *Once Upon a Tide* (PS–K). Illus. by Selina Young. 2006, Random $16.95 (0-385-75100-1). Two small children have an adventurous and imaginative day at the beach searching for buried treasure. (Rev: SLJ 5/06)

619 San Souci, Daniel. *The Amazing Ghost Detectives* (1–4). Illus. by author. Series: Clubhouse Books. 2006, Tricycle $15.95 (978-1-58246-165-6). Danny and the rest of the gang return to find someone has been in their clubhouse but the lock is untouched; could it be a ghost? (Rev: SLJ 4/07)

620 Sauer, Tammi. *Cowboy Camp* (PS–2). Illus. by Mike Reed. 2005, Sterling $14.95 (1-4027-2224-9). 32pp. Avery seems an unlikely candidate for Cowboy Camp, but he eventually proves his worth when he foils an evil scheme by Black Bart. (Rev: BL 2/15/06; SLJ 3/06)

COMMUNITY AND EVERYDAY LIFE

621 Alberto, Daisy. *No Rules for Rex!* (1–3). Illus. by Jerry Smath. Series: Social Studies Connects. 2005, Kane paper $4.99 (1-57565-146-7). 32pp. Rex learns about the importance of following rules in this book designed to support social studies curricula. (Rev: SLJ 9/05)

622 Amado, Elisa. *Tricycle* (PS–2). Illus. by Alfonso Ruano. 2007, Groundwood $17.95 (978-0-88899-614-5). 32pp. When Margarita, a child of privilege, sees her friend Rosario steal her bicycle, she says nothing, keenly aware of the poverty in which her friend lives. (Rev: BL 4/1/07; SLJ 6/07)

623 Anderson, Sara. *A Day at the Market* (PS–2). Illus. by author. 2006, Handprint $14.95 (1-59354-149-X). The sights and sounds of Seattle's Pike Place Market are depicted in rhyme and artistic collages in this large-format board book. (Rev: SLJ 5/06)

624 Ashman, Linda. *Desmond and the Naughtybug* (PS–2). Illus. by Anik McGrory. , Dutton $15.99 (0-525-47203-7). Desmond tries hard to be a good boy, but even his best intentions falter when the Naughtybugs show up. (Rev: HBG 10/06; SLJ 1/06)

625 Baguley, Elizabeth. *Meggie Moon* (PS–2). Illus. by Gregoire Mabire. 2005, Good Bks $16.00 (1-56148-474-1). Digger and Tiger spurn Meggie Moon's overtures because she's a girl, but they change their tune when she constructs a snappy-looking race car from scraps and refuse. (Rev: SLJ 10/05)

626 Bernhard, Durga. *In the Fiddle Is a Song: A Lift-the-Flap Book of Hidden Potential* (PS–1). 2006, Chronicle $10.95 (0-8118-4951-1). 24pp. Flaps reveal the potential within objects — the huge oak tree within a single acorn, the loaf of bread within a sheaf of wheat. (Rev: BL 6/1–15/06; SLJ 6/06)

627 Best, Cari. *Sally Jean, the Bicycle Queen* (K–2). Illus. by Christine Davenier. 2006, Farrar $16.00 (0-374-36386-2). Sally Jean comes up with her own solution when her parents can't afford to buy her a new bike. (Rev: BL 5/1/06; SLJ 5/06*)

628 Brisson, Pat. *Melissa Parkington's Beautiful, Beautiful Hair* (K–2). Illus. by Suzanne Bloom. 2006, Boyds Mills $15.95 (1-59078-409-9). 40pp. Admired for the color and luster of her long, black hair, Melissa Parkington longs to be recognized for something more significant and finds a way to do something for others with her hair. (Rev: SLJ 11/06)

629 Brodt, Burton P. *Four Little Old Men: A (Mostly) True Tale from a Small Cajun Town* (1–4). Illus. by Luc Melanson. 2005, Sterling LB $14.95 (1-4027-2006-8). A Cajun tale in which four old friends adapt to the changing weather during a non-stop card game on a levee beside the Mississippi River. (Rev: SLJ 1/06)

630 Burningham, John. *Edwardo: The Horriblest Boy in the Whole Wide World* (PS–3). Illus. by author. 2007, Knopf $16.99 (978-0-375-84053-1). The power of positive reinforcement is emphasized in this story of Edwardo, whose behavior becomes worse and worse the more he is criticized but improves dramatically when he is praised. (Rev: BL 1/1–15/07; SLJ 2/07*)

631 Carlson, Nancy. *Get Up and Go!* (PS–K). Illus. 2006, Viking $15.99 (0-670-05981-1). 32pp. Carlson emphasizes the importance of exercise and examines its many benefits. (Rev: BL 12/1/05; SLJ 2/06)

632 Cole, Joanna. *My Friend the Doctor* (PS–K). Illus. by Maxie Chambliss. 2005, HarperCollins $5.99 (0-06-050500-1). 32pp. Cartoon illustrations and brief text depict a little girl's visit to the doctor for a checkup that includes getting a shot. (Rev: BL 7/05; SLJ 9/05)

633 Cooper, Elisha. *A Good Night Walk* (PS). 2005, Scholastic $16.99 (0-439-68783-7). 40pp. This gentle picture book captures the ebb and flow of neighborhood life as a parent and child take an evening stroll. (Rev: BCCB 10/05; BL 11/1/05*; HB 11–12/05; HBG 4/06; SLJ 9/05)

634 Cooper, Elisha. *Beach* (K–2). 2006, Scholastic $16.99 (0-439-68785-3). 40pp. Double-page watercolor spreads and a simple text celebrate the joys of a day at the beach. (Rev: BL 6/1–15/06; SLJ 7/06)

635 Cowell, Cressida. *That Rabbit Belongs to Emily Brown* (PS–K). Illus. by Neal Layton. 2007, Hyperion $16.99 (978-1-4231-0645-6). 40pp. Young Emily loves her tattered old stuffed rabbit named Stanley, with whom she has many adventures, and refuses to give him up even when offered much newer toys. (Rev: BL 4/1/07)

636 Crews, Nina. *Below* (PS–K). Illus. 2006, Holt $16.95 (0-8050-7728-6). 32pp. Striking photographs tell the story of Jack's efforts to rescue Guy, his action figure, when Guy falls through a hole in the stairs. (Rev: BL 3/1/06; SLJ 3/06)

637 Cupiano, Ina. *Quinito's Neighborhood / El vecindario de Quinito* (PS–2). Illus. by José Ramírez. 2005, Children's Book Pr. $16.95 (0-89239-209-6). 24pp. Readers meet Quinito's neighbors and find out what they all do in warm illustrations and bilingual text. (Rev: BL 12/1/05; SLJ 10/05*)

638 Curtis, Jamie Lee. *Is There Really a Human Race?* (K–2). Illus. by Laura Cornell. 2006, HarperCollins $16.99 (0-06-075346-3). 40pp. When did this race start? Where is it going? Is it important to win? A mother thoughtfully helps her son unravel these difficult questions. (Rev: BL 9/15/06; SLJ 8/06*)

639 Cuyler, Margery. *Please Play Safe! Penguin's Guide to Playground Safety* (PS). 2006, Scholastic $16.99 (0-439-52832-1). 32pp. Penguin and his friend cleverly demonstrate the do's and don'ts of playground behavior. (Rev: BL 8/06; SLJ 8/06)

640 Dean, Carol Shorey. *The Live Bale of Hay: A Real Maine Adventure* (1–3). Illus. by Sandra Dunn. 2005, Down East $15.95 (0-89272-674-1). A bear that looks like a bale of hay is scared away by their dog's barking and two girls get safely home in this gentle adventure. (Rev: SLJ 8/05)

641 De La Hoya, Oscar. *Super Oscar* (PS–2). Trans. by Andrea Montejo. Illus. by Lisa Kopelke. 2006, Simon & Schuster $15.95 (1-4169-0611-8). Oscar turns into Super Oscar to help his parents get ready for a picnic in this bilingual (Spanish and English) story. (Rev: SLJ 6/06)

642 Doughty, Rebecca. *Lost and Found* (K–2). Illus. 2005, Putnam $12.99 (0-399-24177-6). 32pp. Always in a rush, young Lucy is forever losing things; after looking under her bed, she resolves to take more time in the future. (Rev: BL 8/05)

643 Elya, Susan Middleton. *Bebé Goes Shopping* (K–2). Illus. by Steven Salerno. 2006, Harcourt $16.00 (0-15-205426-X). 40pp. A child's visit to the supermarket with his mother introduces a number of Spanish vocabulary words in the rhyming text, which is enhanced by retro-style illustrations. (Rev: BCCB 6/06; BL 2/15/06*; HBG 10/06; SLJ 5/06)

644 Erlbruch, Wolf. *The Big Question* (K–3). 2005, Europa paper $14.95 (1-933372-03-6). 52pp. A variety of answers to life's biggest question — why am I here? — can be found in the pages of this tall, creative book that won the 2004 Ragazzi Award at the Bologna Book Fair. (Rev: BL 1/1–15/06)

645 Ford, Bernette. *No More Diapers for Ducky!* (PS). Illus. by Sam Williams. 2006, Sterling $12.95 (1-905417-08-X). 32pp. A fluffy duckling makes the transition from wearing diapers to using the potty. (Rev: BL 6/1–15/06; SLJ 8/06)

646 Gershator, Phillis, and David Gershator. *Summer Is Summer* (PS–K). Illus. by Sophie Blackall. 2006, Holt $16.95 (0-8050-7444-9). 32pp. In this gentle picture book, two girls — one African American, the other white — and their brothers make the most of summer, finding countless ways to have fun. (Rev: BL 4/15/06; SLJ 6/06*)

647 Gerstein, Mordicai. *Leaving the Nest* (PS–2). Illus. by author. 2007, Farrar $16.00 (978-0-374-34369-9). In a single backyard youngsters — a kitten, a blue jay, a squirrel, and a girl — experiment with new skills under the watchful eyes of their mothers. (Rev: BL 3/1/07; SLJ 4/07)

648 Godwin, Laura. *The Ring Bearer* (K–2). Illus. by John Wallace. 2006, Hyperion $12.99 (0-7868-5510-X). In this colorful picture book, rhymed couplets outline the responsibilities of the ring bearer during a wedding ceremony; a companion to *The Flower Girl* (2000). (Rev: SLJ 2/06)

649 Gomi, Taro. *My Friends / Mis amigos* (PS–1). Illus. by author. 2006, Chronicle LB $14.50 (0-8118-4849-3); paper $6.95 (0-8118-5204-0). Animals, friends, family, and teachers all have something to teach a little girl in this bilingual book. (Rev: SLJ 6/06)

650 González, Ada Acosta. *Mayte and the Bogeyman / Mayte y el Cuco* (2–4). Illus. by Christina Rodriguez. 2006, Piñata $14.95 (1-55885-442-8). Presented in both Spanish and English, this is an entertaining and colorfully illustrated story about Mayte and Pepito's assumption that Don Aparicio the ice cream man has evil intentions. (Rev: SLJ 6/06)

651 Gray, Rita. *Easy Street* (PS–1). Illus. by Mary Bono. 2006, Dutton $15.99 (0-525-47657-1). Rhyming text and colorful illustrations depict the building of an asphalt street. (Rev: SLJ 6/06)

652 Heide, Iris van der. *The Red Chalk* (PS–2). Illus. by Marije Tolman. 2006, Front St. $15.95 (1-932425-79-9). 32pp. Bored with her red chalk, Sara swaps it with Tim for his marbles, but the marbles soon lose their allure and she continues to trade until she finds something that suits her — red chalk. (Rev: BL 9/1/06; SLJ 1/07)

653 Helmore, Jim. *Letterbox Lil: A Cautionary Tale* (PS–2). Illus. by Karen Wall. 2005, Barron's $12.99 (0-7641-5893-7). The lift-the-flap format suits this story about Letterbox Lil and her love of spying on authors. (Rev: SLJ 3/06)

654 Hindley, Judy. *Baby Talk* (PS). Illus. by Brita Granström. 2006, Candlewick $15.99 (0-7636-2971-5). 32pp. A day in the life of a toddler is chronicled in rhyming verse and appealing illustrations. (Rev: BL 2/15/06; SLJ 3/06)

655 Hoppey, Tim. *Tito, the Firefighter / Tito, el bombero* (1–3). Trans. by Eida de la Vega. Illus. by Kimberly Hoffman. 2005, Raven Tree $16.95 (0-

9724973-3-1). 32pp. In this English/Spanish picture book with appealing illustrations, 8-year-old Tito's ability to speak both languages helps neighborhood firemen and paves the way for a ride on the fire truck. (Rev: SLJ 10/05)

656 Hutchins, Pat. *Bumpety Bump* (PS–K). Illus. 2006, Greenwillow $15.99 (0-06-055999-3). 32pp. A young boy and his grandfather harvest fruits and vegetables from the garden watched by a little red hen that later provides them with an egg; cross-sections show the plants above and below ground. (Rev: BL 2/1/06; SLJ 4/06)

657 Isadora, Rachel. *Yo, Jo!* (PS–K). Illus. 2007, Harcourt $16.00 (978-0-15-205783-1). 40pp. Young Jomar is a street-savvy kind with vocabulary to match in this evocative book. (Rev: BL 2/1/07)

658 Johnson, Adrian. *That's Not Funny!* (K–2). Illus. 2005, Bloomsbury $16.95 (1-58234-966-5). 32pp. *Schadenfreude* — enjoying other's misfortunes — is at the heart of this story about Alfie, who learns the hard way that what's funny to others may not be so funny to him. (Rev: BL 10/15/05; SLJ 9/05)

659 Johnson, Angela. *Lily Brown's Paintings* (K–2). Illus. by E. B. Lewis. 2007, Scholastic LB $16.99 (978-0-439-78225-8). Young Lily Brown's paintbrush takes her from everyday scenes into a world of imagination. (Rev: BL 2/1/07; SLJ 2/07)

660 Johnson, D. B. *Eddie's Kingdom* (PS–2). Illus. 2005, Houghton $16.00 (0-618-56299-0). 32pp. Through his art, young Eddie resolves the complaints of his neighbors and brings peace to their apartment building. (Rev: BL 10/15/05; SLJ 11/05)

661 Johnson, David. *Snow Sounds: An Onomatopoeic Story* (PS–2). Illus. 2006, Houghton $16.00 (0-618-47310-6). 32pp. Illustrations and onomatopoeias tell the story of a young boy's snowy morning. (Rev: BL 9/1/06; SLJ 10/06)

662 Johnston, Tony. *Sticky People* (PS–K). Illus. by Cyd Moore. 2006, HarperCollins $15.99 (0-06-028759-4). Two children spend the day getting as sticky as they can, then have a bath to wash it all away in this book with rhyming text. (Rev: SLJ 7/06)

663 Karns, Marie. *The Incredible Peepers of Penelope Budd* (PS–K). Illus. by Amy Wummer. 2005, Gibbs Smith $15.95 (1-58685-405-4). With one blue eye and one brown eye, young Penelope Budd sees the world around her in a different light. (Rev: SLJ 1/06)

664 Katz, Karen. *Can You Say Peace?* (PS). Illus. by author. 2006, Holt $15.95 (0-8050-7893-2). 32pp. Drawings of children from around the world are featured along with collages representing their country of origin and the word for "peace" in their native language. (Rev: BL 5/15/06; SLJ 9/06)

665 Klinting, Lars. *What Do You Want?* (PS). Illus. 2006, Groundwood $15.95 (0-88899-636-5). 36pp. This import from Sweden with charming, simple illustrations explores the desires of various animate and inanimate objects, including a bird, bee, chair, chicken, and pillow. (Rev: BL 3/1/06; SLJ 4/06)

666 Konnecke, Ole. *Anthony and the Girls* (PS–2). Trans. by Nancy Seitz. 2006, Farrar $15.00 (0-374-30376-2). 32pp. Little Anthony's attempts to win the attention of two girls in a nearby sandbox all fail until he bursts into tears, bringing them running to his side. (Rev: BL 6/1–15/06; SLJ 2/06)

667 Krauss, Ruth. *The Growing Story* (PS–K). Illus. by Helen Osenbury. 2007, HarperCollins $16.99 (0-06-024716-9). 40pp. In this new edition of Krauss's classic story published in 1947, a young boy observes growth everywhere around him and wonders if he is growing too. (Rev: BL 4/1/07; SLJ 7/1/07)

668 Kroll, Virginia. *Cristina Keeps a Promise* (1–3). Illus. by Enrique O. Sánchez. Series: The Way I Act. 2006, Albert Whitman $15.95 (0-8075-1350-4). Cristina gives up a chance to meet her favorite author so she can keep a promise and attend her brother's Special Olympics track meet. (Rev: SLJ 1/07)

669 Kroll, Virginia. *Everybody Has a Teddy* (PS–K). Illus. by Sophie Allsopp. 2007, Sterling $12.95 (978-1-4027-3580-6). 32pp. A little boy describes his classmates' teddy bears in detail and then his own — not a teddy bear but a toy monkey called Muh. (Rev: BL 3/15/07)

670 Kroll, Virginia. *Good Neighbor Nicholas* (1–3). Illus. by Nancy Cote. Series: The Way I Act. 2006, Albert Whitman $15.95 (0-8075-2998-2). Nicholas clashes with his cranky, older neighbor on a number of occasions until he begins to understand some of the reasons the older man is so unhappy. (Rev: SLJ 1/07)

671 Kroll, Virginia. *Jason Takes Responsibility* (1–3). Illus. by Nancy Cote. Series: The Way I Act. 2005, Albert Whitman $15.95 (0-8075-2537-5). Jason loses one of the invitations to his grandmother's birthday party on his way to the post office, but he does his best to make things right on the day. (Rev: SLJ 1/06)

672 Kroll, Virginia. *Makayla Cares About Others* (PS–1). Illus. by Nancy Cote. 2007, Albert Whitman $15.95 (978-0-8075-4945-2). 32pp. Young Makayla overcomes her fear of bugs to help her neighbor Mrs. MacFee dig a memory garden for her cat. (Rev: BL 4/1/07)

673 Lachtman, Ofelia Dumas. *Pepita Packs Up / Pepita empaca* (PS–2). Trans. by Gabriela Baeza Ventura. Illus. by Alex Pardo DeLange. 2005, Piñata $14.95 (1-55885-431-2). In this appealing bilingual picture book, a little girl faces moving day with mixed emotions — sadness at leaving her old friends and neighbors behind but anticipation about what awaits at her new home. (Rev: SLJ 2/06)

674 Larsen, Kirsten. *Tara Pays Up!* (1–3). Illus. by Paige Billin-Frye. 2006, Kane $4.99 (1-57565-187-4). 32pp. Tara learns that the taxes she has to pay in the store go toward many of the services she enjoys. (Rev: BL 8/06)

675 McDonnell, Patrick. *Art* (PS–K). Illus. 2006, Little, Brown $14.99 (0-316-11491-X). 40pp. In this imaginative picture book, an aspiring young artist named Art celebrates art in all its varied forms. (Rev: BL 4/1/06; SLJ 4/06)

676 MacLennan, Cathy. *Chicky Chicky Chook Chook* (PS–1). Illus. by author. 2007, Boxer Bks. LB $12.95 (978-1-905417-40-7). An onomatopoeic story full of animal sounds and creative rhymes, featuring a group of animals as the weather changes from warm sun to rain. (Rev: SLJ 4/07*)

677 McNaughton, Colin. *Potty Poo-Poo Wee-Wee!* (PS). Illus. 2005, Candlewick $9.99 (0-7636-2781-X). 40pp. Littlesaurus, a young dinosaur, is having problems with toilet training and further confounds matters with his potty mouth. (Rev: BL 8/05; SLJ 8/05)

678 McQuinn, Anna. *Lola at the Library* (PS). Illus. by Rosalind Beardshaw. 2006, Charlesbridge paper $6.95 (1-58089-142-X). A trip to the library with her mother is a treat for little Lola. (Rev: SLJ 7/06)

679 Meyers, Susan. *This Is the Way a Baby Rides* (PS–2). Illus. by Hiroe Nakata. 2005, Abrams $15.95 (0-8109-5763-9). 40pp. A lively toddler has fun at a picnic and his many movements are mimicked by animal babies on parallel spreads. (Rev: BL 10/1/05; SLJ 12/05)

680 Milgrim, David. *Time to Get Up, Time to Go* (PS–K). Illus. by author. 2006, Clarion $15.00 (0-618-51998-X). 32pp. A very busy young boy looks after himself and his stuffed doll during an activity-filled day; the minimal text and eye-focusing illustrations work well together. (Rev: SLJ 4/06)

681 Mortensen, Denise Dowling. *Ohio Thunder* (PS–3). Illus. by Kate Kiesler. 2006, Clarion $16.00 (0-618-59542-2). 32pp. Rhyming verse and dramatic artwork describe a summer thunderstorm above the fields of an Ohio farm. (Rev: BL 4/15/06; SLJ 5/06)

682 Munro, Roxie. *Circus* (PS–1). Illus. by author. 2006, Chronicle $15.95 (0-8118-5209-1). This colorful lift-the-flap book captures all the excitement of the circus and incorporates simple seek-and-find features in every elaborate spread. (Rev: SLJ 12/06)

683 Murphy, Stuart J. *Polly's Pen Pal* (PS–3). Illus. by Rémy Simard. Series: MathStart. 2005, Harper-Collins $15.99 (0-06-053168-1); paper $4.99 (0-06-053170-3). 33pp. Polly's (e-mail) pen pal lives in

Canada, and through her Polly learns about the metric system; with cartoon-like illustrations. (Rev: SLJ 7/05)

684 Nakagawa, Hirotaka. *Sumo Boy* (PS–2). Illus. by Yoshifumi Hasegawa. 2006, Hyperion $15.99 (0-7868-3635-0). This rollicking tale of a young sumo wrestler-turned-hero is full of action and information on sumo wrestling moves and terminology. (Rev: SLJ 4/06)

685 Novak, Matt. *Flip Flop Bop* (PS–1). Illus. by author. 2005, Roaring Brook $15.95 (1-59643-049-4). Summertime means flip-flop time for the dancing children in this happy picture book. (Rev: SLJ 7/05)

686 Parr, Todd. *Reading Makes You Feel Good* (PS–K). Illus. 2005, Little, Brown $15.99 (0-316-16004-0). 32pp. This brightly colored picture book examines the many benefits of reading and the many places you can read, alone or with others. (Rev: BL 12/1/05; SLJ 9/05)

687 Patricelli, Leslie. *Binky* (PS). Illus. by author. 2005, Candlewick $6.99 (0-7636-2364-4). A board book about losing a beloved pacifier. Also use *Blankie* (2005). (Rev: SLJ 7/05)

688 Pearson, Debora. *Sophie's Wheels* (PS). Illus. by Nora Hilb. 2006, Annick $18.95 (1-55451-038-4); paper $6.95 (1-55451-037-6). Sophie, the sister of Leo in *Leo's Tree* (2004), appreciates the importance of wheels in her life — on strollers, on supermarket carts, on tricycles and bicycles. (Rev: BL 12/1/06; SLJ 3/07)

689 Phillips, Christopher. *Ceci Ann's Day of Why* (PS–K). Illus. by Shino Arihara. 2006, Tricycle $14.95 (1-58246-171-6). 32pp. Vivid illustrations are paired with questions about everything in a little girl's life. (Rev: BL 1/1–15/07)

690 Pinkney, Sandra L. *Read and Rise* (K–3). Photos by Myles C. Pinkney. Illus. 2006, Scholastic $15.99 (0-439-30929-8). 40pp. Part of the National Urban League's Read and Rise literacy campaign, this blend of verse and color photography emphasizes the importance of reading. (Rev: BL 2/1/06; SLJ 1/06)

691 Portis, Antoinette. *Not a Box* (PS–K). Illus. by author. 2007, HarperCollins $12.99 (0-06-112322-6). 32pp. With a little imagination, a box is not just a box. (Rev: BL 12/1/06; SLJ 1/07)

692 Raschka, Chris. *New York Is English, Chattanooga Is Creek* (1–3). Illus. 2005, Simon & Schuster $16.95 (0-689-84600-2). 40pp. New York City hosts a party for other American cities, each of which arrives in a costume inspired by its name's origins. (Rev: BL 10/1/05; SLJ 10/05)

693 Reed, Lynn Rowe. *Big City Song* (PS). 2006, Holiday $16.95 (0-8234-1988-6). 32pp. Bright illustration and simple rhythms celebrate the sights and sounds of urban life. (Rev: BL 9/15/06)

694 Rosenthal, Amy Krouse. *One of Those Days* (K–3). Illus. by Rebecca Doughty. 2006, Putnam $13.99 (0-399-24365-8). 32pp. This whimsical picture book imagines dozens of ways in which a child's day can take a turn for the worse but holds out hope that things will turn around tomorrow. (Rev: BL 6/1–15/06; SLJ 5/06)

695 Roth, Julie Jersild. *Knitting Nell* (2–4). Illus. by author. 2006, Houghton $16.00 (0-618-54033-4). Nell, a quiet girl, finds added confidence when her knitting talent is recognized at the county fair. (Rev: SLJ 7/06)

696 Ryder, Joanne. *Won't You Be My Hugaroo?* (PS–K). Illus. by Melissa Sweet. 2006, Harcourt $16.00 (0-15-205778-1). 40pp. Hugs of all kinds — from the job-well-done hug to a parent's loving bedtime hug — are shown with happy animal characters. (Rev: BL 3/1/06)

697 Sakai, Komako. *Emily's Balloon* (PS). Illus. by author. 2006, Chronicle $14.95 (0-8118-5219-9). A young girl is saddened when her helium-filled balloon is blown high into the branches of a tree in her backyard. (Rev: SLJ 4/06)

698 Schaefer, Carole Lexa. *The Bora-Bora Dress* (PS–3). Illus. by Catherine Stock. 2005, Candlewick $16.99 (0-7636-1234-0). 32pp. Lindsay is upset when she's told she must wear a dress for a party at her aunt's house, but a brightly colored island frock soon catches her eye. (Rev: BL 8/05*)

699 Schaefer, Lola M. *Toolbox Twins* (PS). Illus. by Melissa Iwai. 2006, Holt $16.95 (0-8050-7733-2). 32pp. Young Vincent and his dad, each with his own toolbox, work on chores around the house. (Rev: BL 9/15/06; SLJ 10/06)

700 Schubert, Leda. *Here Comes Darrell* (PS–2). Illus. by Mary Azarian. 2005, Houghton $16.00 (0-618-41605-6). 32pp. Darrell the handyman spends so much time helping out his neighbors that he overlooks some important chores around home, but when a storm takes the roof off Darrell's barn his neighbors show their appreciation for all he's done. (Rev: BL 10/1/05; SLJ 11/05)

701 Seskin, Steve, and Allen Shamblin. *A Chance to Shine* (PS–2). Illus. by R. Gregory Christie. 2006, Tricycle $16.95 (1-58246-167-0). 32pp. This attractive picture-book version of a 1991 song tells how an African American father's act of kindness helps his son to look beyond color and social status in judging others. (Rev: BL 4/15/06)

702 Shulman, Lisa. *The Moon Might Be Milk* (PS–2). Illus. by Will Hillenbrand. 2007, Dutton $16.99 (0-525-47647-4). 32pp. Rosie asks a number of animals what the moon is made of and they all have different ideas — the cat says milk, the hen says an egg, the dog says butter — and then Rosie's grand-

mother combines all these ingredients to make moon-shaped sugar cookies; includes a recipe. (Rev: BL 2/15/07*)

703 Simon, Charnan. *A Greedy Little Pig* (1–3). Illus. by Marcy Ramsey. Series: Magic Door to Learning. 2006, The Child's World LB $21.36 (1-59296-622-5). 24pp. A lovable but greedy pig learns a valuable lesson; a section on trying new foods follows the story. Also use *Big Bad Buzz, Jeremy Jones, Clumsy Guy,* and *Messy Molly* (all 2006). (Rev: SLJ 4/07)

704 Slingsby, Janet. *Hetty's 100 Hats* (PS–2). Illus. by Emma Dodd. 2005, Good Bks. $16.00 (1-56148-456-3). With some help, Hetty puts together a collection of 100 hats of all types in this book that is perfect for 100th-day-of-school celebrations. (Rev: SLJ 8/05)

705 Spinelli, Eileen. *The Best Time of Day* (PS–2). Illus. by Bryan Langdo. 2005, Harcourt $16.00 (0-15-205051-5). 32pp. In rhyming text, farm residents — both human and animal — muse about their favorites time of day. (Rev: BL 10/15/05; SLJ 1/06)

706 Sturges, Philemon. *I Love Tools!* (PS–1). Illus. by Shari Halpern. 2006, HarperCollins $12.99 (0-06-009287-4). Various tools are introduced as a family works to build a birdhouse. (Rev: SLJ 6/06)

707 Terry, Sonya. *"L" Is for Library* (1–3). Illus. by Nicole Wong. 2006, Upstart $16.95 (1-932146-44-X). A cat conducts a tour of the library, introducing print and nonprint resources for every letter from A to Z. (Rev: SLJ 8/06)

708 Train, Mary. *Time for the Fair* (K–2). Illus. by Karel Hayes. 2005, Down East $15.95 (0-89272-694-6). Grace learns a little about the rhythms of the seasons as she anxiously awaits the arrival of the annual farmer's fair. (Rev: SLJ 12/05)

709 Tripp, Valerie. *Lindy's Happy Ending* (1–2). Illus. by Joy Allen. 2005, American Girl paper $3.99 (1-58485-991-1). 48pp. With some help from her friends, Lindy learns the importance of following through on things. (Rev: SLJ 7/05)

710 Villaseñor, Victor. *The Stranger and the Red Rooster / El forastero y el gallo rojo* (2–4). Trans. by Gabriela Baeza Ventura. Illus. by José Jara. 2006, Piñata $14.95 (1-55885-420-7). Presented in both English and Spanish, this is the story of how a frightening man with a scar is welcomed into his new community once he has a rooster in his arms. (Rev: SLJ 6/06)

711 Viorst, Judith. *Just in Case* (K–2). Illus. by Diana Cain Blumenthal. 2006, Simon & Schuster $15.95 (0-689-87164-3). 40pp. Charlie likes to be prepared for any eventuality, but when his friends throw him a birthday party he discovers that surprises can be fun. (Rev: BL 12/1/05; SLJ 1/06)

712 Wellington, Monica. *Mr. Cookie Baker* (PS–K). 2006, Dutton $15.99 (0-525-47763-2). 32pp. A new edition of the colorful picture book following Mr. Baker through his day, from mixing the dough through enjoying the last of the cookies. (Rev: BL 10/1/06)

713 Wellington, Monica. *Pizza at Sally's* (PS–K). 2006, Dutton $15.99 (0-525-47715-2). 32pp. This brightly illustrated picture book follows Sally the pizzeria owner as she goes through all the steps of making a pizza; a recipe is appended. (Rev: BL 8/06; SLJ 6/06)

714 Whybrow, Ian. *Harry and the Dinosaurs at the Museum* (PS–1). Illus. by Adrian Reynolds. 2005, Puffin $15.95 (0-141-38018-7). When Harry gets lost at a museum, his toy dinosaurs feel right at home. (Rev: SLJ 7/05)

715 Wilson, Karma. *How to Bake an American Pie* (PS–2). Illus. by Raul Colon. 2007, Simon & Schuster $16.99 (0-689-86506-6). 40pp. A cat and a dog whip up a recipe consisting of such ingredients as purple mountain majesty, liberty, courage, and fruited plains. (Rev: BL 4/1/07)

716 Wong, Janet S. *The Dumpster Diver* (1–3). Illus. by David Roberts. 2007, Candlewick $16.99 (978-0-7636-2380-7). 32pp. The children of an apartment complex enjoy helping Steve the electrician dive for buried treasure in the dumpster in the back alley; the group then creates new and inventive objects from the retrieved "junk." (Rev: BL 2/15/07*)

717 Wood, Douglas. *Nothing to Do* (PS–2). Illus. by Wendy Halperin. 2006, Dutton $16.99 (0-525-47656-3). 32pp. Nothing to do? Try reading a book, sailing a toy boat, walking through the woods, or any of the other low-tech activities that children may find unexpectedly satisfying. (Rev: BL 5/1/06; SLJ 5/06)

718 Wood, Douglas. *The Secret of Saying Thanks* (PS–2). Illus. by Greg Shed. 2005, Simon & Schuster $16.95 (0-689-85410-2). 32pp. This beautifully illustrated picture book underlines the importance of showing gratitude for the wonders around us. (Rev: BL 10/15/05; SLJ 10/05)

719 Yee, Wong Herbert. *Who Likes Rain?* (PS–1). Illus. 2007, Holt $14.95 (0-8050-7734-0). 32pp. A little girl heads outdoors on a rainy day and discovers that many plants and animals really like rain — but not all. (Rev: BL 3/1/07*)

720 Yolen, Jane. *How Do Dinosaurs Eat Their Food?* (PS–2). Illus. by Mark Teague. 2005, Scholastic $15.99 (0-439-24102-2). 40pp. In this lively picture-book addition to the humorous series, dinosaurs of various descriptions and temperaments model both good and bad table manners. (Rev: BL 7/05; SLJ 8/05)

721 Ziefert, Harriet. *Circus Parade* (PS–2). Illus. by Tanya Roitman. 2005, Blue Apple $15.95 (1-59354-

088-4). A parade of circus characters, ranging from majorettes and clowns to elephants and horses, march through a colorful town to a lively rhyming chant. (Rev: SLJ 10/05)

FAMILY STORIES

722 Abdullah, Patricia. *Saving Daddy* (K–2). Illus. by Alexandra Cabri. 2007, E C C I $17.95 (1-933193-16-6). 32pp. Daddy's kidneys fail but his life is saved after son James sends out a computer plea for help; the elderly donor, Amina, a white woman, is embraced by James's African American family. (Rev: BL 2/1/07)

723 Anholt, Laurence. *Seven for a Secret* (1–3). Illus. by Jim Coplestone. 2006, Frances Lincoln $15.95 (1-84507-300-2). 32pp. A dying man leaves a treasure for his granddaughter, whose family has been enduring a financial crisis. (Rev: BL 5/1/06; SLJ 6/06)

724 *Are We There Yet?* (K–2). Illus. by Dale Gottlieb. Series: I'm Going to Read! 2005, Sterling $19.95 (1-4027-2714-3); paper $3.95 (1-4027-2713-5). 32pp. This beginning reader portrays a girl and her younger brother pestering their father as he drives them to the toy store. (Rev: BL 10/15/05)

725 Ashman, Linda. *Mama's Day* (PS). Illus. by Jan Ormerod. 2006, Simon & Schuster $15.95 (0-689-83475-6). 32pp. The bond between mothers and their babies is celebrated in a charming blend of verse and ink-and-gouache illustrations. (Rev: BL 3/15/06; SLJ 5/06)

726 Asim, Jabari. *Daddy Goes to Work* (PS–2). Illus. by Aaron Boyd. 2006, Little, Brown $15.99 (0-316-73575-2). 32pp. The story of a young African American girl's day at work with her father is told in rhyming couplets. (Rev: BL 2/1/06; SLJ 6/06)

727 Aska, Warabe. *Tapicero Tap Tap* (PS–2). Illus. 2006, Tundra $16.95 (0-88776-760-5). 24pp. Spanish furniture maker Tapicero Tap Tap tells his grandson how he put aside his boyhood dreams of travel to care for his family after his father was killed. (Rev: BL 3/1/06)

728 Aston, Dianna Hutts. *Mama Outside, Mama Inside* (PS–K). Illus. by Susan Gaber. 2006, Holt $15.95 (0-8050-7716-2). 32pp. This appealing picture book explores the parallels between two expectant mothers — one a bird and the other a human. (Rev: BL 2/15/06; SLJ 3/06)

729 Bang, Molly. *In My Heart* (PS–2). Illus. 2006, Little, Brown $15.99 (0-316-79617-4). 32pp. A mother emphasizes to her child that she is always in her heart, throughout the day. (Rev: BL 1/1–15/06; SLJ 1/06)

730 Banks, Kate. *Max's Words* (K–3). Illus. by Boris Kulikov. 2006, Farrar $16.00 (0-374-39949-2). 32pp. When Max's older brothers refuse to share their stamp and coin collections with him, the young boy starts a very special collection of his own. (Rev: BL 9/1/06; SLJ 9/06*)

731 Bee, William. *Whatever* (K–2). Illus. by author. 2005, Candlewick $12.99 (0-7636-2886-7). Billy is supremely indifferent to his father's amazing efforts to amuse him, always saying "whatever." (Rev: SLJ 1/06)

732 Bergström, Gunilla. *Very Tricky, Alfie Atkins,* (PS–K). Trans. from Swedish by Elisabeth Kallick Dyssegaard. Illus. by author. 2005, Farrar $15.00 (91-29-66152-8). 27pp. Alfie is allowed to play with his father's tools but only gets his father's attention when he needs the forbidden saw; a charming story first published in Sweden in the 1970s. (Rev: SLJ 9/05)

733 Berry, Matt. *Up on Daddy's Shoulders* (PS). Illus. by Lucy Corvino. 2006, Scholastic paper $6.99 (0-439-67045-4). 32pp. This picture book beautifully captures a young boy's joy and feelings of invincibility as he rides tall on his father's shoulders. (Rev: BL 9/1/06; SLJ 6/06)

734 Best, Cari. *Are You Going to Be Good?* (PS–2). Illus. by G. Brian Karas. 2005, Farrar $16.00 (0-374-30394-0). 32pp. With illustrations that show a child's perspective this is the story of Robert's first grown-up party and the number of "don'ts" he has to remember. (Rev: BL 9/1/05; SLJ 9/05)

735 Binch, Caroline. *The Princess and the Castle* (PS–K). Illus. 2006, Red Fox paper $8.99 (0-09-943236-6). 32pp. Her father died at sea when she was young, so Genevieve is wary of the sea and initially cool to the fisherman her mother brings into their life. (Rev: BL 12/15/05; SLJ 2/06)

736 Bootman, Colin. *Fish for the Grand Lady* (PS–2). 2006, Holiday $16.95 (0-8234-1898-7). 32pp. The natural beauty and lilting speech of Trinidad are showcased in this gentle tale of two brothers who set out to catch some fish for their grandmother to cook. (Rev: BL 10/15/06; SLJ 10/06)

737 Bouchard, David. *Nokum Is My Teacher* (K–3). Illus. by Allen Sapp. 2007, Fitzhenry & Whiteside $21.95 (978-0-88995-367-3). 32pp. A young Cree boy's grandmother helps him to understand why he has to go to school with white people; the text is in both Cree and English. (Rev: BL 4/15/07)

738 Briant, Ed. *A Day at the Beach* (PS–1). Illus. by author. 2005, HarperCollins $16.99 (0-06-079981-1). A panda family planning a day at the beach has to go home to pick up forgotten items so many times that before they know it, the entire day is gone. (Rev: SLJ 6/06)

739 Bunge, Daniela. *The Scarves* (1–4). Trans. from German by Kathryn Bishop. Illus. by author. 2006, Minedition $16.99 (0-698-40045-3). Upset when her grandparents separate after decades of marriage,

a little girl devises a scheme to reunite them. (Rev: SLJ 1/07)

740 Bunting, Eve. *My Mom's Wedding* (K–3). Illus. by Lisa Papp. 2006, Sleeping Bear $16.95 (1-58536-288-3). Pinky's mom is getting remarried and Pinky has mixed feelings about the wedding and her new stepfather. (Rev: SLJ 3/07)

741 Bunting, Eve. *My Red Balloon* (PS). Illus. by Kay Life. 2005, Boyds Mills $15.95 (1-59078-263-1). 32pp. With a "Welcome Home" balloon clutched in his tiny hand, a little boy waits on the dock for his father to return from months at sea aboard an aircraft carrier. (Rev: BL 7/05; SLJ 9/05)

742 Busse, Sarah Martin, and Jacqueline Briggs Martin. *Banjo Granny* (PS). Illus. by Barry Root. 2006, Houghton $16.00 (0-618-33603-6). 32pp. A rhythmic tall tale in which a banjo-toting bluegrass-loving grandmother travels far and wide to pay a visit to her newborn grandchild. (Rev: BL 11/1/06; SLJ 12/06*)

743 Cabrera, Jane. *Mommy, Carry Me Please!* (PS–1). Illus. by author. 2006, Holiday House $16.95 (0-8234-1935-5). Shows the many different and special ways in which animal and human mothers carry their babies. (Rev: SLJ 2/06)

744 Caseley, Judith. *In Style with Grandma Antoinette* (K–2). Illus. by author. 2005, Tanglewood $15.95 (0-9749303-4-2). Little Rosie is at first hesitant to spend the day at the hair salon where her grandmother works, but once there she pitches in to help and has a wonderful time. (Rev: SLJ 1/06)

745 Chaconas, Dori. *Dancing with Katya* (K–3). Illus. by Constance R. Bergum. 2006, Peachtree $16.95 (1-56145-376-5). 32pp. When Katya, who has dreamed of being a ballerina, is stricken by polio and forced to wear heavy braces, her older sister Anna tries to keep her from surrendering to despair; set in the early 20th century. (Rev: BL 9/1/06; SLJ 9/06)

746 Cheng, Andrea. *The Lemon Sisters* (PS–2). Illus. by Tatjana Mai-Wyss. 2006, Putnam $16.99 (0-399-24023-3). 32pp. The sight of three young sisters playing together in the snow gladdens the heart of an elderly woman who recalls fun with her own sisters who have long since moved away. (Rev: BL 12/15/05; SLJ 1/06)

747 Child, Lauren. *But Excuse Me That Is My Book* (PS–2). Illus. Series: Charlie and Lola. 2006, Dial $16.99 (0-8037-3096-9). 32pp. Colorful collage-style art portrays the story of little Lola, who is deeply disappointed when she discovers that the book she absolutely loves best has been checked out of the library by somebody else; eventually her big — and very patient — brother Charlie helps her find a substitute. (Rev: BL 4/1/06; SLJ 4/06*)

748 Child, Lauren. *Snow Is My Favorite and My Best* (PS–K). Series: Charlie and Lola. 2006, Dial

$16.99 (0-8037-3174-4). 32pp. Charlie's little sister Lola is so enthusiastic about snow that she's devastated when it melts, and Charlie has to persuade her that snow every day would be boring and inconvenient. (Rev: BCCB 12/06; BL 9/15/06; HBG 4/07; SLJ 11/06)

749 Colato Laínez, René. *Playing Lotería / El juego de la lotería* (1–3). Illus. by Jill Arena. 2005, Luna Rising $15.95 (0-87358-881-9). In this engaging bilingual picture book, a young boy visits his grandmother in Mexico and agrees to teach her some English words if she will tutor him in Spanish. (Rev: SLJ 10/05)

750 Collins, Suzanne. *When Charlie McButton Lost Power* (K–3). Illus. by Mike Lester. 2005, Putnam $15.99 (0-399-24000-4). Charlie surprises himself by having fun playing with his little sister when a power outage puts a stop to his electronic fun. (Rev: SLJ 7/05)

751 Conway, David. *The Most Important Gift of All* (PS–K). Illus. by Karen Littlewood. 2006, School Specialty $15.95 (0-7696-4618-2). 32pp. Excited about the birth of her brother, a young Kenyan girl wanders in search of love, a gift she wants to give to her new sibling; the story is told in a traditional folktale style with large, warm illustrations. (Rev: BL 4/1/06; SLJ 5/06)

752 Cook, Stephen. *Day Out with Daddy* (PS–1). Illus. by author. 2006, Walker $16.95 (0-8027-8059-8). A mischievous boy tells his own version of his special day with his father; the illustrations show something closer to the truth. (Rev: SLJ 5/06)

753 Coste, Marion. *Finding Joy* (PS–2). Illus. by Yong Chen. 2006, Boyds Mills $16.95 (1-59078-192-9). 32pp. This story opens with Chinese parents sadly leaving their baby girl and closes with the same girl, renamed Joy, at home with her new American parents. (Rev: BL 1/1–15/07; SLJ 11/06)

754 Cote, Nancy. *It's All About Me!* (PS–2). Illus. 2005, Putnam $16.99 (0-399-24280-5). 32pp. A young boy used to being the center of attention adjusts to the arrival of a little brother and in turn helps him accept the arrival of a third. (Rev: BL 12/15/05; SLJ 12/05)

755 Coyle, Carmela LaVigna. *Do Princesses Really Kiss Frogs?* (PS–3). Illus. by Mike Gordon and Carl Gordon. 2005, Rising Moon $15.95 (0-87358-880-0). While on a walk with her father and the family dog, a little girl peppers her dad with questions. (Rev: SLJ 11/05)

756 Cruise, Robin. *Little Mamá Forgets* (PS–2). Illus. by Stacey Dressen-McQueen. 2006, Farrar $16.00 (0-374-34613-5). 40pp. Lucy's Mexican American grandmother is losing her memory and Lucy must remind her how to do simple things, but the older woman still manages to remember some of

the important things in life. (Rev: BL 1/1–15/06; HBG 10/06; LMC 1/07; SLJ 8/06)

757 Cunha, Francisco. *My Very Own Lighthouse* (PS–2). Illus. 2006, Winged Chariot $16.95 (1-905341-01-6). 32pp. Worried about her fisherman father out at sea, a young girl builds a lighthouse in her window to help guide her father home. (Rev: BL 11/15/06)

758 Downes, Belinda. *Baby Days: A Quilt of Rhymes and Pictures* (PS–K). Illus. 2006, Candlewick $14.99 (0-7636-2786-0). 32pp. Embroidered into the pages of this picture book, each of which resembles a quilt square, are snippets of poetry and song; game pieces; images of objects children love; and pictures of children at play. (Rev: BL 2/1/06)

759 Driscoll, Laura. *Super Specs* (K–2). Illus. by Barry Gott. 2005, Kane paper $4.95 (1-57565-145-9). 32pp. Molly, fed up with her younger brother's teasing about her new glasses, uses her math skills to convince her sibling that the glasses give her special powers. (Rev: BL 8/05)

760 Duke, Shirley Smith. *No Bows!* (PS). Illus. by Jenny Mattheson. 2006, Peachtree $15.95 (1-56145-356-0). 32pp. A strong-minded little girl makes her preferences quite clear throughout the day. (Rev: BL 7/06; SLJ 4/06)

761 English, Karen. *The Baby on the Way* (PS–2). Illus. by Sean Qualls. 2005, Farrar $16.00 (0-374-37361-2). 32pp. An African American grandmother tells her curious grandson the story of her birth and the traditions of slavery. (Rev: BL 10/1/05; SLJ 11/05)

762 Ericsson, Jennifer A. *Home to Me, Home to You* (PS–2). Illus. by Ashley Wolff. 2005, Little, Brown $15.99 (0-316-60922-6). 32pp. In parallel illustrations and alternating points of view, a little girl at home and a mother returning from a business trip look forward to their reunion. (Rev: BL 9/1/05; SLJ 8/05)

763 Eschbacher, Roger. *Road Trip* (K–3). Illus. by Thor Wickstrom. 2006, Dial $16.99 (0-8037-2927-8). 40pp. A rhyming story about a family's road trip and all its boredom, anticipation, excitement, and surprises. (Rev: BL 5/15/06; SLJ 7/06)

764 Fitzpatrick, Marie-Louise. *Silly Mommy, Silly Daddy* (PS–1). Illus. by author. 2006, Frances Lincoln $15.95 (1-84507-547-1). Young Beth is downcast and all attempts to cheer her up prove unsuccessful until her sister appears starts making faces. (Rev: SLJ 9/06)

765 Funke, Cornelia. *The Wildest Brother* (PS–2). Trans. by Chantal Wright. Illus. by Kerstin Meyer. 2006, Scholastic $16.99 (0-439-82862-7). 32pp. Imaginative young Ben is a brave boy during the day, protecting his sister from dragons and other imaginary creatures, but he still needs her reassurance at night. (Rev: BL 7/06; SLJ 6/06)

766 Gadot, A.S. *The First Gift* (K–2). Illus. by Marie Lafrance. 2006, Lerner $15.95 (1-58013-146-8); paper $6.95 (1-58013-149-2). 24pp. This appealing picture book provides an introduction to the origins of names and also takes a brief look at the diversity of first names found in different parts of the globe; includes information on Jewish naming customs. (Rev: BL 10/1/06)

767 Gay, Marie-Louise. *What Are You Doing, Sam?* (PS). Series: Stella and Sam. 2006, Groundwood $14.95 (0-88899-734-5). 32pp. Stella keeps a close eye on younger brother Sam as the boy tries to teach new tricks to Fred the dog. (Rev: BL 9/1/06; SLJ 9/06)

768 Gold, August. *Does God Hear My Prayer?* (PS–1). Photos by Diane Hardy Waller. 2005, Sky-Light Paths paper $8.99 (1-59473-102-0). A child learns what prayer is — and what it isn't — in this gentle book with rhyming text. (Rev: SLJ 7/05)

769 Goode, Diane. *The Most Perfect Spot* (PS–2). 2006, HarperCollins $16.99 (0-06-072697-0). 32pp. Jack and his Mama try to enjoy a picnic at the park and end up wet, muddy — and the new owners of a stray puppy. (Rev: BL 5/1/06; SLJ 5/06*)

770 Griessman, Annette. *The Fire* (K–3). Illus. by Leonid Gore. 2005, Putnam $16.99 (0-399-24019-5). 32pp. Little Maria safely escapes with her mother, little brother, and teddy bear when a fire breaks out in their home. (Rev: BL 10/1/05; SLJ 11/05)

771 Grimes, Nikki. *Welcome, Precious* (PS–2). Illus. by Bryan Collier. 2006, Scholastic $16.99 (0-439-55702-X). 32pp. A young African American family welcomes a new baby to the many wonders of the world. (Rev: BL 9/1/06; SLJ 11/06)

772 Guy, Ginger Foglesong. *My Grandma / Mi abuelita* (PS–1). Illus. by Vivi Escriva. 2007, HarperCollins $15.99 (0-06-079098-9). 24pp. A father, son, and daughter fly from their city to Grandmother's tropical home in this engagingly illustrated bilingual story. (Rev: BL 1/1–15/07)

773 Hanson, Warren. *Grandpa Has a Great Big Face* (PS–K). Illus. by Mark Elliott. 2006, HarperCollins $16.99 (0-06-078775-9). A child's grandfather seems larger than life — big enough to hold a city in his hands or bridge a river with his foot. (Rev: SLJ 5/06)

774 Harris, Robie H. *I Love Messes!* (PS). Illus. by Nicole Hollander. Series: Just Being Me. 2005, Little, Brown $7.99 (0-316-10946-0). 32pp. A preschool girl can't resist making a mess, particularly when it comes to food, but helps her father clean up afterward; a note to parents gives advice on such situations. (Rev: BL 11/15/05; SLJ 1/06)

775 Harris, Robie H. *I'm All Dressed!* (PS). Illus. by Nicole Hollander. Series: Just Being Me. 2005, Little, Brown $7.99 (0-316-10948-7). 32pp. A toddler dresses himself in an unorthodox manner for an outdoor excursion; a note to parents gives advice on such situations. (Rev: BL 11/15/05; SLJ 1/06)

776 Henderson, Kathy. *Look at You!* (PS). 2007, Candlewick $15.99 (978-0-7636-2745-4). 40pp. Diverse babies and toddlers explore the world, eat, play, crawl, and clap in soft, oversize watercolors. (Rev: BL 2/15/07*)

777 Hoberman, Mary Ann. *I'm Going to Grandma's* (PS–K). Illus. by Tiphanie Beeke. 2007, Harcourt $16.00 (978-0-15-216592-5). 32pp. A gentle story about a child's nervousness the first time she spends the night with Grandma and Grandpa. (Rev: BL 4/1/07)

778 Holt, Kimberly Willis. *Waiting for Gregory* (PS–2). Illus. by Gabi Swiatkowska. 2006, Holt $16.95 (0-8050-7388-4). 32pp. Young Iris eagerly awaits the birth of her new cousin, a boy to be named Gregory. (Rev: BL 2/1/06; SLJ 3/06)

779 Hunter, Jana Novotny. *When Daddy's Truck Picks Me Up* (PS–1). Illus. by Carol Thompson. 2006, Albert Whitman $15.95 (0-8075-8914-4). A little boy at preschool can't concentrate for anticipating the moment when his dad will pick him up in his big tanker truck. (Rev: SLJ 10/06)

780 Isadora, Rachel. *What a Family! A Fresh Look at Family Trees* (2–4). Illus. 2006, Putnam $16.99 (0-399-24254-6). 40pp. Ollie, who is very short, and his grandpa discuss other people in the family who were tall, short, had funny ears, and so forth; appealing illustrations show all these individual characteristics. (Rev: BL 1/1–15/06; SLJ 2/06)

781 Jabar, Cynthia. *Wow! It Sure Is Good to Be You!* (PS–2). Illus. by author. 2006, Houghton $9.95 (0-618-58132-4). Phone calls and letters help a little girl realize that even if the people you love are far away, they can still be with you. (Rev: SLJ 6/06)

782 Jacobs, Julie. *My Heart Is a Magic House* (PS–K). Illus. by Bernadette Pons. 2007, Albert Whitman $15.95 (978-0-8075-5335-0). A young squirrel called Stephanie worries about being supplanted by the new sibling that's on the way, but her mother reassures her that she will simply add another room to her heart. (Rev: SLJ 4/07)

783 Jeffs, Stephanie. *Jenny: Coming to Terms with the Death of a Sibling* (K–4). Illus. by Jacqui Thomas. 2006, Abingdon $14.00 (0-687-49709-4). 29pp. Jenny must cope with her sister's illness and death and asks Jesus to take care of her in heaven. (Rev: SLJ 3/07)

784 Johnson, Lindan Lee. *The Dream Jar* (PS–2). Illus. by Serena Curmi. 2005, Houghton $16.00 (0-618-17698-5). 32pp. With the help of her older sister, a young girl learns the secret of transforming nightmares into pleasant dreams. (Rev: BL 12/1/05; SLJ 12/05)

785 Joosse, Barbara M. *Papa, Do You Love Me?* (PS–2). Illus. by Barbara Lavallee. 2005, Chronicle $15.95 (0-8118-4265-7). 32pp. A Maasai father happily repeats expressions of unconditional love for his son. (Rev: BL 7/05; SLJ 8/05)

786 Knowlton, Laurie Lazzaro. *A Young Man's Dance* (K–3). Illus. by Layne Johnson. 2006, Boyds Mills $15.95 (1-59078-259-3). Now that his beloved grandmother has been institutionalized with Alzheimer's disease, her young grandson is reluctant to visit her, but he discovers that although the old woman no longer remembers much about her earlier life she still loves to dance. (Rev: SLJ 4/06)

787 Kosofsky, Chaim. *Much, Much Better* (PS–3). Illus. by Jessica Schiffman. 2006, Hachai $14.95 (978-1-929628-22-3). The prophet Elijah, who disguises himself as a poor traveler, visits a generous couple and tells them they will be blessed with a baby. (Rev: SLJ 3/07)

788 Krishnaswami, Uma. *Bringing Asha Home* (1–3). Illus. by Jamel Akib. 2006, Lee & Low $16.95 (1-58430-259-3). 32pp. Arun, a young Indian American boy, eagerly awaits the arrival of a new sister, who is being adopted from his father's native country of India. (Rev: BL 10/15/06; SLJ 11/06)

789 Krosoczka, Jarrett J. *Giddy Up, Cowgirl* (PS–K). Illus. 2006, Viking $15.99 (0-670-06050-X). 40pp. Lively illustrations add to the humor of this story about a little girl who is determined to help her mother and the often less-than-helpful results. (Rev: BL 1/1–15/06; SLJ 2/06)

790 LaMarche, Jim. *Up* (PS–3). 2006, Chronicle $16.95 (0-8118-4445-5). 32pp. A magical tale about a boy who discovers he has a special power (levitation) and uses it to prove to his father and older brother that he's big and can be a fisherman too. (Rev: BL 11/15/06)

791 Lawler, Janet. *A Father's Song* (PS). Illus. by Lucy Corvino. 2006, Sterling $12.95 (1-4027-2501-9). 24pp. In rhyming verse, a father expresses love for his son as the two spend a day together in the park. (Rev: BL 3/1/06; SLJ 3/06)

792 Lichtenheld, Tom. *What's with This Room?* (PS–3). Illus. by author. 2005, Little, Brown $15.99 (0-316-59286-2). A little boy assures his parents that everything in his extremely messy room serves an important educational purpose. (Rev: SLJ 11/05)

793 Lindbergh, Reeve. *My Little Grandmother Often Forgets* (PS–2). Illus. by Kathryn Brown. 2007, Candlewick $16.99 (978-0-7636-1989-3). 32pp. A little boy describes his grandmother's forgetfulness with love and understanding. (Rev: BL 4/15/07)

794 Lloyd-Jones, Sally. *How to Be a Baby — By Me, the Big Sister* (K–3). Illus. by Sue Heap. 2007, Random $15.99 (978-0-375-83843-9). An older sister lists the many, many things that babies can't do before realizing that there are a few benefits to babies as well. (Rev: BCCB 4/07; BL 11/15/06*; HB 1–2/07; HBG 10/07; SLJ 2/07)

795 Look, Lenore. *Uncle Peter's Amazing Chinese Wedding* (K–2). Illus. by Yumi Heo. 2006, Simon & Schuster $16.95 (0-689-84458-1). 40pp. As her Chinese American family prepares for Peter's wedding, Jenny worries she will lose her special relationship with her uncle. (Rev: BCCB 1/06; BL 12/15/05*; HBG 10/06; LMC 8–9/06; SLJ 1/06)

796 Lord, Janet. *Here Comes Grandma!* (PS–K). Illus. by Julie Paschkis. 2005, Holt $12.95 (0-8050-7666-2). 32pp. A grandmother goes to great lengths to visit her beloved grandchild. (Rev: BL 10/1/05; SLJ 9/05)

797 Lyon, George Ella. *No Dessert Forever!* (PS–K). Illus. by Peter Catalanotto. 2006, Simon & Schuster $16.95 (1-4169-0385-2). 40pp. A young girl vents her frustrations with life through discussions with her doll; the brief text is amplified by the realistic, warm watercolors. (Rev: BL 11/1/06; SLJ 12/06)

798 McConnell, Sarah. *Don't Mention Pirates* (PS–2). Illus. by author. 2006, Barron's $14.99 (0-7641-5945-3). Although the Silver family has renounced its pirate past, it quickly reconsiders matters after young Scarlet discovers some buried gold. (Rev: SLJ 8/06)

799 McElroy, Lisa Tucker. *Love, Lizzie: Letters to a Military Mom* (1–3). Illus. by Diane Paterson. 2005, Albert Whitman $15.95 (0-8075-4777-8). 32pp. In letters to her mom, a soldier serving overseas, young Lizzie describes her life — the good things and the bad — and includes maps that show details of key events. (Rev: BL 9/1/05; SLJ 10/05)

800 Mack, Todd. *Princess Penelope Takes Charge!* (PS–2). Illus. by Julia Gran. 2006, Scholastic $16.99 (0-439-67380-1). Penelope wanted a baby sister and is not very excited when Dexter arrives instead, until she decides to welcome him into her personal kingdom. (Rev: SLJ 6/06)

801 Mahoney, Daniel J. *A Really Good Snowman* (K–3). Illus. by author. 2005, Clarion $15.00 (0-618-47554-0). 32pp. Happy to be free of his little sister Nancy for a while, Jack enters a snowman-building contest with two of his friends, but he quickly abandons this to come to her aid when older boys harass her. (Rev: SLJ 11/05)

802 Makhijani, Pooja. *Mama's Saris* (PS–2). Illus. by Elena Gomez. 2007, Little, Brown $16.99 (0-316-01105-3). 32pp. A young Indian American girl admires her mother's saris and wants to wear one herself. (Rev: BL 4/15/07)

803 Mayer, Pamela. *The Grandma Cure* (PS–K). Illus. by John Nez. 2005, Dutton $15.99 (0-525-47559-1). 32pp. Two grandmothers disagree over the best way to cure their granddaughter of a cold. (Rev: BL 1/1–15/06; SLJ 1/06)

804 Mercier, Deirdre McLaughlin. *Yesterday We Had a Hurricane / Ayer tuvimos un huracán* (PS–2). Illus. by author. 2006, Bumble Bee $17.95 (0-9754342-9-2). In this reassuring bilingual picture book, a mother comforts a child during and after a frightening storm. (Rev: SLJ 10/06)

805 Michelson, Richard. *Oh No, Not Ghosts!* (1–3). Illus. by Adam McCauley. 2006, Harcourt $16.00 (0-15-205186-4). 44pp. As a boy and his little sister try to settle down to sleep, the brother teasingly escalates all the horrors they might face — ghosts, demons, goblins, giants, and skeletons. (Rev: SLJ 8/06)

806 Milord, Susan. *Love That Baby!* (PS). Illus. 2005, Houghton $7.95 (0-618-56323-7). 16pp. This delightful lift-the-flap book celebrates the interaction between babies and their parents. (Rev: BL 10/1/05; SLJ 11/05)

807 Moser, Lisa. *Watermelon Wishes* (K–2). Illus. by Stacey Schuett. 2006, Clarion $16.00 (0-618-56433-0). 32pp. In this appealing story, a young boy and his grandfather spend the summer tending a watermelon patch they planted together, and the boy hopes to harvest one very special melon that will grant him a wish: to spend another summer of fun with his granddad. (Rev: SLJ 12/06)

808 Nevius, Carol. *Building with Dad* (PS–2). Illus. by Bill Thomson. 2006, Marshall Cavendish $16.99 (0-7614-5312-1). 32pp. Eye-catching vertical spreads illustrate this story about a young boy who accompanies his contractor dad to the construction site of a new school. (Rev: BL 9/1/06; SLJ 10/06)

809 Newman, Marjorie. *Just Like Me* (PS). Illus. by Ken Wilson-Max. 2006, Walker $15.95 (0-8027-8080-6). Tom resents his new baby brother because the infant is suddenly the center of attention, but when his parents explain that the baby will grow up just as he has, the older boy accepts his role as big brother. (Rev: SLJ 4/06)

810 O'Connor, Jane. *The Snow Globe Family* (PS–2). Illus. by S. D. Schindler. 2006, Putnam $16.99 (0-399-24242-2). 40pp. Two families — a large one living in a house and a tiny one living on the mantelpiece within a snow globe — enjoy a winter storm. (Rev: BL 10/1/06; SLJ 12/06)

811 O'Connor, Joe. *Where Did Daddy's Hair Go?* (PS–2). Illus. by Henry Payne. 2006, Random $14.95 (0-375-83571-7). Daddy has "lost" his hair. Where did it go? Did it hurt? Does it matter? (Rev: SLJ 4/06)

812 O'Hair, Margaret. *Star Baby* (PS). Illus. by Erin Eitter Kono. 2005, Clarion $15.00 (0-618-30668-4). 32pp. This gentle picture book chronicles in rhythmic rhyming text and soft acrylic artwork a day in the life of a mother and child. (Rev: BL 10/15/05; SLJ 10/05)

813 Ohi, Ruth. *And You Can Come Too* (PS–2). Illus. 2005, Annick $19.95 (1-55037-905-4); paper $5.95 (1-55037-904-6). 32pp. After her father scolds her for squabbling with her little sister, Sara decides to run away from home but allows her younger sibling to come along, and Dad even helps with building a tent in the backyard. (Rev: BL 10/1/05)

814 Ohi, Ruth. *Me and My Sister* (PS–K). Illus. by author. 2005, Annick LB $19.95 (1-55037-893-7); paper $5.95 (1-55037-892-9). In simple rhyming text, a girl describes the events — good and bad — of a day with her toddler sister. (Rev: BL 7/05; SLJ 10/05)

815 O'Leary, Sara. *When You Were Small* (1–3). Illus. by Julie Morstad. 2006, Simply Read $16.95 (1-894965-36-1). 32pp. When Henry was small, he was *really* small, according to his father, who tells tales of Henry once fitting in his shirt pocket in this imaginatively illustrated book. (Rev: BL 5/1/06; SLJ 10/06)

816 Ormerod, Jan. *Ballet Sisters: The Duckling and the Swan* (PS–2). Illus. by author. 2007, Scholastic paper $5.99 (0-439-82281-5). 32pp. For beginning readers, this is the story of a graceful older sister who takes ballet lessons and an awkward younger sister who wants to dance. (Rev: BL 12/1/06; SLJ 1/07)

817 Orona-Ramirez, Kristy. *Kiki's Journey* (K–2). Illus. by Jonathan Warm Day. 2006, Children's Book Pr. $16.95 (0-89239-214-2). 32pp. A young Native American girl who was born on a reservation but has grown up in Los Angeles travels back to the Taos Pueblo where she learns some important lessons about her heritage. (Rev: BL 9/1/06; SLJ 10/06)

818 Paradis, Susan. *Snow Princess* (PS–2). Illus. 2005, Front St. $16.95 (1-932425-31-4). 32pp. Waiting for her father's return from work on a snowy day, a little girl lets her imagination run wild. (Rev: BL 11/1/05; SLJ 1/06)

819 Park, Frances, and Ginger Park. *The Have a Good Day Cafe* (1–3). Illus. by Katherine Potter. 2005, Lee & Low $16.95 (1-58430-171-6). 32pp. Concerned about his grandmother's homesickness for her native Korea, young Mike suggests her ethnic foods might revive business at their food cart. (Rev: BL 9/1/05; SLJ 8/05)

820 Parr, Todd. *The Grandma Book* (1–4). Illus. by author. 2006, Little, Brown $9.99 (0-316-05802-5). A simple celebration of all kinds of grandmothers and the different ways they show love to their grandchildren. Also use *The Grandpa Book* (2006). (Rev: SLJ 4/06)

821 Pelley, Kathleen T. *Inventor McGregor* (PS). Illus. by Michael Chesworth. 2006, Farrar $16.00 (0-374-33606-7). 32pp. Prolific inventor Hector

McGregor is moved to a new office in the city but finds that without his family and his country home, his muse has deserted him. (Rev: BL 2/15/06; SLJ 4/06)

822 Perez, Amada Irma. *Nana's Big Surprise / Nana, Que Sorpresa!* (1–3). Illus. by Maya Christina Gonzalez. 2007, Children's Book Pr. $16.95 (0-89239-190-1). 24pp. In this brightly illustrated bilingual picture book, Amada and her siblings hope a gift of some baby chicks will lift the spirits of their visiting grandmother who's still grieving the death of her husband. (Rev: BL 3/15/07)

823 Perry, Elizabeth. *Think Cool Thoughts* (PS–2). Illus. by Linda Bronson. 2005, Clarion $16.00 (0-618-23493-4). 32pp. Angel, her mother, and her aunt flee the heat downstairs to spend a lovely summer night watching the stars from the roof of their apartment building. (Rev: BL 7/05; SLJ 8/05)

824 Piven, Hanoch. *The Scary Show of Mo and Jo* (PS–2). Illus. by author. 2005, Running Pr. $18.95 (0-7624-2097-9). Two siblings try to outdo one another with creative disguises that are artfully conceived in Piven's collages. (Rev: SLJ 11/05)

825 Polacco, Patricia. *Rotten Richie and the Ultimate Dare* (1–3). 2006, Philomel $16.99 (0-399-24531-6). 48pp. Tired of her brother Richie's teasing about her ballet classes, Trish challenges her obnoxious sibling to show what he can do on the dance floor; a companion to *My Rotten Redheaded Older Brother* (1999). (Rev: BL 4/15/06; SLJ 5/06)

826 Purmwell, Ann. *Christmas Tree Farm* (PS–2). Illus. by Jill Weber. 2006, Holiday $16.95 (0-8234-1886-3). 32pp. A warm story about a Christmas tree farm, the excitement during the winter holidays, and the work that continues all year round. (Rev: BL 9/1/06; SLJ 10/06)

827 Reiser, Lynn. *You and Me, Baby* (PS–1). Photos by Penny Gentieu. 2006, Knopf $15.95 (0-375-83401-X). Simple text accompanies a collection of appealing photographs of babies from diverse backgrounds and their parents. (Rev: SLJ 10/06)

828 Reynolds, Peter. *The Best Kid in the World* (PS–2). Illus. by author. 2006, Simon & Schuster $15.95 (0-689-87624-6). Jealous that her older brother once received a "Best Kid in the World" award, SugarLoaf sets out to do a number of good deeds, but things don't go exactly as she planned. (Rev: SLJ 8/06)

829 Reynolds, Peter. *My Very Big Little World* (PS–K). Illus. 2006, Simon & Schuster $15.95 (0-689-87621-1). 40pp. SugarLoaf, a captivating middle child, introduces young readers to the important people and places in her life. (Rev: BL 4/15/06; SLJ 1/06)

830 Ries, Lori. *Fix It, Sam* (PS–K). Illus. by Sue Ramá. 2007, Charlesbridge $15.95 (978-1-57091-598-7); paper $6.95 (978-1-57091-722-6). 32pp.

Little Petey relies on big brother Sam for lots of help, but discovers that he can fix things, too; bright mixed media art extends the text. (Rev: BL 1/1–15/07; SLJ 2/07)

831 Robberecht, Thierry. *Back into Mommy's Tummy* (PS–K). Illus. by Philippe Goossens. 2005, Clarion $15.00 (0-618-58106-5). 32pp. A 5-year-old girl whose mother is pregnant says she wants to go back into Mommy's tummy, where the center of attention is. (Rev: BL 12/1/05; SLJ 2/06)

832 Rosenbaum, Andria Warmflash. *A Grandma Like Yours / A Grandpa Like Yours* (PS–1). Illus. by Barb Björnson. 2006, Lerner LB $16.95 (1-58013-167-0); paper $6.95 (1-58013-168-9). One side of this flipbook extols the virtues of Jewish grandmas (in the guise of friendly animals), and the other, Jewish grandpas. (Rev: SLJ 5/06)

833 Ryder, Joanne. *My Mother's Voice* (K–2). Illus. by Peter Catalanotto. 2006, HarperCollins $15.99 (0-06-029509-0). 32pp. This gentle picture book celebrates the role of a mother's voice in a loving relationship with her daughter. (Rev: BL 4/15/06; SLJ 4/06)

834 Sage, James. *Mr. Beast* (K–3). Illus. by Russell Ayto. 2005, Holt $16.95 (0-8050-7730-8). Dad pretends to be a beast when Charlie eats up all the homemade doughnuts. (Rev: SLJ 9/05)

835 Salonen, Roxane Beauclair. *First Salmon* (K–3). Illus. by Jim Fowler. 2005, Boyds Mills $15.95 (1-59078-171-6). 32pp. Charlie, a young Native American boy still grieving over the death of his beloved Uncle Joe, finds it hard to get excited about the annual First Salmon celebration. (Rev: BL 10/15/05; SLJ 11/05)

836 Samuels, Barbara. *Happy Valentines Day, Dolores* (K–2). Illus. 2006, Farrar $16.00 (0-374-32844-7). 32pp. Despite her promise to quit snooping in her older sister's room, Dolores simply can't resist trying on a necklace she finds in a valentine box, with disastrous consequences; the detailed cartoon illustrations add to the fun. (Rev: BL 11/15/05*; HBG 10/06; SLJ 1/06*)

837 Savadier, Elivia. *Time to Get Dressed!* (PS). Illus. 2006, Roaring Brook $14.95 (1-59643-161-X). 32pp. Simple text and charming pictures depict Dad's patience as he struggles to get his toddler dressed for day care. (Rev: BL 4/1/06; SLJ 3/06)

838 Schotter, Roni. *Mama, I'll Give You the World* (1–3). Illus. by S. Saelig Gallagher. 2006, Random $16.95 (0-375-83612-8). 40pp. To repay her mother for all her loving kindness, young Maria plans a very special birthday surprise. (Rev: BL 8/06; SLJ 9/1/06*)

839 Smalls, Irene. *My Nana and Me* (PS–K). Illus. by Cathy Ann Johnson. 2005, Little, Brown $15.99 (0-316-16821-1). 32pp. An African American preschooler tells about a very special day spent with her grandmother. (Rev: BL 11/1/05; SLJ 10/05)

840 Smalls, Irene. *My Pop Pop and Me* (PS–K). Illus. by Cathy Ann Johnson. 2006, Little, Brown $15.99 (0-316-73422-5). 32pp. An African American grandfather and his grandson enjoy baking a lemon cake together. (Rev: BL 2/1/06; SLJ 6/06)

841 Spalding, Andrea. *Bottled Sunshine* (1–3). Illus. by Ruth Ohi. 2005, Fitzhenry & Whiteside $16.95 (1-55041-703-7). A young boy's memories of his last visit with his grandmother provide comfort after her death; the illustrations complement the gentle story. (Rev: SLJ 10/05)

842 Spinelli, Eileen. *When You Are Happy* (PS–2). Illus. by Geraldo Valerio. 2006, Simon & Schuster $16.95 (0-689-86251-2). 40pp. Members of a family reassure a little girl that they love her. (Rev: BL 3/1/06; SLJ 3/06)

843 Stanton, Karen. *Papi's Gift* (PS–2). Illus. by Rene King Moreno. 2007, Boyds Mills $16.95 (978-1-59078-422-8). 32pp. Graciela desperately misses her father, who has left their village in Mexico to pick fruit in California; she treasures their weekly phone calls and prays for his return. (Rev: BL 4/15/07)

844 Struve-Bodeen, Stephanie. *The Best Worst Brother* (K–4). Illus. by Charlotte Fremaux. 2005, Woodbine $14.95 (1-890627-68-2). Emma discovers that it will take hard work to teach Isaac, her little brother who has Down's syndrome, to use sign language in this sequel to *We'll Paint the Octopus Red* (1998). (Rev: SLJ 9/05)

845 Sugarman, Brynn Olenberg. *Rebecca's Journey Home* (PS–2). Illus. by Michelle Shapiro. 2006, Lerner $17.95 (1-58013-157-3). 32pp. This tender story of a Jewish American family adopting a Vietnamese baby girl also provides insight into both cultures. (Rev: BL 1/1–15/07; SLJ 11/06)

846 Sullivan, Sarah. *Dear Baby: Letters from Your Big Brother* (PS–K). Illus. by Paul Meisel. 2005, Candlewick $14.99 (0-7636-2126-9). 40pp. During the first year of his baby sister's life, her big brother records his thoughts about her development and his growing love for her. (Rev: BL 9/15/05; SLJ 9/05)

847 Thiel, Annie. *Chloe's New Baby Brother* (1–4). Illus. by William M. Edwards and Karen Marjoribanks. 2006, Playdate Kids $14.95 (1-933721-01-4). Only child Chloe learns that the arrival of a new sibling will not affect her parents' love for her. (Rev: SLJ 9/06)

848 Thong, Roseanne. *Tummy Girl* (PS–K). Illus. by Sam Williams. 2007, Holt $15.95 (0-8050-7609-3). 32pp. Rhyming text and a photo-album format celebrate a baby growing into a toddler and then into a schoolgirl. (Rev: BL 4/1/07)

849 Toten, Teresa. *Bright Red Kisses* (PS–K). Illus. by Deirdre Betteridge. 2005, Annick LB $19.95 (1-55037-909-7); paper $7.95 (1-55037-908-9). 32pp. A young girl helps her mother prepare for an evening out, from running the bath to choosing the best lipstick, which will kiss her when her mother returns. (Rev: BL 1/1–15/06)

850 Van Leeuwen, Jean. *Benny and Beautiful Baby Delilah* (PS–K). Illus. by LeUyen Pham. 2006, Dial $16.99 (0-8037-2891-3). 32pp. Bennie finds his "beautiful" baby sister very trying until he succeeds in making her smile; excellent artwork adds to the heartwarming story. (Rev: BL 2/1/06; SLJ 3/06*)

851 Voake, Charlotte. *Hello Twins* (PS). Illus. by author. 2006, Candlewick $15.99 (0-7636-3003-9). 32pp. Little Charlotte and Simon may be twins, but they are different and they like it that way. (Rev: BL 5/15/06; SLJ 7/06)

852 Wargin, Kathy-Jo. *A Mother's Wish* (K–3). Illus. by Irena Roman. 2006, HarperCollins $15.99 (0-06-057170-5). A mother and her daughter make wishes—the mother for her daughter's independence, the daughter for closeness with her mother—in this loving story. (Rev: SLJ 5/06)

853 Wigersma, Tanneke. *Baby Brother* (PS–1). Illus. by Nynke Mare Talsma. 2005, Front St. $16.95 (1-932425-55-1). In a letter to her grandmother, little Mia focuses on her cat's delivery of five kittens, only mentioning the birth of her baby brother at the end; illustrations fill in the gaps. (Rev: SLJ 11/05)

854 Williams, Linda E. *The Best Winds* (K–3). Illus. by Eujin Kim Neilan. 2006, Boyds Mills $16.95 (1-59078-274-7). 32pp. Jinho ignores his grandfather's stories of ancient Korean traditions as the two work to create a kite, but when the young boy carelessly damages the kite he learns to appreciate his cultural heritage. (Rev: BL 4/1/06; SLJ 3/06)

855 Yaccarino, Dan. *Every Friday* (PS–K). Illus. 2007, Holt $16.95 (0-8050-7724-3). 32pp. A father and son enjoy their weekly Friday breakfast together. (Rev: BL 2/1/07)

856 Yolen, Jane. *Soft House* (PS–K). Illus. by Wendy Halperin. 2005, Candlewick $15.99 (0-7636-1697-4). 32pp. To fight boredom on a rainy day, a girl and her younger brother use household items to build a cozy fort. (Rev: BL 11/1/05)

857 Young, Ed. *My Mei Mei* (PS–2). Illus. 2006, Philomel $16.99 (0-399-24339-9). 32pp. A moving story about Antonia — who herself was adopted from China — and her difficult adjustment to life with her newly adopted infant sister, also from China. (Rev: BL 1/1–15/06; SLJ 2/06*)

858 Zemach, Margot. *Eating up Gladys* (PS–2). Illus. by Kaethe Zemach. 2005, Scholastic $16.99 (0-439-66490-X). 32pp. When Gladys, their bossy older sister, pushes them just a little too far, younger siblings Rose and Hilda plot a spectacular revenge. (Rev: BL 9/1/05; SLJ 9/05)

859 Ziefert, Harriet. *Bigger than Daddy* (PS). Illus. by Elliot Kreloff. 2006, Blue Apple $15.95 (1-59354-147-3). 36pp. On a trip to the park, Edward wants to switch roles with his daddy and do grown-up things. (Rev: BL 5/1/06; SLJ 8/06)

860 Ziefert, Harriet. *Grandma, It's for You!* (PS–1). Illus. by Lauren Browne. 2006, Blue Apple $15.95 (1-59354-109-0). Little Lulu fashions a very special hat to give to her grandmother. (Rev: SLJ 8/06)

861 Zolotow, Charlotte. *If It Weren't for You* (PS–2). Illus. by G. Brian Karas. 2006, Harper-Collins $15.99 (0-06-027875-7). As big sister fantasizes about what life would be like without her younger sibling, her younger sister behaves with such uncharacteristic kindness that the older girl decides she'd just as soon keep her around. (Rev: SLJ 10/06)

862 Zuckerman, Linda. *I Will Hold You 'til You Sleep* (PS). Illus. by Jon J. Muth. 2006, Scholastic $16.99 (0-439-43420-3). With poetic text and gentle illustrations, this book celebrates parents' love for a child throughout the years. (Rev: SLJ 10/06)

FRIENDSHIP STORIES

863 Atwood, Margaret. *Up in the Tree* (PS–2). Illus. 2006, Groundwood $14.95 (0-88899-729-9). 32pp. In this engaging two-color picture book first published in 1976, the Canadian author tells the story of two boys who make their home in a tree. (Rev: BL 4/1/06)

864 Chodos-Irvine, Margaret. *Best Best Friends* (PS–K). Illus. by author. 2006, Harcourt $16.00 (0-15-205694-7). 40pp. In this charming story for the very young, preschool jealousy briefly interrupts Clare and Mary's best-friendship. (Rev: BCCB 9/06; BL 5/1/06; HB 5–6/06; HBG 10/06; SLJ 6/06)

865 Gleeson, Libby. *Half a World Away* (K–2). Illus. by Freya Blackwood. 2007, Scholastic $15.99 (978-0-439-88977-3). Best friends Louie and Amy are devastated when Amy moves from Australia to New York City, but they find a way to communicate nonetheless. (Rev: BL 3/1/07*; SLJ 2/07)

866 Greenfield, Eloise. *The Friendly Four* (PS–2). Illus. by Jan Spivey Gilchrist. 2006, HarperCollins $16.99 (0-06-000759-1). 48pp. Drum has been dreading a dull summer and is happily surprised when three other African American children move into the neighborhood and they all become friends; an upbeat story told in a series of free-verse poems. (Rev: BL 4/15/06; SLJ 8/06)

867 Grimes, Nikki. *Danitra Brown, Class Clown* (K–3). Illus. by E. B. Lewis. 2005, HarperCollins $15.99 (0-68-817290-3). 32pp. Zuri worries about her ailing mother and about the new school year in

this latest story — presented in simple rhyming verses with expressive watercolors — about her close friendship with Danitra Brown. (Rev: BL 8/05; SLJ 9/05*)

868 Hughes, Susan. *Earth to Audrey* (1–3). Illus. by Stéphane Poulin. 2005, Kids Can $16.95 (1-55337-843-1). Audrey, a summer visitor to Ray's town, is so different that at first he thinks she's an alien, and as time goes by she teaches him a new way of looking at the world. (Rev: SLJ 1/06)

869 Jahn-Clough, Lisa. *Little Dog* (PS–2). Illus. 2006, Houghton $16.00 (0-618-57405-0). 32pp. An artist named Rosa and a hungry Little Dog used to living on the streets find happiness and friendship in the countryside. (Rev: BL 4/15/06; SLJ 5/06)

870 Jeffers, Dawn. *Vegetable Dreams / Huerto soñado* (K–2). Trans. by Eida de la Vega. Illus. by Claude Schneider. 2006, Raven Tree $16.95 (0-9741992-9-X). 32pp. A little girl plants a vegetable garden with the help of a kind, elderly neighbor and together they watch it grow; in Spanish and English. (Rev: SLJ 6/06)

871 Jeffers, Oliver. *Lost and Found* (PS–K). Illus. 2006, Philomel $15.99 (0-399-24503-0). 32pp. Finding a penguin on his doorstep, a little boy decides to take him home to the South Pole; it is only when he has put the penguin ashore that he realizes that all the bird wanted was a friend. (Rev: BL 12/15/05; SLJ 1/06)

872 Kroll, Virginia. *Forgiving a Friend* (PS–K). Illus. by Paige Billin-Frye. Series: The Way I Act. 2005, Albert Whitman $15.95 (1-8075-0618-4). 32pp. Seth, furious with Jacob for damaging his toy truck, refuses to accept his friend's apology, but soon learns an important lesson about forgiveness when he accidentally breaks a lamp himself. (Rev: BL 10/1/05)

873 Krosoczka, Jarrett J. *My Buddy, Slug* (PS–2). Illus. by author. 2006, Knopf $15.95 (0-375-83342-0). Alex upsets his friend the slug and must make an apology. (Rev: SLJ 9/06)

874 Luthardt, Kevin. *You're Weird!* (PS). Illus. by author. 2005, Dial $9.99 (0-8037-2986-3). A turtle and a rabbit learn to get along despite their differences and to refrain from calling each other "weird." (Rev: SLJ 8/05)

875 Michelin, Linda. *Zuzu's Wishing Cake* (PS). Illus. by D. B. Johnson. 2006, Houghton $16.00 (0-618-64640-X). 32pp. Zuzu loves to make things and uses all her creative energies in an effort to make the new boy next door smile. (Rev: BL 10/1/06; SLJ 10/06)

876 Michelson, Richard. *Across the Alley* (1–3). 2006, Putnam $16.99 (0-399-23970-7). 32pp. Abe, a young Jewish boy, and Willie, his African American neighbor across the alley, nurture their friendship and their dreams, and discover unsuspected talents for baseball and the violin. (Rev: BL 9/1/06; SLJ 10/06)

877 Rand, Gloria. *A Pen Pal for Max* (K–3). Illus. by Ted Rand. 2005, Holt $16.95 (0-8050-7586-0). 32pp. Maximiliano, who lives on a Chilean fruit farm, slips a note into a box of grapes bound for the United States and is delighted when he gets a letter from 10-year-old Maggie; their friendship grows and Maggie's school helps when Max's is hit by an earthquake. (Rev: BL 10/15/05; SLJ 10/05)

878 Reiser, Lynn. *My Way / A mi manera: A Margaret and Margarita Story / Un cuento de Margarita y Margaret* (PS–K). Illus. 2007, Greenwillow $15.99 (0-06-084101-X). 32pp. This bilingual picture book focuses on a friendship: although each friend has her own style, each learns from the other; refreshingly, Reiser emphasizes commonalities rather than differences. (Rev: BL 1/1–15/07)

879 Robbins, Jacqui. *The New Girl . . . and Me* (PS–2). Illus. by Matt Phelan. 2006, Simon & Schuster $16.95 (0-689-86468-X). 32pp. Shy Mia hangs back at first but mention of a pet iguana gives her the courage to approach new girl Shakeeta and the two become friends. (Rev: BCCB 9/06; BL 7/06*; SLJ 7/06)

880 Rosenbluth, Roz. *Getting to Know Ruben Plotnick* (K–3). Illus. by Maurie J. Manning. 2005, Flashlight $15.95 (0-972-92255-5). David worries what will happen when his new friend Ruben — the most popular boy in class — meets David's grandmother, whose dementia has made her behavior erratic. (Rev: SLJ 11/05)

881 Teevin, Toni. *What to Do? What to Do?* (PS–2). Illus. by Janet Pedersen. 2006, Clarion $16.00 (0-618-44632-X). 32pp. When too many birds begin clamoring for lonely Sophie's home-baked bread, she consults a fortune teller and makes new friends. (Rev: BL 5/1/06; SLJ 7/06)

HUMOROUS STORIES

882 Ahlberg, Allan. *The Runaway Dinner* (PS–3). Illus. by Bruce Ingman. 2006, Candlewick $15.99 (0-7636-3142-6). A sausage called Melvin decides he does not want to be eaten by young Banjo Cannon and takes flight, setting the stage for a frantic chase as the boy, his parents, the rest of the meal, kitchen furniture, and cutlery follow in pursuit. (Rev: BCCB 11/06; HBG 4/07; SLJ 12/06)

883 Anderson, Derek. *Gladys Goes Out to Lunch* (PS–2). Illus. by author. 2005, Simon & Schuster $15.95 (0-689-85688-1). Gladys the gorilla leaves the zoo in search of the source of a delicious smell, and tests various food (pizza, ice cream) before finding a cart selling banana bread. (Rev: SLJ 8/05)

884 Anderson, Peggy Perry. *Chuck's Truck* (PS–2). Illus. by author. 2006, Houghton $16.00 (0-618-66836-5). 32pp. A rhyming story about a farmer whose truck is overfull of friendly animals, with lively illustrations. (Rev: HB 5–6/06; HBG 10/06; SLJ 5/06)

885 Armstrong, Jennifer. *Once Upon a Banana* (PS–2). Illus. by David Small. 2006, Simon & Schuster $16.95 (0-689-84251-1). 48pp. A hilarious chain of accidents results when a monkey carelessly discards a banana peel on a busy sidewalk; rhyming street signs serve as captions for this wordless story. (Rev: BCCB 12/06; BL 11/1/06; HB 1–2/07; HBG 4/07; LMC 1/07; SLJ 12/06*)

886 Arnold, Marsha Diane. *Roar of a Snore* (PS). Illus. by Pierre Pratt. 2006, Dial $16.99 (0-8037-2936-7). Jack is being kept awake by a loud snoring sound, so he awakens the rest of his family, along with the dog and farm animals, and together they try to find out who's responsible. (Rev: HBG 4/0; SLJ 8/06*)

887 Arnold, Tedd. *Hi! Fly Guy!* (K–2). Illus. by author. 2005, Scholastic $5.99 (0-439-63903-4). 30pp. Buzz enters a fly in a pet competition, and the gifted insect impresses everyone with its multiple talents. (Rev: BCCB 10/05; HBG 4/06; LMC 1/06; SLJ 2/06)

888 Arnold, Tedd. *The Twin Princes* (K–3). Illus. by author. 2007, Dial $16.99 (0-8037-2696-1). 32pp. Twin chicken princes — one good, one bad — compete to inherit the kingdom in this pun-filled story. (Rev: BL 3/1/07*)

889 Atwood, Margaret. *Bashful Bob and Doleful Dorinda* (K–3). Illus. by Dusan Petricic. 2006, Bloomsbury Children's $17.95 (1-59990-004-1). 32pp. Alliteration and clever use of color enhance this Cinderella-like story of two hard-done-by children who wind up heroes. (Rev: BL 11/1/06)

890 Bachelet, Gilles. *My Cat, the Silliest Cat in the World* (PS–2). 2006, Abrams $16.95 (0-8109-4913-X). 32pp. A funny story of a "cat" that's not a cat at all but an elephant with a decidedly feline demeanor. (Rev: BL 6/1–15/06; SLJ 4/06)

891 Becker, Suzy. *Manny's Cows: The Niagara Falls Tale* (PS–2). 2006, HarperCollins $15.99 (0-06-054152-0). 40pp. Disaster strikes when Manny, a farm boy who tends a herd of 500 cows, takes them with him on a vacation trip to Niagara Falls. (Rev: BL 6/1–15/06; SLJ 6/06)

892 Berry, Lynne. *The Curious Demise of a Contrary Cat* (K–2). Illus. by Luke LaMarca. 2006, Simon & Schuster $12.95 (1-4169-0211-2). 40pp. Repetition and predictability are hallmarks of this wacky story about Cat's refusal to pitch in and help Witch with her party. (Rev: BL 11/1/06; SLJ 8/06)

893 Blankenship, Lee Ann. *Mr. Tuggle's Troubles* (K–3). Illus. by Karen Dugan. 2005, Boyds Mills $15.95 (1-59078-196-1). Mr. Tuggle has trouble looking after his clothes and looks stranger and stranger as he devises various replacements. (Rev: SLJ 10/05)

894 Bluemle, Elizabeth. *My Father the Dog* (PS–2). Illus. by Randy Cecil. 2006, Candlewick $15.99 (0-7636-2222-2). 32pp. A girl (convincingly) equates her father's habits with those of her pet dog in this entertaining picture book. (Rev: BL 5/15/06; SLJ 7/06)

895 Bowen, Anne. *What Do Teachers Do (After YOU Leave School?)* (K–3). Illus. by Barry Gott. 2006, Carolrhoda LB $15.95 (1-57505-922-3). Visions of teachers gone wild — dancing in the gym, roller-skating down the corridors, writing on the walls — may convince young children that teachers don't really live in the school. (Rev: SLJ 11/06)

896 Bright, Paul. *I'm Not Going Out There!* (K–2). Illus. by Ben Cort. 2006, Good Bks. $16.00 (1-56148-535-7). A little boy hides beneath his bed and refuses to come out, but he makes it clear that it's not the fearsome creatures in his bedroom that are keeping him there but rather his annoying sister. (Rev: SLJ 11/06)

897 Broach, Elise. *Cousin John Is Coming!* (K–3). Illus. by Nate Lilly. 2006, Dial $16.99 (0-8037-3013-6). Ben and his cat recall the various horrors of Cousin John's last visit while Ben's mother rhapsodizes about John's forthcoming arrival; cartoon illustrations provide much of the humor. (Rev: SLJ 7/06)

898 Brown, Peter. *Chowder* (PS–2). 2006, Little, Brown $15.99 (0-316-01180-0). 32pp. Chowder is a bulldog with unusual talents and has little in common with the other dogs in his neighborhood, but he finally finds friends when a petting zoo opens nearby. (Rev: BL 9/1/06; HBG 4/07; LMC 3–4/07; SLJ 9/06)

899 Brown, Peter. *Flight of the Dodo* (K–2). Illus. by author. 2005, Little, Brown $15.99 (0-316-11038-8). Penguin and a handful of other flightless birds join forces to invent a flying machine; both text and illustrations are full of fun. (Rev: SLJ 12/05)

900 Bruel, Nick. *Who Is Melvin Bubble?* (K–4). Illus. by author. 2006, Roaring Brook $16.95 (1-59643-116-4). This humorous profile of Melvin Bubble contains sometimes contradictory views of Melvin from his parents, dog, teddy bear, Santa Claus, and even a monster that lives in Melvin's closet. (Rev: SLJ 8/06)

901 Bryan, Sean. *A Girl and Her Gator* (K–2). Illus. by Tom Murphy. 2006, Arcade $14.99 (1-55970-798-4). A silly story about Claire, who is unsettled at first when she discovers an alligator on her head, but, assured that the gator should cause no change in her activities, the young girl blithely carries on with her everyday routine. (Rev: SLJ 8/06)

902 Chartrand, Lili. *Taming Horrible Harry* (K–3). Trans. from French by Susan Ouriou. Illus. by Rogé. 2006, Tundra $16.95 (0-88776-772-9). What the monster called Harry enjoys most is scaring children — until he learns to read and discovers the joy of books; offbeat illustrations add to the appeal. (Rev: SLJ 7/06)

903 Christelow, Eileen. *Letters from a Desperate Dog* (PS–2). 2006, Clarion $16.00 (0-618-51003-6). 32pp. Emma the dog feels badly treated by her owner George and seeks the advice of a canine columnist in the *Weekly Bone*. (Rev: BL 10/1/06; SLJ 11/06)

904 Cote, Genevieve. *What Elephant?* (K–3). Illus. by author. 2006, Kids Can $16.95 (1-55337-875-X). When his neighbors express skepticism, George decides that perhaps he was mistaken when he saw an elephant in his house. (Rev: SLJ 12/06)

905 Crandall, Court. *Hugville* (PS–1). Illus. by Joe Murray. 2005, Random $13.95 (0-375-82418-9). The mayor of Hugville proudly conducts a tour of his town, pointing out all the different types of hugs that are practiced there. (Rev: SLJ 1/06)

906 Crimi, Carolyn. *The Louds Move In!* (K–2). Illus. by Regan Dunnick. 2006, Marshall Cavendish $14.95 (0-7614-5221-4). Although the neighbors have been annoyed by the noise created by the Loud family, they become worried when the din suddenly subsides. (Rev: SLJ 5/06)

907 Cronin, Doreen. *Bounce* (PS). Illus. by Scott Menchin. 2007, Simon & Schuster $14.00 (978-1-4169-1627-7). 40pp. In this appealing sequel to *Wiggle* (2005), simple, rhyming text and colorful artwork combine to capture the essence of bouncing. (Rev: BL 3/15/07)

908 Cronin, Doreen. *Diary of a Spider* (PS–3). Illus. by Harry Bliss. 2005, HarperCollins $15.99 (0-06-000153-4). A young spider's diary reveals typical concerns — molting, reassuring unhappy friends, worries about strange food, relations with flies, and vacuum drills. (Rev: SLJ 8/05)

909 Crunk, Tony. *Railroad John and the Red Rock Run* (1–3). Illus. by Michael Austin. 2006, Peachtree $16.95 (1-56145-363-3). 32pp. Train engineer John overcomes some daunting challenges to deliver passenger Lonesome Bob to his wedding on time; illustrations reminiscent of daguerreotypes complement this tall tale. (Rev: BL 4/1/06; SLJ 5/06)

910 Davidson, Ellen Dee. *Princess Justina Albertina: A Cautionary Tale* (PS–1). Illus. by Michael Chesworth. 2007, Charlesbridge $15.95 (978-1-57091-652-6). The willful Princess Justina Albertina wants a pet — a perfect pet — and is satisfied with none until her faithful nanny brings her a gryphon; and then the trouble begins. (Rev: SLJ 3/07)

911 Delaney, Mary. *Mabel O'Leary Put Peas in Her Ear-y* (PS–2). Illus. by Kathy Couri. 2006, Little, Brown $15.99 (0-316-13506-2). Little Mabel's hearing is severely compromised when she hides her detested peas in her ears; rhyming text and detailed illustrations add to the silliness. (Rev: SLJ 3/06)

912 Derby, Sally. *Whoosh Went the Wind!* (K–3). Illus. by Vincent Nguyen. 2006, Marshall Cavendish $16.99 (0-7614-5309-1). 32pp. In this lively picture book, an imaginative little boy explains to his skeptical teacher how the wind made him late for school. (Rev: BL 10/15/06; SLJ 10/06)

913 Durant, Alan. *Burger Boy* (PS–2). Illus. by Mei Matsuoka. 2006, Clarion $16.00 (0-618-71466-9). 32pp. Benny's mother warns him that if he eats nothing but burgers he'll turn into one and that's just what happens in this hilarious picture book. (Rev: BL 11/15/06; SLJ 10/06)

914 Eaton, Maxwell. *Best Buds* (1–3). Illus. by author. 2006, Knopf $12.99 (978-0-375-83803-3). Max (who looks a lot like Charlie Brown) and his best friend Pinky the pig have adventures together on Saturdays, until the week when Pinky disappears; bright cartoon pictures add to the humor. (Rev: SLJ 2/07)

915 Ellis, Sarah. *The Queen's Feet* (K–2). Illus. by Dusan Petricic. 2006, Red Deer $17.95 (0-88995-320-1). 32pp. Queen Daisy's unruly feet finally get totally out of line and she has to rein them in this humorous story full of wordplay. (Rev: BL 5/1/06; SLJ 4/06)

916 Esbaum, Jill. *Estelle Takes a Bath* (PS–2). Illus. by Mary Newell Depalma. 2006, Holt $16.95 (0-8050-7741-3). 32pp. Estelle's comfortable bath is rudely interrupted by a little field mouse. (Rev: BL 1/1–15/07; SLJ 11/06)

917 Fallon, Jimmy. *Snowball Fight!* (PS–1). Illus. by Adam Stower. 2005, Dutton $15.99 (0-525-47456-0). A boy and his younger sister enjoy a snow day off school in this book with action-packed cartoon illustrations. (Rev: SLJ 11/05)

918 Fearnley, Jane. *The Search for the Perfect Child* (PS–K). Illus. by author. 2006, Candlewick $15.99 (0-7636-3231-7). 40pp. The coolest dog in the world is searching for a perfect child and has a number of criteria laid out. (Rev: BL 12/1/06; SLJ 11/06)

919 Feiffer, Kate. *Double Pink* (K–3). Illus. by Bruce Ingman. 2005, Simon & Schuster $15.95 (0-689-87190-2). Young Madison's single-minded love for the color pink gets out of control. (Rev: SLJ 11/05)

920 Fisher, Doris, and Dani Sneed. *One Odd Day* (K–2). Illus. by Karen Lee. 2006, Sylvan Dell $15.95 (0-9768823-3-7). In this humorous story told in rhyming text, a young boy awakens one day to

discover that everything around him is truly odd: his dog has five legs and his shirt has three sleeves. (Rev: SLJ 12/06)

921 Fleming, Candace. *Tippy-Tippy-Tippy, Hide!* (PS–K). Illus. by G. Brian Karas. 2007, Simon & Schuster $16.99 (0-689-87479-0). 40pp. In this sequel to *Muncha! Muncha! Muncha!* (2002), Mr. McGreely is determined to keep the rabbits out of his cozy house and barricades it so thoroughly that he can't get out when spring finally arrives. (Rev: BL 12/15/06; SLJ 1/07)

922 Fox, Mem. *A Particular Cow* (PS–2). Illus. by Terry Denton. 2006, Harcourt $16.00 (0-15-200250-2). Out for her Saturday walk, a cow collides with a clothesline, ends up with a pair of bloomers on her head, and slapstick mayhem follows. (Rev: SLJ 9/06)

923 Frazee, Marla. *Walk On! A Guide for Babies of All Ages* (PS–K). Illus. 2006, Harcourt $16.00 (0-15-205573-8). 40pp. A humorous how-to guide for babies who are just learning to walk. (Rev: BL 4/1/06; SLJ 4/06*)

924 Freedman, Michelle. *The Ravioli Kid: An Original Spaghetti Western* (K–3). Illus. by Jason Abbott. 2005, Gibbs Smith $15.95 (1-58685-438-0). In this rollicking, pun-filled western tale, 7-year-old Stellina Pomodoro faces off against Angel Hair and the Anti-Pasta Gang. (Rev: SLJ 4/06)

925 French, Jackie. *Pete the Sheep-Sheep* (PS–1). Illus. by Bruce Whatley. 2005, Clarion $14.00 (0-618-56862-X). 32pp. Shaun, a newly arrived sheep shearer at Shaggy Gully, shows the old timers that he can easily outperform them and their sheepdogs with the help of Pete, his "sheep-sheep." (Rev: BL 1/1–15/06; SLJ 11/05)

926 Funke, Cornelia. *Princess Pigsty* (K–2). Trans. from German by Chantal Wright. Illus. by Kerstin Meyer. 2007, Scholastic $16.99 (0-439-88554-X). Princess Isabella is bored with her privileged life and longs to be normal; when she throws her crown away and refuses to cooperate, her father punishes her with work that she thoroughly enjoys. (Rev: SLJ 4/07)

927 Graham, Bob. *Dimity Dumpty* (PS–2). Illus. by author. 2007, Candlewick $15.99 (978-0-7636-3078-2). 40pp. Dimity is Humpty Dumpty's diffident little sister who conquers her timidity when her brother needs help. (Rev: BL 12/1/06)

928 Graves, Keith. *The Unexpectedly Bad Hair of Barcelona Smith* (K–3). Illus. by author. 2006, Philomel $16.99 (0-399-24273-2). Barcelona sees dangers all around him and takes all precautions until the day his hair takes over. (Rev: SLJ 6/06)

929 Gray, Kes. *006 and a Half* (K–2). Illus. by Nick Sharratt. 2007, Abrams $10.95 (978-0-8109-1719-4). 32pp. Daisy goes undercover as a secret agent but is frustrated when no one seems to be able to decipher her secret coded language. (Rev: BL 4/1/07)

930 Hamilton, Arlene. *Only a Cow* (PS–2). Illus. by Dean Griffiths. 2006, Fitzhenry & Whiteside $16.95 (1-55041-871-8). 32pp. A boisterous cow called Lucille longs to run, and gets her chance when she finds herself in a horse race at the county fair. (Rev: BL 1/1–15/07)

931 Harrington, Janice N. *The Chicken-Chasing Queen of Lamar County* (PS–2). 2007, Farrar $16.00 (978-0-374-31251-0). 32pp. A young African American girl who enjoys chasing chickens decides to forgo the fun when she finds her main target tending to a flock of new chicks. (Rev: BL 2/1/07)

932 Haseley, Dennis. *The Invisible Moose* (PS–2). Illus. by Steven Kellogg. 2006, Dial $16.99 (0-8037-2892-1). 40pp. A shy Canadian moose in love with a lovely girl moose who is captured by a trapper uses an invisibility potion to follow her to New York City; a funny story of magic, romance, and adventure. (Rev: BL 2/1/06; SLJ 3/06)

933 Hawkes, Kevin. *The Wicked Big Toddlah* (PS–1). Illus. 2007, Knopf $16.99 (978-0-375-82427-2). 40pp. A baby of gargantuan proportions is born in Maine, posing daunting challenges for the normal-sized people who must care for him. (Rev: BL 4/15/07)

934 Hayes, Joe. *The Gum-Chewing Rattler* (K–3). Illus. by Antonio Castro L. 2006, Cinco Puntos $16.95 (0-938317-99-7). In this amusing tall tale, inspired by the author's childhood in small-town Arizona, a young boy is saved from the bite of a rattlesnake by a wad of bubble gum. (Rev: SLJ 1/07)

935 Helakoski, Leslie. *Big Chickens* (PS–4). Illus. by Henry Cole. 2006, Dutton $15.99 (0-525-47575-3). 32pp. When a wolf is spotted in the barnyard, four hens run for their lives but find they gain courage when it's really needed. (Rev: BL 2/1/06; SLJ 2/06)

936 Henkes, Kevin. *Lilly's Big Day* (PS–K). Illus. 2006, Greenwillow $15.99 (0-06-074236-4). 40pp. Lilly is beside herself with excitement at the thought of being flower girl at her teacher's wedding, but there's a slight problem — he hasn't asked her. (Rev: BL 3/1/06*; SLJ 4/06*)

937 Himmelman, John. *Chickens to the Rescue* (PS–2). Illus. 2006, Holt $16.95 (0-8050-7951-3). 32pp. Farmer Greenstalk's chickens come to the rescue of farm residents — both human and animal — in this entertaining romp. (Rev: BL 11/1/06; SLJ 10/06*)

938 Hogg, Gary. *Look What the Cat Dragged In!* (K–3). Illus. by Mike Wohnoutka. 2005, Dutton $15.99 (0-525-46984-2). 32pp. When the slothful Lazybones family begins to talk of replacing their

faithful cat with a dog, the hardworking feline plots revenge. (Rev: BL 11/1/05; SLJ 2/06)

939 Hooper, Meredith. *Celebrity Cat* (K–3). Illus. by Bee Willey. 2006, Frances Lincoln $15.95 (1-84507-290-1). 36pp. Felissima, a cat with a passion for art, creates her own renditions of famous paintings to include cats in each one. (Rev: BL 11/15/06; SLJ 12/06)

940 Hopkins, Jackie Mims. *The Gold Miner's Daughter: A Melodramatic Fairy Tale* (K–2). Illus. by Jon Goodell. 2006, Peachtree $15.95 (1-56145-362-5). 32pp. In this modern-day fable presented in the form of a stage production, Gracie Pearl encounters a series of classic fairy tale characters as she struggles to find a way to save her home and mine from an evil banker. (Rev: BL 2/15/06; SLJ 4/06)

941 Horowitz, Dave. *Five Little Gefiltes* (PS–2). Illus. by author. 2007, Putnam $12.99 (978-0-399-24608-1). In this Yiddish-flavored takeoff on "Five Little Ducklings," five young gefilte fish swim off on their own and explore the delights of New York City in the early 20th century. (Rev: SLJ 2/07)

942 James, Simon. *Baby Brains Superstar* (PS). Illus. 2005, Candlewick $15.99 (0-7636-2894-8). 32pp. In this appealing sequel to *Baby Brains* (2004), young Baby, a musical prodigy because Mom wore earphones on her belly, decides to pursue a career in rock 'n' roll, performing before a massive audience. (Rev: BL 9/15/05; SLJ 11/05)

943 Jinkins, Jim. *Shrinky Pinky!* (1–3). Illus. Series: Pinky Dinky Doo. 2005, Random $12.95 (0-375-83234-3). 48pp. Pinky tells her younger brother a tall tale about how she dealt with a bully named Lane Puppytray. (Rev: BL 12/1/05)

944 Johnson, Paul Brett. *On Top of Spaghetti* (PS–2). Illus. 2006, Scholastic $15.99 (0-439-74944-1). 32pp. The lyrics of Tom Glazer's song about spaghetti provide the framework for this tale of a runaway meatball. (Rev: BL 4/15/06; SLJ 5/06)

945 Joyce, William. *A Day with Wilbur Robinson* (PS–2). 2006, HarperCollins $16.99 (0-06-089098-3). 40pp. A young friend visits Wilbur Robinson at home, meets his extraordinary family, and gets swept up in some unforgettable adventures in this wacky romp, an expanded version of the 1990 title. (Rev: BL 8/06)

946 Kelly, Mij. *Where's My Darling Daughter?* (PS). Illus. by Katharine McEwen. 2006, Good Bks. $16.00 (1-56148-537-3). Certain that he has misplaced his baby daughter (who is on her father's back the whole time), Poppa Bombola sets off on a frantic search. (Rev: SLJ 12/06)

947 Kloske, Geoffrey. *Once Upon a Time, the End (Asleep in 60 Seconds)* (K–3). Illus. by Barry Blitt. 2005, Simon & Schuster $15.95 (0-689-86619-4). 40pp. An exhausted father tells his insatiable child hilariously abbreviated versions of fairy tales and nursery rhymes. (Rev: BCCB 12/05; BL 11/15/05*; HBG 4/06; SLJ 10/05)

948 Kopelke, Lisa. *The Younger Brother's Survival Guide: By Matt* (PS–3). Illus. by author. 2006, Simon & Schuster $15.95 (0-689-86249-0). Matt offers helpful and humorous advice on how to survive life with an older sibling. (Rev: SLJ 3/06)

949 Krensky, Stephen. *Big Bad Wolves at School* (PS–2). Illus. by Brad Sneed. 2007, Simon & Schuster $15.99 (978-0-689-83799-9). 32pp. Rufus, a happy-go-lucky young wolf, finds classes at the Big Bad Wolf Academy a little too challenging for his tastes; energetic illustrations add to the hilarity. (Rev: BL 4/1/07)

950 Lendler, Ian. *An Undone Fairy Tale* (K–3). Illus. by Whitney Martin. 2005, Simon & Schuster $15.95 (0-689-86677-1). 32pp. A fairy tale involving a princess locked in a tower spins out of control when the illustrator and narrator can't keep up. (Rev: BL 1/1–15/06; SLJ 12/05)

951 Levine, Martha Peaslee. *Stop That Nose!* (PS–1). Illus. by Lee White. 2006, Marshall Cavendish $14.95 (0-7614-5280-X). Dad's nose flies off in a sneezing fit and young David chases valiantly after it as it continues to sneeze, ejecting all sorts of things en route. (Rev: SLJ 4/06)

952 Lillegard, Dee. *Balloons Balloons Balloons* (PS–1). Illus. by Bernadette Pons. 2007, Dutton $16.99 (978-0-525-45940-8). Children and adult react in different ways when a town is inundated with colorful balloons. (Rev: SLJ 2/07)

953 Lithgow, John. *Marsupial Sue Presents "The Runaway Pancake"* (K–2). Illus. by Jack Davis. 2005, Simon & Schuster $17.95 (0-689-87847-8). 40pp. Marsupial Sue the kangaroo — here cast in the role of Auntie May — and her friends are staging their version of "The Gingerbread Man"; Lithgow reads the story on an accompanying CD. (Rev: BL 11/1/05; SLJ 10/05)

954 Long, Kathy. *The Runaway Shopping Cart* (PS–2). Illus. by Susan Estelle Kwas. 2007, Dutton $16.99 (978-0-525-47187-5). When the shopping cart Kaleb's sitting in gets loose and starts rolling through town it attracts a train of followers, Gingerbread Man-style. (Rev: SLJ 4/07)

955 Lubner, Susan. *Ruthie Bon Bair, Do Not Go to Bed with Wringing Wet Hair!* (PS–3). Illus. by Bruce Whatley. 2006, Abrams $15.95 (0-8109-5470-2). Little Ruthie refuses to follow her mother's advice and ends up with all kinds of horrid hair problems. (Rev: SLJ 11/06)

956 McAllister, Angela. *Just Like Sisters* (PS–3). Illus. by Sophie Fatus. 2006, Simon & Schuster $15.95 (1-4169-0643-6). Nancy is unfazed when her penpal Ally comes to visit and turns out to be an alligator. (Rev: SLJ 6/06)

957 McAllister, Angela. *Trust Me, Mom!* (PS–2). Illus. by Ross Collins. 2005, Bloomsbury $16.95 (1-58234-955-X). Armed with plenty of advice from his mom, young Ollie sets out on a solo trip to the store, but along the way he encounters some unexpected surprises. (Rev: SLJ 12/05)

958 McElligott, Matthew. *Backbeard and the Birthday Suit: The Hairiest Pirate Who Ever Lived* (K–2). Illus. 2006, Walker $16.95 (0-8027-8065-2). 32pp. Blackbeard the pirate trades his dilapidated buccaneering duds for a stylish new outfit much to the surprise of his crew. (Rev: BL 4/15/06; SLJ 4/06)

959 McElmurry, Jill. *I'm Not a Baby!* (PS–2). 2006, Random $16.95 (0-375-83614-4). 32pp. Leo Leotardi, the youngest member of his family, has difficulty convincing family members that he's no longer a baby; Victorian-era illustrations of Leo bursting out of his baby clothes add to the fun. (Rev: BL 6/1–15/06; HBG 4/07; SLJ 7/06*)

960 McGee, Marni. *Winston the Book Wolf* (PS–2). Illus. by Ian Beck. 2006, Walker $16.95 (0-8027-9569-2). 32pp. In this amusing send-up of the Little Red Riding Hood story, the wolf has an appetite for books, behavior that infuriates the librarian, but he's shown the error of his ways and taught to read — and not eat — the books by a little girl named Rosie who just happens to be wearing a red hood. (Rev: SLJ 12/06)

961 McKy, Katie. *Pumpkin Town! (Or, Nothing Is Better and Worse Than Pumpkins)* (K–3). Illus. by Pablo Bernasconi. 2006, Houghton $16.00 (0-618-60569-X). José and his brothers don't know quite what to do when the pumpkin seeds they discarded at the end of the last growing season take root and threaten to overrun the town. (Rev: SLJ 11/06)

962 McNaughton, Colin. *Captain Abdul's Little Treasure* (K–3). Series: Captain Abdul. 2006, Candlewick $14.99 (0-7636-3045-4). 48pp. The treasure on Captain Abdul's ship is a baby, and his pirate baby-sitters love playing with him despite their gruff appearances. (Rev: BL 5/1/06)

963 Madison, Alan. *The Littlest Grape Stomper* (K–2). Illus. by Giselle Potter. 2007, Random $16.99 (978-0-375-83675-6). This whimsical tall tale describes the story behind the Grape Lakes, in which a boy called Sixto Poblano — disinclined to use the six toes he has on each foot to stomp grapes — squishes a huge vatful and then spills it out, creating a massive flood. (Rev: SLJ 4/07)

964 Madison, Alan. *Pecorino Plays Ball* (K–2). Illus. by AnnaLaura Cantone. 2006, Simon & Schuster $15.95 (0-689-86522-8). 40pp. Although he's never caught or pitched a baseball before, young Pecorino Sasquatch looks forward to his first Little League game. (Rev: BL 2/1/06; SLJ 3/06)

965 Madison, Alan. *Pecorino's First Concert* (K–2). Illus. by AnnaLaura Cantone. 2005, Simon & Schuster $15.95 (0-689-85952-X). Pecorino goes to the orchestra and gets trapped in a tuba in this amusing tale. (Rev: SLJ 8/05)

966 Mahy, Margaret. *Down the Back of the Chair* (PS–2). Illus. by Polly Dunbar. 2006, Clarion $16.00 (0-618-69395-5). 32pp. A family in search of lost car keys discovers lots more under the chair cushions (including a diamond ring, a ski, and a lion) in this rhyming jaunt. (Rev: BL 5/1/06; SLJ 6/06)

967 Manushkin, Fran. *The Shivers in the Fridge* (PS–1). Illus. by Paul Zelinsky. 2006, Dutton $16.99 (0-525-46943-5). 40pp. Readers may take some time to work out that the very cold characters In this fanciful picture book are actually members of a family of refrigerator magnets. (Rev: BCCB 10/06; BL 10/15/06; HB 11–12/06; HBG 4/07; SLJ 10/06)

968 Melling, David. *The Scallywags* (PS–2). Illus. 2007, Barron's $14.99 (978-0-7641-5991-6). 32pp. The wolf family known as the Scallywags decide to reform their behavior after the other animals totally reject them, but they go much too far in the other direction. (Rev: BL 2/1/07)

969 Milgrim, David. *Young MacDonald* (PS–1). Illus. 2006, Dutton $12.99 (0-525-47570-2). 32pp. Young MacDonald is a new-tech enthusiast and has a wonderful time experimenting with new animal combinations (a horse and a pig become a "hig") until his parents come home. (Rev: BL 4/15/06; SLJ 5/06)

970 Mora, Pat. *Doña Flor: A Tall Tale About a Giant Woman with a Great Big Heart* (PS–2). Illus. by Raul Colon. 2005, Knopf $15.95 (0-375-82337-9). 40pp. When the cries of a fearsome beast frighten her fellow villagers, Doña Flor, a woman of monumental stature, sets off to find out what's causing the animal's distress only to discover the perpetrator is much less threatening than expected. (Rev: BL 12/1/05; SLJ 10/05)

971 Newman, Jeff. *Hippo! No, Rhino* (K–2). Illus. by author. 2006, Little, Brown $15.99 (0-316-15573-X). A rhino at the zoo is mistakenly labeled a hippo in this almost-wordless tale. (Rev: SLJ 7/06)

972 Nolen, Jerdine. *Plantzilla Goes to Camp* (1–3). Illus. by David Catrow. 2006, Simon & Schuster $16.95 (0-689-86803-0). 32pp. Mortimer's pet plant is not allowed at his summer camp but manages to sneak in anyway and save him from a bully; a sequel to *Plantzilla* (2002). (Rev: BL 4/15/06; SLJ 3/06)

973 O'Connor, Jane. *Fancy Nancy* (PS–2). Illus. by Robin Preiss Glasser. 2006, HarperCollins $15.99 (0-06-054209-8). 32pp. Nancy, a fashion-obsessed young girl, is determined to give the rest of her fam-

ily a badly needed makeover. (Rev: BL 1/1–15/06; SLJ 2/06)

974 Offill, Jenny. *17 Things I'm Not Allowed to Do Anymore* (PS–K). Illus. by Nancy Carpenter. 2006, Schwartz & Wade $15.99 (0-375-83596-2). 32pp. The mischievous narrator of this appealing picture book recounts some of the things she's been forbidden to do — stapling her brother's hair to the pillow, freezing flies in ice cubes, and so forth. (Rev: BL 11/1/06; SLJ 11/06*)

975 Palatini, Margie. *Three French Hens* (PS–2). Illus. by Richard Egielski. 2005, Hyperion $15.99 (0-7868-5167-8). 40pp. Three French hens — Collette, Poulette, and Fifi — sent as a gift to M. Philippe Renard end up instead in the clutches of Phil Fox, who welcomes the trio as potential food but is soon transformed by their kind attentions. (Rev: BCCB 11/05; BL 11/1/05; HB 11–12/05; HBG 4/06; LMC 11–12/05; SLJ 10/05*)

976 Parpan, Justin. *Gwango's Lonesome Trail* (1–5). Illus. by author. 2006, Red Cygnet $17.95 (1-60108-004-2). Gwango, a lonely dinosaur, wanders the contemporary Southwest in search of a friend; handsome paintings show the landscape and the humorous text has a retro feel. (Rev: SLJ 12/06)

977 Pelletier, Andrew T. *The Amazing Adventures of Bathman!* (K–2). Illus. by Peter Elwell. 2005, Dutton $15.99 (0-525-47164-2). A little boy becomes Bathman, superhero of the tub, in this fun bathtime book. (Rev: SLJ 7/05)

978 Pinkwater, Daniel. *Bad Bear Detectives: An Irving and Muktuk Story* (PS–2). Illus. by Jill Pinkwater. Series: Irving and Muktuk. 2006, Houghton $16.00 (0-618-43125-X). 32pp. Who stole the muffins? Two falsely accused polar bears set out to find the real suspects. (Rev: BL 7/06; SLJ 8/06)

979 Pinkwater, Daniel. *Bad Bears Go Visiting* (K–3). Illus. by Jill Pinkwater. 2007, Houghton $16.00 (978-0-618-43126-7). 32pp. Naughty polar bears Irving and Muktuk break out of the zoo and pay an unexpected and rowdy visit to the Beachball family. (Rev: BL 4/1/07)

980 Pinkwater, Daniel. *Dancing Larry* (K–3). Illus. by Jill Pinkwater. 2006, Marshall Cavendish $16.95 (0-7614-5220-6). 32pp. Larry the polar bear, denied admission to Madame Swoboda's ballet class, forms his own dance company. (Rev: BL 3/15/06; SLJ 6/06)

981 Powell, Anna. *Don't Say That, Willy Nilly!* (K–2). Illus. by David Roberts. 2005, Good Bks. $16.00 (1-56148-488-1). Willy Nilly has an amazing knack for saying the wrong thing at the wrong time. (Rev: SLJ 10/05)

982 Ransom, Jeanie Franz. *What Do Parents Do? (When You're Not Home)* (PS–2). Illus. by Cyd Moore. 2007, Peachtree $16.95 (978-1-56145-409-9). 32pp. Apparently parents get up to all sorts of things in their children's absence — jumping on the bed, dressing up the dog . . . (Rev: BL 4/1/07)

983 Reed, Lynn Rowe. *Please Don't Upset P.U. Zorilla* (PS–1). Illus. by author. 2006, Knopf $15.95 (0-375-83654-3). P.U. Zorilla, a skunk, finds it hard to hold down a job until his stinky spray succeeds in foiling a robbery and Mayor Tootlebee offers him a job as police chief. (Rev: SLJ 10/06)

984 Robertson, M. P. *Hieronymus Betts and His Unusual Pets* (PS–1). Illus. by author. 2005, Frances Lincoln $15.95 (1-84507-289-8). Hieronymus Betts introduces his menagerie of unusually awful pets, but he asserts that there's one thing that's even worse — a little brother! (Rev: SLJ 2/06)

985 Robinson, Fay. *Faucet Fish* (PS–2). Illus. by Wayne Anderson. 2005, Dutton $15.99 (0-525-47166-9). 32pp. Elizabeth can't seem to get her parents' attention, even when all types of fish begin to come out of the bathroom faucet. (Rev: BL 8/05; SLJ 8/05)

986 Rosenthal, Betsy R. *It's Not Worth Making a Tzimmes Over!* (PS–2). Illus. by Ruth Rivers. 2006, Albert Whitman $15.95 (0-8075-3677-6). 32pp. This humorous picture book chronicles a cooking experiment gone wrong and introduces young readers to an unflappable grandmother and a handful of Yiddish terms. (Rev: BL 3/15/06; SLJ 5/06)

987 Ross, Tony. *I Want My Tooth* (K–2). Illus. by author. 2005, Kane/Miller paper $4.95 (1-929132-85-9). When the Little Princess loses one of her teeth, she orders everyone in the castle to search for it. (Rev: SLJ 10/05)

988 Rumford, James. *Don't Touch My Hat* (K–2). Illus. 2007, Knopf $16.99 (0-375-83782-5). 40pp. Sheriff John relies on his lucky 10-gallon hat until the night he rushes off to catch some bad men wearing his wife's fancy plumed chapeau. (Rev: BL 12/15/06; SLJ 1/07)

989 Ruurs, Margriet. *Wake Up, Henry Rooster!* (PS–2). Illus. by Sean Cassidy. 2006, Fitzhenry & Whiteside $16.95 (1-55041-952-8). 32pp. Henry the rooster is no early bird and the farm life gets out of whack as he sleeps off his late nights. (Rev: BL 5/15/06; SLJ 7/06)

990 Scamell, Ragnhild. *Ouch!* (PS–1). Illus. by Michael Terry. 2006, Good Bks. $16.00 (1-56148-511-X). Poor Hedgehog has an apple stuck in her spines and all her friends' efforts to help her backfire until she comes across Goat. (Rev: SLJ 7/06)

991 Schertle, Alice. *The Adventures of Old Bo Bear* (PS–2). Illus. by David Parkins. 2006, Chronicle $16.95 (0-8118-3476-X). 28pp. After his favorite teddy bear loses an ear in a much-needed washing, his owner takes him off for some energetic play that involves quite a lot of dirt plus some potential

explanations for the missing appendage. (Rev: BL 2/1/06; SLJ 2/06)

992 Schotter, Roni. *The Boy Who Loved Words* (2–4). Illus. by Giselle Potter. 2006, Random $16.95 (0-375-83601-2). 40pp. A boy called Selig loves words, and after collecting many on scraps of paper — and suffering the scorn of his classmates — he decides to distribute them around. (Rev: BL 2/1/06; SLJ 4/06*)

993 Schwarz, Viviane. *Shark and Lobster's Amazing Undersea Adventure* (PS–2). 2006, Candlewick $15.99 (0-7636-2910-3). 40pp. Shark and Lobster convince their undersea friends to build a fortress to protect themselves against tigers, then realize the folly of their phobia. (Rev: BL 7/06)

994 Shulman, Mark. *Mom and Dad Are Palindromes* (1–4). Illus. by Adam McCauley. 2006, Chronicle $15.95 (0-8118-4328-9). Once Bob finds out what palindromes are, he sees them everywhere — more than 100 in all. (Rev: SLJ 6/06)

995 Sierra, Judy. *The Secret Science Project That Almost Ate the School* (1–3). Illus. by Stephen Gammell. 2006, Simon & Schuster $16.95 (1-4169-1175-8). A young girl orders a science fair project by mail, but neglects to read the directions on its package carefully. (Rev: SLJ 11/06)

996 Sierra, Judy. *Thelonius Monster's Sky-High Fly Pie: A Revolting Rhyme* (PS–2). Illus. by Edward Koren. 2006, Knopf $16.95 (0-375-83218-1). 40pp. Thelonius invites friends to enjoy a pie of flies, but the fly takes off before he can enjoy it in this funny rhyming story illustrated in cartoonist Koren's signature style. (Rev: BL 5/1/06; SLJ 5/06*)

997 Slater, Dashka. *Baby Shoes* (PS). Illus. by Hiroe Nakata. 2006, Bloomsbury $15.95 (1-58234-684-4). 32pp. Baby's new white shoes are soon covered in multicolor stains as he and his mother take a walk. (Rev: BL 5/1/06; HBG 10/06; SLJ 5/06)

998 Slonim, David. *He Came with the Couch* (K–3). Illus. by author. 2005, Chronicle $15.95 (0-8118-4430-7). A wacky story about a family buys that buys a sofa that's the home of a funny-looking creature suffering from "upholsterosis." (Rev: SLJ 11/05)

999 Smith, Stu. *The Bubble Gum Kid* (K–2). Illus. by Julia Woolf. 2006, Running Pr. $15.95 (0-7624-2046-4). Billy Bob Glum asks his sister to teach him how to blow a bubble so he can impress an annoying bully named Double Chin Dan; a fast-paced story told in rhyming text. (Rev: SLJ 12/06)

1000 Sydor, Colleen. *Camilla Chameleon* (K–2). Illus. by Pascale Constantin. 2005, Kids Can $16.95 (1-55337-482-7). A zany story about Camilla, whose ability to blend in with her surroundings stems from her mother's craving for cream-of-chameleon soup when she was pregnant; then her mother gets pregnant again and develops a taste for cream of pterodactyl soup . . . (Rev: SLJ 6/06)

1001 Taylor, Alastair. *Mr. Blewitt's Nose* (K–2). Illus. by author. 2005, Houghton $16.00 (0-618-42353-2). Primrose and her amazingly smelly dog search for the owner of a lost nose in this amusing book. (Rev: SLJ 7/05)

1002 Tyler, Anne. *Timothy Tugbottom Says No!* (PS). Illus. by Mitra Modaressi. 2005, Putnam $15.99 (0-399-24255-4). 32pp. Toddler Timothy Tugbottom steadfastly refuses to try anything new until an uncomfortable night in his cramped crib convinces him that change can be good. (Rev: BL 11/1/05; SLJ 10/05)

1003 Van Allsburg, Chris. *Probuditi!* (PS–2). 2006, Houghton $18.95 (0-618-75502-0). 32pp. Inspired by the performance of a professional magician, young Calvin hypnotizes his sister and then panics when he can't remember the magic word that will undo the spell; eye-catching sepia illustrations full of humor add to the nostalgic atmosphere. (Rev: BL 11/1/06; SLJ 12/06*)

1004 Vestergaard, Hope. *What Do You Do When a Monster Says Boo?* (PS–K). Illus. by Maggie Smith. 2006, Dutton $15.99 (0-525-47737-3). 32pp. A rhyming picture book about what to do (and what not to do) when your little sister acts like a monster. (Rev: BL 7/06; SLJ 8/06)

1005 Waechter, Philip. *Rosie and the Nightmares* (K–2). Illus. 2005, Handprint $15.95 (1-59354-115-5). 32pp. Tormented by monster-filled nightmares, Rosie the bunny seeks help from a dream specialist and visits a Tunnel of Fear. (Rev: BL 12/1/05; SLJ 11/05)

1006 Weis, Carol. *When the Cows Got Loose* (PS–2). Illus. by Ard Hoyt. 2006, Simon & Schuster $16.95 (0-689-85166-9). 40pp. While Ida Mae is daydreaming about how to get famous, the cows she's been watching wander off, and now she must get busy to round them back up; the illustrations of eccentric cows match the droll tone of the story. (Rev: BL 6/1–15/06; SLJ 8/06)

1007 Whybrow, Ian. *Badness for Beginners: A Little Wolf and Smellybreff Adventure* (K–3). Illus. by Tony Ross. Series: Little Wolf and Smellybreff. 2005, Carolrhoda LB $16.95 (1-57505-861-8). Little Wolf's efforts to be bad fail to impress the rest of his family. (Rev: SLJ 9/05)

1008 Wilson, Karma. *Moose Tracks!* (PS–2). Illus. by Jack E. Davis. 2006, Simon & Schuster $16.95 (0-689-83437-3). 32pp. A thoroughly silly story narrated by the owner of a very untidy house who can identify the sources of much of the mess, but not the culprit who left moose tracks all over the place. (Rev: BL 2/15/06; SLJ 4/06)

1009 Winthrop, Elizabeth. *The Biggest Parade* (K–3). Illus. by Mark Ulriksen. 2006, Holt $16.95 (0-8050-7685-9). Chairman of the town's 250th birthday parade, Harvey wants to include everyone, even his basset hound Fred; Fred refuses but, in the end, it seems that Fred has identified the place he is needed most — as a spectator. (Rev: SLJ 10/06)

1010 Young, Amy. *Belinda and the Glass Slipper* (PS–2). 2006, Viking $15.99 (0-670-06082-8). 32pp. In this sequel to *Belinda the Ballerina*, Belinda faces competition from a formidable — and underhanded — rival. (Rev: BL 10/1/06; SLJ 10/06)

1011 Ziefert, Harriet. *There Was a Little Girl, She Had a Little Curl* (PS). Illus. by Elliot Kreloff. 2006, Blue Apple $9.95 (1-59354-161-9). Preschooler Isabel decides to cut her own hair. (Rev: SLJ 10/06)

NATURE AND SCIENCE

1012 Ayres, Katherine. *Up, Down, and Around* (PS–1). Illus. by Nadine Bernard Westcott. 2007, Candlewick $16.99 (978-0-7636-2378-4). 32pp. This lively picture book captures the excitement of gardening as two young children help a man plant vegetables, some of which grow up while others grow down. (Rev: BL 3/15/07)

1013 Base, Graeme. *Uno's Garden* (2–4). Illus. 2006, Abrams $19.95 (0-8109-5473-7). 40pp. Uno builds a home in a beautiful forest, surrounded by Moopaloops, Lumpybums, and Frinklepods, but the colorful setting attracts more and more people until the plants and animals are almost all gone; the attractive illustrations offer opportunities for counting and finding items. (Rev: BL 11/15/06)

1014 Buell, Janet. *Sail Away, Little Boat* (PS–3). Illus. by Jui Ishida. 2006, Carolrhoda LB $15.95 (1-57505-821-9). From its launching in a brook by a young girl and boy, a plucky toy sailboat heads ever downriver — past fish, deer, and other animals — until it reaches a seashore and is quickly adopted by other children. (Rev: SLJ 4/06)

1015 Clark, Joan. *Snow* (PS–K). Illus. by Kady MacDonald Denton. 2006, Groundwood $16.95 (0-88899-712-4). After a solid month of snow the landscape around Sammy's house is deeply covered, so the young boy climbs to his rooftop to survey the scene and imagine what is going on beneath the blanket of snow. (Rev: SLJ 9/06)

1016 Depalma, Mary Newell. *The Grand Old Tree* (PS–1). Illus. 2005, Scholastic $16.99 (0-439-62334-0). 32pp. The life and death of a grand tree is celebrated in an appealing blend of simple text and art. (Rev: BL 11/15/05; SLJ 12/05)

1017 Fleming, Denise. *The First Day of Winter* (PS–K). Illus. 2005, Holt $15.95 (0-8050-7384-1). 32pp. A snowman receives a nice selection of presents in this twist on "The Twelve Days of Christmas." (Rev: BL 12/15/05; SLJ 12/05)

1018 Ford, Bernette. *First Snow* (PS). Illus. by Sebastien Braun. 2005, Holiday $16.95 (0-8234-1937-1). 32pp. A bunny and his siblings enjoy exploring their first snowfall under the light of the moon. (Rev: BL 11/1/05*; HBG 4/06; SLJ 9/05*)

1019 George, Jean Craighead. *Luck* (PS–2). Illus. by Wendell Minor. 2006, HarperCollins $16.99 (0-06-008201-1). 32pp. Luck is a sandhill crane whose rescue from a plastic six-pack holder, growth, and migration are presented in beautiful artwork and prose in this compelling picture book. (Rev: BL 5/1/06; SLJ 6/06)

1020 Godkin, Celia. *Wolf Island* (1–3). Illus. by author. 2007, Fitzhenry & Whiteside $17.95 (978-1-55455-007-4); paper (1-55455-008-4). 32pp. When a wolf family leaves an island, this sets in motion a chain of events that changes the whole ecology; previously published in 1993, this new edition has more visual appeal. (Rev: BL 2/15/07; SLJ 4/07)

1021 Gomi, Taro. *Spring Is Here / Llegó la primavera* (PS). Illus. by author. 2006, Chronicle $14.50 (0-8118-4759-4); paper $6.95 (0-8118-4760-8). The changing seasons are artfully illustrated using a calf as the background in this book with text in both English and Spanish. (Rev: SLJ 6/06*)

1022 Griessman, Annette. *Like a Hundred Drums* (PS–K). Illus. by Julie Monks. 2006, Houghton $15.00 (0-618-55878-0). 32pp. A summer thunderstorm interrupts a day on a farm in this simple picture book with folk-art illustrations. (Rev: BL 5/1/06; SLJ 6/06)

1023 Horacek, Petr. *Butterfly Butterfly: A Book of Colors* (PS–K). Illus. 2007, Candlewick $12.99 (978-0-7636-3343-1). 16pp. While waiting for a beautifully butterfly to reappear, a little girl enjoys other insects in this rewarding picture book with die-cut holes and a final pop-up of the returning butterfly. (Rev: BL 4/15/07)

1024 Jackson, Ellen. *Earth Mother* (PS–2). Illus. by Leo Dillon and Diane Dillon. 2005, Walker $16.95 (0-8027-8992-7). 32pp. Earth Mother is presented with conflicting requests from Man, Frog, and Mosquito and declares that all is well; excellent illustrations add to the serenity with beautiful scenery. (Rev: BL 8/05*; SLJ 9/05)

1025 Knudsen, Michelle. *A Moldy Mystery* (1–3). Illus. by Barry Gott. Series: Science Solves It! 2006, Kane paper $4.99 (1-57565-167-X). 32pp. Jeff throws out some moldy food containers only to discover that they were part of his older brother's science project and he must work out how to replace them; lots of facts appear in "Did you know?" boxes. (Rev: BL 4/15/06)

1026 Näslund, Corel Kristina. *Our Apple Tree* (PS–2). Illus. by Kristina Digman. 2005, Roaring Brook $15.95 (1-59643-052-4). 32pp. This Swedish import provides an unusual look at the life cycle of

an apple, from the perspective of two small children living in the apple tree. (Rev: BL 8/05; SLJ 11/05) [634]

1027 Paterson, Diane. *Hurricane Wolf* (K–3). Illus. 2006, Albert Whitman $16.95 (0-8075-3438-2). 32pp. Together with his parents, young Noah prepares for the arrival of Hurricane Anna and then assesses the damage after the storm has passed. (Rev: BL 3/1/06; SLJ 3/06)

1028 Pettenati, Jeanne K. *Galileo's Journal: 1609–1610* (1–3). Illus. by Paolo Rui. 2006, Charlesbridge $16.95 (1-57091-879-1); paper $6.95 (1-57091-880-5). 32pp. Galileo records in a fictional journal the events of eight key months in his life, a period during which he developed a telescope and made discoveries about the solar system. (Rev: BL 8/06)

1029 Powell, Consie. *The First Day of Winter* (1–3). Illus. 2005, Albert Whitman $15.95 (0-8075-2450-6). 32pp. In rhyming text that follows the pattern of "The 12 Days of Christmas," this counting picture book celebrates various aspects of the winter season. (Rev: BL 1/1–15/06; SLJ 1/06)

1030 Rotner, Shelley. *Senses at the Seashore* (PS–1). Illus. 2006, Millbrook LB $23.93 (0-7613-2897-1). 32pp. This colorful book shows how children can use their five senses to experience all the joys of a day at the beach. (Rev: BL 4/15/06; SLJ 10/06)

1031 Sabuda, Robert. *Winter's Tale* (K–3). Illus. Series: Classic Collectible Pop-Up. 2005, Simon & Schuster $26.95 (0-689-85363-7). 12pp. Spectacular pop-ups celebrate the winter landscape and wildlife. (Rev: BL 9/1/05; SLJ 9/05)

1032 St. Pierre, Stephanie. *What the Sea Saw* (PS–3). Illus. by Beverly Doyle. 2006, Peachtree $16.95 (1-56145-359-5). Beautiful paintings accompany simple rhyming text about all there is to see at the seaside. (Rev: SLJ 6/06)

1033 Schaefer, Lola M. *An Island Grows* (PS–2). Illus. by Cathie Felstead. 2006, Greenwillow $16.99 (0-06-623930-3). 40pp. The birth of an island (through a volcanic eruption) and its development and habitation by plants, animals, and people are told in simple rhyme; good both for fiction browsers and for science classes. (Rev: BL 7/06; SLJ 7/06)

1034 Schwartz, Amy. *A Beautiful Girl* (PS). 2006, Roaring Brook $16.95 (1-59643-165-2). 32pp. On her way to the market Jenna meets four friendly animals, each of which remarks on one of her physical characteristics. (Rev: BL 8/06; SLJ 8/06)

1035 Stringer, Lauren. *Winter Is the Warmest Season* (PS–2). Illus. 2006, Harcourt $16.00 (0-15-204967-3). 40pp. A young boy lists the many reasons he feels that winter — not summer — is the warmest season of the year. (Rev: BL 9/1/06; HBG 4/07; SLJ 11/06)

1036 Wiesner, David. *Flotsam* (PS–2). Illus. 2006, Clarion $17.00 (0-618-19457-6). 40pp. On a visit to the seaside a young boy finds an old-fashioned camera containing a film full of amazing images among the flotsam tossed on the beach in this inventive wordless book. (Rev: BCCB 9/06; BL 8/06; HB 9–10/06; HBG 4/07; LMC 2/07; SLJ 9/06*)

OTHER TIMES, OTHER PLACES

1037 Addy, Sharon Hart. *Lucky Jake* (PS–2). Illus. by Wade Zahares. 2007, Houghton $17.00 (978-0-618-47286-4). 40pp. Jake's dad is prospecting for gold, barely scratching out a living, but Jake knows how to take the little they have and use it to make them a better life. (Rev: BL 4/15/07)

1038 Alvarez, Julia. *A Gift of Gracias* (1–3). Illus. by Beatriz Vidal. 2005, Knopf $15.95 (0-375-82425-1). 40pp. The patron saint of the Dominican Republic — Nuestra Señora de la Altagracia — features in this story of a family facing a devastating crop failure. (Rev: BL 9/15/05; HBG 4/06; LMC 2/06; SLJ 11/05)

1039 Arrigan, Mary. *Mario's Angels: A Story About the Artist Giotto* (K–3). Illus. by Gillian McClure. 2006, Frances Lincoln $15.95 (1-84507-404-1). 32pp. In this appealing picture-book blend of fact and fiction, young Mario suggests that Italian Renaissance artist Giotto include some angels in the fresco that he's painting and offers to pose. (Rev: BL 11/1/06; SLJ 12/06)

1040 Birtha, Becky. *Grandmama's Pride* (K–3). Illus. by Colin Bootman. 2005, Albert Whitman $16.95 (0-8075-3028-X). 32pp. In 1956, African American Sarah Marie, with her sister and grandmother, travels by bus to the South and learns about segregation. (Rev: BL 11/1/05; SLJ 11/05)

1041 Bryant, Jen. *Call Me Marianne* (K–3). Illus. by David A. Johnson. 2006, Eerdmans $16.00 (0-8028-5242-4). 32pp. In 1940s Brooklyn, young Jonathan encounters poet Marianne Moore at the zoo and the two discuss poetry and the work of poets; a biography of Moore is appended. (Rev: BL 2/15/06; SLJ 3/06)

1042 Bunting, Eve. *Pop's Bridge* (K–3). Illus. by C. F. Payne. 2006, Harcourt $17.00 (0-15-204773-5). 32pp. Robert and Charlie are proud of their fathers, who are working on the construction of San Francisco's Golden Gate Bridge, but Robert secretly thinks his father's role as a "skywalker" is more important. (Rev: BL 4/15/06; SLJ 6/06)

1043 Campbell, Bebe Moore. *Stompin' at the Savoy* (2–4). Illus. by Richard Yarde. 2006, Philomel $16.99 (0-399-24197-3). 40pp. Young Mindy reconsiders her decision to skip an upcoming jazz dance recital after she is magically transported to 1920s Harlem and a night at the Savoy Ballroom. (Rev: BL 8/06; SLJ 3/07)

1044 Castaldo, Nancy. *Pizza for the Queen* (PS–2). Illus. by Melisande Potter. 2005, Holiday $16.95 (0-8234-1865-0). 32pp. This captivating, fact-based tale tells how a Neapolitan pizza maker came up with the recipe for Pizza Margherita — a pie fit for a queen. (Rev: BL 11/15/05; SLJ 9/05)

1045 Chapman, Nancy Kapp. *Tripper's Travels: An International Scrapbook* (K–3). Illus. by Lee Chapman. 2005, Marshall Cavendish $16.95 (0-7614-5240-0). Tripper the dog's round-the-world travels are preserved in a scrapbook with maps and factual information. (Rev: SLJ 12/05)

1046 Charles, Veronica Martenova. *The Birdman* (K–3). Illus. by Annouchka Gravel Galouchko. 2006, Tundra $17.95 (0-88776-740-0). 32pp. Deeply shaken by the unexpected death of his wife and children, Nobi the tailor eases his grief by buying caged birds and setting them free; set in Calcutta, this is based on a true story. (Rev: BL 10/1/06; SLJ 12/06)

1047 Coombs, Kate. *The Secret-Keeper* (1–4). Illus. by Heather Solomon. 2006, Simon & Schuster $16.95 (0-689-83963-4). Keeping the secrets of everyone in the village weighs so heavily on Kalli that she becomes ill, only to recover when she hears some happy news. (Rev: SLJ 7/06)

1048 Cotten, Cynthia. *Abbie in Stitches* (K–3). Illus. by Beth Peck. 2006, Farrar $16.00 (0-374-30004-6). 32pp. In 19th-century New York State, Abbie resists pressure to do needlework, much preferring to read. (Rev: BL 9/1/06; SLJ 9/06)

1049 Cullen, Lynn. *Moi and Marie Antoinette* (1–3). Illus. by Amy Young. 2006, Bloomsbury $16.95 (1-58234-958-4). 32pp. Marie Antoinette's dog Sebastien chronicles his mistress's life from the age of 13 to becoming queen of France. (Rev: BL 11/1/06)

1050 Cumberbatch, Judy. *Can You Hear the Sea?* (PS). Illus. by Ken Wilson-Max. 2006, Bloomsbury $15.95 (1-58234-703-4). 32pp. Sarah is given a shell by her grandfather who promises she will be able to hear the sea if she puts it to her ear and listens carefully, but the sounds of her small West African village are too loud. (Rev: BL 4/15/06; SLJ 8/06)

1051 Cunnane, Kelly. *For You Are a Kenyan Child* (PS–K). Illus. by Ana Juan. 2006, Simon & Schuster $16.95 (0-689-86194-X). 40pp. A young Kenyan boy is forgiven for his inattention to his cattle in this gentle story that conveys lots of information about rural Africa. (Rev: BL 2/1/06; SLJ 1/06*)

1052 Daly, Niki. *Happy Birthday, Jamela* (PS–K). Series: Jamela. 2006, Farrar $16.00 (0-374-32842-0). 32pp. Jamela's mother makes her buy boring, sensible shoes to go with her birthday dress, so Jamela brightens them up with beads in this fourth book about the young South African girl. (Rev: BL 8/06; SLJ 8/06)

1053 Danneberg, Julie. *Cowboy Slim* (PS–2). Illus. by Margot Apple. 2006, Charlesbridge $15.95 (1-58089-045-8). 32pp. Slim, a newcomer to the WJ Ranch, wants nothing more than to be a cowboy, but at first his love for poetry seems to get in the way of his dream. (Rev: BL 2/15/06; SLJ 2/06)

1054 Diakité, Penda. *I Lost My Tooth in Africa* (PS–2). Illus. by Baba Wague Diakité. 2006, Scholastic $16.99 (0-439-66226-5). 32pp. While visiting her extended family in the West African nation of Mali, a young girl loses her tooth and is treated to a visit from the African Tooth Fairy. (Rev: BL 2/1/06; SLJ 1/06)

1055 Dolenz, Micky. *Gakky Two-Feet* (K–2). Illus. by David Clark. 2006, Putnam $16.99 (0-399-24468-9). 32pp. In Africa more than 5 million years ago, Gak, a hominidee, is the object of scorn because he walks on two feet rather than four, but this skill comes in handy in an emergency. (Rev: BL 6/1–15/06)

1056 Elvgren, Jennifer Riesmeyer. *Josias, Hold the Book* (1–3). Illus. by Nicole Tadgell. 2006, Boyds Mills $15.95 (1-59078-318-2). 32pp. Living in rural Haiti, Josias must work in the garden instead of going to school until he realizes that book-learning could improve their crops. (Rev: BL 2/15/06; SLJ 3/06)

1057 Foreman, Michael. *Mia's Story: A Sketchbook of Hopes and Dreams* (1–3). 2006, Candlewick $15.99 (0-7636-3063-2). 32pp. Mia, a young resident of a poverty-stricken Chilean village, beautifies her community with the pretty flowers she finds while searching for a missing puppy. (Rev: BL 8/06; SLJ 8/06)

1058 Francis, Pauline. *Sam Stars at Shakespeare's Globe* (2–4). Illus. by Jane Tattersfield. 2006, Frances Lincoln $15.95 (1-84507-406-8). 32pp. A picture-book account of a boy named Sam who acts in the Globe Theatre and aspires to the role of Juliet. (Rev: BL 11/1/06; SLJ 12/06)

1059 Garland, Sherry. *The Buffalo Soldier* (K–3). Illus. by Ronald Himler. 2006, Pelican $15.95 (1-58980-391-4). 32pp. This overview of the "buffalo soldiers" — members of the all-African American cavalry regiments that served after the Civil War — is told from the viewpoint of a fictional recruit who is a former slave; includes eye-catching illustrations and a historical note. (Rev: BL 11/1/06; SLJ 12/06)

1060 Gershator, Phillis. *Sky Sweeper* (K–3). Illus. by Holly Meade. 2007, Farrar $16.00 (978-0-374-37007-7). 40pp. This is the beautifully illustrated, challenging story of Takeboki, who as a boy takes a job tending the gardens at a Zen temple, work he enjoys despite its simplicity. (Rev: BL 3/15/07)

1061 Gibfried, Diane. *Brother Juniper* (K–2). Illus. by Meilo So. 2006, Clarion $16.00 (0-618-54361-9). Brother Juniper, a follower of Father Francis of Assisi, is so generous that he gives away the monks' church, bit by bit, to the poor; for this he is condemned by his brothers but commended by the saint. (Rev: SLJ 5/06)

1062 Hayes, Joe. *A Spoon for Every Bite / Una cuchara para cada bocado* (1–4). Illus. by Rebecca Leer. 2005, Cinco Puntos paper $8.95 (0-938317-93-8). A bilingual version of the story in which a poor couple fools a rich neighbor into spending his fortune on spoons. (Rev: SLJ 10/05)

1063 Henson, Heather. *Angel Coming* (PS–2). Illus. by Susan Gaber. 2005, Simon & Schuster $15.95 (0-689-85531-1). 40pp. A child living in the Appalachian Mountainous in the early 20th century anxiously awaits the arrival of a member of the Frontier Nursing Service — known by locals as "angels on horseback" — who will help the child's mother through childbirth. (Rev: BL 7/05*; SLJ 7/05)

1064 Herbauts, Anne. *Prince Silencio* (1–3). Trans. from French by Zoe Bedrick. 2006, Enchanted Lion $14.95 (1-59270-055-1). Prince Silencio ("Silence") teaches his noisy subjects the value of occasional quiet times in this story translated from the French. (Rev: SLJ 6/06)

1065 Hoberman, Mary Ann. *Mrs. O'Leary's Cow* (K–2). Illus. by Jenny Mattheson. 2007, Little, Brown $16.99 (978-0-316-14840-5). 32pp. With new verses added to the classic song and a transition to a rural environment, this is the humorous story of firefighters' efforts to save the barn after the cow kicks over the lantern. (Rev: BL 4/1/07)

1066 Hubbard, Crystal. *Catching the Moon* (PS–2). Illus. by Randy DuBurke. 2005, Lee & Low $16.95 (1-58430-243-7). 32pp. In the 1920s, a young African American girl is determined to become a professional baseball player; based on the life of Toni Stone (1921–1996). (Rev: BL 9/1/05; SLJ 11/05)

1067 Hurst, Carol Otis. *Terrible Storm* (K–2). Illus. by S. D. Schindler. 2007, Greenwillow $16.99 (0-06-009001-4). 32pp. Two grandfathers separately share their memories of the blizzard that hit New England in 1888. (Rev: BL 11/15/06; SLJ 1/07)

1068 Ichikawa, Satomi. *My Father's Shop* (K–2). Illus. 2006, Kane/Miller $15.95 (1-929132-99-9). 32pp. Mustafa, son of a Moroccan rug seller, doesn't enjoy learning foreign words from his father but in a romp through the local marketplace he attracts the attention of many tourists and brings them back to the rug shop. (Rev: BL 2/15/06)

1069 Johnson, Angela. *Wind Flyers* (1–3). Illus. by Loren Long. 2007, Simon & Schuster $16.99 (0-689-84879-X). 32pp. A young African American boy proudly describes his great-great-uncle's prowess as a flyer and one of the Tuskegee Airmen. (Rev: BL 12/1/06; SLJ 1/07)

1070 Kessler, Cristina. *The Best Beekeeper of Lalibela: A Tale from Africa* (PS–2). Illus. by Leonard Jenkins. 2006, Holiday $16.95 (0-8234-1858-8). 32pp. Almaz, a young Ethiopian girl, is determined to prove the men wrong and succeed at keeping bees and producing honey. (Rev: BL 8/06; SLJ 8/06)

1071 Krebs, Laurie. *We're Riding on a Caravan: An Adventure on the Silk Road* (1–3). Illus. by Helen Cann. 2005, Barefoot Bks. $16.99 (1-84148-343-5). 32pp. This richly illustrated picture book follows a family of silk traders as they travel China's Silk Road. (Rev: BL 11/1/05; SLJ 1/06)

1072 Lee, Huy Voun. *In the Leaves* (K–3). Illus. 2005, Holt $16.95 (0-8050-6764-7). 32pp. On a trip to a farm, Xiao Ming is eager to introduce his friends to the ten Chinese characters he has learned, and to explain their relationship to the surrounding world; includes effective illustrations and a pronunciation guide. (Rev: BL 8/05; SLJ 8/05)

1073 Lee-Tai, Amy. *A Place Where Sunflowers Grow / Sabaku Ni Saita Himawari* (1–3). Illus. by Felicia Hoshino. 2006, Children's Book Pr. $16.95 (0-89239-215-0). 32pp. In English and Japanese, this is a gentle story of the Japanese internment in World War II, featuring a young Japanese American girl who tries to adjust by painting pictures. (Rev: BL 8/06)

1074 Levine, Ellen. *Henry's Freedom Box* (1–3). Illus. by Kadir Nelson. 2007, Scholastic $16.99 (978-0-439-77733-9). 40pp. A fictionalized account of the dangerous and exciting story of a young slave who escaped to freedom in a packing crate, traveling by train and by steamboat until he arrived in Philadelphia. (Rev: BL 2/1/07)

1075 Lewis, Alan K. *I Grew Up on a Farm* (1–4). Illus. by Bob Fletcher. 2005, Moo Pr. LB $19.95 (0-9766805-2-1). 32pp. Simple text and black-and-white family photographs describe growing up on a farm during the 1950s. (Rev: SLJ 2/06)

1076 Littlesugar, Amy. *Clown Child* (PS–2). Illus. by Kimberly Bulcken Root. 2006, Philomel $15.99 (0-399-23106-4). 32pp. Olivia, who is a clown in a traveling circus in the early 20th century, comes to appreciate her life on the road once she gets a taste of most people's everyday routines. (Rev: BL 7/06; SLJ 7/06)

1077 Lorbiecki, Marybeth. *Jackie's Bat* (1–3). Illus. by Brian Pinkney. 2006, Simon & Schuster $15.95 (0-689-84102-7). 40pp. A young batboy named Joey reveals his prejudice when Jackie Robinson joins the Brooklyn Dodgers and his subsequent growing admiration for the player. (Rev: BL 2/1/06; SLJ 1/06)

1078 Lord, Michelle. *Little Sap and Monsieur Rodin* (2–4). Illus. by Felicia Hoshino. 2006, Lee & Low $16.95 (1-58430-248-8). 32pp. Little Sap, a dancer from Cambodia, is flattered to be noticed by the artist Auguste Rodin in this story based on actual events and illustrated with lovely mixed-media paintings. (Rev: BL 5/1/06)

1079 Lunge-Larsen, Lise. *Noah's Mittens: The Story of Felt* (K–3). Illus. by Matthew Trueman. 2006, Houghton $16.00 (0-618-32950-1). 32pp. In this whimsical picture-book tale, Noah finds a use for the sheep's wool after it becomes thickly matted during the lengthy journey of the ark. (Rev: BL 10/15/06; SLJ 12/06)

1080 McCaughrean, Geraldine. *The Jesse Tree* (2–4). Illus. by Bee Willey. 2005, Eerdmans $20.00 (0-8028-5288-2). 96pp. A curious young boy pesters a crotchety old woodcarver into telling him Bible stories about the Old Testament characters who are the spiritual ancestors of Jesus Christ. (Rev: BL 10/1/05; SLJ 1/06)

1081 McClintock, Barbara. *Adele and Simon* (K–3). Illus. 2006, Farrar $16.00 (0-374-38044-9). 40pp. As Adele escorts her little brother home from school through the streets of 1900s Paris, the boy manages to lose something at every stop along the way; endpaper maps add to this view of the City of Light. (Rev: BL 6/1–15/06; HB 9–10/06; HBG 4/07; LMC 4/07; SLJ 8/06)

1082 McCully, Emily Arnold. *The Escape of Oney Judge: Martha Washington's Slave Finds Freedom* (2–4). Illus. by author. 2007, Farrar $16.00 (978-0-374-32225-0). In this fictionalized account of the escape of one of Martha Washington's slaves, Oney Judge travels with the Washingtons to Philadelphia where she meets free blacks and begins to appreciate the concept of freedom. (Rev: BCCB 6/07; BL 11/15/06; SLJ 2/07)

1083 McDonald, Megan. *Saving the Liberty Bell* (K–3). Illus. by Marsha Carrington. 2005, Simon & Schuster $16.95 (0-689-85167-7). 32pp. In this exciting, fact-based story from the American Revolution, 11-year-old John Jacob Mickley tells how he helped to hide the Liberty Bell from British troops. (Rev: BL 7/05; SLJ 7/05)

1084 McNulty, Faith. *If You Decide to Go to the Moon* (K–3). Illus. by Steven Kellogg. 2005, Scholastic $16.99 (0-590-48359-5). 48pp. McNulty describes how it will feel to travel to the moon in this mock guide for prospective travelers. (Rev: BCCB 11/05; BL 11/1/05; HB 9–10/05; HBG 4/06; LMC 2/06; SLJ 10/05*)

1085 Michelson, Richard. *Happy Feet: The Savoy Ballroom Lindy Hoppers and Me* (K–3). Illus. by E. B. Lewis. 2005, Harcourt $16.00 (0-15-205057-4). 32pp. A young African American boy hears the story of the opening of Harlem's Savoy Ballroom on the night he himself was born; this story beautifully evokes the mood of the 1920s. (Rev: BL 11/1/05; SLJ 11/05)

1086 Mora, Pat. *The Song of Francis and the Animals* (K–3). Illus. by David Frampton. 2005, Eerdmans $16.00 (0-8028-5253-X). 32pp. This poetic narrative celebrates the close bonds between Saint Francis and the animals he encountered throughout his life. (Rev: BL 10/15/05; SLJ 10/05)

1087 Nikola-Lisa, W. *Magic in the Margins: A Medieval Tale of Bookmaking* (K–3). Illus. by Bonnie Christensen. 2007, Houghton $17.00 (978-0-618-49642-6). 32pp. Working as an apprentice in a medieval monastery's scriptorium, Simon, a young orphan, dreams of illuminating manuscripts. (Rev: BL 4/1/07)

1088 O'Neal, Deborah, and Angela Westengard. *The Trouble with Henry: A Tale of Walden Pond* (PS–2). Illus. by S. D. Schindler. 2005, Candlewick $16.99 (0-7636-1828-4). 40pp. A fictional account of Thoreau's efforts to keep Walden Pond free of industry; a note adds biographical information. (Rev: BL 10/15/05; SLJ 10/05)

1089 Ormerod, Jan. *Lizzie Nonsense: A Story of Pioneer Days* (PS–2). Illus. 2005, Clarion $15.00 (0-618-57493-X). 32pp. The power of imagination is shown in this beautifully illustrated story of Lizzie and her mother, pioneers living alone on Australia's frontier while Papa goes away to work. (Rev: BL 9/15/05; SLJ 9/05)

1090 Park, Linda Sue. *Bee-bim Bop!* (PS–2). Illus. by Ho Baek Lee. 2005, Clarion $15.00 (0-618-26511-2). 32pp. A hungry Korean girl helps her mother shop for ingredients and then prepare a favorite meal; the recipe is included. (Rev: BL 10/15/05; SLJ 9/05)

1091 Pendziwol, Jean E. *The Red Sash* (1–3). Illus. by Nicolas Debon. 2005, Groundwood $16.95 (0-88899-589-X). 40pp. A young mixed-race boy, son of a voyageur — fur traders who wore red sashes, describes life in and around Lake Huron in the early 19th century. (Rev: BL 12/1/05; SLJ 1/06)

1092 Perkins, Mitali. *Rickshaw Girl* (2–5). Illus. by Jamie Hogan. 2007, Charlesbridge $13.95 (978-1-58089-308-4). 91pp. Naima is a talented painter of the traditional alpana patterns but she longs to do more to help her poor Bangladeshi family, even driving her father's rickshaw, an occupation forbidden to girls. (Rev: BCCB 5/07; BL 11/1/06; HB 5/6–07; LMC 4–5/07; SLJ 4/07)

1093 Pilegard, Virginia Walton. *The Warlord's Alarm: A Mathematical Adventure* (K–3). Illus. by Nicolas Debon. 2006, Pelican $15.95 (1-58980-378-7). 32pp. In ancient China, Chuan invents a method of measuring time so that he can awaken his master in the middle of the night; a note explains how water clocks work. (Rev: BL 11/1/06; SLJ 11/06)

1094 Pilegard, Virginia Walton. *The Warlord's Messengers* (K–2). Illus. by Nicolas Debon. 2005, Pelican $15.95 (1-58980-271-3). 32pp. Friends Chuan and Jing Jing use their math skills and ingenuity to come up with a plan to satisfy a Chinese emperor's wishes. (Rev: BL 11/15/05; SLJ 12/05)

1095 Prince, April Jones. *Twenty-One Elephants and Still Standing* (1–3). Illus. by François Roca. 2005, Houghton $16.00 (0-618-44887-X). 32pp. Was this new wonder, the Brooklyn Bridge, safe? P. T. Barnum and his 21 elephants crossed in 1884. (Rev: BL 10/15/05; SLJ 11/05*)

1096 Rao, Sandhya. *My Mother's Sari* (PS–K). Illus. by Nina Sabnani. 2006, North-South $14.95 (0-7358-2101-1). 28pp. A little Indian girl shows the many uses for her mother's sari; the endpapers show how a sari is wrapped. (Rev: BL 8/06)

1097 Reed, Jennifer. *The Falling Flowers* (K–3). Illus. by Dick Cole. 2005, Shen's $16.95 (1-885008-28-7). Mayumie and her grandmother enjoy viewing Tokyo's cherry blossoms in this book illustrated with beautiful watercolors. (Rev: SLJ 6/06)

1098 Russell, Margaret Timberlake. *Maggie's Amerikay* (K–3). Illus. by Jim Burke. 2006, Farrar $17.00 (0-374-34722-0). 40pp. An African American boy and an Irish American girl befriend each other while enduring hard times in a late-19th-century New Orleans rich in ragtime. (Rev: BL 5/1/06; SLJ 4/06)

1099 Sasso, Sany Eisenberg. *Butterflies Under Our Hats* (PS–2). Illus. by Joani Keller Rothenberg. 2006, Paraclete $16.95 (1-55725-474-5). 32pp. In the town of Chelm — a place famously without luck — a visitor who believes in hope arrives in a cloud of butterflies. (Rev: BL 6/1–15/06; SLJ 8/06)

1100 Smith, Lane. *John, Paul, George and Ben* (K–3). Illus. 2006, Hyperion $16.99 (0-7868-4893-6). 40pp. A humorous look at the contributions of five of America's founding fathers — John Hancock, Paul Revere, George Washington, Benjamin Franklin, and Thomas Jefferson — with facts appended; best suited to readers who already are familiar with the history. (Rev: BL 2/15/06; SLJ 3/06*)

1101 Sockabasin, Allen. *Thanks to the Animals* (PS–2). Illus. by Rebekah Raye. 2005, Tilbury House $16.95 (0-88448-270-7). When Joo Tum's infant son tumbles off the family's sled, the baby is lovingly tended by an assortment of animals until his father returns for him. (Rev: SLJ 10/05)

1102 Spiotta-Dimare, Loren. *Rockwell: A Boy and His Dog* (1–4). Illus. by Cliff Miller. 2005, Barron's $14.95 (0-7641-5790-6). 28pp. A fictional conversation between the painter and his model, Scotty, gives the reader a feel for the artist's inspirations and times. (Rev: SLJ 8/05)

1103 Stryer, Andrea Stenn. *Kami and the Yaks* (K–3). Illus. by Bert Dodson. 2007, Bay Otter $15.95 (978-0-977896-10-3); paper (978-0-977896-11-0). When a deaf Sherpa boy finds one of his family's herd of yaks in distress in a storm, he must climb all the way down to his village to get help. (Rev: BL 2/1/07; SLJ 4/07)

1104 Thermes, Jennifer. *Sam Bennett's New Shoes* (K–2). 2006, Carolrhoda $15.95 (1-57505-822-7). 32pp. In this story based on an 18th-century custom, Sam Bennett gets new shoes and his father takes the old shoes and hides them in the wall to bring good fortune. (Rev: BL 6/1–15/06; SLJ 3/06)

1105 Villaseñor, Victor. *The Frog and His Friends Save Humanity / La rana y sus amigos salvan a la humanidad* (PS–3). Trans. by Edna Ochoa. Illus. by José Ramírez. 2005, Arte Publico $14.95 (1-55885-429-0). 32pp. In this captivating bilingual children's tale, set at the dawn of creation, other animals puzzle over the role of a human child. (Rev: BL 8/05; SLJ 6/06)

1106 Wells, Rosemary. *The Miraculous Tale of the Two Maries* (K–2). Illus. by Petra Mathers. 2006, Viking $16.99 (0-670-05960-9). 32pp. Two teenage girls, both named Marie, drown in the ocean but persuade God to allow them to return to their town to do good deeds; inspired by a story of 19th-century France. (Rev: BL 3/1/06*; HB 3–4/06; HBG 10/06; SLJ 3/06)

1107 Weston, Anne. *My Brother Needs a Boa* (2–4). Illus. by Cheryl Nathan. 2005, Star Bright $15.95 (1-932065-96-5). To rid his shop of a pesky mouse, Benito heeds his sister's advice and goes in search of a rodent-catching snake. (Rev: SLJ 10/05)

1108 Whitaker, Zai. *Kali and the Rat Snake* (1–3). Illus. by Srividya Natarajan. 2006, Kane/Miller $15.95 (1-933605-10-3). Kali's classmates are unkind because his father is a snake catcher, but Kali wins their respect and gratitude when he captures a six-foot snake that invades their classroom; with handsome illustrations and endpapers. (Rev: SLJ 10/06)

1109 Woodruff, Elvira. *Small Beauties: The Journey of Darcy Heart O'Hara* (K–3). Illus. by Adam Rex. 2006, Knopf $15.95 (0-375-82686-6). 32pp. Darcy's precious mementoes of her home in Ireland — a pebble, a flower, a chip of stone — give her strength during the family's difficult journey to America. (Rev: BL 8/06)

1110 Wormell, Christopher. *The Wild Girl* (PS–1). Illus. by author. 2006, Eerdmans $17.00 (0-8028-5311-0). A young girl who survives a hard and lonely life in a cave with her dog — eating fruit, nuts, and fish — at first tries to chase a bear away, but realizing it has a cub she allows it to come into the cave and they all share what they have. (Rev: SLJ 11/06)

1111 Would, Nick. *The Scarab's Secret* (K–3). Illus. by Christina Balk. 2006, Walker $16.95 (0-8027-9561-7). 32pp. A scarab beetle tells how it saved the life of an Egyptian prince and thus secured for itself an important place in the mythology of ancient Egypt. (Rev: BL 3/15/06; SLJ 4/06)

1112 Xiong, Kim. *Little Stone Lion* (PS–2). Illus. 2005, Heryin $13.99 (0-9762056-1-0). 32pp. A small stone lion reflects on the people and history of the small Chinese village over which he stands guard. (Rev: BL 11/1/05)

1113 Yin. *Brothers* (2–4). Illus. by Chris Soentpiet. 2006, Philomel $16.99 (0-399-23406-3). 40pp. Newly arrived in 19th century San Francisco, Ming ignores his older brothers' warnings not to venture outside Chinatown and strikes up a friendship with Patrick, a young Irish immigrant; a sequel to *Coolies* (2000). (Rev: BL 8/06; SLJ 11/06)

PERSONAL PROBLEMS

1114 Browne, Anthony. *Silly Billy* (PS–2). Illus. 2006, Candlewick $15.99 (0-7636-3124-8). 32pp. Billy's Grandma gives him some Guatemalan worry dolls to help him reduce his burden of fears in this beautifully illustrated picture book. (Rev: BL 10/15/06; SLJ 11/06)

1115 Chapra, Mimi. *Sparky's Bark / El ladrido de Sparky* (PS–2). Illus. by Vivi Escriva. 2006, HarperCollins $15.99 (0-06-053172-X). 32pp. A Hispanic girl visiting relatives in Ohio overcomes her culture shock and begins to learn English in this bilingual picture book. (Rev: BL 5/1/06; SLJ 6/06)

1116 Crocker, Nancy. *Betty Lou Blue* (PS–2). Illus. by Boris Kulikov. 2006, Dial $16.99 (0-8037-2937-5). 32pp. Poor Betty Lou Blue is taunted mercilessly by classmates because of her large feet, but those appendages come to the rescue when an avalanche traps her tormentors in snowdrifts. (Rev: BL 8/06; SLJ 12/06)

1117 Dierssen, Andreas. *The Old Red Tractor* (PS–K). Trans. by Marianne Martens. Illus. by Daniel Sohr. 2006, North-South $16.95 (978-0-7358-2088-3). 32pp. Towhead Tony loves his old red tractor until a friend shows up with a brand-new tractor that has a horn. (Rev: BL 9/15/06; SLJ 10/06)

1118 Durango, Julia. *Dream Hop* (PS–2). Illus. by Jared Lee. 2005, Simon & Schuster $15.95 (0-689-87163-5). 32pp. A pajama-clad boy learns to escape his nightmares by "dream hopping." (Rev: BL 12/1/05; SLJ 10/05)

1119 Fitzpatrick, Marie-Louise. *I Am I* (K–3). Illus. by author. 2006, Roaring Brook $16.95 (1-59643-054-0). Two children compete for dominance and their hateful words destroy the landscape around them; they eventually work out that peaceful coexistence is a much better strategy. (Rev: SLJ 6/06*)

1120 Gilmore, Rachna. *Grandpa's Clock* (2–4). Illus. by Amy Meissner. 2006, Orca $17.95 (1-55143-333-8). Cayley's grandfather promises to make her a special clock, but the project must be put on hold when he has a heart attack and goes to the hospital. (Rev: SLJ 6/06)

1121 Grant, Karima. *Sofie and the City* (PS–2). Illus. by Janet Montecalvo. 2006, Boyds Mills $15.95 (1-59078-273-9). A little girl from Senegal yearns for home but learns to appreciate life in the United States when she makes a friend. (Rev: SLJ 5/06)

1122 Headley, Justina Chen. *The Patch* (PS–2). Illus. by Mitch Vane. 2006, Charlesbridge $15.95 (1-58089-049-0). 32pp. Five-year-old Becca, an aspiring ballerina, at first balks at wearing an eye patch to correct her lazy eye but finds a way to turn the patch into a fashion asset. (Rev: BL 2/1/06; SLJ 2/06)

1123 Johnson, Vincent L. *Of Corn Silk and Black Braids* (K–3). Illus. by Linda Crockett. 2005, Marzetta $17.95 (0-9657033-2-0). Sarah, a young African American girl, envies Mary Beth who has lovely blond hair, but with a little help from her mother and aunt, the girl learns to like herself just the way she is. (Rev: SLJ 12/05)

1124 Kraus, Jeanne R. *Annie's Plan: Taking Charge of Schoolwork and Homework* (2–5). Illus. by Charles Beyl. 2007, Magination $14.95 (978-1-59147-481-4). 47pp. Annie is a smart girl but she has trouble staying focused, so her parents and teacher help her organize herself for more efficient homework; includes a note for adults. (Rev: SLJ 4/07)

1125 Krishnaswami, Uma. *The Closet Ghosts* (PS–2). Illus. by Shiraaz Bhabha. 2006, Children's Book Pr. $16.95 (0-89239-208-8). 32pp. Anu has just moved and is distressed to find ghosts in her closet; with the help of a Hindu god and the friends she finds at her new school, all ends well. (Rev: SLJ 6/06)

1126 Kroll, Virginia. *Ryan Respects* (K–2). Illus. by Paige Billin-Frye. Series: The Way I Act. 2006, Albert Whitman $15.95 (0-8075-6946-1). 24pp. After unkindly teasing his friend Doug, young Ryan gets his comeuppance and also learns some important lessons about the importance of respecting others' feelings. (Rev: BL 4/15/06; SLJ 3/06)

1127 Laguna, Sofie. *Bad Buster* (1–2). Illus. by Leigh Hobbs. Series: Nibbles. 2006, Running Pr. paper $3.95 (978-0-7624-2626-3). 60pp. Buster is very good at being bad but when he stops a burglary and is praised for his good deed, will he decide to change or go back to his bad ways? An easy chapter book that may appeal to reluctant readers. (Rev: SLJ 3/07)

1128 Lears, Laurie. *Nathan's Wish: A Story about Cerebral Palsy* (1–3). Illus. by Stacey Schuett. 2005, Albert Whitman $15.95 (0-8075-7101-6). Nathan, who has cerebral palsy, is encouraged when his neighbor finds a way to help an injured owl. (Rev: SLJ 7/05)

1129 Leonetti, Mike. *Gretzky's Game* (1–3). Illus. by Greg Banning. 2006, Raincoast $15.95 (1-55192-851-5). 32pp. Ryan, a young hockey player who's small for his age, patterns his playing style after that of his idol, Wayne Gretzky. (Rev: BL 2/15/06)

1130 Levy, Janice. *Alley Oops* (1–4). Illus. by Cynthia B. Decker. 2005, Flashlight $15.95 (0-972-92254-7). J.J. has been bullying an overweight boy called Patrick, so J.J.'s father sits down with him and tells him a story about his own behavior as a boy. (Rev: SLJ 8/05)

1131 Liao, Jimmy. *The Sound of Colors: A Journey of the Imagination* (1–5). Adapted by Sarah L. Thomson. Illus. by author. 2005, Little, Brown $16.99 (0-316-93992-7). A blind girl imagines a colorful journey over land and sea as she makes her way through the subway. (Rev: SLJ 9/05)

1132 Ludwig, Trudy. *Just Kidding* (K–3). Illus. by Adam Gustavson. 2006, Tricycle $15.95 (1-58246-163-2). 32pp. D.J. gets help from his father and a teacher when Vince's bullying becomes upsetting; front matter offers advice to adults and back matter provides tips for children. (Rev: BL 4/15/06; SLJ 6/06)

1133 Mayer, Mercer. *There Are Monsters Everywhere* (PS–2). Illus. by author. 2005, Dial $15.99 (0-8037-0621-9). Fearful of the monsters that follow him everywhere he goes, a young boy takes karate lessons. (Rev: SLJ 12/05)

1134 Meddaugh, Susan. *Just Teenie* (PS–2). Illus. 2006, Houghton $16.00 (0-618-68565-0). 32pp. Justine is totally frustrated by her tininess until an out-of-control plant gives her a different perspective on life. (Rev: BL 4/15/06; SLJ 6/06)

1135 Montserrat, Pep. *Ms. Rubinstein's Beauty* (K–3). Illus. 2006, Sterling $14.95 (1-4027-3063-2). 32pp. A bearded lady and a man with an elephantine nose — who appear as freaks in different circuses — discover the inner beauty in each other during an encounter in the park. (Rev: BL 9/15/06; SLJ 1/07)

1136 Prats, Joan de Déu. *Sebastian's Roller Skates* (PS–2). Illus. by Francesc Rovira. 2005, Kane/Miller $15.95 (1-929132-81-6). 40pp. Shy Sebastian finds his self-confidence and ability to express himself growing after he masters roller skating. (Rev: BL 11/1/05; SLJ 10/05)

1137 Raschka, Chris. *The Purple Balloon* (1–3). Illus. 2007, Random $16.99 (978-0-375-84146-0). 32pp. Designed primarily for terminally ill children and their friends and family members, this book deals sensitively with the issues that face those who are dying and the people who love them, emphasizing how many people are there to help. (Rev: BL 4/1/07)

1138 Riggs, Shannon. *Not in Room 204* (1–3). Illus. by Jaime Zollars. 2007, Albert Whitman $15.95 (978-0-8075-5764-8). 32pp. A class about "stranger danger" gives Regina the courage to tell her teacher about her father's inappropriate behavior; a sensitive story that provides no details. (Rev: BL 2/1/07)

1139 Robberecht, Thierry. *Sam Is Never Scared* (PS–2). Illus. by Philippe Goossens. 2006, Clarion $12.00 (0-618-73278-0). 29pp. Sam acts brave in public but hides his fears of monsters and ghosts until the day a huge spider lands on his hand; his father reassures him that everyone is afraid of something. (Rev: SLJ 10/06)

1140 Seeger, Pete, and Paul Dubois Jacobs. *The Deaf Musicians* (K–3). Illus. by R. Gregory Christie. 2006, Putnam $16.99 (0-399-24316-X). When jazz pianist Lee loses his hearing, he has to leave the group he's been playing with, but while studying sign language at a school for the deaf he meets Max, a sax player, and together they start up a sign-language band. (Rev: SLJ 11/06*)

1141 Shin, Sun Yung. *Cooper's Lesson* (PS–3). Trans. by Min Paek. Illus. by Kim Cogan. 2004, Children's Book $16.95 (0-89239-193-6). In Korean and English, this picture book tells the story of Cooper, the son of a Korean mother and a white American father, and his difficulties in establishing a cultural identity. (Rev: BL 8/05; SLJ 5/04)

1142 Soto, Gary. *My Little Car* (PS–2). Illus. by Pam Paparone. 2006, Putnam $15.99 (0-399-23220-6). 32pp. Teresa loves the low-rider pedal-car that her grandfather gives her, but over time its allure fades and she starts to neglect it. (Rev: BL 3/1/06; SLJ 6/06)

1143 Thiel, Annie. *Danny Is Moving* (1–4). Illus. by William M. Edwards. 2006, Playdate Kids $14.95 (1-933721-02-2). Danny worries about leaving his old friends and moving to a new neighborhood, but he soon discovers how easy it is to make new friends. (Rev: SLJ 9/06)

1144 Vettiger, Susanne. *Basghetti Spaghetti* (K–2). Illus. by Marie-Anne Räber. 2005, North-South $15.95 (0-7358-1991-2). Oscar, a crab, has some trouble pronouncing words correctly when he's nervous but improves after visiting Doctor Octopus. (Rev: SLJ 8/05)

1145 Winter, Jeanette. *Angelina's Island* (PS–2). 2007, Farrar $16.00 (978-0-374-30349-5). 320pp. Living in New York City with her parents, Angelina longs for the sun, food, and friends of her former home in Jamaica. (Rev: BL 2/1/07)

REAL AND ALMOST REAL ANIMALS

1146 Anderson, Sara. *Octopus Oyster Hermit Crab Snail: A Poem of the Sea* (1–3). Illus. by author. 2005, Handprint $16.95 (1-59354-079-5). Eye-catching illustrations and rhyming text introduce a variety of marine creatures. (Rev: HBG 4/06; SLJ 12/05)

1147 Arnosky, Jim. *Babies in the Bayou* (PS–2). Illus. by author. 2007, Putnam $16.99 (0-399-22653-2). 32pp. A look at the young animals of the bayou and their mothers, with simple text and lush illustrations. (Rev: BL 12/1/06; SLJ 1/07)

1148 Arnosky, Jim. *Grandfather Buffalo* (PS–2). Illus. 2006, Putnam $16.99 (0-399-24169-8). 32pp. A heartwarming story about an aging buffalo, unable to keep up with the herd, that finds renewed interest in life when he saves a newborn calf in a dust storm. (Rev: BL 2/1/06; HBG 10/06; SLJ 2/06*)

1149 Aruego, Jose, and Ariane Dewey. *The Last Laugh* (PS). Illus. 2006, Dial $12.99 (0-8037-3093-4). 24pp. A bullying snake gets his comeuppance from a clever duck in this nearly wordless humorous story. (Rev: BCCB 5/06; BL 2/1/06; HBG 10/06; SLJ 3/06)

1150 Bailey, Linda. *Stanley's Wild Ride* (PS–2). Illus. by Bill Slavin. 2006, Kids Can $14.95 (1-55337-960-8). 32pp. Stanley the dog escapes from his backyard and liberates his canine friends for a wild time on the town. (Rev: BL 3/1/06; SLJ 6/06)

1151 Bennett, Dean. *Finding a Friend in the Forest: A True Story* (PS–3). Illus. by author. 2005, Down East $15.95 (0-89272-662-8). A beagle and a doe become fast friends in this appealing picture book set in northern Maine. (Rev: SLJ 1/06)

1152 Blackstone, Stella. *I Dreamt I Was a Dinosaur* (PS–2). Illus. by Clare Beaton. 2005, Barefoot Bks. $15.99 (1-84148-238-2). A child dreams of being a dinosaur and cavorting with all sorts of prehistoric creatures; factual information is appended. (Rev: SLJ 1/06)

1153 Bradley, Kimberly Brubaker. *The Perfect Pony* (K–2). Illus. by Shelagh McNicholas. 2007, Dial $16.99 (978-0-8037-2851-6). 32pp. A young girl talks about learning to ride and her search for just the right pony. (Rev: BL 4/1/07)

1154 Broach, Elise. *Wet Dog!* (PS–2). Illus. by David Catrow. 2005, Dial $16.99 (0-8037-2809-3). After he is turned away from nearly every source of water in town, a very hot dog interrupts a wedding party by a cool lake. (Rev: SLJ 7/05)

1155 Bruel, Robert O. *Bob and Otto* (PS–K). Illus. by Nick Bruel. 2007, Roaring Brook $15.95 (978-1-59643-203-1). 32pp. In their early years, worms Bob and Otto are inseparable, but the two must part ways when Bob's metamorphosis into a butterfly approaches. (Rev: BL 4/1/07)

1156 Burke, Tina. *Fly, Little Bird* (PS–K). Illus. by author. 2006, Kane/Miller $14.95 (1-933605-02-2). 32pp. A nearly wordless book that depicts a little girl, accompanied by her puppy, capturing and then setting free a baby wild parrot. (Rev: BL 5/15/06)

1157 Cartwright, Reg. *What We Do* (PS–1). Illus. by author. 2005, Holt $7.95 (0-8050-7671-9). In rhyming text and bright illustrations, a variety of animals explain the way the move and behave. (Rev: SLJ 10/05)

1158 Chess, Victoria. *The Costume Party* (K–2). Illus. 2005, Kane/Miller $15.95 (1-929132-87-5). 32pp. Trapped indoors by several days of bad weather, Madame Coco throws a costume party to entertain her five pet dogs. (Rev: BL 10/15/05; SLJ 9/05)

1159 Clark, Emma Chichester. *Piper* (PS–2). Illus. 2007, Eerdmans $17.00 (978-0-8028-5314-1). 32pp. Piper, a good-natured black dog, angers his new owner by cavorting with rabbits instead of getting rid of them; running away after a beating, he helps an old woman who provides him with a happy new home. (Rev: BL 1/1–15/07)

1160 Clark, Emma Chichester. *Will and Squill* (PS–2). Illus. 2006, Carolrhoda $15.95 (1-57505-936-3). 32pp. A boy named Will and a squirrel called Squill are great friends despite their mothers' disapproval. (Rev: BL 3/1/06; SLJ 3/06)

1161 Clayton, Elaine. *A Blue Ribbon for Sugar* (K–2). 2006, Roaring Brook $16.95 (1-59643-157-1). 32pp. When Bonnie's beloved rocking horse breaks, she's treated to riding lessons on a real pony and eventually wins a blue ribbon at a horse show. (Rev: BL 6/1–15/06; SLJ 5/06)

1162 Clements, Andrew. *Slippers at School* (PS–2). Illus. by Janie Bynum. 2005, Dutton $12.99 (0-525-47189-8). 32pp. Slippers, Laura's puppy, hides in the girl's backpack on her first day at school and manages to evade ejection through a series of funny misunderstandings. (Rev: BL 8/05; SLJ 9/05)

1163 Clements, Andrew. *Slippers Loves to Run* (PS–2). Illus. by Janie Bynum. Series: Slippers. 2006, Dutton $12.99 (0-525-47648-2). 32pp. Restless puppy Slippers runs from his back yard to explore the big world before running home for a hug from his owners. (Rev: SLJ 6/06)

1164 Cochran, Bill. *The Forever Dog* (PS–2). Illus. by Dan Andreasen. 2007, HarperCollins $15.99 (978-0-06-053939-9). 32pp. A young boy tries to forgive his dead dog for deserting him. (Rev: BL 4/1/07; SLJ 3/07)

1165 Day, Alexandra. *Carl's Sleepy Afternoon* (K–2). Illus. 2005, Farrar $12.95 (0-374-31088-2). 40pp. Rottweiler Carl is left at home for a good nap

but ends up having a very busy afternoon. (Rev: BL 9/1/05; SLJ 10/05)

1166 Denslow, Sharon Phillips. *In the Snow* (PS–K). Illus. by Nancy Tafuri. 2005, Greenwillow $15.99 (0-06-059683-X). 40pp. A young child puts out seeds to feed hungry woodland animals in this gentle story that introduces animals and the idea of animal footprints. (Rev: BL 10/15/05; SLJ 3/06)

1167 Díaz, Katacha. *Badger at Sandy Ridge Road* (K–3). Illus. by Kristin Kest. Series: Smithsonian's Backyard. 2005, Soundprints $15.95 (1-59249-420-X). 31pp. The story of a desert badger looking for a place to give birth is followed by facts about the North American badger. (Rev: SLJ 7/05)

1168 Diehl, Jean Heilprin. *Loon Chase* (1–3). Illus. by Kathryn Freeman. 2006, Sylvan Dell $15.95 (0-9764943-8-8). When their bird dog's hunting instincts send it in pursuit of a mother loon and her babies, a boy and his mother worry that their pet will hurt the endangered birds. (Rev: SLJ 4/06)

1169 Drachman, Eric. *A Frog Thing* (PS–2). Illus. by James Muscarello. 2006, Kidwick Books $18.95 (0-9703809-3-3). A frog named Frank who longs to fly finally gets his chance but comes to recognize that flying really isn't a frog thing; with beautiful illustrations and CD. (Rev: SLJ 6/06)

1170 Ehlert, Lois. *Wag a Tail* (PS–2). 2007, Harcourt $16.00 (978-0-15-205843-2). 40pp. Ehlert's colorful paper collages portray happy dogs as they first visit a farmer's market with their humans, then cavort leash-free at a dog park. (Rev: BL 1/1–15/07)

1171 Elschner, Géraldine. *Fritz's Fish* (1–3). Trans. by Kathryn Bishop. Illus. by Daniela Bunge. 2005, Putnam $14.99 (0-698-40028-3). 32pp. Downcast because his parents can't have a pet, young Fritz brings home a fish he finds swimming in the street after a flood. (Rev: BL 1/1–15/06; SLJ 1/06)

1172 Elschner, Géraldine. *Mark's Messy Room* (PS–2). Trans. from German by Charise Myngheer. Illus. by Alexandra Junge. 2006, Minedition $16.99 (0-698-40047-X). Carlo the cat has had enough of Mark's messy room and decides to leave home, only to discover that tidiness its limitations. (Rev: SLJ 1/07)

1173 Gannij, Joan. *Elusive Moose* (PS–2). Illus. by Clare Beaton. 2006, Barefoot Bks. $15.99 (1-905236-75-1). 32pp. An invisible narrator lists all the animals he has seen in the north woods, except for the moose that's hiding in each scene. (Rev: BL 11/15/06; SLJ 11/06)

1174 George, Lindsay Barren. *In the Garden: Who's Been Here?* (PS–2). Illus. 2006, Greenwillow $16.99 (0-06-078762-7). 48pp. While picking vegetables in the garden, Christina and Jeremy wonder about the animals that got there first. (Rev: BL 4/15/06; SLJ 5/06)

1175 George, Margaret, and Christopher J. Murphy. *Lucille Lost: A True Adventure* (PS–2). Illus. by Debra Bandelin. 2006, Viking $16.99 (0-670-06093-3). 32pp. Pet turtle Lucille has frightening adventures when she is mistakenly released into the wild; based on true events, this also includes facts about tortoises. (Rev: BL 5/1/06; SLJ 8/06)

1176 Gray, Rita. *The Wild Little Horse* (PS–2). Illus. by Ashley Wolff. 2005, Dutton $15.99 (0-525-47455-2). A young colt takes pleasure in his surroundings — and in his independence — as his parents allow him the freedom to run and explore. (Rev: SLJ 9/05)

1177 Greco, Francesca. *Cyril the Mandrill* (PS–2). Illus. by author. 2005, Star Bright $16.95 (1-932065-92-X). Lonely Cyril, derided by other animals in the zoo who are jealous of his bright, distinctive markings, finally wins them over. (Rev: SLJ 7/05)

1178 Grimes, Nikki. *When Gorilla Goes Walking* (PS–2). Illus. by Shane Evans. 2007, Scholastic $16.99 (978-0-439-31770-2). 32pp. Cecelia, a young African American girl, describes in interconnected poems the exploits of her assertive cat called Gorilla. (Rev: BL 4/15/07; HBG 10/07)

1179 Guilloppe, Antoine. *One Scary Night* (2–4). Illus. 2005, Milk & Cookies $15.95 (0-689-04636-7). 32pp. In this scary, wordless picture book, a young boy wandering through the snowy woods alone at night is being followed by a creature that in the last spread turns out to be a friendly dog. (Rev: BL 11/1/05; SLJ 11/05)

1180 Hammerle, Susa. *Let's Try Horseback Riding* (PS–2). Trans. by Marisa Miller. Illus. by Kyrima Trapp. 2006, North-South $12.95 (0-7358-2093-7). 24pp. Rebecca is thrilled to receive riding lessons for her birthday, and learns all about caring for horses, horseback riding, and equine behavior. (Rev: BL 9/15/06; SLJ 11/06)

1181 Hatkoff, Isabella, and Craig Hatkoff. *Owen and Mzee: The Language of Friendship* (K–4). Photos by Peter Greste. 2007, Scholastic $16.99 (978-0-439-89959-8). This appealing sequel to *Owen and Mzee: The True Story of a Remarkable Friendship* continues the story of the bond between the baby hippo orphaned by the Indian Ocean tsunami and an ancient tortoise, focusing on how the two creatures communicate with one another. (Rev: BL 12/15/06*; SLJ 2/07*) [599.63]

1182 Henkes, Kevin. *A Good Day* (PS–K). Illus. by author. 2007, Greenwillow $16.99 (978-0-06-114018-1). 32pp. Four animals start off having a bad day, but luckily things turn around before the day is over. (Rev: BL 12/15/06; SLJ 3/07*)

1183 Herman, R. A. *Gomer and Little Gomer* (PS). Illus. by Steve Haskamp. 2005, Dutton $14.99 (0-525-47359-9). Gomer the dog loses his favorite toy,

Little Gomer, and his friend Chi Chi, who initially mocked the toy, helps him find it. (Rev: SLJ 9/05)

1184 Hobbs, Leigh. *Old Tom, Man of Mystery* (K–2). Illus. by author. 2005, Peachtree $16.95 (1-56145-346-3). Angry when his mistress assigns him a number of chores, Old Tom the cat decides to play a trick on her; a sequel to *Old Tom's Holiday* (2004). (Rev: SLJ 12/05)

1185 Hodgkins, Fran. *The Cat of Strawberry Hill: A True Story* (PS–2). Illus. by Lesia Sochor. 2005, Down East $15.95 (0-89272-684-9). 32pp. A playful kitten that goes astray from its owners at a highway rest stop is adopted by innkeepers and has a satisfying life thereafter. (Rev: BL 12/15/05; SLJ 3/06)

1186 Hornsey, Chris. *Why Do I Have to Eat off the Floor?* (PS–1). Illus. by Gwyn Perkins. 2007, Walker $15.95 (978-0-8027-9617-2). 24pp. Murphy, a fun-loving beagle, poses all sorts of questions about his life to his young owner. (Rev: BL 4/1/07; SLJ 3/07)

1187 Huggins-Cooper, Lynn. *Alien Invaders / Invasores extraterrestres* (1–3). Trans. by Eida de la Vega. Illus. by Bonnie Leick. 2005, Raven Tree $16.95 (0-9724973-9-0). 32pp. In this attractive bilingual picture book, a little boy becomes convinced that the insects he sees all around him are alien invaders from outer space. (Rev: SLJ 10/05)

1188 Huneck, Stephen. *Sally's Snow Adventure* (PS–2). 2006, Abrams $15.95 (0-8109-7061-9). 32pp. While on a ski trip to a dog-friendly resort, Sally the black Labrador retriever gets lost but is finally saved by a pair of rescue dogs that she befriended earlier. (Rev: BL 9/1/06; SLJ 10/06)

1189 Janisch, Heinz. *Heave Ho!* (PS–K). Illus. by Carola Holland. 2006, North-South $16.95 (0-7358-2091-0). In only 12 sentences, this entertaining tale shows a dog, a cat, and a few mice banding together to raid the refrigerator. (Rev: SLJ 11/06)

1190 Jennings, Sharon. *Bearcub and Mama* (PS). Illus. by Melanie Watt. 2005, Kids Can $15.95 (1-55337-566-1). Bearcub learns to separate from his beloved mama in this story about growing into independence. (Rev: SLJ 8/05)

1191 Johnson, Rebecca. *The Proud Pelican's Secret* (K–2). Photos by Steve Parish. Series: Animal Storybooks. 2005, Gareth Stevens LB $20.67 (0-8368-5974-X). 24pp. A pelican who seems more interested in his looks than in fishing nonetheless always seems well fed; facts and photographs round out this nice combination of fiction and nonfiction. (Rev: SLJ 2/06)

1192 Johnson, Rebecca. *Sea Turtle's Clever Plan* (K–2). Photos by Steve Parish. 2005, Gareth Stevens LB $20.67 (0-8368-5975-8). 24pp. A clever, newly hatched sea turtle finds a way to avoid danger on her trip to the sea; facts and photographs round out this nice combination of fiction and non-fiction. (Rev: SLJ 2/06)

1193 Johnson, Rebecca. *Tree Frog Hears a Sound* (K–2). Photos by Steve Parish. Series: Animal Storybooks. 2005, Gareth Stevens LB $20.67 (0-8368-5976-6). 24pp. A female tree frog hops through the forest in search of the male whose call she has heard; facts and photographs round out this nice combination of fiction and nonfiction. (Rev: SLJ 2/06)

1194 Jones, Jolie. *Little Kisses* (K–2). Illus. by Julie Downing. Series: The Julie Andrews Collection. 2005, HarperCollins $15.99 (0-06-058698-2). Bejinhos the dog and Jolie enjoy each other's company and know the rules, but Bejinhos gets into trouble while his mistress is spending at school; appealing illustrations enhance the meandering text. (Rev: SLJ 1/06)

1195 Joosse, Barbara M. *Wind-Wild Dog* (1–3). Illus. by Kate Kiesler. 2006, Holt $16.95 (0-8050-7053-2). 32pp. Sled-dog Ziva faces a difficult choice between remaining with the man who has shown his faith in her and running free with the wolves she hears at night. (Rev: BL 10/1/06; SLJ 11/06)

1196 Karon, Jan, and Melanie Cecka. *Violet Comes to Stay* (K–2). Illus. by Emily Arnold McCully. 2006, Viking $15.99 (0-670-06073-9). Violet the kitten fails to remember her mother's mousing advice and has problems finding a suitable home. (Rev: SLJ 11/06)

1197 Kasza, Keiko. *The Dog Who Cried Wolf* (PS–2). Illus. 2005, Putnam $15.99 (0-399-24247-3). 32pp. When his owner reads him a book about wolves, Moka the dog decides to run away to the wilds and live free, but eventually discovers a wolf's life is not quite what he expected. (Rev: BL 9/1/05; SLJ 12/05*)

1198 Kelly, Irene. *A Small Dog's Big Life: Around the World with Owney* (PS–2). Illus. 2005, Holiday $16.95 (0-8234-1863-4). 32pp. This engaging picture book chronicles in fictionalized letters and newspaper accounts the story of Owney, a stray dog that became a post office mascot in the late 19th century and traveled around the world. (Rev: BL 7/05; SLJ 8/05)

1199 Kerr, Judith. *Goose in a Hole* (PS–2). Illus. by author. 2006, Collins $15.99 (0-00-720793-X). In search of the water that has mysteriously gone missing from the village pond, Katerina the goose fearlessly sets off down a hole, family in tow. (Rev: SLJ 7/06)

1200 King, Stephen Michael. *Mutt Dog!* (PS–2). Illus. 2005, Harcourt $16.00 (0-15-205561-4). 32pp. Mutt Dog struggles to survive on the city streets until he is adopted by a worker at the local homeless shelter. (Rev: BL 10/1/05; SLJ 11/05)

1201 Koldofsky, Eleanor. *Clip-Clop* (K–3). Illus. by David Parkins. 2005, Tundra $15.95 (0-88776-681-1). In this nostalgia-filled picture book set in the early 20th century, young Consuela lives for her encounters with the workhorses that pass through her neighborhood each day; an Author's Note provides additional information. (Rev: SLJ 11/05)

1202 Kwon, Yoon-duck. *My Cat Copies Me* (K–3). Illus. 2007, Kane/Miller $15.95 (978-1-933605-26-5). 32pp. A young girl and her cat have fun together, copying each other's movements at play. (Rev: BL 4/15/07)

1203 Lareau, Kara. *Ugly Fish* (1–4). Illus. by Scott Magoon. 2006, Harcourt $16.00 (0-15-205082-5). Ugly Fish, who would rather eat other fish than make friends, gets his comeuppance when Shiny Fish is introduced into his tank. (Rev: SLJ 7/06)

1204 Lee, Spike, and Tonya Lewis Lee. *Please, Puppy, Please* (PS–1). Illus. by Kadir Nelson. 2005, Simon & Schuster $16.95 (0-689-86804-9). 32pp. Two African American children give their high-energy puppy lots of instructions he fails to heed. (Rev: BL 11/1/05; SLJ 11/05)

1205 Lewis, Kim. *A Puppy for Annie* (PS–2). Illus. by author. 2006, Candlewick $15.99 (978-0-7636-3200-7). Annie loves her Border collie Bess and gradually learns to understand what Bess is trying to convey as the two roam together in the English countryside. (Rev: BL 11/15/06; SLJ 2/07)

1206 Litty, Julie. *Chloe and the Magic Baton* (K–3). Trans. from French by Charise Myngheer. Illus. by author. 2006, Minedition $15.99 (0-698-40039-9). Young Chloe, wary about the pony she will be riding in the jumping competition, does very well when her uncle gives her a baton that he says is magical; when this talisman goes missing and her nerves return, it is the pony itself that saves the day. (Rev: SLJ 8/06)

1207 Loupy, Christophe. *Wiggles* (K–2). Illus. by Eve Tharlet. 2005, North-South $15.95 (0-7358-1980-7). Lirrle Wiggles, a farm dog, enjoys helping out with the chores very early one morning in this picture book with watercolor illustrations. (Rev: SLJ 7/05)

1208 McBratney, Sam. *I Love It When You Smile* (PS–1). Illus. by Charles Fuge. 2006, HarperCollins $15.99 (0-06-084245-8). Lively illustrations incorporating an onlooking mouse and duck add to the simple text about a mother kangaroo trying to cheer up her grumpy child. (Rev: SLJ 5/06)

1209 McCarty, Peter. *Fabian Escapes* (PS–K). Illus. 2007, Holt $16.95 (978-0-8050-7713-1). 32pp. In this colorful sequel to *Hondo and Fabian* (2002), Fabian the cat leads a canine trio on a merry chase while Hondo the dog is stuck at home playing with the toddler. (Rev: BL 3/15/07)

1210 McGrory, Anik. *Kidogo* (PS–1). Illus. by author. 2005, Bloomsbury $15.95 (1-58234-974-6). Kidogo, a young elephant, is feeling very small until he encounters a colony of ants. (Rev: SLJ 9/05*)

1211 McKinlay, Penny. *Flabby Tabby* (PS–1). Illus. by Britta Teckentrup. 2006, Frances Lincoln $15.95 (1-84507-090-9). 32pp. Tabby, an overweight cat, embarks on a secret fitness program when a new kitten arrives in the house and keeps beating her to the food bowl. (Rev: BL 1/1–15/06; SLJ 2/06)

1212 Manuel, Lynn. *The Trouble with Tilly Trumble* (K–2). Illus. by Diane Greenseid. 2006, Abrams $16.95 (0-8109-5972-0). 32pp. Tilly Trumble is preoccupied by chairs and particularly by finding the right one for the comfortable spot by her fire, but the stray dog that appears on her doorstep seems to solve the problem. (Rev: BL 4/15/06; SLJ 12/06)

1213 Markle, Sandra. *Little Lost Bat* (2–4). Illus. by Alan Marks. 2006, Charlesbridge $15.95 (1-57091-656-X). 32pp. This picture-book tale about a newborn bat left to fend for itself after its mother is killed by a predator is full of bat facts and lore. (Rev: BL 6/1–15/06; HB 7–8/07; HBG 4/07; LMC 2/07; SLJ 8/06*)

1214 Masurel, Claire. *¡No, Tito, no! / No, No, Titus!* (K–2). Trans. by Diego Lasconi. Illus. by Shari Halpern. 2006, North-South LB $16.50 (0-7358-2074-0); paper $6.95 (0-7358-2075-9). An endearing puppy, newly adopted by a farm family, tries to figure out where he fits in the overall scheme of things. (Rev: SLJ 10/06)

1215 Meister, Cari. *My Pony Jack at Riding Lessons* (PS–K). Illus. by Amy Young. Series: Viking Easy-to-Read. 2005, Viking $13.99 (0-670-05918-8). 32pp. In this sequel to *My Pony Jack* (2005) suitable for beginning readers, Lacy takes riding lessons. (Rev: BL 10/15/05; SLJ 10/05)

1216 Meister, Cari. *My Pony Jack at the Horse Show* (PS–2). Illus. by Amy Young. Series: Viking Easy-to-Read. 2006, Viking $13.99 (0-670-05919-6). 32pp. Lacy gets her pony Jack ready for a show, suffers some nerves when she arrives at the ring, and comes home with second prize; for beginning readers. (Rev: SLJ 8/06)

1217 Meyers, Susan. *Kittens! Kittens! Kittens!* (PS–K). Illus. by David Walker. 2007, Abrams $15.95 (978-0-8109-1218-2). 32pp. Rhyming text and cheerful pictures track kittens as they play, explore, and grow. (Rev: BL 1/1–15/07)

1218 Miles, Victoria. *Old Mother Bear* (PS–3). Illus. by Molly Bang. 2007, Chronicle $16.95 (978-0-8118-5033-9). 32pp. This strikingly illustrated picture book based on true events follows an aging female grizzly bear as she guides her final set of cubs along the path to adulthood. (Rev: BL 4/15/07)

1219 Murphy, Yannick. *Ahwooooooooo!* (PS–2). 2006, Clarion $16.00 (0-618-11762-8). 32pp. Little

Wolf's parents are too busy to teach him how to howl, so he turns to his grandfather for help. (Rev: BL 8/06; SLJ 6/06)

1220 Niland, Deborah. *Annie's Chair* (PS–K). Illus. by author. 2006, Walker $16.95 (0-8027-8082-2). Annie initially has a very big problem when she finds the dog sitting in her special chair, but a kindly lick reminds her how to share. (Rev: SLJ 6/06)

1221 Page, Gail. *How to Be a Good Dog* (PS–2). Illus. by author. 2006, Bloomsbury $15.95 (1-58234-683-6). Bobo wants to be a good dog, so the cat teaches him how to behave, with mixed results. (Rev: SLJ 6/06)

1222 Pitzer, Susanna. *Not Afraid of Dogs* (PS–2). Illus. by Larry Day. 2006, Walker $16.95 (0-8027-8067-9). 32pp. Daniel is not scared of dogs although he does everything he can to avoid them, but when he finds his visiting aunt's dog cowering in the bathroom during a thunderstorm, he can't resist offering comfort. (Rev: BL 6/1–15/06; SLJ 7/06*)

1223 Poppenhäger, Nicole. *Snow Leopards* (K–3). Trans. from German by J. Alison James. Illus. by Ivan Gantschev. 2006, North-South $15.95 (0-7358-2087-2). Two young snow leopards separated by an avalanche search for each other and are eventually reunited; a moving story with dramatic artwork. (Rev: SLJ 11/06)

1224 Prince, Joshua. *I Saw an Ant on the Railroad Track* (PS–1). Illus. by Macky Pamintuan. 2006, Sterling $14.95 (1-4027-2183-8). 24pp. Jack, a brawny switchman, tries to avoid a collision between an oncoming train and an ant that's on the tracks. (Rev: BL 2/1/06; SLJ 7/06)

1225 Rammell, S. Kelly. *City Beats: A Hip-Hoppy Pigeon Poem* (PS–2). Illus. by Jeanette Canyon. 2006, Dawn $16.95 (1-58469-076-3); paper $8.95 (1-58469-077-1). A hip-hop-style poem describes a city pigeon's life from dawn to dusk. (Rev: SLJ 8/06)

1226 Rankin, Laura. *Fluffy and Baron* (PS–1). Illus. by author. 2006, Dial $16.99 (0-8037-2953-7). The story of an unlikely friendship between a large dog and a wild duck, with beautiful illustrations. (Rev: SLJ 7/06)

1227 Raye, Rebekah. *The Very Best Bed* (PS–2). Illus. by author. 2006, Tilbury House $16.95 (0-88448-284-7). A squirrel searching for the perfect place to sleep tries out various other animals' solutions. (Rev: SLJ 1/07)

1228 Rockwell, Anne. *Backyard Bear* (PS–2). Illus. by Megan Halsey. 2006, Walker $15.95 (0-8027-9573-0). 32pp. A young bear finds itself roaming through a human neighborhood in this realistic story about the effects of development on animal habitats. (Rev: BL 10/15/06; SLJ 10/06)

1229 Romanova, Yelena. *The Perfect Friend* (PS–2). Illus. by Boris Kulikov. 2005, Farrar $15.00 (0-374-35821-4). 32pp. Archie the dog is upset when his owners bring home a new baby, but over time the child grows into a perfect playmate. (Rev: BL 11/15/05; SLJ 10/05)

1230 Root, Phyllis. *Looking for a Moose* (PS–K). Illus. by Randy Cecil. 2006, Candlewick $15.99 (0-7636-2005-X). 32pp. Bouncy text and appealing hide-and-seek illustrations follow a group of children on an adventurous search for an elusive moose. (Rev: BL 10/1/06; SLJ 10/06)

1231 Ruepp, Krista. *Anna's Prince* (K–3). Trans. from German by J. Alison James. Illus. by Ulrike Heyne. 2006, North-South $15.95 (0-7358-2081-3). Young Anna trains her beloved pony, Prince, to carry a rider in this sequel, set in Iceland, to *Winter Pony* (2002) and *Runaway Pony* (2005). (Rev: SLJ 11/06)

1232 Saltzberg, Barney. *I Love Cats* (PS). Illus. by author. 2005, Candlewick $8.99 (0-7636-2588-4). Good reasons to love cats, in rhyming text with sweet illustrations. (Rev: SLJ 8/05)

1233 Saltzberg, Barney. *I Love Dogs* (PS). Illus. by author. 2005, Candlewick $8.99 (0-7636-2587-6). Good reasons to love dogs, in rhyming text with sweet illustrations. (Rev: SLJ 8/05)

1234 Schmidt, Karen Lee. *Carl's Nose* (PS–2). Illus. by author. 2006, Harcourt $16.00 (0-15-205049-3). Carl the dog has a nose for bad weather and provides reliable forecasts to the citizens of Grimsville until the climate suddenly turns sunny and he must seek a new occupation, now using his nose to search for lost souls. (Rev: SLJ 11/06)

1235 Seeger, Laura Vaccaro. *Dog and Bear* (PS–K). Illus. 2007, Roaring Brook $12.95 (978-1-59643-053-2). 32pp. Three simple stories with minimal text depict the friendship between Dog, a fun-loving dachshund, and Bear, a stuffed animal. (Rev: BCCB 6/07; BL 3/15/07; HB 5–6/07; HBG 10/07; LMC 8–9/07)

1236 Shannon, David. *Good Boy, Fergus!* (K–2). Illus. 2006, Scholastic $15.99 (0-439-49027-8). 40pp. West Highland terrier Fergus has a great day, encouraged in his chasing and scratching and munching by his young master. (Rev: BL 1/1–15/06; SLJ 3/06)

1237 Sloat, Teri. *I'm a Duck!* (PS–2). Illus. 2006, Putnam $15.99 (0-399-24274-0). 32pp. A happy duck celebrates its duck-ness and in the process introduces readers to its life cycle. (Rev: BL 3/1/06; SLJ 2/06)

1238 Smith, Linda. *Mrs. Crump's Cat* (2–4). Illus. by David Roberts. 2006, HarperCollins $15.99 (0-06-028302-5). When a stray cat shows up on her porch, the life of cranky Mrs. Crump takes a turn for the better. (Rev: SLJ 4/06)

1239 Spinelli, Eileen. *Hero Cat* (PS–2). Illus. by Jo Ellen McAllister Stammen. 2006, Marshall Cavendish $16.95 (0-7614-5223-0). 32pp. A mother cat rescues her kittens from a fire in this story based on truth. (Rev: BL 3/1/06; SLJ 4/06)

1240 Spirin, Gennady. *Martha* (PS–K). Illus. 2005, Philomel $14.99 (0-399-23980-4). 32pp. In this picture book illustrated with warm watercolors, Russian-born Spirin tells how he and his family nursed an injured crow back to health. (Rev: BL 7/05; SLJ 4/05)

1241 Stainton, Sue. *I Love Cats* (PS–1). Illus. by Anne Mortimer. 2007, HarperCollins $15.99 (978-0-06-085154-5). 24pp. A colorful celebration of cats of all kinds. (Rev: BL 3/15/07; SLJ 3/07)

1242 Stanley, Mandy. *What Do You Do?* (PS). Illus. by author. 2005, Simon & Schuster $7.99 (1-4169-0499-9). A number of animals answer the title's question in this book, which is similar to the author's *What Do You Say?* (2003). (Rev: SLJ 7/05)

1243 Stevens, Janet, and Susan Stevens Crummel. *The Great Fuzz Frenzy* (PS–2). Illus. 2005, Harcourt $17.00 (0-15-204626-7). 56pp. Chaos erupts when a green tennis ball drops into a prairie dog burrow; an exciting read with inventive illustrations enhanced by the oversize format. (Rev: BL 9/1/05; SLJ 9/05*)

1244 Stohner, Anu. *Brave Charlotte* (PS–2). Illus. by Henrike Wilson. 2005, Bloomsbury $16.95 (1-58234-690-9). 32pp. Charlotte, an adventurous sheep, comes to the rescue when the shepherd breaks his leg in this picture book featuring excellent illustrations. (Rev: BL 8/05; SLJ 1/06)

1245 Tafuri, Nancy. *Five Little Chicks* (PS). Illus. 2006, Simon & Schuster $14.95 (0-689-87342-5). 32pp. A mother hen teaches her five newborn chicks where to find a good meal. (Rev: BL 12/15/05; SLJ 2/06)

1246 Tafuri, Nancy. *Whose Chick Are You?* (PS–K). Illus. by author. 2007, HarperCollins $16.99 (978-0-06-082514-0). When a baby swan hatches, nobody seems to know who it belongs to. (Rev: BL 12/15/06; SLJ 2/07)

1247 Turner, Sandy. *Cool Cat, Hot Dog* (PS–2). Illus. by author. 2005, Simon & Schuster $16.95 (0-689-84946-X). Imaginative torn-paper artwork is the highlight of this discussion — between a dog and cat — of their different characteristics. (Rev: SLJ 8/05)

1248 Von Buhler, Cynthia. *The Cat Who Wouldn't Come Inside: Based on a True Story* (PS–2). Photos by author. Illus. by author. 2006, Houghton $16.00 (0-618-56314-8). In an effort to convince a stray cat to stay, a woman adds more and more attractions to her front porch, until it's just as nice outside as inside. (Rev: SLJ 11/06)

1249 Votaw, Carol. *Good Morning, Little Polar Bear* (PS–2). Illus. by Susan Banta. 2005, North-Word $15.95 (1-55971-932-X). In this appealing picture book, a young Inuit child celebrates the arrival of summer by making the rounds of the creatures that call the Arctic home. (Rev: SLJ 11/05)

1250 Waldron, Kathleen Cook. *Roundup at the Palace* (K–3). Illus. by Alan Daniel and Lea Daniel. 2006, Red Deer $17.95 (0-88995-319-8). A bull escapes from a truck on the way to a stock show in Denver, and Zack and Alice must coax him back to safety in this story based on an actual event. (Rev: SLJ 7/06)

1251 Walsh, Melanie. *Do Lions Live on Lily Pads?* (PS). 2006, Houghton $15.00 (0-618-47300-9). 32pp. Using questions and answers, this simple picture book reveals the distinctive habitats of animals including lions, parakeets, giraffes, and crocodiles. (Rev: BL 6/1–15/06; SLJ 7/06)

1252 Winstead, Rosie. *Ruby and Bubbles* (K–2). Illus. by author. 2006, Dial $15.99 (0-8037-3024-1). Ruby's love for her pet bird Bubbles is shaken when bullies mock the bird and its inability to fly. (Rev: SLJ 2/06)

1253 Wright, Cliff. *Bear and Ball* (PS). Illus. by author. 2005, Chronicle $5.95 (0-8118-4819-1). A simple board book rhyming story about two bear cubs playing with a ball. Also use *Bear and Kite* (2005). (Rev: SLJ 7/05)

1254 Ziefert, Harriet. *Beach Party!* (PS). Illus. by Simms Taback. 2005, Blue Apple $8.95 (1-59354-067-1). A board book featuring adorable sea animals on their way to the ocean for a swim. (Rev: SLJ 8/05)

1255 Ziefert, Harriet. *Murphy Jumps a Hurdle* (K–3). Illus. by Emily Bolam. 2006, Blue Apple $15.95 (1-59354-174-0). 40pp. Murphy the yellow Lab and his owner Cheryl tackle agility training in this entertaining book with cartoonlike illustrations. (Rev: BL 11/1/06)

SCHOOL STORIES

1256 Abercrombie, Barbara. *The Show-and-Tell Lion* (K–2). Illus. by Lynne Cravath. 2006, Simon & Schuster $16.95 (0-689-86408-6). 32pp. Unprepared for show-and-tell, young Matthew makes up a story about having a lion but faces a real dilemma when his classmates want to see it. (Rev: BL 9/15/06; HBG 4/07; SLJ 7/06)

1257 Aliki. *A Play's the Thing* (2–4). Illus. 2005, HarperCollins $16.99 (0-06-074355-7). 32pp. José is less than thrilled when his teacher, Miss Brilliant, decides the class will put on a dramatization of "Mary Had a Little Lamb"; cartoon panels and a running narrative tell the story. (Rev: BL 10/15/05; HB 9–1/05; HBG 4/06; LMC 4–5/06; SLJ 8/05*)

1258 Borden, Louise. *The Last Day of School* (1–3). Illus. by Adam Gustavson. 2006, Simon & Schuster $15.95 (0-689-86869-3). 40pp. It's the last day of school, and one of Mrs. Mallory's third-grade students has a special surprise for her. (Rev: BL 2/1/06; SLJ 3/06)

1259 Bowen, Anne. *The Great Math Tattle Battle* (1–3). Illus. by Jaime Zollars. 2006, Albert Whitman $15.95 (0-8075-3163-4). 32pp. Math whiz Harley Harrison is the scourge of his second-grade class, constantly tattling on his classmates until a newcomer called Emma Jean turns the tables on him. (Rev: BL 4/15/06; SLJ 6/06)

1260 Brisson, Pat. *I Remember Miss Perry* (K–3). Illus. by Stephane Jorisch. 2006, Dial $16.99 (0-8037-2981-2). 32pp. Stevie fondly remembers Miss Perry — his first teacher — when she is killed in a car accident. (Rev: BL 2/1/06; SLJ 3/06)

1261 Bunting, Eve. *One Green Apple* (1–3). Illus. by Ted Lewin. 2006, Clarion $16.00 (0-618-43477-1). 32pp. Farah, a young Muslim immigrant, feels uncomfortable in her new school until she joins classmates on a field trip to an apple orchard where she discovers that some things are the same no matter where you are. (Rev: BL 6/1–15/06; HBG 10/06; LMC 8–9/06; SLJ 6/06)

1262 Carson, Jana. *Stop Teasing Taylor!* (K–2). Illus. by Meryl Treatner. Series: We Both Read. 2005, Treasure Bay $7.99 (1-891327-61-5); paper $3.99 (1-891327-62-3). Designed to be read in tandem by a beginning reader and one who's more advanced, this is a simple story about a young boy's first day at school. (Rev: SLJ 4/06)

1263 Choldenko, Gennifer. *How to Make Friends with a Giant* (K–2). Illus. by Amy Walrod. 2006, Putnam $16.99 (0-399-23779-8). Tiny Jake and giant Jacomo become unlikely friends in this story about the advantages of being different. (Rev: SLJ 7/06)

1264 Cohen, Miriam. *First Grade Takes a Test* (K–1). Illus. by Ronald Himler. 2006, Star Bright $15.95 (1-59572-054-5); paper $5.95 (1-59572-055-3). 32pp. A newly illustrated version of Cohen's story about a first-grade class and what they learn about aptitude when they take an intelligence test. (Rev: BL 11/15/06)

1265 Cox, Judy. *Don't Be Silly, Mrs. Millie!* (PS–K). Illus. by Joe Mathieu. 2005, Marshall Cavendish $14.95 (0-7614-5166-8). 32pp. Kindergarten teacher Mrs. Millie is prone to confusing her words — "coats" become "goats" — and the illustrations add to the general zaniness. (Rev: BL 8/05; SLJ 10/05)

1266 Danneberg, Julie. *Last Day Blues* (K–2). Illus. by Judy Love. 2006, Charlesbridge $16.95 (1-58089-046-6); paper $6.95 (1-58089-104-7). 32pp. Mrs. Hartwell's class worries that she will be lonely during the summer and tries to think of a suitable gift; meanwhile, Mrs. Hartwell can be seen celebrating the end of school with other teachers. (Rev: BL 1/1–15/06; SLJ 2/06)

1267 Davis, Katie. *Kindergarten Rocks!* (PS–K). Illus. by author. 2005, Harcourt $15.00 (0-15-204932-0). Dexter isn't nervous at all during his first day of kindergarten, but his stuffed dog Rufus is quite apprehensive. (Rev: SLJ 9/05)

1268 Derby, Sally. *The Wacky Substitute* (K–3). Illus. by Jennifer Herbert. 2005, Marshall Cavendish $14.95 (0-7614-5219-2). When substitute teacher Mr. Wuerst loses his eyeglasses, it sets the stage for some entertaining mishaps in the classroom. (Rev: SLJ 10/05)

1269 DiPucchio, Kelly S. *Mrs. McBloom, Clean Up Your Room!* (K–2). Illus. by Guy Francis. 2005, Hyperion $15.99 (0-7868-0932-9). 32pp. Mrs. McBloom is retiring after a half century of teaching, and her students help to clean up the amazingly diverse clutter in her classroom. (Rev: BL 8/05; SLJ 9/05)

1270 Dodds, Daye Ann. *Teacher's Pets* (PS–2). Illus. by Marylin Hafner. 2006, Candlewick $15.99 (0-7636-2252-4). 40pp. Miss Fry's classroom becomes home to her students' pets in this story of a happy menagerie. (Rev: BL 5/15/06; SLJ 5/06)

1271 Dubosarsky, Ursula. *Rex* (K–2). Illus. by David Mackintosh. 2006, Roaring Brook $16.95 (1-59643-186-5). 32pp. In words and art, various students describe what happened when they took Rex the class chameleon home for the night. (Rev: BL 11/15/06; SLJ 9/06)

1272 Finchler, Judy, and Kevin O'Malley. *Miss Malarkey Leaves No Reader Behind* (1–3). Series: Miss Malarkey. 2006, Walker $16.95 (0-8027-8084-9). 32pp. Miss Malarkey finally finds a book that's just right for a guy who's not too fond of reading. (Rev: BL 7/06; SLJ 8/06)

1273 Grindley, Sally. *It's My School* (PS–2). Illus. by Margaret Chamberlain. 2006, Walker $15.95 (0-8027-8086-5). 32pp. Tom is not pleased when his little sister starts school but he is quick to protect her when necessary. (Rev: BL 8/06; SLJ 7/06*)

1274 Harper, Jessica. *A Place Called Kindergarten* (PS–K). Illus. by G. Brian Karas. 2006, Putnam $15.99 (0-399-24226-0). 32pp. The barnyard animals worry when Tommy doesn't turn up as usual, but he has only gone to kindergarten and returns to tell them all about it. (Rev: BL 8/06; SLJ 8/06)

1275 Hays, Anna Jane. *Ready, Set, Preschool!* (PS). Illus. by True Kelley. 2005, Knopf $16.95 (0-375-82519-3). 40pp. This collection of rhymes, stories, and interactive games offers lots of concepts and ideas for preschoolers and their parents. (Rev: BL 8/05; SLJ 9/05)

1276 Heck, Ed. *Monkey Lost* (PS–2). Illus. by author. 2005, Milk & Cookies $15.95 (0-689-04633-2). Eric's teacher and classmates pitch in to help find the monkey he brought to school for show-and-tell, unaware that it is only a stuffed animal. (Rev: SLJ 11/05)

1277 Hennessy, B. G. *Mr. Ouchy's First Day* (K–2). Illus. by Paul Meisel. 2006, Putnam $15.99 (0-399-24248-1). 32pp. Mr. Ouchy is nervous about his first day as a teacher until he actually interacts with the class. (Rev: BL 8/06; SLJ 7/06)

1278 Hobbie, Nathaniel. *Priscilla Superstar!* (1–3). Illus. by Jocelyn Hobbie. 2006, Little, Brown $16.99 (0-316-01386-2). 32pp. Even though Priscilla doesn't get the lead in her roller-skating school's play she still shows off her talent and learns what it means to be a real star. (Rev: BL 2/1/07; SLJ 10/06)

1279 Kelley, True. *School Lunch* (K–2). Illus. 2005, Holiday $16.95 (0-8234-1894-4). 32pp. When Harriet, the school cook, takes a vacation, students and faculty are disappointed in her replacements and write letters begging her to return. (Rev: BL 9/15/05; SLJ 11/05)

1280 Kline, Suzy. *Herbie Jones Sails into Second Grade* (1–3). Illus. by Sami Sweeten. 2006, Putnam $14.99 (0-399-22665-6). 64pp. On his first day of second grade, Herbie Jones meets a new friend and learns that his teacher is a man who has a sense of humor. (Rev: BL 8/06)

1281 Koster, Gloria. *The Peanut-Free Café* (K–2). Illus. by Maryann Cocca-Leffler. 2006, Albert Whitman $16.95 (0-8075-6386-2). 32pp. Food allergies take center stage in this story about the steps a classmate takes to make life more comfortable for a student with a peanut allergy. (Rev: BL 2/1/06; SLJ 9/06)

1282 Krishnaswami, Uma. *The Happiest Tree: A Yoga Story* (PS–2). Illus. by Ruth Jeyaveeran. 2005, Lee & Low $16.95 (1-58430-237-2). 32pp. Meena signs up for a children's yoga class that she hopes will help her to overcome her clumsiness. (Rev: BL 10/1/05; SLJ 11/05)

1283 Laminack, Lester L. *Jake's 100th Day of School* (1–3). Illus. by Judy Love. 2006, Peachtree $16.95 (1-56145-355-2). 32pp. Jake has prepared 100 family photographs for the 100th day of school but leaves them at home in his excitement; his principal and a 100-year-old woman rescue the day. (Rev: BL 2/1/06; SLJ 3/06)

1284 Levert, Mireille. *Eddie Longpants* (K–1). Illus. by author. 2005, Groundwood $16.95 (0-88899-671-3). Teased by his classmates about being so tall, Eddie Longpants must decide whether to retaliate in kind or show his tormentors that he knows a better way to behave. (Rev: SLJ 10/05)

1285 McNaughton, Colin. *When I Grow Up* (PS–1). Illus. by author. 2005, Candlewick $12.99 (0-7636-

2675-9). Children putting on a school play tell what they want to be one day — except for one little boy, who is reassured when he says he doesn't want to grow up. (Rev: SLJ 7/05)

1286 Mills, Claudia. *Ziggy's Blue-Ribbon Day* (K–3). Illus. by R. W. Alley. 2005, Farrar $16.00 (0-374-32352-6). 32pp. Ziggy's artistic talent makes up for his lack of athletic ability at the track-and-field meet. (Rev: BL 9/1/05; SLJ 11/05)

1287 Northway, Jennifer. *See You Later, Mom!* (PS). Illus. by author. 2006, Frances Lincoln $15.95 (1-84507-537-4). William takes his time separating from Mom and making friends at preschool. (Rev: SLJ 6/06)

1288 Pattison, Darcy. *19 Girls and Me* (PS–2). Illus. by Steven Salerno. 2006, Philomel $16.99 (0-399-24336-4). John Hercules is dismayed to learn he is the only boy in his kindergarten class, but soon sets aside his assumptions about girls and thinks of his 19 classmates as friends. (Rev: SLJ 7/06)

1289 Plourde, Lynn. *Book Fair Day* (1–3). Illus. by Thor Wickstrom. 2006, Dutton $16.99 (0-525-47696-2). 40pp. It's Book Fair Day in the school library, and Dewey Booker is worried that all the good books will be gone by the time his class gets its turn. (Rev: BL 8/06; SLJ 7/06)

1290 Poydar, Nancy. *The Bad-News Report Card* (K–3). Illus. 2006, Holiday $16.95 (0-8234-1992-4). 32pp. Stricken by an attack of report card anxiety, Isabel hides the card away and tries to forget about it; when she finally checks it out, she discovers that all her worries were unwarranted. (Rev: BL 9/1/06)

1291 Poydar, Nancy. *The Biggest Test in the Universe* (1–3). Illus. by author. 2005, Holiday House $16.95 (0-8234-1944-4). Sam is apprehensive about taking the "big test" after hearing horror stories about it from the older kids, but he discovers these stories are exaggerated. (Rev: SLJ 9/05)

1292 Rodman, Mary Ann. *First Grade Stinks!* (PS–1). Illus. by Beth Spiegel. 2006, Peachtree $15.95 (1-56145-377-3). 32pp. Haley pretty quickly decides that first grade is no fun in comparison with kindergarten. (Rev: BL 8/06; SLJ 8/06)

1293 Rosen, Michael. *Totally Wonderful Miss Plumberry* (PS–K). Illus. by Chinlun Lee. 2006, Candlewick $15.99 (0-7636-2744-5). 40pp. Molly's teacher recognizes Molly's huge disappointment when Russell's stegosaurus seems to be stealing the show and she refocuses the class on Molly's crystal. (Rev: BL 8/06)

1294 Slate, Joseph. *Miss Bindergarten Celebrates the Last Day of Kindergarten* (PS–K). Illus. by Ashley Wolff. 2006, Button $16.99 (0-525-47744-6). 48pp. The school year comes to an end for Miss Bindergarten and her 26 alphabetical kindergarten students. (Rev: BL 2/15/06; SLJ 3/06)

1295 Trice, Linda. *Kenya's Word* (1–3). Illus. by Pamela Johnson. 2006, Charlesbridge $16.95 (1-57091-887-2); paper $6.95 (1-57091-888-0). 32pp. After a series of homework assignments that went awry, Kenya is determined to impress her teacher and classmates with her "favorite describing word." (Rev: BL 2/1/06; SLJ 3/06)

1296 Wells, Rosemary. *Yoko's World of Kindness: Golden Rules for a Happy Classroom* (PS–2). Illus. by John Nez and Jody Wheeler. 2005, Hyperion $19.99 (0-7868-5109-0). 154pp. An anthology of previously published stories about Yoko, Noisy Nora, and other children in Mrs. Jenkins's class. (Rev: SLJ 10/05)

TRANSPORTATION AND MACHINES

1297 Freymann, Saxton, and Joost Elffers. *Fast Food* (PS–2). Illus. by Saxton Freymann. 2006, Scholastic $12.99 (0-439-11019-X). 32pp. In this volume, Freymann and Effers turn their ordinary fruits and vegetables into a variety of modes of transportation. (Rev: BL 2/1/06*; LMC 4–5/06; SLJ 4/06) [641.8]

1298 Hubbell, Patricia. *Trains: Huffing! Puffing! Pulling!* (1–3). 2005, Marshall Cavendish $14.95 (0-7614-5194-3). 32pp. With an appealing blend of rhyming text and intricate collage illustrations, this picture book introduces young readers to different types of trains. (Rev: BL 10/1/05; SLJ 9/05)

1299 London, Jonathan. *A Truck Goes Rattley-Bumpa* (PS). Illus. by Denis Roche. 2005, Holt $14.95 (0-8050-7233-0). 32pp. Trucks of all shapes and sizes performing different tasks are shown in simple illustrations with short rhyming couplets. (Rev: BL 10/1/05; SLJ 9/05)

1300 London, Jonathan. *My Big Rig* (PS–K). Illus. by Viviana Garofoli. 2007, Marshall Cavendish $14.99 (978-0-7614-5346-8). 32pp. Inspired by his toy truck, a young boy imagines a cross-country trip at the wheel of a tractor-trailer. (Rev: BL 4/15/07)

1301 McCarty, Peter. *Moon Plane* (PS–K). 2006, Holt $16.95 (0-8050-7943-2). 32pp. Gazing up at a plane in the sky, a young boy imagines what it would be like to board such an aircraft and fly all the way to the moon; the simple, effective text and illustrations encourage imagination. (Rev: BL 9/1/06; HBG 4/07)

1302 McMullen, Kate. *I'm Dirty!* (PS–2). Illus. by Jim McMullen. 2006, HarperCollins $16.99 (0-06-009293-9). 40pp. A spirited backhoe loader groans aloud as it works, counting the items it is moving and generally enjoying getting good and dirty. (Rev: BCCB 10/06; BL 9/15/06; HB 11–12/06; HBG 4/07)

1303 Mitton, Tony. *Cool Cars* (PS–K). Illus. by Ann Parker. Series: Amazing Machines. 2005,

Kingfisher $9.95 (0-7534-5802-0). 24pp. Introduces all kinds of cars — family cars, taxis, race cars, and so forth — with an appealing blend of rhyming text and dynamic artwork. (Rev: BL 7/05; SLJ 6/05)

1304 Moore, Patrick. *The Mighty Street Sweeper* (PS). Illus. 2006, Holt $15.95 (0-8050-7789-8). 32pp. A colorful celebration of the street sweeper, a little truck with a very big responsibility. (Rev: BL 10/15/06; SLJ 10/06)

1305 Piper, Watty. *The Little Engine That Could* (PS–1). Illus. by Loren Long. 2005, Philomel $17.99 (0-399-24467-0). 48pp. This new edition of the beloved children's classic about a diminutive but determined train engine is beautifully illustrated in rich, warm colors. (Rev: BL 9/1/05; SLJ 9/05)

1306 Pulver, Robin. *Axle Annie and the Speed Grump* (K–3). Illus. 2005, Dial $16.99 (0-8037-2787-9). 32pp. Axle Annie, Burskyville's beloved and very skilled school bus driver, saves the life of dangerous driver Rush Hotfoot with the help of her passengers. (Rev: BL 11/1/05; SLJ 12/05)

1307 Ransom, Candice. *Tractor Day* (PS). Illus. by Laura J. Bryant. 2007, Walker $16.95 (978-0-8027-8090-4). 32pp. This cozy, rhyming tribute to farming depicts a cheerful family hard at work, with dad and daughter riding the big red tractor all day. (Rev: BL 1/1–15/07; SLJ 3/07)

1308 Suen, Anastasia. *Red Light, Green Light* (PS). Illus. by Ken Wilson-Max. 2005, Harcourt $16.00 (0-15-202582-0). 40pp. Minimal text and bold illustrations blend to depict a toddler deploying his toy vehicles on a busy traffic grid. (Rev: BL 11/15/05; SLJ 10/05)

1309 Willems, Mo. *The Pigeon Loves Things That Go!* (PS). Illus. by author. 2005, Hyperion $6.99 (0-7868-3651-2). A board book featuring the beloved pigeon from *Don't Let the Pigeon Drive the Bus* and another children's favorite: things that move. (Rev: SLJ 8/05)

Stories About Holidays and Holy Days

BIRTHDAYS

1310 Baker, Roberta. *Olive's Pirate Party* (PS–2). Illus. by Debbie Tilley. 2005, Little, Brown $15.99 (0-316-16792-4). 32pp. When Olive learns that her birthday party will be held at her elderly aunt's house, she fears her plans for pirate fun will be ruined. (Rev: BL 8/05; SLJ 11/05)

1311 Foreman, George, and Fran Manushkin. *Let George Do It!* (K–3). Illus. by Whitney Martin. 2005, Simon & Schuster $15.95 (0-689-87807-9). Big George, his five sons — all named George, and the family dog also named George all prepare for Dad's birthday party. (Rev: SLJ 1/06)

1312 Kromhout, Rindert. *Little Donkey and the Birthday Present* (K–2). Trans. from Dutch by Marianne Martens. Illus. by Annemarie van Haeringen. 2007, North-South $15.95 (978-0-7358-2132-3). Little Donkey chooses a beautiful kite as a present for his friend Jackie the yak, but then decides he wants to keep it himself. (Rev: SLJ 4/07)

1313 Schaefer, Carole Lexa. *Dragon Dancing* (PS–1). Illus. by Pierr Morgan. 2007, Viking $16.99 (978-0-670-06084-9). For Mei Lin's birthday, the class decorates dragons and enjoys a boisterous and colorful dragon dance. (Rev: BL 1/1–15/07; SLJ 3/07*)

1314 Sperring, Mark. *The Fairytale Cake* (PS–K). Illus. by Jonathan Langley. 2005, Scholastic $15.95 (0-439-68329-7). 32pp. Detailed drawings add to the fun in this story of a parade of nursery rhyme and fairy tale characters delivering a little boy's birthday cake. (Rev: BL 7/05; SLJ 9/05)

1315 Stein, David Ezra. *Cowboy Ned and Andy* (PS–2). Illus. by author. 2006, Simon & Schuster $14.95 (1-4169-0041-1). Andy, a horse, wants to get Cowboy Ned a cake for his birthday, but when he can't find one in the desert, he gives Ned a hug instead. (Rev: SLJ 7/06)

1316 Weninger, Brigitte. *Double Birthday* (PS–K). Trans. from German by Charise Myngheer. Illus. by Stephanie Roehe. Series: Miko. 2005, Minedition $10.99 (0-698-40015-1). Miko the mouse tries to share his birthday gifts with Mimiki, his stuffed toy friend. (Rev: SLJ 10/05)

CHRISTMAS

1317 Alsenas, Linas. *Mrs. Claus Takes a Vacation* (K–3). Illus. by author. 2006, Scholastic $16.99 (0-439-77978-2). Feeling restricted, Mrs. Claus decides to take a world tour of her own, leaving Mr. Claus at home to worry about her. (Rev: HB 11–12/06; HBG 4/07; SLJ 10/06)

1318 Appelt, Kathi. *Merry Christmas, Merry Crow* (PS–2). Illus. by Jon Goodell. 2005, Harcourt $16.00 (0-15-202651-7). 32pp. In this charming rhyming Christmas tale, a clever crow flies around town collecting odds and ends with which to decorate a Christmas tree. (Rev: BL 10/15/05; HBG 4/06; SLJ 10/05)

1319 Bauer, Marion Dane. *Christmas Lights* (PS–1). Illus. by Susan Mitchell. 2006, Simon & Schuster $14.95 (0-689-86942-8). This colorful light-up book celebrates the joys of Christmas. (Rev: SLJ 10/06)

1320 Bedford, David. *I've Seen Santa!* (PS–1). Illus. by Tim Warnes. 2006, Tiger Tales $15.95 (1-58925-058-3). Little Bear, Big Bear, and Mommy Bear try to stay awake for Santa. (Rev: SLJ 10/06)

1321 Bond, Rebecca. *A City Christmas Tree* (PS–2). Illus. 2005, Little, Brown $15.99 (0-316-53731-4).

32pp. For Maggie Laroche and her siblings, the arrival of the Christmas tree vendor in their bustling city neighborhood is a sure sign that the holiday season is here. (Rev: BL 10/15/05; SLJ 10/05)

1322 Brown, Margaret Wise. *The Little Fir Tree* (K–2). Illus. by Jim LaMarche. 2005, HarperCollins $15.99 (0-06-028189-8). 32pp. LaMarche's art breathes new life into the classic tale, first published in 1954, of a little fir tree and how it helped to brighten Christmas for a lame boy. (Rev: BL 9/15/05; SLJ 10/05)

1323 Buehner, Caralyn. *Snowmen at Christmas* (PS–K). Illus. by Mark Buehner. 2005, Dial $16.99 (0-8037-2995-2). 32pp. First seen in *Snowmen at Night* (2002), these jolly characters return to show how snow families celebrate Christmas. (Rev: BL 9/1/05; SLJ 10/05)

1324 Chaconas, Dori. *Christmas Mouseling* (PS–2). Illus. by Susan Kathleen Hartung. 2005, Viking $15.99 (0-670-05984-6). 32pp. When a wintry wind destroys their nest, a mother mouse finds shelter for her newborn in the manger in which Jesus Christ was just born. (Rev: BL 10/15/05; SLJ 10/05)

1325 Chaconas, Dori. *When Cows Come Home for Christmas* (PS–2). Illus. by Lynne Chapman. 2005, Albert Whitman $15.95 (0-8075-8877-6). 32pp. In this romp of a Christmas tale, members of an extended bovine family try to squeeze together in a small house to celebrate the holiday. (Rev: BL 10/15/05; SLJ 10/05)

1326 Chen, Chih-Yuan. *The Best Christmas Ever* (PS–2). Illus. 2005, Heryin $13.99 (0-9762056-2-9). In this gentle Christmas tale, Little Bear works behind the scenes to ensure that the holiday is a happy one for everyone in his family despite the lack of money. (Rev: BL 12/1/05)

1327 Clark, Emma Chichester. *Melrose and Croc: A Christmas Story to Remember* (PS–2). Illus. 2006, Walker $16.95 (0-8027-9597-8). 32pp. A simple, beautifully illustrated story about Melrose the dog and Croc the crocodile, lonely souls who meet in the big city on Christmas Eve. (Rev: BL 11/1/06; SLJ 10/06)

1328 Cotten, Cynthia. *This Is the Stable* (PS–2). Illus. by Delana Bettoli. 2006, Holt $16.95 (0-8050-7556-9). 32pp. Using a "This Is the House that Jack Built" style, this rhyming retelling of the Nativity story is a good choice for read-alouds. (Rev: BL 11/1/06; SLJ 10/06)

1329 Cowley, Joy. *Mrs. Wishy-Washy's Christmas* (PS–1). Illus. by Elizabeth Fuller. 2005, Philomel $15.99 (0-399-24344-5). 32pp. When Mrs. Wishy-Washy orders the farm animals to get cleaned up for Christmas, the creatures balk at using the icy tub in the barnyard and instead go inside to use her tub. (Rev: BL 9/15/05; SLJ 10/05)

1330 Crisp, Marty. *The Most Precious Gift: A Story of the Nativity* (PS–2). 2006, Philomel $16.99 (0-399-24296-1). 32pp. A poor boy named Ameer joins a caravan to go see the baby Jesus and must decide what gift he can offer the newborn king. (Rev: BL 11/15/06; SLJ 10/06)

1331 Demas, Corinne. *Two Christmas Mice* (PS–2). Illus. by Stephanie Roth. 2005, Holiday $16.95 (0-8234-1785-9). 32pp. Neighbors Annamouse and Willamouse join forces to celebrate Christmas. (Rev: BL 10/15/05; SLJ 10/05)

1332 Duval, Kathy. *The Three Bears' Christmas* (PS–K). Illus. by Paul Meisel. 2005, Holiday $16.95 (0-8234-1871-5). 32pp. The three bears return from a Christmas Eve walk to find that someone has been in their house — even tried out the beds — and left a red coat and presents under the tree. (Rev: BL 9/1/05*; HB 11–12/05; HBG 4/06; SLJ 10/05)

1333 Elschner, Géraldine. *Pashmina the Little Christmas Goat* (PS–2). Illus. by Angela Kehlenbeck. 2006, Penguin $16.99 (0-698-40046-1). 32pp. When father brings home a small white goat to eat for Christmas dinner the family decides instead to keep it and raise it, and the rewards continue year after year; rich illustrations add to the warmth of the story. (Rev: BL 12/1/06; SLJ 10/06)

1334 Engelbreit, Mary. *Mary Engelbreit's A Merry Little Christmas: Celebrate from A to Z* (PS–3). Illus. by author. 2006, HarperCollins $16.99 (0-06-074158-9). Celebrates a mouse family's Christmas, and all the delights from A to Z. (Rev: SLJ 10/06)

1335 Fine, Edith Hope. *Cricket at the Manger* (PS–2). Illus. by Winslow Pels. 2005, Boyds Mills $15.95 (1-56397-993-4). 32pp. Awakened by strange noises, an initially grouchy cricket witnesses the birth of Jesus in a manger. (Rev: BL 9/1/05; SLJ 10/05)

1336 Frazee, Marla. *Santa Claus: The World's Number One Toy Expert* (PS–K). Illus. 2005, Harcourt $16.00 (0-15-204970-3). 40pp. A portrait of Santa hard at work, taking requests and testing toys. (Rev: BCCB 12/05; BL 11/1/05*; HB 11–12/05; HBG 4/06; SLJ 10/05*)

1337 Harley, Bill. *Dear Santa: The Letters of James B. Dobbins* (PS–2). Illus. by R. W. Alley. 2005, HarperCollins $15.99 (0-06-623778-5). 32pp. In a series of letters to Santa Claus, Jimmy Dobbins places orders for some pretty outrageous Christmas gifts and also offers explanations for some of his lapses in behavior over the past year. (Rev: BL 10/1/05; SLJ 10/05)

1338 Hassett, Ann, and John Hassett. *The Finest Christmas Tree* (K–2). Illus. 2005, Houghton $16.00 (0-618-50901-1). 32pp. Things look bleak for Farmer Tuttle when the demand for his Christmas trees drops as more and more of his customers opt for the artificial variety. (Rev: BL 11/1/05; SLJ 10/05)

1339 Helmer, Marilyn. *One Splendid Tree* (K–2). Illus. by Dianne Eastman. 2005, Kids Can $15.95 (1-55337-683-8). With their father off fighting in World War II, siblings Junior and Hattie try to give their tiny apartment a bit of Christmas spirit by decorating a discarded plant; the illustrations offer lots of period details. (Rev: SLJ 10/05)

1340 Holland, Trish, and Christine Ford. *The Soldiers' Night Before Christmas* (K–3). Illus. by John Manders. 2006, Random $8.99 (0-375-83795-7). Using the structure of Clement Moore's classic Christmas poem, this story in rhyme is set on a U.S. Army base in the desert, and the gifts arrive not in a sleigh but by Humvee. (Rev: SLJ 10/06)

1341 Johns, Barbara L. *Christmas at the Candle Factory* (K–2). Illus. by Carolyn R. Stich. 2006, Steeple Ridge $16.95 (0-9762862-1-1). Despite her irritation with the kitten called Elvis, Midnight the candle factory cat finds herself missing him when he's gone. (Rev: SLJ 10/06)

1342 Kidslabel. *Spot 7 Christmas* (1–4). 2006, Chronicle $12.95 (0-8118-5323-3). Readers are challenged to identify what's out of place in each of these 13 Christmas-themed photo spreads. (Rev: SLJ 10/06)

1343 Knott, Anthony. *An Angel Came to Nazareth: A Story of the First Christmas* (K–5). Illus. by Maggie Kneen. 2005, Chronicle $15.95 (0-8118-4798-5). An angel offers four beasts of burden — horse, donkey, camel, and ox — the option of choosing their riders for a trip from Nazareth to Bethlehem; a simple story with lush illustrations. (Rev: SLJ 10/05)

1344 Kroll, Steven. *Pooch on the Loose: A Christmas Adventure* (PS–1). Illus. by Michael Garland. 2005, Marshall Cavendish $14.95 (0-7614-5239-7). 32pp. Bart the dog escapes from his master and visits the sights of New York City; Photoshop art gives a realistic view of the city and Christmas. (Rev: BL 9/1/05; SLJ 10/05)

1345 Kroll, Virginia. *Uno, Dos, Tres, Posada! Let's Celebrate Christmas* (PS–2). Illus. by Loretta Lopez. 2006, Viking $15.99 (0-670-05923-3). Readers learn vocabulary and numbers in Spanish as a little girl introduces each step of a posada, a Hispanic holiday tradition celebrated on the nine nights before Christmas. (Rev: SLJ 10/06)

1346 Krykorka, Ian. *Carl, the Christmas Carp* (K–3). Illus. by Vladyana Krykorka. 2006, Orca $17.95 (1-55143-329-X). 32pp. Radim's Czech family usually eats carp for Christmas but when he feels sorry for the fish and releases it into the river, his family learns a new tradition for the holiday. (Rev: BL 11/15/06)

1347 Leuck, Laura. *Santa Claws* (1–4). Illus. by Gris Grimly. 2006, Chronicle $16.95 (0-8118-4992-9). In this offbeat Christmas tale, Mack and Zack, two young monsters, prepare for the arrival of Santa Claws. (Rev: SLJ 10/06)

1348 Lloyd-Jones, Sally. *Little One, We Knew You'd Come* (PS). Illus. by Jackie Morris. 2006, Little, Brown $16.99 (0-316-52391-7). This artful depiction of the Nativity story celebrates the joy of the new parents. (Rev: SLJ 10/06)

1349 Love, Maryann Cusimano. *You Are My Miracle* (PS–K). Illus. by Satomi Ichikawa. 2005, Philomel $15.99 (0-399-24037-3). A mother bear and her child celebrate Christmas in rhyming text that emphasizes togetherness. (Rev: SLJ 10/05)

1350 McCaughrean, Geraldine. *Father and Son: A Nativity Story* (K–2). Illus. by Fabian Negrin. 2006, Hyperion $16.99 (1-4231-0344-0). 32pp. In this attractive picture book, McCaughrean imagines Joseph's thoughts about his newly born son. (Rev: BL 10/15/06; SLJ 10/06)

1351 McCutcheon, John. *Christmas in the Trenches* (2–4). Illus. by Henri Sorenson. 2006, Peachtree $18.95 (1-56145-374-9). 32pp. On Christmas Day, a World War I veteran tells his grandchildren about the incredible Christmas truce of 1914; McCutcheon's song by the same name is printed at the end. (Rev: BL 8/06; SLJ 10/06)

1352 Major, Kevin. *Aunt Olga's Christmas Postcards* (K–3). Illus. by Bruce Roberts. 2005, Groundwood $18.95 (0-88899-593-8). 40pp. Anna and her 95-year-old great-great-Aunt Olga write Christmas verses together and share historic postcards and memories. (Rev: BL 11/1/05; SLJ 10/05)

1353 Martín, Hugo C. *Pablo's Christmas* (K–4). Illus. by Lee Chapman. 2006, Sterling LB $14.95 (1-4027-2560-4). Left behind to watch over his expectant mother when his father leaves Mexico to find work in the United States, Pablo does his best to prepare for Christmas. (Rev: SLJ 10/06)

1354 Mayer, Mercer. *The Little Drummer Mouse* (K–3). Illus. by author. 2006, Dial $16.99 (0-8037-3147-7). A little mouse, playing on his acorn drum, helps to celebrate the birth of Jesus Christ. (Rev: SLJ 10/06)

1355 Minor, Wendell, and Florence Minor. *Christmas Tree!* (PS–2). Illus. by authors. 2005, HarperCollins $15.99 (0-06-056034-7). Christmas trees of all kinds and sizes are celebrated in rhyming text and colorful illustrations. (Rev: SLJ 10/05)

1356 Moore, Clement C., and Carter Goodrich. *A Creature Was Stirring: One Boy's Night Before Christmas* (PS–2). Illus. by Carter Goodrich. 2006, Simon & Schuster $16.95 (0-689-86399-3). 40pp. Moore's classic Christmas poem is presented here along with a young boy's account of what he did that night when he could not sleep. (Rev: BL 11/15/06; SLJ 10/06)

1357 Pallotta, Jerry. *Who Will Guide My Sleigh Tonight?* (PS–2). Illus. by David Biedrzycki. 2006, Scholastic paper $5.99 (0-439-85369-9). Santa Claus, searching for animals to pull his gift-laden sleigh, considers a wide array of possibilities — from skunks and giraffes to kangaroos and snakes — before finally settling on reindeer. (Rev: SLJ 10/06)

1358 Recorvits, Helen. *Yoon and the Christmas Mitten* (PS–2). Illus. by Gabi Swiatkowska. 2006, Farrar $16.00 (0-374-38688-9). 32pp. Yoon, a young Korean American girl, learns about the Christmas holiday in her American school and tries to persuade her family that they can celebrate the holiday and still be true to their Korean customs; a sequel to *My Name Is Yoon* (2003). (Rev: BL 12/1/06; SLJ 10/06)

1359 Reiss, Mike. *Merry Un-Christmas* (1–3). Illus. by David Catrow. 2006, HarperCollins $15.99 (0-06-059126-9). Noelle and her family live in Texmas, where it's Christmas 364 days of the year and the one day they look forward to eagerly is Un-Christmas, when there are no gifts and the kids can go to school. (Rev: SLJ 10/06)

1360 Rox, John. *I Want a Hippopotamus for Christmas* (K–3). Illus. by Bruce Whatley. 2005, HarperCollins $16.99 (0-06-052942-3). A girl's Christmas wish is granted when a hippo arrives at her house in this funny version of a 1953 song. (Rev: SLJ 10/05)

1361 Ryan, Pam Muñoz. *There Was No Snow on Christmas Eve* (K–2). Illus. by Dennis Nolan. 2005, Hyperion $15.99 (0-786-85492-8). 32pp. A beautifully illustrated reminder that the Nativity took place in a hilly desert where snow is very rare, unlike the wintry setting that Christmas has become for many. (Rev: BL 10/15/05; SLJ 10/05)

1362 Santiago, Esmeralda. *A Doll for Navidades* (K–2). Illus. by Enrique O. Sánchez. 2005, Scholastic $16.99 (0-439-55398-9). 32pp. Seven-year-old Esmeralda desperately wants a doll for Three Kings' Day and she is deeply disappointed when her younger sister receives one instead in this picture book set in Puerto Rico. (Rev: BL 11/1/05; SLJ 10/05)

1363 Schneider, Antonie. *Advent Storybook: 24 Stories to Share Before Christmas* (K–3). Trans. by Marisa Miller. Illus. by Maja Dusikova. 2005, North-South $17.95 (0-7358-1963-7). Benjamin Bear's mother tells him a Christmas-related story for each of the 24 days in the little bear's Advent calendar; each parable features Little Bear and ends with a moral. (Rev: SLJ 10/05)

1364 Sharkey, Niamh. *Santasaurus* (PS–2). Illus. by author. 2005, Candlewick $15.99 (0-7636-2671-6). Full of Christmas spirit, dinosaur siblings Milo,

Mollie, and Ollie eagerly await the arrival of Santasaurus. (Rev: SLJ 10/05)

1365 Slate, Joseph. *What Star Is This?* (K–2). Illus. by Alison Jay. 2005, Putnam $15.99 (0-399-24014-4). 32pp. In this story of the Nativity, a small comet lights the way to the scene of Christ's birth. (Rev: BL 12/1/05; SLJ 10/05)

1366 Smith, Cynthia Leitich, and Greg Leitich Smith. *Santa Knows* (K–3). Illus. by Steven Björkman. 2006, Dutton $16.99 (0-525-47757-8). Alfie F. Snorklepuss is convinced there's no Santa, so it's an eye-opening experience for this Santa-doubter when the man himself shows up to take Alfie on a trip to the North Pole. (Rev: SLJ 10/06)

1367 Van Steenwyk, Elizabeth. *Prairie Christmas* (K–3). Illus. by Ronald Himler. 2006, Eerdmans $17.00 (0-8028-5280-7). 32pp. In 1880s Nebraska, 11-year-old Emma experiences a very special Christmas on a trip with her mother to deliver a new baby. (Rev: BL 9/15/06; SLJ 10/06)

1368 Weigelt, Udo. *Little Donkey's Wish* (K–2). Trans. by Marianne Martens. Illus. by Pirkko Vainio. 2005, North-South $15.95 (0-7358-2031-7). A shy donkey gets her Christmas wish when Santa chooses her to fill in for one of his reindeer. (Rev: SLJ 10/05)

1369 Willey, Margaret. *A Clever Beatrice Christmas* (PS–2). Illus. by Heather Solomon. 2006, Simon & Schuster $16.95 (0-689-87017-5). 40pp. To prove the existence of Père Noël to some skeptical friends, clever Beatrice promises to bring some irrefutable evidence, such as a clipping from his beard or a bell from his sleigh. (Rev: BL 10/15/06; SLJ 10/06)

1370 Wilson, Karma. *Mortimer's Christmas Manger* (PS–2). Illus. by Jane Chapman. 2005, Simon & Schuster $15.95 (0-689-85511-7). Tired of his home in a dark hole under the stairs, Mortimer the mouse takes up residence in a Nativity scene. (Rev: SLJ 10/05)

1371 Winthrop, Elizabeth. *The First Christmas Stocking* (2–4). Illus. by Bagram Ibatoulline. 2006, Random $15.95 (0-385-32804-4). 40pp. On Christmas Eve, Claire gives the stockings she's knitted to a poor boy on the street instead of to the rich customer who ordered them, and wakes up on Christmas morning to find a miracle of her own. (Rev: BL 11/15/06)

EASTER

1372 deGroat, Diane. *Last One in Is a Rotten Egg!* (PS–2). Illus. by author. 2007, HarperCollins $15.99 (978-0-06-089294-4). A much-anticipated visit from their cousin turns out to be far less fun than expected for Gilbert the opossum and his sister. (Rev: BL 1/1–15/07; SLJ 2/07)

1373 Engelbreit, Mary. *Queen of Easter* (PS–K). Illus. by author. Series: Ann Estelle Stories. 2006, HarperCollins $15.99 (0-06-008184-8). Disappointed with the plain straw hat she is given for the Easter parade, Ann Estelle leaves it outside, where robins adopt it as a nest; Ann Estelle enjoys redecorating last year's hat and the new family in this year's. (Rev: SLJ 2/06)

1374 Krensky, Stephen. *Milo the Really Big Bunny* (PS–2). Illus. by Melissa Suber. 2006, Simon & Schuster $14.95 (0-689-87345-X). Milo, an oversized bunny, capitalizes on his unique stature as he helps Easter Bunny on a blustery Easter Sunday. (Rev: SLJ 2/06)

1375 Stoeke, Janet Morgan. *Minerva Louise and the Colorful Eggs* (PS–2). 2006, Dutton $15.99 (0-525-47633-4). It's spring, but Minerva Louise the chicken doesn't know what to make of the brightly colored eggs she discovers hidden in odd places around the farmyard. (Rev: BL 2/1/06; SLJ 2/06)

1376 Wells, Rosemary. *Max Counts His Chickens* (PS–K). Illus. 2007, Viking $15.99 (978-0-670-06222-5). 32pp. Combining a counting lesson with Max and Ruby's familiar sibling tussles, this charming tale features a marshmallow chick hunt and a special delivery from the Easter bunny. (Rev: BL 1/1–15/07)

HALLOWEEN

1377 Atwell, Debby. *The Warthog's Tail* (K–3). 2005, Houghton $16.00 (0-618-50781-7). 32pp. When a young witch is unable to conjure up a spell powerful enough to remove a sleeping warthog from her path, she decides instead to try her powers of persuasion. (Rev: BL 10/1/05; SLJ 11/05)

1378 Bauer, Marion Dane. *I'm Not Afraid of Halloween! A Pop-up and Flap Book* (PS–K). Illus. by Rusty Fletcher. 2006, Simon & Schuster $7.99 (0-689-85050-6). This colorful pop-up book, which includes lift-the-flap features, showcases a host of costumed trick-or-treaters who come calling at a young vampire's door on Halloween night. (Rev: SLJ 9/06)

1379 Bollinger, Peter. *Algernon Graves Is Scary Enough* (K–2). Illus. by author. 2005, HarperCollins $14.99 (0-06-052268-2). Algernon can't decide between spooky costumes for Halloween and decides to combine them all. (Rev: SLJ 8/05)

1380 Cazet, Denys. *The Perfect Pumpkin Pie* (PS–2). Illus. 2005, Simon & Schuster $15.95 (0-689-86467-1). 32pp. In this lively Halloween tale, a boy and his grandmother are visited by a ghost who's searching for some pumpkin pie. (Rev: BL 10/15/05; SLJ 10/05)

1381 Choi, Yangsook. *Behind the Mask* (K–3). Illus. 2006, Farrar $16.00 (0-374-30522-6). 40pp. A young Korean American boy, still grieving over his grandfather's death, gains cachet among his classmates when he wears his grandfather's scary mask dance costume for Halloween. (Rev: BL 10/15/06; SLJ 12/06)

1382 Cuyler, Margery. *The Bumpy Little Pumpkin* (PS–2). Illus. by Will Hillenbrand. 2005, Scholastic $15.95 (0-439-52835-6). 32pp. Her older siblings scoff when Little Nell (first seen in *The Biggest, Best Snowman*, published in 1998) selects an ugly little pumpkin at harvest time, but the girl manages to transform the gourd into a nice-looking jack-o'-lantern with the help of a few animal friends. (Rev: BL 9/1/05; SLJ 8/05)

1383 Desimini, Lisa. *Trick-or-Treat, Smell My Feet!* (PS–2). Illus. 2005, Scholastic $16.95 (0-439-23323-2). 40pp. Delia and Ophelia, twin witches, cast a spell over the neighborhood trick-or-treaters. (Rev: BL 9/15/05; SLJ 8/05)

1384 Friedman, Laurie. *I'm Not Afraid of This Haunted House* (K–2). Illus. by Teresa Murfin. 2005, Carolrhoda $15.95 (1-57505-751-4). 32pp. In this spine-tingling Halloween tale, told in rhyming couplets, young Simon Lester Henry Strauss takes friends on a tour of a haunted house. (Rev: BL 9/1/05; SLJ 9/05)

1385 Grambling, Lois G. *T. Rex Trick-or-Treats* (K–2). Illus. by Jack E. Davis. 2005, HarperCollins $12.99 (0-06-050252-5). 32pp. T. Rex can't decide what he wants to wear when he goes trick-or-treating. (Rev: BL 9/1/05; SLJ 8/05)

1386 Hatch, Elizabeth. *Halloween Night* (PS–1). Illus. by Jimmy Pickering. 2005, Doubleday $15.95 (0-385-74622-9). A cumulative, mildly scary story in which a timid little mouse winds up with the treats. (Rev: SLJ 8/05)

1387 Horowitz, Dave. *The Ugly Pumpkin* (K–2). Illus. by author. 2005, Putnam $15.99 (0-399-24267-8). A misshapen pumpkin feels out of place as Halloween nears. (Rev: SLJ 8/05)

1388 Kimball, Linda Hoffman. *Come with Me on Halloween* (PS–1). Illus. by Mike Reed. 2005, Albert Whitman $16.95 (0-8075-3132-4). The father-son relationship is reversed as the two meet fearsome characters while trick-or-treating. (Rev: SLJ 10/05)

1389 Kovalski, Maryann. *Omar's Halloween* (PS–K). 2006, Fitzhenry & Whiteside $16.95 (1-55041-559-X). 32pp. As Halloween nears, Omar the bear has terrible trouble with costume selection, but on the day his ghost outfit finally comes into its own. (Rev: BL 9/1/06; SLJ 9/06)

1390 Krieb, Mr. *We're Off to Find the Witch's House* (PS–2). Illus. by R. W. Alley. 2005, Dutton $12.99 (0-525-47003-4). 32pp. In this fun-filled Halloween tale told in rhyming text, four trick-or-treaters encounter all sorts of frightening ghosts and ghouls when they set off in search of a witch's house. (Rev: BL 9/15/05; SLJ 8/05)

1391 McGhee, Alison. *A Very Brave Witch* (K–2). Illus. by Harry Bliss. 2006, Simon & Schuster $12.95 (0-689-86730-1). On Halloween night, a young witch has an eye-opening encounter with some colorfully costumed trick-or-treaters. (Rev: SLJ 8/06)

1392 McGrath, Barbara Barbieri. *The Little Green Witch* (K–2). Illus. by Martha Alexander. 2005, Charlesbridge $14.95 (1-58089-042-3). In a Halloween twist on "The Little Red Hen," a little witch grows a pumpkin and no one wants to help her until it's time to eat pumpkin pie. (Rev: SLJ 8/05)

1393 Montes, Marissa. *Los Gatos Black on Halloween* (K–2). Illus. by Yuyi Morales. 2006, Holt $16.95 (0-8050-7429-5). 32pp. There's a Monster's Ball at Haunted Hall and a rhythmic English/Spanish text describes the antics of los gatos, los muertos, las brujas, and their friends, all enjoying themselves until the arrival of the scary trick-or-treaters. (Rev: BL 8/06)

1394 Neitzel, Shirley. *Who Will I Be? A Halloween Rebus Story* (PS–2). Illus. by Nancy Winslow Parker. 2005, Greenwillow $12.99 (0-06-056067-3). 32pp. In this engaging rebus tale, a young girl tries to decide what sort of costume to wear for Halloween. (Rev: BL 8/05; SLJ 9/05)

1395 Spurr, Elizabeth. *Halloween Sky Ride* (PS–3). Illus. by Ethan Long. 2005, Holiday House $16.95 (0-8234-1870-7). A not-too-scary witch takes too many friends on a broom ride to a Halloween party. (Rev: SLJ 8/05)

1396 Spurr, Elizabeth. *Pumpkin Hill* (PS–2). Illus. by Whitney Martin. 2006, Holiday House $16.95 (0-8234-1869-3). There's an orange avalanche in this rollicking Halloween tale as hundreds of plump pumpkins roll down a hill into town, causing confusion at first but paving the way for festive holiday decorations. (Rev: SLJ 10/06)

JEWISH HOLY DAYS

1397 Adler, Tzivia. *The Sefer Torah Parade* (PS). Illus. by Ito Esther Perez. 2005, Hachai $11.95 (1-929628-26-9). A Jewish girl describes the festivities as a new Torah is brought into her family's temple. (Rev: HBG 4/06; SLJ 9/05)

1398 Cleary, Brian P. *Eight Wild Nights: A Family Hanukkah Tale* (K–3). Illus. by David Udovic. 2006, Lerner LB $16.95 (1-58013-152-2). The members of an extended and rambunctious family gather for Festival of Lights. (Rev: SLJ 10/06)

1399 Hanft, Josh. *The Miracles of Passover* (K–3). Illus. by Seymour Chwast. 2007, Blue Apple $15.95 (978-1-59354-600-7). This is an attractive book that

explains Passover traditions in engaging text and imaginative lift-the-flaps. (Rev: SLJ 4/07) [296.4]

1400 Krensky, Stephen. *Hanukkah at Valley Forge* (2–4). Illus. by Greg Harlin. 2006, Dutton $17.99 (0-525-47738-1). 32pp. In this fact-based historical tale, a young Jewish soldier explains to General George Washington the meaning of the Hanukkah celebration. (Rev: BL 9/1/06; SLJ 10/06)

1401 Kropf, Latifa Berry. *Happy Birthday, World: A Rosh Hashanah Celebration* (PS). Illus. by Lisa Carlson. 2005, Lerner $5.95 (0-929371-32-1). This attractive board book introduces young readers to Rosh Hashanah by comparing the rituals of the Jewish holiday to those of a child's birthday. (Rev: SLJ 11/05)

1402 Newman, Leslea. *The Eight Nights of Chanukah* (K–2). Illus. by Elivia Savadier. 2005, Abrams $12.95 (0-8109-5785-X). 24pp. Newman gives "The Twelve Days of Christmas" a new twist with a version that celebrates Hanukkah; a note and a glossary follow the text. (Rev: BL 10/15/05; SLJ 10/05)

1403 Rauchwerger, Diane Levin. *Dinosaur on Passover* (PS–K). Illus. by Jason Wolff. 2006, Lerner LB $15.95 (1-58013-156-5); paper $6.95 (1-58013-161-1). A dinosaur joins in the Passover seder in this story with rhyming text that covers all the usual rituals. (Rev: SLJ 4/06)

1404 Schotter, Roni. *Passover!* (PS–1). Illus. by Erin Eitter Kono. 2006, Little, Brown $12.99 (0-316-93991-9). 32pp. A Jewish family's preparations for Passover are described in rhyming text with cartoon illustrations. (Rev: BL 2/15/06; SLJ 4/06)

1405 Shulman, Goldie. *Way Too Much Challah Dough* (PS–2). Illus. by Vitaliy Romanenko. 2006, Hachai $11.95 (1-929628-23-4). 32pp. When Mindy uses too much yeast, her challah dough grows out of control and her grandmother must come to the rescue. (Rev: BL 10/1/06)

1406 Terwilliger, Kelly. *Bubbe Isabella and the Sukkot Cake* (PS–K). Illus. by Phyllis Hornung. 2005, Kar-Ben $15.95 (1-58013-187-5); paper $6.95 (1-58013-128-X). 24pp. A Jewish grandmother makes a lemon cake and a beautiful sukkah for the Sukkot holiday, but at first the only guests are animals that prefer the decoration to the cake. (Rev: BL 9/1/05; SLJ 10/05)

THANKSGIVING

1407 Anderson, Derek. *Over the River: A Turkey's Tale* (PS–K). Illus. 2005, Simon & Schuster $14.95 (0-689-87635-1). 40pp. The popular Thanksgiving song is given a new twist in this tale of a turkey family on its way to celebrate the holiday with Grandma. (Rev: BL 9/15/05; HBG 4/06; SLJ 10/05)

1408 Archer, Peggy. *Turkey Surprise* (PS–K). Illus. by Thor Wickstrom. 2005, Dial $10.99 (0-8037-

2969-3). 32pp. A turkey succeeds in eluding two Pilgrim brothers, who settle for a vegetarian Thanksgiving feast. (Rev: BL 9/1/05; HBG 4/06)

1409 Reed, Lynn Rowe. *Thelonius Turkey Lives!* (PS–2). Illus. by author. 2005, Knopf $15.95 (0-375-83126-6). The other farm animals gang up on their keeper when Thelonious becomes convinced she wants to eat him for Thanksgiving. (Rev: SLJ 8/05)

1410 Spurr, Elizabeth. *The Peterkins' Thanksgiving* (2–4). Illus. by Wendy Halperin. 2005, Simon & Schuster $17.95 (0-689-84142-6). 32pp. A Victorian era Thanksgiving dinner at the Peterkins gets off to a shaky start when the turkey and fixings get stuck in the dumbwaiter. (Rev: BL 10/15/05; SLJ 10/05)

VALENTINE'S DAY

1411 Friedman, Laurie. *Love, Ruby Valentine* (K–4). Illus. by Lynne Cravath. 2006, Carolrhoda $15.95 (1-57505-899-5). Ruby Valentine works so hard to prepare for Valentine's Day that when the big day comes, she sleeps through it and must deliver her gifts a day late. (Rev: SLJ 11/06)

1412 Weeks, Sarah. *Be Mine, Be Mine, Sweet Valentine* (PS–K). Illus. by Fumi Kosaka. 2005, HarperCollins $9.99 (0-694-01514-8). A rhyming guessing game in which the reader must supply the name of the Valentine's Day gift. (Rev: SLJ 1/06)

Books for Beginning Readers

1413 Adler, David A. *Bones and the Dinosaur Mystery* (K–2). Illus. by Barbara Johansen Newman. 2005, Viking $13.99 (0-670-06010-0). 32pp. When his toy dinosaur disappears on a trip to the museum, boy detective Jeffrey Bones resolves to find out what happened. (Rev: BL 10/1/05; HBG 4/06; SLJ 10/05)

1414 Adler, David A. *Young Cam Jansen and the Substitute Mystery* (K–2). Illus. by Susanna Natti. Series: Puffin Easy to Read. 2005, Viking $13.99 (0-670-05988-9). 32pp. Cam Jansen uses her photographic memory and deductive skills to help the substitute teacher in this easy-to-read mystery. (Rev: BL 9/1/05; HBG 4/06)

1415 Arnold, Tedd. *Shoo, Fly Guy!* (K–2). Illus. by author. 2006, Scholastic $5.99 (0-439-63905-0). 30pp. Fly Guy, Buzz's pet fly, goes in search of something good to eat but keeps getting shooed away from potential treats. (Rev: HBG 4/07; LMC 2/07; SLJ 9/06)

1416 Arnold, Tedd. *Super Fly Guy* (K–3). Illus. 2006, Scholastic paper $5.99 (0-439-63904-2).

32pp. Buzz and his pet fly, Fly Guy, conspire to get the school lunchroom's new cook fired so that her more talented predecessor can win back the job in this easy chapter book. (Rev: BCCB 7–8/06; BL 4/1/06; HBG 10/06; LMC 4–5/06; SLJ 3/06)

1417 Baker, Keith. *On the Go with Mr. and Mrs. Green* (PS–2). Series: Mr. and Mrs. Green. 2006, Harcourt $16.00 (0-15-205762-5). 72pp. The further adventures of the affectionate alligators include magic tricks and high technology. (Rev: BL 5/1/06; SLJ 6/06)

1418 Berenstain, Stan, and Jan Berenstain. *The Berenstain Bears' New Pup* (K–2). Illus. by authors. Series: Berenstain Bears. 2005, HarperCollins paper $3.99 (0-06-058344-4). 32pp. A rhyming easy-reader about a new pet, in the Berenstain tradition. (Rev: SLJ 7/05)

1419 Blackaby, Susan. *Bess and Tess* (K–2). Illus. by Ronnie Roonie. Series: Read-it! Readers. 2005, Picture Window LB $18.60 (1-4048-1013-7). 24pp. This very easy beginning reader reinforces the concept of opposites by comparing Lucy's two dogs. (Rev: SLJ 9/05)

1420 Blackwood, Gary. *The Just-So-Woman* (1–3). Illus. by Jane Manning. 2006, HarperCollins $15.99 (0-06-057727-4). 48pp. Once upon a time in the days before electricity, the Just-So Woman ran out of soap, butter, and other farm essentials and asked her neighbor, the Any-Way Man, for help, learning an important lesson in the process; a funny book for beginning readers. (Rev: BL 12/1/06; SLJ 11/06)

1421 Bottner, Barbara, and Gerald Kruglik. *Pish and Posh Wish for Fairy Wings* (K–2). Illus. by Barbara Bottner. 2006, HarperCollins $15.99 (0-06-051419-1). 48pp. Trainee fairies Pish and Posh learn to cooperate (with a little help from the Monster Under the Bed) in order to make a wise wish and earn their fairy wings. (Rev: BL 12/1/06)

1422 Brimner, Larry Dane. *Twelve Plump Cookies* (1–2). Illus. by Sharon Holm. Series: Magic Door to Learning. 2005, The Child's World LB $21.36 (1-59296-523-7). 24pp. A young boy bakes a dozen cookies for guests, but when more people than expected show up, he must use his ingenuity to see that everyone gets at least part of a cookie. (Rev: SLJ 12/05)

1423 Byars, Betsy. *Boo's Dinosaur* (1–3). Illus. by Erik Brooks. 2006, Holt $15.95 (0-8050-7958-0). 41pp. Boo convinces her older brother to join in the fun as she entertains a dinosaur that only she can see in this appealing early chapter book. (Rev: SLJ 9/06)

1424 *Can You Play?* (PS–1). Illus. by Emily Bolam. Series: I'm Going to Read! 2005, Sterling LB $11.95 (1-4027-2072-6); paper $3.95 (1-4027-2094-7). Stella and her dog romp through the pages of this curriculum-oriented beginning reader. (Rev: SLJ 9/05)

1425 Carris, Joan. *Welcome to the Bed and Biscuit* (1–3). Illus. by Noah Z. Jones. 2006, Candlewick $15.99 (0-7636-2151-X). 128pp. Grandpa Bender runs an animal boardinghouse but his personal pets — a mynah, a cat, and a small pig — have extra privileges and are miffed when Grandpa brings home a tiny puppy. (Rev: BL 10/1/06; SLJ 10/06)

1426 Cazet, Denys. *A Snout for Chocolate* (K–2). Illus. by author. Series: Grandpa Spanielson's Chicken Pox Stories. 2006, HarperCollins $15.99 (0-06-051093-5). 48pp. To distract his grandson from a continuing itchy case of chicken pox, Grandpa Spanielson tells the boy how he saved Mrs. Piggerman's life when he was fire chief. Also use *The Shrunken Head* (2007). (Rev: SLJ 1/06)

1427 Cazet, Denys. *The Case of the Missing Jelly Donut* (1–3). Illus. Series: An I Can Read Book. 2005, HarperCollins $15.99 (0-06-073007-2). 48pp. Minnie and Moo, bovine detectives, go undercover to track down a suspected donut thief in this entertaining easy chapter book. (Rev: BL 9/1/05; SLJ 10/05)

1428 Cazet, Denys. *Minnie and Moo: Wanted Dead or Alive* (K–2). Series: I Can Read. 2006, HarperCollins $15.99 (0-06-073010-2). 48pp. Cows Minnie and Moo go to the bank to try to arrange a loan for Mr. Farmer but are mistaken for notorious bank robbers. (Rev: BL 8/06; SLJ 8/06)

1429 Chaconas, Dori. *Cork and Fuzz: Short and Tall* (PS–2). Illus. by Lisa McCue. Series: Viking Easy-to-Read. 2006, Viking $13.99 (0-670-05985-4). 32pp. The friendship between Cork the muskrat and Fuzz the possum is tested over their differences in size. Also use *Cork and Fuzz: Good Sports* (2007). (Rev: BL 1/1–15/06; SLJ 4/06)

1430 Ciencin, Scott. *Batman: Green Gotham* (2–4). Illus. by Rick Burchett. Series: Scholastic Reader. 2005, Scholastic paper $3.99 (0-439-47102-8). 40pp. In this easy-reader chapter book, rendered in comic-book format, Batman tries to recover a rare black orchid that was stolen from the Gotham City Botanical Gardens by Poison Ivy. (Rev: SLJ 3/06)

1431 *A Class Play with Ms. Vanilla* (PS–2). Illus. by Martha Gradisher. Series: I'm Going to Read! 2005, Sterling LB $11.95 (1-4027-2087-4); paper $3.95 (1-4027-2108-0). A class production of Little Red Riding Hood doesn't turn out quite as the students expected in this easy reader. (Rev: SLJ 9/05)

1432 Cushman, Doug. *Dirk Bones and the Mystery of the Haunted House* (K–2). Series: I Can Read! 2006, HarperCollins $15.99 (0-06-073764-6). 32pp. Dirk Bones, a skeleton reporter for the "Ghostly Tombs," investigates a haunted house whose ghostly residents are spooked by unexplained noises. (Rev: BL 8/06; SLJ 7/06)

1433 Dahl, Michael. *The Tall, Tall Slide* (K–2). Illus. by Sara Gray. Series: Read It! Readers. 2006, Picture Window LB $18.60 (1-4048-1186-9). 32pp. On a hot summer day, new friends help Tina to overcome her fears of the tall slide at the local swimming pool. (Rev: BL 3/1/06)

1434 Denton, Kady MacDonald. *Watch Out, William!* (K–2). Series: I Am Reading. 2006, Kingfisher paper $3.95 (0-7534-5960-4). 48pp. Three short chapters recount everyday adventures of William and his little sister Jane. (Rev: BL 5/1/06; SLJ 8/06)

1435 DiCamillo, Kate. *Mercy Watson Fights Crime* (PS–2). Illus. by Chris Van Dusen. 2006, Candlewick $12.99 (0-7636-2590-6). 70pp. Mercy Watson, the crime-fighting pig, nabs a toaster thief red-handed. (Rev: SLJ 11/06*)

1436 DiCamillo, Kate. *Mercy Watson to the Rescue* (PS–2). Illus. by Chris Van Dusen. 2005, Candlewick $12.99 (0-7636-2270-2). 80pp. The Watsons love Mercy, their pig, so much that they invite her to share their bed, a decision with disastrous consequences; the first in a new series of chapter books for beginning readers. (Rev: BCCB 12/05; BL 8/05*; HBG 4/06; LMC 2/06; SLJ 10/05)

1437 Eastman, Peter. *Fred and Ted Go Camping* (PS–2). Illus. by author. Series: Beginner Books. 2005, Random $8.99 (0-375-82965-2). Two dog friends enjoy each other's company on a camping trip in this book for beginning readers. (Rev: SLJ 7/05)

1438 Eaton, Deborah. *My Wild Woolly* (K–2). Illus. by G. Brian Karas. Series: Green Light Readers. 2005, Harcourt $12.95 (0-15-205148-1). 24pp. A young boy spends an entertaining afternoon playing in his backyard with a "wild woolly," a creature the boy's mother claims does not exist. (Rev: BL 11/1/05)

1439 Florie, Christine. *Lara Ladybug* (PS–1). Illus. by Danny Brooks Dalby. Series: Rookie Reader. 2005, Children's Pr. LB $17.00 (0-516-25137-6); paper $4.95 (0-516-25281-X). 23pp. Lara has lost her spots in this book for beginning readers illustrated with collages. (Rev: SLJ 7/05)

1440 Freeman, Martha. *Mrs. Wow Never Wanted a Cow* (K–2). Illus. by Steven Salerno. 2006, Random $8.99 (0-375-83418-4). Mrs. Wow's pets change their ways when a cow becomes a member of the family in this humorous brightly illustrated book for beginning readers. (Rev: SLJ 6/06)

1441 *Go Away, Crows!* (PS–2). Illus. by Santiago Cohen. Series: I'm Going to Read! 2005, Sterling LB $11.95 (1-4027-2080-7); paper $3.95 (1-4027-2103-X). A brother and sister find a way to scare the crows away from their garden in this easy reader. (Rev: SLJ 9/05)

1442 Gorbachev, Valeri. *Ms. Turtle the Babysitter* (K–1). Illus. by author. 2005, HarperCollins $15.99

(0-06-058073-9). 64pp. Simple chapters describe the ways three little frogs try their turtle babysitter's patience. (Rev: SLJ 8/05)

1443 Greenburg, Dan. *Dude, Where's My Spaceship?* (2–3). Illus. by Dave Calver. Series: Weird Planet. 2006, Random LB $11.99 (0-375-93344-1); paper $3.99 (0-375-83344-7). 81pp. After crashing their spaceship on Earth, alien Klatu and his brother Lek try to rescue their sister Ploo, who's been taken captive by a band of earthlings; humor and large print make this suitable for emerging readers. (Rev: SLJ 3/06)

1444 Greene, Stephanie. *Moose Crossing* (1–3). Illus. by Joe Mathieu. Series: Moose and Hildy. 2005, Marshall Cavendish $14.95 (0-7614-5233-8). 56pp. In this easy-reader chapter book, Moose finds that celebrity is not as much fun as he expected. (Rev: SLJ 3/06)

1445 Greene, Stephanie. *Moose's Big Idea* (1–3). Illus. by Joe Mathieu. Series: Moose and Hildy. 2005, Marshall Cavendish $14.95 (0-7614-5212-5). 51pp. In this easy-reader chapter book, Moose bemoans his lost antlers, draws pictures at home during hunting season, and later sells puts on a disguise and sells doughnuts, coffee, and original artwork to unsuspecting hunters; all this in the company of his pig friend Hildy. (Rev: SLJ 10/05)

1446 Gregorich, Barbara. *Waltur Buys a Pig in a Poke and Other Stories* (2–4). Illus. by Kristin Sorra. 2006, Houghton $15.00 (0-618-47306-8). 64pp. In this easy-reader chapter book full of wordplay, Waltur the bear learns the truth behind three widely held maxims. (Rev: BL 6/1–15/06; SLJ 7/06)

1447 Guest, Elissa Haden. *Iris and Walter and the Birthday Party* (1–3). Illus. by Christine Davenier. Series: Iris and Walter. 2006, Harcourt $15.00 (0-15-205015-9). 44pp. Walter and Iris's friends will get to ride Walter's horse on his birthday, but there is a surprise — a foal — awaiting them. (Rev: BL 2/1/06; SLJ 3/06)

1448 Gutierrez, Akemi. *The Mummy and Other Adventures of Sam and Alice* (K–2). Illus. by author. 2005, Houghton $16.00 (0-618-50761-2). Siblings Sam and Alice show — in three short stories — how the power of imagination can turn a humdrum day into a fascinating adventure. (Rev: SLJ 11/05)

1449 Hapka, Cathy, and Ellen Titlebaum. *How Not to Babysit Your Brother* (K–3). Illus. by Debbie Palen. Series: Step into Reading. 2005, Random LB $11.99 (0-375-92856-1); paper $3.99 (0-375-82856-7). 48pp. A humorous early chapter book about two brothers who create quite a stir while their grandmother is sleeping. (Rev: SLJ 8/05)

1450 *Harry's Bath* (K–1). Illus. by Seymour Chwast. Series: I'm Going to Read! 2005, Sterling LB $11.95 (1-4027-2077-7); paper $3.95 (1-4027-2100-

5). Harry claims he can't get in the tub because it's already full of animals in this beginning reader. (Rev: SLJ 9/05)

1451 Hay, Samantha. *Creepy Customers* (K–2). Illus. by Sarah Warburton. Series: I Am Reading. 2005, Kingfisher paper $3.95 (0-7534-5857-8). 46pp. One creepy customer after another shows up in Steve's father's store in this beginning chapter book. (Rev: SLJ 9/05)

1452 Hay, Samantha. *Hocus-Pocus Hound* (1–3). Illus. by Nathan Reed. Series: I Am Reading. 2006, Kingfisher paper $3.95 (0-7534-5957-4). 48pp. A scruffy-looking hound becomes an unexpectedly helpful assistant to Marvo the Magician. (Rev: SLJ 1/07)

1453 Hays, Anna Jane. *The Secret of the Circle-K Cave* (2–4). Illus. by Jerry Smath. Series: Science Solves It. 2006, Kane paper $4.99 (1-57565-189-0). 32pp. While visiting his aunt and uncle in New Mexico, Rick and his cousins explore a cave where they discover clues to an unsolved 19th-century robbery; scientific aspects are covered in sidebars. (Rev: BL 8/06)

1454 Hill, Karen. *Finding the Golden Ruler* (K–2). Illus. by Felicia Hoshino. 2005, Simon & Schuster $9.99 (1-4169-0513-8); paper $3.99 (1-4169-0317-8). 24pp. In this faith-based story for beginning readers, a little boy learns that it just makes sense to treat others as you want to be treated. (Rev: BL 10/1/05)

1455 Hill, Susan. *Ruby's Perfect Day* (PS–K). Illus. by Margie Moore. 2006, HarperCollins $15.99 (0-06-008982-2). 32pp. Ruby Raccoon learns that playing by herself can be just as much fun as playing with all her woodland friends. (Rev: BL 12/1/06; SLJ 10/06)

1456 Howe, James. *Houndsley and Catina* (2–4). Illus. by Marie-Louise Gay. 2006, Candlewick $14.99 (0-7636-2404-7). 40pp. Best friends Houndsley the dog and Catina the cat try to find goals that fit their talents; an early chapter book with watercolor-and-pencil illustrations. (Rev: BL 2/15/06; SLJ 5/06)

1457 Howe, James. *Houndsley and Catina and the Birthday Surprise* (PS–2). Illus. by Marie-Louise Gay. 2006, Candlewick $14.99 (0-7636-2405-5). 48pp. Houndsley the dog and Catina the cat are sad that they do not know their birthdays but they find a creative way to get around this; an easy-reader sequel to *Houndsley and Catina* (2006). (Rev: BL 10/1/06; SLJ 11/06)

1458 Hsu, Stacey W. *Old Mo* (PS–1). Illus. by Adam Ritter. Series: Rookie Reader. 2006, Children's Pr. LB $19.50 (0-516-24981-9). 32pp. A boy and his beloved pet cat enjoy each other's company throughout the day in this easy reader. (Rev: SLJ 6/06)

1459 Hulme, Joy N. *Mary Clare Likes to Share: A Math Reader* (K–1). Illus. by Lizzy Rockwell. Series: Step into Reading. 2006, Random LB $11.99 (978-0-375-93421-6); paper $3.99 (978-0-375-83421-9). 32pp. A humorous, rhyming easy-reader that uses Mary Clare's sharing of food to introduce fractions. (Rev: SLJ 2/07)

1460 Jacobson, Jennifer Richard. *Andy Shane and the Pumpkin Trick* (1–3). Illus. by Abby Carter. 2006, Candlewick $13.99 (0-7636-2605-8). 64pp. Andy is reluctant to spend so much time on bossy Dolores's birthday party, especially as it's on Halloween, but in the end he saves the day, confounding pranksters. (Rev: BL 9/1/06; SLJ 10/06)

1461 Jensen, Patricia. *I Am Sick* (K–2). Illus. by Johanna Hantel. Series: My First Reader. 2005, Children's Pr. LB $18.50 (0-516-24878-2); paper $3.95 (0-516-24970-3). 32pp. A young girl is nervous about going to the doctor, but her father goes with her and the doctor is kind, giving her medicine that makes her headache and sore throat better; for beginning readers. (Rev: SLJ 1/06)

1462 Jinkins, Jim. *Pinky Dinky Doo: Back to School Is Cool* (K–3). Illus. by author. Series: Step into Reading. 2005, Random $12.95 (0-375-83236-X); paper $3.99 (0-375-83237-8). 48pp. Pinky makes up a funny story about picture day at school to tell to her little brother. (Rev: SLJ 9/05)

1463 Kenah, Katharine. *The Best Seat in Second Grade* (K–2). Illus. by Abby Carter. Series: I Can Read! 2005, HarperCollins $15.99 (0-06-000734-6). 64pp. Sam, a second grader, gets more than he bargained for when he takes the class hamster along on a school field trip. (Rev: BL 8/05; SLJ 7/05)

1464 Kenah, Katharine. *The Best Teacher in Second Grade* (K–2). Illus. by Abby Carter. Series: I Can Read! 2006, HarperCollins $15.99 (0-06-053564-4). 48pp. Luna's teacher supports the new girl's idea for a special night sky program even though her classmates are cool to the suggestion. (Rev: BL 6/1–15/06; SLJ 7/06)

1465 Kerrin, Jessica Scott. *Martin Bridge on the Lookout!* (2–4). Illus. by Joseph Kelly. 2005, Kids Can $14.95 (1-55337-689-7); paper $4.95 (1-55337-773-7). 142pp. In this beginning chapter book, Martin Bridge returns in a trio of short stories about minor misadventures that turn out well. (Rev: SLJ 11/05)

1466 Kimmelman, Leslie. *In the Doghouse* (K–2). Illus. by True Kelley. Series: Holiday House Reader. 2006, Holiday $14.95 (0-8234-1882-0). 32pp. Emma's dog Bo disappears after she is angry with him, causing much anguish but ending in a joyous reunion in this well-rounded book for beginning readers. (Rev: BL 4/15/06; SLJ 5/06)

1467 Klein, Adria F. *Max Goes to School* (PS–1). Illus. by Mernie Gallagher-Cole. Series: Read-it!

Readers. 2005, Picture Window LB $18.60 (1-4048-1179-6). 24pp. Max, a young African American boy, spends an enjoyable first day at school in this simple easy-reader. Also use *Max Goes to the Barber* and *Max Goes to the Dentist* (both 2005). (Rev: SLJ 1/06)

1468 Kline, Suzy. *Horrible Harry Takes the Cake* (1–3). Illus. by Frank Remkiewicz. Series: Horrible Harry. 2006, Viking $13.99 (0-670-06075-5). 64pp. Harry tries to find out who their teacher is marrying; the nineteenth book in this humorous series. (Rev: BL 2/1/06; SLJ 5/06)

1469 Knudsen, Michelle. *Fish and Frog* (PS). Illus. by Valeria Petrone. Series: Brand New Readers. 2005, Candlewick $14.99 (0-7636-2456-X); paper $5.99 (0-7636-2457-8). 40pp. An enjoyable beginning reader with a simple story line and bright illustrations portraying a fish and frog that live in the same pond. (Rev: SLJ 8/05)

1470 Kroll, Virginia. *Honest Ashley* (K–3). Illus. by Nancy Cote. Series: The Way I Act. 2005, Albert Whitman $15.95 (0-8075-3371-8). 32pp. The virtues of honesty are explored in this tale of a girl trying to decide whether to copy an old essay of her brother's or to do the school assignment on her own. (Rev: BL 6/1–15/06; SLJ 3/06)

1471 Kvasnosky, Laura McGee. *Zelda and Ivy: The Runaways* (K–3). 2006, Candlewick $14.99 (0-7636-2689-9). 48pp. Fox sisters Zelda and Ivy decide to run away from home, bury a time capsule, and experiment with a creative juice. (Rev: BL 6/1–15/06; SLJ 7/06*)

1472 Labatt, Mary. *A Parade for Sam* (PS–2). Illus. by Marisol Sarrazin. Series: Kids Can Read. 2005, Kids Can $14.95 (1-55337-787-7); paper $3.95 (1-55337-788-5). 32pp. Not content to watch the carnival parade from the sidelines, Sam, a fluffy puppy, wants to be a part of it; suitable for beginning readers. (Rev: BL 10/15/05)

1473 Labatt, Mary. *Sam at the Seaside* (PS–2). Illus. by Marisol Sarrazin. Series: Kids Can Read. 2006, Kids Can $14.95 (1-55337-876-8); paper $3.95 (1-55337-876-8). 32pp. On a visit to the seashore with her owners, Sam the puppy's exuberance gets her into all sorts of problems. Also use *Sam Goes Next Door* (2006). (Rev: SLJ 11/06)

1474 Lucas, Sally. *Dancing Dinos Go to School* (PS–K). Illus. by Margeaux Lucas. Series: Step into Reading. 2006, Random LB $11.99 (0-375-93241-0); paper $Random,.00 (0-375-83241-6). 32pp. A group of dinosaurs leap from the pages of a book and spend a wild day disrupting the school. (Rev: BL 8/06; SLJ 10/06)

1475 McEwan, Jamie. *Whitewater Scrubs* (K–2). Illus. by John Margeson. 2005, Darby Creek $14.99 (1-58196-038-7). 64pp. Accustomed to athletic success, Clara must conquer her fears when she joins

Willie and the football scrubs for a kayaking class; suitable for beginning chapter-book readers. (Rev: BL 9/1/05; SLJ 11/05)

1476 McKenna, Colleen O'Shaughnessy. *Third Grade Wedding Bells* (2–4). Illus. by Stephanie Roth. Series: Third Grade. 2006, Holiday $15.95 (0-8234-1943-6). 160pp. Gordie, Lucy, and Lamont are distressed to hear their teacher is getting married — will they lose her? (Rev: BL 5/1/06; SLJ 4/06)

1477 McNamara, Margaret. *Fall Leaf Project* (PS–K). Illus. by Mike Gordon. Series: Ready-to-Read. 2006, Simon & Schuster LB $11.89 (1-4169-1538-9); paper $3.99 (1-4169-1537-0). 32pp. Mrs. Connor's class collects leaves in a variety of fall colors and sends them to a first-grade class in the Southwest. (Rev: BL 1/1–15/07)

1478 McNamara, Margaret. *The First Day of School* (K–2). Illus. by Mike Gordon. Series: Ready-to-Read. 2005, Aladdin LB $11.89 (0-689-86915-0); paper $3.99 (0-689-86914-2). 32pp. Michael can't wait to start first grade until he learns that he won't be able to take his dog to class; suitable for beginning readers. (Rev: BL 8/05; SLJ 8/05)

1479 Medearis, Angela Shelf. *On the Way to the Pond* (K–2). Illus. by Lorinda Bryan Cauley. 2006, Harcourt $12.95 (0-15-205599-1); paper $3.95 (0-15-205623-8). Tess Tiger and Herbert Hippo have a picnic by a cool pond in this easy reader. (Rev: SLJ 6/06)

1480 Meister, Cari. *Tiny Goes Camping* (PS). Illus. by Rich Davis. Series: Viking Easy-to-Read. 2006, Viking $13.99 (0-670-89250-5). 32pp. A boy and his huge dog ("Tiny" of the title) plan to camp out in their back yard in this easy reader. (Rev: BL 5/1/06; SLJ 6/06)

1481 Morris, Jennifer E. *May I Please Have a Cookie?* (K–1). Illus. Series: Scholastic Reader. 2005, Scholastic paper $3.99 (0-439-73819-9). 32pp. A young alligator learns the right way to get a cookie from his mother in this beginning reader. (Rev: BL 1/1–15/06)

1482 Parish, Herman. *Amelia Bedelia, Rocket Scientist?* (K–2). Illus. by Lynn Sweat. 2005, Greenwillow $15.99 (0-06-051887-1). 64pp. Chaos ensues when housekeeper Amelia Bedelia offers to help out at the school's science fair. (Rev: BL 7/05; SLJ 7/05)

1483 Parish, Herman. *Amelia Bedelia Under Construction* (K–2). Illus. by Lynn Sweat. Series: Amelia Bedelia. 2006, Greenwillow $15.99 (0-06-084344-6). 64pp. When Amelia Bedelia baby-sits for the Hardys, some unexpected construction work gets under way. (Rev: BL 6/1–15/06; SLJ 5/06)

1484 Paul, Ann Whitford. *Hop! Hop! Hop!* (PS–K). Illus. by Jan Gerardi. Series: Step into Reading. 2005, Random LB $11.99 (0-375-92857-X); paper $3.99 (0-375-82857-5). 32pp. An early reader featuring Little Rabbit, who tries to do what Big Rabbit does but can't always keep up. (Rev: SLJ 8/05)

1485 Pierce, Terry. *Tae Kwon Do!* (PS–K). Illus. by Todd Bonita. Series: Step into Reading. 2006, Random $3.99 (0-375-83448-6). 32pp. For beginning readers, this is a simple rhyming account of a brother and sister's tae kwon do class. (Rev: SLJ 5/06)

1486 Platt, Kin. *Big Max and the Mystery of the Missing Giraffe* (K–2). Illus. by Lynne Cravath. Series: I Can Read. 2005, HarperCollins $15.99 (0-06-009918-6). 64pp. Big Max continues his detective work in this entertaining mystery for beginning readers. (Rev: SLJ 7/05)

1487 *The Prince Has a Boo-Boo!* (K–1). Illus. by R. W. Alley. Series: I'm Going to Read. 2005, Sterling $11.95 (1-4027-2067-X); paper $3.95 (1-4027-2089-0). 28pp. This beginning reader featuring a cumulative story about a prince in need of a bandage introduces 50 basic vocabulary words. (Rev: BL 9/1/05; SLJ 9/05)

1488 Proimos, James, and Andy Rheingold. *When Guinea Pigs Fly!* (2–5). Illus. by James Proimos. 2005, Scholastic $14.95 (0-439-51899-7); paper $3.99 (0-439-51902-0). 105pp. Brooks the guinea pig dreams of freedom from his pet shop, so he is initially ecstatic when he and friends Leone and Allen are accidentally set free in a park; a beginning chapter book with black-and-white cartoon drawings. (Rev: SLJ 11/05)

1489 Reggier, DeMar. *Gooci Food* (K–2). Illus. by David Austin Clar. Series: My First Reader. 2005, Children's Pr. LB $18.50 (0-516-24879-0); paper $3.95 (0-516-24969-X). 32pp. In this easy-reader, a young boy accompanies his father to the grocery store where they buy ingredients for a special meal for Mom. (Rev: SLJ 1/06)

1490 Ries, Lori. *Aggie and Ben: Three Stories* (K–2). Illus. by Frank W. Dormer. 2006, Charlesbridge $12.95 (1-57091-594-6). 48pp. A beginning chapter book in which Ben takes home a new pet dog, Aggie, and the two get to know each other. (Rev: SLJ 7/06)

1491 Rylant, Cynthia. *Annie and Snowball and the Dress-up Birthday* (K–2). Illus. by Sucie Stevenson. Series: Ready-to-Read. 2007, Simon & Schuster $14.99 (978-1-4169-0938-5). 40pp. Annie (cousin of Henry of Henry and Mudge) likes wearing nice ribbons and bows, so she and her pet rabbit Snowball invite Henry and Mudge to a "Dress-up Birthday," but that term can be misinterpreted . . . . (Rev: SLJ 4/07)

1492 Rylant, Cynthia. *The Case of the Desperate Duck* (1–3). Illus. by G. Brian Karas. Series: The High-Rise Private Eyes. 2005, HarperCollins $14.99 (0-06-053451-6). 48pp. A rabbit and a raccoon solve the mystery of the missing sugar cubes in this easy-reader. (Rev: SLJ 8/05)

1493 Rylant, Cynthia. *Henry and Mudge and the Big Sleepover* (K–2). Illus. by Sucie Stevenson. 2006, Simon & Schuster $14.95 (0-689-81171-3). 40pp. Henry and his dog Mudge enjoy a variety of typical sleepover activities at Patrick's house. (Rev: BL 8/06; SLJ 7/06)

1494 Rylant, Cynthia. *Henry and Mudge and the Tumbling Trip* (1–3). Illus. by Carolyn Bracken. Series: Ready-to-Read. 2005, Simon & Schuster $14.95 (0-689-81180-2). 40pp. Henry and his dog Mudge take a trip out west. (Rev: BL 2/1/06)

1495 Rylant, Cynthia. *Mr. Putter and Tabby Make a Wish* (PS–2). Illus. by Arthur Howard. Series: Mr. Putter and Tabby. 2005, Harcourt $14.00 (0-15-202426-3). Mr. Putter invites friends for tea to celebrate his birthday, but they seem to be taking a very long time to arrive. (Rev: SLJ 10/05*)

1496 Rylant, Cynthia. *Mr. Putter and Tabby Spin the Yarn* (PS–2). Illus. by Arthur Howard. 2006, Harcourt $14.00 (0-15-205067-1). 44pp. To reward Mrs. Teaberry for all her kindnesses, Mr. Putter decides to serve tea at her knitting club, but things go awry when Mr. Putter's cat and Mrs. Teaberry's dog run amok. (Rev: SLJ 10/06)

1497 Schaefer, Lola M. *Mittens* (PS–K). Illus. by Susan Kathleen Hartung. Series: My First I Can Read. 2006, HarperCollins $14.99 (0-06-054659-X). 32pp. A simple book for beginning readers about Mittens the kitten's fears about his new home. (Rev: BL 4/15/06; SLJ 6/06)

1498 Schmauss, Judy Kentor. *Parade Day* (K–1). Illus. by Randy Chewning. Series: Reader's Clubhouse. 2006, Barron's paper $3.99 (0-7641-3293-8). 24pp. This simple tale of friends gathering for a parade is designed to help children practice their phonics skills, focusing in this title on the long "a" sound. Part of a series that includes *Too, Too Hot!* and *Luke's Mule* (both 2006). (Rev: SLJ 11/06)

1499 Schulte, Mary. *Who Do I Look Like?* (PS–1). Illus. by Maryn Roos. Series: A Rookie Reader. 2006, Children's Pr. LB $19.50 (0-516-24978-9). 32pp. An easy reader that features a child in a racially mixed family wondering whom he most resembles. (Rev: SLJ 6/06)

1500 Sharmat, Marjorie Weinman, and Mitchell Sharmat. *Nate the Great Talks Turkey* (K–2). Illus. by Jody Wheeler. 2006, Delacorte $11.95 (0-385-73336-4). 80pp. Boy detective Nate the Great decides to pass on the case of the missing turkey until he uncovers a clue that just cannot be ignored; his cousin Olivia meanwhile is doing her own sleuthing. (Rev: BL 10/15/06; SLJ 10/06)

1501 Silverman, Erica. *Partners* (1–3). Illus. by Betsy Lewin. 2006, Harcourt $15.00 (0-15-202125-6). 44pp. Kate and her faithful horse Cocoa continue their happy friendship in four new episodes; a sequel to *Cowboy Kate and Cocoa* (2005). (Rev: BL 2/15/06; SLJ 8/06)

1502 Silverman, Erica. *School Days* (PS–2). Illus. by Betsy Lewin. Series: Cowgirl Kate and Cocoa. 2007, Harcourt $15.00 (978-0-15-205378-9). 48pp. Cocoa the horse suffers separation anxiety when Kate starts school and seems to be preoccupied with homework and her new friend. (Rev: BL 3/15/07)

1503 Smith, Charles R., Jr. *Let's Play Baseball!* (PS–1). Illus. by Terry Widener. 2006, Candlewick $8.99 (0-7636-1646-X). A little boy can't resist the call of a baseball wanting to play. (Rev: SLJ 7/06)

1504 Stauffacher, Sue. *Bessie Smith and the Night Riders* (2–4). Illus. by John Holyfield. 2006, Putnam $16.99 (0-399-24237-6). 32pp. A fictionalized, dramatically illustrated account of a real-life confrontation between singer Bessie Smith and Ku Klux Klan members in 1927. (Rev: BL 2/1/06; SLJ 1/06)

1505 Sudduth, Brent. *Penny Star*, vol. 4 (1–3). Illus. by Stu Harrison. Series: Phonics Comics. 2005, Innovative paper $4.99 (1-58476-321-3). Young fashion designer Penny Star tries to solve a trio of mysteries in this comic-book volume with carefully selected vocabulary for beginning readers. (Rev: SLJ 1/06)

1506 Sudduth, Brent. *The Smart Boys*, vol. 3 (1–3). Illus. by Geo Parkin. Series: Phonics Comics. 2005, Innovative paper $4.99 (1-58476-320-5). In this trio of comic book stories, the young Smart brothers — who enjoy outwitting their parents — show their ingenuity by creating a turbo shopping cart, shrinking themselves, and extending daylight. (Rev: SLJ 1/06)

1507 Taylor-Butler, Christine. *Step-by-Step* (K–2). Illus. by Susan Miller. Series: My First Reader. 2005, Children's Pr. LB $18.50 (0-516-24875-8); paper $3.95 (0-516-24974-6). 32pp. A young boy makes a beautiful bouquet for his grandmother by dyeing white flowers using bright colors. (Rev: SLJ 1/06)

1508 Taylor-Butler, Christine. *Who Needs Friends?* (PS–1). Illus. by Susan Havice. Series: A Rookie Reader. 2006, Children's Pr. LB $19.50 (0-516-24979-7). 32pp. A young boy decides to throw himself a birthday party when it seems no one has remembered the special day. (Rev: SLJ 6/06)

1509 Thiesing, Lisa. *A Dark and Noisy Night* (PS–1). Illus. Series: Dutton Easy Reader. 2005, Dutton $13.99 (0-525-47388-2). 32pp. Peggy the Pig cannot fall asleep because of the scary noises that seem to be everywhere. (Rev: BL 9/15/05; SLJ 1/06)

1510 Thomas, Shelley Moore. *Happy Birthday, Good Knight* (K–2). Illus. by Jennifer Plecas. Series: Dutton Easy Reader. 2006, Dutton $13.99 (0-525-47184-7). 48pp. Things go badly when the

Good Knight's three little dragon friends try to create a birthday gift.. (Rev: BL 1/1–15/06; SLJ 3/06)

1511 Torrey, Richard. *Beans Baker's Best Shot* (1–3). Series: Step into Reading. 2006, Random LB $11.99 (0-375-92839-1); paper $3.99 (0-375-82839-7). 48pp. An injury sidelines Beans Baker from his soccer team's championship game, but he tries to do his part by cheering on his teammates. (Rev: BL 8/06; SLJ 10/06)

1512 Twain, Mark. *The Best Fence Painter*. Book 2 (K–2). Adapted by Catherine Nichols. Illus. by Amy Bates. Series: The Adventures of Tom Sawyer. 2006, Sterling paper $3.95 (1-4027-3288-0). 32pp. For beginning readers, this chapter book with simple vocabulary and short sentences retells the fence-painting episode. Also use *A Song for Aunt Polly* (2006). (Rev: SLJ 8/06)

1513 Underwood, Deborah. *Pirate Mom* (PS–2). Illus. by Stephen Gilpin. Series: Step into Reading. 2006, Random LB $11.99 (0-375-93323-9); paper $3.99 (0-375-83323-4). 48pp. When Pete's mother is hypnotized into thinking she is a pirate, it's up to

Pete to try to stop her zany behavior. (Rev: BL 5/1/06)

1514 Van Leeuwen, Jean. *Oliver Pig and the Best Fort Ever* (K–2). Illus. by Ann Schweninger. Series: Dial Easy-to-Read. 2006, Dial $15.99 (0-8037-2888-3). 40pp. Oliver Pig calls on his friends to help him build "the best fort ever" in four chapters suited to beginning readers. (Rev: BL 4/15/06; SLJ 7/06)

1515 Wallace, Carol. *Turkeys Together* (K–2). Illus. by Jacqueline Rogers. Series: Holiday House Reader. 2005, Holiday House $15.95 (0-8234-1895-2). 40pp. A hunting dog befriends two mother turkeys in this easy-reader. (Rev: SLJ 8/05)

1516 Ziefert, Harriet. *Sometimes I Share* (PS–1). Illus. by Carol Nicklaus. Series: I'm Going to Read! 2005, Sterling $11.95 (1-4027-2068-8); paper $3.95 (1-4027-2090-4). 28pp. Simple first-person text chronicles the ups and downs of a girl's relationship with her little brother; suitable for early beginning readers. (Rev: BL 8/05)

Fiction for Older Readers

General

1517 Amesse, Susan. *Kissing Brendan Callahan* (4–6). 2005, Roaring Brook $15.95 (1-59643-015-X). 160pp. Twelve-year-old Sarah, an aspiring romance writer, is devastated when her mother won't let her enter a writing contest to be judged by the girl's favorite author; meanwhile kissable Brendan offers a questionable alternative. (Rev: BL 11/15/05; HBG 4/06; SLJ 12/05; VOYA 12/05)

1518 Anderson, M. T. *Me, All Alone, at the End of the World* (4–6). Illus. by Kevin Hawkes. 2005, Candlewick $16.99 (0-7636-1586-2). 40pp. A boy's solitary but idyllic life at the End of the World is threatened by the arrival of an elderly entrepreneur who proposes to turn the area into a massive theme park. (Rev: BL 11/15/05; HBG 4/06; LMC 2/06; SLJ 12/05)

1519 Bair, Sheila. *Rock, Brock, and the Savings Shock* (3–5). Illus. by Barry Gott. 2006, Albert Whitman $15.95 (0-8075-7094-X). While Brock saves his money, his twin brother Rock squanders it, and learns a lesson about the value of a dollar; saving tips and a brief math lesson at the end explain the underlying concepts. (Rev: SLJ 7/06)

1520 Bateson, Catherine. *Stranded in Boringsville* (5–8). 2005, Holiday House $16.95 (0-8234-1969-X). 138pp. Twelve-year-old Rain's life is turned upside down when she and her mother move from cosmopolitan Melbourne to a small Australian town in the middle of nowhere; but she finds a good friend in her neighbor Daniel. (Rev: BL 12/1/05; SLJ 2/06; VOYA 2/06)

1521 Bell, Alison. *Zibby Payne and the Wonderful, Terrible Tomboy Experiment* (3–5). Series: Zibby Payne. 2006, Lobster paper $6.95 (1-897073-39-9). 96pp. When her longtime friend Sarah shows more interest in fashion and boy-watching than sports, 6th-grader Zibby reacts by becoming a total tomboy. (Rev: SLJ 12/06)

1522 Bell, Joanne. *Breaking Trail* (5–7). 2005, Groundwood $15.95 (0-88899-630-6); paper $6.95 (0-88899-662-4). 135pp. Becky's dreams of training a dog team to participate in the Junior Quest fade when her father grows increasingly depressed, but a sled trip back to the family's cabin offers a chance to make those dreams come true. (Rev: SLJ 10/05)

1523 Boles, Philana Marie. *Little Divas* (5–8). 2006, HarperCollins LB $16.89 (0-06-073300-4). 176pp. Twelve-year-old Cass is facing a lot of change in her life: her parents' divorce, living with her father, a new friend, a first kiss, and perhaps a new school. (Rev: BL 4/1/06; SLJ 1/06)

1524 Bonk, John J. *Dustin Grubbs: Take Two!* (5–8). 2006, Little, Brown $15.99 (0-316-15637-X). 243pp. In this humorous sequel to *Dustin Grubbs: One-Man Show*, the 12-year-old aspiring actor deals with the school production of *Oliver!*, bullying classmates, his parents' divorce, and the chance to act in a commercial. (Rev: SLJ 2/07)

1525 Bonners, Susan. *The Vanishing Point* (5–8). 2005, Farrar $16.00 (0-374-38081-3). 336pp. Kate, a quiet girl who is spending the summer at the beach with family friends who have a daughter about her age, concentrates on her interest in art and a mystery about a painting. (Rev: BL 9/1/05; SLJ 10/05)

1526 Butler, Don Hillestad. *Tank Talbott's Guide to Girls* (4–6). 2006, Albert Whitman $15.95 (0-8075-7761-8). 178pp. As part of his effort to move on to 6th grade, Tank Talbott writes a guide to girls, filled with advice he'll need himself if he's to survive a summer-long visit from his stepsisters; a sequel to *Trading Places with Tank Talbott* (2003). (Rev: BL 4/15/06; SLJ 5/06)

1527 Byrd, Sandra. *Island Girl* (5–8). Series: Friends for a Season. 2005, Bethany House paper $9.99 (0-7642-0020-8). 125pp. Confused by changes in her family situation, 13-year-old Meg spends a summer with her grandparents on an Oregon island where she meets and befriends Tia. (Rev: BL 10/1/05)

1528 Cassidy, Cathy. *Scarlett* (5–8). 2006, Viking $15.99 (0-670-06068-2). 272pp. Much to her surprise (and with some help from a mysterious boy), 12-year-old Scarlett actually enjoys living in Ireland with her father and his new family. (Rev: BL 12/1/06)

1529 Charlton-Trujillo, E. E. *Prizefighter en mi casa* (5–8). 2006, Delacorte $15.95 (0-385-73325-9). 210pp. The visit of a Mexican prizefighter to her family's home in South Texas triggers a chain of life-changing events for 12-year-old Chula Sanchez, who suffers from epilepsy caused by an accident. (Rev: SLJ 12/06)

1530 Clinton, Cathryn. *Simeon's Fire* (4–7). 2005, Candlewick $15.99 (0-7636-2707-0). 128pp. Simeon, a young Amish farm boy, struggles with guilt and fear after he witnesses the torching of his family's barn by two men who threaten to exact revenge if he tells what he's seen. (Rev: BL 11/1/05; SLJ 12/05)

1531 Codell, Esmé Raji. *Vive la Paris* (4–6). 2006, Hyperion $15.99 (0-7868-5124-4). 192pp. Paris McCray, an African American fifth grader, develops a very special relationship with her piano teacher, a Holocaust survivor; a companion to *Sahara Special* (2003). (Rev: BL 9/15/06; SLJ 10/06)

1532 De Alcantara, Pedro. *Befiddled* (4–7). 2005, Delacorte LB $17.99 (0-385-90281-6). 179pp. Mr. Freeman, the superintendent in her apartment building, turns out to be the person to pull 13-year-old Becky out of her dismal doldrums and lift her violin playing to its proper level. (Rev: SLJ 2/06; VOYA 4/06)

1533 de Guzman, Michael. *The Bamboozlers* (5–8). 2005, Farrar $16.00 (0-374-30512-9). 167pp. Twelve-year-old Albert Rosegarden is in for the adventure of his life when he accompanies his ex-con grandfather on a trip to Seattle. (Rev: HB 11–12/05; SLJ 12/05)

1534 *Dexter the Tough* (2–5). Illus. by Mark Elliott. 2007, Simon & Schuster $15.99 (1-4169-1159-6). 139pp. After getting off on the wrong foot at his new school, Dexter puts on a tough exterior to hide his anxieties, but a persistent teacher and a would-be friend manage to break through to the uncertain young boy inside. (Rev: SLJ 1/07)

1535 Draper, Sharon M. *The Space Mission Adventure* (3–6). Illus. by Jesse Joshua Watson. Series: Ziggy and the Black Dinosaurs. 2006, Simon & Schuster LB $11.89 (1-4169-2458-2); paper $4.99 (0-689-87914-8). 121pp. While attending Space Camp in Huntsville, Alabama, Ziggy and his friends (African American boys from Ohio) cooperate with other campers and experience the weightlessness of space travel during a simulated shuttle mission; lots of scientific information is interwoven. (Rev: SLJ 1/07)

1536 Durkee, Sarah. *The Fruit Bowl Project* (5–8). 2006, Delacorte LB $17.99 (0-385-90310-3). 160pp. Both an entertaining novel and an inspiration for a writing class, this is the story of a rock star, Nick Thompson, who challenges each member of an 8th-grade writing workshop to write a story or poem containing seven common elements. (Rev: BL 12/1/05; HB 3–4/06; SLJ 1/06; VOYA 4/06)

1537 Ekeland, Ivar. *The Cat in Numberland* (3–5). Illus. by John O'Brien. 2006, Cricket $19.95 (0-8126-2744-X). 59pp. Is zero a number? What is infinity? The answers are found at Hotel Infinity, where there is always room . . . even though all the rooms are full; a clever book introducing complex ideas. (Rev: SLJ 7/06)

1538 Ellison, James Whitfield. *Akeelah and the Bee* (4–6). 2006, Newmarket paper $6.95 (1-55704-729-4). 186pp. A novelization of the movie about Akeelah, an 11-year-old student at a middle school in South Central Los Angeles, who is pushed into participating in her school's spelling bee and wins, qualifying her for the district competition. (Rev: SLJ 11/06)

1539 Fast, Natalie. *The Secret Apartment* (4–6). 2005, Delacorte $14.95 (0-385-74671-7). 192pp. Eleven-year-old Jillian's life isn't happy when her widowed mother marries a publishing executive and moves the family to a ritzy apartment in New York, but when she meets Emily things look up. (Rev: BL 11/1/05; SLJ 12/05)

1540 Friedman, Laurie. *Heart to Heart with Mallory* (2–4). Illus. by Barbara Pollak. 2006, Carolrhoda LB $15.95 (1-57505-932-0). 159pp. In diary format, Mallory worries that Joey's father and Mary Ann's mother will get married, and that Joey and Mary Ann will forget about Mallory. (Rev: SLJ 1/07)

1541 Givner, Joan. *Ellen Fremedon, Journalist* (5–7). 2005, Groundwood $15.95 (0-88899-668-3). 192pp. In this appealing sequel to *Ellen Fremedon* (2004), young Ellen uncovers some shocking stories when she starts a newspaper in quiet Partridge Cove. (Rev: BL 11/1/05; SLJ 2/06)

1542 Hächler, Bruno. *Hubert and the Apple Tree* (2–4). Trans. by Rosemary Lanning. Illus. by Albrecht Rissler. 2006, North-South $15.95 (0-7358-2044-9). 32pp. Hubert loves the apple tree he has grown up with, and is distressed when it is hit by lightning; a challenging, beautifully illustrated, picture book for older children. (Rev: BL 4/15/06)

1543 Hahn, Mary Downing. *Janey and the Famous Author* (2–4). Illus. by Timothy Bush. 2005, Clarion $15.00 (0-618-35408-5). 48pp. Devastated when she gets separated from her class and misses an opportunity to meet her favorite author at a literary festival, Janey is comforted by a kindly older woman. (Rev: BL 12/1/05)

1544 Halpern, Sue. *Introducing . . . Sasha Abramowitz* (5–8). 2005, Farrar $17.00 (0-374-38432-0). 288pp. Eleven-year-old Sasha Marie Curie Abramowitz longs more than anything for a normal life, but her family circumstances — including a brother with Tourette's — make that seem to be an unattainable goal. (Rev: BL 10/1/05; SLJ 12/05; VOYA 12/05)

1545 Han, Jenny. *Shug* (5–8). 2006, Simon & Schuster $14.95 (1-4169-0942-7). 256pp. Annemarie Wilcox, a 7th-grader better known as Shug, faces numerous challenges in addition to the usual middle-school problems: a gorgeous older sister, squabbling parents, a fight with her best friend, and a crush on Mark that doesn't seem to be reciprocated. (Rev: BL 2/15/06; SLJ 5/06)

1546 Harley, Bill. *The Amazing Flight of Darius Frobisher* (4–6). 2006, Peachtree $14.95 (1-56145-381-1). 160pp. When his father disappears on a hot-air balloon trip and is presumed dead, 11-year-old Darius Frobisher is sent to live with his cranky Aunt Inga, a situation lightened when he meets a man who may have built a bicycle that will fly. (Rev: SLJ 12/06)

1547 Harrington, Jane. *Four Things My Geeky-Jock-of-a-Best-Friend Must Do in Europe* (5–8). 2006, Darby Creek LB $15.95 (1-58196-041-7). 160pp. From the European cruise she is taking with her mother, 13-year-old Brady reports via letter on her progress in meeting her must-dos — which include wearing a revealing bikini and meeting a "code-red Euro-hottie." (Rev: SLJ 6/06)

1548 Hemphill, Helen. *Runaround* (5–8). 2007, Front St. $16.95 (978-1-932425-83-3). 117pp. In 1960s Kentucky, motherless 11-year-old Sassy needs more information about love but has trouble finding a source as her Dad is busy with other things, her housekeeper wants her just to act like a young lady, and her sister may be involved with the same handsome neighbor. (Rev: BL 3/1/07*)

1549 Hiaasen, Carl. *Flush* (5–8). 2005, Knopf LB $18.99 (0-375-92182-6). 272pp. Noah Underwood and his younger sister Abbey set out to prove their father was justified in sinking a floating casino because it was polluting. (Rev: BL 8/05; SLJ 9/05)

1550 Hill, David. *Running Hot* (5–8). 2007, Simply Read paper $9.95 (978-1-894965-52-1). 116pp. A group of students clearing forest trees in rural New Zealand suddenly find themselves threatened by a raging fire. (Rev: SLJ 4/07)

1551 Hirsch, Odo. *Have Courage, Hazel Green!* (4–7). 2006, Bloomsbury $15.95 (1-58234-659-3). 256pp. Independent-minded Hazel Green and her friends must mend some fences when her plan to shame a neighbor into apologizing for a blatant act of ethnic prejudice backfires. (Rev: BL 6/1–15/06; SLJ 8/06)

1552 Hobbs, Valerie. *Defiance* (4–7). 2005, Farrar $16.00 (0-374-30847-0). 128pp. An elderly neighbor named Pearl — and her cow — become valuable friends to 11-year-old Toby, who does not want to tell his parents that his cancer is back. (Rev: BL 8/05; SLJ 9/05)

1553 Jaramillo, Ann. *La Línea* (5–8). 2006, Roaring Brook $16.95 (1-59643-154-7). 144pp. Miguel, 15, and his sister Elena, 13, survive a terrifying journey across the border (la linea) from Mexico to California to join their parents. (Rev: BCCB 5/06; BL 3/15/06*; HBG 10/06; LMC 10/06; SLJ 4/06; VOYA 4/06)

1554 Jennings, Richard W. *Stink City* (5–8). 2006, Houghton $16.00 (0-618-55248-0). 192pp. Cade Carlsen, heir to his family's successful — but smelly — catfish bait business, becomes an anti-fishing activist. (Rev: BL 10/15/06)

1555 Kehret, Peg. *Trapped* (4–6). 2006, Dutton $16.99 (0-525-47728-4). 192pp. A cat called Pete participates in this exciting story about efforts to track down the man who's setting illegal traps. (Rev: BL 12/1/06; SLJ 11/06)

1556 Kerrin, Jessica Scott. *Martin Bridge Blazing Ahead!* (2–4). Illus. by Joseph Kelly. 2006, Kids Can $14.95 (1-55337-961-6); paper $4.95 (1-55337-962-4). 109pp. Martin Bridge is back in a funny early chapter book with two new slice-of-life tales: an overnight camping trip with the Junior Badgers and a lawnmower repair session with his dad. (Rev: SLJ 11/06)

1557 Kimmel, Elizabeth Cody. *Lily B. on the Brink of Paris* (5–8). 2006, HarperCollins $15.99 (0-06-083948-1). 192pp. Lily B.'s latest diary entries record the cultural sights of Paris, where the 13-year-old travels with her French class. (Rev: BL 1/1–15/07; SLJ 1/07)

1558 King-Smith, Dick. *The Catlady* (3–5). Illus. by John Eastwood. 2006, Knopf $15.95 (0-375-82985-7). 80pp. In 1901 England, Muriel Ponsonby has a house full of cats, many of whom she believes are reincarnated — including Queen Victoria. (Rev: BL 1/1–15/06; SLJ 1/06)

1559 Kompaneyets, Marc. *The Squishiness of Things* (2–5). Illus. 2005, Knopf $15.95 (0-375-82750-1). 40pp. Hieronymus, an eccentric scholar, embarks on an epic journey to discover the origin of a single strand of hair that appears one morning on his desktop. (Rev: BL 7/05; SLJ 8/05)

1560 Lee, Milly. *Landed* (3–5). Illus. by Yangsook Choi. 2006, Farrar $16.00 (0-374-34314-4). 40pp. Twelve-year-old Sun must study hard to prepare for the tests he will face from American immigration officials. (Rev: BCCB 5/06; BL 1/1–15/06*; HBG 10/06; LMC 11–12/06; SLJ 2/06)

1561 Lord, Cynthia. *Rules* (4–7). 2006, Scholastic $15.99 (0-439-44382-2). 208pp. Catherine is a likable 12-year-old struggling to cope with the family challenges posed by her younger autistic brother. (Rev: BL 2/15/06; SLJ 4/06)

1562 Lowery, Linda. *Truth and Salsa* (4–7). 2006, Peachtree $14.95 (1-59145-366-8). 176pp. Staying with her grandmother in Mexico after her parents separate, Haley makes a new friend and learns about people living on the edge of poverty. (Rev: SLJ 7/06)

1563 Mason, Jane B., and Sarah Hines Stephens. *Bella Baxter and the Itchy Disaster* (2–4). Illus. by John Shelley. 2005, Simon & Schuster paper $3.95 (0-689-86281-4). 80pp. Bella Baxter's special preparations for the arrival of a visiting botanist at the Sea Inn take a dangerous turn. (Rev: BL 12/15/05)

1564 Matthews, L. S. *A Dog for Life* (5–7). 2006, Delacorte $14.95 (0-385-73366-6). 144pp. Tom is sick and Mouse the dog is banished on grounds of possible infection, so John and Mouse, who can communicate psychically, set out to find Mouse a new home. (Rev: BL 12/1/06*; SLJ 10/06)

1565 Morpurgo, Michael. *I Believe in Unicorns* (3–5). Illus. by Gary Blythe. 2006, Candlewick $12.99 (0-7636-3050-0). 80pp. A moving story about a boy's love of books and storytelling and his and others' efforts to save the contents of the library when war arrives. (Rev: BL 12/1/06; SLJ 12/06)

1566 Naylor, Phyllis Reynolds. *Anyone Can Eat Squid!* (2–4). Illus. by Marcy Ramsey. Series: Simply Sarah. 2005, Marshall Cavendish $14.95 (0-7614-5182-X). 76pp. Sarah, hoping to be recognized as "special," tries to help a classmate whose parents own a Chinese restaurant. (Rev: SLJ 7/05)

1567 Naylor, Phyllis Reynolds. *Roxie and the Hooligans* (3–5). Illus. by Alexandra Boiger. 2006, Simon & Schuster $15.95 (1-4169-0243-0). 128pp. Fantasy and reality become blurred in this multilayered story about 9-year-old Roxie Warbler, who applies her book-learned knowledge to survive and conquer when stranded on a desert island with bullies and robbers. (Rev: BL 2/15/06; SLJ 4/06)

1568 Paratore, Coleen Murtagh. *The Cupid Chronicles* (5–9). 2006, Simon & Schuster $15.95 (978-1-4169-0867-8). 207pp. Now that her mother is married, Willa puts her considerable energies into the campaign to save the town library, and somehow romance keeps intruding; a sequel to *The Wedding Planner's Daughter* (2005). (Rev: SLJ 4/07)

1569 Park, Linda Sue. *Project Mulberry* (5–8). 2005, Clarion $16.00 (0-618-47786-1). Working on a silkworm project with her friend Patrick, Korean American Julia also learns about prejudices and friendship. (Rev: BL 8/05; SLJ 5/05)

1570 Parkinson, Siobhan. *Something Invisible* (4–7). 2006, Roaring Brook $16.95 (1-59643-123-7). 160pp. Jake, a self-absorbed 11-year-old, learns a lot about family and friendship over a summer that involves tragedy. (Rev: BL 3/1/06; SLJ 4/06; VOYA 6/06)

1571 Patterson, Nancy Ruth. *The Winner's Walk* (3–5). Illus. by Thomas F. Yezerski. 2006, Farrar $16.00 (0-374-38445-2). 128pp. Nine-year-old Case Callahan, fearful he'll be a loser all his life, takes in a stray dog so talented that it makes the boy look good, but Case soon discovers that the dog's rightful owner is a disabled girl. (Rev: BL 8/06; SLJ 10/06)

1572 Rahlens, Holly-Jane. *Prince William, Maximilian Minsky and Me* (5–8). 2005, Candlewick $15.99 (0-7636-2704-6). 320pp. Thirteen-year-old Nelly, a brainy schoolgirl living in Berlin with her German father and American Jewish mother and totally smitten by Britain's dashing Prince William, is planning her bat mitzvah, worrying about her parents' marriage, and getting her friend Max to teach her basketball; has a glossary of German, Hebrew, and Yiddish words. (Rev: BL 11/1/05; SLJ 1/06)

1573 Regan, Dian Curtis. *The World According to Kaley* (3–5). 2005, Darby Creek $14.99 (1-58196-039-5). 112pp. Kaley's fourth-grade World History assignments include a lot of commentary about her personal life, plus some rather hazy understanding of world history with an emphasis on interpretation. (Rev: BL 11/1/05)

1574 Richter, Jutta. *The Summer of the Pike* (4–7). Trans. by Anna Brailovsky. Illus. by Quint Buchholz. 2006, Milkweed $16.95 (1-57131-671-X); paper $6.95 (1-57131-672-8). 91pp. Anna, Daniel, and Lucas, who live on the grounds of a German manor, spend a difficult summer as Anna wishes for a closer relationship with her mother and the boys' mother is slowly dying of cancer. (Rev: BL 1/1–15/07; SLJ 12/06)

1575 Roberts, Diane. *Puppet Pandemonium* (3–5). 2006, Delacorte $15.95 (0-385-73309-7). 115pp. Still recovering from the trauma of moving from Seattle to small-town Texas, fifth-grader Baker gains recognition with his ventriloquist skills. (Rev: SLJ 12/06)

1576 Robinson, Sharon. *Safe at Home* (4–7). 2006, Scholastic $16.99 (0-439-67197-3). 151pp. Still shaken by the sudden death of his father, 10-year-old Elijah Breeze must cope with culture shock when his mother moves him from suburban Connecticut to New York City's Harlem and he attends a coed summer baseball camp. (Rev: SLJ 10/06)

1577 Sachar, Louis. *Small Steps* (5–8). 2006, Delacorte LB $18.99 (0-385-90333-2). 272pp. Two years after being released from Camp Green Lake, African American 17-year-old Armpit is home in Texas and trying to find good work, which is hard when you have a record, when X-Ray turns up with an interesting proposal; a sequel to *Holes* (1998). (Rev: BL 1/1–15/06*; SLJ 1/06; VOYA 2/06)

1578 San Souci, Daniel. *Space Station Mars* (1–4). Illus. by author. Series: A Clubhouse Book. 2005, Tricycle $15.95 (1-58246-142-2). When they find a strange-looking rock in their neighbor's yard, the San Souci brothers and their friends become convinced that it's a meteor from Mars; a sequel to *The Dangerous Snake and Reptile Club* (2004). (Rev: SLJ 10/05)

1579 Schwartz, Ellen. *Stealing Home* (4–7). 2006, Tundra $8.95 (0-88776-765-6). 217pp. Joey, a biracial 9-year-old baseball fan living in the Bronx, is orphaned with his mother's death and moved to live with his Jewish maternal grandparents in Brooklyn, where he must cope with a startlingly different world. (Rev: BL 9/1/06; SLJ 10/06)

1580 Shafer, Audrey. *The Mailbox* (5–7). 2006, Delacorte $15.95 (0-385-73344-5). 178pp. Twelve-year-old Gabe, who has been happy with Uncle Vernon after years in foster care, is shocked when he comes home to find Uncle Vernon dead. (Rev: SLJ 11/06)

1581 Wallace, Karen. *Something Slimy on Primrose Drive* (2–4). Illus. by Helen Flook. 2006, Stone Arch LB $15.95 (1-59889-113-8). 65pp. Pearl Wolfbane hopes life will become more normal when her Munsters-like family moves to Primrose Drive, but her new, conservative neighbors surprise her when they all join forces to track down a thief. (Rev: BL 11/15/06)

1582 Whitehouse, Howard. *The Strictest School in the World: Being the Tale of a Clever Girl, a Rubber Boy and a Collection of Flying Machines, Mostly Broken* (5–8). Illus. by Bill Slavin. 2006, Kids Can $16.95 (1-55337-882-2); paper $6.95 (1-55337-883-0). 252pp. Raised in India where her father is a British colonial official, Emmaline Cayley is upset when her parents send her to a strict school in England, so she hatches a plan to escape; an appealing blend of humor, fantasy, and Gothic atmosphere. (Rev: SLJ 11/06)

1583 Woodson, Jacqueline. *Feathers* (4–6). 2007, Putnam $15.99 (978-0-399-23989-2). 118pp. When a white boy joins Frannie's 1971 sixth-grade class, and is sometimes called the "Jesus Boy," Frannie examines her own faith and the problems in her home. (Rev: BL 0-399-23989-8; SLJ 4/07*)

Adventure and Mystery

1584 Abela, Deborah. *Mission: The Nightmare Vortex* (4–6). Illus. by George O'Connor. Series: Spy Force. 2005, Simon & Schuster $9.95 (0-689-87359-X). 246pp. Eleven-year-old Max Remy and her best friend Linden, Spy Force agents, spring into action to foil the evil plans of Mr. Blue to activate a dormant volcano and destroy all the spies at a secret awards ceremony. (Rev: HBG 4/06; SLJ 4/06)

1585 Adler, David A. *Cam Jansen and the Secret Service Mystery* (2–4). Illus. by Susanna Natti. 2006, Viking $13.99 (0-670-06092-5). 64pp. When the pearls belonging to a school donor are stolen, Cam Jansen, girl detective, teams up with the Secret Service to try to track them down. (Rev: BL 10/15/06; HBG 4/07)

1586 Adler, David A. *Cam Jansen and the Valentine Baby Mystery* (2–4). Illus. by Susanna Natti. Series: Cam Jansen. 2005, Viking $13.99 (0-670-06009-7). 80pp. Girl detective Cam Jansen and her friend Eric investigate the disappearance of Eric's mother's purse from a hospital waiting room; the 25th installment in this popular series. (Rev: BL 1/1–15/06; HBG 4/06)

1587 Allison, Jennifer. *Gilda Joyce: The Ladies of the Lake* (5–8). 2006, Dutton $15.99 (0-525-47693-8). 256pp. Thirteen-year-old Gilda Joyce — introduced in *Gilda Joyce: Psychic Investigator* (2005) — uses all her psychic abilities to unravel the mystery surrounding a drowning death at her school. (Rev: BL 10/15/06; HBG 4/07; SLJ 9/06)

1588 Baccalario, Pierdomenico. *The Door to Time* (4–6). Illus. by Iacopo Bruno. Series: Ulysses Moore. 2006, Scholastic $12.99 (0-439-77438-1). 240pp. After moving to a home on the English coast, Jason and Julia, 11-year-old twins, along with a new friend, try to unravel the mysteries surrounding their new house. (Rev: BL 12/15/05; SLJ 1/06)

1589 Bateman, Colin. *Bring Me the Head of Oliver Plunkett* (4–7). 2005, Delacorte LB $17.99 (0-385-90269-7). 272pp. In this zany sequel to *Running with the Reservoir Pups* (2004), set in Belfast, Northern Ireland, 12-year-old Eddie deals with school, young romance, some loony adults, and a missing preserved head of a martyr. (Rev: BL 10/15/05; SLJ 11/05)

1590 Biedrzycki, David. *Ace Lacewing: Bug Detective* (2–4). Illus. 2005, Charlesbridge $15.95 (1-57091-569-5). 40pp. Full of funny wordplay and cartoon-style art, this is the story of bug detective Ace Lacewing's efforts to find the missing Queenie Bee. (Rev: BL 9/1/05; SLJ 8/05)

1591 Bruchac, Joseph. *The Return of Skeleton Man* (5–8). Illus. by Sally Comport. 2006, HarperCollins $15.99 (0-06-058090-9). 144pp. Molly, the Mohawk teen who survived a terrifying kidnapping in *Skeleton Man* (2001), discovers her nemesis is back. (Rev: BL 9/15/06; SLJ 8/06)

1592 Buckey, Sarah Masters. *The Stolen Sapphire: A Samantha Mystery* (2–4). Series: American Girl Mysteries. 2006, American Girl paper $6.95 (1-59369-099-1). 181pp. Traveling to Europe on an ocean liner in the early 1900s, Samantha and her adopted sister Nellie try to prove the innocence of their French tutor, who's been accused of stealing a valuable gem. (Rev: SLJ 4/06)

1593 Buckley, Michael. *The Sisters Grimm: The Unusual Suspects* (4–6). Illus. by Peter Ferguson. 2005, Abrams $14.95 (0-8109-5926-7). 290pp. Sabrina and Daphne Grimm, descendants of Wilhelm and living in a community full of fairy-tale figures, investigate the mysterious death of Sabrina's teacher; a multilayered, fast-paced second installment in the series. (Rev: SLJ 1/06; VOYA 8/06)

1594 Byars, Betsy. *The Black Tower* (4–6). 2006, Viking $10.99 (0-670-06174-3). 144pp. Herculeah Jones tries to unravel the suspenseful mystery surrounding the dark past of a neighborhood mansion. (Rev: BL 10/15/06; SLJ 12/06)

1595 Byars, Betsy. *King of Murder* (4–6). Series: A Herculeah Jones Mystery. 2006, Sleuth $10.99 (0-670-06065-8). 115pp. Herculeah finds herself in grave danger as she tries to unmask suspected murderer Mathias King. (Rev: SLJ 6/06)

1596 Casanova, Mary. *Jess* (3–5). Series: American Girl Today. 2005, Pleasant paper $6.95 (1-59369-016-9). 126pp. While accompanying her parents on an archaeological expedition to Belize, 10-year-old Jess meets a new friend who invites her on an eco-adventure in the nearby rain forest; factual information is interwoven and an afterword adds relevance. (Rev: SLJ 9/06)

1597 Catanese, P. W. *The Thief and the Beanstalk* (4–6). 2005, Simon & Schuster paper $4.99 (0-689-87173-2). 272pp. An exciting adventure in which Nick, with greed in his heart, climbs a giant beanstalk and finds at the top the giant's wife and her evil sons — and a moral dilemma. (Rev: SLJ 7/05)

1598 Cirrone, Dorian. *The Missing Silver Dollar* (2–4). Illus. by Liza Woodruff. Series: Lindy Blues. 2006, Marshall Cavendish $14.95 (0-7614-5284-2). 74pp. Lindy Blues, a fourth grader and self-appointed investigative reporter for her neighborhood, tracks down a neighbor's missing silver dollar. (Rev: SLJ 9/06)

1599 Clements, Andrew. *Room One* (3–5). Illus. by Chris Blair. 2006, Simon & Schuster $15.95 (0-689-86686-0). 176pp. Ted, the only 6th grader in his one-room school, discovers a mystery while delivering papers one morning in this story set in rural Nebraska. (Rev: BL 5/1/06; SLJ 7/06)

1600 Colfer, Eoin. *Half Moon Investigations* (4–6). 2006, Hyperion $16.95 (0-7868-4957-6). 304pp. Fletcher ("Half") Moon, an aspiring private investigator, finds himself in all sorts of trouble when pretty April Devereux asks him to nab a thief in their Irish town; this story is full of jargon and humor. (Rev: BL 5/1/06; SLJ 4/06)

1601 Copeland, Mark. *The Bundle at Blackthorpe Heath* (4–7). 2006, Houghton $15.00 (0-618-56302-4). 224pp. With the help of a spyglass he receives as a birthday present, 12-year-old Arthur Piper uncovers a conspiracy to undermine his grandfather's traveling insect circus. (Rev: BL 6/1–15/06; SLJ 7/06)

1602 Couloumbis, Audrey. *Maude March on the Run! or, Trouble Is Her Middle Name* (5–7). 2007, Random $15.99 (0-375-83246-7). 308pp. In this action-packed sequel to *The Misadventures of Maude March*, 16-year-old Maude and her 12-year-old sister, both orphans, are pursued by the law after Maude is unjustly accused of multiple crimes. (Rev: SLJ 1/07)

1603 Curtis, Christopher Paul. *Mr. Chickee's Funny Money* (4–6). Series: Flint Future Detectives. 2005, Random $15.95 (0-385-32772-2). 160pp. Nine-year-old Steven and his friends try to find out if the quadrillion dollar bill he was given by his blind neighbor is the real thing in this fast-paced and humorous mystery. A sequel is *Mr. Chickee's Messy Mission* (2007). (Rev: BL 8/05; SLJ 10/05*)

1604 Dale, Anna. *Dawn Undercover* (4–7). 2005, Bloomsbury $16.95 (1-58234-657-7). 350pp. Although she longs to have others notice her, 11-year-old Dawn Buckle discovers that her virtual invisibility makes her an ideal spy for the S.H.H. (Strictly Hush-Hush) agency. (Rev: BL 10/15/05; SLJ 12/05)

1605 Doder, Joshua. *A Dog Called Grk* (5–8). 2007, Delacorte $14.99 (978-0-385-73359-5). 272pp. In this fast-paced adventure, 12-year-old Londoner Tim, trying to help the Stanislavian ambassador's family — and dog — becomes enmeshed in international political intrigue. (Rev: BL 1/1–15/07)

1606 Doyle, Bill. *Nabbed! The 1925 Journal of G. Codd Fitzmorgan* (4–8). Illus. by Anthony Lewis. Series: Crime Through Time. 2006, Little, Brown paper $5.99 (0-316-05737-1). 125pp. When the groom-to-be disappears from an engagement party on a secluded island during Prohibition, 14-year-old G. Codd Fitzmorgan takes it upon himself to find him and also bust up a bootlegging ring; short chapters resemble journals, with sketches, clippings, and photographs. (Rev: SLJ 8/06)

1607 Doyle, Bill. *Swindled! The 1906 Journal of Fitz Morgan* (4–8). Illus. by Brian Dow. Series: Crime Through Time. 2006, Little, Brown paper $5.99 (0-316-05736-3). 139pp. While traveling by train from New York City to San Francisco in 1906, 14-year-old Fitz Morgan and his traveling companion, Justine Pinkerton, try to figure out why so many of their fellow passengers are being poisoned; the short chapters resemble journals, with sketches, clippings, and photographs. (Rev: SLJ 8/06)

1608 Draper, Penny. *Terror at Turtle Mountain* (4–7). 2006, Coteau paper $7.95 (1-55050-343-X). 160pp. In Canada's Northwest Territory in 1903, a 13-year-old girl participates in frantic efforts to rescue victims of a rock slide; an action-packed novel based on a real-life incident. (Rev: SLJ 10/06)

1609 Ernst, Kathleen. *Secrets in the Hills: A Josefina Mystery* (4–7). Series: American Girl Mystery. 2006, Pleasant $10.95 (1-59369-098-3); paper $6.95 (1-59369-097-5). 184pp. In 1820s New Mexico, Josefina decides to investigate the possibility that there is treasure buried near her home. (Rev: BL 5/15/06; SLJ 4/06)

1610 Fardell, John. *The Flight of the Silver Turtle* (5–8). 2006, Putnam $15.99 (0-399-24382-8). 256pp. The same crew from *The 7 Professors of the Far North* (2005) must find an antigravity machine before the villains discover it, in an exciting chase around Europe. (Rev: BL 12/15/06; SLJ 10/06)

1611 Fardell, John. *The 7 Professors of the Far North* (5–8). Illus. 2005, Penguin $14.99 (0-399-24381-X). 224pp. Three plucky British children are on a mission to rescue six elderly scientists — and the human race — and they have only three days to get to the island fortress in the middle of the Arctic Ocean. (Rev: BL 1/1–15/06; SLJ 12/05)

1612 Freeman, Martha. *Who Stole Halloween?* (4–6). 2005, Holiday $16.95 (0-8234-1962-2). 232pp. Alex, boy detective, asks his friend Yasmeen to help him track down a missing cat named Halloween. (Rev: BL 8/05; SLJ 10/05)

1613 Gaetz, Dayle Campbell. *Alberta Alibi* (4–6). 2005, Orca paper $6.95 (1-55143-404-0). When Sheila's divorced father is accused of sabotaging a housing development near his Canadian ranch, the 12-year-old and her friends Katie and Rusty try to prove him innocent and identify the real culprits; the third installment in a series. (Rev: SLJ 4/06; VOYA 4/06)

1614 Givner, Joan. *Ellen Fremedon, Volunteer* (4–6). 2007, Groundwood $16.95 (978-0-88899-743-2). 184pp. Thirteen-year-old Ellen, at loose ends with her best friend away at summer camp, volunteers to help out a local retirement center and gets drawn into the mystery surrounding the disappearance of a new friend's mother. (Rev: BL 4/1/07)

1615 Gliori, Debi. *Pure Dead Batty* (4–7). Series: Pure Dead. 2006, Knopf $15.95 (0-375-83316-1). 304pp. In the fifth volume of this popular series, Mrs. McLachlan, the Strega-Borgia family's nanny,

disappears, and Don Luciano is falsely accused of her murder. (Rev: BL 8/06; SLJ 8/06)

1616 Gold, Maya. *Harriet the Spy, Double Agent* (4–7). Series: Harriet the Spy. 2005, Delacorte LB $17.99 (0-385-90294-8). 160pp. Harriet the Spy is back, spying on her mysterious new classmate Annie in this installment by Gold. (Rev: BL 9/1/05; SLJ 1/06)

1617 Gordon, Amy. *Return to Gill Park* (5–8). Series: Gill Park. 2006, Holiday $16.95 (0-8234-1998-3). 234pp. This oddball sequel to *The Gorillas of Gill Park* (2006) finds Willy Wilson on the trail of vandals determined to destroy the beauty of the park he now owns. (Rev: BL 5/15/06; SLJ 4/06)

1618 Graf, Mike. *Bryce and Zion: Danger in the Narrows* (5–8). Illus. by Marjorie Leggitt. Series: Adventures with the Parkers. 2006, Fulcrum paper $9.95 (1-55591-532-9). 94pp. On a vacation in the national parks of southern Utah, 10-year-old twins James and Morgan Parker learn about the delicate ecology of the area, rescue an injured hiker, and come to the aid of their father when he slips and falls in the Narrows; a fact-filled adventure story with full-color photographs and nature sketches. (Rev: SLJ 12/06)

1619 Greenburg, Dan. *Treachery and Betrayal at Jolly Days* (4–6). Illus. by Scott M. Fischer. Series: Secrets of the Dripping Fang. 2006, Harcourt $11.95 (0-15-205463-4). 144pp. Once again fleeing the evil Mandible sisters, the Schluffmuffin twins find themselves in a swamp and encounter a zombie who just might be their long-lost father. (Rev: BL 2/15/06; SLJ 6/06)

1620 Higson, Charlie. *Blood Fever: A James Bond Adventure* (5–8). Series: Young Bond. 2006, Hyperion $16.95 (0-7868-3662-8). 347pp. Even at 13, Bond is having adventures: this one finds him on the island of Sardinia, caught up in an art-theft mystery and rescuing a girl in peril. (Rev: SLJ 6/06)

1621 Hirsch, Odo. *Something's Fishy, Hazel Green* (4–6). 2005, Bloomsbury $15.95 (1-58234-928-2). 208pp. Hazel Green comes to the aid of the local fishmonger when two of his prized lobsters are stolen; a funny sequel to *Hazel Green* (2003). (Rev: BL 7/05; SLJ 8/05)

1622 Holm, Jennifer, and Jonathan Hamel. *You Only Have Nine Lives* (3–5). Illus. by Brad Weinman. Series: The Stink Files. 2005, HarperCollins $14.99 (0-06-052985-7). 128pp. Traveling to France as the winner of a cat food competition, cat sleuth Mr. Stink is mistaken as a prince and uncovers secrets about his own origins. (Rev: SLJ 12/05)

1623 Horowitz, Anthony. *Alex Rider: The Gadgets* (5–8). Illus. by John Lawson. 2006, Philomel $15.99 (0-399-24486-7). 44pp. A look at all the gadgets used in the first five Alex Rider mysteries — including such wonders as a radio mouth brace, exploding ear stud, and pizza delivery assassin kit — with diagrams and details of how they were used. (Rev: BL 4/1/06; SLJ 4/06)

1624 Horowitz, Anthony. *South by Southeast: A Diamond Brothers Mystery* (4–7). Series: Diamond Brothers. 2005, Philomel $16.99 (0-399-24155-8); paper $5.99 (0-14-240374-1). 148pp. Hapless private eye Tim Diamond and his brother Nick find themselves drawn into a labyrinthine mystery after a visit from a stranger. (Rev: BL 12/1/05; SLJ 12/05)

1625 Ibbotson, Eva. *The Beasts of Clawstone Castle* (5–8). Illus. by Kevin Hawkes. 2006, Dutton $16.99 (0-525-47719-5). 243pp. In this suspenseful story set at Britain's Clawstone Castle, famous for its herd of white cattle but facing hard times, siblings Madlyn and Rollo suggest adding a few ghosts to attract tourists; then just as things seem about to take a turn for the better, the cattle are kidnapped. (Rev: SLJ 11/06)

1626 Johns, Linda. *Hannah West in Deep Water* (5–8). 2006, Puffin/Sleuth paper $5.99 (0-14-240700-3). 160pp. Hannah investigates environmental shenanigans while she and her mother are house-sitting a houseboat and a dog. (Rev: BL 12/15/06)

1627 Johns, Linda. *Hannah West in the Belltown Towers: A Mystery* (5–8). 2006, Sleuth Puffin paper $5.99 (0-14-240637-6). 160pp. Hannah, an adopted Chinese girl with lots of nerve and curiosity, moves with her mother to Seattle and soon finds herself embroiled in an art theft. (Rev: BL 5/1/06)

1628 Johnson, Henry, and Paul Hoppe. *Travis and Freddy's Adventures in Vegas* (5–8). 2006, Dutton $15.99 (0-525-47646-6). 176pp. A lighthearted, fast-paced adventure in which preteens Travis and Freddy head to Las Vegas to win enough money to save Travis's home; there they win big but soon find they have the mob at their heels. (Rev: BL 2/15/06; SLJ 4/06; VOYA 4/06)

1629 Joosse, Barbara M. *Dead Guys Talk: A Wild Willie Mystery* (3–5). Illus. by Abby Carter. 2006, Clarion $15.00 (0-618-30666-8). 112pp. A puzzle at the cemetery tasks the nerve and sleuthing skills of Scarface Detectives Willie, Lucy, and Kyle. (Rev: BL 5/1/06; SLJ 9/06)

1630 Keane, Dave. *The Haunted Toolshed* (2–5). Illus. by author. Series: Joe Sherlock, Kid Detective. 2006, HarperCollins $15.99 (0-06-076189-X); paper $3.99 (0-06-076188-1). 120pp. Goofy boy detective Joe Sherlock gets to the bottom of a tricky mystery in this first installment in a series that will entertain the flatulence gang. (Rev: SLJ 7/06)

1631 Korman, Gordon. *The Abduction* (4–7). Series: Kidnapped. 2006, Scholastic paper $4.99 (0-439-84777-X). 138pp. A fast-paced thriller, the opening volume of a new series, in which 15-year-old Aiden works with the FBI to rescue his 11-year-old sister

Meg, who was abducted while on her way home from school and is meanwhile resisting her captors. The second volume is *The Search* (2006). (Rev: BL 8/06; SLJ 9/06)

1632 Lafevers, R. L. *Theodosia and the Serpents of Chaos* (5–8). Illus. by Yoko Tanaka. 2007, Houghton $16.00 (978-0-618-75638-4). 344pp. In the early 20th century, precocious 11-year-old Theodosia finds herself embroiled in a supernatural mystery involving Egyptian artifacts. (Rev: BL 5/1/07*; SLJ 4/07)

1633 Lalicki, Tom. *Danger in the Dark: A Houdini and Nate Mystery* (3–6). 2006, Farrar $14.95 (0-374-31680-5). 192pp. With the help of Harry Houdini, 12-year-old Nate plans to uncover suspected swindling by the strange man who's been holding séances with Nate's rich great-aunt in this historical mystery set in 1911 Manhattan. (Rev: BL 11/15/06; SLJ 10/06)

1634 Lasky, Kathryn. *Born to Rule* (3–6). Series: Camp Princess. 2006, HarperCollins $15.99 (0-06-058761-X). 143pp. This first book in the Camp Princess series has Princess Alicia of All the Belgravias reluctantly attending princess training camp and stumbling upon a ghost story. (Rev: SLJ 5/06)

1635 Latta, Sara. *Stella Brite and the Dark Matter Mystery* (2–4). Illus. by Meredith Johnson. 2006, Charlesbridge paper $6.95 (1-57091-884-8). 32pp. To give their fledgling detective agency a higher profile, Stella Brite and her brother Max try to unravel the mystery of invisible dark matter in the universe. (Rev: SLJ 4/06)

1636 McCall, Josh. *The Blackout Gang* (5–8). 2006, Penguin paper $10.99 (1-59514-050-6). 192pp. An exciting New York City mystery in which three young sleuths must combat an evil schemer who has plunged the city into darkness. (Rev: BL 7/06; SLJ 7/06)

1637 McCall Smith, Alexander. *The Cowgirl Aunt of Harriet Bean* (2–4). Illus. by Laura Rankin. 2006, Bloomsbury $9.95 (1-58234-977-0). 67pp. Out West to meet her Aunt Formica for the first time, girl detective Harriet Bean, accompanied by Aunts Thessalonika and Japonica, uses her sleuthing skills to help track down some cattle rustlers. (Rev: SLJ 1/07)

1638 McFadden, Deanna. *Robinson Crusoe: Retold from the Daniel Defoe Original* (4–7). Illus. by Jamel Akib. Series: Classic Starts. 2006, Sterling $4.95 (1-4027-2664-3). 160pp. The 1719 original text is retold in brief, accessible sentences that portray Crusoe and Friday as equals. (Rev: BL 2/15/06)

1639 Mack, Tracy, and Michael Citrin. *The Fall of the Amazing Zalindas* (4–7). Illus. by Greg Ruth. Series: Sherlock Holmes and the Baker Street Irregulars. 2006, Scholastic $16.99 (0-439-82836-8). 256pp. Sherlock Holmes calls on a gang of street children to help him investigate the mysterious deaths of a family of trapeze artists. (Rev: BL 11/1/06; SLJ 1/07)

1640 Marsh, Carole. *The Case of the Crybaby Cowboy* (1–3). Illus. by Cecil Anderson. Series: Three Amigos. 2006, Gallopade paper $3.99 (0-635-06166-X). 54pp. The Three Amigos, boy detectives, try to find out why one of their classmates — dressed like a cowboy — cries all the time. Also use *The Riddle of the Ooglie Booglie* (2006). (Rev: SLJ 11/06)

1641 Mason, Jane B., and Sarah Hines Stephens. *Bella Baxter and the Lighthouse Mystery* (2–4). Illus. by John Shelley. Series: Bella Baxter. 2006, Simon & Schuster paper $3.99 (0-689-86282-2). 80pp. Bella Baxter, excited when a popular filmmaker pays a visit to her family's inn, volunteers to guide him to a local lighthouse that may be haunted. (Rev: BL 2/15/06)

1642 Mass, Wendy. *Jeremy Fink and the Meaning of Life* (5–8). 2006, Little, Brown $15.99 (0-316-05829-7). 290pp. Just before his 13th birthday, Jeremy Fink receives a package from his dead father containing a locked box but no keys; Jeremy and Liz set off on a tour of New York City in search of the keys and meet a number of characters with different views on the meaning of life. (Rev: BL 12/15/06; SLJ 12/06)

1643 Melville, Herman. *Moby-Dick* (5–9). Illus. by Patrick Benson. 2006, Candlewick $21.99 (978-0-7636-3018-8). 192pp. The classic whaling adventure story in a beautifully illustrated, abridged version. (Rev: SLJ 4/07)

1644 Miller, Kirsten. *Kiki Strike: Inside the Shadow City* (5–8). 2006, Bloomsbury $16.95 (1-58234-960-6). 250pp. A complex story featuring adventurous and multitalented 12-year-old girls exploring the subterranean levels of New York City. (Rev: BL 7/06; HBG 10/06; LMC 10/06; SLJ 6/06; VOYA 8/06)

1645 Moodie, Craig. *The Sea Singer* (5–8). 2005, Roaring Brook $16.95 (1-59643-050-8). 176pp. Upset that his father left him behind, 12-year-old Finn stows away on Leif Eriksson's ship, which will follow his father's route to Vineland. (Rev: BL 8/05; SLJ 8/05; VOYA 2/06)

1646 Mowll, Joshua. *Operation Typhoon Shore* (5–8). Illus. by Joshua Mowll, et al. Series: The Guild of Specialists. 2006, Candlewick $15.99 (978-0-7636-3122-2). 277pp. In 1920, siblings Doug and Becca sail through a typhoon on their uncle's ship while seeking the gyrolabe that may offer a clue to their parents' disappearance; the second installment in the series. (Rev: SLJ 3/07)

1647 Nordin, Sofia. *In the Wild* (4–7). Trans. from Swedish by Maria Lundin. 2005, Groundwood $15.95 (0-88899-648-9). 119pp. Set in Sweden, this is an adventure story featuring 6th-grade outcast Amanda and bully Philip, who become lost and must rely on their own resources to survive. (Rev: SLJ 10/05)

1648 Obrist, Jürg. *Complex Cases: Three Major Mysteries for You to Solve* (3–6). Illus. by author. Series: Mini-Mysteries. 2006, Millbrook LB $23.93 (0-7613-3419-X); paper $6.95 (0-8225-5975-7). 93pp. This new volume in the series presents three longer mysteries, challenging readers to solve them using deduction and the clues in the many illustrations. (Rev: SLJ 6/06)

1649 Oliver, Andrew. *If Photos Could Talk* (4–7). Series: A Sam and Stephanie Mystery. 2005, Adams-Pomeroy paper $12.95 (0-9661009-6-4). 259pp. Twelve-year-olds Sam and Stephanie investigate the disappearance of an elderly man in their small Wisconsin town in this well-plotted novel. (Rev: SLJ 1/06)

1650 Potter, Ellen. *Pish Posh* (4–6). 2006, Philomel $15.99 (0-399-23995-2). 240pp. Eleven-year-old Clara Frankofile is a horrible snob who rules the roost at her parents' posh New York City restaurant, but she finds herself in new territory when she investigates a mystery about the soup chef. (Rev: BL 2/1/06; SLJ 4/06)

1651 Pullman, Philip. *The Scarecrow and His Servant* (4–6). Illus. by Peter Bailey. 2005, Knopf $15.95 (0-375-81531-7). 240pp. A multilayered tale in which a scarecrow and his orphan-boy servant embark on a series of adventures. (Rev: BCCB 9/05; BL 9/1/05*; HB 9–10/05; LMC 2/06; SLJ 9/05)

1652 Quattlebaum, Mary. *Jackson Jones and the Curse of the Outlaw Rose* (3–5). 2006, Delacorte $14.95 (0-385-73349-6). 112pp. Jackson and friends, who garden in an inner-city community patch, tussle with mystery when a rose twig, removed from an old cemetery, seems to bring bad luck; the third installment in the series. (Rev: BL 1/1–15/07; SLJ 11/06)

1653 Richards, Justin. *Shadow Beast* (5–8). Series: Invisible Detectives. 2005, Putnam $10.99 (0-399-24314-3). 192pp. Parallel stories feature exciting adventures in the sewers of 1930s London and contemporary beasts that may be related. (Rev: BL 8/05; SLJ 10/05)

1654 Richardson, V. A. *The Moneylender's Daughter* (5–8). 2006, Bloomsbury $17.95 (1-58234-885-5). 300pp. In this exciting sequel to *The House of Windjammer* (2003), Adam Windjammer sets sail for America, finds himself burdened with more responsibility on the death of his uncle, and is preoccupied with thoughts of Jade van Helsen, daughter of the man who brought his family to the brink of ruin. (Rev: BL 6/1–15/06; SLJ 9/06)

1655 Roberts, Willo Davis. *The One Left Behind* (4–7). 2006, Simon & Schuster $16.95 (0-689-85075-1). 144pp. Mandy, an 11-year-old mourning her dead twin sister, is accidentally left home alone for the weekend and pluckily investigates when there's a break-in downstairs. (Rev: BL 4/1/06; SLJ 5/06)

1656 Rossell, Judith. *Jack Jones and the Pirate Curse* (4–7). 2007, Walker $15.95 (978-0-8027-9661-5). 176pp. Jack inherits the family curse and finds himself suddenly facing a band of vengeful pirates he knows he must fight with brain rather than brawn. (Rev: BL 4/1/07)

1657 Selznick, Brian. *The Invention of Hugo Cabret* (4–9). Illus. by author. 2007, Scholastic $22.99 (978-0-439-81378-5). 531pp. In 1930s Paris a young apprentice clock keeper, an orphan who struggles to make his way in life, finds himself drawn into a complex mystery that threatens the anonymity he treasures; part graphic novel, part flip book, the design is as compelling as the story. (Rev: BL 1/1–15/07; SLJ 3/07*)

1658 Shahan, Sherry. *Death Mountain* (5–8). 2005, Peachtree $15.95 (1-56145-353-6). 178pp. In this gripping thriller, 14-year-old Erin uses her survival skills to rescue her new friend Mae and navigate their way through a mountain wilderness to safety. (Rev: SLJ 11/05; VOYA 2/06)

1659 Simmons, Alex, and Bill McCay. *Buffalo Bill Wanted!* (4–6). Series: The Raven League. 2007, Sleuth $10.99 (978-1-59514-073-9). 202pp. When a police officer is shot and scalped during a London visit by Buffalo Bill's Wild West show and suspicion falls on Cody and members of his troupe, the mystery-solving Raven League — children who assist Sherlock Holmes — takes on the case. (Rev: SLJ 2/07)

1660 Simmons, Alex, and Bill McCay. *The Raven League* (4–6). 2006, Sleuth $10.99 (1-59514-072-7). 188pp. Sherlock Holmes is missing and Archie Wiggins has been kicked out the Baker Street Irregulars - the gang of street urchins who assist the great detective — in this mystery set in the gritty streets of London. (Rev: SLJ 7/06)

1661 Simner, Janni Lee. *Secret of the Three Treasures* (3–5). 2006, Holiday $16.95 (0-8234-1914-2). 134pp. The irrepressible Tiernay, emulating her novelist father's heroes, sets out with her mother's boyfriend's son in search of buried treasure and finds herself in real danger; a humorous multilayered story that also tackles bullying and genealogy. (Rev: BL 5/1/06; SLJ 8/06)

1662 Singh, Vandana. *Younguncle Comes to Town* (3–5). Illus. by B. M. Kamath. 2006, Viking $14.99 (0-670-06051-8). 112pp. Three siblings in northern India are captivated by the real-life adventures of Younguncle, their father's youngest brother. (Rev: BL 4/1/06; SLJ 5/06)

1663 Smith, Roland. *Jack's Run* (5–8). 2005, Hyperion $15.99 (0-7868-5592-4). 288pp. Last seen adapting to being in the witness protection program in *Zach's Lie* (2001), Jack and Joanne are now in danger after Joanne has blown their cover in this fast-paced, suspenseful story. (Rev: BL 8/05; SLJ 12/05; VOYA 10/05)

1664 Snyder, Zilpha Keatley. *The Treasures of Weatherby* (4–6). 2007, Simon & Schuster $15.95 (978-1-4169-1398-6). 213pp. Harleigh J. Weatherby, IV, an undersized 12-year-old, makes friends with Allegra, a mysterious stranger, and together they set out to foil a plot to steal the long-lost Weatherby treasure. (Rev: SLJ 2/07)

1665 Springer, Nancy. *The Case of the Missing Marquess: An Enola Holmes Mystery* (5–8). 2006, Philomel paper $10.99 (0-399-24304-6). 224pp. Enola Holmes, the much younger sister of Sherlock and Mycroft, embarks on a search for her mother, who disappears on Enola's 14th birthday. (Rev: BCCB 2/06; BL 12/1/05*; HBG 10/06; SLJ 2/06*)

1666 Stenhouse, Ted. *Murder on the Ridge* (5–8). 2006, Kids Can $16.95 (1-55337-892-X); paper $6.95 (1-55337-893-8). 240pp. Will and Arthur, a white boy and an Indian boy who are friends despite the prejudices of 1950s Canada, investigate a World War I mystery in the latest installment in the series that started with *Across the Steel River* (2001) and *A Dirty Deed* (2003). (Rev: BL 5/15/06)

1667 Stevenson, Robert Louis. *Treasure Island* (5–9). Adapted and illus. by Tim Hamilton. Series: Puffin Graphics. 2005, Puffin paper $9.99 (0-142-40470-5). 176pp. Robert Louis Stevenson's adventure classic springs to life in this striking graphic novel adaptation that remains faithful to the original text. (Rev: SLJ 11/05)

1668 Strickland, Brad. *The House Where Nobody Lived* (5–8). Series: Lewis Barnavelt. 2006, Dial $16.99 (0-8037-3148-5). 176pp. Lewis befriends David, whose family has moved into a creepy, long-abandoned house, which may be haunted; with help from Uncle Jonathan and a neighborhood witch, Lewis confronts magic and danger. (Rev: BL 1/1–15/07; SLJ 1/07)

1669 Taylor, Cora. *Murder in Mexico* (4–7). Series: The Spy Who Wasn't There. 2007, Coteau paper $7.95 (978-1-55050-353-1). 162pp. In this second, fast-paced installment in the mystery series, twins Jennifer and Maggie are visiting ruins in the Yucatan when Jennifer must use her ability to become invisible to solve a crime. (Rev: SLJ 4/07)

1670 Trout, Richard E. *Czar of Alaska: The Cross of Charlemagne* (5–8). Series: MacGregor Family Adventure. 2005, Pelican $15.95 (1-58980-328-0). 248pp. In volume four of the series, the five Mac-

Gregors travel to Alaska to assess the environmental impact of drilling for oil and become entangled with ecoterrorists and priests seeking an ancient cross. (Rev: SLJ 12/05)

1671 Umansky, Kaye. *The Silver Spoon of Solomon Snow* (4–6). 2005, Candlewick $14.99 (0-7636-2792-5). 304pp. Ten-year-old Solomon Snow, left as a foundling at the home of Ma and Pa Scubbins, sets out to unravel the mystery surrounding his birth and acquires some new and eccentric friend along the way. (Rev: BL 11/1/05; SLJ 12/05)

1672 Umansky, Kaye. *Solomon Snow and the Stolen Jewel* (4–7). 2007, Candlewick $12.99 (978-0-7636-2793-5). 256pp. In this sequel to *Solomon Snow and the Silver Spoon* (2005), Solomon and Prudence set out to help Prudence's father escape from a prison ship and become caught up in a plot to steal a cursed ruby. (Rev: BL 4/15/07)

1673 Van Draanen, Wendelin. *Sammy Keyes and the Dead Giveaway* (5–8). 2005, Knopf LB $17.99 (0-375-92350-0). 304pp. Seventh-grade sleuth Sammy tackles personal problems — should she make a confession that would exonerate her archenemy? — and community ones as she investigates abuse of eminent domain. (Rev: BL 9/1/05; SLJ 11/05)

1674 Van Draanen, Wendelin. *Shredderman: Enemy Spy* (3–5). Illus. by Brian Biggs. 2005, Knopf $12.95 (0-375-82354-9). 176pp. Nolan Byrd — in the guise of his secret alter ego, Shredderman the superhero — goes after an international spy ring in this fourth book in the series. (Rev: BL 8/05; SLJ 7/05)

1675 Walden, Mark. *H.I.V.E: The Higher Institute of Villainous Education* (5–8). 2007, Simon & Schuster $15.99 (1-4169-3571-1). 320pp. Kidnapped along with three of his friends and enrolled in an academy that grooms students in the villainous arts, 13-year-old brilliant orphan Otto maps a plan to escape, a feat never before accomplished. (Rev: BL 4/1/07)

1676 Wright, Betty Ren. *Princess for a Week* (3–5). Illus. by Jacqueline Rogers. 2006, Holiday $16.95 (0-8234-1945-2). 105pp. Roddy is already stressed when an overbearing girl called Princess comes to stay; she persuades him to investigate the goings-on at an abandoned house nearby. (Rev: BL 5/1/06; SLJ 5/06)

Animal Stories

1677 Bunting, Eve. *Reggie* (1–3). Illus. by D. Brent Burkett. 2006, Cricket $16.95 (0-8126-2746-6). 112pp. Alex keeps a toy mouse he finds even though he knows another child is looking for it, but

when his own dog Patch disappears, he questions his decision. (Rev: BL 10/1/06; SLJ 11/06)

1678 Feiffer, Jules. *A Room with a Zoo* (3–5). Illus. 2005, Hyperion $16.95 (0-7868-3702-0). 192pp. Julie (daughter of author and cartoonist Feiffer) wants a dog, and the procession of intervening pets do not assuage this need. (Rev: BL 9/15/05; SLJ 11/05)

1679 Fine, Anne. *The Diary of a Killer Cat* (2–4). Illus. by Steve Cox. 2006, Farrar $15.00 (0-374-31779-8). 64pp. Tuffy the cat cannot understand the reactions of his humans to what he views as totally normal feline behavior. (Rev: BL 1/1–15/06; SLJ 2/06)

1680 Fine, Anne. *Notso Hotso* (2–4). Illus. by Tony Ross. 2006, Farrar $15.00 (0-374-35550-9). 96pp. Anthony, a British dog with a sense of dignity but a bad skin condition, is initially mortified when his fur is shaved off, but then decides he looks like a lion; an easy chapter book that will appeal to reluctant readers. (Rev: BL 1/1–15/06; SLJ 3/06)

1681 Haas, Jessie. *Jigsaw Pony* (2–4). Illus. by Ying-Hwa Hu. 2005, Greenwillow $14.99 (0-06-078245-5). 112pp. Sharing isn't easy for twins Fran and Kiera, but they eventually come together over their adopted pony Jigsaw. (Rev: BL 9/1/05; SLJ 12/05)

1682 Heinz, Brian. *Cheyenne Medicine Hat* (4–8). Illus. by Gregory Manchess. 2006, Creative Editions $18.95 (1-56846-181-X). 32pp. The story of a summer in the life of a wild mustang mare as she tries to keep her band safe from predators — both animal and human. (Rev: SLJ 11/06)

1683 Hobbs, Valerie. *Sheep* (4–6). 2006, Farrar $16.00 (0-374-36777-9). 128pp. A poignant tale of a smart and sensitive border collie desperately searching for a home and the chance to herd sheep. (Rev: BL 2/1/06; SLJ 3/06)

1684 Kadohata, Cynthia. *Cracker! The Best Dog in Vietnam* (5–8). 2007, Simon & Schuster $16.99 (978-1-4169-0637-7). 309pp. In this action-packed, fact-based tale of canine heroism partly narrated by the dog, Cracker the German shepherd saves the lives of countless soldiers during the Vietnam War. (Rev: SLJ 2/07)

1685 Loizeaux, William. *Wings* (4–6). Illus. by Leslie Bowman. 2006, Farrar $16.00 (0-374-34802-2). 160pp. In 1960, 10-year-old Nick finds a baby mockingbird that's been abandoned by its mother and nurses it back to health. (Rev: BL 9/1/06; SLJ 9/06)

1686 Martin, Ann M. *A Dog's Life: The Autobiography of a Stray* (4–6). 2005, Scholastic $16.99 (0-439-71559-8). 192pp. Squirrel the dog looks back on the difficult years she spent as a stray before she was finally adopted by a loving human family. (Rev: BL 12/1/05; SLJ 11/05; VOYA 12/05)

1687 Mitchard, Jacquelyn. *Rosalie, My Rosalie: The Tale of a Duckling* (2–4). Illus. by John Bendall-Brunello. 2005, HarperCollins $15.99 (0-06-072219-3). 128pp. A young girl with the unlikely name of Henry is overjoyed when her father brings home a tiny duckling for her to raise in this warm beginning chapter book. (Rev: BL 7/05; SLJ 6/05)

1688 Naylor, Phyllis Reynolds. *Cuckoo Feathers* (3–5). Illus. by Marcy Ramsey. 2006, Marshall Cavendish $14.95 (0-7614-5285-0). 96pp. When the two pigeons Sarah has regarded as her own decamp for a neighboring Chicago apartment, she is reluctant to give them up. (Rev: BL 5/1/06; SLJ 6/06)

1689 Nolan, Lucy. *On the Road* (1–3). Illus. by Mike Reed. 2005, Marshall Cavendish $14.95 (0-7614-5234-6). 64pp. The dog who thinks her name is Down Girl relates an exciting car ride to the beach with her friend Sit, fun camping in the woods, and a trip to the vet, all the while commenting on life and owners. (Rev: BL 11/15/05; SLJ 3/06)

1690 Platt, Chris. *Moon Shadow* (4–7). 2006, Peachtree $14.95 (1-56145-382-X). 176pp. When a wild mustang mare dies giving birth near her Nevada home, 13-year-old Callie vows to raise and train the foal. (Rev: BL 11/1/06; SLJ 1/07)

1691 Reinhart, Matthew. *The Jungle Book: A Pop-up Adventure* (2–4). Illus. by author. 2006, Simon & Schuster $26.95 (1-4169-1824-8). The stories of Mowgli, Shere Khan, and other jungle inhabitants unfold in dramatic fold-outs and pop-ups. (Rev: SLJ 11/06)

1692 Tolan, Stephanie S. *Listen!* (4–7). 2006, HarperCollins $15.99 (0-06-057925-8). 208pp. Lonely after the death of her mother and the departure of her best friend for the summer, 12-year-old Charley finds solace in a stray dog. (Rev: BL 4/1/06)

Ethnic Groups

1693 Banerjee, Anjali. *Looking for Bapu* (3–6). 2006, Random $15.95 (0-385-74657-1). 160pp. Devastated by the death of his grandfather, Bapu, 8-year-old Anu, an Indian American living in Seattle, tries desperately to reconnect with the spirit of Bapu. (Rev: BL 9/1/06; SLJ 10/06)

1694 Bernardo, Anilú. *Un día con mis tías / A Day with My Aunts* (2–4). Illus. by Christina Rodriguez. 2006, Piñata $15.95 (1-55885-374-X). A young Latina girl spends a fun-filled day with her aunts in this appealing bilingual book that includes empanada recipes. (Rev: SLJ 10/06)

1695 Bertrand, Diane Gonzales. *The Ruiz Street Kids / Los muchachos de la calle Ruiz* (3–6). 2006, Piñata paper $9.95 (1-55885-321-9). 240pp. Joe

Silva and his friends shun David until they realize he's just insecure; Spanish text follows the English. (Rev: SLJ 10/06)

1696 Cheng, Andrea. *Eclipse* (5–8). 2006, Front St. $16.95 (1-932425-21-7). 136pp. In 1952 Cincinnati, 8-year-old immigrant Peti is disappointed when his relatives arrive to live with them; his cousin is a bully and his mother still worries about her father, who cannot get out of Hungary. (Rev: BL 11/1/06)

1697 Cheng, Andrea. *Shanghai Messenger* (4–6). Illus. by Ed Young. 2005, Lee & Low $17.95 (1-58430-238-0). 40pp. Xiao Mei, an 11-year-old Chinese American girl, learns about the Chinese half of her heritage on a summer trip to Shanghai. (Rev: BL 8/05; SLJ 9/05)

1698 Cummings, Mary. *Three Names of Me* (2–5). Illus. by Lin Wang. 2006, Albert Whitman $15.95 (0-8075-7903-3). A young Chinese American girl tells the story behind her three names — one from her birth mother, another she received at the orphanage, and a third given by her adoptive parents. (Rev: SLJ 10/06)

1699 Herrera, Juan Felipe. *Downtown Boy* (5–8). 2005, Scholastic $16.90 (0-439-64489-5). 304pp. This poignant free-verse novel, narrated by 10-year-old Juanito, offers an unflinching look at what life was like for Chicano migrant workers and their families in 1950s California. (Rev: BL 12/15/05; SLJ 1/06; VOYA 4/06)

1700 Himelblau, Linda. *The Trouble Begins* (4–8). 2005, Delacorte LB $16.99 (0-385-90288-3). 200pp. Du Nguyen, 11 years old and a refugee from Vietnam via the Philippines, initially longs for his former freedom and chafes against the expectations of his relatives and elders in America. (Rev: BCCB 12/05; HB 1–2/06; SLJ 2/06)

1701 Hobbs, Will. *Crossing the Wire* (5–8). 2006, HarperCollins $15.99 (0-06-074138-4). 224pp. Victor, a teenage Mexican boy who is the sole support for his family, decides to risk the dangerous crossing into the United States in search of work. (Rev: BL 5/1/06; SLJ 5/06; VOYA 4/06)

1702 Lester, Julius. *The Old African* (4–7). Illus. by Jerry Pinkney. 2005, Dial $19.99 (0-8037-2564-7). 80pp. An elderly slave who never speaks uses his acute mental powers to relieve the pain of his people on a Georgia plantation. (Rev: BL 7/05*; SLJ 9/05; VOYA 12/05)

1703 Lin, Grace. *The Year of the Dog* (3–5). Illus. 2006, Little, Brown $14.99 (0-316-06000-3). 136pp. A 12-year-old Taiwanese American girl chronicles the events of a year that includes a new friend, academic achievements, growing awareness of cultural differences, and a touch of romance. (Rev: BCCB 2/06; BL 1/1–15/06*; HB 3–4/06; HBG 10/06; SLJ 3/06)

1704 Look, Lenore. *Ruby Lu, Empress of Everything* (2–4). Illus. by Anne Wilsdorf. 2006, Simon & Schuster $15.95 (0-689-86460-4). 176pp. Ruby Lu faces new challenges as she helps her deaf cousin Flying Duck, newly arrived from China, to adjust to school and life in America; a sequel to *Ruby Lu, Brave and True* (2004). (Rev: BL 2/15/06; SLJ 7/06*)

1705 Ly, Many. *Home Is East* (4–7). 2005, Delacorte LB $17.99 (0-385-73223-6). 224pp. When Amy's mother leaves, the young Cambodian American struggles to get on with her father and to make friends and fit in when they move from Florida to San Diego. (Rev: BL 8/05; SLJ 8/05)

1706 Marsden, Carolyn, and Virginia Shin-Mui Loh. *The Jade Dragon* (2–4). 2006, Candlewick $15.99 (0-7636-3012-8). 176pp. Ginny, a young Chinese American girl, and Stephanie, adopted by a Caucasian American couple, become friends after a few false starts. (Rev: BL 11/1/06; SLJ 11/06)

1707 Mobin-Uddi, Asma. *My Name Is Bilal* (4–7). Illus. by Barbara Kiawk. 2005, Boyds Mills $15.95 (1-59078-175-9). 32pp. When they start at a new school, Muslim Bilal and his sister Ayesha balance pride in their own heritage and their desire to blend in. (Rev: BL 8/05; SLJ 8/05)

1708 Nislick, June Levitt. *Zayda Was a Cowboy* (4–7). 2005, Jewish Publication Soc. paper $9.95 (0-8276-0817-9). 128pp. A Jewish grandfather tells his grandchildren about his exploits as a cowboy when he first arrived in America from Eastern Europe; an epilogue gives background and there is a glossary and a bibliography. (Rev: BL 8/05*)

1709 O'Connell, Rebecca. *Penina Levine Is a Hard-Boiled Egg* (4–6). Illus. by Marjella Lue Sue. 2007, Roaring Brook $16.95 (978-1-59643-140-9). 176pp. Penina, a feisty Jewish sixth grader troubled by a school assignment involving the Easter bunny, worries that confiding in her parents will only cause more trouble. (Rev: BL 3/15/07)

1710 Parker, Toni Trent. *Sienna's Scraphook: Our African American Heritage Trip* (3–6). Illus. by Janell Genovese. 2005, Chronicle $15.95 (0-8118-4300-9). 61pp. Sienna, a young African American girl, keeps a scrapbook of her family's summer trip to important sites in the history of black Americans; Sienna's humorous comments, varied ephemera, and appealing illustrations add to the appeal. (Rev: SLJ 1/06)

1711 Robles, Anthony D. *Lakas and the Makibaka Hotel* (2–4). Trans. by Eloisa D. de Jesus. Illus. by Carl Angel. 2006, Children's Book Pr. $16.95 (0-89239-213-4). 32pp. Based on a real-life incident, this lively bilingual (English and Tagalog) picture book tells the story of a group of Filipino Americans fighting to prevent the sale of the hotel in which they live. (Rev: BL 2/15/06; SLJ 4/06)

1712 Weatherford, Carole Boston. *Dear Mr. Rosenwald* (2–4). Illus. by R. Gregory Christie. 2006, Scholastic $16.99 (0-439-49522-9). 32pp. In this fact-based tale from the rural South of the 1920s, 10-year-old Ovella describes her community's efforts to build a new school with seed money from Julius Rosenwald, president of Sears, Roebuck. (Rev: BL 10/1/06; SLJ 10/06*)

Family Stories

1713 Bauer, Jutta. *Grandpa's Angel* (1–3). Illus. 2005, Candlewick $12.99 (0-7636-2743-7). 48pp. The illustrations — most notably the images of a guardian angel — add another dimension to this captivating tale about an elderly man telling his grandson about the ups and downs of his life; a German import, this includes stories of World War II. (Rev: BL 10/15/05; SLJ 10/05)

1714 Birdseye, Tom. *A Tough Nut to Crack* (3–5). 2006, Holiday $16.95 (0-8234-1967-3). 124pp. Cassie, sent from the city to help out at her grandfather's farm after he's injured, is determined to mend a long-standing feud between her father and grandfather. (Rev: BL 1/1–15/07; SLJ 1/07)

1715 Cassidy, Cathy. *Indigo Blue* (5–8). 2005, Viking $15.99 (0-670-05927-7). 256pp. As her family life slowly disintegrates, 11-year-old Indigo tries her best to conceal the truth from her friends at school in this realistic story set in Britain. (Rev: BL 10/1/05; SLJ 11/05)

1716 Cotten, Cynthia. *Fair Has Nothing to Do with It* (4–7). 2007, Farrar $16.00 (978-0-374-39935-1). 160pp. Upset by the death of his grandfather, 12-year-old Michael focuses his energies on an art project to honor his memory. (Rev: BL 4/1/07)

1717 Creech, Sharon. *Replay* (4–7). 2005, HarperCollins LB $16.89 (0-06-054020-6). 240pp. Twelve-year-old Leo untangles some of the secrets of his boisterous Italian American family when he finds his father's boyhood journal. (Rev: BCCB 11/05; BL 9/1/05*; HBG 4/06; LMC 3–4/06; SLJ 9/05; VOYA 12/05)

1718 Davies, Jacqueline. *The Lemonade War* (3–5). 2007, Houghton $16.00 (978-0-618-75043-6). 192pp. Evan and his younger sister Jessie — who has just skipped third grade and will be in Evan's class next year — now find themselves in constant conflict, even over their money-raising activities; includes tips for running a lemonade stand. (Rev: BL 3/15/07)

1719 Edwards, Nancy. *Mom for Mayor* (3–5). Illus. by Michael Chesworth. 2006, Cricket $15.95 (0-8126-2743-1). 144pp. In a last-ditch effort to prevent the sale of a local playground to developers, fifth-grader Eric convinces his mother to run for mayor against the man who engineered the sale plan; an entertaining chapter book with humorous illustrations. (Rev: BL 3/15/06; SLJ 3/06)

1720 Ellis, Sarah. *Odd Man Out* (4–6). 2006, Groundwood $16.95 (0-88899-702-7). 160pp. Twelve-year-old Kip spends a summer with his grandmother and five female cousins and learns — from a binder he finds in the attic — about the father he never knew. (Rev: BL 12/1/06; SLJ 12/06)

1721 Flood, Pansie Hart. *Sometimey Friend* (3–5). Illus. by Felicia Marshall. 2005, Carolrhoda $15.95 (1-57505-866-9). 128pp. While the aunt who raised her travels to Florida, 10-year-old Sylvia Freeman stays in South Carolina with her elderly great-grandmother, an arrangement that suits her fine until her classmates begin poking fun at the old woman. (Rev: BL 11/15/05; SLJ 12/05)

1722 Gay, Marie-Louise, and David Homel. *Travels with My Family* (3–5). 2006, Groundwood $15.95 (0-88899-688-8). 80pp. Adventures are guaranteed in this family, which takes unusual (and sometimes dangerous) vacations — observed by an older brother with a dry sense of humor. (Rev: BL 5/15/06; SLJ 8/06)

1723 Goobie, Beth. *Something Girl* (5–8). 2005, Orca paper $7.95 (1-55143-347-8). 112pp. Fifteen-year-old Sophie tries to hide the fact that her mother is an alcoholic and her father abusive in this book for reluctant readers. (Rev: BL 7/05; SLJ 12/05)

1724 Greene, Stephanie. *Sophie Hartley, on Strike* (3–5). 2006, Clarion $15.00 (978-0-618-71960-0). 152pp. Ten-year-old Sophie and her older sister Nora feel their share of the household chores is too heavy and decide to go on strike. (Rev: BL 1/1–15/07; SLJ 1/07)

1725 Grimes, Nikki. *Dark Sons* (5–8). 2005, Hyperion $15.99 (0-7868-1888-3). 218pp. Alternating between biblical times and contemporary New York, free-verse narratives express the frustrations of Ishmael — son of Abraham, who must wander the desert with his rejected mother — and of Sam, whose father has left his mother for a young white woman. (Rev: BL 8/05*; SLJ 11/05; VOYA 10/05)

1726 Hermes, Patricia. *Emma Dilemma and the New Nanny* (3–5). 2006, Marshall Cavendish $15.95 (0-7614-5286-9). 112pp. Accident-prone Emma, 8, is trying to keep her ferret under control and the new nanny from being fired, but somehow things keep going wrong. (Rev: BL 4/15/06; SLJ 5/06)

1727 Hermes, Patricia. *Emma Dilemma and the Two Nannies* (2–4). 2007, Marshall Cavendish $15.99 (978-0-7614-5353-6). 116pp. Emma's nanny is taking a three-week vacation and, worried that her parents may prefer the substitute nanny, Emma plots against this eventuality while also coping with

crises such as her ferret eating a classmate's book. (Rev: SLJ 4/07)

1728 Hicks, Betty. *Out of Order* (4–7). 2005, Roaring Brook $15.95 (1-59643-061-3). 176pp. In alternating chapters, four new stepsiblings relate the problems — and the fun — they have had adjusting to life together. (Rev: BL 9/15/05; SLJ 10/05; VOYA 12/05)

1729 Johnston, Tony. *Angel City* (2–4). Illus. by Carole Byard. 2006, Philomel $16.99 (0-399-23405-5). 40pp. An elderly African American man discovers a Latino baby abandoned in a dumpster and takes the child home to raise as his own. (Rev: BL 6/1–15/06; SLJ 6/06)

1730 Jones, Kimberly K. *Sand Dollar Summer* (5–8). 2006, Simon & Schuster $15.95 (1-4169-0362-3). 224pp. Annalise's summer in Maine with her mother and younger, often-mute brother Free takes a dramatic turn when a hurricane hits their island. (Rev: BL 5/15/06; HBG 10/06; LMC 1/07; SLJ 6/06*)

1731 Kelly, Katy. *Lucy Rose: Big on Plans* (2–4). Illus. by Adam Rex. 2005, Delacorte $12.95 (0-385-73204-X). 128pp. Lucy Rose, a precocious 8-year-old, chronicles her busy plans for the summer in her journal. (Rev: BL 8/05; SLJ 6/05)

1732 Kelly, Katy. *Lucy Rose: Busy Like You Can't Believe* (2–4). Illus. by Adam Rex. Series: Lucy Rose. 2006, Delacorte $12.95 (0-385-73319-4). 176pp. Now in fourth grade, Lucy Rose reveals in her diary her struggles with her mother's romantic life and learns some important lessons about the perils of eavesdropping. (Rev: BL 10/15/06; SLJ 10/06)

1733 Klise, Kate. *Far from Normal* (5–8). 2006, Scholastic $16.99 (0-439-79447-1). 256pp. In this sequel to *Deliver Us from Normal* (2005), the Harrisong family makes a deal with the devil when a retailing giant threatens to sue over disparaging remarks made about the chain in a book written by Charles. (Rev: BL 10/15/06; VOYA 4/07)

1734 Lupica, Mike. *Miracle on 49th Street* (5–8). 2006, Philomel $17.99 (0-399-24488-3). 288pp. The life of pro basketball star Josh Cameron is turned upside down when 12-year-old Molly Parker turns up claiming to be his daughter. (Rev: BL 9/1/06; SLJ 11/06)

1735 Mazer, Norma Fox. *What I Believe* (5–8). 2005, Harcourt $16.00 (0-15-201462-4). 176pp. When Vicki's father loses his job and the family's fortunes go into free fall, Vicki finds the resulting changes hard to accept and reveals in her poems and journal her coping strategies. (Rev: BL 9/15/05; SLJ 10/05)

1736 Mead, Alice. *Isabella's Above-Ground Pool* (2–4). Illus. by Maryann Cocca-Leffler. 2006, Farrar $16.00 (0-374-33617-2). 112pp. Nine-year-old

Isabella learns some important lessons about sharing after a tornado sweeps through her small Texas town. (Rev: BL 4/1/06; SLJ 5/06)

1737 Meehl, Brian. *Out of Patience* (4–6). 2006, Delacorte $15.95 (0-385-73299-6). 304pp. Twelve-year-old Jake's dream of escaping his boring Kansas hometown, where his plumber father hopes to open a toilet museum, is put on the back burner when his dad brings home a cursed toilet plunger. (Rev: BL 4/1/06; SLJ 11/06; VOYA 6/06)

1738 Mills, Claudia. *Trading Places* (4–6). 2006, Farrar $16.00 (0-374-31798-4). 138pp. Twins Todd and Amy must relinquish their familiar roles when things get tough at home and at school. (Rev: BL 2/1/06; SLJ 5/06)

1739 Moss, Marissa. *Amelia's Longest, Biggest, Most-Fights-Ever Family Reunion* (3–5). Illus. Series: Amelia. 2006, Simon & Schuster $9.95 (0-689-87447-2). 80pp. Amelia first steels herself for a reunion with her father's extended family and then records her experiences. (Rev: BL 8/06; SLJ 9/06)

1740 Mourlevat, Jean-Claude. *The Pull of the Ocean* (5–8). Trans. by Y. Mauder. 2006, Delacorte $15.95 (0-385-73348-8). 208pp. In this modern version of "Tom Thumb," Yann — the smallest and youngest of seven — leads his six older brothers (three sets of twins) away from their dismal home to the ocean that's far to the west, meeting many characters along the way. (Rev: BL 12/1/06; SLJ 1/07*)

1741 Paros, Jennifer. *Violet Bing and the Grand House* (2–4). Illus. 2007, Viking $14.99 (0-670-06151-4). 112pp. Despite her determination not to, Violet Bing finds some things that pique her interest during a summer stay with her Great-Aunt Astrid. (Rev: BL 3/15/07)

1742 Ransom, Candice. *Finding Day's Bottom* (4–6). 2006, Carolrhoda $15.95 (1-57505-933-9). 168pp. In this poignant tale set in the Blue Ridge Mountains of Virginia, 11-year-old Jane-Ery slowly comes to appreciate her Grandpap's love after her father's death in an accident. (Rev: BL 10/15/06; SLJ 9/06)

1743 Rodowsky, Colby. *Ben and the Sudden Too-Big Family* (3–5). 2007, Farrar $16.00 (978-0-374-30658-8). 120pp. Ben, 10, likes to divide events in his life into "all right" and "not all right," and although his new stepmother and even the arrival of his new adopted sister from China fell into the former category, he's not at all sure about the prospect of a houseful of his stepmother's relatives. (Rev: SLJ 4/07)

1744 Rubel, Nicole. *It's Hot and Cold in Miami* (3–5). Illus. 2006, Farrar $16.00 (0-374-33611-3). 208pp. Fifth-grade twin sisters Rachel and Rebecca look just alike, but Rachel finds herself living in her perfect sister's shadow until a teacher recognizes her unique talents. (Rev: BL 4/15/06; SLJ 5/06)

1745 Schirripa, Steven R., and Charles Fleming. *Nicky Deuce: Home for the Holidays* (5–8). 2006, Random $15.95 (0-385-90276-X). 208pp. In this entertaining sequel to *Nicky Deuce: Welcome to the Family* (2005), Nicky – worried about being bored — is happy to entertain family and friends from Brooklyn (Grandma Tutti, Uncle Frankie, and friend Tommy) at his fancy home in New Jersey. (Rev: BL 12/1/06; SLJ 1/07)

1746 Schirripa, Steven R., and Charles Fleming. *Nicky Deuce: Welcome to the Family* (4–6). 2005, Delacorte $15.95 (0-385-73257-0). 176pp. When his summer camp is abruptly closed, Nicholas Borelli II is sent to Brooklyn for a two-week stay with his Grandma Tutti and learns about his Italian American roots. (Rev: BL 10/1/05; SLJ 8/05)

1747 Smith, Emily. *Joe vs. the Fairies* (2–4). Illus. by Georgie Birkett. 2006, Trafalgar paper $7.50 (0-552-55174-0). 92pp. Joe isn't pleased when his cousins arrive and monopolize his sisters with girlish games, but then he meets a girl who enjoys climbing trees. (Rev: BL 1/1–15/06)

1748 Thomas, Jane Resh. *Blind Mountain* (4–7). 2006, Clarion $15.00 (0-618-64872-0). 128pp. Forced to go on a hiking trip with his bossy father in the mountainous Montana wilderness, 12-year-old Sam finds himself in charge of their survival when his father is temporarily blinded by a branch. (Rev: BL 12/1/06; SLJ 12/06)

1749 Thomson, John. *A Small Boat at the Bottom of the Sea* (5–7). 2005, Milkweed $16.95 (1-57131-657-4); paper $6.95 (1-57131-656-6). 148pp. Upset and angry when he's sent to spend the summer with his ex-con uncle and dying aunt on Puget Sound, 12-year-old Donovan begins to develop a closer relationship with his uncle as his vacation progresses. (Rev: SLJ 10/05; VOYA 4/06)

1750 Trueit, Trudi. *Julep O'Toole: Confessions of a Middle Child* (4–6). 2005, Dutton $15.99 (0-525-47619-9). 144pp. Eleven-year-old Julep O'Toole, sandwiched between a perfect older sister and an asthmatic little brother, is suffering from low self-esteem. (Rev: BL 10/1/05; SLJ 10/05)

1751 Williams, Dar. *Lights, Camera, Amalee* (5–7). 2006, Scholastic $16.99 (0-439-80352-7). 311pp. A modest inheritance from a grandmother she barely knew gives 12-year-old Amalee the funds she needs to make a documentary about endangered species. (Rev: SLJ 9/06)

1752 Woodworth, Chris. *When Ratboy Lived Next Door* (4–8). 2005, Farrar $16.00 (0-374-34677-1). 192pp. Twelve-year-old Lydia takes an instant dislike to her new neighbor Willis and his pet raccoon, but as she gains a better understanding of the family dynamics that make the boy who he is, she also gains valuable insights into her strained relationship with her mother. (Rev: BCCB 2/05; BL 1/1–15/05; SLJ 3/05)

Fantasy and the Supernatural

1753 Abbott, Tony. *Kringle* (5–8). 2005, Scholastic $14.99 (0-439-74942-5). 352pp. In early Britain a 12-year-old orphan named Kringle battles dark forces and discovers his true destiny. (Rev: BCCB 12/05; BL 10/15/05; HBG 4/06; SLJ 10/05; VOYA 2/06)

1754 Alter, Stephen. *The Phantom Isles* (4–7). Illus. 2007, Bloomsbury $16.95 (978-1-58234-738-7). 224pp. Sixth-graders Courtney, Orion, and Ming join with the librarian of their Massachusetts town in an effort to free ghosts that have become trapped in books. (Rev: BL 2/1/07; SLJ 3/07)

1755 Andersen, Jodi. *May Bird and the Ever After* (4–7). Illus. by Leonid Gore. 2005, Simon & Schuster $15.95 (0-689-86923-1). 336pp. After falling into a lake near her home, 10-year-old May Bird finds herself in Ever After, a fantasy underworld inhabited by the souls of the dead. (Rev: BCCB 12/05; BL 10/15/05; HBG 4/06; SLJ 12/05; VOYA 12/05)

1756 Anderson, Jodi Lynn. *May Bird Among the Stars* (4–7). 2006, Simon & Schuster $16.95 (0-689-86924-X). 272pp. In this sequel to *May Bird and the Ever After*, 10-year-old May Bird and her cat Somber Kitty remain trapped in the Afterlife torn between finding a way home and helping to save Ever After from the villainous Bo Cleevil. (Rev: BL 12/1/06; SLJ 11/06)

1757 Arnold, Louise. *Golden and Grey: The Nightmares That Ghosts Have* (4–6). 2006, Simon & Schuster $15.95 (0-689-87586-X). 304pp. In this sequel to *Golden and Grey: An Unremarkable Boy and a Rather Remarkable Ghost*, 11-year-old Tom Golden and his ghostly friend Grey Arthur try to figure out what's causing ghosts to disappear. (Rev: BL 10/15/06; HBG 4/07; LMC 2/07; SLJ 9/06)

1758 Avi. *Strange Happenings: Five Tales of Transformation* (4–7). 2006, Harcourt $15.00 (0-15-205790-0). 160pp. Shape-shifting and invisibility are among the transformations in this collection of five fantasy tales. (Rev: BL 3/15/06; SLJ 5/06)

1759 Baccalario, Pierdomenico. *The Long-Lost Map* (4–6). Trans. by Leah Janeczko. Series: Ulysses Moore. 2006, Scholastic $12.99 (0-439-77439-X). 272pp. Jason and Rick are investigating in ancient Egypt while Jason's twin Julia, back in Cornwall, deals with Oblivia Newton in this exciting, fast-paced sequel to *Door to Time* (2005). (Rev: BL 7/06; SLJ 8/06)

1760 Ball, Justin, and Evan Croker. *Space Dogs* (4–7). 2006, Knopf $15.95 (0-375-83256-4). 250pp. When a powerful force threatens to destroy Gersbach, the planet's inhabitants dispatch dog-shaped vehicles to Earth in a desperate attempt to head off disaster; they end up battling in the front yard of Amy and Lucy Buckley in this humorous, action-packed story. (Rev: BL 6/1–15/06; SLJ 8/06)

1761 Banks, Lynne Reid. *Harry the Poisonous Centipede Goes to Sea* (3–5). Illus. by Tony Ross. 2006, HarperCollins $15.99 (0-06-077548-3). 208pp. Out for a day of fun, centipede pals Harry and George find themselves packed into a banana crate and shipped off to a big city where nothing is familiar. (Rev: BL 10/15/06; SLJ 9/06)

1762 Barrows, Annie. *Ivy and Bean* (1–3). Illus. by Sophie Blackall. 2006, Chronicle $14.95 (0-8118-4903-1). 116pp. Seven-year-old Bean takes an instant dislike to Ivy when she moves in across the street, but when Ivy comes to Bean's rescue the two begin to develop a friendship; excellent artwork adds to the story. (Rev: BCCB 6/06; BL 4/1/06*; HBG 10/06; LMC 2/07; SLJ 7/06)

1763 Barrows, Annie. *Ivy and Bean and the Ghost That Had to Go* (1–3). Illus. by Sophie Blackall. 2006, Chronicle $14.95 (978-0-8118-4910-4). 102pp. Best friends Ivy and Bean try to run off the ghost that's haunting the girls' bathroom at school. (Rev: BL 10/15/06; SLJ 2/07)

1764 Barry, Dave, and Ridley Pearson. *Peter and the Shadow Thieves* (5–8). Illus. by Greg Call. 2006, Hyperion $18.99 (0-7868-3787-X). 464pp. In this sequel to *Peter and the Starcatchers* (2005), the for-ever-young Peter and Tinker Bell race to foil the evil plans of Lord Ombra. (Rev: BL 6/1–15/06; SLJ 8/06; VOYA 8/06)

1765 Batson, Wayne Thomas. *The Door Within* (4–7). 2005, Thomas Nelson $16.99 (1-4003-0659-0). 320pp. Aidan Thomas, upset by his family's sudden move from Maryland to Colorado, finds himself drawn toward another world after he discovers three ancient scrolls in the basement of his grandfather's home in this first volume of a fantasy trilogy with a strong religious base. (Rev: BL 12/1/05; SLJ 1/06)

1766 Bauer, Marion Dane. *The Blue Ghost* (2–4). Illus. by Suling Wang. 2005, Random $11.95 (0-375-83179-7). 96pp. Nine-year-old Liz is summoned into the past to help a family of children and a blue ghost. (Rev: BL 9/1/05; SLJ 8/05)

1767 Baum, L. Frank. *The Wonderful Wizard of Oz* (2–7). Illus. by Michael Foreman. 2005, Sterling LB $12.95 (1-4027-2535-3). 160pp. The lustrous watercolor artwork of Michael Foreman brings new life and humorous details to this classic fantasy. (Rev: SLJ 12/05)

1768 Beck, Ian. *The Secret History of Tom True-heart* (4–7). Illus. 2007, HarperCollins $16.99 (978-0-06-115210-8). 341pp. Twelve-year-old Tom Trueheart must try to track down his six older brothers when they mysteriously disappear, suspected victims of the enemy of storytelling. (Rev: SLJ 2/07)

1769 Becker, Bonny. *Holbrook: A Lizard's Tale* (4–6). Illus. by Abby Carter. 2006, Clarion $15.00 (0-618-71458-8). 148pp. Holbrook the lizard takes his best painting to the city in hopes of artistic recognition; this complex animal adventure features take-offs on art world luminaries, the outwitting of the carnivorous Count Rumolde, and revelations about city life. (Rev: BL 1/1–15/07; SLJ 12/06)

1770 Berkeley, Jon. *The Palace of Laughter: The Wednesday Tales No. 1* (4–7). Illus. by Brandon Dorman. Series: Julie Andrews Collection. 2006, HarperCollins $16.99 (0-06-075507-5). 418pp. Miles Wednesday, an 11-year-old orphan, joins forces with a talking tiger and a diminutive angel named Little to rescue Little's mentor from the Palace of Laughter. (Rev: SLJ 8/06)

1771 Berryhill, Shane. *Chance Fortune and the Out-laws* (5–8). Series: Adventures of Chance Fortune. 2006, Tom Doherty Assoc. $17.95 (0-765-31468-1). 269pp. Despite his lack of superpowers, 14-year-old Josh Blevins manages to bluff his way into Burlington Academy for the Superhuman, and there discovers that evil is afoot. (Rev: SLJ 1/07)

1772 Bildner, Phil, and Loren Long. *The Barnstorm-ers: Tales of Travelin' Nine Game 1* (4–7). Illus. by Loren Long. 2007, Simon & Schuster $9.99 (1-4169-1863-9). 144pp. On the road with their late father's traveling baseball team, siblings Griffith, Ruby, and Graham discover a ragged baseball with magical powers. (Rev: BL 4/1/07)

1773 Bode, N. E. *The Somebodies* (5–8). Illus. by Peter Ferguson. 2006, HarperCollins $16.99 (0-06-079111-7). 284pp. Fern and her best friend Howard are determined to foil the Blue Queen's plan to destroy the home of the Anybodies who live in a city beneath Manhattan; the final book in a fast-paced trilogy. (Rev: SLJ 9/06)

1774 Boniface, William. *The Hero Revealed* (3–5). Illus. by Stephen Gilpin. Series: Extraordinary Adventures of Ordinary Boy. 2006, HarperCollins $15.99 (0-06-077464-9). 320pp. Ordinary Boy is the only resident with no superpowers, but when Superopolis is threatened by the evil Professor Brain-Drain it looks as if Ordinary Boy may be the only one who can save the day. (Rev: BL 6/1–15/06; SLJ 6/06)

1775 Bruchac, Joseph. *Whisper in the Dark* (5–8). 2005, HarperCollins $15.99 (0-06-058087-9). 192pp. A frightening Native American legend seems to be coming true for 13-year-old Maddie,

descended from a Narragansett chief. (Rev: BL 9/1/05; SLJ 8/05)

1776 Buckley, Michael. *The Sisters Grimm: The Fairy-Tale Detectives* (4–6). Illus. by Peter Ferguson. Series: Sisters Grimm. 2005, Abrams $14.95 (0-8109-5925-9). 304pp. Sent to live with their grandmother after their parents disappear, sisters Daphne and Sabrina Grimm find themselves in a magical town full of fairy tale characters known as Everafters. (Rev: BL 11/15/05; SLJ 1/06; VOYA 8/06)

1777 Byng, Georgia. *Molly Moon's Hypnotic Time Travel Adventure* (4–6). 2005, HarperCollins $16.99 (0-06-075032-4). 392pp. When her beloved dog is kidnapped, Molly Moon travels back in time to late 19th-century India where she matches wits with the villainous Maharaja of Waqt and meets former versions of herself. (Rev: SLJ 1/06)

1778 Carman, Patrick. *Beyond the Valley of Thorns* (4–6). Series: The Land of Elyon. 2005, Scholastic $11.99 (0-439-70094-9). 221pp. In the second installment of this fantasy series, Alexa and her companions confront a host of new dangers as they battle the ogre Abaddon. (Rev: SLJ 10/05; VOYA 12/05)

1779 Carman, Patrick. *The Tenth City* (4–6). Series: The Land of Elyon. 2006, Scholastic $11.99 (0-439-70095-7). 186pp. In the conclusion of this fantasy series, Alexa and her band of supporters face off against Grindall who has kidnapped Yipes, Alexa's diminutive friend. (Rev: SLJ 8/06)

1780 Carmody, Isobelle. *Little Fur: The Legend Begins* (3–5). 2006, Random $12.95 (0-375-83854-6). 208pp. Little Fur (who is half elf, half troll) sets out on a journey through the human world to save the trees that she calls home as well as the earth spirit. (Rev: BL 11/15/06; SLJ 11/06)

1781 Carroll, Lewis. *Alice Through the Looking-Glass* (4–7). Illus. by Helen Oxenbury. 2005, Candlewick $24.99 (0-7636-2892-1). 226pp. Faithful to the original text, Oxenbury's inviting artwork will draw young readers; a companion to her award-winning *Alice's Adventures in Wonderland* (1999). (Rev: BL 12/15/05*; HBG 4/06; SLJ 12/05)

1782 Carroll, Lewis. *Alice's Adventures in Wonderland* (3–5). Illus. by Alison Jay. 2006, Dial $25.99 (0-8037-2940-5). 224pp. A handsomely illustrated, faithful retelling of the classic story, with glowing paintings of diverse sizes. (Rev: BL 11/1/06)

1783 Catanese, P. W. *The Mirror's Tale: A Further Tales Adventure* (4–7). 2006, Simon & Schuster paper $4.99 (1-4169-1251-7). 274pp. When their father decides to separate his mischievous 13-year-old twin sons for the summer, they switch places and one is sent to the castle of his aunt and uncle where he discovers and falls under the spell of a bewitching mirror. (Rev: SLJ 8/06)

1784 Codell, Esmé Raji. *Diary of a Fairy Godmother. Drazen Kozjan* (4–6). Illus. 2005, Hyperion $14.99 (0-7868-0965-5). 176pp. Hunky Dory, a witch in training, is conflicted about her future and wonders if she must devote her life to evil. (Rev: BL 8/05; SLJ 7/05)

1785 Collins, Suzanne. *Gregor and the Curse of the Warmbloods* (4–6). Series: Underland Chronicles. 2005, Scholastic $16.95 (0-439-65623-0). 368pp. In this third volume in the series, Gregor, his sister Boots, and his mother travel to the Underland to deal with the terrible plague spreading there. (Rev: BL 7/05; SLJ 7/05; VOYA 10/05)

1786 Collins, Suzanne. *Gregor and the Marks of Secret* (5–8). Series: The Underland Chronicles. 2006, Scholastic $16.99 (0-439-79145-6). 341pp. Gregor, accompanied by his little sister Boots, joins forces with Queen Luxa to defend Underland from attacks by the rat army. (Rev: SLJ 9/06; VOYA 8/06)

1787 Collodi, Carlo. *The Adventures of Pinocchio.* Rev. ed. (4–10). Trans. from Italian by M. A. Murray. Illus. by Roberta Innocenti. 2005, Creative Editions $19.95 (1-56846-190-9). 191pp. Nineteenth-century European landscapes provide the backdrop for this appealing retelling of the classic story about the puppet that longed to become a little boy; a revision of the 1988 edition. (Rev: SLJ 12/05)

1788 Corder, Zizou. *Lionboy: The Truth* (5–8). 2005, Dial $16.99 (0-8037-2985-5). 240pp. In the final installment in the trilogy, Charlie Ashanti, reunited with his parents in Morocco, is kidnapped by the Corporacy and put on a boat bound for the Caribbean, but the boy wonder calls on his animal friends for help. (Rev: BL 10/1/05; SLJ 9/05; VOYA 12/05)

1789 Cowell, Cressida. *How to Speak Dragonese: By Hiccup Horrendous Haddock III* (3–5). Illus. by author. 2006, Little, Brown $10.99 (0-316-15600-0). 221pp. Young Viking Hiccup is joined by a friend and his dragon as they fight Roman invaders in this entertaining sequel to *How to Train Your Dragon* (2004) and *How to Be a Pirate* (2005). (Rev: SLJ 6/06)

1790 Crane, Jordan. *The Clouds Above* (2–4). Illus. 2005, Fantagraphics $18.95 (1-56097-627-6). 216pp. Simon skips school and with his cat, Jack, climbs a magic staircase into a world of adventure. (Rev: BL 10/1/05) [741.5]

1791 Crilley, Mark. *Rogmasher Rampage* (3–5). Illus. 2005, Delacorte $10.95 (0-385-73112-4). 176pp. Billy Clikk — no ordinary sixth grader but a secret trainee in the Allied Forces for the Management of Extraterritorial Creatches — is on a mission to China; a fast-paced sequel to *Creatch Battler* (2004). (Rev: BL 9/1/05; SLJ 10/05)

1792 Daley, Michael J. *Space Station Rat* (4–6). 2005, Holiday $15.95 (0-8234-1866-9). 182pp. An escaped lab rat and a lonely boy, both residents of an orbiting space station, become friends and together face many challenges; the fast-paced texts switches from one character to the other. (Rev: BL 8/05; SLJ 8/05)

1793 Delaney, Joseph. *The Last Apprentice: Revenge of the Witch* (5–8). Illus. by Patrick Arrasmith. 2005, Greenwillow LB $15.89 (0-06-076619-0). 336pp. A scary story in which young Tom, seventh son of a seventh son, takes on the job of spook and must protect the people from ghouls, boggarts, and beasties. (Rev: BCCB 10/05; BL 8/05*; HB 11–12/05; HBG 4/06; LMC 3/06; SLJ 11/05; VOYA 8/06)

1794 De Mari, Silvana. *The Last Dragon* (5–8). Trans. by Shaun Whiteside. 2006, Hyperion $16.95 (0-7868-3636-9). 320pp. To fulfill a prophecy in which he will play a key role, a young elf named Yorsh, the last of his kind in a world hostile to elves, sets off in search of the last dragon. (Rev: BL 11/1/06; SLJ 1/07)

1795 DeMatteis, J. M. *The Road to Inconceivable* (4–7). Illus. by Mike Ploog. Series: Abadazad. 2006, Hyperion paper $9.99 (1-4231-0062-X). 160pp. Kate follows her brother, who's been missing for five years, into the mystical land of Abadazad; Kate's diary entries alternate with illustrations and tales of the magical land. (Rev: BL 7/06; SLJ 11/06)

1796 Desplechin, Marie. *Poor Little Witch Girl* (4–6). 2006, Bloomsbury $15.95 (1-58234-898-7). 128pp. Eleven-year-old Verbena is learning to deal with the fact that she's a witch even though she longs for a normal life, but when one of her Grandma's spell lessons involves the cutest boy at school she feels her social life is doomed. (Rev: BL 12/1/06; SLJ 12/06)

1797 Deutsch, Stacia, and Rhody Cohon. *King's Courage* (2–4). Illus. by David Wenzel. Series: Blast to the Past. 2006, Simon & Schuster paper $3.99 (1-4169-1269-X). 112pp. Abigail and her friends travel back in time on a mission to convince Dr. Martin Luther King, Jr. to continue his civil rights campaign. (Rev: BL 2/1/06)

1798 DiCamillo, Kate. *The Miraculous Journey of Edward Tulane* (2–4). Illus. by Bagram Ibatoulline. 2006, Candlewick $18.99 (0-7636-2589-2). 200pp. Edward Tulane, a china rabbit, learns the meaning of love on an odyssey that begins when he falls into the sea during an ocean voyage. (Rev: BCCB 4/06; BL 1/1–15/06*; HB 3–4/06; LMC 4–5/06; SLJ 2/06*)

1799 DiTerlizzi, Tony, and Holly Black. *Arthur Spiderwick's Field Guide to the Fantastical World Around You* (4–6). Illus. 2005, Simon & Schuster

$24.95 (0-689-85941-4). 122pp. This large-format, beautifully illustrated volume is the guide to the inhabitants of the "Invisible World" that is featured in the Spiderwick series. (Rev: BL 2/1/06; SLJ 3/06)

1800 Divakaruni, Chitra Banerjee. *The Mirror of Fire and Dreaming* (5–8). 2005, Roaring Brook $16.95 (1-59643-067-2). 336pp. In this sequel to *The Conch Bearer* (2003), 12-year-old Anand continues his magic studies and travels back to Moghul times, where he encounters powerful sorcerers and evil jinns. (Rev: BL 9/1/05; SLJ 12/05)

1801 D'Lacey, Chris. *The Fire Within* (5–8). 2005, Scholastic $12.95 (0-439-67343-0). 340pp. A multi-layered fantasy in which British college student David Rain comes to board at the home of Liz Pennykettle and her daughter, Lucy, and discovers that the clay dragons crafted by Liz have magical properties. (Rev: SLJ 10/05)

1802 Donaldson, Julia. *The Giants and the Joneses* (3–5). Illus. by Greg Swearingen. 2005, Holt $14.95 (0-8050-7805-3). 215pp. In this twist on the tale of Jack and the Beanstalk, filled with invented words, Jumbeelia, a young giantess who lives in Groil, climbs down a "bimplestonk" to a miniature world below where she kidnaps three "iggly plops." (Rev: SLJ 10/05)

1803 Downer, Ann. *The Dragon of Never-Was* (4–7). Illus. by Omar Ryyan. 2006, Simon & Schuster $16.95 (0-689-85571-0). 305pp. In this lively sequel to *Hatching Magic* (2003), 12-year-old Theodora Oglethorpe accompanies her father to Scotland to investigate the origin of a mysterious scale and there learns more about her own magical powers. (Rev: BL 6/1–15/06; SLJ 12/06)

1804 Driscoll, Laura. *Beck and the Great Berry Battle* (1–3). Illus. by Judith Holmes Clarke. Series: Disney Fairies. 2006, Random paper $5.99 (0-7364-2373-7). 128pp. When conflict breaks out between the hummingbirds and the chipmunks in Never Land's Pixie Hollow, Beck the fairy steps in to mediate the dispute. (Rev: BL 2/1/06; SLJ 3/06)

1805 Driscoll, Laura. *Vidia and the Fairy Crown* (2–3). Illus. by Judith Holmes Clarke and the Disney Storybook Artists. Series: Disney Fairies. 2006, Random paper $5.99 (0-7364-2372-9). 128pp. Vidia, a temperamental fairy who lives in Never Land's Pixie Hollow, struggles to clear her name after she's falsely accused of stealing Queen Clarion's crown. (Rev: SLJ 3/06)

1806 Dunmore, Helen. *Ingo* (5–8). 2006, HarperCollins $16.99 (0-06-081852-2). 336pp. As they search for their missing father, 11-year-old Sapphire and her brother Conor find themselves torn between their home on England's Cornish coast and the Mer people and magical sea world of Ingo. (Rev: BCCB

10/06; BL 9/1/06; HBG 4/07; SLJ 8/06; VOYA 4/06)

1807 Dunrea, Olivier. *Hanne's Quest* (2–4). Illus. 2006, Philomel $16.99 (0-399-24216-3). 112pp. Hanne, a young hen in Mem Pockets's henhouse, sets off on a heroic quest to save her owners' farm; excellent illustrations enhance this chapter book. (Rev: BCCB 4/06; BL 2/1/06*; HB 3–4/06; HBG 10/06; SLJ 2/06)

1808 DuPrau, Jeanne. *The Prophet of Yonwood* (4–7). Series: Embers. 2006, Random $15.95 (0-375-87526-3). 304pp. About 50 years before the time of the Embers series, 11-year-old Nickie hides out at her great-grandfather's estate in Yonwood, North Carolina, and thinks about good an evil as she watches her neighbors react to predictions of doom. (Rev: BL 5/15/06; SLJ 6/06; VOYA 4/06)

1809 Dyer, Heather. *The Girl with the Broken Wing* (2–4). Illus. by Peter Bailey. 2005, Scholastic $15.99 (0-439-74827-5). 160pp. An angel with a broken wing leads twins James and Amanda on some merry adventures. (Rev: BL 11/1/05; SLJ 1/06)

1810 Edwards, Julie Andrews, and Emma Walton Hamilton. *The Great American Mousical* (4–6). Illus. by Tony Walton. 2006, HarperCollins $15.99 (0-06-057918-8). 160pp. In this spoof by actress Julie Andrews and her daughter, a troupe of mice in a condemned Broadway theater are feverishly rehearsing a musical revue when their star goes missing. (Rev: BL 1/1–15/06; SLJ 2/06)

1811 Enthoven, Sam. *The Black Tattoo* (5–8). 2006, Penguin $19.99 (1-59514-114-6). 512pp. In this action-packed fantasy epic set in London and Hell, three teenage friends — Esme, Charlie, and Jack — work together to defeat a demonic entity that has taken possession of Charlie. (Rev: BL 9/1/06; SLJ 1/07)

1812 Farland, David. *Of Mice and Magic* (5–8). Illus. by Howard Lyon. Series: Ravenspell. 2005, Covenant Communications $16.95 (1-57734-918-0). 276pp. Ben's magical mouse Amber turns Ben into a mouse and together the two set out to rescue the animals from the pet store. (Rev: SLJ 1/06)

1813 Fischbein, Dina. *Really Raoulino* (4–6). Illus. by Bill Crews. 2006, Handprint $15.95 (1-59354-151-1). 150pp. Neither Raoulino, a newcomer at the Metropolitan Zoo, nor his keepers know what kind of animal he is, but he knows that what really matters is getting out of the zoo and back to his island home. (Rev: BL 4/15/06; SLJ 6/06)

1814 Flanagan, John. *The Burning Bridge* (5–8). Series: Ranger's Apprentice. 2006, Philomel $16.99 (0-399-24455-7). 256pp. Will and his friend Horace again face war and find the safety of the kingdom depends on them. (Rev: BL 5/15/06; SLJ 8/06)

1815 Fox, Helen. *Eager's Nephew* (5–8). 2006, Random $15.95 (0-385-74673-3). 208pp. In this sequel to *Eager* (2004), Eager the robot and his nephew Jonquil pay a forbidden visit to Eager's human friends, the Bells; mystery and adventure ensue. (Rev: BL 10/15/06; SLJ 1/07)

1816 Frederick, Heather. *For Your Paws Only* (4–6). Illus. by Sally Comport. Series: Spy Mice. 2005, Simon & Schuster $9.95 (1-4169-0573-1). 258pp. Morning Glory Goldenleaf, lead operative of the Spy Mice Agency, uncovers a plot by evil rat leader Roquefort Dupont to rid the world of mice. (Rev: SLJ 12/05)

1817 Frederick, Heather. *Spy Mice: The Black Paw* (4–6). Illus. by Sally Comport. 2005, Simon & Schuster $9.95 (0-689-87753-6). 240pp. Fifth grader Oz Levinson is having trouble adjusting to his new life in Washington, D.C., but things take a turn for the better after he meets a mouse spy who draws him into a whole new world of espionage and adventure. (Rev: BL 7/05; SLJ 10/05)

1818 Garcia, Laura Gallego. *The Valley of the Wolves* (5–8). Trans. by Margaret Sayers Peden. 2006, Scholastic $16.99 (0-439-58553-8). 248pp. Dana, 10, learns to use her magical powers at an academy of sorcery and wonders about the origins of her best friend and constant companion Kai, visible only to Dana. (Rev: BL 5/15/06; SLJ 6/06; VOYA 6/06)

1819 Garza, Xavier. *Juan and the Chupacabras / Juan y el Chupacabras* (2–4). Trans. by Carolina Villarroel. Illus. by April Ward. 2006, Piñata $15.95 (1-55885-454-1). Cousins Luz and Juan don't know whether to believe their grandfather's tales of confrontations with the dreaded Chupacabras, so they decide to search out one of the bloodsucking demons themselves. (Rev: SLJ 10/06)

1820 Gilliland, Judith Heide. *Strange Birds* (4–7). 2006, Farrar $17.00 (0-374-37275-6). 240pp. Anna, 11, finds solace in a herd of tiny magical horses after her parents die. (Rev: BL 5/15/06; SLJ 5/06)

1821 Gliori, Debi. *Pure Dead Trouble* (4–7). Series: Pure Dead. 2005, Knopf LB $17.99 (0-375-93311-5). 304pp. Nanny MacLachlan plays a key role in this fourth, darker and more complex, installment in the series. (Rev: BL 10/1/05; SLJ 8/05; VOYA 8/05)

1822 Gopnik, Adam. *The King in the Window* (5–8). 2005, Hyperion $19.95 (0-7868-1862-X). 416pp. Mistaken by window wraiths as their king, 11-year-old Oliver Parker struggles to resist their efforts to pull him into their world. (Rev: BL 10/1/05; SLJ 11/05; VOYA 2/06)

1823 Greenburg, Dan. *Secrets of Dripping Fang: The Onts* (3–5). Illus. by Scott M. Fischer. Series: The Onts. 2005, Harcourt $11.95 (0-15-205457-X). 131pp. Despite significant hygiene issues, the orphaned Shluffmuffin twins are adopted by the elderly Mandible sisters and welcomed to the old ladies' mansion in Dripping Fang Forest, where they discover that all is not as it seems. (Rev: SLJ 12/05)

1824 Griggs, Terry. *Invisible Ink* (4–7). Series: Cat's Eye Corner. 2006, Raincoast paper $7.95 (1-55192-833-7). 257pp. The third installment in a humorous, pun-filled series finds 10-year-old Olivier visiting his grandparents' unusual home and being whisked off into another zany adventure. (Rev: SLJ 9/06)

1825 Gutman, Dan. *Satch and Me* (4–7). Series: Baseball Card Adventure. 2005, HarperCollins LB $16.89 (0-06-059492-6). 173pp. Stosh travels back to 1942 to establish whether Satchel Paige was the fastest pitcher in history and learns about racial discrimination in the process. (Rev: SLJ 2/06; VOYA 4/06)

1826 Hahn, Mary Downing. *Deep and Dark and Dangerous* (5–8). 2007, Clarion $16.00 (978-0-618-66545-7). 192pp. While spending the summer at her aunt's cottage in Maine, 13-year-old Ali meets a mysterious girl named Sissie who seems to know a great deal about a tragic accident that occurred three decades earlier. (Rev: BL 3/15/07)

1827 Hahn, Mary Downing. *Witch Catcher* (4–7). 2006, Clarion $16.00 (0-618-50457-5). 240pp. When Jen and her widowed father move into a rambling old mansion, the 12-year-old girl disregards warnings and investigates an old stone tower behind the house. (Rev: BL 6/1–15/06; SLJ 8/06)

1828 Hanson, Mary. *How to Save Your Tail* (2–4). Illus. by John Hendrix. 2007, Random $15.99 (0-375-83755-8). 112pp. Captured by palace cats Brutus and Muffin, Bob the rat uses his baking and storytelling skills to keep himself off the dinner menu. (Rev: BL 4/1/07)

1829 Helgerson, Joseph. *Horns and Wrinkles* (4–7). 2006, Houghton $16.00 (0-618-61679-9). 368pp. Mysterious events are taking place in Blue Wing, Minnesota — the nose of a bully named Duke turns into a rhino horn, and his parents turn to stone — and 12-year-old Claire is drawn into an adventure involving fairies and trolls. (Rev: BL 9/1/06; SLJ 9/06)

1830 Herbauts, Anne. *Monday* (3–5). Illus. by author. 2006, Enchanted Lion $16.95 (1-59270-057-8). 36pp. This unusual, almost-wordless book will appeal to thoughtful readers who follow a creature called Monday through a cycle of seasons, some shared with his friends Lester Day and Tom Morrow. (Rev: SLJ 4/07)

1831 Holm, Jennifer L., and Matthew Holm. *Babymouse: Beach Babe* (4–6). Illus. Series: Babymouse. 2006, Random LB $12.99 (0-375-93231-3); paper $5.95 (0-375-83231-9). 96pp. School is over for the year, and the lively Babymouse is headed to the beach for a summer of fun and adventure. (Rev: BL 3/15/06; SLJ 7/06)

1832 Holm, Jennifer L., and Matthew Holm. *Babymouse: Rock Star* (2–4). 2006, Random LB $12.99 (0-375-93232-1); paper $5.95 (0-375-83232-7). 91pp. Babymouse may play the flute at school but in her dreams she's a wildly popular rock star. (Rev: SLJ 9/06)

1833 Horowitz, Anthony. *Evil Star* (5–8). Series: Gatekeepers. 2006, Scholastic $17.99 (0-439-67996-6). 320pp. In the second installment of this action-packed fantasy series, 14-year-old Matt Freeman travels to Peru to learn more about the possible opening of another gate to the underworld. (Rev: BL 6/1–15/06; SLJ 7/06)

1834 Horowitz, Anthony. *Raven's Gate* (5–8). Series: Gatekeepers. 2005, Scholastic $17.95 (0-439-67995-8). 256pp. Faced with a choice between jail and life in a remote Yorkshire village, 14-year-old Matt chooses the latter, unaware that he's about to enter a world of frightening evil. (Rev: BL 7/05*; SLJ 7/05; VOYA 10/05)

1835 Hughes, Carol. *Dirty Magic* (5–8). 2006, Random $17.95 (0-375-83187-8). 432pp. In a desperate attempt to save his little sister's life, 10-year-old Joe Brooks enters a shadowy world where ill children are held captive. (Rev: BL 10/1/06)

1836 Ingpen, Robert. *The Dreamkeeper: A Letter to Alice Elizabeth from Her Grandfather, Robert Ingpen* (2–4). Illus. 2006, Penguin $15.99 (0-698-40036-4). 32pp. The author writes to his granddaughter, telling her about the Dreamkeeper, a man who captures the creatures that have escaped from dreams. (Rev: BL 3/1/06)

1837 Jacques, Brian. *High Rhulain* (5–8). Illus. by David Elliot. Series: Redwall. 2005, Philomel $23.99 (0-399-24208-2). 384pp. In this eighteenth installment, ottermaid Tiria bravely journeys to the Green Isle to rescue otter kinsmen from evil wildcats. (Rev: BL 9/1/05; SLJ 9/05)

1838 Jarvis, Robin. *Thomas: Book Three of the Deptford Histories* (5–8). 2006, Chronicle $17.95 (0-8118-5412-4). 400pp. This prequel to the Deptford Mice trilogy, written as the memoirs of an old sea mouse, contains plenty of battles, storms and heroic deeds and can be read as a stand-alone novel. (Rev: BL 1/1–15/07)

1839 Jarvis, Robin. *The Whitby Witches* (4–7). Illus. by Jess Petersen. 2006, Chronicle $17.95 (0-8118-5413-2). 296pp. Sent to live with their elderly Aunt Alice in the English seaside village of Whitby, 8-year-old Ben — who can see the invisible — and 12-year-old Jennet find themselves swept up in a struggle between good and evil. (Rev: BL 10/1/06; SLJ 10/06)

1840 Jenkins, Emily. *Toys Go Out: Being the Adventures of a Knowledgeable Stingray, a Toughy*

Little Buffalo, and Someone Called Plastic (1–3). Illus. by Paul Zelinsky. 2006, Random $16.95 (0-375-83604-7). 128pp. Three toys that belong to Little Girl have adventures, embarrassing situations, and scary moments that will be very familiar to young readers; a beginning chapter book. (Rev: BCCB 11/06; BL 10/1/06; HBG 10/07; SLJ 9/06*)

1841 Jennings, Patrick. *Wish Riders* (5–8). 2006, Hyperion $15.99 (1-4231-0010-7). 288pp. Combining historical fiction and fantasy, this tale of transformation focuses on Edith, 15, who slaves with four other foster children, cooking and cleaning in a Depression-era logging camp until a mysterious seed pod grows into five horses that spirit the children away to forest adventures. (Rev: BL 1/1–15/07)

1842 Johansen, K. V. *Nightwalker* (5–8). 2007, Orca paper $8.95 (978-1-55143-481-0). 144pp. Thrown into the dungeon when it's discovered that he possesses a powerful magical ring, young Maurey escapes with the help of a baroness and travels to Talverdin in an effort to find out if he is a nightwalker. (Rev: BL 4/1/07)

1843 Johnson, Crockett. *Magic Beach* (1–3). Illus. 2005, Front St. $18.95 (1-932425-27-6). 64pp. A boy and his sister conjure up a magical kingdom by writing words in the sand of a very special beach; originally published as *Castles in the Sand* in 1965. (Rev: BL 11/1/05; SLJ 6/06)

1844 Johnson, Gillian. *Thora: A Half-Mermaid Tale* (4–6). Illus. 2005, HarperCollins $15.99 (0-06-074378-6). 256pp. Ten-year-old Thora, half girl and half mermaid, on dry land after spending the first ten years of her life at sea, tries to foil the villainous plans of a fat-cat tycoon named Frooty de Mare. (Rev: BL 8/05)

1845 Johnson, Jane. *The Secret Country* (4–7). Illus. by Adam Stower. Series: Eidolon Chronicles. 2006, Simon & Schuster $14.95 (1-4169-0712-2). 336pp. When 12-year-old Ben Arnold adopts a talking cat, he learns he is the Prince of Eidolon and that Mr. Dodds, owner of the Pet Emporium, is kidnapping creatures from his kingdom. (Rev: BL 6/1–15/06; SLJ 4/06; VOYA 8/06)

1846 Jones, Diana Wynne. *The Game* (5–8). 2007, Penguin $11.99 (978-0-14-240718-9). 192pp. Hayley, an orphan who has been raised by her difficult grandparents, now finds herself amid a large, happy family in Ireland with cousins who love to play in the mythosphere, a land of stories where secrets about her past reside. (Rev: BL 12/1/06; SLJ 3/07)

1847 Jones, Diana Wynne. *The Pinhoe Egg* (5–8). Series: Chrestomanci. 2006, Greenwillow $18.89 (0-06-113125-3). 528pp. In this compelling addition to the Chrestomanci series, Marianne Pinhoe and Cat Chant find a strange egg with magical properties. (Rev: BL 9/15/06; SLJ 10/06)

1848 Kerr, P. B. *The Blue Djinn of Babylon* (5–8). Series: Children of the Lamp. 2006, Scholastic $16.99 (0-439-67021-7). 384pp. Philippa Gaunt, 12, is wrongly convicted of cheating and her twin John must rescue her in this action-packed sequel to *The Akhenatan Adventure* (2005). (Rev: BL 3/15/06; SLJ 3/06; VOYA 2/06)

1849 Kessler, Liz. *Emily Windsnap and the Monster from the Deep* (4–7). Series: Emily Windsnap. 2006, Candlewick $15.99 (0-7636-2504-3). 224pp. Half-human and half-mermaid, Emily Windsnap enjoys an idyllic life on Allpoints Island until she inadvertently awakens an evil monster named Kraken; a sequel to *The Tail of Emily Windsnap* (2004). (Rev: BL 6/1–15/06; SLJ 7/06)

1850 Kladstrup, Kristin. *The Book of Story Beginnings* (4–6). 2006, Candlewick $15.99 (0-7636-2609-0). 362pp. In this multilayered fantasy, 12-year-old Lucy tries with the help of a mysterious notebook to unravel the mystery surrounding the disappearance of her great-uncle Oscar in 1914. (Rev: BL 3/1/06; SLJ 4/06)

1851 Langrish, Katherine. *Troll Mill* (5–8). 2006, HarperCollins LB $16.89 (0-06-058308-8). 288pp. In this sequel to *Troll Fell* (2004), 15-year-old Peer Ulfsson, who still worries about his cruel uncles and is increasingly involved with Hilde, must help protect a half-selkie baby from trolls and other threats. (Rev: BCCB 3/06; BL 2/1/06*; HBG 10/06; LMC 2/07; SLJ 3/06; VOYA 2/06)

1852 Larson, Kirsten. *Lily's Pesky Plant* (2–3). Illus. by Judith Holmes Clarke and the Disney Storybook Artists. Series: Disney Fairies. 2006, Random paper $5.99 (0-7364-2374-5). 128pp. Lily, a fairy who lives in Never Land's Pixie Hollow, has a green thumb, but the new plant in her garden has her neighbors very worried. (Rev: SLJ 3/06)

1853 Lethcoe, Jason. *Amazing Adventures from Zoom's Academy* (3–6). Illus. by author. 2005, Ballantine paper $12.95 (0-345-48355-3). 151pp. Thirteen-year-old Summer Jones is amazed to find out that her father is a professor at Zoom's Academy for the Super-Gifted; while Summer's powers are being assessed, a move is afoot to attack the academy. (Rev: SLJ 1/06)

1854 Levine, Gail Carson. *Fairy Dust and the Quest for the Egg* (3–5). Illus. by David Christiana. Series: Disney Fairies. 2005, Disney $18.99 (0-7868-3491-9). 208pp. Prilla, a new arrival in the fairy community of Never Land, has trouble fitting in until she's assigned to help repair the magic egg that keeps the inhabitants of Never Land forever young. (Rev: BL 8/05*; HBG 10/06; SLJ 10/05)

1855 Lowry, Lois. *Gossamer* (5–8). 2006, Houghton $16.00 (0-618-68550-2). 144pp. A spirit called Littlest One learns to mix memories that will heal peo-

ple while they sleep. (Rev: BL 2/15/06; SLJ 5/06*; VOYA 8/06)

1856 Lubar, David. *True Talents* (5–8). 2007, Tor $17.95 (978-0-7653-0977-8). 320pp. In this sequel to *Hidden Talents* (1999), the paranormally gifted student friends from Edgeview Alternative School flex their extraordinary powers in a series of interconnected adventures; memos, e-mails, and illustrations add to the action-packed narrative. (Rev: BL 3/15/07)

1857 McAllister, Angela. *Digory the Dragon Slayer* (3–5). Illus. by Ian Beck. 2006, Bloomsbury $14.95 (1-58234-722-0); paper $5.95 (1-58234-912-6). 124pp. Digory is a gentle poetry-loving lad who is mistakenly considered knight material and sent off to slay dragons and marry princesses. (Rev: SLJ 8/06)

1858 McAllister, M. I. *Urchin and the Heartstone* (4–7). Illus. by Omar Rayyan. Series: The Mistmantle Chronicles. 2006, Hyperion $17.95 (0-7868-5488-X). 297pp. The animal inhabitants of Mistmantle eagerly prepare for the coronation of Crispin the squirrel as king, but things go awry when Urchin, Crispin's companion, is kidnapped and taken to the island of Whitewings. (Rev: SLJ 12/06)

1859 McAllister, M. I. *Urchin of the Riding Stars* (5–8). Series: Mismantle Chronicles. 2005, Hyperion $17.95 (0-7868-5486-3). 288pp. When his mentor, Captain Crispin, is unjustly accused of slaying the infant prince of Mismantle, Urchin the squirrel is determined to find out who actually is responsible for the crime. (Rev: BL 10/1/05; SLJ 11/05; VOYA 2/06)

1860 McCartney, Paul, and Philip Ardagh. *High in the Clouds* (2–4). Illus. by Geoff Dunbar. 2005, Dutton $19.99 (0-525-47733-0). 96pp. In his first outing as a children's author, singer/composer Paul McCartney spins a tale about an orphaned squirrel that sets off to find the tropical animal sanctuary that his mother told him about before she died. (Rev: SLJ 3/06)

1861 MacHale, D. J. *The Rivers of Zadaa* (5–8). Series: Pendragon. 2005, Simon & Schuster $14.95 (1-4169-0710-6). 405pp. Bobby Pendragon teams up with Loor to foil the villainous Saint Dane's plan to cut off the water supply to Loor's people in Zadaa. (Rev: SLJ 7/05)

1862 McNish, Cliff. *Breathe: A Ghost Story* (4–8). 2006, Carolrhoda LB $15.95 (0-8225-6443-2). 261pp. After the death of his father, young Jack moves with his mother to an old farmhouse in the English countryside, a home that they share with the spirits of four children and the Ghost Mother who enslaved them. (Rev: SLJ 11/06)

1863 McNish, Cliff. *Silver City* (5–8). Series: Silver Sequence. 2006, Carolrhoda $15.95 (1-57505-926-6). 256pp. As the fearsome Roar draws closer to the

Earth, Milo, Thomas, Helen, and their friends use their magical powers to keep the threat at bay; a sequel to *The Silver Child* (2005). (Rev: BL 6/1–15/06; SLJ 9/06)

1864 Martin, George R. R. *The Ice Dragon* (3–5). Illus. by Yvonne Gilbert. 2006, Tom Doherty Assoc. $12.95 (978-0-7653-1631-8). 106pp. Seven-year-old Adara is a child who loves the cold, and her bond with the ice dragon allows her to rescue her home and family from marauding invaders. (Rev: SLJ 2/07)

1865 Martin, Rafe. *Birdwing* (5–8). 2005, Scholastic $16.99 (0-459-21167-0). 359pp. This appealing fantasy picks up where "The Six Swans" by the Brothers Grimm ends, chronicling the story of Ardwin, the prince who was turned into a swan and then restored to human form apart from his left arm, which remains a swan's wing. (Rev: BCCB 12/05 ; BL 11/15/05; HB 1–2/06; SLJ 12/05; VOYA 12/05)

1866 Mayes, Walter M. *Walter the Giant Storyteller's Giant Book of Giant Stories* (3–5). Illus. by Kevin O'Malley. 2005, Walker $18.95 (0-8027-8974-9). Captured by the tiny inhabitants of a Lilliputian-like island, Walter the Giant Storyteller tells a series of stories to convince his captors that giants are not bloodthirsty and mean but rather the victims of character assassination; an oversize volume with dramatic illustrations. (Rev: SLJ 11/05)

1867 Meyer, Kai. *The Stone Light* (5–7). Trans. from German by Elizabeth D. Crawford. Series: The Dark Reflections Trilogy. 2006, Simon & Schuster $16.95 (0-689-87789-7). 350pp. Desperately searching for help in their fight to free Venice from the evil Egyptian pharaoh, Merle travels on Vermithrax, the flying lion, to Hell in hopes of convincing Lucifer to ally himself with their cause; the sequel to *The Water Mirror* (2005). (Rev: BL 3/15/07; SLJ 1/07)

1868 Meyer, Kai. *The Water Mirror* (4–7). Trans. by Elizabeth D. Crawford. Series: Dark Reflections. 2005, Simon & Schuster $15.95 (0-689-87787-0). 256pp. In an alternate Venice in danger of destruction, 14-year-old Merle, a plucky orphan, finds herself playing a central role; the first volume in a series noted for its setting. (Rev: BL 1/1–15/06; SLJ 11/05*; VOYA 12/05)

1869 Miéville, China. *Un Lun Dun* (5–9). 2007, Del Rey $17.95 (978-0-345-49516-7). 425pp. In contemporary London, Zanna and her friend Deeba find themselves on the edge of a strange Unlondon that is awaiting a chosen one. (Rev: SLJ 4/07*)

1870 Mishkin, Dan. *The Forest King: Woodlark's Shadow* (5–8). Illus. by Tom Mandrake. 2006, Komikwerks $12.95 (0-9742803-5-6). 126pp. Justin is convinced that there's something evil lurking in the woods surrounding his home; this action-packed

suspense story will attract reluctant readers. (Rev: SLJ 1/07)

1871 Moloney, James. *The Book of Lies* (4–6). 2007, HarperCollins $16.99 (0-06-057842-4). 368pp. Kidnapped and brought to Mrs. Timmons's Home for Orphans and Foundlings, a young boy awakens with no memory of his former life, but a young girl offers him a single clue that sets him on the trail to his past. (Rev: BL 4/15/07)

1872 Moonshower, Candie. *The Legend of Zoey* (4–6). 2006, Delacorte $15.95 (0-385-73280-5). 224pp. A multilayered story told in part through the diary entries of Zoey, a modern girl of Native American heritage, who travels back in time to 1811 and meets Prudence, the daughter of white settlers; the two endure the New Madrid earthquakes together. (Rev: BL 7/06; SLJ 12/06)

1873 Morrison, P. R. *Wind Tamer* (4–6). 2006, Bloomsbury $16.95 (1-58234-781-6). 336pp. A visit from his uncle convinces 10-year-old Archie Stringweed, who lives in a remote Scottish village, to confront the curse that has hung over his family for generations. (Rev: BL 10/15/06; SLJ 11/06)

1874 Nesbit, E. *Lionel and the Book of Beasts* (2–4). Illus. by Michael Hague. 2006, HarperCollins $15.95 (0-688-14006-8). 48pp. This abridged retelling of Nesbit's classic book tells the story of new young king Lionel, who accidentally unleashes a dragon upon the land. (Rev: BL 12/1/06; SLJ 1/07)

1875 Nigg, Joseph. *How to Raise and Keep a Dragon* (5–10). Illus. by Dan Malone. 2006, Barron's $18.99 (0-7641-5920-8). 128pp. This whimsical guide to the care and feeding of dragons offers tips for selecting just the right type of dragon, finding the correct equipment and supplies, establishing good modes of communication, and training for competitions. (Rev: SLJ 11/06)

1876 Nimmo, Jenny. *Charlie Bone and the Castle of Mirrors* (4–6). Series: Children of the Red King. 2005, Scholastic $9.95 (0-439-54528-5). 432pp. Back for another year at Bloor's Academy, Charlie Bone enlists the help of friends to save Billy Raven from his new adoptive parents. (Rev: BL 9/1/05; SLJ 10/05; VOYA 10/05)

1877 Nimmo, Jenny. *Emlyn's Moon* (3–5). Series: Magician Trilogy. 2007, Scholastic $9.99 (0-439-84676-5). 152pp. In this second installment in the trilogy, young magician Gwyn and his friend Nia find they hold the fate of Emlyn Llewelyn in their hands. (Rev: BL 12/15/06)

1878 Nimmo, Jenny. *The Snow Spider* (3–5). Series: Magician Trilogy. 2006, Scholastic $9.99 (0-439-84675-7). 128pp. On Gwyn's 9th birthday his grandmother reveals to him that he's a magician, giving him five gifts to help him with his powers;

set in Wales, this story incorporates elements of the local folklore. (Rev: BL 11/15/06)

1879 Nix, Garth. *Drowned Wednesday* (5–8). Series: The Keys to the Kingdom. 2005, Scholastic $15.95 (0-439-70086-8). 389pp. In the third volume of the Keys to the Kingdom fantasy series, Arthur Penhaligon faces multiple challenges as he struggles to win the third key to the kingdom. (Rev: BL 7/05; SLJ 7/05; VOYA 8/05)

1880 Nyoka, Gail. *Mella and the N'anga: An African Tale* (5–8). 2006, Sumach paper $9.95 (1-894549-49-X). 160pp. Mella, the daughter of a king in ancient Zimbabwe, with the help of the magical powers she learns from the spiritual adviser called N'anga, strives to save her father's life and realm. (Rev: BL 3/1/06; SLJ 7/06)

1881 Ogburn, Jacqueline. *The Bake Shop Ghost* (1–3). Illus. by Marjorie Priceman. 2005, Houghton $16.00 (0-618-44557-9). 32pp. The ghost of Cora Lee Merriweather, the bad-tempered owner of a bake shop, scares away all of the bakery's new owners until Annie Washington arrives, determined to stand her ground. (Rev: BCCB 9/05; BL 9/1/05*; HBG 4/06; LMC 4–5/06; SLJ 10/05)

1882 Okorafor-Mbachu, Nnedi. *Zahrah the Windseeker* (5–8). 2005, Houghton $16.00 (0-618-34090-4). 320pp. In this appealing debut novel, 13-year-old Zahrah, a "dada girl" readily identifiable by her telltale vine-entwined dreadlocks, struggles to come to terms with her magical powers. (Rev: BL 11/15/05; SLJ 12/05)

1883 Osborne, Mary Pope. *Night of the New Magicians* (2–4). Illus. by Sal Murdocca. Series: Magic Tree House. 2006, Random $11.95 (0-375-83035-9). 116pp. Jack and Annie are sent on a magician-searching mission at the 1889 World's Fair. (Rev: BL 5/1/06)

1884 Park, Linda Sue. *Archer's Quest* (4–7). 2006, Clarion $16.00 (0-618-59631-3). 176pp. An ancient Korean ruler suddenly appears in the New York State bedroom of 12-year-old Kevin and the two must work out how to get him back home before the Year of the Tiger ends. (Rev: BL 3/15/06; SLJ 5/06)

1885 Pilkey, Dav. *Ricky Ricotta's Mighty Robot vs. the Uranium Unicorns from Uranus* (1–3). Illus. by Martin Ontiveros. Series: Ricky Ricotta. 2005, Scholastic $16.99 (0-439-37646-7); paper $3.99 (0-439-37647-5). 125pp. Ricky the mouse and his Mighty Robot must foil Uncle Unicorn's evil plot to take over the world. (Rev: SLJ 1/06)

1886 Pratchett, Terry. *Johnny and the Dead* (5–8). Series: Johnny Maxwell. 2006, HarperCollins LB $16.89 (0-06-054189-X). 224pp. In the funny second volume of this trilogy, ghosts of the "post-senior citizens" buried in a local cemetery ask the title character to help block plans to bulldoze their final

resting place. (Rev: BL 12/15/05; HB 1–2/06; SLJ 12/05; VOYA 2/06)

1887 Primavera, Elise. *The Secret Order of the Gumm Street Girls* (4–7). Illus. 2006, HarperCollins $16.99 (0-06-056946-8). 464pp. Four girls who live on Gumm Street have little in common until a series of incidents appear to threaten their picturesque town of Sherbet and Franny, Pru, Cat, and Ivy find themselves on a very Oz-like adventure. (Rev: BL 12/15/06; SLJ 12/06)

1888 Quinn, Zoe. *The Caped 6th Grader: Happy Birthday, Hero!* (4–6). Illus. by Brie Spangler. 2006, Random LB $11.99 (0-385-90304-9); paper $4.99 (0-440-42079-2). 135pp. Zoe Richards has just turned 12 when she finds out she has inherited a gene that gives her super powers; she now must work out how to keep this secret and live her normal life. (Rev: SLJ 9/06)

1889 Radunsky, Vladimir. *I Love You Dude* (2–4). Illus. 2005, Harcourt $16.00 (0-15-205176-7). 48pp. Dude, a young girl's doodle of a blue elephant on the wall of a New York City building, escapes cleanup by the anti-graffiti squad and sets off to find acceptance and a home. (Rev: BL 12/1/05; SLJ 10/05)

1890 Ransom, Candice. *Bones in the Badlands* (2–4). Illus. by Greg Call. Series: Time Spies. 2006, Wizards of the Coast paper $4.99 (978-0-7869-4028-8). (111pp. In the second volume of this time-travel series, Alex, Mattie, and Sophie find themselves in the Badlands at the close of the 19th century and help a paleontologist protect a cache of dinosaur bones from thieves. (Rev: SLJ 2/07)

1891 Ransom, Candice. *Secret in the Tower* (2–4). Illus. by Greg Call. Series: Time Spies. 2006, Wizards of the Coast paper $4.99 (978-0-7869-4027-1). 112pp. In the opening book of this time-travel fantasy series, siblings Alex, Mattie, and Sophie find an antique spyglass that transports them back in time to the Revolutionary Battle of Yorktown in 1781. (Rev: SLJ 2/07)

1892 Reiche, Dietlof. *Freddy to the Rescue: Book Three in the Golden Hamster Saga* (3–5). Trans. from German by John Brownjohn. Illus. by Joe Cepeda. Series: Golden Hamster Saga. 2005, Scholastic $16.95 (0-439-53157-8). 235pp. It's up to talented golden hamster Freddy (and his cat and a few guinea pigs) to save a tribe of field hamsters in the third book in this funny series. (Rev: SLJ 9/05)

1893 Rogers, Jonathan. *The Secret of the Swamp King* (4–6). 2005, Broadman & Holman $15.99 (0-8054-3132-2). 229pp. Worried that the giant-slaying hero Aidan may be growing too popular, King Darrow dispatches the teenager on an impossible mission. (Rev: SLJ 11/05)

1894 Rowling, J. K. *Harry Potter and the Half-Blood Prince* (5–12). Illus. by Mary GrandPré.

2005, Scholastic LB $34.99 (0-439-78677-0). 672pp. In this sixth and penultimate volume, Harry, now 16, begins mapping a strategy to defeat the evil Lord Voldemort. (Rev: BL 8/05*; SLJ 9/05; VOYA 10/05)

1895 Ruby, Laura. *The Wall and the Wing* (5–8). 2006, HarperCollins LB $17.89 (0-06-075256-4). 336pp. An offbeat fantasy set in a future New York in which 12-year-old Gurl finds she can make herself invisible, a rare talent in a population where most people can fly. (Rev: BL 2/1/06; SLJ 2/06; VOYA 2/06)

1896 Runton, Andy. *Flying Lessons* (3–5). Illus. Series: Owly. 2005, Top Shelf paper $10.00 (1-891830-76-7). 140pp. A flying squirrel at first resists Owly's overtures of friendship but later offers to teach the young bird to fly. (Rev: BL 3/15/06)

1897 Runton, Andy. *Owly: Just a Little Blue* (3–5). Illus. Series: Owly. 2005, Top Shelf paper $10.00 (1-891830-64-3). 128pp. Owly and his friend Wormy try to help a bluebird whose habitat is endangered, but their overtures of friendship are at first rebuffed. (Rev: BL 7/05; SLJ 3/06)

1898 Rupp, Rebecca. *Journey to the Blue Moon: In Which Time Is Lost and Then Found Again* (5–8). 2006, Candlewick $15.99 (0-7636-2544-2). 264pp. A multilayered story in which Alex loses his grandfather's pocket watch and takes a trip to the blue moon, where all things lost go; there he finds other searchers and a group that threatens his chances of returning home. (Rev: BL 12/1/06; SLJ 10/06)

1899 Rupp, Rebecca. *The Return of the Dragon* (3–6). 2005, Candlewick $15.99 (0-7636-2377-6). 160pp. In this engaging sequel to *The Dragon of Lonely Island* (1998), the Davis siblings return to the island and discover that their friend Fafnyr, a three-headed dragon, is being pursued by an unscrupulous billionaire named J. P. King. (Rev: BL 9/1/05; SLJ 12/05)

1900 Sage, Angie. *Flyte* (5–8). Illus. by Mark Zug. Series: Septimus Heap. 2006, HarperCollins $17.99 (0-06-057734-7). 544pp. In this fast-paced sequel to *Magyk* (2005), wizard Septimus must protect Princess Jenna from numerous dangers; a CD includes games. (Rev: BL 5/15/06; SLJ 6/06; VOYA 2/06)

1901 Sage, Angie. *My Haunted House* (2–4). Illus. by Jimmy Pickering. Series: Araminta Spookie. 2006, HarperCollins $8.99 (978-0-06-077481-3). 132pp. Living in a haunted house suits Araminta Spookie just fine, so she's understandably upset when her Aunt Tabby announces she plans to sell the house. (Rev: SLJ 2/07)

1902 Sage, Angie. *Physik* (5–8). 2007, Harper-Collins $17.99 (0-06-057737-1). 560pp. When Septimus Heap, apprenticed to a wizard, inadvertently releases the spirit of an evil queen who lived centuries earlier, the ill-tempered monarch unleashes chaos in the kingdom; the third book in the series. (Rev: BL 4/1/07)

1903 Sage, Angie. *The Sword in the Grotto* (2–4). Illus. by Jimmy Pickering. Series: Araminta Spookie. 2006, HarperCollins $8.99 (978-0-06-077484-4). 146pp. In the second book in the series, Araminta and her friend Wanda Wizzard run into trouble when they try to retrieve a sword from a grotto to present to the ghostly Sir Horace for his 500th birthday. (Rev: SLJ 2/07)

1904 Said, S. F. *The Outlaw Varjak Paw* (4–6). Illus. by Dave McKean. 2006, Random $16.95 (0-385-75044-7). 256pp. In this action-packed sequel to *Varjak Paw* (2003), the talented cat is forced into a confrontation with Sally Bones, who, like Varjak, is skilled in the martial arts. (Rev: BL 4/1/06; SLJ 2/06)

1905 Scieszka, Jon. *Oh Say, I Can't See* (3–5). Illus. by Adam McCauley. Series: Time Warp Trio. 2005, Viking $14.99 (0-670-06025-9). 80pp. The three young time travelers play a key role in George Washington's decision to cross the Delaware River on Christmas Day in 1776. (Rev: BL 11/15/05; SLJ 11/05)

1906 Scieszka, Jon. *You Can't, but Genghis Khan* (2–5). Adapted by Jennifer Frantz. Illus. Series: Time Warp Trio. 2006, HarperTrophy paper $4.99 (0-06-111636-X). 74pp. The Time Warp Trio — Fred, Joe, and Sam — return in an adaptation from the TV series, in which they travel back to 13th-century Mongolia and are rescued from a battle by a young Genghis Khan. (Rev: SLJ 1/07)

1907 Shalant, Phyllis. *Bartleby of the Big Bad Bayou* (4–6). 2005, Dutton $16.99 (0-525-47366-1). 160pp. Bartleby the turtle and his alligator friend Seezer, both former pets, return to bayou country but find there have been some unwelcome changes while they were away; a sequel to *Bartleby of the Mighty Mississippi* (2000). (Rev: BL 7/05; SLJ 8/05)

1908 Shalant, Phyllis. *The Great Cape Rescue* (3–5). Series: The Society of Super Secret Heroes. 2007, Dutton $15.99 (978-0-525-47404-3). 128pp. A scruffy-looking cape gives Finch and his three best friends the power to deal with school bullies and family problems, so when the cape begins talking and suggests they use its powers to help others, the boys heed its message. (Rev: BL 4/1/07)

1909 Shan, Darren. *Lord of the Shadows* (5–10). Series: Cirque du Freak. 2006, Little, Brown $15.99 (0-316-15628-0). 220pp. In the 11th book in the series, part-vampire Darren faces off against Steve Leopard, leader of the Vampaneze, in a battle to determine who will be the next Lord of the Shadows. (Rev: SLJ 9/06)

1910 Sherman, Delia. *Changeling* (5–8). 2006, Viking $16.99 (0-670-05967-6). 292pp. Neef, kidnapped as a baby by fairies, faces exile from her home in New York Between — an alternate Manhattan inhabited by elves, pixies, fairies, and other spirits — when she breaks the rules. (Rev: SLJ 10/06)

1911 *Showcase Presents Superman*, vol. 1 (3–8). 2005, DC Comics paper $9.99 (1-4012-0758-8). 560pp. This impressive volume collects 29 Superman comics published between 1959 and 1963. (Rev: SLJ 1/06)

1912 Sierra, Judy. *The Gruesome Guide to World Monsters* (5–8). Illus. by Henrik Drescher. 2005, Candlewick $17.99 (0-7636-1727-X). 64pp. A wonderfully ghoulish field guide to more than 60 monsters from world folklore, complete with Gruesomeness Ratings and Survival Tips if appropriate. (Rev: BCCB 9/05; BL 9/15/05*; HBG 4/06; LMC 2/06; SLJ 9/05)

1913 Silberberg, Alan. *Pond Scum* (4–7). 2005, Hyperion $15.99 (0-7868-5634-3). 304pp. Ten-year-old Oliver gains a whole new appreciation for his animal neighbors after he finds a magical gem that allows him to assume the shape of various creatures. (Rev: BL 12/1/05; SLJ 11/05)

1914 Sleator, William. *Hell Phone* (5–8). 2006, Abrams $16.95 (0-8109-5479-6). 238pp. In this dark, suspenseful novel, 17-year-old Nick discovers that the cell phone he bought at a bargain price constantly rings with frightening requests. (Rev: BL 10/1/06; SLJ 11/06)

1915 Smallcomb, Pam. *The Trimoni Twins and the Shrunken Treasure* (3–6). 2005, Bloomsbury $15.95 (1-58234-656-9). 229pp. In Amsterdam to put on a magic show, the 11-year-old Trimoni twins try to unravel the mystery of the shrinking coin. (Rev: SLJ 12/05)

1916 Smith, Sherwood. *Trouble Under Oz* (4–6). Illus. by William Stout. 2006, HarperCollins $16.99 (0-06-029609-7). 239pp. When Princess Ozma asks for their help, Em and Dori, descendants of Dorothy Gale, have to decide how to come to Ozma's aid while still keeping peace on the home front. (Rev: SLJ 12/06)

1917 Snow, Alan. *Here Be Monsters!* (4–6). Illus. by author. 2006, Simon & Schuster $17.95 (0-689-87047-7). 512pp. A complex, inventive, and humor-filled fantasy involving an amazing cast of eccentric characters and a resourceful hero called Arthur. (Rev: BL 5/15/06; SLJ 8/06)

1918 Stanley, Diane. *Bella at Midnight* (5–8). Illus. by Bagram Ibatoulline. 2006, HarperCollins LB $16.89 (0-06-077574-2). 288pp. A fine retelling of the Cinderella story featuring a plucky Bella and a storytelling format. (Rev: BCCB 4/06; BL 2/1/06*; HB 3–4/06; HBG 10/06; LMC 2/07; SLJ 3/06*; VOYA 2/06)

1919 Stanley, Diane. *The Trouble with Wishes* (2–4). Illus. by author. 2007, HarperCollins $16.99 (978-0-06-055451-4). In this humorous variation on the legend of Pygmalion, a sculptor named Pyg falls in love with a statue of a goddess and wishes she were real; his wish is granted and he soon comes to regret this. (Rev: BL 11/1/06; SLJ 2/07)

1920 Stead, Rebecca. *First Light* (5–8). 2007, Random $15.99 (978-0-375-84017-3). 336pp. On a scientific expedition to Greenland with his parents, 12-year-old Peter meets 14-year-old Thea, a member of a secret society that lives beneath the ice. (Rev: BL 4/15/07)

1921 Steer, Dugald A. *The Dragon's Eye* (5–8). Series: Dragonology Chronicles. 2006, Candlewick $15.99 (0-7636-2810-7). 256pp. In the late 19th century, Daniel Cook, 12, and his sister Beatrice attend a dragon school run by Dr. Ernest Drake and accompany him on search for the important Dragon's Eye. (Rev: BL 1/1–15/07; SLJ 1/07)

1922 Stewart, Paul. *Freeglader* (4–6). Illus. by Chris Riddell. Series: Edge Chronicles. 2006, Random $12.95 (0-385-75083-8). 416pp. Librarian knight Rook Barkwater and his friends face daunting challenges on their journey to reach a new home in the Free Glades; the final volume in this fast-paced and complex fantasy. (Rev: BL 12/1/05; SLJ 2/06; VOYA 12/05)

1923 Stewart, Paul, and Chris Riddell. *Fergus Crane* (3–5). 2006, Random $14.95 (0-385-75088-9). 240pp. Nine-year-old Fergus Crane embarks on a series of magical adventures after a flying box and a winged horse enter his life. (Rev: BL 2/15/06; SLJ 6/06)

1924 Stewart, Paul, and Chris Riddell. *Hugo Pepper* (3–5). Illus. Series: Far-Flung Adventures. 2007, Random $14.99 (978-0-385-75092-9). 272pp. Ten-year-old Hugo Pepper, son of explorers who were eaten by polar bears, sets off on his parents' sled to learn more about his roots and finds himself in Firefly Square, where he finds adventure, intrigue, and eccentricity. (Rev: BL 4/1/07; SLJ 2/07)

1925 Stewart, Sharon. *Raven Quest* (5–8). 2005, Carolrhoda LB $15.95 (1-57505-894-4). 320pp. Tok the raven seeks to restore his good name after being falsely accused of murder and sets off to find the legendary Grey Lords. (Rev: SLJ 1/06; VOYA 12/05)

1926 Stewart, Trenton Lee. *The Mysterious Benedict Society* (4–7). Illus. by Carson Ellis. 2007, Little, Brown $16.99 (978-0-316-05777-6). 485pp. Orphan Reynie Muldoon is one of a number of gifted children selected to take part in an effort to infiltrate the Learning Institute for the Very Enlightened; a complex story of mystery and adventure. (Rev: BL 1/1–15/07; SLJ 3/07*)

1927 Strickland, Brad. *Grimoire: The Curse of the Midions* (5–8). 2006, Dial $11.99 (0-8037-3060-8). 160pp. A trip to London with his parents goes terribly awry when Jarvey Midion finds himself transported to an alternate universe where he must confront the villainous wizard Tantalus Mideon. (Rev: BL 6/1–15/06; SLJ 11/06)

1928 Thorpe, Kiki. *The Trouble with Tink* (2–3). Illus. by Judith Holmes Clarke and the Disney Storybook Artists. Series: Disney Fairies. 2006, Random paper $5.99 (0-7364-2371-0). 128pp. When Tinker Bell loses her hammer, she also loses her ability to mend the battered pots and pans of Never Land's Pixie Hollow. (Rev: SLJ 3/06)

1929 Townley, Roderick. *The Constellation of Sylvie* (5–8). Series: Sylvie Cycle. 2006, Simon & Schuster $16.95 (0-689-85713-6). 208pp. In this third installment in the series, Princess Sylvie and her literary entourage find themselves on a spacecraft bound for Jupiter. (Rev: BL 6/1–15/06; SLJ 8/06)

1930 Tripp, Jenny. *Pete and Fremont* (4–6). Illus. by John Manders. 2007, Harcourt $16.00 (978-0-15-205629-2). 192pp. Circus performers Pete the poodle and Fremont the grizzly bear form a mutually beneficial friendship in this story full of circus lore. (Rev: BL 3/15/07)

1931 Ullman, Barb Bentler. *The Fairies of Nutfolk Wood* (3–5). 2006, HarperCollins $15.99 (0-06-073614-3). 256pp. After her parents divorce, 10-year-old Willa and her mother move into a trailer in the woods; here Willa recovers from her stress and, with her elderly neighbor Hazel, befriends the local fairies. (Rev: BL 5/15/06; HBG 10/06; SLJ 7/06)

1932 Ursu, Anne. *The Shadow Thieves* (5–8). 2006, Simon & Schuster $16.95 (1-4169-0587-1). 416pp. A plot to reanimate the dead using the essence of living children is foiled by cousins Charlotte and Zee in this story of heroism and mythology that ranges from the Midwest to England to Hades. (Rev: BL 3/1/06; SLJ 4/06)

1933 Van Belkom, Edo. *Lone Wolf* (5–8). 2005, Tundra paper $8.95 (0-88776-741-9). 177pp. The four teen werewolves adopted by Ranger Brock in *Wolf Pack* (2004) defend their beloved woods against a corrupt developer. (Rev: SLJ 1/06; VOYA 4/06)

1934 Vande Velde, Vivian. *Three Good Deeds* (3–5). 2005, Harcourt $16.00 (0-15-205382-4). 160pp. Transformed into a goose by a witch's curse, Howard must perform three good deeds to return to human form. (Rev: BL 10/15/05; SLJ 10/05)

1935 Vande Velde, Vivian. *Witch Dreams* (5–8). 2005, Marshall Cavendish $15.95 (0-7614-5235-4). 128pp. Nyssa, a 16-year-old witch, seeks justice for

her parents, who were murdered six years earlier. (Rev: BL 12/15/05; SLJ 11/05; VOYA 12/05)

1936 Velmans, Hester. *Isabel of the Whales* (4–6). 2005, Delacorte $15.95 (0-385-73202-3). 181pp. An informative fantasy in which a girl becomes a whale and learns about diving, feeding, and communication while she teaches the whales about such dangers as nets and ships. (Rev: SLJ 8/05)

1937 Voake, Steve. *The Dreamwalker's Child* (5–8). 2006, Bloomsbury $16.95 (1-58234-661-5). 300pp. After being hit by a car, Sam Palmer finds himself in the alternate world of Aurobon, where he learns of a deadly plot to wipe out human life on Earth using a virus transmitted by mosquitoes. (Rev: SLJ 8/06; VOYA 6/06)

1938 Wade, Rebecca. *The Theft and the Miracle* (5–8). 2007, HarperCollins $16.99 (0-06-077493-2). 368pp. Mystery and supernatural are combined in this story of Hannah, a plain, overweight 12-year-old with artistic abilities, who — with her friend Sam — finds herself on a hunt for a missing religious statue. (Rev: BL 11/15/06; SLJ 1/07)

1939 Wallace, Bill. *The Legend of Thunderfoot* (3–5). 2006, Simon & Schuster $15.95 (1-4169-0691-6). 160pp. In this appealing animal fantasy, a young roadrunner finds ways to make the most of his oversized feet, swollen out of proportion by a snakebite. (Rev: BL 11/1/06; SLJ 10/06)

1940 Warner, Sally. *Twilight Child* (5–8). 2006, Viking $17.99 (0-670-06076-3). 304pp. Finnish Eleni finds romance and danger on a Scottish island in this story set in the 18th century and filled with elements of fantasy. (Rev: BCCB 9/06; BL 5/15/06; HBG 10/06; SLJ 7/06)

1941 Watts, Leander. *Ten Thousand Charms* (5–7). 2005, Houghton $16.00 (0-618-44897-7). 228pp. In this historical fantasy set in the 19th century, Roddy, an 11-year-old apprentice to a ropemaker in Pharaoh, New York, joins forces with a deposed European king to rescue the king's daughter from the villainous Scalander. (Rev: BCCB 5/05; SLJ 8/05; VOYA 2/06)

1942 Weatherill, Cat. *Barkbelly* (4–7). Illus. by Peter Brown. 2006, Knopf $15.95 (0-375-83327-7). 320pp. A wooden boy being raised by normal parents flees after he accidentally causes a tragedy and searches for his own family. (Rev: BL 5/15/06; SLJ 7/06)

1943 Welvaert, Scott R. *The Curse of the Wendigo: An Agate and Buck Adventure* (5–9). Illus. by Brann Garvey. 2006, Stone Arch LB $22.60 (1-59889-066-2). 105pp. Searching for their parents in the vast Canadian wilderness in the late 19th century, 16-year-old Buck and his younger sister Agate find themselves being pursued by the mythical Wendigo; suitable for reluctant readers. (Rev: SLJ 1/07)

1944 Wersba, Barbara. *Walter: The Story of a Rat* (4–7). Illus. by Donna Diamond. 2005, Front St. $16.95 (1-932425-41-1). 64pp. Miss Pomeroy, a children's author, develops a friendship with a literary rat named Walter who shares her house in this thoughtful and sophisticated book. (Rev: BCCB 2/06; BL 11/15/05; SLJ 12/05)

1945 Westera, Marleen. *Sheep and Goat* (1–3). Illus. by Sylvia van Ommen. 2006, Front St. $16.95 (1-932425-81-0). 99pp. Sheep and Goat are very fond of each other despite their differences in these 18 short stories in an early-chapter-book format. (Rev: BL 2/1/07; SLJ 11/06)

1946 Whittemore, JoAnne. *Escape from Arylon* (5–8). Series: The Silverskin Legacy. 2006, Llewellyn paper $8.95 (0-7387-0869-0). 360pp. Ainsley and Megan, neighbors with an uneasy friendship, find themselves transported through a portal to Arylon, where they meet many magical characters and must save the Staff of Lexiam from thieves. (Rev: SLJ 6/06; VOYA 6/06)

1947 Whybrow, Ian. *The Unvisibles* (4–6). 2006, Holiday $16.95 (0-8234-1972-X). 184pp. Oliver Gasper and Nicky Chew are 12-year-old boys with almost nothing in common, but their lives intersect when Oliver desperately needs a friend to help him reverse the magical chant that rendered him invisible. (Rev: BL 4/15/06; SLJ 5/06)

1948 Williams, Maiya. *The Hour of the Cobra* (4–7). 2006, Abrams $16.95 (0-8109-5970-4). 300pp. Xanthe, Xavier, Rowan, and Nina time-travel to ancient Egypt and narrowly avoid altering history in this sequel to *The Golden Hour* (2004). (Rev: BL 5/15/06; SLJ 7/06; VOYA 6/06)

1949 Williams, Mark London. *Trail of Bones* (5–8). Series: Danger Boy. 2005, Candlewick $9.99 (0-7636-2154-4). 300pp. Eli, Thea, and Clyne — three characters of very different backgrounds — travel back in time from 2019 to early-19th-century America and become involved with Lewis and Clark and the plight of escaping slaves. (Rev: SLJ 7/05)

1950 Winterson, Jeanette. *Tanglewreck* (4–7). 2006, Bloomsbury $16.95 (1-58234-919-3). 415pp. After "time tornadoes" upset the delicate balance of time and space in and around London, 11-year-old Silver embarks on a fantastic odyssey in search of the Timekeeper that, hopefully, can set things right again. (Rev: BL 10/1/06; SLJ 10/06; VOYA 8/06)

1951 Wojtowicz, Jen. *The Boy Who Grew Flowers* (1–3). Illus. by Steve Adams. 2005, Barefoot Bks. $16.99 (1-84148-686-8). 32pp. In this story of differences and self-acceptance, Rink Bowagon, a boy who sprouts flowers from his body during the full moon, courts Angelina Quiz, a new girl at school who has a short right leg. (Rev: BL 10/15/05; SLJ 2/06)

1952 Wood, Beverley, and Chris Wood. *Jack's Knife* (5–9). Series: A Sirius Mystery. 2006, Raincoast paper $7.95 (1-55192-709-8). 293pp. This sequel to *Dog Star* (1998) finds Jack time-traveling with bull terrier Patsy Ann to 1930s Alaska to help solve a mystery at sea. (Rev: SLJ 5/06)

1953 Worley, Rob. *Heir to Fire: Gila Flats* (5–8). Illus. by Mike Dubisch. 2006, Komikwerks $12.95 (0-9742803-7-2). 169pp. Fourteen-year-old Ryan Morales realizes he has extraordinary powers and uses them to combat the strange forces attacking the remote Arizona town in which he lives; this fast-paced novel will attract reluctant readers. (Rev: SLJ 1/07)

1954 Wright, Randall. *The Silver Penny* (4–7). 2005, Holt $16.95 (0-8050-7391-4). 197pp. In this compelling fantasy set in the 19th century, Jacob — after breaking his leg and facing disability — receives from his great-grandfather a lucky silver penny that gives him access to a supernatural world. (Rev: BCCB 7–8/05; SLJ 8/05; VOYA 10/05)

1955 Young, Steve. *15 Minutes* (5–8). 2006, HarperCollins $15.99 (0-06-072508-7). 172pp. Casey, a seventh grader who's always late for almost everything, discovers that his grandfather's watch gives him the power to go back 15 minutes. (Rev: SLJ 9/06)

1956 Zahn, Timothy. *Dragon and Herdsman: The Fourth Dragonback Adventure* (5–8). 2006, Tom Doherty Assoc. $17.95 (0-765-31417-7). 299pp. With the help of a shape-changing dragon and his friend Alison, 14-year-old Jack Morgan escapes from the Malison Ring. (Rev: SLJ 9/06; VOYA 6/06)

1957 Zappa, Ahmet. *The Monstrous Memoirs of a Mighty McFearless* (4–7). Illus. by author. 2006, Random $12.95 (0-375-83287-4). 224pp. Written and illustrated by the son of Frank Zappa, this rollicking fantasy follows Mini and Max McFearless, monsterminators who must rescue their father from kidnappers. (Rev: BL 5/15/06; SLJ 7/06)

Friendship Stories

1958 Abbott, Tony. *Firegirl* (5–8). 2006, Little, Brown $15.99 (0-316-01171-1). 145pp. Tom, already an outsider at his Catholic school, bravely befriends a girl scarred by burns even when his classmates ostracize and ridicule her. (Rev: BL 7/06; SLJ 7/06)

1959 Blume, Lesley M. M. *Cornelia and the Audacious Escapades of the Somerset Sisters* (4–6). 2006, Knopf $15.95 (0-375-83523-7). 272pp. Cornelia befriends the elderly woman who moves in next door and finds her loneliness abated by the woman's fascinating stories of her life. (Rev: BL 7/06; SLJ 9/06)

1960 Campbell, Ellen Langas. *Raising the Roof* (3–6). Illus. by April D'Angelo. Series: Girls Know How. 2005, NouSoma paper $4.95 (0-9743604-1-4). 121pp. A group of fifth-grade girls decide to build a clubhouse with the help of a local construction firm's female CEO. (Rev: SLJ 1/06)

1961 Denman, K. L. *Mirror Image* (5–8). Series: Currents. 2007, Orca $14.95 (978-1-55143-667-8); paper $8.95 (978-1-55143-667-4). 112pp. Sable, an immigrant to Canada from Bosnia who is a loner, and popular Lacey could not be more different, and the girls are initially disappointed to be paired for an art project. (Rev: BL 3/15/07)

1962 Friedman, Laurie. *Happy Birthday, Mallory!* (2–4). Illus. by Tamara Schmitz. Series: Mallory. 2005, Carolrhoda LB $15.95 (1-57505-823-5). 159pp. As a special treat, Mallory is allowed to have an old friend come to visit for her ninth birthday in this beginning chapter book. (Rev: SLJ 9/05)

1963 Greenwald, Sheila. *Rosy Cole's Memoir Explosion: A Heartbreaking Story About Losing Friends, Annoying Family, and Ruining Romance* (3–5). Series: Rosy Cole. 2006, Farrar $16.00 (0-374-36347-1). 112pp. Rosy sets out to write a memoir and, in an effort to be entertaining, portrays her friends in a less-than-flattering light. (Rev: BL 5/1/06; SLJ 4/06)

1964 Grindley, Sally. *Dear Max* (2–4). Illus. by Tony Ross. 2006, Simon & Schuster $14.95 (1-4169-0392-5). 144pp. Max, a 9-year-old aspiring writer, sends a letter to his favorite author, D. J. Lucas, and the two develop an unusual friendship, sharing their problems with writing and life in often-humorous exchanges. Also use *Bravo, Max!* (2007). (Rev: BL 8/06; SLJ 8/06*)

1965 Lombard, Jenny. *Drita, My Homegirl* (3–5). 2006, Putnam $15.99 (0-399-24380-1). 112pp. Drita, a refugee from Kosovo, and Maxie, a motherless African American girl, connect despite their differences in this story set in a Brooklyn neighborhood. (Rev: BL 5/1/06; SLJ 3/06*)

1966 McDonald, Megan. *Judy Moody: Around the World in 8 1/2 Days* (3–4). Illus. by Peter Reynolds. 2006, Candlewick $15.99 (0-7636-2832-8). 157pp. In this new easy-chapter-book adventure, third-grader Judy Moody becomes so obsessed with new friend Amy Namey that she neglects some of her longtime pals. (Rev: SLJ 11/06)

1967 Myracle, Lauren. *The Fashion Disaster That Changed My Life* (5–8). 2005, Dutton $15.99 (0-525-47222-3). 160pp. Through her diary and instant messages, Allison relates the turmoil of 7th grade, from her humiliating first-day arrival with her mother's underwear clinging to her pants to her problems

making and keeping friends. (Rev: BL 9/15/05; SLJ 7/05)

1968 Nemeth, Sally. *The Heights, the Depths, and Everything in Between* (5–8). 2006, Knopf $15.95 (0-375-83458-3). 272pp. Jake Little, a dwarf, and Lucy Small, who despite her name is unusually tall, become friends and navigate the rough waters of middle school and dealing with parents in this story set in the 1970s. (Rev: BL 7/06)

1969 Pennypacker, Sara. *Clementine* (2–4). Illus. by Marla Frazee. 2006, Hyperion $14.99 (0-7868-3882-5). 144pp. Eight-year-old Clementine means well but seems to find herself spending a lot of time in the school principal's office. (Rev: BL 10/15/06; SLJ 10/06*)

1970 Seuling, Barbara. *Robert and the Happy Endings* (2–4). Illus. by Paul Brewer. 2007, Cricket $16.95 (978-0-8126-2748-0). 160pp. This perceptive chapter book explores the nature of friendship as Robert befriends the new girl who's deaf, gets help from Lester in recovering his stolen bike, and teams up with his erstwhile archenemy Susanne on a school activity. (Rev: BL 1/1–15/07)

1971 Spinelli, Jerry. *Eggs* (4–7). 2007, Little, Brown $15.99 (978-0-316-16646-1). 240pp. Two troubled children — 9-year-old David and 13-year-old Primrose — forge an unlikely friendship. (Rev: BL 4/1/07)

1972 Stauffacher, Sue. *Donutheart* (4–6). 2006, Knopf $15.95 (0-375-83275-0). 208pp. In this sequel to *Donuthead* (2003), Franklin is having trouble making the adjustment to middle school but he sets aside his own preoccupations (hygiene and safety, among them) to come to the aid of Sarah, his best friend. (Rev: BL 11/1/06; SLJ 1/07)

1973 Tarshis, Lauren. *Emma-Jean Lazarus Fell Out of a Tree* (4–6). 2007, Dial $16.99 (978-0-8037-3164-6). 208pp. Emma-Jean Lazarus is persuaded to use her analytical mind to help a classmate cope with a bully and discovers that social relationships are not always logical. (Rev: BL 3/15/07)

1974 Warner, Sally. *Not So Weird Emma* (2–4). Illus. by Jamie Harper. 2005, Viking $14.99 (0-670-06005-4). 128pp. The friendship of third graders Emma McGraw and Cynthia Harbison is fractured when the two start calling each other unflattering names; a sequel to *Only Emma* (2005). (Rev: BL 9/1/05; SLJ 11/05)

1975 Yee, Lisa. *So Totally Emily Ebers* (5–8). 2007, Scholastic $16.99 (978-0-439-83847-4). 281pp. In this companion to *Millicent Min, Girl Genius* (2003) and *Stanford Wong Flunks Big-Time* (2005), Emily writes a series of letters to her absent father, telling him about her friends Millicent and Stanford and their tutoring arrangement. (Rev: BL 3/15/07)

Graphic Novels

1976 Akimoto, Nami. *Ultra Cute. Vol. 1* (5–8). Trans. from Japanese by Emi Onishi. Illus. by author. 2006, TokyoPop paper $9.99 (1-59532-956-0). 179pp. Ami and Noa, more rivals than friends, compete with each other over two guys who are not as nice as they seem. (Rev: SLJ 7/06)

1977 Austen, Chuck. *Superman: The Wrath of Gog* (5–12). Illus. by Ivan Reis, et al. 2005, DC Comics paper $14.99 (1-4012-0450-3). Superman is gravely injured in a battle with Gog and returns to his boyhood home to recuperate. (Rev: SLJ 9/05)

1978 Baltazar, Art, and Franco Aureliani. *Patrick the Wolf Boy. Vol. 1* (2–8). Illus. by Art Baltazar. 2005, DDP paper $10.95 (1-932796-27-4). A graphic novel about the hilarious adventures of a young werewolf. (Rev: SLJ 7/05)

1979 Baum, L. Frank. *The Wizard of Oz* (3–5). Adapted by Michael Cavallero. 2005, Puffin paper $9.99 (0-14-240471-3). 152pp. In this graphic adaptation that retains original dialogue, Dorothy wears jeans, the Good Witch of the North sports sunglasses, and the Tin Woodman has traded his ax for a buzz saw. (Rev: SLJ 11/05)

1980 Blackman, Haden, and others. *Clone Wars Adventures* (4–7). Series: Star Wars Clone Wars Adventures. 2006, Dark Horse paper $6.95 (1-59307-483-2). 96pp. This fifth volume of the fantasy series, based on the TV cartoon show, includes four fast-paced stories of graphic-novel action and adventure. (Rev: BL 6/1–15/06)

1981 Clugston, Chynna. *Queen Bee* (5–8). Illus. 2005, Scholastic paper $8.99 (0-439-70987-3). 112pp. In this humorous graphic novel about school cliques, Haley and Alexa, two middle school students with psychokinetic powers, battle each other to become the school's most popular girl. (Rev: BL 9/15/05; SLJ 1/06; VOYA 12/05)

1982 *Creepy Creatures* (3–5). Illus. by Gabriel Hernandez, et al. Series: Goosebumps Graphix. 2006, Scholastic $16.99 (0-439-84124-0); paper $8.99 (0-439-84125-9). 144pp. Three Goosebumps stories — "The Werewolf of Fever Swamp," "The Scarecrow Walks at Midnight," and "The Abominable Snowman of Pasadena" — are presented in black-and-white graphic-novel format. (Rev: BL 10/1/06; SLJ 11/06)

1983 de Campi, Alex. *Kat and Mouse: Tripped* (3–5). Illus. by Federica Manfredi. 2007, TokyoPop paper $5.99 (978-1-59816-549-4). 96pp. In this second installment in the manga mystery series, Kat and Mouse are on a field trip to the art museum when a famous painting is stolen. (Rev: BL 3/15/07)

1984 Dezago, Todd. *Spider-Man: The Terrible Threat of the Living Brain!* (5–8). Illus. by Jonboy Meyers, et al. Series: Spider-Man. 2006, ABDO LB $21.35 (1-59961-008-6). Spider-Man, with a little help from Flash, foils the theft of the Living Brain, a powerful robot-like computer. (Rev: SLJ 11/06)

1985 Dezago, Todd. *Spider-Man and Captain America: Stars, Stripes, and Spiders!* (5–8). Series: Spider-Man Team Up. 2006, ABDO LB $21.35 (1-59961-001-9). In this action-packed comic-book fantasy, superheroes Spider-Man and Captain America team up to battle the Grey Gargoyle. (Rev: SLJ 11/06)

1986 Fisher, Jane Smith. *WJHC: Hold Tight* (4–7). Illus. 2005, Wilson Place paper $11.95 (0-9744235-1-3). 96pp. This graphic-novel sequel to *WJHC: On the Air* (2003) continues the adventures of six diverse teenage friends who launched a high school radio station, following them through a reality TV show, a celebrity fashion show, and a trip to a rock concert. (Rev: BL 11/1/05; SLJ 1/06)

1987 Frampton, Otis. *Oddly Normal. v.1* (4–7). Illus. 2006, Viper paper $11.95 (0-9777883-0-X). 128pp. Half-human and half-witch, unhappy 10-year-old Oddly Normal struggles to find a place where she fits in; a collection of four issues of a mini-series published by Viper Comics. (Rev: BL 11/1/06)

1988 Friesen, Ray. *A Cheese Related Mishap and Other Stories* (5–8). Illus. 2005, Don't Eat Any Bugs paper $8.95 (0-9728177-6-X). 96pp. This collection of zany tales full of entertaining characters and situations was created by a teenage author/illustrator. (Rev: BL 11/15/05; SLJ 3/06)

1989 Friesen, Ray. *Yarg!* (3–5). Illus. Series: Lookit! 2007, Don't Eat Any Bugs paper $11.95 (978-0-972817-79-0). 102pp. Back for a new round of adventures in this madcap sequel to *A Cheese Related Mishap* (2005), Melville the penguin and his friends scramble for gold in an effort to pay the back rent on the castle of Pellmellia. (Rev: BL 3/15/07)

1990 Fujino, Moyamu. *The First King Adventure*, Vol. 1 (4–8). Trans. from Japanese by Kay Bertrand. Illus. by author. 2004, ADV paper $9.99 (1-4139-0194-8). Prince Tiltu cannot succeed his father as king until he's made contracts with all of the spirit masters that inhabit the kingdom. (Rev: SLJ 7/05)

1991 Grayson, Devin. *X-Men: Evolution: Hearing Things* (5–8). Illus. by UDON, et al. Series: X-Men Evolution. 2006, ABDO LB $21.35 (1-59961-053-1). In this comic-book adventure from the early years of the X-Men series, Jean Grey comes to grips with her telepathic and telekinetic powers. (Rev: SLJ 11/06)

1992 *Green Lantern* (4–10). Series: Showcase Presents. 2005, DC Comics paper $9.99 (1-4012-0759-6). 526pp. A collection of black-and-white reprints of the early comics about the handsome crime fighter. (Rev: SLJ 5/06)

1993 Holm, Jennifer L., and Matthew Holm. *Babymouse: Our Hero* (4–6). Illus. 2005, Random LB $12.99 (0-375-93230-5); paper $5.95 (0-375-83230-0). 96pp. Babymouse dreads competing in her class's annual dodgeball tournament, but when her best friend is threatened she surprises herself and saves the day for her team. (Rev: BL 12/1/05; SLJ 3/06)

1994 Holm, Jennifer L., and Matthew Holm. *Babymouse: Queen of the World* (4–6). Illus. 2005, Random LB $12.99 (0-375-93229-1); paper $5.95 (0-375-83229-7). 96pp. Babymouse learns some important lessons about the true meaning of friendship after she slights Wilson Weasel to win an invitation to Felicia Furrypaws' slumber party. (Rev: BL 12/1/05; SLJ 3/06)

1995 Huey, Debbie. *Bumperboy and the Loud, Loud Mountain* (2–4). 2006, AdHouse paper $8.95 (0-9766610-1-2). 128pp. Bumperboy and his faithful canine sidekick try to unravel the mysteries surrounding the disappearance of the Grums and an endangered talking mountain called Jumbra; the second installment in a graphic-novel series. (Rev: BL 8/06)

1996 Ikezawa, Satomi. *Guru Guru Pon-Chan*, Vol. 1 (5–12). Trans. from Japanese by Douglas Varenas. Illus. by author. 2005, Del Rey paper $10.95 (0-345-48095-3). 171pp. In this whimsical shape-changing story, Ponta, a Labrador retriever puppy, nibbles on a newly invented "chit-chat" bone and turns into a human girl who comically retains doggy behavior. (Rev: SLJ 11/05)

1997 Ikumi, Mia. *Tokyo Mew Mew a la Mode*, Vol. 1 (5–8). Trans. from Japanese by Yoohae Yang. Illus. by author. 2005, TokyoPop paper $9.99 (1-59532-789-4). 197pp. In the opening volume of the Tokyo Mew Mew a la Mode series, 12-year-old Berry Shirayuki is shanghaied into a team of girl superheroes and soon finds herself doing battle with dragons and the evil Saint Rose Crusaders. (Rev: SLJ 11/05)

1998 Johns, Geoff, et al. *Teen Titans: The Future Is Now* (5–8). Illus. Series: Teen Titans. 2005, DC Comics paper $9.99 (1-4012-0475-9). 224pp. In volume four of the series, the title characters return from a mission into the future to learn that Robin's father died while they were away. (Rev: BL 3/15/06) [741.5]

1999 Kennedy, Mike. *Superman: Infinite City* (5–12). Illus. by Carlos Meglia. 2005, DC Comics $24.99 (1-4012-0067-2). 96pp. Superman and Lois become enmeshed in a power struggle in an alternate world known as Infinite City. (Rev: SLJ 9/05)

2000 Kobayashi, Makoto. *Planet of the Cats* (5–8). Series: What's Michael? 2006, Dark Horse paper $9.95 (1-59307-525-1). 104pp. In this 11th, concluding volume of the graphic novel series first published in Japan, Hanako, a human exobiologist, and her spaceship crew find themselves stranded on a planet ruled by house cats. (Rev: BL 9/1/06)

2001 Kobayashi, Makoto. *Sleepless Nights* (5–8). Illus. Series: What's Michael? 2005, Dark Horse paper $8.95 (1-59307-337-2). 88pp. Volume ten of the continuing adventures of the house cat who has been described as "Japan's version of Garfield, Heathcliff, and Krazy Kat all rolled into one." (Rev: BL 9/1/05)

2002 McKeever, Sean. *Marvel Adventures Spider-Man: Power Struggle* (4–6). Illus. by Patrick Scherberger. 2006, Marvel paper $6.99 (0-7851-1903-5). A Spider-Man for modern readers, well-drawn and lots of fun for fans of superheroes. (Rev: SLJ 7/06)

2003 Martin, Ann M., and Raina Telgemeier. *Kristy's Great Idea* (4–6). Illus. by Raina Telgemeier. Series: Baby-Sitters Club. 2006, Scholastic paper $16.99 (0-439-80241-5). 192pp. The first volume in the popular Baby-Sitters Club series returns in graphic-novel format. Also in this series: *The Truth About Stacey* (2006). (Rev: BL 3/15/06; SLJ 7/06)

2004 Masters, Anthony. *Joker* (2–4). Illus. by Michael Reid. Series: Graphic Trax. 2006, Stone Arch LB $19.93 (1-59889-024-7). 66pp. In this easy-to-read graphic novel, Mel's magic performances in the classroom have fallen flat, but the boy comes to the rescue when his dad — a bank manager — is seized by would-be robbers. (Rev: SLJ 9/06)

2005 *Metamorpho, the Element Man* (5–9). 2005, DC Comics paper $16.99 (1-4012-0762-6). 559pp. A retro black-and-white comic book, first published in the mid-1960s and featuring the adventures of Rex Mason (aka Metamorpho), transformed into "a walking chemistry set" superhero. (Rev: SLJ 5/06) [741.5]

2006 Misako Rocks!. *Biker Girl* (5–8). Illus. 2006, Hyperion paper $7.99 (0-78683-676-8). 112pp. Aki, a shy, bookish girl, is transformed into a superhero after finding a discarded bicycle in her grandfather's garage. (Rev: BL 3/15/06; SLJ 9/06) [741.5]

2007 O'Brien, Anne Sibley. *The Legend of Hong Kil Dong: The Robin Hood of Korea* (3–5). 2006, Charlesbridge $14.95 (1-58089-302-3). 48pp. In graphic novel format, this is a Korean tale — perhaps the first novel written in the Korean alphabet — that features a strong character seeking to undo injustices. (Rev: BL 7/06; SLJ 9/06)

2008 Petrucha, Stefan. *Nancy Drew: The Demon of River Heights* (4–9). Series: Nancy Drew, Girl Detective. 2005, Papercutz $12.95 (1-59707-004-1). The familiar heroine returns in graphic-novel format with this story in which Nancy, Bess, George discover the secret behind a legendary monster. (Rev: SLJ 8/05)

2009 Raicht, Mike. *Spider-Man: Kraven the Hunter* (5–8). Illus. by Jamal Igle, et al. Series: Spider-Man. 2006, ABDO LB $21.35 (1-59961-009-4). Spider-Man once again does battle with Kraven the Hunter, one of his oldest enemies. (Rev: SLJ 11/06)

2010 Renier, Aaron. *Spiral Bound: Top Secret Summer* (4–7). Illus. 2005, Top Shelf paper $14.95 (1-891830-50-3). 180pp. This delightful graphic novel chronicles the summer adventures of the animal residents of the Town, a community with a monster in its pond. (Rev: BL 11/1/05)

2011 Scieszka, Jon. *Nightmare on Joe's Street* (2–4). Ed. by Zachary Rau. Illus. by Peter K. Hirsch. Series: Time Warp Trio. 2006, paper $6.99 (0-06-111639-4). 96pp. In the opening volume of this graphic-novel adaptation of the Time Warp Trio television series, Joe and Sam transport Frankenstein's monster back in time so that he can reconcile his differences with his creator, Mary Shelley. (Rev: BL 10/1/06; SLJ 1/07)

2012 Shanower, Eric. *Adventures in Oz* (4–7). Illus. by author. 2007, IDW $47.25 (1-60010-071-6); paper $39.99 (1-933239-61-1). 256pp. Dorothy and her friends from Oz return in this beautifully drawn collection of five graphic novel adventures. (Rev: BL 3/15/07; SLJ 3/07; VOYA 4/07) [741.5]

2013 *Showcase Presents the House of Mystery*, vol. 1 (5–9). 2006, DC Comics paper $16.99 (1-4012-0786-3). 552pp. A collection of relatively tame horror comics that first appeared in the 1960s, in black and white. (Rev: SLJ 7/06)

2014 Smith, Jeff. *Eyes of the Storm*, vol. 3 (4–8). Illus. by author. Series: Bone. 2006, Scholastic $18.95 (0-439-70625-4); paper $9.99 (0-439-70638-6). 192pp. The final book in the first Bone trilogy, this comic-book fantasy has funny moments, suspense and dream sequences that fans will love. (Rev: SLJ 7/06)

2015 Stewart, Paul. *Joust of Honor* (3–6). Illus. by Chris Riddell. Series: A Knight's Story. 2005, Simon & Schuster $9.95 (0-689-87240-2). 137pp. In this second volume of the humorous, action-packed adventures of a medieval knight, Free Lance must choose between pleasing a beautiful lady and earning a sack of gold. (Rev: SLJ 8/05)

2016 Team, Marathon. *The O. P.* (3–5). Illus. 2006, Papercutz paper $7.95 (1-59707-043-2). 96pp. Based on the Cartoon Network's "Totally Spies" series, this slight but enjoyable graphic novel features teen girls who spy for the World Organization of Human Protection. (Rev: BL 1/1–15/07)

2017 *Teen Titans: Jam Packed Action!* (4–8). 2005, DC Comics paper $7.99 (1-4012-0902-5). 96pp.

Two exciting technology-oriented stories are drawn from the Cartoon Network show. (Rev: SLJ 5/06)

2018 Trondheim, Lewis. *Tiny Tyrant* (4–7). Illus. by Fabrice Parme. 2007, Roaring Brook paper $12.95 (978-1-59643-094-5). 128pp. Ethelbert, the diminutive and willful 6-year-old child-king of Portocristo, is used to getting his own way in this series of funny episodes. (Rev: BL 3/15/07)

2019 Wilson, Bob. *Fearless Dave* (2–6). Illus. by author. 2006, Frances Lincoln $15.95 (1-84507-496-3). This is an enjoyably silly story about a reluctant knight named Dave whose mother succeeds in bringing him glory — and the princess. (Rev: SLJ 12/06)

2020 Zirkel, Huddleston. *A Bit Haywire* (4–7). Illus. 2006, Viper paper $11.95 (978-0-977788-35-4). 64pp. Owen has many extraordinary powers, but he's having trouble figuring out how to control them. (Rev: BL 3/15/07)

Growing into Maturity

Family Problems

2021 Brown, Susan Taylor. *Hugging the Rock* (5–8). 2006, Tricycle $15.95 (1-58246-180-5). 171pp. In this poignant novel told in free-verse poetry, Rachel describes the difficulties she and her dad have in coping after her mother's departure. (Rev: SLJ 9/06)

2022 Cardenas, Teresa. *Letters to My Mother* (5–8). Trans. by David Unger. 2006, Groundwood $15.95 (0-88899-720-5); paper $6.95 (0-88899-721-3). 104pp. In unhappy letters to her dead mother, a 10-year-old Cuban girl describes cruelty and prejudice at the hands of her relatives. (Rev: BL 5/1/06; SLJ 8/06)

2023 Cheaney, J. B. *The Middle of Somewhere* (5–8). 2007, Knopf $15.99 (978-0-375-83790-6). 256pp. Put in charge of her learning disabled brother while her mother recovers from knee surgery, 12-year-old Ronnie Sparks comes under even greater pressure when she and her brother accompany their grandfather on a trip to Kansas. (Rev: BL 3/15/07)

2024 Day, Karen. *Tall Tales* (5–8). 2007, Random $15.99 (978-0-375-83773-9). 240pp. As she starts school in yet another new town, 12-year-old Meg conceals her father's alcoholism and abuse, afraid it will frighten off potential friends. (Rev: BL 4/1/07)

2025 Ferber, Brenda. *Julia's Kitchen* (5–8). 2006, Farrar $16.00 (0-374-39932-8). 160pp. Eleven-year-old Cara Segal's faith is tested when her mother and sister die in a house fire while Cara is sleeping over at a friend's home. (Rev: BL 2/1/06; SLJ 4/06)

2026 Gallagher, Mary Collins. *Ginny Morris and Dad's New Girlfriend* (3–5). Illus. by Whitney Martin. 2006, Magination $14.95 (978-1-59147-386-2);

paper $8.95 (978-1-59147-387-9). 64pp. Ginny is distressed to discover that her divorced father has a girlfriend in this story written to help children dealing with divorce. (Rev: SLJ 2/07)

2027 Gingras, Charlotte. *Emily's Piano* (4–6). Illus. by Stephane Jorisch. 2005, Firefly $18.95 (1-55037-913-5); paper $7.95 (1-55037-912-7). 64pp. Shaken by the breakup of her parents' marriage, Emily remembers the piano as a symbol of happiness and tracks it down. (Rev: BL 1/1–15/06; SLJ 5/06)

2028 Gregory, Nan. *I'll Sing You One-O* (5–8). 2006, Clarion $16.00 (0-618-60708-0). 220pp. Twelve-year-old Gemma is overwhelmed when relatives — including a twin brother — turn up to take her from the foster home she's come to love, and she becomes convinced that an angel will save the day. (Rev: BL 8/06; SLJ 10/06*)

2029 Grimes, Nikki. *The Road to Paris* (4–7). 2006, Putnam $15.99 (0-399-24537-5). 160pp. Half-white and half-black, 9-year-old Paris suddenly finds herself separated from her older brother Malcolm and living with a foster family in a mostly white neighborhood. (Rev: BL 8/06; SLJ 12/06)

2030 Harness, Cheryl. *Just for You to Know* (5–8). 2006, HarperCollins $16.99 (0-06-078313-3). 308pp. Life is turned upside down for 13-year-old Carmen Cathcart, an aspiring artist, when her mother dies during childbirth. (Rev: SLJ 9/06)

2031 Hest, Amy. *Remembering Mrs. Rossi* (3–5). Illus. by Heather Maione. 2007, Candlewick $14.99 (978-0-7636-2163-6). 192pp. The sudden death of 8-year-old Annie's mother, a sixth-grade teacher, shocks those left behind, and while Annie and her father move toward healing, they take comfort in a scrapbook created by her mother's class. (Rev: BL 1/1–15/07)

2032 Love, D. Anne. *Semiprecious* (4–6). 2006, Simon & Schuster $16.95 (0-689-85638-5). 304pp. Garnet and her sister Opal are left at an aunt's house in small-town Oklahoma while their mother goes off in pursuit of stardom in this novel set in the 1960s. (Rev: BL 7/06; SLJ 9/06)

2033 Martine, Carmela A. *Rosa, Sola* (4–6). 2005, Candlewick $15.99 (0-7636-2395-4). 256pp. Rosa is bereft when the baby brother she's dreamed about is stillborn. (Rev: BCCB 1/06; BL 12/1/05*; HBG 4/06; LMC 11–12/05; SLJ 10/05)

2034 O'Connor, Barbara. *How to Steal a Dog* (4–6). 2007, Farrar $16.00 (0-374-33497-8). 176pp. Desperate to restore some sense of order to her life, in tatters since her father left the family, young Georgina decides to steal a dog and collect a reward. (Rev: BL 3/15/07)

2035 Olson, Gretchen. *Call Me Hope* (4–7). 2007, Little, Brown $15.99 (978-0-316-01236-2). 288pp. Beaten down by her mother's verbal abuse, 11-year-old Hope screws up the courage to confront her

mother and tell her how badly she has been hurt by the name calling. (Rev: BL 3/15/07)

2036 Russo, Marisabina. *A Portrait of Pia* (5–8). 2007, Harcourt $17.00 (978-0-15-205577-6). 240pp. Overwhelmed by her brother's schizophrenia and her mother's new boyfriend, 12-year-old Pia, already a talented artist, travels to Italy to meet her long-absent father and learns how to love her family despite its flaws. (Rev: BL 4/1/07)

2037 Trueit, Trudi. *Julep O'Toole: Miss Independent* (4–6). Illus. 2006, Dutton $15.99 (0-525-47637-7). 160pp. Eleven-year-old Julep and her mother have differing views on Julep's abilities to make her own decisions; a sequel to *Julep O'Toole: Confessions of a Middle Child* (2005). (Rev: BL 4/15/06; SLJ 3/06)

2038 Villareal, Ray. *My Father, the Angel of Death* (5–8). 2006, Piñata paper $9.95 (1-55885-466-5). 192pp. Newly relocated to Texas and unhappy with his home life, Jesse Baron wonders what life would be like if his dad were not the well-known wrestler called the Angel of Death; suitable for reluctant readers. (Rev: SLJ 10/06)

2039 Weeks, Sarah. *Jumping the Scratch* (4–6). 2006, HarperCollins $15.99 (0-06-054109-1). 176pp. Burdened with a dark secret and in shock after some radical changes in his home life, Jamie Reardon focuses his attention on helping his recently injured aunt to recover her short-term memory. (Rev: BL 2/1/06; SLJ 5/06)

2040 Zimmer, Tracie Vaughn. *Sketches from a Spy Tree* (3–5). Illus. by Andrew Glass. 2005, Clarion $16.00 (0-618-23479-9). 64pp. In a series of poems, a young girl with an identical twin who doesn't always share her views recounts her family's attempts to regain its footing after a devastating divorce. (Rev: BL 8/05; SLJ 8/05)

Personal Problems

2041 Brugman, Alyssa. *Being Bindy* (5–8). 2006, Delacorte $15.95 (0-385-73294-5). 208pp. In this coming-of-age novel set in Australia, Bindy finds eighth grade a torturous experience that is further complicated by her divorced father's romance with the mother of her former best friend. (Rev: BL 6/1–15/06; SLJ 3/06*; VOYA 4/06)

2042 Bulion, Leslie. *Uncharted Waters* (4–8). 2006, Peachtree $14.95 (1-56145-365-X). 185pp. Jonah's summer of self-discovery following a dismal school year includes a heroic rescue at sea and excelling at his true talent. (Rev: SLJ 6/06)

2043 Caldwell, V. M. *Runt* (5–7). 2006, Milkweed $16.95 (1-57131-662-0); paper $6.95 (1-57131-661-2). 196pp. Runt, a 13-year-old who is trying to cope with his mother's death and his new living arrangements, becomes close to Mitch, who is dying of cancer. (Rev: SLJ 7/06)

2044 Collard, Sneed B., III. *Dog Sense* (5–8). 2005, Peachtree $14.95 (1-56145-351-X). 192pp. Unhappy after moving from sunny California to a small town in Montana, 13-year-old Guy Martinez finds solace in time spent with his dog, Streak, and a newfound friend named Luke. (Rev: BL 10/15/05; SLJ 11/05)

2045 Crilley, Mark. *Spring* (4–7). Illus. Series: Miki Falls. 2007, HarperTempest paper $7.99 (978-0-06-084616-9). 176pp. In this manga-style romance novel, high school senior Miki is determined to break through the defenses of the gorgeous but secretive new boy called Hiro. (Rev: BL 3/15/07)

2046 Dee, Barbara. *Just Another Day in My Insanely Real Life* (4–7). 2006, Simon & Schuster $15.95 (1-4169-0861-7). 256pp. Cassie must deal with the fallout from her parents' divorce, with her irresponsible older sister and demanding little brother, and with her former best friends in this novel about an all-too-real situation. (Rev: BL 5/15/06; SLJ 8/06)

2047 de Guzman, Michael. *Finding Stinko* (5–8). 2007, Farrar $16.00 (0-374-32305-4). 144pp. On the run from his latest and worst set of foster parents, Newboy, an elective mute, finds new voice with a ventriloquist's dummy; a compelling book of survival on the streets. (Rev: BL 4/15/07)

2048 Deriso, Christine Hurley. *Do-Over* (5–8). 2006, Delacorte $15.95 (0-385-73333-X). 183pp. Between the recent death of her mother and the move to a new school, seventh-grader Elsa is having a hard time of it, but things look up when her mother mysteriously appears one night and grants her do-over power. (Rev: SLJ 8/06)

2049 Evangelista, Beth. *Gifted* (5–8). 2005, Walker $16.95 (0-8027-8994-3). 192pp. George R. Clark is gifted and colossally unpopular with most of his classmates, so he is uneasy about going on his 8th-grade science field trip without his principal-father to protect him from the bullies; funny and real. (Rev: BL 12/15/05*; HBG 4/06; LMC 11–12/05; SLJ 1/06; VOYA 10/05)

2050 Friedman, Laurie. *In Business with Mallory* (2–4). Illus. by Barbara Pollak. 2006, Carolrhoda LB $15.95 (1-57505-925-8). 159pp. Mallory comes up with a scheme to earn the money she needs to buy a coveted purse, then isn't sure if that's the wisest use of her cash. (Rev: SLJ 6/06)

2051 Gorman, Carol. *Games: A Tale of Two Bullies* (4–7). 2007, HarperCollins $15.99 (0-06-057027-X). 288pp. Instead of suspending Mick and Boot for fighting, their principal requires them to play board games together; after a rocky start punctuated with petty crimes, the boys explore a hidden tunnel together, discovering that they both cope with alco-holic, abusive fathers. (Rev: BL 1/1–15/07; SLJ 1/07)

2052 Grant, Vicki. *Pigboy* (5–9). Series: Orca Currents. 2006, Orca $14.95 (1-55143-666-3); paper $8.95 (1-53143-643-4). 101pp. Certain that his classmates' teasing will reach a new high, Dan Hogg dreads the field trip to a pig farm, but he deals well with the challenges that await him as he faces off with an escaped convict; suitable for reluctant readers and gripping enough for others. (Rev: SLJ 12/06)

2053 Grindley, Sally. *Bravo, Max!* (3–5). Illus. by Tony Ross. 2007, Simon & Schuster $15.99 (978-1-4169-0393-2). 160pp. In his continuing correspondence with his favorite author, 11-year-old Max — first seen in *Dear Max* (2006) — writes about his dislike of his mother's boyfriend, the play Max has written that parallels events in his life, and the joys and agonies of growing up. (Rev: BL 3/15/07)

2054 Holmes, Sara. *Letters from Rapunzel* (5–8). 2007, HarperCollins $15.99 (978-0-06-078073-9). 184pp. In letters to an unknown correspondent, Cadence — who calls herself Rapunzel — describes her father's depression and her sense of being alone. (Rev: SLJ 2/07)

2055 Horrocks, Anita. *Almost Eden* (5–8). 2006, Tundra paper $9.95 (0-88776-742-7). 288pp. Elsie is a Mennonite girl who must deal with her mother's depression, the onset of puberty, and religious doubts in this story set in Canada in the 1960s. (Rev: BL 5/15/06)

2056 Horvath, Polly. *The Vacation* (5–7). 2005, Farrar $16.00 (0-374-30870-8). 197pp. When his parents go to Africa as missionaries, 12-year-old Henry is taken on an eye-opening, cross-country trip by his eccentric maiden aunts, Magnolia and Pigg; comedy and weirdness ensue. (Rev: BCCB 10/05; BL 6/05; HB 7–8/05; SLJ 8/05*)

2057 Kimmel, Elizabeth Cody. *Lily B. on the Brink of Love* (5–8). 2005, HarperCollins LB $16.89 (0-06-075543-1). 224pp. In this charming sequel to *Lily B. on the Brink of Cool* (2003), the title character, an aspiring writer and advice columnist for her school paper, needs counsel herself when she falls in love. (Rev: BL 10/1/05; SLJ 7/05)

2058 Ludwig, Trudy. *Sorry!* (2–5). Illus. by Maurie J. Manning. 2006, Tricycle $15.95 (1-58246-173-2). Jack learns about insincere apologies when he makes friends with the popular Charlie; appended are an author's note, discussion questions, and "Apology Dos and Don'ts." (Rev: SLJ 12/06)

2059 MacLean, Christine Cole. *Mary Margaret, Center Stage* (3–5). Illus. by Vicky Lowe. 2006, Dutton $15.99 (0-525-47597-4). 176pp. Longtime teacher's pet Mary Margaret is jealous when a new girl joins her fourth-grade class and begins to steal the spotlight. (Rev: BL 2/1/06; SLJ 6/06)

2060 Olmstead, Kathleen, retel. *Anne of Green Gables* (3–4). Illus. by Lucy Corvino. 2005, Sterling $4.95 (1-4027-1130-1). 153pp. A pared-down version of the well-loved story for younger readers, with black-and-white illustrations and a large typeface. (Rev: SLJ 7/05)

2061 Patron, Susan. *The Higher Power of Lucky* (4–6). Illus. by Matt Phelan. 2006, Simon & Schuster $16.95 (1-4169-0194-9). 144pp. In a tiny California hamlet called Hard Pan, 10-year-old Lucky feels constantly uncertain about her life and seeks a "higher power" that will bring her some peace. (Rev: BL 12/1/06; SLJ 12/06)

2062 Paulsen, Gary. *The Amazing Life of Birds: (The Twenty-Day Puberty Journal of Duane Homer Leech)* (5–7). 2006, Random $13.95 (0-385-74660-1). 84pp. Having a bad time with the onset of puberty and its accompanying embarrassments — amusingly confided in his journal, 12-year-old Duane identifies with a baby bird developing in a nest outside his window. (Rev: SLJ 10/06)

2063 Pearce, Jacqueline. *Dog House Blues* (4–6). 2005, Orca paper $6.95 (1-55143-360-5). 150pp. Dog-loving Erika, tired of being teased and bullied by a former friend, learns how to stand up for herself. (Rev: SLJ 4/06)

2064 Schumacher, Julie. *The Book of One Hundred Truths* (5–8). 2006, Delacorte $15.95 (0-385-73290-2). 192pp. While spending the summer with her grandparents at the Jersey shore, 12-year-old Thea finds herself baby-sitting her younger cousin Jocelyn and struggling to keep private the truths she is listing in her diary. (Rev: BL 11/1/06)

2065 Shreve, Susan. *Kiss Me Tomorrow* (5–8). 2006, Scholastic $16.99 (0-439-68047-6). 160pp. Alyssa (aka Blister) is not having a good seventh grade; she feels abandoned by best friend Jonah although she's quick to help him when he's in trouble; she is unhappy about her mother's new boyfriend; and she worries about everything else from clothes to sex. (Rev: BL 9/15/06; SLJ 10/06)

2066 Siebold, Jan. *My Nights at the Improv* (4–8). 2005, Whitman $14.95 (0-8075-5630-0). 98pp. Lizzie, a shy 8th-grader whose father died two years before, learns how to speak out by eavesdropping on an improvisational theater class, in the process also learning about bullying Vanessa. (Rev: BCCB 7–8/05; SLJ 11/05)

2067 Soto, Gary. *Mercy on These Teenage Chimps* (5–8). 2007, Harcourt $16.00 (978-0-15-206022-0). 147pp. Friends Ronnie Gonzalez and Joey Rios have just turned 13 and are wrestling with physical and emotional changes. (Rev: BL 12/1/06; SLJ 2/07)

2068 Timberlake, Amy. *That Girl Lucy Moon* (5–8). 2006, Hyperio $15.99 (0-7868-5298-4). 294pp. When her mother takes off on an extended photog-

raphy assignment, Lucy Moon is left without her biggest ally in her campaigns for animal rights, social justice, and, now, for the liberation of a sledding hill. (Rev: SLJ 9/06)

2069 Whittenberg, Allison. *Sweet Thang* (5–8). 2006, Delacorte $15.95 (0-385-73292-9). 192pp. Set in 1970s Pennsylvania, this story follows the trials of 14-year-old Charmaine, who must deal with her little orphaned cousin, Tracy John, as well as with problems at school — the darkness of her skin and her infatuation for a boy. (Rev: BL 5/1/06; SLJ 4/06)

2070 Wolfson, Jill. *Home, and Other Big, Fat Lies* (5–7). 2006, Holt $16.95 (0-8050-7670-0). 281pp. Shuttled through the foster care system for much of her life, 11-year-old Whitney isn't expecting much out of her latest stop with a family in remote northern California, but her interest in nature — and some new friendships — open her eyes to the importance of fighting for what you believe in. (Rev: SLJ 12/06)

2071 Wolfson, Jill. *What I Call Life* (5–8). 2005, Holt $16.95 (0-8050-7669-7). 272pp. Five young girls — all refugees from troubled families — find friendship and strength during their stay in a group home run by a wise Knitting Lady. (Rev: BCCB 9/05; BL 11/1/05; HBG 4/06; LMC 4–5/06; SLJ 9/05; VOYA 12/05)

Physical and Emotional Problems

2072 Auch, Mary Jane. *One-Handed Catch* (4–6). 2006, Holt $16.95 (0-8050-7900-9). 256pp. In this inspiring novel set just after World War II, 11-year-old Norm strives to live a normal life after he loses a hand in an accident, succeeding not only in music and art but also baseball. (Rev: BL 10/1/06; SLJ 11/06)

2073 Baskin, Nora Raleigh. *In the Company of Crazies* (5–8). Illus. by Henry P. Raleigh. 2006, HarperCollins $15.99 (0-06-059607-4). 170pp. Shaken to her core by the sudden death of a classmate, 13-year-old Mia Singer is sent to a school for emotionally disturbed teenagers where she begins to learn some important lessons about what makes her tick. (Rev: SLJ 8/06)

2074 Deans, Sis. *Rainy* (4–6). 2005, Holt $16.95 (0-8050-7831-2). 208pp. Rainy, an energetic 10-year-old girl with attention deficit hyperactivity disorder whose parents reject medication, has trouble at summer camp. (Rev: BL 8/05; SLJ 10/05; VOYA 10/05)

2075 Graff, Lisa. *The Thing About Georgie* (3–5). 2007, HarperCollins $15.99 (0-06-087589-5). 224pp. Nine-year-old Georgie's school and family problems, compounded by his dwarfism, are sensitively explored in this upbeat, often funny novel. (Rev: BL 1/1–15/07; SLJ 2/07)

2076 MacKall, Dandi Daley. *Larger-Than-Life Lara* (4–6). 2006, Dutton $16.99 (0-525-47726-8). 192pp. Ten-year-old Laney uses the writing skills she has learned to recount fat Lara's arrival at school and her amazing ability to shrug off slights. (Rev: BL 8/06; SLJ 9/06)

2077 Matlin, Marlee, and Doug Cooney. *Nobody's Perfect* (4–6). 2006, Simon & Schuster $15.95 (0-689-86986-X). 240pp. Fourth-grader Megan, who is deaf, has a hard time understanding why the new girl at school seems unfriendly in this sequel to *Deaf Child Crossing* (2002). (Rev: BL 7/06; SLJ 8/06)

2078 Zimmer, Tracie Vaughn. *Reaching for the Sun* (5–8). 2007, Bloomsbury $14.95 (1-59990-037-8). 192pp. Seventh-grader Josie faces daunting troubles: school, loneliness, cerebral palsy, and her rural area's development; a new, science-loving neighbor becomes a friend and Josie redefines her relationship with her mother in this appealing verse novel. (Rev: BL 1/1–15/07)

Historical Fiction and Foreign Lands

General and Miscellaneous

2079 Broome, Errol. *Gracie and the Emperor* (4–6). 2005, Annick $18.95 (1-55037-891-0); paper $7.95 (1-55037-890-2). 123pp. Life changes dramatically for 11-year-old Gracie when Napoleon Bonaparte is exiled to the island of St. Helena, where the girl lives with her widowed father. (Rev: SLJ 12/05)

2080 Campbell, Nicola I. *Shi-shi-etko* (2–4). Illus. by Kim LaFave. 2005, Groundwood $16.95 (0-88899-659-4). 32pp. A young Canadian Indian girl savors the final few days before she is to be sent away to residential school, far from her family. (Rev: BL 11/1/05; SLJ 11/05)

2081 Crosbie, Duncan. *Life on a Famine Ship: A Journal of the Irish Famine, 1845–1850* (4–6). Illus. by Brian Lee and Peter Bull Studios. 2006, Barron's $16.99 (0-7641-6004-4). 25pp. Informative and illustrative flaps and pop-ups of the ship add to 9-year-old Michael's account of flight from Ireland and a long and dangerous journey to the United States. (Rev: SLJ 12/06)

2082 Dowswell, Paul. *Prison Ship: Adventures of a Young Sailor* (5–9). 2006, Bloomsbury $16.95 (1-58234-676-3). 313pp. In this action-packed sequel to *Powder Monkey* set at the beginning of the 19th century, 13-year-old English sailor Sam Witchall is falsely convicted of theft and sent off to prison in Australia, where he escapes into the Outback. (Rev: SLJ 12/06)

2083 Gregory, Kristiana. *Catherine: The Great Journey* (4–7). Series: Royal Diaries. 2005, Scholastic $10.99 (0-439-25385-3). 169pp. The imagined diary of Catherine the Great's teenage years and her engagement to the Grand Duke of Russia; plenty of historical background gives readers a sense of Catherine's times. (Rev: SLJ 5/06)

2084 Hartnett, Sonya. *The Silver Donkey* (5–8). Illus. by Don Powers. 2006, Candlewick $15.99 (0-7636-2937-5). 272pp. Two young French children find and help a wounded World War I soldier in the woods near their home, and as he heals he tells them stories about the tiny silver donkey he carries with him. (Rev: BL 11/15/06; SLJ 12/06)

2085 Miles, Victoria. *Magnifico* (4–6). 2006, Fitzhenry & Whiteside $15.95 (1-55041-960-9). 262pp. Mariangela Benitti must endure teasing and torturous practice to master the accordion, an instrument foisted upon her by her immigrant Italian family, in this story set in Canada in 1939. (Rev: BL 7/06; SLJ 7/06)

2086 Polisar, Barry Louis. *Stolen Man: The Story of the Amistad Rebellion* (3–5). 2006, Rainbow Morning Music paper $7.95 (978-0-938663-50-8). 7.95pp. An account of the *Amistad* slave rebellion of 1839 from the perspective of a slave named Sengbe Pieh (later known at Joseph Cinque). (Rev: BL 2/1/07)

2087 Provensen, Alice. *Klondike Gold* (2–4). Illus. 2005, Simon & Schuster $17.95 (0-689-84885-4). 40pp. A fictionalized story about William Howell, a young prospector who made the difficult journey from Boston to the Yukon Territory in search of gold in the Klondike River valley in the late 19th century. (Rev: BL 12/1/05; SLJ 12/05*)

2088 Reynolds, Susan. *The First Marathon: The Legend of Pheidippides* (2–4). Illus. by Daniel Minter. 2006, Albert Whitman $16.95 (0-8075-0867-5). 32pp. The role of long-distance runner Pheidippides in the important Battle of Marathon is told in a dramatic, fictionalized text with large illustrations and an informative afterword. (Rev: BL 2/15/06; SLJ 3/06)

2089 Russell, Christopher. *Dogboy* (4–6). 2006, Greenwillow $15.99 (0-06-084116-8). 272pp. Twelve-year-old Brind, who was raised with dogs and now is renowned for his talent as a kennel boy, faces many challenges and finds a new friend, Aurelie, in this novel set amid the Hundred Years War between France and England. (Rev: BL 4/15/06; SLJ 8/06; VOYA 8/06)

2090 Skrypuch, Marsha Forchuk. *Aram's Choice* (3–5). Illus. by Muriel Wood. 2006, Fitzhenry & Whiteside $14.95 (1-55041-352-X); paper $8.95 (1-55041-354-6). 72pp. Aram, a 12-year-old refugee from the Armenian genocide in Turkey in the early 1900s, travels with other orphans to a new home in

Canada; based on truth, this compelling story contains many interesting facts and a historical note follows the text. (Rev: BL 8/06; SLJ 9/06)

2091 Steer, Dugald A., ed. *Pirateology: The Sea Journal of Captain William Lubber* (4–7). Illus. by Yvonne Gilbert. 2006, Candlewick $19.99 (0-7636-3143-4). 32pp. An authentic-looking large-format scrapbook chronicling the pirate-chasing adventures of a sea captain of old, complete with treasure maps and a working compass. (Rev: BL 7/06; SLJ 12/06)

Africa

2092 Farmer, Nancy. *Clever Ali* (2–4). Illus. by Gail de Marcken. 2006, Scholastic $17.99 (0-439-37014-0). 40pp. This beautifully written and illustrated picture book for older children, based on a true story of medieval Egypt, features 7-year-old Ali, who must find a way to outwit an evil sultan. (Rev: BL 10/1/06; SLJ 10/06)

2093 Hawes, Louise. *Muti's Necklace: The Oldest Story in the World* (2–4). Illus. by Rebecca Guay. 2006, Houghton $16.00 (0-618-53583-7). 32pp. In ancient Egypt, servant Muti risks everything to retrieve her treasured necklace and receives a proposal of marriage from the pharaoh in return; based on an ancient Egyptian story. (Rev: BL 7/06; SLJ 6/06)

2094 Mwangi, Meja. *The Mzungu Boy* (5–8). 2005, Groundwood $15.95 (0-88899-653-5). 160pp. In 1950s Kenya, a 12-year-old Kenyan boy becomes friendly with the white landowner's son despite both families' disapproval. (Rev: BL 8/05; SLJ 11/05)

2095 Platt, Richard. *Egyptian Diary: The Journal of Nakht* (4–6). Illus. by David Parkins. 2005, Candlewick $17.99 (0-7636-2756-9). 64pp. Nakht, a 9-year-old Egyptian boy training to become a scribe like his father, records in his journal observations about life in ancient Memphis, giving readers a good idea of Egyptian culture that is bolstered by the back matter. (Rev: BL 11/15/05; SLJ 2/06)

2096 Ross, Stewart. *Egypt in Spectacular Cross-Section* (2–4). Illus. by Stephen Biesty. 2005, Scholastic $18.99 (0-439-74537-3). 32pp. Illustrator Biesty's detailed cross-sections provide lots of ways to inform readers of interesting facts within the framework of Ross's story about a trip down the Nile family wedding in the Egypt of Ramses II. (Rev: BL 9/1/05; SLJ 9/05) [932]

2097 Smith, Alexander McCall. *Akimbo and the Elephants* (3–5). Illus. by LeUyen Pham. 2005, Bloomsbury $9.95 (1-58234-686-0). 80pp. Ten-year-old Akimbo, who lives with his ranger father on an African game preserve, helps to track down poachers who are killing full-grown elephants for their ivory tusks. Also use *Akimbo and the Lions*

(2005), in which he adopts a lion cub. (Rev: BL 9/1/05; SLJ 11/05)

2098 Watson, Pete. *The Heart of the Lion* (3–5). Illus. by Mary Watson. 2005, Shenanigan $15.95 (0-9726614-1-7). 32pp. A young American boy visits a West African village, meets a new friend, and learns about the region's distinctive culture. (Rev: BL 8/05; SLJ 10/05)

Asia

2099 Alexander, Lloyd. *Dream-of-Jade: The Emperor's Cat* (3–5). Illus. by D. Brent Burkett. 2005, Cricket $16.95 (0-8126-2736-9). 48pp. Dream-of-Jade, a talking cat, develops a close friendship with a lonely Chinese emperor. (Rev: BL 9/15/05; HBG 4/06; SLJ 11/05)

2100 Fleischman, Sid. *The White Elephant* (3–5). Illus. by Robert McGuire. 2006, Greenwillow $15.99 (0-06-113136-9). 112pp. Run Run, a young elephant trainer, angers Prince Noi and as a punishment is given a white elephant that he must care for but cannot put to work because of its rarity. (Rev: BL 9/1/06; SLJ 10/06)

2101 Louis, Catherine. *Liu and the Bird: A Journey in Chinese Calligraphy* (2–4). Trans. by Sibylle Kazeroid. Illus. by Feng Xiao Min. 2006, North-South $16.95 (0-7358-2050-3). 40pp. A young Chinese girl draws for her grandfather the things she saw on her journey to visit him in this introduction to calligraphic symbols. (Rev: BL 4/15/06; SLJ 4/06)

2102 Noyes, Deborah. *When I Met the Wolf Girls* (3–5). Illus. by August Hall. 2007, Houghton $17.00 (978-0-618-60567-5). 40pp. An orphan girl named Bulu narrates this story, based on truth, about two young girls raised by wolves and their difficulties adapting to life at an Indian orphanage. (Rev: BL 3/15/07)

2103 Say, Allen. *Kamishibai Man* (1–3). Illus. 2005, Houghton $17.00 (0-618-47954-6). 32pp. An elderly Japanese man who once made the rounds selling candy and telling stories to children revisits the magic of a bygone era. (Rev: BCCB 11/05; BL 9/15/05*; HB 11–12/05; HBG 4/06; LMC 3/06; SLJ 10/05*)

2104 Vejjajiva, Jane. *The Happiness of Kati* (4–7). Trans. by Prudence Borthwick. 2006, Simon & Schuster $15.95 (1-4169-1788-8). 144pp. Nine-year-old Kati's mother is dying and the identity of her father is a mystery in this story set in Thailand. (Rev: BL 5/15/06; SLJ 6/06)

2105 Young, Ed. *Beyond the Great Mountains: A Visual Poem About China* (4–6). Illus. 2005, Chronicle $17.95 (0-8118-4343-2). 36pp. The vastness and beauty of China are celebrated in an appealing but challenging blend of simple poetry and paper collage artwork. (Rev: BL 11/1/05; SLJ 10/05)

Europe

2106 Bradley, Kimberly Brubaker. *The Lacemaker and the Princess* (4–8). 2007, Simon & Schuster $16.99 (978-1-4169-1920-9). 208pp. As the French Revolution gathers strength, a young lace maker becomes the companion of Princess Marie-Thérèse, daughter of Marie Antoinette and King Louis XVI, and witness the growing social unrest. (Rev: BL 4/15/07)

2107 Comora, Madeleine. *Rembrandt and Titus: Artist and Son* (4–6). Illus. by Thomas Locker. 2005, Fulcrum $17.95 (1-55591-490-X). 32pp. Titus, son of Dutch artist Rembrandt, describes his father's life and vision; the full-page illustrations are based on Rembrandt's paintings or etchings. (Rev: BL 9/1/05; SLJ 10/05)

2108 French, Jackie. *Rover* (5–8). 2007, Harper-Collins $16.99 (0-06-085078-7). 304pp. When Vikings raid Hekja's Scottish village, she and her puppy are taken to Greenland, where she's enslaved to Freydis, Leif Erikson's sister; Hekja's dog can spot icebergs, and the two accompany Freydis on her voyage to North America in this compelling, historically accurate story. (Rev: BL 1/1–15/07)

2109 Gilman, Laura Anne. *Grail Quest: The Camelot Spell* (5–8). Series: Grail Quest. 2006, Harper-Collins LB $14.89 (0-06-077280-8). 304pp. On the eve of King Arthur's quest for the Holy Grail, three young teens of different backgrounds — Gerard, Newt, and Ailias — must reverse a spell crippling all adults. (Rev: BL 2/1/06; SLJ 6/06)

2110 Glaser, Linda. *Bridge to America* (3–5). 2005, Houghton $16.00 (0-618-56301-6). 208pp. Fivel, a young Jew from Poland, describes his life in the shtetl, the agonizing wait for money to fund his family's journey to join his father in the United States, and the difficulties in adjusting when he arrives. (Rev: BL 8/05; SLJ 11/05)

2111 Glatshteyn, Yankev. *Emil and Karl* (5–8). Ed. by Jeffrey Shandler. 2006, Roaring Brook $16.95 (1-59643-119-9). 208pp. Two 9-year-old friends — one Jewish, one Aryan — try to elude the Nazis on the streets of Vienna shortly after Germany's invasion; a fast-paced, moving story initially published in 1940. (Rev: BL 4/15/06; SLJ 6/06*; VOYA 4/06)

2112 Jacobson, Rick. *The Mona Lisa Caper* (2–4). Illus. 2005, Tundra $15.95 (0-88776-726-5). 24pp. This fact-based tale chronicles the 1911 theft of Leonardo da Vinci's *Mona Lisa* from the Louvre in Paris. (Rev: BL 7/05; SLJ 8/05)

2113 Lasky, Kathryn. *Dancing Through Fire* (4–7). Series: Portraits. 2005, Scholastic paper $9.99 (0-439-71009-X). 160pp. The Franco-Prussian War interrupts the dreams of 13-year-old Sylvie, a student at the Paris Opera Ballet in the 1870s. (Rev: BCCB 1/06; BL 12/1/05; SLJ 11/05)

2114 Lawrence, Caroline. *Gladiators from Capua* (5–8). Series: Roman Mysteries. 2005, Roaring Brook $16.95 (1-59643-074-5). 198pp. In their search for Jonathan, who may be alive after all, Flavia, Lupus, and Nubia venture into the coliseum and witness gladiator fights. (Rev: BL 12/1/05; SLJ 2/06)

2115 Littlesugar, Amy. *Willy and Max: A Holocaust Story* (2–4). Illus. by William Low. 2006, Philomel $15.99 (0-399-23483-7). 40pp. When the Nazis invade Belgium, Jewish boy Max and his family must flee, leaving a precious painting with the gentile family of Max's friend Willy; many years later, the painting — which was taken by the Nazis — is returned to Max's son in America; an author's note discusses the wholesale theft of artworks by the Germans. (Rev: BL 1/1–15/06; SLJ 3/06)

2116 McDonough, Yona Zeldis. *The Doll with the Yellow Star* (3–5). Illus. by Kimberly Bulcken Root. 2005, Holt $16.95 (0-8050-6337-4). 64pp. Claudine, an 8-year-old Jewish girl living in France during the Nazi occupation, is sent to safety in America. (Rev: BL 9/1/05; SLJ 10/05)

2117 Mitchell, Jack. *The Roman Conspiracy* (5–9). 2005, Tundra paper $8.95 (0-88776-713-3). 164pp. In this compelling historical thriller set in the Roman Empire, young Aulus Spurinna travels to Rome in a desperate attempt to protect his homeland of Etruria from military pillagers. (Rev: SLJ 11/05)

2118 Morpurgo, Michael. *War Horse* (5–8). 2007, Scholastic $16.99 (978-0-439-79663-7). 176pp. This gripping tale of World War I and all its horrors is told from the point of view of Joey, an English farm horse that's been drafted for service on the battlefront. (Rev: BL 4/1/07)

2119 Napoli, Donna Jo. *Fire in the Hills* (5–8). 2006, Dutton $16.99 (0-525-47751-9). 256pp. In this fact-based sequel to *Stones in Water* (1997), 14-year-old Roberto returns to Italy after escaping from a Nazi prison camp and joins the resistance movement. (Rev: BL 9/1/06; SLJ 9/06)

2120 Pausewang, Gudrun. *Dark Hours* (5–8). Trans. from German by John Brownjohn. 2006, Annick $21.95 (978-1-55451-042-9). 208pp. In Germany during the closing days of World War II, Gisela and her younger siblings become trapped in an air raid shelter after being separated from their mother and grandmother. (Rev: BL 11/1/06; SLJ 2/07)

2121 Roy, Jennifer. *Yellow Star* (5–8). 2006, Marshall Cavendish $16.95 (0-7614-5277-X). 256pp. The fictionalized story, told in first-person free-verse chapters introduced by historical notes, of the author's aunt Syvia, a Holocaust survivor who spent much of her childhood in the grim Lodz ghetto. (Rev: BL 4/15/06; SLJ 7/06*; VOYA 6/06)

2122 Spring, Debbie. *The Righteous Smuggler* (4–6). Series: Holocaust Remembrance. 2006, Second Story paper $5.95 (1-896764-97-5). 160pp. Hendrik, the 12-year-old son of a Dutch fisherman, helps his father to smuggle Jews out of the country after Germany invades the Netherlands. (Rev: BL 1/1–15/06; SLJ 4/06)

2123 Toksvig, Sandi. *Hitler's Canary* (5–8). 2007, Roaring Brook $16.95 (978-1-59643-247-5). 191pp. A Danish family decides to risk everything in order to help Jews escape the Nazis. (Rev: BL 1/1–15/07; SLJ 4/07)

2124 Winter, Jonah. *The 39 Apartments of Ludwig van Beethoven* (3–5). Illus. by Barry Blitt. 2006, Random $15.95 (0-375-83602-0). 40pp. A funny "mockumentary" about Beethoven's constant moving from one apartment to another — along with his five legless pianos — and the putative reasons for these moves. (Rev: BL 8/06; SLJ 10/06)

Great Britain and Ireland

2125 Avi. *Crispin: At the Edge of the World* (5–8). 2006, Hyperion $16.99 (0-7868-5152-X). 240pp. In this compelling sequel to *Crispin: The Cross of Lead*, Bear, who Crispin now regards as a father, is seriously wounded and they make friends with a disfigured girl named Troth; Crispin now finds himself making decisions for the three. (Rev: BCCB 1/07; BL 9/15/06; HB 9–10/06; HBG 4/07; LMC 2/07; SLJ 10/06*; VOYA 10/06)

2126 Cooper, Susan. *Victory* (4–7). 2006, Simon & Schuster $16.95 (1-4169-1477-3). 208pp. Homesick Molly finds her fate is intertwined with that of Sam, a child sailor of the 19th century who fought in the Battle of Trafalgar; chapters alternate between the present and the past. (Rev: BL 5/1/06; LMC 11/12/06; SLJ 7/06)

2127 Cottrell Boyce, Frank. *Framed* (4–7). 2006, HarperCollins $16.99 (0-06-073402-7). 320pp. Life changes dramatically for 9-year-old Dylan Hughes and his quiet Welsh village when priceless art from London's National Gallery is temporarily stored in a nearby quarry. (Rev: BL 9/1/06; SLJ 8/06*)

2128 Dowswell, Paul. *Powder Monkey: Adventures of a Young Sailor* (5–9). 2005, Bloomsbury $16.95 (1-58234-675-5). 276pp. In this stirring historical novel set in the opening years of the 19th century, 13-year-old Sam Witchall begins his career at sea as a "powder monkey," assisting the gun crews on a warship. (Rev: SLJ 11/05; VOYA 10/05)

2129 Duey, Kathleen. *Lara at the Silent Place* (4–6). Series: Hoofbeats. 2005, Dutton $15.99 (0-525-47341-6). 128pp. In the fourth and final installment in this historical fiction series, Lara and her horse

return home, where she is reunited with her father but must decide where her future lies. (Rev: BL 7/05)

2130 Fine, Anne. *Frozen Billy* (4–6). Illus. by Georgina McBain. 2006, Farrar $16.00 (0-374-32481-6). 192pp. In this historical novel set in Edwardian England, Clarrie and Will are left in the care of their uncle, a vaudeville ventriloquist who drinks and gambles away the little money he makes; the two come up with a scheme to improve their uncle's act. (Rev: BL 9/1/06; SLJ 11/06)

2131 Finney, Patricia. *Feud* (4–7). Series: Lady Grace Mysteries. 2006, Delacorte $7.95 (0-385-73323-2); paper $9.99 (0-385-90342-1). 208pp. Lady Grace, maid of honor to Queen Elizabeth I, attempts to unravel the mystery surrounding the poisoning of another maid of honor. (Rev: BL 10/15/06)

2132 Grant, K. M. *Green Jasper* (5–9). Series: The de Granville Trilogy. 2006, Walker $16.95 (0-8027-8073-7). 249pp. Will and Gavin, introduced in *Blood Red Horse* (2005), come home from the crusade to find England in chaos and Gavin's beloved Ellie abducted by Constable de Scabious; a multilayered medieval adventure story. (Rev: SLJ 6/06; VOYA 8/06)

2133 Heneghan, James. *Safe House* (5–8). 2006, Orca paper $7.95 (1-55143-640-X). 160pp. Twelve-year-old Liam Fogarty is forced to go on the run after he sees the face of one of the gunmen who killed his mother and father in their Belfast home. (Rev: BL 11/1/06; SLJ 1/07)

2134 Hinton, Nigel. *Time Bomb* (5–8). 2006, Tricycle $15.95 (1-58246-186-4). 284pp. Coming of age in post-World War II London, four 12-year-old friends who have lost their trust in adults discover an unexploded German bomb and set in motion a chain of events. (Rev: SLJ 12/06)

2135 Holmes, Victoria. *Heart of Fire* (5–8). 2006, HarperCollins $15.99 (0-06-052037-X). 352pp. Maddie has lived with her grandparents since her parents' death and is pleased when her long-absent older brother Theo arrives along with a beautiful horse; but Theo seems strange, and Maddie's suspicions are confirmed when he turns out to be an impostor. (Rev: BL 10/1/06; SLJ 12/06)

2136 Morris, Gerald. *The Quest of the Fair Unknown* (5–8). 2006, Houghton $16.00 (0-618-63152-6). 272pp. To fulfill the deathbed plea of his mother, Beaufils sets off to find his long-absent father, a knight in the court of King Arthur. (Rev: BL 10/15/06; SLJ 11/06)

2137 Priestley, Chris. *The White Rider* (5–8). 2005, Corgi paper $8.99 (0-440-86608-1). 192pp. In this riveting sequel to *Death and the Arrow*, 16-year-old Tom Marlowe is swept up in a series of intrigues in early-18th-century London. (Rev: BL 10/15/05)

2138 Thomas, Jane Resh. *The Counterfeit Princess* (5–8). 2005, Clarion $15.00 (0-395-93870-8). 198pp. Iris, a young English girl with an uncanny resemblance to Princess Elizabeth (soon to be Elizabeth I), finds herself embroiled in intrigue in this novel set in the 16th century. (Rev: BL 11/15/05; SLJ 10/05)

2139 Toews, Marj. *Black-and-White Blanche* (1–3). Illus. by Dianna Bonder. 2006, Fitzhenry & Whiteside $16.95 (1-55005-132-6). The Witherspoons, a Victorian family that rigidly adheres to the social ban on colored clothing, are forced to relax their standards when the family's youngest member insists on wearing pink. (Rev: SLJ 8/06)

2140 Zucker, Jonny. *The Bombed House* (5–8). Illus. by Paul Savage. Series: Keystone Books. 2006, Stone Arch LB $19.93 (1-59889-092-1). 33pp. This fast-paced story, will attract reluctant readers, features brothers Ned and Harry Jennings, who find a German soldier hiding in London during World War II. (Rev: SLJ 1/07)

Latin America

2141 Ramírez, Antonio. *Napí Goes to the Mountain* (1–3). Trans. from Spanish by Elisa Amado. Illus. by Domi. 2006, Groundwood $18.95 (978-0-88899-713-5). A young Mexican girl and her younger brother go upriver into the jungle in search of their father, and during the course of their search are transformed into deer and meet a series of folkloric creatures; a sequel to *Napí* (2004). (Rev: SLJ 2/07)

United States

NATIVE AMERICANS

2142 Bruchac, Marge. *Malian's Song* (2–4). Illus. by William Maughan. 2006, Vermont Folklife Center $16.95 (0-916718-26-3). 32pp. Malian, a young Abenaki girl, tells how she fled to safety while her father died defending the family's home in 1759; the story of this British raid was passed from generation to generation. This text includes Abenaki words as well as details of Abenaki life. (Rev: BL 8/06; SLJ 1/07)

2143 Sneve, Virginia Driving Hawk. *Bad River Boys: A Meeting of the Lakota Sioux with Lewis and Clark* (2–4). Illus. by Bill Farnsworth. 2005, Holiday $16.95 (0-8234-1856-1). 32pp. Based on an entry from William Clark's journal, this fictional story tells of an encounter between three Lakota boys and members of Lewis and Clark's Corps of Discovery expedition. (Rev: BL 11/15/05; SLJ 11/05)

2144 Wyss, Thelma Hatch. *Bear Dancer: The Story of a Ute Girl* (4–7). 2005, Simon & Schuster $15.95 (1-4169-0285-6). 192pp. In this fact-based historical

novel, life is turned upside down for Elk Girl, a member of the Tabaguache Ute, when she is kidnapped by a rival tribe. (Rev: BL 10/15/05; SLJ 10/05)

COLONIAL PERIOD

2145 Hermes, Patricia. *Salem Witch* (5–8). Series: My Side of the Story. 2006, Kingfisher paper $7.95 (978-0-7534-5991-1). 172pp. Two teenage friends develop different views during the witch trials in 17th-century Salem, and readers can flip the book to read each person's opinion. (Rev: SLJ 2/07)

2146 Ketchum, Liza. *Where the Great Hawk Flies* (4–7). 2005, Clarion $16.00 (0-618-40085-0). 272pp. The Coombs family and the Tuckers have trouble getting along — even the young boys — because Mrs. Tucker is a Pequot Indian and the Coombs suffered mightily during an Indian raid seven years before. (Rev: BCCB 12/05; BL 9/15/05*; HB 1–2/06; LMC 1/06; SLJ 1/06; VOYA 4/06)

2147 Kimmel, Eric A. *Blackbeard's Last Fight* (2–4). Illus. by Leonard Everett Fisher. 2006, Farrar $17.00 (0-374-30780-6). 32pp. In the early 18th century, cabin boy Jeremy Hobbs hears conflicting reports about Blackbeard the pirate and witnesses his capture and execution; vivid paintings (avoiding the final scene) add to the exciting story. (Rev: BL 3/1/06; SLJ 5/06)

2148 Schwabach, Karen. *A Pickpocket's Tale* (5–8). 2006, Random $15.95 (0-375-93379-4). 240pp. After being caught picking pockets on the streets of London in 1730, 10-year-old orphan Molly is exiled to America where she learns many new things from the Jewish family to which she is indentured. (Rev: BL 11/15/06; SLJ 11/06)

THE REVOLUTION

2149 Carlson, Drew. *Attack of the Turtle* (4–6). Illus. by David A. Johnson. 2007, Eerdmans $16.00 (978-0-8028-5308-0). 149pp. Based on actual events, this Revolutionary War novel highlights the secret construction of the *Turtle*, the first submarine used in warfare; Nate, 14, conquers his fear of water to work on the project. (Rev: BL 1/1–15/07)

2150 Elliott, L. M. *Give Me Liberty* (5–8). 2006, HarperCollins $16.99 (0-06-074421-9). 384pp. Nathaniel Dunn, a 13-year-old indentured servant in colonial Virginia, is taken under the wing of an elderly schoolmaster and watches as the revolutionary movement grows and affects his own behavior. (Rev: BL 10/1/06; SLJ 9/06)

2151 Jones, Elizabeth McDonald. *Peril at King's Creek: A Felicity Mystery* (3–5). Series: American Girl Mysteries. 2006, Pleasant $10.95 (1-59369-102-5); paper $6.95 (1-59369-101-7). 168pp. Spending the summer of 1776 at her family's Virginia plantation, Felicity hears reports that British troops are raiding the farms of patriots and becomes suspicious of a visitor who shows a lot of interest in her horse. (Rev: BL 6/1–15/06; SLJ 4/06)

2152 Tripp, Valerie. *Very Funny, Elizabeth!* (3–5). Illus. by Dan Andreasen. Series: American Girl. 2005, American Girl paper $6.95 (1-59369-061-4). 81pp. Ten-year-old Elizabeth Cole and her friend Felicity, who are growing up in Revolutionary-era Williamsburg, enjoy teasing Elizabeth's older sister Annabelle in this volume that provides historical detail. (Rev: SLJ 3/06)

THE YOUNG NATION, 1789–1861

2153 Blos, Joan W. *Letters from the Corrugated Castle: A Novel of Gold Rush California, 1850–1852* (4–8). 2007, Simon & Schuster $17.99 (0-689-87077-4). 320pp. Reunited with a mother long believed to be dead, 13-year-old Eldora must learn to adjust to living a life of comfort in San Francisco; newspaper articles and her correspondence with Luke, who hopes to find a fortune, reveal much about life during the Gold Rush. (Rev: BL 4/15/07)

2154 Dahlberg, Maurine F. *The Story of Jonas* (4–7). 2007, Farrar $16.00 (978-0-374-37264-4). 148pp. In the mid-1800s, Jonas, a 13-year-old slave, is sent on an expedition to find gold in the Kansas Territory and realizes that freedom is not beyond his grasp. (Rev: BL 4/07; SLJ 4/07)

2155 DeFelice, Cynthia. *Bringing Ezra Back* (4–6). 2006, Farrar $16.00 (0-374-39939-5). 160pp. In this sequel to *Weasel* (1990), 12-year-old Nathan travels from Ohio to Pennsylvania in 1840 in an attempt to locate and help Ezra, the man grievously injured by Weasel. (Rev: BL 8/06; SLJ 9/06)

2156 Duble, Kathleen Benner. *Hearts of Iron* (5–8). 2006, Simon & Schuster $15.95 (1-4169-0850-1). 256pp. In a Connecticut iron-working community in the early 19th century, two young lovers rebel against their families' plans for their future. (Rev: BL 9/15/06; SLJ 11/06)

2157 Giblin, James Cross. *The Boy Who Saved Cleveland* (3–6). Illus. by Michael Dooling. 2006, Holt $15.95 (0-8050-7355-8). 64pp. This fact-based story recounts the trials of 10-year-old Seth Doan who helped to nurse early settlers of Cleveland, Ohio, through a malaria outbreak in the late 18th century. (Rev: BL 4/15/06; SLJ 5/06)

2158 Howard, Ellen. *The Log Cabin Wedding* (2–4). Illus. by Ronald Himler. 2006, Holiday $15.95 (0-8234-1989-4). 48pp. Elvirey is upset when her widowed father falls in love with the Widow Aiken in this chapter-book sequel to the picture books *Log Cabin Quilt* (1996), *The Log Cabin Christmas* (2000), and *The Log Cabin Church* (2002). (Rev: BL 9/15/06; SLJ 12/06)

2159 Lyons, Mary E. *Letters from a Slave Boy: The Story of Joseph Jacobs* (4–8). 2007, Simon & Schuster $15.99 (978-0-689-87867-1). 198pp. In letters to relatives and friends, Joseph Jacobs tells the story of his flight north and his subsequent adventures, always seeking a safe, free life; based on truth, this is a companion to *Letters from a Slave Girl: The Story of Harriet Jacobs* (1992). (Rev: SLJ 2/07)

2160 Raven, Margot Theis. *Night Boat to Freedom* (1–3). Illus. by E. B. Lewis. 2006, Farrar $16.00 (0-374-31266-4). 40pp. Twelve-year-old Christmas John, urged on by Granny Judith, helps dozens of slaves escape to freedom, but when she tells the boy that he, too, must flee, he refuses to go without her; text and illustrations blend to make this a touching story. (Rev: BCCB 12/06; BL 10/15/06; SLJ 11/06)

2161 Tingle, Tim. *Crossing Bok Chitto* (2–4). Illus. by Jeanne Rorex Bridges. 2006, Cinco Puntos $17.95 (0-938317-77-6). 40pp. Martha Tom, a young Choctaw girl in 1800s Mississippi, befriends a slave boy and his family and leads them to freedom when they face a crisis. (Rev: BCCB 7–8/06; BL 4/15/06*; LMC 11–12/06)

2162 Wait, Lea. *Finest Kind* (4–7). 2006, Simon & Schuster $16.95 (1-4169-0952-4). 256pp. When his family falls on hard times and is forced to move from Boston to Maine in the 1830s, 12-year-old Jake Webber finds himself shouldering new responsibilities, including looking after his disabled younger brother. (Rev: BL 10/15/06; SLJ 11/06)

2163 Woods, Brenda. *My Name Is Sally Little Song* (4–7). 2006, Putnam $15.99 (0-399-24312-7). 176pp. Eleven-year-old Sally, a slave on a Georgia plantation at the beginning of the 19th century, escapes with her family and heads south to seek refuge with the Seminole Indians. (Rev: BCCB 11/06; BL 8/06; HBG 4/07; SLJ 9/06)

2164 Woodson, Jacqueline. *Show Way* (3–5). Illus. by Hudson Talbott. 2005, Putnam $16.99 (0-399-23749-6). 48pp. Woodson looks back in her own family history to tell the story of seven generations of women who pass down secret "Show Way" quilt patterns and a tradition of fighting for freedom. (Rev: BCCB 1/06; BL 9/15/05*; HB 11–12/05; HBG 4/06; SLJ 11/05*)

PIONEERS AND WESTWARD EXPANSION

2165 Couloumbis, Audrey. *The Misadventures of Maude March, or, Trouble Rides a Fast Horse* (5–8). 2005, Random LB $17.99 (0-375-93245-3). 291pp. When their aunt and sole guardian is killed, Maude and Sallie March rebel against their new foster family and set off on their own in this rollicking tale of the Old West. (Rev: SLJ 9/05)

2166 Ferris, Jean. *Much Ado About Grubstake* (5–8). 2006, Harcourt $17.00 (978-0-15-205706-0).

265pp. Sixteen-year-old Arley, owner of her family's mine and boarding house in 1888 Grubstake, Colorado, becomes suspicious when a stranger takes an unusual interest in the rundown mining town; adventure, romance, and humor are combined in this mystery. (Rev: BL 8/06; SLJ 11/06)

2167 Hart, Alison. *Anna's Blizzard* (3–5). Illus. by Paul Bachem. 2005, Peachtree $12.95 (1-56145-349-8). 141pp. Twelve-year-old Anna Vail loves life on the prairie although she lacks confidence at school, but when a blizzard traps children in the schoolhouse, it's Anna and her faithful pony who guide them all to safety. (Rev: SLJ 10/05)

2168 Kent, Deborah. *Blackwater Creek* (4–6). Series: Saddles, Stars, and Stripes. 2005, Kingfisher $8.95 (0-7534-5885-3). 152pp. In 1849 California, Hungarian immigrant Erika looks after horses for a local rancher while her brother and father search for gold. (Rev: SLJ 3/06)

2169 Kent, Deborah. *Riding the Pony Express* (3–7). Series: Saddles, Stars, and Stripes. 2006, Kingfisher $8.95 (0-7534-6001-7). 149pp. Despite the fact that her father has died and her brother is accused of robbery, 15-year-old Lexie has no intention of being shipped back East and, disguising herself as a boy, sets off on her own along the Pony Express trail to prove her brother innocent. (Rev: SLJ 8/06)

2170 MacLachlan, Patricia. *Grandfather's Dance* (4–6). Series: Sarah Plain and Tall. 2006, Harper-Collins $14.99 (0-06-027560-X). 96pp. At Anna's wedding, Cassie, the fourth-grade daughter of Sarah (of *Sarah Plain and Tall*), mulls over her bonds with the rest of the family in this closing installment in the series. (Rev: BL 7/06; SLJ 11/06)

2171 Paulsen, Gary. *The Legend of Bass Reeves* (5–8). 2006, Random $15.95 (0-385-74661-X). 160pp. This fictionalized biography profiles the little-known life and career of Bass Reeves, the former slave who became one of the West's most effective lawmen. (Rev: BCCB 10/06; BL 6/1–15/06; HBG 10/07; SLJ 8/06)

2172 Schultz, Jan Neubert. *Battle Cry* (5–9). 2006, Carolrhoda LB $15.95 (1-57505-928-2). 240pp. Native American Chaska and white settler Johnny are drawn into the bloody 1862 Dakota Conflict in this dramatic tale. (Rev: SLJ 7/06)

2173 Sommerdorf, Norma. *Red River Girl* (4–7). 2006, Holiday $16.95 (0-8234-1903-7). 216pp. In 1846 after her Ojibwa mother dies, 12-year-old Metis girl Josette starts a journal that documents her family's journey by wagon train from Canada to St. Paul, Minnesota, where they settle and she becomes a teacher. (Rev: BL 11/15/06; SLJ 12/06)

THE CIVIL WAR

2174 Durrant, Lynda. *My Last Skirt* (5–8). 2006, Clarion $16.00 (0-618-57490-5). 208pp. After migrating from Ireland to America, Jennie Hodgers, who prefers wearing pants to skirts, adopts the persona of Albert Cashier and joins the Union army in this novel based on a true story. (Rev: BL 2/15/06; SLJ 4/06*)

2175 Ernst, Kathleen. *Hearts of Stone* (5–8). 2006, Dutton $16.99 (0-525-47686-5). 256pp. Fifteen-year-old Hannah and her three younger siblings struggle to survive after they're orphaned in Civil War Tennessee. (Rev: BL 11/1/06; SLJ 12/06)

2176 Fleischner, Jennifer. *Nobody's Boy* (5–8). Illus. 2006, Missouri Historical Soc. $12.95 (1-883982-58-8). 96pp. George's mother buys freedom for herself and her son; she goes on to work for Mrs. Lincoln in the White House while George chooses the more dangerous avenue of helping slaves find freedom. (Rev: BL 2/1/07)

2177 Hopkinson, Deborah. *From Slave to Soldier: Based on a True Civil War Story* (2–4). Illus. by Brian Floca. Series: Ready-to-Read. 2005, Simon & Schuster $14.95 (0-689-83965-0). 48pp. Inspired by real events, this book for beginning readers chronicles the experiences of a slave boy who runs off to join the Union army and works as a mule driver; an afterword adds context. (Rev: BL 1/1–15/06; SLJ 10/05)

2178 Hurst, Carol Otis. *Torchlight* (4–7). 2006, Houghton $16.00 (0-618-27601-7). 160pp. As tension mounts between the Yankee and Irish immigrant settlers in a Massachusetts town in 1864, Charlotte and Maggie struggle to maintain their friendship. (Rev: BL 12/1/06; SLJ 1/07)

2179 Kent, Deborah. *Chance of a Lifetime* (4–6). Series: Saddles, Stars, and Stripes. 2005, Kingfisher $8.95 (0-7534-5884-5). 173pp. In 1849, 14-year-old Jacquetta May Logan enlists the help of a slave girl to hide her family's Morgan horses from advancing Union forces. (Rev: SLJ 3/06)

2180 Noble, Trinka Hakes. *The Last Brother: A Civil War Tale* (2–4). Illus. by Robert Papp. 2006, Sleeping Bear $17.95 (1-58536-253-0). 48pp. Eleven-year-old Gabe, who has lost two brothers in battle, joins the Union Army with older brother Davy and learns to be a bugler. (Rev: BL 9/1/06; SLJ 12/06)

2181 Rappaport, Doreen. *Freedom Ship* (2–4). Illus. by Curtis James. 2006, Hyperion $15.99 (0-7868-0645-1). 40pp. Slaves seize control of a Confederate steamship and turn it over to Union forces in this fictionalized version of a real event that is followed by a fascinating historical note. (Rev: BL 10/1/06; SLJ 11/06)

2182 Spain, Susan Rosson. *The Deep Cut* (5–8). 2006, Marshall Cavendish $16.99 (0-7614-5316-4). 224pp. Thirteen-year-old Lonzo, often considered "slow," finally gains the respect of his father for his actions during the hostilities. (Rev: BL 12/1/06*; SLJ 12/06)

RECONSTRUCTION TO WORLD WAR II, 1865–1941

2183 Arato, Rona. *Ice Cream Town* (5–8). Illus. 2007, Fitzhenry & Whiteside paper $11.95 (978-1-55041-591-9). 186pp. Ten-year-old Sammy Levin, a recent Jewish immigrant from Poland, finds it tough to adjust to his new life on the streets of New York City's Lower East Side in the early 1900s. (Rev: BL 4/1/07)

2184 Birney, Betty. *The Seven Wonders of Sassafras Springs* (3–6). Illus. by Matt Phelan. 2005, Simon & Schuster $16.95 (0-689-87136-8). 224pp. It's 1923 and Eben McAllister longs to travel but first he must meet his father's challenge to find the hidden wonders in his small farming community. (Rev: BL 9/1/05; SLJ 8/05)

2185 Blegvad, Lenore. *Kitty and Mr. Kipling: Neighbors in Vermont* (3–5). Illus. by Erik Blegvad. 2005, Simon & Schuster $16.95 (0-689-87363-8). 131pp. Eight-year-old Kitty learns about the world outside her small Vermont town when famed author Rudyard Kipling and his family move into a nearby home. (Rev: SLJ 12/05)

2186 Celenza, Anna Harwell. *Gershwin's Rhapsody in Blue* (2–4). Illus. by JoAnn E. Kitchel. 2006, Charlesbridge $19.95 (1-57091-556-3). 32pp. The story of Gershwin's struggle to produce a concerto in a few short weeks in 1924 is accompanied by CD of the resulting classic. (Rev: BL 11/1/06; SLJ 7/06)

2187 Dotty, Kathryn Adams. *Wild Orphan* (5–8). 2006, Edinborough $14.95 (1-889020-20-6). 144pp. In the Midwest in the 1920s, Lizbeth's friendship with an independent-minded orphan named Georgiana gives her courage. (Rev: BL 6/1–15/06)

2188 Dudley, David L. *The Bicycle Man* (5–8). 2005, Clarion $16.00 (0-618-54233-7). 256pp. In this poignant portrait of African American life in the rural South during the late 1920s, 12-year-old Carissa develops a mutually beneficial relationship with Bailey, an elderly jack-of-all-trades to whom she and her mother offer a home. (Rev: BL 11/15/05; SLJ 11/05)

2189 Durbin, William. *El Lector* (4–6). 2006, Random $15.95 (0-385-74651-2). 160pp. Thirteen-year-old Bella dreams of one day becoming a *lector* like her grandfather, who reads books and newspapers to workers in a Florida cigar factory. (Rev: BL 2/1/06; SLJ 2/06)

2190 Giff, Patricia Reilly. *Water Street* (5–8). 2006, Random $15.95 (0-385-73068-3). 176pp. In this poignant sequel to *Nory Ryan's Song* (2000) and *Maggie's Door* (2003), set in late-19th-century Brooklyn and told from alternating points of view, 13-year-old Bird Ryan and her new upstairs neighbor Thomas develop a close friendship. (Rev: BCCB 1/07; BL 8/06; HB 9–10/06; HBG 4/07; LMC 2/07; SLJ 9/06)

2191 Haas, Jessie. *Chase* (5–9). 2007, HarperCollins $16.99 (978-0-06-112850-9). 256pp. In mid-19th-century Pennsylvania, Phin Chase witnesses a murder and flees, pursued by a stranger and a horse that seems to have tracking abilities. (Rev: SLJ 4/07)

2192 Harper, Jo, and Josephine Harper. *Finding Daddy: A Story of the Great Depression* (1–3). Illus. by Ron Mazellan. 2005, Turtle Bks. $16.95 (1-890515-31-0). 42pp. Young Bonnie is bereft when her father must leave home to find work, and she sets out to find him; a timeline, glossary, and song lyrics provide more information about the Great Depression. (Rev: SLJ 9/05)

2193 Hill, Kirkpatrick. *Dancing at the Odinochka* (4–7). 2005, Simon & Schuster $15.95 (0-689-87388-3). 272pp. An atmospheric life of Erinia — daughter of a Russian father and Athabascan mother — growing up in the 1860s in what is now Alaska. (Rev: BL 8/05; SLJ 8/05)

2194 Hopkinson, Deborah. *Into the Firestorm: A Novel of San Francisco, 1906* (5–8). 2006, Knopf $15.95 (0-375-83652-7). 208pp. Recently orphaned, Nick Bray leaves Texas and travels to San Francisco where he must help his new neighbors cope with the devastating earthquake and resulting fires. (Rev: BL 9/1/06; SLJ 12/06)

2195 Hopkinson, Deborah. *Sky Boys: How They Built the Empire State Building* (2–4). Illus. by James E. Ransome. 2006, Random $16.95 (0-375-83610-1). 48pp. A young boy and his unemployed father watch as daring workers defy gravity in the construction of New York City's Empire State Building; dramatic illustrations highlight the heights. (Rev: BL 12/1/05; SLJ 2/06)

2196 Hurst, Carol Otis. *You Come to Yokum* (3–5). Illus. by Life Kay. 2005, Houghton $15.00 (0-618-55122-0). 144pp. The Carlyle family's move to rural western Massachusetts does nothing to dampen Mrs. Carlyle's enthusiastic — and sometimes embarrassing — support for the women's suffrage movement. (Rev: BL 9/1/05; SLJ 1/06)

2197 Jocelyn, Marthe. *How It Happened in Peach Hill* (5–9). 2007, Random $15.99 (978-0-375-83701-2). 232pp. Fifteen-year-old Annie, who does research for her "clairvoyant" mother mainly by pretending she is stupid, longs for a normal life in this compelling novel set in the 1920s. (Rev: BL 1/1–15/07; SLJ 4/07*)

2198 Kirwan, Anna. *Of Flowers and Shadows* (4–6). Series: Portraits. 2005, Scholastic $9.99 (0-439-71010-3). 182pp. This appealing fictional tale, inspired by Winslow Homer's "Girl and Laurel" painting, tells how Aurelia, an orphan and servant for a family in Townsend, Massachusetts, came to pose for the artist. (Rev: BL 11/15/05; SLJ 11/05)

2199 Laskas, Gretchen Moran. *The Miner's Daughter* (5–8). 2007, Simon & Schuster $15.99 (978-1-4169-1262-0). 249pp. In the coal country of 1930s West Virginia, 16-year-old Willa looks after her ailing and pregnant mother and three younger siblings while dreaming of a better life. (Rev: SLJ 2/07)

2200 Paterson, Katherine. *Bread and Roses, Too* (5–8). 2006, Clarion $16.00 (0-618-65479-8). 288pp. Jake and Rosa, children from different backgrounds, suffer the effects of the textile workers' strike in early 20th-century Massachusetts. (Rev: BCCB 3/07; BL 8/06; HB 9–10/06; HBG 4/07; LMC 2/07; SLJ 9/06; VOYA 12/06)

2201 Peck, Richard. *Here Lies the Librarian* (5–8). 2006, Dial $16.99 (0-8037-3080-2). 208pp. Four young female librarians arrive in a small town in Indiana in 1914 and inspire 14-year-old Peewee McGrath to consider her future in different ways. (Rev: BL 3/1/06; SLJ 4/06*; VOYA 2/06)

2202 Porter, Tracey. *Billy Creekmore* (5–7). 2007, HarperCollins $16.99 (0-06-077570-X). 320pp. From a grim orphanage to the mines of West Virginia and on to a life in the circus, 10-year-old Billy describes in picaresque style the difficult life of the young and poor in the early 20th century. (Rev: BL 4/15/07)

2203 Reich, Susanna. *Penelope Bailey Takes the Stage* (4–7). 2006, Marshall Cavendish $16.95 (0-7614-5287-7). 208pp. A frustrated Penny takes a role in the school play against the wishes of her aunt in this novel set in Victorian San Francisco. (Rev: BL 5/15/06; SLJ 5/06)

2204 Rubright, Lynn. *Mama's Window* (4–6). Illus. by Patricia C. McKissack. 2005, Lee & Low $16.95 (1-57480-160-0). 96pp. Sugar, an 11-year-old African American orphan living with his uncle on the Mississippi Delta, fights to ensure that his late mother's dream of a stained-glass window for the local church becomes a reality. (Rev: BL 7/05; SLJ 8/05)

2205 Tate, Eleanora. *Celeste's Harlem Renaissance* (4–7). 2007, Little, Brown $15.99 (978-0-316-52394-3). 288pp. In the early 1920s Celeste arrives in New York from North Carolina and discovers that her aunt is not the famous singer and dancer she was told but that the lively spirit of the Harlem Renaissance brings her rewards. (Rev: BL 2/1/07)

2206 Waldman, Neil. *Say-Hey and the Babe: Two Mostly True Baseball Stories* (4–6). Illus. by author. 2006, Holiday $16.95 (0-8234-1857-X). 40pp. Two

stories based on fact link a baseball autographed by Babe Ruth and subsequently lost with a stickball player's discovery in a sewer grate 14 years later; sidebars add lots of baseball lore and separate fact from fiction. (Rev: BL 5/15/06; SLJ 7/06)

2207 Yep, Laurence. *The Earth Dragon Awakes: The San Francisco Earthquake of 1906* (3–5). 2006, HarperCollins $15.99 (0-06-027524-3). 128pp. Best friends Henry and Ching, both fans of "penny dreadful" adventure novels, live through the earthquake and realize that their fathers are heroes. (Rev: BL 3/1/06; SLJ 5/06)

World War II and After

2208 Borden, Louise. *Across the Blue Pacific* (3–5). Illus. by Robert Andrew Parker. 2006, Houghton $17.00 (0-618-33922-1). 48pp. In this poignant fictional memoir, a woman recalls her concern as a fourth grader for the welfare of a neighbor who served on a submarine in the Pacific during World War II; watercolor paintings evoke the mood and time period. (Rev: BCCB 6/06; BL 4/1/06*; HB 5–6/06; HBG 10/06; LMC 1/07; SLJ 5/06)

2209 Giff, Patricia Reilly. *Willow Run* (4–6). 2005, Random $15.95 (0-385-73067-5). 176pp. Life changes dramatically for 11-year-old Meggie Dillon when her immediate family moves to Michigan so that her father can work in a airplane factory in World War II. (Rev: BCCB 12/05; BL 7/05*; HB 9–10/05; HBG 4/06; LMC 1/06; SLJ 9/05; VOYA 2/06)

2210 Gwaltney, Doris. *Homefront* (5–8). 2006, Simon & Schuster $15.95 (0-689-86842-1). 320pp. A young girl must cope with the diverse effects of World War II on her Virginia farming family. (Rev: BCCB 10/06; BL 7/06; SLJ 7/06*)

2211 Harrar, George. *The Wonder Kid* (4–7). Illus. by Anthony Winiarski. 2006, Houghton $16.00 (978-0-618-56317-3). 245pp. As a kid growing up in the 1950s, Jesse contracts polio and with the encouragement of a friend passes the time creating a comic strip hero called the Wonder Kid. (Rev: SLJ 3/07)

2212 Hostetter, Joyce Moyer. *Blue* (4–7). 2006, Boyds Mills $16.95 (1-59078-389-1). 200pp. When her father leaves for World War II, Ann Fay, the oldest of four children, struggles to keep up with the chores in their North Carolina home until polio strikes the community. (Rev: BL 2/15/06; SLJ 6/06)

2213 Kadohata, Cynthia. *Weedflower* (5–8). 2006, Simon & Schuster $16.95 (0-689-86574-0). 260pp. Sumiko and her Japanese American family are moved from their California flower farm to an internment camp in Arizona after the attack on Pearl Harbor; there she grows a garden and befriends a local Mojave boy. (Rev: BCCB 6/06; BL 4/15/06*;

HB 7–8/06; HBG 10/06; LMC 1/07; SLJ 7/06*; VOYA 2/06)

2214 Kerley, Barbara. *Greetings from Planet Earth* (4–6). 2007, Scholastic $16.99 (978-0-439-80203-1). 246pp. In 1977, as he considers a class project on space exploration, 12-year-old Theo is more preoccupied with family questions — why can he never discuss his father, who never returned from Vietnam? (Rev: BL 4/15/07)

2215 Klages, Ellen. *The Green Glass Sea* (4–7). 2006, Viking $16.99 (0-670-06134-4). 272pp. In 1943, talented 10-year-old Dewey goes to live with her father at the Los Alamos compound, a tense place where she initially has trouble making friends. (Rev: BL 11/15/06; SLJ 11/06)

2216 Lawrence, Iain. *Gemini Summer* (4–7). 2006, Delacorte $15.95 (0-385-73089-6). 224pp. In the mid-1960s, soon after Danny's brother Beau dies in an accident, a stray dog appears and adopts Danny; Danny becomes devoted to the dog and, because he sees much of Beau in Rocket, he and Rocket set off for Cape Canaveral to realize Beau's dream of seeing the Gemini mission. (Rev: BL 12/15/06; SLJ 11/06)

2217 McKissack, Patricia C. *Away West* (3–6). Illus. by Gordon C. James. Series: Scraps of Time. 2006, Viking $14.99 (0-670-06012-7). 112pp. In this second volume in the series, the Webster children learn the story of Everett Turner, who works in a livery stable after the Civil War and dreams of living in the African American town of Nicodemus, Kansas. (Rev: BL 4/15/06; SLJ 5/06)

2218 Peck, Richard. *On the Wings of Heroes* (4–6). 2007, Dial $16.99 (978-0-8037-3081-6). 148pp. Life before and during World War II is presented from the perspective of Davy Bowman, who lives in small-town America and has an older brother in the Air Force. (Rev: BL 12/1/06; SLJ 4/07*; VOYA 4/07)

2219 Ray, Delia. *Singing Hands* (4–7). 2006, Clarion $16.00 (0-618-65762-2). 256pp. Gussie's parents are deaf, which means she can be even more mischievous than the average child in this book set in the 1940s American South. (Rev: BL 5/1/06; SLJ 7/06)

2220 Smith, D. James. *Probably the World's Best Story About a Dog and the Girl Who Loved Me* (5–8). 2006, Simon & Schuster $15.95 (1-4169-0542-1). 240pp. In 1951 California, 12-year-old Paolo's beloved dog Rufus is dognapped and he enlists the help of his younger brother and a deaf cousin to unravel the mystery while also coping with a new paper route and a budding romance; this sequel to *The Boys of San Joaquin* (2004) introduces a sign language word with each chapter. (Rev: BL 9/1/06; SLJ 8/06)

2221 Tripp, Valerie. *Brave Emily* (2–4). Illus. by Nick Backes. 2006, Pleasant $12.95 (1-59369-211-0); paper $6.95 (1-59369-210-2). 78pp. Sent to live with an American family to escape the bombing of London in World War II, shy third grader Emily has trouble adjusting to the dramatic changes in her life. (Rev: BL 11/1/06; SLJ 2/07)

2222 Waters, Zack C. *Blood Moon Rider* (5–8). 2006, Pineapple $13.95 (1-56164-350-5). 126pp. Abandoned by his stepmother after his father is killed in World War II, 14-year-old Harley Wallace survives an eventful journey to the home of a grandfather he's never met and there finds more excitement waiting. (Rev: SLJ 8/06)

2223 Weston, Elise. *The Coastwatcher* (5–8). 2005, Peachtree $14.95 (1-56145-350-1). 160pp. Vacationing on the South Carolina coast with his family in 1943, 11-year-old Hugh sees some signs that Germans are nearby and is determined to convince the doubting adults that he is right. (Rev: BL 11/1/05; SLJ 3/06)

2224 White, Ruth. *Way Down Deep* (4–7). 2007, Farrar $16.00 (978-0-374-38251-3). 197pp. In 1944 West Virginia, the arrival of a new family in a town called Way Down Deep suddenly raises questions about the origins of Ruby June, a foundling who has lived there for 10 years. (Rev: BL 3/1/07; SLJ 4/07)

2225 Woodworth, Chris. *Georgie's Moon* (5–8). 2006, Farrar $16.00 (0-374-33306-8). 176pp. Seventh-grader Georgie Collins lives her life waiting for her father to return from Vietnam, and is unable to accept his death at first. (Rev: BL 3/1/06; SLJ 4/06)

Holidays and Holy Days

2226 Chaikin, Miriam. *Angel Secrets: Stories Based on Jewish Legend* (4–6). Illus. by Leonid Gore. 2005, Holt $18.95 (0-8050-7150-4). 80pp. In this collection of six short stories based on Jewish folklore, angels do God's work on Earth as well as in Heaven. (Rev: BL 10/1/05; SLJ 9/05) [296.3]

2227 Codell, Esmé Raji. *Hanukkah, Shmanukkah!* (3–5). Illus. by LeUyen Pham. 2005, Hyperion $16.99 (0-7868-5197-1). 48pp. Dickens's *A Christmas Carol* is retold as a Hanukkah tale full of humor and Yiddish phrases; a glossary is provided. (Rev: BL 9/1/05)

2228 Dickens, Charles. *A Christmas Carol* (5–10). Illus. by P. J. Lynch. 2006, Candlewick $19.99 (0-7636-3120-5). 159pp. Watercolor-and-gouache illustrations give a Victorian flavor to this attractive volume. (Rev: SLJ 10/06)

2229 Funke, Cornelia. *When Santa Fell to Earth* (3–5). 2006, Scholastic $15.99 (0-439-78204-X).

176pp. With the help of his new friends Charlotte and Ben, a good Santa must try to save Christmas from the evil schemes of Gerold Geronimus Goblynch. (Rev: BL 11/15/06; SLJ 10/06)

2230 Gerstein, Mordicai. *The White Ram: A Story of Abraham and Isaac* (3–5). 2006, Holiday $16.95 (0-8234-1897-9). 32pp. This beautifully illustrated retelling of the Old Testament story of Abraham and Isaac focuses on the white ram that ultimately takes the place of Isaac on the sacrificial altar. (Rev: BL 10/1/06; SLJ 9/06*)

2231 Jacobs, Laurie A. *A Box of Candles* (2–4). Illus. by Shelly Schonebaum Ephraim. 2005, Boyds Mills $17.95 (1-59078-169-4). 40pp. Given a silver candlestick and a year's worth of candles for her birthday, 7-year-old Ruthie faithfully observes Shabbat and other Jewish holidays as she struggles to adjust to changes in her family life. (Rev: BL 10/15/05; SLJ 9/05)

2232 Marunas, Nathaniel. *Manga Claus: The Blade of Kringle* (5–8). Illus. by Erik Craddock. 2006, Penguin $12.99 (1-59514-134-0). 80pp. In this graphic-novel Christmas tale, a disgruntled elf triggers a series of events that wrecks Santa's North Pole workshop and threatens to ruin Christmas for millions of children around the world. (Rev: BL 10/15/06; SLJ 10/06)

2233 Papineau, Lucie. *Christmas Eve Magic* (2–5). Trans. from French by Brigitte Shapiro. Illus. by Stéphane Poulin. 2006, Kids Can $16.95 (1-55337-953-5). In this story inspired by Dickens's *A Christmas Carol*, animals take the leading roles, led by a greedy pig called Barton. (Rev: SLJ 10/06)

2234 Ross, Richard. *Arctic Airlift* (1–3). Illus. 2005, Blue Fox $17.00 (0-9763119-0-9). 40pp. Santa's workshop is threatened by a flood, and young ham radio operator Robert picks up the distress call. (Rev: BL 10/15/05; SLJ 10/05)

2235 Sawyer, Ruth. *The Wee Christmas Cabin of Carn-na-ween* (3–5). Illus. by Max Grafe. 2005, Candlewick $14.99 (0-7636-2553-1). 40pp. Life holds little hope for Oona, who was abandoned by tinkers as a baby and has spent her life caring for others, until she pays a Christmas visit to the Gentle People of Carn-na-ween. (Rev: BL 11/15/05; SLJ 10/05)

2236 *A Simply Wonderful Christmas: A Literary Advent Calendar* (3–6). Illus. by Silke Leffler. 2006, North-South $25.00 (0-7358-2100-3). 133pp. Arranged like an advent calendar, this collection of stories and poems contains a special literary treat for each night in December leading up to Christmas. (Rev: SLJ 10/06)

2237 Steinhofel, Andreas. *An Elk Dropped In* (2–4). Illus. by Kerstin Meyer. 2006, Boyds Mills $16.95 (1-932425-80-2). 79pp. In a German village, an elk named Mr. Moose takes Santa's sleigh out for a

practice run and ends up crashing into Billy Wagner's house, where they happily care for him until he recuperates. (Rev: BL 11/15/06; SLJ 10/06)

Humorous Stories

2238 Ahlberg, Allan. *The Children Who Smelled a Rat* (2–4). Illus. by Katharine McEwen. 2005, Candlewick $15.99 (0-7636-2870-0). 80pp. In this action-packed tale about the Gaskitt family, twins Gus and Gloria try to figure out what caused their teacher's weird behavior, taxi driver Mom finds strange packages, and Dad chases after the baby's runaway shopping cart. (Rev: BCCB 11/05; BL 11/1/05; HBG 4/06; LMC 2/06; SLJ 10/05*)

2239 Amato, Mary. *Drooling and Dangerous: The Riot Brothers Return!* (3–5). Illus. by Ethan Long. Series: The Riot Brothers. 2006, Holiday $16.95 (0-8234-1986-X). 177pp. Wilbur and Orville Riot return for more zany adventures — as spies, as movie stars, and as school principals. (Rev: BL 5/15/06; HBG 10/06; SLJ 10/06)

2240 Anderson, M. T. *The Clue of the Linoleum Lederhosen: M. T. Anderson's Thrilling Tales* (4–7). Illus. by Kurt Cyrus. 2006, Harcourt $15.00 (0-15-205352-2). 256pp. Jasper Dash, Boy Technonaut, Katie, and Lily are caught up in an exciting mystery at Moose Tongue Lodge in this zany sequel to *Whales on Stilts* (2005). (Rev: BCCB 7–8/06; BL 5/1/06*; HB 5–6/06; HBG 10/06; SLJ 6/06; VOYA 6/06)

2241 Asch, Frank. *Star Jumper: Journal of a Cardboard Genius* (3–5). 2006, Kids Can $14.95 (1-55337-886-5); paper $5.95 (1-55337-887-3). 128pp. Intending to escape his little brother, Alex goes about building a spaceship and a duplicator, with some unintended consequences. (Rev: BL 7/06; HBG 10/06; LMC 1/07; SLJ 6/06)

2242 Benton, Jim. *The Fran That Time Forgot* (2–4). Illus. by author. Series: Franny K. Stein, Mad Scientist. 2005, Simon & Schuster $14.95 (0-689-86294-6). 102pp. Franny travels back in time in an attempt to change her middle name (Kissypie) in this half-funny, half-scary story. (Rev: SLJ 8/05)

2243 Benton, Jim. *Frantastic Voyage* (2–4). Illus. Series: Franny K. Stein, Mad Scientist. 2005, Simon & Schuster $14.95 (1-4169-0229-5). 112pp. When her canine assistant swallows a tiny doomsday device, girl scientist Franny shrinks herself so she can go and retrieve it; gross scenes will attract reluctant readers to this beginning chapter book with black-and-white cartoons. (Rev: BL 1/1–15/06; SLJ 4/06)

2244 Birney, Betty G. *Trouble According to Humphrey* (2–4). 2007, Putnam $14.99 (978-0-399-

24505-3). 176pp. Humphrey the class hamster describes his concerns about Paul's grades, Mandy's family's financial problems, and other woes in this third, funny installment in the series. (Rev: BL 1/1–15/07; SLJ 2/07)

2245 Brockmeier, Kevin. *Grooves: A Kind of Mystery* (4–7). 2006, HarperCollins LB $16.89 (0-06-073692-5). 208pp. In this funny mystery with science fiction overtones, unprepossessing 7th-grader Dwayne Ruggles finds out that the sounds coming from his blue jeans are really cries for help from imprisoned factory workers. (Rev: BL 2/1/06; SLJ 3/06)

2246 Child, Lauren. *Clarice Bean Spells Trouble* (3–5). 2005, Candlewick $15.99 (0-7636-2813-1). 192pp. Vowing to be more like Ruby Redfort, a character in books and a TV series, Clarice Bean tries to prepare for an upcoming spelling bee while also vying for a leading part in a school production of *The Sound of Music*. (Rev: BL 9/1/05; SLJ 8/05)

2247 Cibos, Lindsay, and Jared Hodges. *Peach Fuzz*, vol. 1 (3–5). Illus. by authors. 2005, TokyoPop paper $9.99 (1-59532-599-9). The story of a girl and her pet ferret, told from both pet's and owner's point of view. (Rev: SLJ 7/05)

2248 Dunbar, Fiona. *The Truth Cookie* (4–7). 2005, Scholastic $15.99 (0-439-74022-3). 224pp. Twelve-year-old Lulu's campaign to keep her father from marrying a supermodel gets an unexpected boost when Lulu discovers a recipe for Truth Cookies in this entertaining novel set in London. (Rev: BL 11/15/05; SLJ 12/05)

2249 Elliott, David. *Evangeline Mudd and the Great Mink Escapade* (3–5). 2006, Candlewick $15.99 (0-7636-2295-8). 192pp. Evangeline Mudd, enthusiastic warrior for animal rights, sets out to free a number of minks before they are turned into ballet costumes. (Rev: BL 2/15/06; SLJ 3/06)

2250 Fine, Anne. *The Return of the Killer Cat* (3–5). Illus. by Steve Cox. 2007, Farrar $16.00 (0-374-36248-3). 74pp. In this sequel to *The Diary of a Killer Cat* (2006), Tuffy plans to do as he pleases while his family vacations, but his hopes are dashed when he learns that the vicar is coming to cat-sit him. (Rev: BL 3/15/07; SLJ 2/07)

2251 Gervais, Ricky. *More Flanimals* (3–5). Illus. by Rob Steen. 2006, Putnam $15.99 (0-399-24605-3). 64pp. A silly guide to Flanimal species as the Skwunt and the Swog Monglet and their evolution, anatomy, and behavior. (Rev: SLJ 10/06)

2252 Gleitzman, Morris. *Toad Away* (4–6). 2006, Random $14.95 (0-375-82766-8). 208pp. Limpy, the Australian cane toad, journeys to the Amazon in his quest to find a way to peacefully coexist with humans. (Rev: BL 2/15/06; SLJ 4/06)

2253 Goscinny, René. *Nicholas,* (4–6). Trans. from French by Anthea Bell. Illus. by Jean-Jacques

Sempé. 2005, Phaidon $19.95 (0-7148-4529-9). 128pp. Nicholas, a mischievous schoolboy, and his friends get into one scrape after another in this collection of tales by the author of the *Asterix* comics. (Rev: SLJ 10/05)

2254 Goscinny, René. *Nicholas on Vacation* (2–5). Trans. from French by Anthea Bell. Illus. by Jean-Jacques Sempé. 2006, Phaidon $19.95 (978-0-7148-4678-1). 126pp. Follow Nicholas on his summer vacations as he travels to the beach with his parents and goes to a camp to stay overnight for the first time. (Rev: SLJ 3/07)

2255 Hagerup, Klaus. *Markus and Diana* (4–6). Trans. from Norwegian by Tara Chace. 2006, Front St. $17.95 (1-932425-59-4). 188pp. Markus, a Norwegian sixth grader, strikes up a correspondence with a beautiful soap-opera actress by pretending to be a mountain-climbing millionaire, but things threaten to get out of control when she insists on meeting him in person. (Rev: SLJ 12/06)

2256 Hamilton, Richard. *Cal and the Amazing Anti-Gravity Machine* (3–5). 2006, Bloomsbury $14.95 (1-58234-714-X); paper $5.95 (1-58234-714-X). 128pp. In this funny chapter book for new readers, 10-year-old Cal — accompanied by his talking dog Frankie — investigates his neighbor's newly developed antigravity machine with unsettling results. (Rev: BL 4/15/06; SLJ 7/06)

2257 Harper, Charise Mericle. *Just Grace* (2–4). Illus. 2007, Houghton $15.00 (978-0-618-64642-5). 144pp. Just Grace (misnamed by her teacher to set her apart from the other three Graces in her class) deals successfully with the usual third-grade problems in this funny chapter book, but her well-intentioned efforts to find a neighbor's cat go awry. (Rev: BL 3/1/07*)

2258 Howe, James. *Bunnicula Meets Edgar Allan Crow* (4–7). Illus. by Eric Fortune. 2006, Simon & Schuster $15.95 (978-1-4169-1458-7). 138pp. When world-famous author M. T. Graves and his pet, Edgar Allan Crow, come to stay with the Monroe family, Bunnicula the vampire bunny suspects that the household guests are up to no good. (Rev: BL 1/1–15/07; SLJ 2/07)

2259 Keehn, Sally M. *Magpie Gabbard and the Quest for the Buried Moon* (5–8). 2007, Philomel $16.99 (978-0-399-24340-2). 206pp. Thirteen-year-old Magpie Gabbard must fulfill a prophecy and put aside her cussedness in order to save the moon in this exuberant and complex tall tale. (Rev: BL 4/15/07; SLJ 2/07)

2260 Klise, Kate. *Regarding the Bathrooms: A Privy to the Past* (4–6). Illus. by M. Sarah Klise. Series: Regarding the . . . 2006, Harcourt $15.00 (0-15-205164-3). 160pp. The principal of Geyser Creek Middle School grows increasingly frustrated as unexpected events delay progress on the school's bathroom remodeling project in this multilayered, funny story involving a dollop of Roman/bathroom history and told through letters, memos, newspaper articles, and police reports. (Rev: BL 9/1/06; SLJ 8/06)

2261 Klise, Kate. *Regarding the Trees: A Splintered Saga Rooted in Secrets* (4–6). Illus. by M. Sarah Klise. 2005, Harcourt $15.00 (0-15-205163-5). 160pp. In a scrapbook format using letters, news articles, and illustrations, this is the funny, pun-filled, and complex story of a dispute over trimming the trees at the middle school and a community's various interests. (Rev: BL 11/1/05; SLJ 11/05)

2262 Kurzweil, Allen. *Leon and the Champion Chip* (3–6). Illus. by Bret Bertholf. 2005, Greenwillow $15.99 (0-06-053933-X). 336pp. Leon Zeisel starts fifth grade, plans revenge on bully Henry Lumpkin, and discovers to his amazement that his science class will spend a semester researching the potato chip, his favorite snack food; a funny sequel to *Leon and the Spitting Image* (2003). (Rev: BL 11/1/05; SLJ 3/06)

2263 Lubar, David. *Punished!* (4–7). 2006, Darby Creek $15.95 (1-58196-042-5). 96pp. Thanks to a curse, Logan becomes a non-stop punster and must uncover oxymorons, anagrams, and palindromes to break the spell. (Rev: BL 5/1/06; SLJ 5/06*)

2264 McDonald, Megan. *Stink and the Incredible Super-Galactic Jawbreaker* (2–4). Illus. by Peter Reynolds. Series: Stink. 2006, Candlewick $12.99 (0-7636-2158-7). 128pp. When he discovers that a letter of complaint can yield free candy, Stink — Judy Moody's younger brother — embarks on a letter-writing campaign. (Rev: BL 4/15/06; SLJ 7/06)

2265 Mason, Simon. *The Quigleys in a Spin* (3–5). Illus. by Helen Stephens. 2006, Random $14.95 (0-385-75098-6). 192pp. Lucy painting her sleeping dad's toenails and having a dreadful birthday party are only two of the funny episodes in this British chapter book. (Rev: BL 1/1–15/06; SLJ 4/06)

2266 Montgomery, Claire, and Monte Montgomery. *Hubert Invents the Wheel* (4–7). Illus. by Jeff Shelly. 2005, Walker $16.95 (0-8027-8990-0). 184pp. Hubert, a struggling 15-year-old inventor in ancient Sumeria, finally finds success when he invents the wheel, but things quickly spin out of control. (Rev: SLJ 11/05)

2267 Naylor, Phyllis Reynolds. *Boys Rock!* (4–6). 2005, Delacorte $15.95 (0-385-73140-X). 144pp. To earn extra reading credits over the summer, the Hatford brothers decide to publish a newspaper, an undertaking that becomes even more complicated when they reluctantly ask the Malloy sisters to join them. (Rev: BL 10/1/05; SLJ 1/06)

2268 Naylor, Phyllis Reynolds. *Who Won the War?* (4–7). 2006, Delacorte LB $17.99 (0-385-90172-0). 160pp. In the last weeks before they return to Ohio

(and the last volume in the series), the Malloy sisters mount a last-ditch campaign to prove their superiority over the Hatford boys. (Rev: BL 11/1/06; SLJ 9/06)

2269 Ogden, Charles. *Pet's Revenge* (4–6). Illus. by Rick Carton. Series: Edgar and Ellen. 2006, Simon & Schuster $9.95 (1-4169-1408-0). 192pp. Edgar has to act by himself to save their house when Ellen undergoes a character change and endorses a neat, tidy life.. (Rev: BL 5/15/06)

2270 Paulsen, Gary. *Lawn Boy* (5–8). 2007, Random $12.99 (978-0-385-74686-1). 96pp. Given his late grandfather's somewhat battered riding mower as a gift, a 12-year-old entrepreneur launches a phenomenally successful lawn care business in this zany, tongue-in-cheek story. (Rev: BL 4/15/07; HB 7–8/07)

2271 Pennypacker, Sara. *The Talented Clementine* (2–4). Illus. by Marla Frazee. 2007, Hyperion $14.99 (978-0-7868-3870-7). 144pp. Third-grader Clementine views the forthcoming talent show with nothing but dread in this funny chapter book. (Rev: BL 3/15/07)

2272 Petty, J. T. *The Squampkin Patch: A Nasselrogt Adventure* (4–7). Illus. by David Michael Friend. 2006, Simon & Schuster $15.95 (1-4169-0274-0). 251pp. A funny, far-fetched fantasy about two children who escape hard labor at the zipper factory/orphanage (their parents are tied up in tanning beds) and find themselves pursued by squampkins — pumpkin-like creatures — that are out for blood. (Rev: SLJ 7/06)

2273 Pilkey, Dav. *Captain Underpants and the Preposterous Plight of the Purple Potty People* (2–5). Illus. by author. 2006, Scholastic $16.99 (0-439-37613-0); paper $4.99 (0-439-37614-3). 175pp. George and Harold find themselves in an alternate universe inhabited by evil versions of themselves. (Rev: SLJ 12/06)

2274 Rumble, Chris. *Moby Stink* (3–5). Illus. by author. Series: The Adventures of Uncle Stinky. 2005, Tricycle paper $5.95 (1-58246-145-7). 89pp. After landing a huge catfish in his hometown's annual fishing derby, Uncle Stinky frees the creature, infuriating celebrity angler Barry Cooter, who then plots to destroy the town and everyone in it; a wacky, pun-filled tall tale. (Rev: SLJ 1/06)

2275 Scroggs, Kirk. *Dracula vs. Grampa at the Monster Truck Spectacular* (2–5). Illus. by author. Series: Wiley and Grampa's Creature Features. 2006, Little, Brown $12.99 (0-316-05902-1); paper $2.99 (0-316-05941-2). 106pp. Grampa provokes Gramma's ire when he takes grandson Wiley to Colonel Dracula's Monster Truck Spectacular on Halloween night; an exciting evening that includes a strong tornado. Also use *Grampa's Zombie BBQ* (2006). (Rev: SLJ 10/06)

135

2276 Smith, Greg Leitich. *Tofu and T. Rex* (5–8). 2005, Little, Brown $15.99 (0-316-77722-6). 162pp. Cousins Freddie, a militant vegan, and Hans-Peter, who sometimes slices meat at his grandfather's deli, clash when both enroll at Chicago's prestigious Peshtigo School. (Rev: SLJ 9/05)

2277 Snicket, Lemony. *The End* (5–8). Illus. by Brett Helquist. Series: A Series of Unfortunate Events. 2006, HarperCollins $12.99 (0-06-441016-1). 357pp. The Baudelaire orphans find themselves stranded on an island with none other than the villainous Count Olaf; will this be the last installment in the series? (Rev: BL 10/15/06)

2278 Snicket, Lemony. *The Penultimate Peril* (5–8). Illus. by Brett Helquist. Series: A Series of Unfortunate Events. 2005, HarperCollins $15.89 (0-06-029643-7). 360pp. In the next-to-last volume of the popular series, the Baudelaire orphans seek respite from their earlier adventures and meet up with many previous characters at the mysterious Hotel Denouement. (Rev: BL 12/1/05)

2279 Spearman, Andy. *Barry, Boyhound* (4–7). 2005, Knopf LB $17.99 (0-375-93264-X). 240pp. Barry, a fairly ordinary human boy, is transformed overnight into a boyhound, and while he still looks like a boy, he now thinks more like a dog. (Rev: BL 12/1/05; SLJ 9/05)

2280 Standford, Natalie. *Blonde at Heart* (5–8). Series: Elle Woods. 2006, Hyperion $4.99 (0-7868-3843-4). 240pp. How Elle Woods, the central character of the 2001 movie *Legally Blonde*, became a blond bombshell in her effort to attract the attention of her crush. (Rev: BL 7/06; SLJ 5/06)

2281 Tacang, Brian. *Bully-Be-Gone* (3–6). Series: The Misadventures of Millicent Madding. 2006, HarperCollins $15.99 (0-06-073911-8). 216pp. Twelve-year-old Millicent Madding, an inventor with an uneven level of success, comes up with a fragrance that's designed to repel bullies; full of alliteration and wacky characters. (Rev: SLJ 1/06)

2282 Tayleur, Karen. *Excuses! Survive and Succeed with David Mortimore Baxter* (3–6). Illus. by Brann Garvey. 2006, Stone Arch LB $23.93 (978-1-59889-073-0). 71pp. David is good avoiding work and shares all his excuses for getting out of homework, chores, eating veggies, and more in this hilarious story. (Rev: SLJ 3/07)

2283 Tayleur, Karen. *Secrets! The Secret Life of David Mortimore Baxter* (3–6). Illus. by Brann Garvey. 2006, Stone Arch LB $23.93 (978-1-59889-077-8). 82pp. When a well-known wrestler acknowledges Davey as a trustworthy friend on national TV, Davey gets lots more attention and confidences than he needs. (Rev: SLJ 3/07)

2284 Trine, Greg. *Melvin Beederman, Superhero: The Curse of the Bologna Sandwich* (2–4). Illus. by Rhode Montijo. Series: Melvin Beederman, Superhero. 2006, Holt $15.95 (0-8050-7928-9); paper $5.99 (0-8050-7836-3). 138pp. Hapless superhero Melvin is almost defeated by his love for bologna in this installment in the laugh-out-loud series. The adventures continue in *Melvin Beederman, Superhero: The Revenge of the McNasty Brothers* (2005). (Rev: SLJ 5/06)

2285 Tulloch, Richard. *Weird Stuff* (5–8). Illus. by Shane Nagle. 2006, Walker $16.95 (0-8027-8058-X). 195pp. A borrowed pen gives school soccer star Brian Hobble amazing new writing abilities, but they're limited to a single genre — romantic fiction. (Rev: SLJ 8/06)

2286 Yee, Lisa. *Stanford Wong Flunks Big-Time* (4–7). 2005, Scholastic $16.99 (0-439-62247-6). 256pp. In this rollicking sequel to *Millicent Minn, Girl Genius*, Stanford Wong is upset when his parents hire Millicent, his arch-nemesis, to tutor him in English. (Rev: BL 11/15/05; SLJ 12/05)

School Stories

2287 Amato, Mary. *Please Write in This Book* (2–5). Illus. by Eric Brace. 2006, Holiday House $16.95 (978-0-8234-1932-6). 97pp. A teacher's effort to get children writing is only successful after hurtful slurs and rivalries run their course. (Rev: BCCB 3/07; BL 12/15/06; HBG 4/07; SLJ 4/07)

2288 Bagert, Brod. *Hormone Jungle: Coming of Age in Middle School* (5–8). Illus. 2006, Maupin House $23.95 (0-929895-87-8). 121pp. The scrapbook of Christina Curtis's middle-school years tells the story of the poetry war that erupted in sixth grade and of the changing relationships between the young people as they learned more about each other. (Rev: SLJ 6/06)

2289 Bonk, John J. *Dustin Grubbs: One-Man Show* (4–6). 2005, Little, Brown $15.99 (0-316-15636-1). 256pp. Eleven-year-old Dustin Grubbs, an aspiring actor, tells the funny story of the trouble-plagued production of a school play. (Rev: BL 12/1/05; SLJ 12/05)

2290 Buzzeo, Toni. *Our Librarian Won't Tell Us Anything!* (2–5). Illus. by Sachiko Yoshikawa. 2006, Upstart $17.95 (978-1-932146-73-8). Robert, a new student at Liberty Elementary, discovers that the conventional wisdom is awry and the librarian is in fact very helpful. (Rev: SLJ 2/07)

2291 Catalanotto, Peter, and Pamela Schembri. *The Secret Lunch Special* (1–3). Illus. by Peter Catalanotto. Series: Second Grade Friends. 2006, Holt $15.95 (0-8050-7838-X). 64pp. Misunderstanding a classmate's remarks, young Emily — new to coping with second grade — worries about the consequences of leaving her lunch bag on the school bus. (Rev: BL 9/1/06; SLJ 9/06)

2292 Clements, Andrew. *Lunch Money* (4–6). Illus. by Brian Selznick. 2005, Simon & Schuster $15.95 (0-689-86683-6). 222pp. Greg comes up with a great idea to make money but runs into setbacks when the school bans his product and another student develops a competing one. (Rev: SLJ 8/05)

2293 Copeland, Cynthia L. *Dilly for President* (3–5). Illus. by author. 2006, Millbrook LB $21.90 (0-7613-2442-9); paper $6.95 (0-7613-2442-9). 64pp. In her diary, Dilly describes her classmates and teachers as she enters fourth grade and decides to run for class president. (Rev: SLJ 4/06)

2294 Disalvo-Ryan, DyAnne. *The Sloppy Copy Slipup* (3–5). Illus. 2006, Holiday $16.95 (0-8234-1947-9). 103pp. Brian Higman complains that he can't find anything interesting to write about, but his teacher and classmates show him that the stuff of his everyday life provides plenty of inspiration. (Rev: BL 3/1/06; SLJ 5/06)

2295 Dowell, Frances O'Roark. *Phineas L. MacGuire . . . Erupts! The First Experiment* (3–5). Illus. by Preston McDaniels. Series: From the Highly Selective Notebooks of Phineas L. MacGuire. 2006, Simon & Schuster $15.95 (1-4169-0195-7). 176pp. Science fair success seems unlikely when Phineas L. MacGuire is paired with the obnoxious new kid to work on a fourth-grade science project. (Rev: BL 6/1–15/06; SLJ 6/06)

2296 Edwards, Michelle. *Stinky Stern Forever* (1–3). Illus. Series: Jackson Friends. 2005, Harcourt $14.00 (0-15-216389-1). 56pp. Pa Lia Vang and her second-grade classmates have complex reactions when the class bully dies in an accident. (Rev: BL 9/1/05; SLJ 10/05*)

2297 Fitzgerald, Dawn. *Soccer Chick Rules* (5–8). 2006, Roaring Brook $16.95 (1-59643-137-7). 160pp. When her school's sports program is threatened, Tess Munro, a talented 13-year-old soccer player, joins the campaign to win approval for the school levy. (Rev: BL 9/1/06; SLJ 10/06)

2298 Flood, Pansie Hart. *Tiger Turcotte Takes on the Know-It-All* (2–4). Illus. by Amy Wummer. 2005, Carolrhoda LB $14.95 (1-57505-814-6); paper $6.95 (1-57505-900-2). 71pp. A beginning chapter book about a second-grade boy-girl rivalry. (Rev: SLJ 7/05)

2299 Fredericks, Mariah. *In the Cards: Love* (5–8). Illus. 2007, Simon & Schuster $15.99 (0-689-87654-8). 288pp. Three eighth-grade girls in Manhattan use tarot cards to discover whether Anna will succeed in turning her crush on Declan into a romance; likable, believable characters populate this funny novel. (Rev: BL 1/1–15/07; SLJ 4/07)

2300 Friedman, D. Dina. *Playing Dad's Song* (4–7). 2006, Farrar $16.00 (0-374-37173-3). 144pp. After

two years 11-year-old Gus is still dealing with his father's death in the World Trade Center, along with problems at school, but finds comfort in taking oboe lessons with an elderly neighbor. (Rev: BL 11/15/06; LMC 4–5/07; SLJ 9/06)

2301 Gilson, Jamie. *Gotcha!* (2–4). Illus. by Amy Wummer. 2006, Clarion $15.00 (0-618-54356-2). 68pp. Information on spiders is interwoven into a story about second-grader Richard and his relationship with a bully named Patrick; an easy, humorous chapter book with line drawings. (Rev: BL 4/1/06; SLJ 4/06)

2302 Gutman, Dan. *The Homework Machine* (4–6). 2006, Simon & Schuster $15.95 (0-689-87678-5). 160pp. A magical homework machine creates an unlikely alliance between a fifth-grade computer geek, a teacher's pet, the class clown, and a slacker. (Rev: BCCB 3/06; BL 2/1/06*; HBG 10/06; LMC 10/06; SLJ 4/06*)

2303 Jacobson, Jennifer Richard. *Andy Shane and the Very Bossy Dolores Starbuckle* (1–3). Illus. by Abby Carter. 2005, Candlewick $15.99 (0-7636-1940-X). 64pp. A bully is making life at school miserable for Andy Shane until his Granny Webb pays a visit to the classroom. (Rev: BL 7/05; SLJ 8/05*)

2304 Jacobson, Jennifer Richard. *Winnie at Her Best* (2–4). Illus. by Alissa Imre Geis. 2006, Houghton $16.00 (0-618-47277-0). 112pp. Winnie must choose between helping out a young friend in need or pursuing her newfound interest in art. (Rev: BL 8/06; SLJ 9/06)

2305 Kinney, Jeff. *Diary of a Wimpy Kid* (5–8). 2007, Abrams $14.95 (0-8109-9313-9); paper $14.95 (978-0-8109-9313-6). 224pp. Greg Heffley writes in his very funny journal about the highlights — and the frequent low moments — of his first year in middle school. (Rev: BL 4/1/07; VOYA 4/07)

2306 LeBlanc, Louise. *Maddie's Big Test* (2–4). Illus. by Marie-Louise Gay. 2007, Formac paper $4.95 (978-0-8878-0714-5). 64pp. Maddie, who's much more interested in becoming a star than in math, is so nervous about her test that she decides to cheat. (Rev: BL 4/1/07)

2307 Lowry, Lois. *Gooney the Fabulous* (2–4). Illus. by Middy Thomas. 2007, Houghton $15.00 (978-0-618-76691-8). 96pp. In this third outing, second-grader Gooney Bird Green leads her classmates in writing their own fables after Miss Pidgeon reads them an Aesop's tale. (Rev: BL 1/1–15/07)

2308 Luddy, Karon. *Spelldown: The Big-Time Dreams of a Small-Town Word Whiz* (5–8). 2007, Simon & Schuster $15.99 (978-1-4169-1610-9). 211pp. Mentored by her Latin teacher, 13-year-old Karlene manages to win the spelling championship in her rural South Carolina county and moves on to competitions at the state and national levels. (Rev: SLJ 2/07)

2309 McDonald, Megan. *Stink and the World's Worst Super-Stinky Sneakers* (2–4). Illus. by Peter Reynolds. 2007, Candlewick $12.99 (978-0-7636-2834-5). 144pp. Stink, who got his name as a baby, had been intent on winning the smelly sneaker contest but is willing to give up this chance to become one of the judges instead. (Rev: BL 4/15/07)

2310 Marsden, Carolyn. *The Quail Club* (3–5). 2006, Candlewick $15.99 (0-7636-2635-X). 144pp. Thai American fifth-grader Oy faces a cultural dilemma when her school schedules a talent show: honor her heritage with a traditional Thai dance or succumb to her classmate's demand that Oy join her in an American dance; a sequel to *The Gold-Threaded Dress* (2002). (Rev: BL 3/1/06; SLJ 4/06)

2311 Mills, Claudia. *Being Teddy Roosevelt* (3–5). Illus. by R. W. Alley. 2007, Farrar $16.00 (978-0-374-30657-1). 96pp. In this funny school story, fourth-grader Riley, assigned to research and depict Theodore Roosevelt, employs some of T.R.'s enterprising zeal to obtain an unaffordable saxophone to play in the school band. (Rev: BL 1/1–15/07; SLJ 3/07)

2312 Moss, Marissa. *Amelia's Book of Notes and Note Passing* (3–5). Series: Amelia. 2006, Simon & Schuster $9.95 (0-689-87446-4). 80pp. Amelia's world is jarred off-orbit when a new girl joins her class at school and Amelia starts receiving hateful anonymous notes. (Rev: BL 5/1/06)

2313 Moss, Marissa. *Amelia's Most Unforgettable Embarrassing Moments* (3–5). Illus. by author. 2005, Simon & Schuster $9.95 (0-689-87041-8). Faced with a three-day class field trip, Amelia worries about whether her bedtime apparel will pass muster; her older sister's presence as a teaching aide adds to her angst but ends up helping her realize she's not alone in her fears. (Rev: SLJ 11/05)

2314 Moss, Marissa. *Amelia's 6th-Grade Notebook* (4–6). Illus. 2005, Simon & Schuster $10.95 (0-689-87040-X). 80pp. Entering middle school, Amelia has to deal with the presence of her older sister and a really mean English teacher. (Rev: BL 7/05; SLJ 10/05)

2315 Pearsall, Shelley. *All of the Above* (5–8). 2006, Little, Brown $15.99 (0-316-11524-X). 242pp. In this inspiring, fact-based novel, a seventh-grade math teacher challenges his students to build the world's largest tetrahedron and ends up involving the whole community; alternating chapters are narrated by the teacher and four of the students. (Rev: BL 9/1/06; SLJ 9/06)

2316 Schwartz, Virginia Frances. *The 4 Kids in 5E and 1 Crazy Year* (3–5). 2006, Holiday $16.95 (0-8234-1946-0). 261pp. A fifth-grade ESL teacher helps each of her four students find themselves through reading and writing; the story is told through the students' journal entries. (Rev: BL 12/1/06; SLJ 11/06)

2317 Seuling, Barbara. *Robert and the Practical Jokes* (2–4). Illus. by Paul Brewer. 2006, Cricket $15.95 (0-8126-2741-5). 136pp. In addition to getting in trouble at school and being fooled into eating a worm, Robert attends a wedding and learns to dance. (Rev: BL 5/1/06; SLJ 3/06)

2318 Walker, Kate. *I Hate Books!* (2–4). Illus. by David Cox. 2007, Cricket $16.95 (978-0-8126-2745-8). 88pp. Hamish is so skilled at telling stories that his teachers are slow to realize he has not learned to read. (Rev: BL 3/15/07)

2319 Warner, Sally. *Super Emma* (2–3). Illus. by Jamie Harper. 2006, Viking $14.99 (0-670-06140-9). 90pp. When Emma rescues EllRay from the clutches of a school bully, the reactions of her classmates — including EllRay — are not at all what she expected. (Rev: SLJ 10/06)

2320 Winkler, Henry, and Lin Oliver. *My Secret Life as a Ping-Pong Wizard* (3–5). Illus. Series: Hank Zipzer. 2005, Grosset & Dunlap $12.99 (0-448-43877-1); paper $4.99 (0-448-43749-X). 158pp. When his fifth-grade classmates begin to get serious about sports, dedicated underachiever Hank Zipzer takes up ping-pong and discovers, much to his surprise, that sports can be fun. (Rev: BL 1/1–15/06)

2321 Wojciechowski, Susan. *Beany and the Meany* (2–4). Illus. by Susanna Natti. 2005, Candlewick $15.99 (0-7636-2630-9). 112pp. Beany is upset when she's teamed up with the class bully for an upcoming science fair project. (Rev: BL 9/1/05; SLJ 7/05)

Science Fiction

2322 Cole, Steve. *Riddle of the Raptors* (3–5). Illus. by Charlie Fowkes. Series: Astrosaurs. 2006, Simon & Schuster paper $4.99 (0-689-87841-9). 126pp. In the opening installment of this humorous science fiction series, Teggs, an Earth-orbiting dinosaur, and his crew of astrosaurs, set out to rescue a couple of their plant-eating athletes who were taken captive by meat-eating velociraptors. (Rev: SLJ 8/06)

2323 Crilley, Mark. *Akiko: The Training Master* (3–6). Illus. by author. Series: Akiko. 2005, Delacorte $9.95 (0-385-73043-8). 207pp. Fifth-grader Akiko is in outer space at the Intergalactic Space Patrollers Training Camp in this latest installment in the humorous, lively series. (Rev: SLJ 7/05)

2324 Fields, Bryan W. *Lunchbox and the Aliens* (3–6). Illus. by Kevan Atteberry. 2006, Holt $16.95 (0-8050-7995-5). 185pp. Two dimwitted aliens — Frazz and Grunfloz — kidnap Lunchbox the basset hound and program him to convert garbage into food; a funny, complex story. (Rev: SLJ 10/06)

2325 Guibert, Emmanuel. *Sardine in Outer Space* (3–5). Trans. by Sasha Watson. Illus. by Joann Sfar. Series: Sardine in Outer Space. 2006, Roaring Brook paper $12.95 (1-5964-3126-1). 128pp. In this comic book space fantasy, an import from France, a young girl named Sardine enlists the help of her cousin and uncle to foil the villainous plans of Supermuscleman. (Rev: BL 3/15/06; SLJ 7/06)

2326 Guibert, Emmanuel. *Sardine in Outer Space 2* (4–6). Illus. by Joann Sfar. Series: Sardine in Outer Space. 2006, Roaring Brook paper $12.95 (1-59643-127-X). 128pp. In the second volume of this graphic novel series, the redheaded Sardine and her fellow space pirates duel once again with the villainous — but slow-witted — Supermuscleman. (Rev: BL 9/1/06; SLJ 11/06)

2327 Guibert, Emmanuel, and Joann Sfar. *Sardine in Outer Space 3* (5–8). Trans. by Elisabeth Brizzi. Illus. 2007, Roaring Brook paper $12.95 (978-1-59643-128-7). 112pp. Sardine and her space-pirate friends tackle Supermuscleman among others in this series of zany adventures. (Rev: BL 3/15/07)

2328 Haddix, Margaret P. *Among the Free* (5–8). Series: Shadow Children. 2006, Simon & Schuster $16.95 (0-689-85798-5). 208pp. Illegal third child Luke inadvertently sets off an uprising that leads to the overthrow of his country's oppressive government. (Rev: BL 6/1–15/06; SLJ 8/06)

2329 Haddix, Margaret P. *Double Identity* (5–8). 2005, Simon & Schuster $15.95 (0-689-87374-3). 224pp. In this science fiction page-turner, 12-year-old Bethany Cole, left with her aunt after her mother suffers a nervous breakdown, uncovers some shocking family secrets. (Rev: BL 10/1/05; SLJ 11/05; VOYA 10/05)

2330 Johansen, K. V. *The Cassandra Virus* (5–8). 2006, Orca paper $7.95 (1-55143-497-0). 153pp. Computer geek Jordan designs a powerful computer program that takes on a life of its own, spreading via the Internet to other computers and taking control of their operations. (Rev: SLJ 11/06; VOYA 8/06)

2331 Luzzatto, Caroline. *Interplanetary Avenger* (4–6). 2005, Holiday House $16.95 (0-8234-1933-9). 120pp. Transported to a school on another planet after he opens a mysterious package, middle-schooler Sam must chase after a shape-shifting ne'er-do-well who is threatening Earth; full of gross humor and zany situations. (Rev: SLJ 12/05)

2332 McKinty, Adrian. *The Lighthouse Land* (5–8). 2006, Abrams $16.95 (0-8109-5480-X). 388pp. In this first installment in an action-packed science fiction series, Jamie (a 13-year-old who is mute after losing his left arm to bone cancer) and his mother move to an Irish island, where he and a new friend discover an artifact that transports them to a far-off planet in time to help a girl named Wishaway. (Rev: BL 11/15/06; SLJ 1/07)

2333 McNamee, Eoin. *The Navigator: Chosen to Save the World* (5–8). 2007, Random $15.99 (978-0-375-83910-8). 352pp. Owen finds himself suddenly in a different world where he and a girl named Cati must battle the Harsh, evil beings who freeze all that they touch and have set time running backward. (Rev: BL 12/1/06; SLJ 3/07)

2334 Miller, Wiley. *The Extraordinary Adventures of Ordinary Basil: The Impossible Flight to Helios* (3–5). 2006, Scholastic $14.99 (0-439-85665-5). 128pp. When a man appears outside bored Basil's window in a floating balloon, he hops in and goes on an adventure to Helios, a secret city in the sky where he has exciting adventures in this well-illustrated book set in the late 19th century. (Rev: BL 2/15/07; SLJ 2/07)

2335 Powell, J. *Big Brother at School* (5–8). Illus. by Paul Savage. Series: Keystone Books. 2006, Stone Arch LB $19.93 (1-59889-091-3). 33pp. At a school where cameras watch students' every move, Lee becomes convinced that the principal and a visiting doctor are aliens and takes step to save his fellow students from abduction. (Rev: SLJ 1/07)

2336 Reeve, Philip. *Larklight, or, The Revenge of the White Spiders!, or, To Saturn's Rings and Back!* (5–8). Illus. by David Wyatt. 2006, Bloomsbury $16.95 (1-59990-020-3). 384pp. Art and Myrtle Mumby, who live with their father in a Victorian mansion orbiting the earth, become embroiled in a plot to destroy the solar system; a science fiction romp with a touch of romance and a dollop of Victorian manners. (Rev: BCCB 2/07; BL 10/1/06; HB 11–12/06; HBG 4/07; LMC 2/07; SLJ 11/06*; VOYA 12/06)

2337 Skurzynski, Gloria. *The Choice* (5–8). Series: The Virtual War Chronologs. 2006, Simon & Schuster $16.95 (0-689-84267-8). 228pp. In the fast-paced concluding installment in the series, 16-year-old Corgan has a final confrontation with the murderous Brigand. (Rev: SLJ 10/06)

2338 Valentine, James. *Rule No. 2: Don't Even Think About It* (5–8). Series: Jumpman. 2006, Simon & Schuster $14.95 (0-689-87353-0). 288pp. In their second adventure full of neat gadgets and humorous cultural tidbits, Australian 13-year-olds Jules and Gen are again involved with young people from the far future. (Rev: BL 4/1/06; SLJ 3/06)

Short Stories and Anthologies

2339 Asher, Sandy, and David L. Harrison, eds. *Dude! Stories and Stuff for Boys* (4–7). 2006, Dutton $17.99 (0-525-47684-9). 224pp. Selections for boys — poems, short stories, and other works — offer diverse experiences; authors include Sneed B. Collard III, Clyde Robert Bulla, Jane Yolen, and Ron Koertge. (Rev: BL 7/06; HBG 4/07; LMC 1/07; SLJ 8/06; VOYA 12/06)

2340 Avi, sel. *Best Shorts: Favorite Short Stories for Sharing* (5–9). Ed. by Carolyn Shute. Illus. by Chris Raschka. 2006, Houghton $16.95 (0-618-47603-2). 397pp. The 24 short stories in this anthology provide a sampling of some of the best writing in a wide variety of genres. (Rev: SLJ 10/06)

2341 *The Big Book of Horror: 21 Tales to Make You Tremble* (5–7). Illus. by Pedro Rodriguez. 2007, Sterling $12.95 (978-1-4027-3860-9). 112pp. This collection of 21 horror tales includes stories by Edgar Allan Poe, Charles Dickens, Robert Louis Stevenson, and H. P. Lovecraft. (Rev: BL 3/15/07)

2342 Crebbin, June, ed. *Horse Tales* (4–7). Illus. by Inga Moore. 2005, Candlewick $18.99 (0-7636-2657-0). 152pp. Diverse short stories about horses, with color illustrations. (Rev: BL 9/1/05; SLJ 8/05)

2343 Davis, Donald. *Mama Learns to Drive and Other Stories: Stories of Love, Humor, and Wisdom* (4–7). 2005, August House $17.95 (0-87483-745-6). 119pp. Brief, slow-paced short stories based on his mother, who grew up in the Smoky Mountains in the 1930s, are mixed with tales about the author's own youth in the 1950s. (Rev: BL 8/05; SLJ 10/05)

2344 Editors of McSweeney's. *Noisy Outlaws, Unfriendly Blobs, and Some Other Things* (4–7). Illus. 2005, McSweeney's $22.00 (1-932416-35-8). 208pp. Kid-friendly stories by well-known authors including Nick Hornby, Neil Gaiman, and Jon Scieskza. (Rev: BL 9/1/05)

2345 Evans, Douglas. *Mouth Moths: More Classroom Tales* (2–4). Illus. by Larry Di Fiori. 2006, Front St. $15.95 (1-932425-23-3). 112pp. The short stories in this collection showcase eccentric students in a third grade classroom. (Rev: BL 11/1/06; SLJ 11/06)

2346 Hart, Sue. *Tales of the Full Moon* (2–4). Illus. by Chris Harvey. 2006, Fulcrum $16.95 (1-55591-582-5). 93pp. Facts about African animals are interwoven into folktale-like stories told by Spinosa the spider. (Rev: BL 7/06)

2347 Holt, Kimberly Willis. *Part of Me: Stories of a Louisiana Family* (5–8). 2006, Holt $16.95 (0-8050-6360-9). 224pp. Reading is the thread that links this collection of short stories that spans four generations of a Louisiana family, from 1939 to the early 21st century. (Rev: BL 9/1/06; SLJ 9/06)

2348 Jocelyn, Marthe, sel. *Secrets* (5–8). 2005, Tundra paper $8.95 (0-88776-723-0). 175pp. A collection of 12 short stories that reveal the importance of secrets. (Rev: SLJ 2/06)

2349 Lubar, David. *Invasion of the Road Weenies and Other Warped and Creepy Tales* (4–7). 2005, Tor $16.95 (0-765-31447-9). 192pp. Entertaining stories about how things don't always work out how you hope or expect; suitable for reluctant readers. (Rev: BL 8/05; SLJ 9/05; VOYA 10/05)

2350 McKissack, Patricia C. *Porch Lies: Tales of Slicksters, Tricksters, and Other Wily Characters* (3–5). Illus. by Andre Carrilho. 2006, Random $18.95 (0-375-83619-5). 160pp. Ten funny and spooky original stories full of bad characters are based on stories McKissack heard on her grandparents' porch. (Rev: BCCB 10/06; BL 5/15/06; HB 9–10/06; HBG 4/07; LMC 1/07; SLJ 9/06)

2351 Martin, Ann M., and David Levithan, eds. *Friends: Stories About New Friends, Old Friends, and Unexpectedly True Friends* (4–6). 2005, Scholastic $16.95 (0-439-72991-2). 208pp. The many faces of friendship are reflected in this collection of short stories by such well-known authors as Meg Cabot, Pam Muñoz Ryan, and Brian Selznick. (Rev: BL 11/15/05; SLJ 1/06)

2352 Oldfield, Jenny, comp. *The Kingfisher Book of Horse and Pony Stories* (4–7). Illus. 2005, Kingfisher $16.95 (0-7534-5850-0). 127pp. The special relationship between horses and humans is celebrated in this collection of 12 contemporary, fantasy, and historical short stories. (Rev: SLJ 12/05)

2353 *Sports Shorts* (4–7). 2005, Darby Creek $15.99 (1-58196-040-9). 128pp. Eight writers contribute "semi-autobiographical" tales about their sporting achievements at school, many humorously revealing failings rather than triumphs. (Rev: BL 9/1/05; SLJ 11/05)

2354 Wells, H. G. *The Magic Shop* (4–6). Illus. by François Roca. 2005, Purple Bear $15.95 (1-933327-02-2). 32pp. Atmospheric artwork brings to life H. G. Wells's short story about a father and son's visit to a very special magic shop. (Rev: BL 10/15/05; SLJ 3/06)

2355 Williams, Laura E., ed. *Unexpected: 11 Mysterious Stories* (4–6). 2005, Scholastic paper $5.99 (0-439-45585-5). 292pp. The short stories in this anthology range from straight mystery to those featuring the supernatural and fantasy, and include the work of such popular children's authors as Gail Carson Levine, Norma Fox Mazer, and Marion Dane Bauer. (Rev: SLJ 1/06)

Sports Stories

2356 Bildner, Phil. *The Greatest Game Ever Played* (1–3). Illus. by Zachary Pullen. 2006, Putnam $16.99 (0-399-24171-X). 40pp. The legendary 1958 NFL championship game between the New York

Giants and the Baltimore Colts comes to life in this appealing story about a father and son struggling to adjust to the loss of their hometown baseball team. (Rev: BL 9/1/06; SLJ 8/06)

2357 Corbett, Sue. *Free Baseball* (4–7). 2006, Dutton $15.99 (0-525-47120-0). 152pp. An endearing 11-year-old called Felix, who loves baseball and is annoyed that his mother won't tell him more about his Cuban outfielder father, is thrilled when he gets the chance to be batboy for a minor league Florida team. (Rev: BCCB 2/06; SLJ 2/06; VOYA 4/06)

2358 Coy, John. *Around the World* (1–4). Illus. by Antonio Reonegro and Tom Lynch. 2005, Lee & Low $17.95 (1-58430-244-5). A fast-paced game of basketball moves from one location to another around the world; the art adds to the energy. (Rev: SLJ 1/06)

2359 Fitzgerald, Dawn. *Getting in the Game* (4–7). 2005, Roaring Brook $15.95 (1-59643-044-3). 136pp. In first-person narrative, Joanna Giordano describes her difficult experiences as the only girl on a 7th-grade ice hockey team that doesn't want her, plus her problems with peers, parents, and ailing grandfather. (Rev: BCCB 9/05; BL 3/1/05; SLJ 7/05; VOYA 6/05)

2360 Garza, Xavier. *Lucha Libre: The Man in the Silver Mask: A Bilingual Cuento* (2–5). Trans. by Luis Humberto Crosthwaite. Illus. by author. 2005, Cinco Puntos $17.95 (0-938317-92-X). Young Carlitos goes to a professional wrestling match ("lucha libre") in Mexico City and is thrilled by the sight of his favorite masked wrestler; can it be someone Carlitos knows? (Rev: SLJ 10/05)

2361 Harkrader, L. D. *Airball: My Life in Briefs* (4–7). 2005, Roaring Brook $15.95 (1-59643-060-5). 208pp. Kirby's middle school basketball team begins to improve when their coach — whom Kirby secretly believes is his father — insists the boys practice in their underwear. (Rev: BL 9/1/05; SLJ 11/05; VOYA 10/05)

2362 Haven, Paul. *Two Hot Dogs with Everything* (4–7). Illus. by Tim Jessell. 2006, Random LB $17.99 (0-375-93350-6). 320pp. Danny, 11, follows many superstitious rituals each time the Sluggers play, but his efforts seem to have no effect until he chews some 108-year-old gum that belonged to the team's founder. (Rev: BL 4/1/06)

2363 King, Donna. *Double Twist* (5–8). 2007, Kingfisher paper $5.95 (978-0-7534-6023-8). 144pp. When her ice-dancing partner injures his knee, 12-year-old Laura Lee scrambles to replace him just one month before the Junior Grand Prix. (Rev: BL 1/1–15/07)

2364 Levy, Elizabeth. *Tackling Dad* (5–8). 2005, HarperCollins LB $16.89 (0-06-000050-3). 144pp. Cassie, 13, has won a place on the football team but

her father won't sign the consent form. (Rev: BL 9/1/05; SLJ 8/05)

2365 Lupica, Mike. *Summer Ball* (5–8). 2007, Philomel $17.99 (978-0-399-24487-2). 256pp. Even though his coach offers little encouragement, Danny Walker's determination helps him lead his summer basketball team to victory. (Rev: BL 4/15/07)

2366 Richardson, Charisse K. *The Real Lucky Charm* (3–5). 2005, Dial $16.99 (0-8037-3105-1); paper $4.99 (0-14-240431-4). 96pp. Ten-year-old Mia attributes her basketball skill to the new charm for her bracelet, and is happy to play on the team with her twin brother Marcus; but when she loses the charm her confidence evaporates. (Rev: BL 9/1/05; SLJ 10/05)

2367 Roberts, Ken. *Thumb on a Diamond* (3–5). Illus. by Leanne Franson. 2006, Groundwood $15.95 (0-88899-629-2); paper $6.95 (0-88899-705-1). 128pp. The children of a remote fishing village on the coast of British Columbia form a baseball team and enter a regional tournament as part of their scheme to visit a big city. (Rev: BL 6/1–15/06; SLJ 8/06)

2368 Rodriguez, Alex. *Out of the Ballpark* (2–4). Illus. by Frank Morrison. 2007, HarperCollins $16.99 (978-0-06-115194-1). 32pp. The Yankees player draws on his childhood experiences in this story of a determined young athlete who succeeds through hard work. (Rev: BL 3/15/07)

2369 Rud, Jeff. *In the Paint* (5–8). 2005, Orca paper $7.95 (1-55143-337-0). 128pp. Matt is glad to make the basketball team but soon finds there are pressures he would prefer to avoid. (Rev: BL 7/05)

2370 Scudamore, Beverly. *Misconduct* (4–6). Series: Sports Stories. 2005, Lorimer paper $5.50 (1-55028-854-7). 107pp. Matthew is influenced by a new kid on his hockey team and must figure out if the friendship is worth his integrity. (Rev: SLJ 8/05)

2371 Wallace, Rich. *Dunk Under Pressure* (4–6). Series: Winning Season. 2006, Viking $14.99 (0-670-06095-X). 119pp. Sixth-grader Dunk (Cornell Duncan), free-throw star, learns about being a team player. (Rev: SLJ 6/06)

2372 Wallace, Rich. *Southpaw* (4–6). Series: Winning Season. 2006, Viking $14.99 (0-670-06053-4). 128pp. Jimmy Fleming, who has moved to Hudson City with his recently divorced father, joins his school's baseball team and manages to win the acceptance of his teammates after a shaky start. (Rev: BL 2/15/06; SLJ 3/06; VOYA 2/06)

2373 Weatherford, Carole Boston. *Champions on the Bench: The Cannon Street YMCA All-Stars* (2–4). Illus. by Leonard Jenkins. 2007, Dial $16.99 (0-8037-2987-1). 32pp. In 1955 South Carolina, 61 white Little League teams refuse to play against an African American team. (Rev: BL 2/1/07; SLJ 1/07)

Fairy Tales

2374 Abeya, Elisabet. *Hansel and Gretel / Hansel y Gretel* (K–3). Illus. by Cristina Losantos. 2005, Chronicle $14.95 (0-8118-4793-4); paper $6.95 (0-8118-4794-2). 32pp. An entertaining, bilingual (Spanish and English) retelling of the classic fairy tale with ink-and-watercolor illustrations. (Rev: BL 8/05; HBG 4/06; SLJ 10/05) [398.2]

2375 Andersen, Hans Christian. *The Little Match Girl* (2–4). Illus. by Kveta Pacovska. 2005, Putnam $18.99 (0-698-40027-5). 32pp. Avant-garde illustrations enliven this retelling of Andersen's beloved fairy tale. (Rev: BL 10/1/05; SLJ 11/05) [398.2]

2376 Andersen, Hans Christian. *The Princess and the Pea* (PS). Illus. by Rachel Isadora. 2007, Putnam $16.99 (978-0-399-24611-1). 32pp. The classic tale is relocated to a beautifully illustrated East Africa. (Rev: BL 4/15/07) [398.2]

2377 Andersen, Hans Christian. *The Ugly Duckling* (K–4). Illus. by Roberta Angaramo. 2006, Purple Bear $15.95 (1-933327-09-X). A beautifully illustrated retelling that is faithful to the details but less wordy than the original. (Rev: SLJ 9/06) [398.2]

2378 Begin, Mary Jane. *The Sorcerer's Apprentice* (PS–K). Illus. 2005, Little, Brown $15.99 (0-316-73611-2). 32pp. In this lively adaptation of the classic story, a young girl apprenticed to a powerful magician is horrified when her attempt to cast a spell goes awry. (Rev: BL 12/15/05; SLJ 2/06) [398.2]

2379 Bofill, Francesc. *Rapunzel* (K–3). Illus. by Joma. 2006, Chronicle $14.95 (0-8118-5059-5); paper $6.95 (0-8118-5060-9). 32pp. A nicely illustrated bilingual retelling of the classic tale, with enjoyable twists. (Rev: BL 3/1/06; SLJ 6/06) [398.2]

2380 Bonning, Tony. *Snog the Frog* (PS–2). Illus. by Rosalind Beardshaw. 2005, Barron's $12.95 (0-7641-5824-4). Snog the frog is no prince, but he's lucky enough to be kissed by a princess in this exuberantly illustrated book. (Rev: SLJ 8/05)

2381 Calhoun, Dia. *The Phoenix Dance* (4–7). 2005, Farrar $17.00 (0-374-35910-5). 272pp. Phoenix Dance, apprentice to the royal shoemaker and subject to emotional extremes, tries to find out what magic compels 12 princesses to wear out their shoes by dancing every night. (Rev: BL 12/15/05; SLJ 11/05; VOYA 10/05) [398.2]

2382 Child, Lauren. *The Princess and the Pea* (K–3). Illus. by Polly Borland. 2006, Hyperion $16.99 (0-7868-3886-8). 40pp. The queen puts a potential bride for her son to the pea-under-the-mattress test in this fractured fairy tale. (Rev: BL 2/15/06; SLJ 3/06*) [398.2]

2383 Collodi, Carlo. *Pinocchio* (3–5). Illus. by Robert Ingpen. 2005, Purple Bear $19.95 (1-933327-00-6). 136pp. A handsome, large-format version of the classic tale about the puppet who wants to become a real boy. (Rev: BL 11/15/05; SLJ 12/05) [398.2]

2384 Coombs, Kate. *The Runaway Princess* (4–7). 2006, Farrar $17.00 (0-374-35546-0). 288pp. In this entertaining takeoff on traditional fairy tales, 15-year-old Princess Meg, angry over being sequestered while princes from far and wide compete for her hand in marriage, escapes and takes matters into her own hands. (Rev: BL 9/1/06; SLJ 9/06) [398.2]

2385 Copper, Melinda. *Snow White* (K–2). Illus. 2005, Dutton $16.99 (0-525-47474-9). 40pp. Animals play the leading roles in this beautifully illustrated version of the classic fairy tale from the Brothers Grimm. (Rev: BL 8/05; SLJ 11/05) [398.2]

2386 Doyle, Malachy. *The Barefoot Book of Fairy Tales* (K–3). Illus. by Nicoletta Ceccoli. 2005, Barefoot Bks. $19.99 (1-84148-798-8). 160pp. Twelve fairy tales from around the world are collected in this quirky and accessible anthology. (Rev: BL 12/1/05; SLJ 2/06) [398.2]

2387 Eilenberg, Max. *Beauty and the Beast* (2–4). Illus. by Angela Barrett. 2006, Candlewick $17.99 (0-7636-3160-4). 64pp. A wonderful retelling of the classic tale of Beauty and the Beast, set in the nineteenth century and accompanied by lovely, expressive watercolor illustrations. (Rev: BL 12/1/06; SLJ 12/06*) [398.2]

2388 Ensor, Barbara. *Cinderella (As If You Didn't Already Know the Story)* (3–6). Illus. 2006, Random $12.95 (0-375-83620-9). 109pp. Cinderella and her prince end up living happily ever after in this retelling, each finding a fulfilling career; Cinderella's letters to her deceased mother tell part of the story. (Rev: SLJ 7/06) [398.2]

2389 Escardo i Bas, Merce. *The Three Little Pigs / Los tres cerditos* (K–2). Illus. by Pere Joan. 2006, Chronicle $14.95 (0-8118-5063-3). 24pp. The familiar story is told in both English and Spanish, with comic-book style illustrations. (Rev: BL 5/1/06; SLJ 6/06) [398.2]

2390 *Fairy Tales of Hans Christian Andersen* (2–6). Trans. by Neil Philip. Illus. by Isabelle Brent. 2005, Reader's Digest $27.95 (0-276-42830-7). 351pp. Excellent new translations of 40 Andersen fairy tales are accompanied by handsome watercolors with gold leaf. (Rev: SLJ 12/05) [398.2]

2391 Foreman, Michael, retel. *Classic Fairy Tales* (PS–3). Illus. by reteller. 2006, Sterling LB $12.95 (1-4027-2865-4). 176pp. These beautifully illustrated retellings of 14 classic fairy tales reduce the violence level and will suit a younger, more sensitive audience. (Rev: SLJ 4/06) [398.2]

2392 Garland, Michael. *King Puck* (K–3). Illus. by author. 2007, HarperCollins $16.99 (978-0-06-084809-5). Father Seamus is lonely on his mountaintop with only one book, so the fairies give the gift of speech to his goat, who goes on to win the grand prize at the fair — king for a day plus the granting of a wish; and the goat asks for books. (Rev: SLJ 2/07) [398.2]

2393 Gordon, David. *Hansel and Diesel* (PS–K). 2006, HarperCollins $15.99 (0-06-058122-0). 32pp. Hansel and Diesel are two little trucks facing the Wicked Winch in this strikingly illustrated twist on the well-known fairy tale. (Rev: BL 5/1/06; SLJ 7/06) [398.2]

2394 Grimm, Jacob, and Wilhelm Grimm. *Rapunzel* (K–3). Trans. by Anthea Bell. Illus. by Dorothee Duntze. 2005, North-South $16.95 (0-7358-2013-9). 32pp. Sunny artwork gives this large-format retelling a more lighthearted feel than usual. (Rev: BL 12/1/05; SLJ 11/05) [398.2]

2395 Ketteman, Helen. *Waynetta and the Cornstalk: A Texas Fairy Tale* (K–3). Illus. by Diane Greenseid. 2007, Albert Whitman $16.95 (978-0-8075-

8687-7). In this fractured version of "Jack and the Beanstalk" set in Texas, life on the ranch changes for the better when cowgirl Waynetta plants some magic corn and scales a huge cornstalk to find a gigantic ranch inhabited by a giant. (Rev: SLJ 4/07) [398.2]

2396 LaRochelle, David. *The End* (PS–3). Illus. by Richard Egielski. 2007, Scholastic $16.99 (978-0-439-64011-4). From the beginning — "And they all lived happily ever after" — to the final "Once upon a time" this zany fairy tale keeps up its topsy-turvy nature. (Rev: BL 1/1–15/07; HB 5–6/07; HBG 10/07; LMC 4–5/07; SLJ 4/07*) [398.2]

2397 McClintock, Barbara. *Cinderella* (K–3). Illus. 2005, Scholastic $15.99 (0-439-56145-0). 32pp. This beautifully illustrated adaptation of the classic Cinderella fairy tale is set in the Paris of Louis XIV. (Rev: BL 1/1–15/06; SLJ 10/05*) [398.2]

2398 Mitchell, Stephen. *The Tinderbox* (2–4). Illus. by Bagram Ibatoulline. 2007, Candlewick $17.99 (978-0-7636-2078-3). 48pp. A soldier, after both gaining and losing riches, uses a magic tinderbox to summon three huge-eyed dogs, secretly court a princess, and, ultimately, escape death; this rich retelling is enhanced by Ibatoulline's ink illustrations that portray the period setting, people, and creatures. (Rev: BL 1/1–15/07) [398.2]

2399 Moses, Will. *Hansel and Gretel: A Retelling from the Original Tale by the Brothers Grimm* (K–3). Illus. 2006, Philomel $16.99 (0-399-24234-1). 40pp. Moses adheres to the darker side of the Grimm story, adding detailed and lush folk-art illustrations. (Rev: BL 2/1/06; SLJ 3/06) [398.2]

2400 Napoli, Donna Jo. *Ugly* (3–5). Illus. by Lita Judge. 2006, Hyperion $14.99 (0-7868-3753-5). 192pp. Ugly, who is different and therefore not accepted by his duck colony, roams Tasmania meeting lots of different animals before finally discovering he is a black swan in this variant of the Andersen "Ugly Duckling" tale that includes lots of background information. (Rev: BL 1/1–15/06; SLJ 3/06) [398.2]

2401 Nesbit, E. *Jack and the Beanstalk* (K–3). Illus. by Matt Tavares. 2006, Candlewick $16.99 (0-7636-2124-2). 48pp. Large illustrations with eye-catching perspectives illustrate this retelling that features a lazy, clumsy Jack who succeeds in the end. (Rev: BL 9/15/06; SLJ 11/06*) [398.2]

2402 Osborne, Mary Pope. *Sleeping Bobby* (PS–2). Illus. by Giselle Potter. 2005, Simon & Schuster $16.95 (0-689-87668-8). 40pp. In this gender-swapping adaptation of "Sleeping Beauty," a handsome prince is awakened from a deep slumber by the spell-breaking kiss of a lovely princess. (Rev: BL 1/1–15/06; SLJ 10/05) [398.2]

2403 Pienkowski, Jan. *The Fairy Tales* (K–3). Trans. by David Walser. Illus. by author. 2006,

Viking $19.99 (0-670-06189-1). 192pp. This handsome collection includes four of the genre's best-known stories — "Cinderella," "Hansel and Gretel," "Sleeping Beauty," and "Snow White" — translated from German and illustrated with dramatic silhouettes filled with color. (Rev: BL 11/1/06; SLJ 11/06) [398.2]

2404 Pirotta, Saviour. *The McElderry Book of Grimm's Fairy Tales* (K–3). Illus. by Emma Chichester Clark. 2006, Simon & Schuster $19.95 (1-4169-1798-5). 128pp. Ten classic Grimm tales are retold in appealing text and illustrations. (Rev: BL 11/1/06; SLJ 11/06) [398.2]

2405 Prokofiev, Sergei. *The Love for Three Oranges* (2–4). Illus. by Elzbieta Gaudasinska. 2006, Pumpkin House $16.95 (0-9646010-3-6). 40pp. The story, based on the libretto for Prokofiev's opera, of a prince who is cursed to fall in love with three oranges and must steal them from a faraway castle, in the process finding his true love. (Rev: BL 11/15/06; SLJ 10/06)

2406 Puttapipat, Niroot. *Musicians of Bremen* (PS–2). Illus. 2005, Candlewick $15.99 (0-7636-2758-5). 32pp. The focus is on music in this retelling that features realistic animals who end up not in Bremen but happily ensconced in a comfortable cottage. (Rev: BL 11/15/05; SLJ 12/05) [398.2]

2407 Reinhart, Matthew. *Cinderella: A Pop-Up Fairy Tale* (K–2). Illus. Series: Classic Collectible Pop-Up. 2005, Simon & Schuster $24.95 (1-4169-0501-4). 12pp. Inventive paper engineering makes this Cinderella memorable. (Rev: BL 11/1/05) [398.2]

2408 Roberts, Lynn. *Little Red: A Fizzingly Good Yarn* (2–4). Illus. by David Roberts. 2005, Abrams $16.95 (0-8109-5783-3). 32pp. In this variation on the story of Little Red Riding Hood, the heroine is replaced by a little boy named Thomas who tricks the wolf into gulping down a ginger ale and belching up the boy's recently devoured grandmother. (Rev: BL 10/15/05; SLJ 11/05)

2409 Ros, Roser. *Musicians of Bremen / Los musicos de Bremner* (2–4). Illus. by Pep Montserrat. 2005, Chronicle $14.95 (0-8118-4795-0); paper $6.95 (0-8118-4796-9). 32pp. This strikingly illustrated bilingual adaptation of the Grimm tale — in which four aging animals, cast out by their owners, travel to Bremen to join the city band — uses European Spanish. (Rev: BL 11/1/05; SLJ 10/05) [398.2]

2410 Ruskin, John. *The King of the Golden River* (3–5). Illus. by Iassen Ghiuselev. 2005, Simply Read $19.95 (1-894965-16-9). 64pp. In this brightly illustrated adaptation of Ruskin's fairy tale, Gluck, a kindhearted lad of 12, is badly treated by his older siblings Hans and Schwartz who are eventually undone by their greed and misanthropy. (Rev: BL 12/1/05) [398.2]

2411 San José, Christine, retel. *Six Swans: A Folktale* (1–4). Illus. by Jes Cole. 2006, Boyds Mills $16.95 (1-59078-056-6). Full-page illustrations offering changing perspectives add to the appeal of this retelling, which the princess herself narrates, of the story of the six brothers who have been changed into swans. (Rev: SLJ 12/06) [398.2]

2412 Setterington, Ken, retel. *Clever Katarina: A Tale in Six Parts* (2–6). Illus. by Nelly Hofer and Ernst Hofer. 2006, Tundra $17.95 (0-88776-764-8). 40pp. The artwork shines in this retelling of a Grimm fairy tale originally called "The Peasant's Clever Daughter," in which a beautiful peasant girl called Katarina must solve a riddle to win the king's hand and save her father from being cast into prison. (Rev: SLJ 12/06) [398.2]

2413 Shepard, Aaron. *One-Eye! Two-Eyes! Three-Eyes! A Very Grimm Fairy Tale* (K–2). Illus. by Gary Clement. 2006, Atheneum $16.95 (0-689-86740-9). 32pp. A girl with two eyes is the butt of much derision from her one-eyed and three-eyed sisters. (Rev: BL 1/1–15/07; SLJ 1/07) [398.2]

2414 Smith, Scudder, retel. *Jack and the Beanstalk* (PS–2). Illus. by Felipe López Salán. 2006, Purple Bear $15.95 (1-933327-11-1). This retelling of the classic fairy tale is fairly faithful to the original but a bit kinder and gentler in tone. (Rev: SLJ 8/06) [398.2]

2415 Willard, Nancy. *The Flying Bed* (2–4). Illus. by John Thompson. 2007, Scholastic $17.99 (978-0-590-25610-0). A Florentine baker's business booms after he buys a very special bed, but his greed jeopardizes his luck. (Rev: BCCB 5/07; BL 1/1/07; LMC 8–9/07; SLJ 4/07) [398.2]

Folklore

General

2416 Ada, Alma Flor, and F. Isabel Campoy. *Tales Our Abuelitas Told: A Hispanic Folktale Collection* (3–5). Illus. by Felipe Davalos. 2006, Simon & Schuster $19.95 (0-689-82583-8). 128pp. The 12 folk tales in this collection have their roots in Hispanic culture but touch on universal themes; interesting notes add relevance. (Rev: BL 9/1/06; SLJ 9/06) [398.2]

2417 Blackstone, Stella. *Storytime: First Tales for Sharing* (PS–K). Illus. by Anne Wilson. 2005, Barefoot Bks. $19.99 (1-84148-345-1). 96pp. Seven familiar tales — including such classics as "Goldilocks and the Three Bears" and "The Gingerbread Man" — are faithfully retold and accompanied by attractive collage and acrylic illustrations. (Rev: BL 1/1–15/06; SLJ 11/05) [398.2]

2418 Hausman, Gerald, and Loretta Hausman. *Horses of Myth* (4–6). Illus. by Robert Florczak. 2005, Dutton $19.99 (0-525-46964-8). 96pp. Five short stories adapt traditional tales about horses from around the world, including Russia, Tahiti, and the United States. (Rev: BL 10/1/05; SLJ 12/05) [398.2]

2419 Henderson, Kathy. *Lugalbanda: The Boy Who Got Caught Up in a War* (2–4). Illus. by Jane Ray. 2006, Candlewick $16.99 (0-7636-2782-8). 80pp. This retelling of an ancient Sumerian legend recounts how a young prince named Lugalbanda receives the strength he needs for war. (Rev: BL 5/1/06; SLJ 4/06*) [398.2]

2420 Jones, Christianne C. *Chicken Little* (K–1). Illus. by Kyle Hermanson. Series: Read-It! Readers/FolkTales. 2005, Picture Window LB $18.60 (1-4048-0972-4). 32pp. The familiar story is retold for beginning readers, with colorful illustrations. (Rev: SLJ 7/05) [398.2]

2421 Krensky, Stephen. *Vampires* (4–7). Illus. Series: Monster Chronicles. 2006, Lerner LB $26.60 (0-8225-5891-2). 48pp. Krensky's conversational style will attract readers to this overview (which is marred by a few errors) of vampires' history, role in literature and film, and of our continuing fascination with them. (Rev: BL 10/15/06) [398.2]

2422 Maddern, Eric. *The Cow on the Roof* (PS). Illus. by Paul Hess. 2006, Frances Lincoln $15.95 (1-84507-374-6). Convinced that he does the lion's share of work, a farmer switches jobs for a day with his wife, only to learn that her chores are not nearly as easy as he had imagined; a traditional tale reset in Wales. (Rev: SLJ 10/06) [398.2]

2423 Shah, Idries. *The Man and the Fox* (K–3). Illus. by Sally Mallam. 2006, Hoopoe Bks. $18.00 (1-883536-43-X); paper $7.99 (1-883536-60-X). A clever fox outwits a man's plot to capture him. (Rev: SLJ 12/06) [398.2]

2424 Villaseñor, Victor. *Little Crow to the Rescue / El cuervito al rescate* (PS–3). Trans. by Elizabeth Cummins Munoz. Illus. by Felipe Ugalde Alcántara. 2005, Arte Publico $15.95 (1-55885-430-4). 32pp. In Spanish and English, this is a pourquoi tale about the reasons for crows' disdain for humans. (Rev: BL 10/1/05; SLJ 2/06) [398.2]

2425 Yolen, Jane. *Meow: Cat Stories from Around the World* (1–3). Illus. by Hala Wittwer. 2005, HarperCollins $16.99 (0-06-029161-3). 40pp. Ten beautifully illustrated cat stories look at cat — and human — behavior around the world. (Rev: BL 8/05; SLJ 8/05) [398.24]

Africa

2426 Ahmed, Said Salah. *The Lion's Share / Qayb Libaax: A Somali Folktale* (PS–2). Illus. by Kelly Dupre. 2006, Minnesota Humanities Commission $15.95 (1-931016-12-7); paper $7.95 (1-931016-13-5). 32pp. After cooperating to kill a camel, the hungry animals must divide the loot, but as always the "lion's share is not fair." (Rev: BL 1/1–15/07; SLJ 1/07) [398.2]

2427 Paye, Won-Ldy, and Margaret H. Lippert, retels. *The Talking Vegetables* (K–4). Illus. by Julie Paschkis. 2006, Holt $16.95 (0-8050-7742-1). In this spirited retelling of a Liberian folk tale, Spider is lazy and chooses not to join with his neighbors in planting a field of vegetables, so when he tries to pick some for his own use the vegetables turn him away. (Rev: SLJ 11/06) [398.2]

Asia

General and Miscellaneous

2428 Conger, David, et al., retels. *Asian Children's Favorite Stories: A Treasury of Folktales from China, Japan, Korea, India, the Philippines, Thailand, Indonesia and Malaysia* (K–4). Illus. by Patrick Yee. 2006, Tuttle $24.95 (978-0-8048-3669-2). 112pp. A collection of 13 tales from different Asian countries including "The Lucky Farmer Becomes King" and "The Crane's Gratitude." (Rev: SLJ 3/07) [398.2]

2429 Otsuka, Yuzo. *Suho's White Horse: A Mongolian Legend* (PS–3). Trans. by Richard McNamara. Illus. by Suekichi Akaba. 2007, R.I.C. $17.95 (1-74126-021-3). 48pp. The sad legend of the invention of the Mongolian fiddle, in which a young shepherd boy's champion horse is seized by an evil ruler. (Rev: BL 4/1/07) [398.2]

2430 Park, Janie Jaehyun. *The Love of Two Stars: A Korean Legend* (K–2). Illus. 2005, Groundwood $16.95 (0-88899-672-1). 32pp. An accessible retelling of the Korean folktale in which two lovers, punished for neglecting their work, win support from the birds when they cannot reunite. (Rev: BL 10/15/05; SLJ 11/05) [398.2]

China

2431 Compestine, Ying Chang. *The Real Story of Stone Soup* (PS–2). Illus. by Stephane Jorisch. 2007, Dutton $16.99 (0-525-47493-5). 32pp. An officious, lazy fisherman gets his comeuppance when his young assistants convince him that the flavor in the soup comes from carefully chosen stones, while the pictures show the truth. (Rev: BL 1/1–15/07; SLJ 1/07) [398.2]

2432 Hong, Chen Jiang. *The Magic Horse of Han Gan* (PS–2). Trans. by Claudia Zoe Bedrick. Illus. 2006, Enchanted Lion $16.95 (1-59270-063-2). 38pp. This attractive picture book recounts the moving and dramatic legend of a magical horse created by 9th-century Chinese artist Han Gan. (Rev: BL 11/1/06; SLJ 12/06*) [398.2]

2433 Storrie, Paul B. *Yu the Great: Conquering the Flood* (4–7). Illus. by Sandy Carruthers. Series: Graphic Myths and Legends. 2007, Lerner LB $26.60 (978-0-8225-3088-6). 48pp. In this graphic-novel adaptation of an ancient Chinese folk tale, the emperor Shun asks Yu to save China and its people from the floods that are ravaging the land. (Rev: BL 3/15/07) [398.2]

India

2434 Fusek-Peters, Andrew. *The Tiger and the Wise Man* (PS–2). Illus. by Diana Mayo. 2005, Child's Play paper $7.99 (1-904550-07-X). 32pp. In this brightly illustrated retelling of a traditional Indian folktale, a wise man may have to pay a very high price for foolishly releasing a vicious tiger from its cage. (Rev: BL 8/05; SLJ 6/05) [398.2]

Southeast Asia

2435 Ha, Song. *Indebted as Lord Chom / No Nhu Chua Chom: The Legend of the Forbidden Street* (1–4). Trans. from Vietnamese by William Smith. Illus. by Ly Thu Ha. 2006, East West Discovery $16.95 (0-9701654-6-3). 32pp. This engaging Vietnamese folk tale, presented in both English and Vietnamese, explains the origins of two Hanoi street names. (Rev: SLJ 1/07) [398.2]

2436 MacDonald, Margaret Read. *Go to Sleep, Gecko! A Balinese Folktale* (PS–2). Illus. by Geraldo Valerio. 2006, August House $16.95 (0-87483-780-4). Gecko complains repeatedly to Elephant, the village chief, that fireflies are keeping him awake at night, but realizes eventually that it's all part of the natural order. (Rev: SLJ 10/06) [398.2]

2437 Quoc, Minh. *Tam and Cam / Tam Cam: The Ancient Vietnamese Cinderella Story* (1–4). Trans. from Vietnamese by William Smith. Illus. by Mai Long. 2006, East West Discovery $16.95 (0-9701654-4-7). 32pp. Reminiscent of the Cinderella story, this Vietnamese folk tale, offered here in both English and Vietnamese, features a young girl who is mistreated by her stepsister and stepmother but eventually wins the heart of the king. (Rev: SLJ 1/07) [398.2]

2438 Quoc, Tran. *The Tet Pole / Su Tich Cay Neu Ngay Tet: The Story of the Tet Festival* (1–4). Trans.

from Vietnamese by William Smith. Illus. by Nguyen Bich. 2006, East West Discovery $16.95 (0-9701654-5-5). 32pp. In this charming bilingual Vietnamese folk tale that explains the origins of the Tet festival, Buddha helps a group of poor farmers outwit the demons that have seized control of their fields. (Rev: SLJ 1/07) [398.2]

2439 Scott, Nathan Kumar. *Mangoes and Bananas* (2–4). Illus. by T. Balaji. 2006, Tara $14.95 (81-86211-06-3). 32pp. In this retelling of an Indonesian folk tale, clever deer Kanchil and a greedy monkey called Monyet plant a fruit garden together on the agreement that they will share equally; an endnote describes the methods used to create the textile-based illustrations. (Rev: BL 4/1/06; SLJ 6/06) [398.2]

Europe

Central and Eastern Europe

2440 Hasler, Eveline. *A Tale of Two Brothers* (K–3). Trans. by Marianne Martens. Illus. by Kathi Bhend. 2006, North-South $16.95 (0-7358-2102-X). 40pp. Hunchbacked brothers Morris and Boris have opposite outlooks on life, and Morris is rewarded for his sunny good nature and enjoyment of all around him. (Rev: BL 9/1/06; SLJ 9/06) [398.2]

2441 Keding, Dan. *Stories of Hope and Spirit: Folktales from Eastern Europe* (3–6). Illus. 2004, August House $18.95 (0-87483-727-8). 77pp. A collection of stories that show the diversity of Eastern Europe and entertain while providing life lessons. (Rev: SLJ 7/05) [398.2]

France

2442 Seeger, Pete, and Paul Dubois Jacobs. *Some Friends to Feed: The Story of Stone Soup* (K–2). Illus. by Michael Hays. 2005, Putnam $16.99 (0-399-24017-9). 48pp. This nicely illustrated retelling of the classic story of a hungry soldier and the children who come to his aid is packaged with an audio CD and musical notation. (Rev: BL 9/1/05; SLJ 10/05) [398.2]

Germany

2443 Daly, Niki. *Pretty Salma: Little Red Riding Hood Story from Africa* (PS–2). Illus. 2007, Clarion $16.00 (978-0-618-72345-4). 32pp. In Ghana, pretty Salma disobeys her grandmother and talks to a strange Mr. Dog, who takes her clothes and tricks Granny into thinking he's Salma. (Rev: BL 2/1/07) [398.2]

2444 Sweet, Melissa. *Carmine: A Little More Red* (PS–2). Illus. by author. 2005, Houghton $16.00 (0-618-38794-3). A fresh and amusing take on the tale of Little Red Riding Hood, told in the form of a sophisticated alphabet book that highlights a different word in the alphabet on each page. (Rev: SLJ 8/05*) [398.2]

Great Britain and Ireland

2445 Artell, Mike. *Three Little Cajun Pigs* (K–3). Illus. by Jim Harris. 2006, Dial $16.99 (0-8037-2815-8). The classic tale is given a funny Cajun spin when a hungry gator fills in for the big, bad wolf. (Rev: HBG 4/07; SLJ 12/06) [398.2]

2446 Blair, Eric. *The Gingerbread Man* (K–1). Illus. by Ben Peterson. Series: Read-It! Readers, Folk Tales Series. 2005, Picture Window LB $18.60 (1-4048-0969-4). 32pp. The familiar story is retold for beginning readers, with colorful illustrations. (Rev: SLJ 7/05) [398.2]

2447 Buehner, Caralyn. *Goldilocks and the Three Bears* (PS–1). Illus. by Mark Buehner. 2007, Dial $16.99 (978-0-8037-2939-1). Three well-behaved bears live in a lovely little log cabin in the woods that a boisterous rope-jumping Goldilocks invades in their absence. (Rev: BL 3/1/07; SLJ 4/07) [398.2]

2448 Ernst, Lisa Campbell. *The Gingerbread Girl* (PS–2). 2006, Dutton $16.99 (0-525-47667-9). 32pp. In this whimsical twist on the story of the Gingerbread Boy, his sister proves much more resourceful than her ill-fated sibling. (Rev: BL 9/1/06; SLJ 11/06) [398.2]

2449 Forest, Heather, retel. *The Little Red Hen: An Old Fable* (PS–2). Illus. by Susan Gaber. 2006, August House $16.95 (0-87483-795-2). A charming, rhyming version of the classic story featuring a black-and-white cat, a Corgi with a blanket, and a literary mouse as the hen's friends. (Rev: SLJ 11/06) [398.2]

2450 Hassett, John, and Ann Hassett. *Can't Catch Me* (PS–2). Illus. by John Hassett. 2006, Houghton $16.00 (0-618-70490-6). 32pp. In this lively adaptation of "The Gingerbread Man," an ice cube escapes from the freezer and makes a dash for the sea. (Rev: SLJ 10/06) [398.2]

2451 Hodges, Margaret. *Dick Whittington and His Cat* (PS–2). Illus. by Melisande Potter. 2006, Holiday $16.95 (0-8234-1987-8). 32pp. Retells the British legend of the orphan who became Lord Mayor of London. (Rev: BL 5/1/06; SLJ 5/06) [398.2]

2452 MacDonald, Margaret Read. *Teeny Weeny Bop* (K–2). Illus. by Diane Greenseid. 2006, Albert Whitman $16.95 (0-8075-7992-0). 32pp. When Teeny Weeny Bop makes a series of bad decisions, she ends up with a slug as a pet in this silly story that incorporates folkloric features. (Rev: BL 5/15/06; SLJ 8/06) [398.2]

2453 Murphy, Jim. *Fergus and the Night-Demon: An Irish Ghost Story* (1–3). Illus. by John Manders. 2006, Clarion $16.00 (0-618-33955-8). 32pp. Out for a night of fun, Fergus O'Mara, a lazy young Irishman, encounters the towering Night-Demon and must try to talk himself out of deep trouble. (Rev: BL 9/1/06; SLJ 8/06)

2454 Pinkney, Jerry. *The Little Red Hen* (PS–K). Illus. 2006, Dial $16.99 (0-8037-2935-9). 32pp. Pinkney's colorful artwork breathes new life into the classic tale. (Rev: BL 3/1/06; SLJ 5/06*) [398.2]

2455 Squires, Janet. *The Gingerbread Cowboy* (PS–K). Illus. by Holly Berry. 2006, HarperCollins $16.99 (0-06-077863-6). 32pp. The familiar tale of the runaway gingerbread boy is given a lively, western twist. (Rev: BL 4/15/06; SLJ 8/06) [398.21]

2456 Vivian, French. *Henny Penny* (PS–2). Illus. by Sophie Windham. 2006, Bloomsbury $16.95 (1-58234-706-9). 32pp. On their way to tell the king that the sky is falling, Henny Penny and her feathered friends fall into the clutches of Foxy Loxy. (Rev: BL 8/06; SLJ 7/06) [398.2]

Greece and Italy

2457 Egielski, Richard. *Saint Francis and the Wolf* (PS–2). Illus. 2005, HarperCollins $15.99 (0-06-623870-6). 40pp. St. Francis communicates with a wolf that has been terrorizing an Italian town and strikes a compromise that satisfies all parties. (Rev: BL 10/1/05*; SLJ 10/05) [398.2]

2458 Hennessy, B. G., reteller. *The Boy Who Cried Wolf* (PS–1). Illus. by Boris Kulikov. 2006, Simon & Schuster $15.95 (0-689-87433-2). 40pp. The fable about the shepherd boy who cried wolf is given vivid new life in this beautifully illustrated, funny picture book. (Rev: BL 2/1/06; SLJ 3/06*) [398.2]

2459 Valeri, Maria Eulalia. *The Hare and the Tortoise / La liebre y la tortuga* (4–6). Illus. by Max. 2006, Chronicle $14.95 (0-8118-5057-9); paper $6.95 (0-8118-5058-7). 32pp. A bilingual retelling of the classic fable. (Rev: BL 9/1/06; SLJ 10/06) [398.2]

2460 Wormell, Christopher. *Mice, Morals and Monkey Business: Lively Lessons from Aesop's Fables* (K–3). Illus. 2005, Running Pr. $18.95 (0-7624-2404-4). 64pp. The moral messages contained in some of Aesop's most memorable fables are highlighted in striking woodcut illustrations; concise versions of the stories are given at the back of the book. (Rev: BL 9/15/05; SLJ 11/05*) [395]

Russia

2461 Ransome, Arthur. *Little Daughter of the Snow* (K–3). Ed. by Shena Guild. Illus. by Tom Bower. 2005, Frances Lincoln $15.95 (1-84507-297-9). 32pp. An enchanting adaptation of Ransome's telling of a traditional Russian tale about a childless couple who create a snow girl who magically comes to life. (Rev: BL 12/1/05; SLJ 1/06) [398.2]

Scandinavia

2462 Coville, Bruce. *Thor's Wedding Day* (4–7). 2005, Harcourt $15.00 (0-15-201455-1). 128pp. A hilarious retelling of an ancient Norse poem, in which Thor's goat boy describes how he helped Thor to retrieve his stolen magic hammer. (Rev: BL 8/05) [398.2]

2463 Del Negro, Janice M. *Willa and the Wind* (1–3). Illus. by Heather Solomon. 2005, Marshall Cavendish $16.95 (0-7614-5232-X). 40pp. In this adaptation of an old Norwegian folktale adorned with airy, swirling illustrations, courageous Willa confronts the North Wind and a wicked innkeeper. (Rev: BL 9/1/05; SLJ 12/05) [398.2]

Spain and Portugal

2464 Montejo, Victor. *White Flower: A Maya Princess* (K–3). Illus. by Rafael Yockteng. 2005, Groundwood $16.95 (0-88899-599-7). 36pp. In this reinterpretation of a Spanish folk tale, White Flower, daughter of a Mayan king, uses her magical powers to help a young nobleman and win his heart. (Rev: BL 12/1/05; SLJ 1/06) [398.2]

Jewish Folklore

2465 Kushner, Lawrence, and Gary Schmidt. *In God's Hands* (1–3). Illus. by Matthew J. Baek. 2005, Jewish Lights $16.99 (1-58023-224-8). 32pp. Jacob, a rich man who believes he is following a divine mandate, bakes loaves of bread and takes them to the synagogue where they are gratefully retrieved by David, a man so poor he can't afford to feed his family. (Rev: BL 10/1/05*; SLJ 10/05) [398.2]

2466 Oberman, Sheldon. *Solomon and the Ant* (5–8). 2006, Boyds Mills $19.95 (1-59078-307-7). 168pp. Nearly 50 traditional Jewish stories are arranged chronologically and accompanied by notes and commentary. (Rev: BL 2/1/06; SLJ 3/06) [398.2]

2467 Philip, Neil. *The Pirate Princess and Other Fairy Tales* (4–6). Illus. by Mark Weber. 2005,

Scholastic $19.99 (0-590-10855-7). 96pp. A large, handsome collection of seven compelling fairy tales/parables written by Nahman ben Simha, a 19th-century Hasidic rabbi — tales that cover themes of true love, adventure, fortune, and health and happiness. (Rev: BL 1/1–15/06; SLJ 3/06) [398.2]

2468 Rogasky, Barbara. *Dybbuk: A Version* (4–6). Illus. by Leonard Everett Fisher. 2005, Holiday $16.95 (0-8234-1616-X). 64pp. In this dark tale based on Jewish folklore, a girl is possessed by the spirit of the boy she was destined to marry. (Rev: BL 10/15/05; SLJ 12/05) [398.2]

2469 Souhami, Jessica. *The Little, Little House* (PS–2). Illus. 2006, Frances Lincoln $15.95 (1-84507-108-5). 32pp. Collage artwork breathes new life into the classic rabbinical fable about a poor man who looks for a way to make his family's crowded dwelling more comfortable. (Rev: BL 2/1/06; SLJ 3/06) [309.2]

2470 Stampler, Ann Redisch. *Shlemazel and the Remarkable Spoon of Pohost* (PS–2). Illus. by Jacqueline M. Cohen. 2006, Clarion $16.00 (0-618-36959-7). 40pp. In this adaptation of a traditional Yiddish folk tale, the shtetl's miller uses trickery to transform lazy Shlemazel into a hardworking member of the community. (Rev: BL 6/1–15/06; SLJ 7/06) [398.2]

2471 Taback, Simms. *Kibitzers and Fools: Tales My Zayda Told Me* (K–3). Illus. by author. 2005, Viking $16.99 (0-670-05955-2). 48pp. Set in the shtetls of Eastern Europe during the late 19th and early 20th centuries, these 13 tales, each of which spotlights a word or two in Yiddish, offer valuable life lessons. (Rev: BL 10/15/05; SLJ 10/05) [398.2]

2472 Waldman, Debby. *A Sack Full of Feathers* (PS–2). Illus. by Cindy Revell. 2006, Orca $19.95 (1-55143-332-X). 32pp. In this vividly portrayed retelling of a Jewish folktale, Yankel learns about the dangers of spreading hurtful gossip. (Rev: BL 10/15/06; SLJ 2/07) [398.2]

Middle East

2473 Ganeri, Anita. *Islamic Stories* (1–6). Illus. by Rebecca Wallis. Series: Traditional Religious Tales. 2006, Picture Window LB $23.95 (1-4048-1313-6). 32pp. Most of the Islamic stories in this collection recount incidents from the life of Muhammad, but they also touch on Abraham, Hagar, Ishmael, and Moses. (Rev: SLJ 4/06) [297.1]

2474 MacDonald, Margaret. *Tunjur! Tunjur! Tunjur! A Palestinian Folktale* (PS–2). Illus. by Alik Arzoumanian. 2006, Marshall Cavendish $16.95 (0-7614-5225-7). 32pp. A woman's prayers for a child

to love are rewarded with the arrival of a little cooking pot with unfortunate larcenous tendencies. (Rev: BL 3/1/06; SLJ 4/06) [398.2]

2475 Shah, Idries. *Fatima the Spinner and the Tent* (PS–2). Illus. by Natasha Delmar. 2006, Hoopoe $18.00 (1-883536-42-1); paper $7.99 (1-883536-61-8). 32pp. Fatima, daughter of a well-to-do spinner, suffers a series of tragedies that turn out to have taught her useful skills in this retelling of an 18th-century Turkish tale. (Rev: BL 9/15/06; SLJ 11/06) [398.2]

2476 Vallverdu, Josep. *Aladdin and the Magic Lamp / Aladino y la lampara maravillosa* (4–6). Illus. by Pep Montserrat. 2006, Chronicle $14.95 (0-8118-5061-7); paper $6.95 (0-8118-5062-5). 32pp. An attractive bilingual retelling. (Rev: BL 9/1/06; SLJ 10/06) [398.22]

North America

Native Americans

2477 *Beaver Steals Fire: A Salish Coyote Story* (PS–2). Illus. by Sam Sandoval. 2005, Univ. of Nebraska $14.95 (0-8032-4323-5). 64pp. Based on traditional Salish folklore and illustrated by tribal artist Sandoval, this tale explores the origin of fire on Earth and the important role that fire plays in Native American life, plus information on fire ecology. (Rev: BL 3/1/06) [398.2]

2478 Duvall, Deborah L. *The Opossum's Tale: A Grandmother Story* (PS–2). Illus. by Murv Jacob. 2005, Univ. of New Mexico $15.95 (0-8263-3694-9). 32pp. Based on Cherokee folklore, this richly illustrated picture book tells how the opossum got its distinctive hairless tail. (Rev: BL 3/15/06; SLJ 2/06) [398.2]

2479 Powell, Patricia Hruby. *Ch'at Tó Yinílo' / Frog Brings Rain* (K–3). Ed. by Jessie Ruffenach. Trans. from Navajo by Peter A. Thomas. Illus. by Kendrick Benally. 2006, Salina Bookshelf $17.95 (1-893354-08-3). A bilingual retelling of a Navajo story about a frog that helps douse a fire and save the First People. (Rev: SLJ 7/06) [398.2]

2480 *Tatanka and the Lakota People: A Creation Story* (1–4). Illus. by Donald F. Montileaux. 2006, South Dakota State Historical Soc. $16.95 (0-9749195-8-6). This creation story tells how the Lakota people were tricked into leaving their Underworld with promises of easy living; English and Lakota words are side by side and the illustrations draw on traditional art. (Rev: SLJ 2/07) [398.2]

2481 Taylor, C. J. *All the Stars in the Sky: Native Stories from the Heavens* (2–4). Illus. by author. 2006, Tundra $17.95 (0-88776-759-1). 40pp. A collection of seven diverse stories about the night sky from various Native American groups. (Rev: BL 12/1/06)

United States

2482 Blair, Eric. *Paul Bunyan* (K–1). Illus. by Micah Chambers-Coldberg. Series: Read-It! Readers Tall Tales. 2005, Picture Window LB $18.60 (1-4048-0976-7). 32pp. The familiar tall tale is retold for beginning readers, with colorful illustrations. (Rev: SLJ 7/05) [398.2]

2483 Davis, David. *Texas Zeke and the Longhorn* (PS–3). Illus. by Alan Fearl Stacy. 2006, Pelican $15.95 (1-58980-348-5). Set in Texas, this version of "The Old Woman and Her Pig" features Old Zeke, who buys a longhorn steer that refuses to be corralled and must turn to a parade of others for help. (Rev: SLJ 9/06) [398.2]

2484 Hamilton, Martha, and Mitch Weiss. *The Hidden Feast: A Folktale from the American South* (PS–2). Illus. by Don Tate. 2006, August House $16.95 (0-87483-758-8). 32pp. Rooster learns an important lesson when he rejects what he believes is cornbread at a party. (Rev: BL 3/1/06; SLJ 4/06) [398.2]

2485 Hurston, Zora Neale. *Lies and Other Tall Tales* (PS–2). Illus. by Christopher Myers. 2005, HarperCollins $15.99 (0-06-000655-2). 40pp. Imaginative illustrations enhance the irreverence of these tall tales collected by Hurston in the 1930s. (Rev: BL 9/15/05*; SLJ 11/05) [398.2]

2486 Hurston, Zora Neale. *The Six Fools* (PS–2). Ed. by Joyce Carol Thomas. Illus. by Ann Tanksley. 2006, HarperCollins $15.99 (0-06-000646-3). 40pp. In this story drawn from the collection of folk tales collected by Zora Neale Hurston during the 1930s, a young groom-to-be travels the world in search of fools as big as his fiancee and her parents. (Rev: BL 2/1/06; SLJ 1/06*) [398.2]

2487 Hurston, Zora Neale, and Joyce Carol Thomas. *The Three Witches* (2–4). Illus. by Faith Ringgold. 2006, HarperCollins $32.00 (0-06-000649-8). 32pp. In this adaptation of an African American tale first collected by Zora Neale Hurston, two young siblings escape the clutches of three witches with a little help from their grandmother, three hound dogs, and a snake. (Rev: BL 6/1–15/06; SLJ 8/06) [398.2]

2488 Kimmel, Eric A. *The Frog Princess: A Tlingit Legend from Alaska* (PS–2). Illus. by Rosanne Litzinger. 2006, Holiday $16.95 (0-8234-1618-6).

32pp. A beautiful girl falls in love with and marries a frog, much to the dismay of her Tlingit family. (Rev: BL 5/1/06; SLJ 6/06) [398.2]

2489 Krensky, Stephen. *John Henry* (2–4). Illus. by Mark Oldroyd. Series: On Your Own Folklore. 2006, Lerner $23.93 (1-57505-887-1). 48pp. Tall tales chronicle some of the amazing feats attributed to John Henry in American railroading folklore. (Rev: BL 9/1/06; SLJ 8/06) [398.2]

2490 Krensky, Stephen, adapt. *Paul Bunyan* (1–4). Illus. by Craig Orback. Series: On My Own Folklore. 2006, Millbrook LB $23.93 (1-57505-888-X). 48pp. For beginning readers, this is an introduction to lumberjack Paul Bunyan and his amazing feats. Also use *Pecos Bill* (2006). (Rev: SLJ 8/06) [398.2]

2491 Quattlebaum, Mary. *Sparks Fly High: The Legend of Dancing Point* (PS–2). Illus. by Leonid Gore. 2006, Farrar $16.00 (0-374-34452-3). 40pp. In this spirited retelling of a Virginia folktale, Colonel Lightfoot competes with the devil in a dance contest. (Rev: BL 10/15/06; SLJ 12/06) [398.2]

2492 San Souci, Robert D., retel. *Sister Tricksters: Rollicking Tales of Clever Females* (3–6). Illus. by Daniel San Souci. 2006, August House $19.95 (0-87483-791-X). 69pp. Molly Cottontail, Miz Grasshopper, and Miz Goose are among the characters in this collection of retold tales about memorable female tricksters. (Rev: SLJ 9/06*) [398.2]

South and Central America

Mexico and Other Central American Lands

2493 MacDonald, Margaret Read. *Conejito: A Folktale from Panama* (K–3). Illus. by Geraldo Vaério. 2006, August House $16.95 (0-87483-779-0). 32pp. In this rhyming folktale from Panama, Conejito, a little rabbit, sets off to visit his aunt and along the way cleverly manages to escape the clutches of three fearsome predators. Conejito's song is included, tempting young children to sing along. (Rev: BL 3/15/06; SLJ 4/06) [398.2]

2494 Menchú, Rigoberta, and Dante Liano. *The Honey Jar* (4–6). Trans. by David Unger. Illus. by Domi. 2006, Groundwood $18.95 (0-88899-670-5). 64pp. Menchú, winner of the Nobel Peace Prize, recounts Guatemalan folktales she learned as a child; illustrations reflect the text in folk-art style. (Rev: BL 3/15/06; SLJ 6/06) [398.2]

Mythology

General and Miscellaneous

2495 Baynes, Pauline. *Questionable Creatures: A Bestiary* (4–6). 2006, Eerdmans $18.00 (978-0-8028-5284-7). 48pp. A great introduction to the mythical animals and creatures that were thought to have existed in medieval times such as unicorns, satyrs, and the phoenix. (Rev: BL 11/15/06; SLJ 4/07) [398.24]

2496 Boughn, Michael. *Into the World of the Dead: Astonishing Adventures in the Underworld* (5–8). Illus. 2006, Annick LB $24.95 (1-55037-959-3); paper $12.95 (1-55037-958-5). 56pp. This illustrated collection of myths and legends from diverse cultures includes a variety of gods, monsters, and heroes who survived travels to the Underworld. (Rev: SLJ 1/07) [398.2]

2497 Daning, Tom. *Mesoamerican Mythology: Quetzalcoatl* (3–6). Illus. 2006, Rosen LB $22.50 (978-1-4042-3401-7). 24pp. A graphic-novel version of the myth about the gods Quetzalcoatl and Tezcatlipoca and how they put their differences aside to defeat the demon caiman of the sea, resulting in the creation of the land and sky. (Rev: SLJ 3/07) [398.2]

2498 Limke, Jeff. *Isis and Osiris: To the Ends of the Earth* (4–6). Illus. Series: Graphic Myths and Legends. 2006, Lerner $26.60 (0-8225-3086-4). 48pp. The lives of ancient Egyptian deities Isis and Osiris are chronicled in graphic-novel format. (Rev: BL 10/15/06; SLJ 11/06) [398.2]

2499 Lorenz, Albert, and Joy Schleh. *The Trojan Horse* (3–5). Illus. 2006, Abrams $17.95 (0-8109-5986-0). 40pp. Learn all about the Trojan War in this humorous, visual approach to the Trojan War that offers conversational text, cartoon panels, and cross-sections of the Greek ships, the Trojan horse,

and the city of Troy. (Rev: BL 11/15/06; SLJ 11/06) [398.2]

2500 Lupton, Hugh, and Daniel Morden. *The Adventures of Odysseus* (3–5). Illus. by Christina Balit. 2006, Barefoot Bks. $19.99 (1-84148-800-3). 128pp. A large-format picture-book retelling of Homer's classic story, with bright, attractive illustrations and fast-paced, sometimes challenging text. (Rev: BL 12/1/06; SLJ 11/06*) [398.20938]

2501 Tchana, Katrin Hyman. *Changing Woman and Her Sisters* (5–8). Illus. by Trina Schart Hyman. 2006, Holiday $18.95 (0-8234-1999-1). 80pp. An illustrated collection of traditional stories about ten goddesses from a variety of lesser-known cultures, including Celtic, ancient Mayan, Shinto, Buddhist, and Navajo. (Rev: BCCB 9/06; BL 6/1–15/06; HB 7–8/06; HBG 10/06; LMC 1/07; SLJ 8/06) [398.2]

2502 Thomson, Ruth. *Myths* (2–6). Illus. Series: A First Look at Art. 2005, Chelsea Clubhouse $15.95 (0-7910-8316-0). 32pp. A look at the portrayal of mythological beings and stories in artwork from around the world. Also use *Weather* (2005). (Rev: SLJ 11/05) [398.2]

2503 West, David. *Mesoamerican Myths* (5–9). Illus. by Mike Taylor. Series: Graphic Mythology. 2006, Rosen LB $26.50 (1-4042-0802-X). 48pp. Presented in graphic-novel format are three tales from the mythology of Mexico and Central America — two creation stories and a hero tale. (Rev: SLJ 9/06) [398.2]

Classical

2504 Byrd, Robert. *The Hero and the Minotaur: The Fantastic Adventures of Theseus* (2–4). 2005, Dutton $17.99 (0-525-47391-2). 40pp. Byrd succeeds in retelling the complex adventures of Theseus in child-friendly narrative and compelling, detailed illustrations. (Rev: BL 7/05; SLJ 8/05*) [398.2]

2505 Harris, John. *Strong Stuff: Herakles and His Labors* (4–7). Illus. by Gary Baseman. 2005, Getty $16.95 (0-89236-784-9). 32pp. A lively, tongue-in-cheek account of the 12 labors of ancient Greece's mythical strongman, Herakles (known to the ancient Romans as Hercules). (Rev: BL 11/15/05; SLJ 11/05) [398.2]

2506 Marzollo, Jean, retel. *Let's Go, Pegasus!* (K–3). Illus. by reteller. 2006, Little, Brown $12.99 (0-316-74136-1). The Greek myth of the creation of Pegasus, retold for young children in an accessible format and featuring owls in a repetitive chorus. (Rev: SLJ 7/06) [398.2]

2507 Marzollo, Jean, retel. *Little Bear, You're a Star! A Greek Myth* (PS–2). Illus. by reteller. 2005, Little, Brown $12.99 (0-316-74135-3). This retelling of the Greek myth about Callisto and Arcas offers a colorful explanation for the origin of the constellations Ursa Major and Minor. (Rev: SLJ 1/06) [398.2]

2508 Shone, Rob. *Greek Myths* (5–9). Illus. by author. Series: Graphic Mythology. 2006, Rosen LB $26.50 (1-4042-0801-1). 48pp. "Jason and the Golden Fleece," "Icarus," and "The Labors of Hercules" are the three tales presented here in graphic-novel format. (Rev: SLJ 9/06) [292.1]

Poetry

General

2509 Agard, John. *Half-Caste and Other Poems* (4–7). 2005, Hodder $16.99 (0-340-89382-6). 80pp. Guyana-born Agard offers a collection of his saucy, Caribbean-flavored poetry dealing with topics such as tolerance and diversity that young people will recognize. (Rev: BL 10/15/05; HB 1–2/06; HBG 4/06; SLJ 1/06; VOYA 2/06) [811]

2510 Alarcón, Francisco X. *Poems to Dream Together / Poemas para soñar juntos* (3–5). Illus. by Paula Barragán. 2005, Lee & Low $16.95 (1-58430-233-X). 32pp. A collection of short, bilingual poems about aspirations. (Rev: BL 7/05; HBG 10/05; LMC 1/06; SLJ 10/05) [811]

2511 Argueta, Jorge. *Talking with Mother Earth / Hablando con Madre Tierra: Poems / Poemas* (3–8). Illus. by Lucía Angela Pérez. 2006, Groundwood $15.95 (0-88899-626-8). These beautiful bilingual poems give voice to a young Central American Indian's feelings of kinship with nature. (Rev: HBG 4/07; LMC 1/07; SLJ 10/06) [811]

2512 Bagert, Brod. *Shout! Little Poems That Roar* (K–2). Illus. by Sachiko Yoshikawa. 2007, Dial $16.99 (978-0-8037-2972-8). This appealing collection of 21 energetic rhyming poems celebrates the wonders — and occasional disappointments — of childhood. (Rev: BL 2/1/07; SLJ 2/07) [811]

2513 Barbe, Walter B., sel. *A School Year of Poems: 180 Favorites from Highlights* (K–3). Illus. by Dennis Hockerman. 2005, Boyds Mills paper $11.95 (1-59078-395-6). 116pp. The poems in this anthology are divided into nine child-friendly categories, including animals, weather, and holidays. (Rev: SLJ 10/05) [811]

2514 Brand, Dionne. *Earth Magic* (4–7). Illus. by Eugenie Fernandes. 2006, Kids Can $14.95 (1-

55337-706-0). 32pp. In her first collection of poetry for young people, Brand writes about life in Trinidad, the island of her birth. (Rev: BL 4/1/06; SLJ 7/06) [811]

2515 Chorao, Kay, comp. *The Baby's Playtime Book* (PS). 2006, Dutton $16.99 (0-525-47576-1). 40pp. The rhymes, songs, and poems in this appealing collection focus on different aspects of child's play, including toys, games, and imaginative play. (Rev: SLJ 3/06) [811.008]

2516 Creech, Sharon. *Who's That Baby? New-Baby Songs* (PS–2). Illus. by David Diaz. 2005, HarperCollins $15.99 (0-06-052939-3). 32pp. In this collection of short poems and songs, Creech chronicles the early days of a newborn baby and its interaction with the world around it. (Rev: BL 8/05) [811]

2517 Dahl, Roald. *Vile Verses* (5–8). Illus. 2005, Viking $25.00 (0-670-06042-9). 192pp. New illustrations adorn the poems in this aptly titled collection. (Rev: BL 11/1/05; SLJ 11/05*) [811]

2518 Field, Rachel. *Grace for an Island Meal* (PS–1). Illus. by Cynthia Jabar. 2006, Farrar $16.00 (0-374-32759-9). 32pp. A family expresses thanks for an idyllic day spent on an island off the coast of Maine. (Rev: BL 4/1/06; SLJ 5/06) [811]

2519 Fletcher, Ralph. *Moving Day* (3–6). Illus. by Jennifer Emery. 2006, Boyds Mills $17.95 (1-59078-339-5). Free-verse poems give voice to the feelings of a 12-year-old who is leaving behind the only world he's known and moving to a new and unfamiliar place. (Rev: SLJ 12/06*) [811]

2520 Gilchrist, Jan Spivey. *My America* (K–2). Illus. by Ashley Bryan. 2007, HarperCollins $16.99 (978-0-06-079104-9). 40pp. Celebrates the diversity of America in its landscape, animal life, and people. (Rev: BL 4/15/07) [813]

2521 Greenfield, Eloise. *When the Horses Ride By: Children in the Times of War* (2–4). Illus. by Jan

153

Spivey Gilchrist. 2006, Lee & Low $17.95 (1-58430-249-6). 40pp. The poems in this collection celebrate the resiliency of children and their ability to rise above the horrors of war and conflict around the world. (Rev: BL 6/1–15/06; SLJ 9/06) [811]

2522 Hayford, James. *Knee-Deep in Blazing Snow: Growing Up in Vermont* (4–7). Illus. by Michael McCurdy. 2005, Boyds Mills $17.95 (1-59078-338-7). 64pp. Hayford's simple, quiet poems evoke a simpler country life. (Rev: BL 1/1–15/06; SLJ 11/05) [811]

2523 Hollyer, Belinda, sel. *She's All That! Poems About Girls* (4–7). Illus. by Susan Hellard. 2006, Kingfisher $14.95 (0-7534-5852-7). 128pp. Poems celebrate today's diverse girls and their interests and concerns, with breezy, hip illustrations. (Rev: SLJ 7/06) [811]

2524 Hopkins, Lee Bennett, ed. *Behind the Museum Door* (K–3). Illus. by Stacey Dressen-McQueen. 2007, Abrams $16.95 (0-8109-1204-X). 32pp. The poems in this anthology celebrate the sights and sensations found within the walls of a museum. (Rev: BL 4/1/07) [811]

2525 Hopkins, Lee Bennett, ed. *Got Geography!* (4–7). Illus. by Philip Stanton. 2006, Greenwillow LB $16.89 (0-06-055602-1). 32pp. Poems celebrate the joys of travel and the maps that guide the way. (Rev: BL 2/1/06; SLJ 5/06) [811]

2526 Janeczko, Paul B., sel. *Hey, You! Poems to Skyscrapers, Mosquitoes, and Other Fun Things* (1–4). 2007, HarperCollins $15.99 (0-06-052347-6). 40pp. These short poems — which include works by Ogden Nash, Nikki Grimes, Douglas Florian — directly address a diverse range of animals, inanimate objects, and concepts, from the lowly dust mite to black holes. (Rev: BL 4/15/07) [811]

2527 Katz, Bobbi. *Once Around the Sun* (K–2). Illus. by LeUyen Pham. 2006, Harcourt $16.00 (0-15-216397-2). 40pp. Simple, happy poems celebrate the highlights of each month in an urban neighborhood. (Rev: BL 4/15/06; SLJ 5/06) [811]

2528 Kennedy, Caroline, ed. *A Family of Poems: My Favorite Poetry for Children* (4–7). Illus. by Jon J Muth. 2005, Hyperion $19.95 (0-7868-5111-2). 144pp. This collection of poems for children includes a number of Kennedy family favorites. (Rev: BL 10/15/05; SLJ 12/05*) [811]

2529 Kipling, Rudyard. *If: A Father's Advice to His Son* (4–6). Photos by Charles R. Smith Jr. 2007, Simon & Schuster $14.99 (978-0-689-87799-5). Kipling's classic poem is given new life in this attractive volume full of photographs of boys and young men competing in a wide array of athletic events. (Rev: SLJ 2/07) [811]

2530 Lewis, J. Patrick. *Blackbeard: The Pirate King* (3–5). 2006, National Geographic $16.95 (0-7922-5585-2). 26pp. Poems about the infamous pirate are

accompanied by diverse artwork. (Rev: BL 5/1/06; SLJ 12/06) [811]

2531 Lewis, J. Patrick. *Vherses: A Celebration of Outstanding Women* (4–7). Illus. by Mark Summers. 2005, Creative $18.95 (1-56846-185-2). 32pp. The accomplishments of 14 notable and diverse women — including Emily Dickinson, Georgia O'Keeffe, and Venus and Serena Williams — are celebrated in an appealing blend of poetry and art. (Rev: BL 12/15/05) [811]

2532 Lewis, J. Patrick, and Rebecca Kai Dotlich. *Castles: Old Stone Poems* (4–7). Illus. by Dan Burr. 2006, Boyds Mills $18.95 (1-59078-380-8). 48pp. The poems in this attractive collection celebrate castles of past and present. (Rev: BL 10/1/06; SLJ 10/06) [811]

2533 Lillegard, Dee. *Go!* (PS). Illus. 2006, Knopf $14.95 (0-375-82387-5). 32pp. The short rhyming poems in this collection celebrate motion and things that move, ranging from skateboards and lawnmowers to garbage trucks and school buses. (Rev: BL 11/1/06; SLJ 12/06) [811]

2534 Maynard, John, ed. *Poetry for Young People: William Blake* (4–6). Illus. by Alessandra Cimatoribus. 2007, Sterling $14.95 (978-0-8069-3647-5). 48pp. A selection of Blake's poems follow a brief biography and a review of his literary importance. (Rev: BL 4/1/07) [811]

2535 Micklos, John, Jr. *No Boys Allowed: Poems About Brothers and Sisters* (PS–3). Illus. by Kathleen O'Malley. 2006, Boyds Mills $15.95 (1-59078-051-5). 31pp. A collection of poems that address with love and humor the sometimes-tricky relationship between brothers and sisters. (Rev: SLJ 5/06) [811]

2536 Miller, Kate. *Poems in Black and White* (4–7). Illus. 2007, Boyds Mills $17.95 (978-1-59078-412-9). 40pp. The poems and striking artwork in this slim volume explore images in black and white. (Rev: BL 4/1/07) [811]

2537 Moore, Lilian. *Beware, Take Care: Fun and Spooky Poems* (PS–1). Illus. by Howard Fine. 2006, Holt $16.95 (0-8050-6917-8). 32pp. Fifteen creepy poems about ghosts and monsters were first published more than 30 years ago. (Rev: BL 9/1/06; SLJ 10/06) [811]

2538 Mordhorst, Heidi. *Squeeze: Poems from a Juicy Universe* (2–4). Illus. by Jesse Torrey. 2005, Boyds Mills $16.95 (1-59078-292-5). 32pp. Twenty-four free-form poems and color photographs celebrates the experiences that are the essence of childhood. (Rev: BL 10/15/05; SLJ 3/06) [811]

2539 Morgenstern, Constance. *Waking Day* (4–7). Illus. 2006, North Word $17.95 (1-55971-919-2). 32pp. In a picture book for older readers, Morgenstern melds Impressionist works with lines from her own poetry. (Rev: BL 2/15/06) [811]

2540 Morris, Jackie, comp. *The Barefoot Book of Classic Poems* (3–9). Illus. by comp. 2006, Barefoot Bks. $19.99 (1-905236-56-5). 128pp. A handsomely illustrated anthology of nearly 75 classic poems, with works by such well-known writers as Robert Frost, John Donne, Robert Louis Stevenson, and William Wordsworth. (Rev: SLJ 1/07) [811]

2541 Mozelle, Shirley. *The Kitchen Talks* (PS–2). Illus. by Petra Mathers. 2006, Holt $15.95 (0-8050-7143-1). 32pp. This collection of short poems — often involving riddles — reveals the innermost thoughts of inanimate objects from the kitchen. (Rev: BL 3/15/06; SLJ 4/06) [811]

2542 Myers, Walter Dean. *Jazz* (3–5). Illus. by Christopher Myers. 2006, Holiday $18.95 (0-8234-1545-7). 48pp. This vibrant blend of poetry and artwork celebrates jazz and the musicians who helped to shape this uniquely American brand of music. (Rev: BCCB 2/07; BL 9/1/06; HBG 4/07; SLJ 9/06) [811]

2543 Norman, Lissette. *My Feet Are Laughing* (K–3). Illus. by Frank Morrison. 2006, Farrar $16.00 (0-374-35096-5). 32pp. In this collection of 16 energetic free-verse poems with evocative illustrations, a young Dominican American girl describes her family and life in New York City's Harlem. (Rev: BL 4/1/06; SLJ 5/06) [811]

2544 Paschen, Elise, ed. *Poetry Speaks to Children* (3–5). Illus. 2005, Sourcebooks $19.95 (1-4022-0329-2). 112pp. A broad selection of poems (nearly 100) representing many genres and poets, with an accompanying CD. (Rev: BL 12/15/05; SLJ 1/06) [811]

2545 Podwal, Mark. *Jerusalem Sky: Stars, Crosses, and Crescents* (3–5). Illus. 2005, Doubleday $15.95 (0-385-74689-X). 32pp. In poems and paintings, Podwal celebrates the power and majesty of Jerusalem, a city sacred to three religions: Christianity, Islam, and Judaism. (Rev: BL 10/1/05*; SLJ 9/05) [811]

2546 Pomerantz, Charlotte. *Thunderboom! Poems for Everyone* (PS–2). Illus. by Rob Shepperson. 2006, Front St. $17.95 (1-932425-40-3). 48pp. There's something for everyone in this diverse collection of poems ranging from boisterous to playful to quiet. (Rev: BL 4/1/06; SLJ 5/06) [811]

2547 Prelutsky, Jack. *Me I Am!* (PS–2). Illus. by Christine Davenier. 2007, Farrar $16.00 (0-374-34902-9). 32pp. Prelutsky's previously published poem about individuality and diversity is shown in dynamic illustrations of three different children. (Rev: BL 4/1/07) [811]

2548 Prelutsky, Jack, ed. *Read a Rhyme, Write a Rhyme* (3–5). Illus. by Meilo So. 2005, Knopf $16.95 (0-375-82286-0). 32pp. Organized in themes — dogs, bugs, birthdays, and so forth — this anthology groups poems on spreads and on each encour-

ages readers to finish an uncompleted "poemstart." (Rev: BL 11/15/05; SLJ 11/05) [811]

2549 Rowden, Justine. *Paint Me a Poem: Poems Inspired by Masterpieces of Art* (4–7). Illus. 2005, Boyds Mills $16.95 (1-59078-289-5). 32pp. Each of the 14 poems in this collection is inspired by a famous painting from the National Gallery of Art. (Rev: BL 11/1/05; SLJ 10/05) [811.54]

2550 Rylant, Cynthia. *The Stars Will Still Shine* (PS–1). Illus. by Tiphanie Beeke. 2005, HarperCollins $15.99 (0-06-054639-5). 40pp. In rhyming text, the author celebrates the continuity of life and such constants as the sky, stars, birds, and church bells. (Rev: BL 10/15/05; SLJ 10/05) [811]

2551 Siebert, Diane. *Tour America: A Journey Through Poems and Art* (4–7). 2006, Chronicle $17.95 (0-8118-5056-0). 64pp. Natural and manmade sights across America are celebrated in this appealing collection of poetry and art. (Rev: BL 6/1–15/06; SLJ 6/06*) [811]

2552 Tennyson, Alfred Lord. *The Lady of Shalott* (5–7). Illus. by Genevieve Cote. 2005, Kids Can $16.95 (1-55337-874-1). 48pp. The setting of Tennyson's "The Lady of Shalott" is moved from the England of King Arthur to the streets of an early-20th-century city in this beautifully illustrated adaptation. (Rev: BL 10/1/05; SLJ 12/05) [821]

2553 Thaler, Mike. *Pig Little* (PS–1). Illus. by Paige Miglio. 2006, Holt $16.95 (0-8050-6977-1). A little pig describes all the fun of a day at the beach with his mommy. (Rev: SLJ 7/06) [811]

2554 Wong, Janet S. *Twist: Yoga Poems* (3–5). Illus. by Julie Paschkis. 2007, Simon & Schuster $17.99 (978-0-689-87394-2). 32pp. Short, accessible poems, each focusing on a familiar pose, consider both physical and philosophical aspects of yoga, while illustrations feature multiethnic practitioners and colorful borders of animals and plants. (Rev: BL 1/1–15/07) [811]

2555 Yolen, Jane, and Andrew Fusek Peters, eds. *Here's a Little Poem* (PS). Illus. by Polly Dunbar. 2007, Candlewick $21.99 (978-0-7636-3141-3). 112pp. This appealing anthology of more than 60 diverse poems includes works by Jack Prelutsky, Langston Hughes, Rosemary Wells, Gertrude Stein, A. A. Milne, Robert Louis Stevenson. (Rev: BL 4/1/07) [811]

African American Poetry

2556 Brooks, Gwendolyn. *Bronzeville Boys and Girls* (K–4). Illus. by Faith Ringgold. 2007, HarperCollins $16.99 (978-0-06-029505-9). 41pp. This newly illustrated collection of poems by Pulitzer Prize-winner Gwendolyn Brooks, originally published in 1956, celebrates the universal joys of childhood. (Rev: BL 2/1/07; SLJ 2/07) [811]

2557 Forman, Ruth. *Young Cornrows Callin Out the Moon* (PS). Illus. by Cbabi Bayoc. 2007, Children's Book Pr. $16.95 (978-0-89239-218-6). 32pp. A happy poem about summer life among the brownstones of South Philadelphia. (Rev: BL 2/1/07) [811]

2558 Grimes, Nikki. *Thanks a Million* (1–3). Illus. by Cozbi A. Cabrera. 2006, Greenwillow $15.99 (0-688-17292-X). 32pp. Poetry in various forms celebrates the joys of showing gratitude for everyday kindnesses and pleasures. (Rev: BL 3/15/06; SLJ 3/06) [811]

2559 Gunning, Monica. *America, My New Home* (2–5). Illus. by Ken Condon. 2004, Boyds Mills $15.95 (1-59078-057-4). In a series of poems, a young Jamaican girl, newly arrived in the United States, tells about her initial reactions to life in America and her homesickness for her native Caribbean island. (Rev: BL 8/05) [811]

2560 Muse, Daphne, ed. *The Entrance Place of Wonders: Poems of the Harlem Renaissance* (3–5). Illus. by Charlotte Riley-Webb. 2006, Abrams $16.95 (0-8109-5997-6). 32pp. Lively oil paintings illustrate this collection of 20 child-friendly poems from the Harlem Renaissance. (Rev: BL 2/1/06; SLJ 3/06) [811]

2561 Richards, Beah E. *Keep Climbing, Girls* (K–3). Illus. by R. Gregory Christie. 2006, Simon & Schuster $15.95 (1-4169-0264-3). 32pp. "Keep climbing" is the recommendation for girls in this beautifully illustrated poem written by the late African American actress. (Rev: BL 2/1/06; SLJ 2/06*) [811]

Animals

2562 Chernaik, Judith, ed. *Carnival of the Animals: Poems Inspired by Saint-Saëns' Music* (K–3). Illus. by Satoshi Kitamura. 2006, Candlewick $16.99 (0-7636-2960-X). 32pp. In this brightly illustrated title, which is bundled with an audio CD, poets offer their profiles of animal characters portrayed musically in the Saint-Saëns classic. (Rev: BCCB 5/06; BL 3/15/06*; HBG 10/06; LMC 10/06; SLJ 4/06) [811]

2563 Cox, Kenyon. *Mixed Beasts* (3–5). Illus. by Wallace Edwards. 2005, Kids Can $17.95 (1-55337-796-6). Nonsense poems about beasts such as the kangarooster and bumblebeaver are accompanied by full-page, detailed illustrations. (Rev: SLJ 1/06) [811]

2564 Harley, Avis. *Sea Stars* (1–5). Photos by Margaret Butschler. 2006, Boyds Mills $16.95 (1-59078-429-4). 35pp. Short poems of varied constructions

and close-up color photographs introduce a number of sea creatures. (Rev: SLJ 10/06) [811]

2565 Horton, Joan. *Hippopotamus Stew: And Other Silly Animal Poems* (PS–2). Illus. by JoAnn Adinolfi. 2006, Holt $16.95 (0-8050-7350-7). 32pp. A menagerie of wacky animals — and humans — is introduced in this collection of 21 nonsense poems illustrated with lively, funny collages. (Rev: BL 2/1/06; SLJ 3/06) [811]

2566 Jackson, Rob. *Animal Mischief* (2–4). Illus. by Laura Jacobsen. 2006, Boyds Mills $15.95 (1-59078-254-2). 32pp. The oddities of animal behavior and appearance are celebrated from a biologist's point of view in this collection of 18 amusing poems. (Rev: BL 4/1/06; SLJ 5/06) [811]

2567 Kumin, Maxine. *Mites to Mastodons: A Book of Animal Poems* (2–4). Illus. by Pamela Zagarenski. 2006, Houghton $16.00 (0-618-50753-1). 32pp. Animals large and small are celebrated in poems that both appeal and convey information; the whimsical collage illustrations add another dimension. (Rev: BL 10/1/06; SLJ 10/06) [811]

2568 Kuskin, Karla. *Toots the Cat* (PS–2). Illus. by Lisze Bechtold. 2005, Holt $16.95 (0-8050-6841-4). 32pp. Poems celebrate the life and adventures of Toots, an independent-minded cat. (Rev: BL 9/1/05; SLJ 1/06) [811.54]

2569 Larios, Julie. *Yellow Elephant: A Bright Bestiary* (K–3). Illus. by Julie Paschkis. 2006, Harcourt $16.00 (0-15-205422-7). 32pp. Using vivid, folk-art illustrations of animals and nature, this collection of poems looks at colors and animals. (Rev: BCCB 5/06; BL 3/15/06*; HBG 10/06; LMC 11–12/06; SLJ 4/06) [811]

2570 MacLachlan, Patricia, and Emily MacLachlan Charest. *Once I Ate a Pie* (2–4). Illus. by Katy Schneider. 2006, HarperCollins $15.99 (0-06-073531-7). 40pp. An appealing bunch of dogs reveal in poems things they love and various doggy characteristics. (Rev: BL 5/1/06; SLJ 5/06) [811.54]

2571 Ruddell, Deborah. *Today at the Bluebird Cafe: A Branchful of Birds* (1–3). Illus. by Joan Rankin. 2007, Simon & Schuster $15.99 (0-689-87153-8). 40pp. Paired with light-filled watercolors, these playful poems combine imaginative anthropomorphizing with facts about birds. (Rev: BL 1/1–15/07; SLJ 2/07*) [811]

2572 Ryder, Joanne. *Toad by the Road: A Year in the Life of These Amazing Amphibians* (2–4). Illus. by Maggie Kneen. 2007, Holt $16.95 (978-0-8050-7354-6). 32pp. This collection of poems chronicles a year in the life of a toad. (Rev: BL 4/1/07; SLJ 4/07) [811]

2573 Sidman, Joyce. *Meow Ruff: A Story in Concrete Poetry* (1–3). Illus. by Michelle Berg. 2006, Houghton $16.00 (0-618-44894-2). 32pp. Recounted in concrete — or visual — poetry, this simple tale with creative graphics tells how a friendship develops between a cat and dog seeking shelter from a storm. (Rev: BCCB 5/06; BL 3/15/06*; HB 5–6/06; HBG 10/06; SLJ 7/06) [811]

2574 Worth, Valerie. *Animal Poems* (4–7). Illus. 2007, Farrar $17.00 (0-374-38057-0). 48pp. A diverse, sometimes challenging collection of poems highlighting animals' individual characteristics. (Rev: BL 4/1/07) [811]

2575 Yang, Huan. *Homes* (PS–K). Illus. by Hsiao-yen Huang. 2005, Heryin $13.99 (0-9762056-3-7). 32pp. A brief, gentle poem about nature and the homes of diverse animals ends with a final spread of parents and children in a comfortable, sunlit home. (Rev: BL 12/1/05) [895.1]

2576 Yolen, Jane. *Count Me a Rhyme: Animal Poems by the Numbers* (3–5). Illus. by Jason Stemple. 2006, Boyds Mills $17.95 (1-59078-345-X). 32pp. Poet mother and photographer son team up to create this attractive combination of counting book (nonet, novena, IX, and so forth) and nature study. (Rev: BL 4/1/06; SLJ 4/06) [811]

Haiku

2577 Issa, Kobayashi. *Today and Today* (K–3). Illus. by G. Brian Karas. 2007, Scholastic $16.99 (0-439-59078-7). 40pp. Issa's haiku are woven together to create a poetic tapestry chronicling a year in the life of a family. (Rev: BL 4/1/07) [895.6]

2578 Janeczko, Paul B., and J. Patrick Lewis. *Wing Nuts: Screwy Haiku* (2–4). Illus. by Tricia Tusa. 2006, Little, Brown $14.99 (0-316-60731-2). 32pp. This picture book introduces readers to *senryu,* a poetic form similar to haiku but generally humorous and focused more on people than nature. (Rev: BL 3/15/06; SLJ 5/06) [811]

2579 Lin, Grace, and Robert Mercer, eds. *Robert's Snowflakes: Artists' Snowflakes for Cancer's Cure* (PS–K). Illus. 2005, Viking $10.99 (0-670-06044-5). 40pp. Children's book illustrators — including Mark Teague, Eric Carle, Denise Fleming, and David Shannon — created the imaginative snowflakes shown in this volume as part of an effort to fight cancer; short haiku accompany the art. (Rev: BL 11/15/05; SLJ 11/05) [811]

Holidays

2580 Hopkins, Lee Bennett, sel. *Halloween Howls: Holiday Poetry* (K–3). Illus. by Stacey Schuett. 2005, HarperCollins $15.99 (0-06-008060-4). 32pp. A dozen previously published poems celebrate the sights, sounds, and smells of Halloween; suitable for beginning readers. (Rev: SLJ 10/05) [811]

2581 Johnston, Tony. *Noel* (K–4). Illus. by Cheng-Khee Chee. 2005, Carolrhoda LB $15.95 (1-57505-752-2). A church bell's chimes summon humans and animals to worship on Christmas Eve in this lyrical poem accompanied by beautiful impressionistic watercolors. (Rev: SLJ 10/05) [811]

2582 Moore, Clement C. *The Night Before Christmas* (PS–2). Illus. by Will Moses. 2006, Philomel $16.99 (0-399-23745-3). 40pp. Folk artist Will Moses portrays the traditional poem in nostalgic paintings full of welcoming houses lit by candles. (Rev: BL 9/15/06; SLJ 10/06) [811]

2583 Moore, Clement C. *The Night Before Christmas* (PS–2). Illus. by Gennady Spirin. 2006, Marshall Cavendish $16.99 (0-7614-5298-2). 32pp. Spirin's interpretation of the poem is set in a quaint European village of days gone by, with illustrations full of contrasting light. (Rev: BL 9/15/06; SLJ 10/06) [811]

2584 Moore, Clement C. *The Night Before Christmas* (PS–2). Illus. by Richard Jesse Watson. 2006, HarperCollins $16.99 (0-06-075741-8). 40pp. Moore's classic poem features a high-tech sleigh complete with a fully equipped cockpit, multicultural elves, and dynamic, realistic art. (Rev: BL 9/15/06; SLJ 10/06) [811]

2585 Moore, Clement C. *The Night Before Christmas* (K–3). Illus. by Lisbeth Zwerger. 2005, Penguin $15.99 (0-698-40030-5). 32pp. The immortal Christmas poem is given new life in the dream-like blue and green artwork accented by the red suit. (Rev: BL 10/15/05; SLJ 10/05) [811]

Humorous Poetry

2586 Brown, Calef. *Flamingos on the Roof* (3–5). Illus. 2006, Houghton $16.00 (0-618-56298-2). 64pp. A delightful collection of nonsense poems accompanied by funky illustrations. (Rev: BL 4/15/06; SLJ 7/06) [811]

2587 Greenberg, David. *Don't Forget Your Etiquette! The Essential Guide to Misbehavior* (1–3). Illus. by Nadine Bernard Westcott. 2006, Farrar $16.00 (0-374-34990-8). 40pp. In humorous poems, "Miss Information" dispenses advice that turns proper etiquette on its head. (Rev: BL 10/1/06; SLJ 10/06) [811]

2588 Gutman, Dan. *Casey Back at Bat* (2–4). Illus. by Steve Johnson. 2007, HarperCollins $16.99 (0-06-056025-8). 32pp. Gutman playfully extends Thayer's classic poem as Casey wallops the baseball around the world and back in time, bumping against the poor Leaning Tower of Pisa and knocking the nose off the Sphinx; glowing, textured illustrations borrowed from 19th-century art extend the fun. (Rev: BL 1/1–15/07; SLJ 1/07*) [811]

2589 Lear, Edward. *The Owl and the Pussycat* (PS–4). Illus. by Anne Mortimer. 2006, Harper-Collins $15.99 (0-06-027228-7). The beloved old rhyme, illustrated in a lush, lovely style. (Rev: SLJ 7/06) [811]

2590 Lewis, J. Patrick. *Once Upon a Tomb: Gravely Humorous Verses* (2–4). Illus. by Simon Bartram. 2006, Candlewick $16.99 (0-7636-1837-3). 32pp. This collection of amusing epitaphs marks the passing of such diverse individuals as an underwear salesman, dairy farmer, schoolteacher, food critic, and fortune teller. (Rev: BL 8/06; SLJ 8/06) [811]

2591 Lewis, J. Patrick. *Tulip at the Bat* (K–3). Illus. by Amiko Hirao. 2007, Little, Brown $16.99 (978-0-316-61280-7). 32pp. The Boston Beasts are up against the New York Pets in this silly, pun-filled World Series championship game. (Rev: BL 4/1/07) [811]

2592 Perry, Andrea. *The Snack Smasher: And Other Reasons Why It's Not My Fault* (2–5). Illus. by Alan Snow. 2007, Simon & Schuster $16.99 (978-0-689-85469-9). 33pp. These humorous poems provide whimsical explanations for some of life's most puzzling mysteries. (Rev: SLJ 2/07) [811]

2593 Prelutsky, Jack. *Behold the Bold Umbrellaphant and Other Poems* (3–5). Illus. by Carin Berger. 2006, Greenwillow LB $17.89 (0-06-054318-3). 32pp. Combinations of animals and objects — alarmadillo, spatuloon, panthermometer, tubaboon, to name just a few — star in these 17 silly poems. (Rev: BL 9/1/06; SLJ 10/06*) [811]

2594 Prelutsky, Jack. *What a Day It Was at School!* (K–2). Illus. by Doug Cushman. 2006, Greenwillow $15.99 (0-06-082335-6). 40pp. This collection of poems — some fantastical and some realistic but all humorous — celebrates the school experience. (Rev: BL 8/06; SLJ 7/06) [811]

2595 Rex, Adam. *Frankenstein Makes a Sandwich* (2–5). Illus. by author. 2006, Harcourt $16.00 (0-15-205766-8). 40pp. Laugh-out-loud poems reveal untold episodes in the lives of some favorite monsters. (Rev: SLJ 9/06*) [811]

Nature and the Seasons

2596 Florian, Douglas. *Comets, Stars, the Moon and Mars* (3–5). Illus. 2007, Harcourt $16.00 (978-0-15-205372-7). 56pp. Large-format, double-page spreads combine mixed-media illustrations with

lyrical poems about celestial bodies. (Rev: BL 4/1/07) [811]

2597 Florian, Douglas. *Handsprings* (K–3). Illus. 2006, Greenwillow $15.99 (0-06-009280-7). 48pp. Florian follows *Winter Eyes* (1999), *Summersaults* (2002), and *Autumnblings* (2003) with a volume of breezy poems about the joys of spring. (Rev: BL 3/15/06; SLJ 4/06) [811]

2598 Havill, Juanita. *I Heard It from Alice Zucchini: Poems About the Garden* (K–3). Illus. by Christine Davenier. 2006, Chronicle $15.95 (0-8118-3962-1). 32pp. The science and magic of gardening are celebrated in this collection of poems illustrated with pen-and-ink and watercolor sketches. (Rev: BL 4/1/06; SLJ 4/06*) [811]

2599 Hines, Anna Grossnickle. *Winter Lights: A Season in Poems and Quilts* (1–3). Illus. 2005, Greenwillow $16.99 (0-06-000817-2). 32pp. The lights and warmth of various winter holidays are celebrated in a collection of poems and quilts. (Rev: BL 9/1/05*; SLJ 10/05*) [811]

2600 Livingston, Myra Cohn. *Calendar* (PS–K). Illus. by Will Hillenbrand. 2007, Holiday $16.95 (978-0-8234-1725-4). 32pp. This simple poem, colorfully illustrated with mixed-media artwork, highlights the special features of the months of the year. (Rev: BL 4/1/07) [811.54]

2601 Prelutsky, Jack. *It's Snowing! It's Snowing! Winter Poems* (K–3). Illus. by Yossi Abolafia. Series: I Can Read. 2006, HarperCollins $15.99 (0-06-053715-9). 48pp. Sixteen loosely connected, easily read poems celebrate the joys of winter. (Rev: BL 1/1–15/06; SLJ 7/06) [811]

2602 Quattlebaum, Mary. *Winter Friends* (PS–2). Illus. by Hiroe Nakata. 2005, Doubleday $15.95 (0-385-74626-1). 32pp. In 16 brief poems, a young girl describes the fun of a snowy day. (Rev: BCCB 11/05; BL 11/1/05; HBG 4/06; SLJ 10/05) [811]

2603 Shakespeare, William. *Winter Song: A Poem by William Shakespeare* (K–4). Illus. by Melanie Hall. 2006, Boyds Mills $15.95 (1-59078-275-5). Wintry illustrations depict an Elizabethan scene as the backdrop for the poem that appears at the conclusion of his play, *Love's Labor's Lost*. (Rev: SLJ 11/06) [821.3]

2604 Shannon, George. *Busy in the Garden* (PS–2). Illus. by Sam Williams. 2006, Greenwillow $15.99 (0-06-000464-9). 40pp. This collection of 24 lively poems celebrates the joys — and headaches — of a backyard garden. (Rev: BL 1/1–15/06; SLJ 2/06) [811]

2605 Sidman, Joyce. *Butterfly Eyes and Other Secrets of the Meadow* (3–5). Illus. by Beth Krommes. 2006, Houghton $16.00 (0-618-56313-X). 48pp.

The diversity of life in and around a country meadow is celebrated in poems that include both scientific facts and riddles. (Rev: BL 10/1/06; SLJ 10/06*) [811]

2606 Spinelli, Eileen. *Polar Bear, Arctic Hare: Poems of the Frozen North* (PS–2). Illus. by Eugenie Fernandes. 2007, Boyds Mills $16.95 (978-1-59078-344-3). 48pp. Twenty-four poems about the animals of the Arctic are paired with large acrylic paintings. (Rev: BL 4/15/07) [811]

2607 Stevenson, Robert Louis. *The Moon* (PS–1). Illus. by Tracey Campbell Pearson. 2006, Farrar $16.00 (0-374-35046-9). 40pp. Stevenson's poem "The Moon" becomes a story of a boy and his father viewing the moon and nocturnal animals on a private nighttime boat trip. (Rev: BL 7/06; HBG 4/07; SLJ 9/06*) [821]

2608 Walker, Alice. *There Is a Flower at the Tip of My Nose Smelling Me* (K–3). Illus. by Stefano Vitale. 2006, HarperCollins $16.99 (0-06-057080-6). 32pp. Brief poems celebrate the interconnectedness between nature and humanity. (Rev: BL 4/1/06; SLJ 5/06) [811]

Sports

2609 Prelutsky, Jack. *Good Sports: Rhymes About Running, Jumping, Throwing, and More* (K–5). Illus. by Chris Raschka. 2007, Knopf $16.99 (978-0-375-83700-5). The rhyming poems in this collection celebrate the excitement of participating in a wide variety of sports and other physical activities. (Rev: BL 3/1/07*; SLJ 2/07) [811]

2610 Thayer, Ernest L. *Casey at the Bat* (5–10). Illus. by Joe Morse. Series: Visions in Poetry. 2006, Kids Can $16.95 (1-55337-827-X). The famous poem is reimagined in a contemporary setting, with a multicultural crowd and modern technology grounding the poem in the here-and-now. (Rev: SLJ 6/06) [811]

Plays

General

2611 Almond, David. *Two Plays: Skellig, Wild Girl, Wild Boy* (5–8). 2005, Delacorte LB $14.99 (0-385-90101-1). 240pp. Grief and hope are strong themes in both the dramatization of Almond's successful novel *Skellig* and the shorter *Wild Girl, Wild Boy* in which a girl, grieving over her father's death, retreats into a world of fantasy. (Rev: BL 10/1/05; HB 1–2/06; HBG 4/06; SLJ 12/05) [822]

2612 Shepard, Aaron. *Stories on Stage: Children's Plays for Reader's Theater (or Readers Theatre) with 15 Play Scripts from 15 Authors.* 2nd ed. (1–6). 2005, Shepard paper $15.00 (0-938497-22-7). 160pp. The 15 story scripts in this collection represent the work of 15 popular writers including Roald Dahl, Louis Sachar, and Harold Courlander. (Rev: SLJ 2/06) [812.5408]

Shakespeare

2613 Kindermann, Barbara. *William Shakespeare's Romeo and Juliet* (4–7). Trans. by J. Alison James. Illus. by Christa Unzner. 2006, North-South $17.95 (0-7358-2090-2). 36pp. This well-phrased prose retelling of the ill-fated romance is enhanced by the Renaissance-style illustrations. (Rev: BL 8/06; SLJ 12/06)

2614 Mayer, Marianna. *William Shakespeare's The Tempest* (3–5). Illus. by Lynn Bywaters. 2005, Chronicle $16.95 (0-8118-5054-4). 40pp. A handsome retelling of Shakespeare's comedy. (Rev: BL 11/1/05; SLJ 2/06) [813]

Biography

Adventurers and Explorers

Collective

2615 Atkins, Jeannine. *How High Can We Climb? The Story of Women Explorers* (5–8). Illus. by Dusan Petricic. 2005, Farrar $17.00 (0-374-33503-6). 224pp. Atkins celebrates the lives and achievements of 12 women adventurers and explorers in this attention-grabbing volume that unfortunately mixes fact and fiction. (Rev: BL 10/15/05; SLJ 9/05) [910]

2616 Clements, Gillian. *The Picture History of Great Explorers* (2–4). Illus. 2005, Frances Lincoln $19.95 (1-84507-075-5). 96pp. A comprehensive and very visual guide, suitable for browsers, to explorers from prehistory through space travel. (Rev: BL 1/1–15/06) [920]

2617 Rooney, Frances. *Extraordinary Women Explorers* (5–8). Illus. Series: Women's Hall of Fame. 2005, Second Story paper $7.95 (1-896764-98-3). 118pp. Women endowed with curiosity and courage are celebrated in this text-dense volume. (Rev: BL 3/1/06; SLJ 12/05) [910]

2618 St. George, Judith. *So You Want to Be an Explorer?* (2–4). Illus. by David Small. 2005, Philomel $16.99 (0-399-23868-9). 56pp. This light-hearted overview of explorers celebrates the accomplishments of diverse figures and distinguishes between "good" and "bad" explorers according to their treatment of native peoples. (Rev: BL 9/15/05; SLJ 9/05) [910]

Individual

BURTON, RICHARD FRANCIS

2619 Young, Serinity. *Richard Francis Burton: Explorer, Scholar, Spy* (5–9). Series: Great Explorations. 2006, Benchmark LB $22.95 (0-7614-2222-6). 80pp. This biography chronicles the English adventurer's explorations in Africa, the Middle East, South Asia, and South America and looks at his interest in the cultures of the people he encountered there. (Rev: SLJ 1/07) [921]

EARHART, AMELIA

2620 Feinstein, Stephen. *Read About Amelia Earhart* (2–4). Series: I Like Biographies! 2006, Enslow LB $21.26 (0-7660-2582-9). 24pp. For early researchers, this is an introductory biography that includes information on Earhart's youth and her work during World War I. (Rev: SLJ 4/06) [921]

HENSON, MATTHEW

2621 Hoena, B. A. *Matthew Henson: Arctic Adventurer* (4–7). Illus. by Phil Miller. Series: Graphic Biographies. 2005, Capstone LB $18.95 (0-7368-4634-4). 32pp. The life of the African American explorer is presented in speedy, user-friendly, classic comic book format. (Rev: BL 11/1/05) [910]

2622 Johnson, Dolores. *Onward: A Photobiography of African-American Polar Explorer Matthew Hen-*

son (5–8). Illus. Series: National Geographic Photobiography. 2005, National Geographic LB $27.90 (0-7922-7915-8). 64pp. The extraordinary life and achievements of African American explorer Matthew Henson are beautifully documented in this volume that also discusses the racism that Henson faced. (Rev: BCCB 5/06; BL 12/15/05*; HB 5–6/06; HBG 10/06; LMC 8–9/06; SLJ 3/06*; VOYA 6/06) [910]

LIVINGSTONE, DAVID

2623 Otfinoski, Steven. *David Livingstone: Deep in the Heart of Africa* (5–9). Series: Great Explorations. 2006, Benchmark LB $22.95 (0-7614-2226-9). 79pp. This biography focuses on the three decades during which the Scottish-born adventurer explored central Africa. (Rev: SLJ 1/07) [921]

OCHOA, ELLEN

2624 Iverson, Teresa. *Ellen Ochoa* (4–8). Series: Hispanic-American Biographies. 2005, Raintree LB $32.86 (1-4109-1299-X). 64pp. The personal and professional life of the first Hispanic American woman astronaut. (Rev: SLJ 1/06) [921]

2625 Johnston, Lissa. *Ellen Ochoa: Pioneering Astronaut* (2–4). Illus. Series: Fact Finders Biographies: Great Hispanics. 2006, Capstone LB $16.95 (0-7368-5438-X). 32pp. A brief profile of the life and career of America's first Hispanic woman to travel into space; NASA and personal photographs

are included, along with timelines and research resources. (Rev: BL 4/1/06) [921]

2626 Latham, Donna. *Ellen Ochoa: Reach for the Stars!* (2–4). Series: Defining Moments. 2005, Bearport LB $22.60 (1-59716-076-8). 32pp. A clearly written account of Ochoa's life, with information on her childhood and education. (Rev: SLJ 2/06) [921]

SELKIRK, ALEXANDER

2627 Kraske, Robert. *Marooned: The Strange but True Adventures of Alexander Selkirk, the Real Robinson Crusoe* (5–8). Illus. by Robert Andrew Parker. 2005, Clarion $15.00 (0-618-56843-3). 128pp. The adventurous life of Alexander Selkirk, the Scottish navigator who served as the model for Daniel Defoe's *Robinson Crusoe*. (Rev: BL 11/15/05; SLJ 12/05) [996.1]

SMITH, JOHN

2628 Schanzer, Rosalyn. *John Smith Escapes Again!* (4–6). 2006, National Geographic $16.95 (0-7922-5930-0). 64pp. While the accuracy of Smith's writings, used as the basis for Schanzer's account, is controversial (and examined in an author's note), this volume's stellar design and compelling writing combine to illuminate a poorly understood figure in the history of colonial America. (Rev: BL 1/1–15/07; SLJ 11/06) [921]

Artists, Composers, Entertainers, and Writers

Collective

2629 Ball, Heather. *Magnificent Women in Music* (4–7). Series: The Women's Hall of Fame. 2006, Second Story paper $7.95 (1-897187-02-5). 108pp. Ten women from different times and with different musical gifts are profiled here, including Clara Schumann, Marian Anderson, and k.d. lang. (Rev: SLJ 7/06)

2630 George-Warren, Holly. *Honky-Tonk Heroes and Hillbilly Angels: The Pioneers of Country and Western Music* (4–6). Illus. by Laura Levine. 2006, Houghton $16.00 (0-618-19100-3). 32pp. Loretta Lynn, Gene Autry, Patsy Cline, and the Carter family are just some of the artists covered in short biographies. (Rev: BL 6/1–15/06; SLJ 6/06) [920]

2631 Gourse, Leslie. *Sophisticated Ladies: The Great Women of Jazz* (5–8). Illus. by Martin French. 2007, Dutton $19.99 (0-525-47198-7). 64pp. Profiles 14 female jazz singers, with full-color portraits, biographical details, and comments on vocal style and importance. (Rev: BL 12/15/06) [920]

2632 Govenar, Alan. *Extraordinary Ordinary People: Five American Masters of Traditional Arts* (5–8). 2006, Candlewick $19.99 (0-7636-2047-5). 96pp. Five American artists, recipients of National Endowment for the Arts fellowships, who practice unique — but traditional — art forms are profiled here. (Rev: BL 9/1/06; SLJ 8/06*) [920]

2633 Marcus, Leonard. *Pass It Down: Five Picture-Book Families Make Their Mark* (5–8). 2007, Walker $19.95 (0-8027-9600-1). 56pp. Multigenerational families of picture book authors/illustrators are featured here: Donald Crews, Ann Jonas, and Nina Crews; Clement, Edith, and Thacher Hurd; Walter Dean and Christopher Myers; Jerry and Brian Pinkney; and Harlow, Anne, and Lizzy Rockwell. (Rev: BL 12/15/06; SLJ 1/07) [920]

Artists

CÉZANNE, PAUL

2634 Burleigh, Robert. *Paul Cézanne: A Painter's Journey* (4–7). Illus. 2006, Abrams $17.95 (0-8109-5784-1). 32pp. A lavishly illustrated and thoughtfully written profile of Cézanne's life and art. (Rev: BL 2/15/06; SLJ 3/06) [759.4]

CHAGALL, MARC

2635 Landmann, Bimba. *I Am Marc Chagall* (2–4). Illus. 2006, Eerdmans $18.00 (0-8028-5305-6). 40pp. Loosely inspired by Chagall's *My Life*, this first-person narrative describes Chagall's life from childhood through emigration to the United States and features painterly illustrations. (Rev: BL 1/1–15/06; SLJ 4/06) [921]

2636 Markel, Michelle. *Dreamer from the Village: The Story of Marc Chagall* (K–3). Illus. by Emily Lisker. 2005, Holt $16.95 (0-8050-6373-0). 40pp. This excellent profile traces the artist's life and career and introduces the importance of his work; browsers may find this more useful than report writers. (Rev: BL 8/05; SLJ 9/05) [709]

DA VINCI, LEONARDO

2637 Krull, Kathleen. *Leonardo da Vinci* (5–8). Illus. by Boris Kulikov. Series: Giants of Science. 2005, Viking $15.99 (0-670-05920-X). 128pp. The less attractive features of da Vinci's times are covered here, along with the artist's childhood and adolescence and his development into both an artist and a scientist, drawing connections between the two disciplines and incorporating much from da Vinci's notebooks. (Rev: BL 9/1/05; SLJ 10/05*) [921]

ELLABAD, MOHIEDDIN

2638 Ellabbad, Mohieddin. *The Illustrator's Notebook* (5–10). Trans. from French by Sarah Quinn. Illus. by author. 2006, Groundwood $16.95 (0-88899-700-0). 30pp. In this fascinating journal printed from right to left, Egyptian-born illustrator Ellabbad reflects on the influences that led him to a life in art and offers valuable insights into Arabic cultural sensibilities. (Rev: SLJ 8/06) [921]

KAHLO, FRIDA

2639 Guzman, Lila, and Rick Guzman. *Frida Kahlo: Painting Her Life* (3–5). Series: Famous Latinos. 2006, Enslow LB $16.95 (0-7660-2643-4). 32pp. A brief, accessible portrait of the Mexican artist, chronicling her personal life and artistic accomplishments in text for young readers that will also suit older reluctant readers. (Rev: BL 10/15/06; SLJ 2/07) [759.972]

LEE, STAN

2640 Miller, Raymond H. *Stan Lee: Creator of Spider-Man* (4–8). Series: Inventors and Creators. 2006, Gale LB $23.70 (0-7377-3447-7). 48pp. Superhero fans will enjoy this biography of the man behind Spider-Man and other comic-book characters. (Rev: SLJ 6/06) [921]

O'KEEFFE, GEORGIA

2641 Rodríguez, Rachel Victoria. *Through Georgia's Eyes* (K–3). Illus. by Julie Paschkis. 2006, Holt $16.95 (0-8050-7740-5). 32pp. O'Keeffe's life — including her childhood — and work are presented in compelling text and vibrant illustrations. (Rev: BCCB 4/06; BL 2/15/06*; HB 5–6/06; HBG 10/06; LMC 10/06; SLJ 3/06) [921]

PARKS, GORDON

2642 Parr, Ann. *Gordon Parks: No Excuses* (3–5). Illus. by Kathryn Breidenthal. 2006, Pelican $15.95 (1-58980-411-2). 32pp. African American photographer Parks's camera work takes center stage in this brief, large-format biography. (Rev: BL 7/06; SLJ 6/06) [770.92]

PEI, I. M.

2643 Englar, Mary. *I. M. Pei* (3–5). Illus. Series: Asian-American Biographies. 2005, Raintree LB $23.00 (1-4109-1056-3). 64pp. Profiles the life and career of the Chinese American architect who designed many notable structures, with sidebars that add historical context. (Rev: BL 10/15/05; SLJ 3/06) [921]

REAM, VINNIE

2644 Fitzgerald, Dawn. *Vinnie and Abraham* (2–4). Illus. by Catherine Stock. 2007, Charlesbridge $15.95 (978-1-57091-658-8). 32pp. This charmingly illustrated picture-book biography illuminates the life of Vinnie Ream, who was not only one of the U.S. Postal Service's first female workers but was also a talented artist and did a life-size sculpture of President Lincoln. (Rev: BL 1/1–15/07) [921]

RIVERA, DIEGO

2645 Guzman, Lila, and Rick Guzman. *Diego Rivera: Artist of Mexico* (3–4). Series: Famous Latinos. 2006, Enslow LB $22.60 (0-7660-2641-8). 32pp. The Mexican artist's life is described in easy-to-understand language, focusing in particular on his vibrantly colored murals. (Rev: SLJ 2/07) [921]

WARHOL, ANDY

2646 Rubin, Susan G. *Andy Warhol: Pop Art Painter* (4–7). Illus. 2006, Abrams $18.95 (0-8109-5477-X). 48pp. This picture-book biography chronicles Warhol's life and career, focusing in particular on his art and his childhood in Pittsburgh; there are many reproductions plus a timeline and a glossary. (Rev: BL 11/1/06; SLJ 11/06) [700]

Composers

FOSTER, STEPHEN

2647 Pancella, Peggy. *Stephen Foster: The Man Behind Our Best-Loved Songs* (1–3). Series: Lives and Times. 2005, Heinemann LB $24.21 (1-4034-6748-X). 32pp. Profiles the composer's life and examines the qualities that made his songs so popular with Americans. (Rev: SLJ 2/06) [921]

GUIDO D'AREZZO

2648 Roth, Susan L. *Do Re Mi: If You Can Read Music, Thank Guido d'Arezzo* (K–5). Illus. by author. 2007, Houghton $17.00 (978-0-618-46572-9). This colorful fictionalized biography of Guido d'Arezzo focuses on the 11th-century Italian monk's development of a musical notation system. (Rev: BL 12/1/06; SLJ 2/07) [921]

JOPLIN, SCOTT

2649 Gillis, Jennifer Blizin. *Scott Joplin: The King of Ragtime* (2–4). Illus. Series: Lives and Times. 2005, Heinemann LB $16.95 (1-4034-6789-8).

32pp. Brief, large text and illustrations cover Joplin's childhood, musical career, death, and later popularity. (Rev: BL 11/1/05) [921]

MESSIAEN, OLIVIER

2650 Bryant, Jen. *Music for the End of Time* (4–7). Illus. by Beth Peck. 2005, Eerdmans $17.00 (0-8028-5229-7). 32pp. This fictionalized picture-book biography tells how French soldier Olivier Messiaen composed and performed music while in a German prison camp during World War II. (Rev: BL 9/1/05; SLJ 12/05) [921]

MOZART, WOLFGANG AMADEUS

2651 Ekker, Ernst A. *Wolfgang Amadeus Mozart: A Musical Picture Book* (3–6). Illus. by Doris Eisenburger. 2006, North-South $20.00 (0-7358-2056-2). A musical CD accompanies this biography that covers the composer's life and career and adds personal details. (Rev: SLJ 5/06) [921]

2652 Sís, Peter. *Play, Mozart, Play!* (K–3). Illus. 2006, Greenwillow $16.99 (0-06-112181-9). 32pp. This beautifully illustrated picture-book biography with a simple text focuses on the musical prodigy's childhood. (Rev: BL 3/15/06; SLJ 5/06*) [780.92]

SAINT-GEORGE, JOSEPH BOLOGNE

2653 Brewster, Hugh. *The Other Mozart: The Life of the Famous Chevalier de Saint-George* (4–6). Illus. by Eric Velasquez. 2006, Abrams $18.95 (0-8109-5720-5). 32pp. A captivating picture-book biography of Joseph Bologne Saint-George, a famous 18th-century composer who was the son of a white plantation owner in Guadeloupe and a black slave. (Rev: BL 2/1/07) [921]

SOUSA, JOHN PHILIP

2654 Gillis, Jennifer Blizin. *John Philip Sousa: The King of March Music* (1–3). Series: Lives and Times. 2005, Heinemann LB $24.21 (1-4034-6751-X). 32pp. The youth and adult accomplishments of the composer of marches are covered in this interesting volume. (Rev: SLJ 2/06) [921]

Entertainers

CISNEROS, EVELYN

2655 Krohn, Katherine. *Evelyn Cisneros: Prima Ballerina* (1–3). Series: Fact Finders, Biographies, Great Hispanics. 2006, Capstone LB $22.60 (0-7368-6416-4). 32pp. Large, easy-to-read print recounts the life of the Mexican American ballerina from childhood until her retirement from the San Francisco Ballet. (Rev: SLJ 1/07) [921]

DAVIS, MILES

2656 Dell, Pamela. *Miles Davis: Jazz Master* (5–8). Series: Journey to Freedom. 2005, Child's World LB $28.50 (1-59296-232-7). 40pp. An easy-to-read biography that deals frankly with the trumpeter's addiction to heroin and his difficult personality. (Rev: SLJ 8/05) [921]

GILLESPIE, DIZZY

2657 Winter, Jonah. *Dizzy* (2–4). Illus. by Sean Qualls. 2006, Scholastic $16.99 (0-439-50737-5). 48pp. This compelling account of trumpeter Dizzy Gillespie's life and career is enhanced by vivid, eye-catching illustrations. (Rev: BL 11/1/06*; SLJ 10/06*) [921]

HOUDINI, HARRY

2658 Fleischman, Sid. *Escape! The Story of the Great Houdini* (4–8). 2006, HarperCollins $18.99 (0-06-085694-9). 210pp. A lively and entertaining biography by a great writer and professional magician, who reveals just enough of the magic behind the tricks; includes many photographs. (Rev: SLJ 8/06*; VOYA 6/06) [921]

2659 MacLeod, Elizabeth. *Harry Houdini: A Magical Life* (4–6). Illus. 2005, Kids Can $14.95 (1-55337-769-9); paper $6.95 (1-55337-770-2). 32pp. This concise biography separates fact from fiction in describing Houdini's life and feats. (Rev: BL 10/15/05; SLJ 4/06) [793.8]

LEE, BRUCE

2660 Mochizuki, Ken. *Be Water, My Friend: The Early Years of Bruce Lee* (2–4). Illus. by Dom Lee. 2006, Lee & Low $16.95 (1-58430-265-8). 32pp. This picture-book biography focuses on the actor's childhood in Hong Kong and his early interest in martial arts. (Rev: BL 9/1/06; SLJ 11/06) [921]

LIMÓN, JOSÉ

2661 Reich, Susanna. *José! Born to Dance: The Story of José Limón* (2–4). Illus. by Raul Colon. 2005, Simon & Schuster $16.95 (0-689-86576-7). 32pp. This biography of the Mexican-born dancer and choreographer emphasizes how the music and events of his childhood impacted his later career. (Rev: BCCB 9/05; BL 8/05*; HBG 4/06; LMC 2/06; SLJ 10/05) [921]

MILLER, NORMA

2662 Govenar, Alan, ed. *Stompin' at the Savoy: The Story of Norma Miller* (5–8). Illus. by Martin French. 2006, Candlewick $16.99 (0-7636-2244-3). 56pp. The energy of Norma Miller, who was still going strong in her early 80s, infuses the pages of this brief biography, made up largely of excerpts from interviews with the legendary African American swing dancer. (Rev: BL 2/1/06; SLJ 3/06) [792.8]

OAKLEY, ANNIE

2663 Feinstein, Stephen. *Read About Annie Oakley* (2–4). Series: I Like Biographies. 2006, Enslow $15.99 (0-7660-2583-7). 24pp. The fascinating life of the sharpshooter is told in simple text and photographs and illustrations. (Rev: BL 7/06; SLJ 4/06) [799.3]

2664 Whiting, Jim. *Annie Oakley* (2–4). Series: A Robbie Reader: What's So Great About? 2006, Mitchell Lane LB $16.95 (1-58415-477-2). 32pp. With large text and lots of white space, this introductory biography chronicles the life of the female sharpshooter who became a star attraction with Buffalo Bill's Wild West show. (Rev: SLJ 1/07) [921]

REEVE, CHRISTOPHER

2665 Apte, Sunita. *Christopher Reeve: Don't Lose Hope!* (3–4). Series: Defining Moments. 2005, Bearport LB $22.60 (1-59716-074-1). 32pp. This easy-to-read biography looks at Reeve's childhood as well as his achievements and the challenges he faced. (Rev: SLJ 1/06) [921]

SIEGEL, SIENA CHERSON

2666 Siegel, Siena Cherson. *To Dance: A Ballerina's Graphic Novel* (5–8). Illus. by Mark Siegel. 2006, Simon & Schuster $17.95 (0-689-86747-6). 64pp. In graphic-novel format, Siegel tells the story of her dance career, from her introduction to ballet at the age of 6 to her stage debut with the New York City Ballet. (Rev: BCCB 1/07; BL 9/1/06; LMC 1/07; SLJ 11/06*; VOYA 4/07) [921]

WINFREY, OPRAH

2667 Westen, Robin. *Oprah Winfrey: "I Don't Believe in Failure"* (5–8). Series: African-American Biography Library. 2005, Enslow LB $31.93 (0-7660-2462-8). 128pp. Winfrey's phenomenal rise to success in the worlds of business and entertainment is placed in social context. (Rev: SLJ 11/05; VOYA 6/06) [921]

Writers

ANDERSEN, HANS CHRISTIAN

2668 Hesse, Karen. *The Young Hans Christian Andersen* (3–5). Illus. by Erik Blegvad. 2005, Scholastic $16.99 (0-439-67990-7). 48pp. This biography focuses on the Danish storyteller's trou-

bled childhood and how it is reflected in some of his memorable fairy tales. (Rev: BL 11/1/05; SLJ 10/05*) [921]

2669 Varmer, Hjordis. *Hans Christian Andersen: His Fairy Tale Life* (4–7). Trans. by Tina Nunnally. Illus. by Lilian Bregger. 2005, Groundwood $19.95 (0-88899-670-X). 112pp. This large-format, lively biography presents the Danish storyteller's single-minded struggle to rise above adversity. (Rev: BL 11/1/05) [839.81]

CRUTCHER, CHRIS

2670 Summers, Michael A. *Chris Crutcher* (5–8). Series: The Library of Author Biographies. 2005, Rosen LB $26.50 (1-4042-0325-7). 112pp. An interview with Crutcher is an interesting addition to this description of the author's life — including his experiences as a novelist, educator, therapist, and child protection advocate — and his works for children. (Rev: SLJ 9/05) [921]

DAHL, ROALD

2671 Cooling, Wendy. *D Is for Dahl: A Gloriumptious A–Z Guide to the World of Roald Dahl* (5–8). Illus. by Quentin Blake. 2005, Viking $15.99 (0-670-06023-2). 160pp. For Dahl fans, this is an alphabetically arranged collection of trivia about his life and writings. (Rev: BL 8/05; SLJ 10/05) [823]

DANZIGER, PAULA

2672 Reed, Jennifer. *Paula Danziger: Voice of Teen Troubles* (5–8). Series: Authors Teens Love. 2006, Enslow $31.93 (0-7660-2444-X). 104pp. This profile of the popular author includes interviews in which she discusses her dysfunctional family and her struggles with depression and bulimia. (Rev: BL 9/15/06) [921]

DEPAOLA, TOMIE

2673 Braun, Eric. *Tomie dePaola* (K–2). Series: First Biographies. 2004, Capstone LB $15.93 (0-7368-3641-1). 24pp. Very basic information on the author/illustrator's life and work for beginning readers and report writers, with photographs and a timeline. (Rev: SLJ 7/05) [921]

2674 dePaola, Tomie. *Christmas Remembered* (5–8). 2006, Putnam $19.99 (0-399-24622-3). 96pp. Folk artist dePaola recalls some of the most memorable Christmases from his past. (Rev: BL 10/1/06; SLJ 10/06) [813]

2675 dePaola, Tomie. *I'm Still Scared: The War Years* (2–4). Illus. 2006, Putnam $13.99 (0-399-24502-2). 80pp. DePaola recalls the fears and uncertainties of children growing up in America during World War II in this installment of his autobiographical series. (Rev: BL 4/15/06; SLJ 11/06) [813.54]

2676 dePaola, Tomie. *Why? The War Years: A 26 Fairmount Avenue Book* (2–4). Illus. 2007, Putnam $14.99 (978-0-399-24692-0). 80pp. Continuing his autobiographical series, dePaola includes many child-appealing vignettes, but focuses on the impact of World War II, concluding with his much-loved cousin's death. (Rev: BL 1/1–15/07) [921]

DICKENS, CHARLES

2677 Rosen, Michael. *Dickens: His Work and His World* (4–7). Illus. by Robert Ingpen. 2005, Candlewick $19.99 (0-7636-2752-6). 96pp. Before reviewing Dickens's major works, Rosen discusses the author's difficult childhood and the social conditions of his times. (Rev: BCCB 3/06; BL 9/15/05*; HBG 4/06; LMC 3/06; SLJ 11/05*) [921]

FLETCHER, RALPH

2678 Fletcher, Ralph. *Marshfield Dreams: When I Was a Kid* (3–5). 2005, Holt $16.95 (0-8050-7242-X). 192pp. Children's author Fletcher recalls growing up in coastal Massachusetts as the oldest of nine siblings. (Rev: BL 10/1/05; SLJ 9/05; VOYA 8/05) [921]

FROST, ROBERT

2679 Wooten, Sara McIntosh. *Robert Frost: The Life of America's Poet* (5–8). Series: People to Know Today. 2006, Enslow LB $31.93 (0-7660-2627-2). 128pp. A fine introduction to the New England poet whose poetry is loved by young people and adults, with information on his difficult childhood and continuing struggles with depression and financial woes. (Rev: SLJ 1/07) [921]

HANDLER, DANIEL

2680 Haugen, Hayley Mitchell. *Daniel Handler: The Real Lemony Snicket* (3–6). Illus. Series: Inventors and Creators. 2005, Gale LB $23.70 (0-7377-3117-6). 48pp. The author of the popular A Series of Unfortunate Events books is profiled (and pictured), with discussion of his books. (Rev: SLJ 8/05) [921]

LEWIS, C. S.

2681 Parker, Vic. *C. S. Lewis* (4–7). Series: Writers Uncovered. 2006, Heinemann LB $23.00 (1-4034-7336-6). 48pp. In addition to providing biographical information on Lewis, Parker looks at his books, especially the Narnia series, giving plot outlines and discussing the stories and themes. (Rev: BL 8/06) [921]

MARKHAM, BERYL

2682 Markham, Beryl. *The Good Lion* (K–3). Illus. by Don Brown. 2005, Houghton $16.00 (0-618-56306-7). 32pp. In this excerpt from her autobiography, author/pilot/adventurer Markham recalls how as a girl she was attacked by a supposedly tame lion on an East African farm. (Rev: BL 9/15/05; SLJ 10/05) [921]

MISTRAL, GABRIELA

2683 Brown, Monica. *My Name Is Gabriela / Me llamo Gabriela: The Life of Gabriela Mistral / La vida de Gabriela Mistral* (K–2). Illus. by John Parra. 2005, Luna Rising $15.95 (0-87358-859-2). Lyrical first-person text tells the story of the life and writing career of Nobel Prize–winning Chilean poet Gabriela Mistral. (Rev: SLJ 2/06*) [921]

MONTGOMERY, LUCY MAUD

2684 Wallner, Alexandra. *Lucy Maud Montgomery: The Author of Anne of Green Gables* (1–3). 2006, Holiday $16.95 (0-8234-1549-X). 32pp. A picture-book life of the author, from her childhood on Prince Edward Island to her marriage to a minister and her success with *Anne*. (Rev: BL 9/15/06; SLJ 12/06) [921]

NERUDA, PABLO

2685 DeLano, Poli. *When I Was a Boy Neruda Called Me Policarpo* (4–6). Trans. by Sean Higgins. Illus. by Manuel Monroy. 2006, Groundwood $15.95 (0-88899-726-4). 96pp. The author presents his childhood memories of Chilean poet Pablo Neruda along with a number of Neruda's poems. (Rev: BL 7/06; SLJ 5/06) [861]

2686 Ray, Deborah Kogan. *To Go Singing Through the World: The Childhood of Pablo Neruda* (3–5). Illus. 2006, Farrar $17.00 (0-374-37627-1). 40pp. A picture-book biography of poet Pablo Neruda, describing his childhood in a Chilean rain forest town and how it shaped his views and writings. (Rev: BL 11/15/06; SLJ 11/06) [921]

PATERSON, KATHERINE

2687 McGinty, Alice B. *Katherine Paterson* (5–8). Series: The Library of Author Biographies. 2005, Rosen LB $26.50 (1-4042-0328-1). 112pp. An interview with Paterson is an interesting addition to this description of the author's life and works for children. (Rev: SLJ 9/05) [921]

POE, EDGAR ALLAN

2688 Frisch, Aaron. *Edgar Allan Poe* (5–9). Photos by Tina Mucci. Illus. by Gary Kelley. Series: Voices in Poetry. 2005, Creative Education LB $31.35

(1-58341-344-8). 45pp. A brief biography that adds atmospheric paintings and photographs to a chronological narrative and excerpts from Poe's works. (Rev: SLJ 3/06) [921]

REY, MARGRET AND H. A.

2689 Borden, Louise. *The Journey That Saved Curious George: The True Wartime Escape of Margret and H. A. Rey* (3–6). Illus. by Allan Drummond. 2005, Houghton $17.00 (0-618-33924-8). 80pp. This handsome large-format volume chronicles the escape from Nazism of Margret and H. A. Rey, the creators of the Curious George books for children. (Rev: BL 10/15/05; SLJ 10/05) [813]

ROWLING, J. K.

2690 Harmin, Karen Leigh. *J. K. Rowling: Author of Harry Potter* (4–7). Series: People to Know Today. 2006, Enslow LB $23.95 (0-7660-1850-4). 128pp. An attractive and accessible biography of the creator of the wildly popular series, with details of her youth, career, and the impact success has had on her life; plus information on aspects of British life that will interest young readers. (Rev: BL 11/1/06) [921]

SENDAK, MAURICE

2691 Braun, Eric. *Maurice Sendak* (K–2). Series: First Biographies. 2004, Capstone LB $15.93 (0-7368-3640-3). 24pp. Very basic information on the author/illustrator's life and work for beginning readers and report writers, with photographs and a timeline. (Rev: SLJ 7/05) [921]

SEUSS, DR.

2692 Carlson, Cheryl. *Dr. Seuss* (K–2). Series: First Biographies. 2004, Capstone LB $15.93 (0-7368-3639-X). 24pp. Very basic information on the author's life and work for beginning readers and report writers, with photographs and a timeline. (Rev: SLJ 7/05) [921]

SHAKESPEARE, WILLIAM

2693 Hilliam, David. *William Shakespeare: England's Greatest Playwright and Poet* (5–8). Illus. Series: Rulers, Scholars, and Artists of the Renaissance. 2005, Rosen LB $23.95 (1-4042-0318-4). 112pp. Information on Shakespeare's life and on the theater scene in 16th-century London is interwoven with quotes from the plays and poems. (Rev: BL 8/05) [822.3]

STINE, R. L.

2694 Parker-Rock, Michelle. *R. L. Stine: Creator of Creepy and Spooky Stories* (5–8). Series: Authors Teens Love. 2005, Enslow LB $26.60 (0-7660-2445-8). 104pp. Stine's writing career is the main focus of this biography that includes an interview. (Rev: SLJ 1/06) [921]

STOWE, HARRIET BEECHER

2695 Griskey, Michèle. *Harriet Beecher Stowe* (5–7). Series: Classic Storytellers. 2005, Mitchell Lane LB $19.95 (1-58415-375-X). 48pp. Good historical and social context makes clear the importance of Stowe's achievements. (Rev: SLJ 11/05) [921]

TAYLOR, MILDRED

2696 Houghton, Gillian. *Mildred Taylor* (5–8). Series: The Library of Author Biographies. 2005, Rosen LB $26.50 (1-4042-0330-3). 112pp. An interview with Taylor is an interesting addition to this description of the African American author's life and writings. (Rev: SLJ 9/05) [921]

TWAIN, MARK

2697 Sherman, Josepha. *Mark Twain* (4–6). Series: Classic Storytellers. 2005, Mitchell Lane LB $19.95 (1-58415-374-1). 48pp. In addition to recounting Twain's life and career as an author, this volume touches on the pressing social issues of the day. (Rev: SLJ 2/06) [921]

WHITE, E. B.

2698 Bernard, Catherine. *E. B. White: Spinner of Webs and Tales* (5–8). Series: Authors Teens Love. 2005, Enslow LB $26.60 (0-7660-2350-8). 104pp. An introductory chapter that gives a good overview of White's life is followed by chapters that delve into more detail plus a timeline and an excerpt from a 1969 interview that adds a more personal dimension. (Rev: BCCB 12/05; SLJ 10/05) [921]

WILDER, LAURA INGALLS

2699 Wilder, Laura Ingalls. *A Little House Traveler: Writings from Laura Ingalls Wilder's Journeys Across America* (5–8). 2006, HarperCollins $16.99 (0-06-072491-9). 352pp. Three of Wilder's diaries — one never before published — chronicle the Little House author's travels with her husband Almanzo and daughter Rose. (Rev: BL 12/15/05; VOYA 4/06) [813]

Contemporary and Historical Americans

Collective

2700 Bausum, Ann. *Our Country's First Ladies* (4–8). 2007, National Geographic $19.95 (1-4263-0006-9). 128pp. These profiles of America's first ladies provide material for report writers and enough interest for browsers. (Rev: SLJ 1/07) [920]

2701 Delano, Marfé Ferguson. *American Heroes* (5–8). Illus. 2005, National Geographic LB $45.90 (0-7922-7215-3). 192pp. Fifty men and women whose heroism has helped to shape America are profiled in this attractive large-format volume. (Rev: BL 12/1/05; SLJ 2/06) [920.073]

2702 Fradin, Dennis Brindell. *The Founders: The 39 Stories Behind the U.S. Constitution* (4–7). Illus. by Michael McCurdy. 2005, Walker $22.95 (0-8027-8972-2). 176pp. The 39 men who signed the Constitution are profiled in brief chapters that include information on their home states. (Rev: BL 10/15/05; SLJ 9/05) [973.3]

2703 Kimmel, Elizabeth Cody. *Ladies First: 40 Daring American Women Who Were Second to None* (4–7). 2006, National Geographic $18.95 (0-7922-5393-0). 192pp. From well-known women such as Sacagawea and Helen Keller to racing driver Shirley Muldowney and rabbi Sally Priesand, this is a well-written and informative resource. (Rev: SLJ 10/06; VOYA 8/06) [920]

2704 Masters, Nancy Robinson. *Extraordinary Patriots of the United States of America: Colonial Times to Pre-Civil War* (5–8). Series: Extraordinary People. 2005, Children's Pr. LB $40.00 (0-516-24404-3). 288pp. Interesting 3- to 5-page profiles are arranged chronologically by year of birth. (Rev: SLJ 2/06) [920]

2705 Time For Kids Eds., and Lisa DeMauro. *Presidents of the United States* (3–6). Illus. Series: Time

for Kids. 2006, HarperCollins $17.99 (0-06-081554-X). 70pp. Following a discussion of the three branches of government, this browsable volume covers the presidents in chronological order, giving basic personal information and a portrait, political cartoons, notable quotations, and so forth; several presidents are selected for more in-depth information. (Rev: SLJ 10/06) [920]

African Americans

ARMSTRONG, LOUIS

2706 Kimmel, Eric. *A Horn for Louis* (2–4). Illus. by James Bernardin. Series: Stepping Stones. 2005, Random $11.95 (0-375-83252-1). 96pp. This beginning chapter book tells the story of how jazz musician Louis Armstrong got his first cornet and evokes New Orleans in the early 1900s. (Rev: BL 2/1/06; SLJ 2/06) [921]

COLEMAN, BESSIE

2707 Braun, Eric. *Bessie Coleman* (K–2). Series: First Biographies. 2005, Capstone LB $15.93 (0-7368-4229-2). 24pp. With its simple sentences and clear black-and-white photographs, this profile of the first African American woman to earn a pilot's license gives basic, introductory information. (Rev: SLJ 2/06) [921]

HAMER, FANNIE LOU

2708 Fiorelli, June Estep. *Fannie Lou Hamer: A Voice for Freedom* (5–10). Series: Avisson Young Adult. 2005, Avisson paper $19.95 (1-888105-62-3). 117pp. Hamer's life, including her youth, are described and placed in the context of events in the United States at the time. (Rev: SLJ 2/06) [921]

JEMISON, MAE

2709 Braun, Eric. *Mae Jemison* (K–2). Series: First Biographies. 2005, Capstone LB $15.93 (0-7368-4231-4). 24pp. With its simple sentences and clear black-and-white photographs, this profile of the first African American woman to become an astronaut gives basic, introductory information. (Rev: SLJ 2/06) [921]

2710 Kraske, Robert. *Mae Jemison: Space Pioneer* (1–3). Series: Fact Finders Biographies. 2006, Capstone LB $22.60 (0-7368-6420-0). 32pp. Large, easy-to-read print recounts the life of the first African American astronaut from her childhood through her resignation from NASA in 1994. (Rev: SLJ 1/07) [921]

2711 Raum, Elizabeth. *Mae Jemison* (3–5). Illus. Series: American Lives. 2005, Heinemann LB $18.75 (1-4034-6942-3). 32pp. This is a brief but thorough and easily understood of the first African American woman to become an astronaut. (Rev: BL 2/15/06) [921]

KING, MARTIN LUTHER, JR.

2712 Bolden, Tonya. *M. L. K: Journey of a King* (5–8). 2007, Abrams $19.95 (978-0-8109-5476-2). 128pp. Bolden's excellent biography focuses on King's private life and strongly held beliefs rather than on his public life. (Rev: SLJ 2/07*) [921]

LAW, WESTLEY WALLACE

2713 Haskins, Jim. *Delivering Justice: W. W. Law and the Fight for Civil Rights* (2–4). Illus. by Benny Andrews. 2005, Candlewick $16.99 (0-7636-2592-2). 32pp. A picture-book biography of Westley Wallace Law that chronicles the mail carrier's campaign to win equal treatment for African Americans in his hometown of Savannah, Georgia. (Rev: BL 9/15/05) [921]

LEWIS, JOHN

2714 Haskins, Jim, and Kathleen Benson. *John Lewis in the Lead: A Story of the Civil Rights Movement* (3–5). Illus. by Benny Andrews. 2006, Lee & Low $17.95 (1-58430-250-X). 40pp. This picture-book biography for older readers covers Lewis's civil rights activism, including his role in "Bloody Sunday" in Selma, Alabama, and his political career. (Rev: BL 10/1/06; SLJ 12/06) [921]

MARSHALL, THURGOOD

2715 Taylor-Butler, Christine. *Thurgood Marshall* (1–2). Series: Rookie Biographies. 2006, Children's Pr. LB $19.50 (0-516-25015-9); paper $4.95 (0-516-27099-0). 32pp. For beginning readers, this is a simple introduction to the life of the African Ameri-

can jurist from his childhood in Baltimore to his appointment to the U.S. Supreme Court. (Rev: SLJ 9/06) [921]

MASON, BIDDY

2716 Williams, Jean Kinney. *Bridget "Biddy" Mason: From Slave to Businesswoman* (4–6). Illus. Series: Signature Lives: American Frontier Era. 2005, Compass Point $22.95 (0-7565-1001-5). 112pp. A life of Bridget "Biddy" Mason, who was born a slave in 1818, traveled west with her Mormon master, gained her freedom, and died in 1891 as one of the richest women in Los Angeles. (Rev: BL 10/15/05; SLJ 3/06; VOYA 6/06) [921]

PARKS, ROSA

2717 Collard, Sneed B., III. *Rosa Parks: The Courage to Make a Difference* (3–5). Series: American Heroes. 2006, Benchmark LB $19.95 (978-0-7614-2163-4). 40pp. Parks's life and contributions are clearly described in large typeface and illustrations. (Rev: SLJ 3/07) [921]

2718 Dubowski, Cathy East. *Rosa Parks: Don't Give In!* (2–4). Series: Defining Moments. 2005, Bearport LB $22.60 (1-59716-078-4). 32pp. A clearly written account of Parks's life and contribution to the civil rights movement. (Rev: SLJ 2/06) [921]

2719 Schraff, Anne. *Rosa Parks: "Tired of Giving In"* (4–8). Series: African-American Biography Library. 2005, Enslow LB $31.93 (0-7660-2463-6). 128pp. An accessible profile of Parks and her importance. (Rev: SLJ 10/05) [921]

RICE, CONDOLEEZZA

2720 Ditchfield, Christin. *Condoleezza Rice: America's Leading Stateswoman*. Rev. ed. (5–8). Series: Great Life Stories. 2006, Watts LB $30.50 (978-0-531-13874-8). 111pp. An updated version of the 2003 biography, adding information on Rice's role as secretary of state and the continuing events in Iraq. (Rev: SLJ 2/07) [921]

RUDOLPH, WILMA

2721 Braun, Eric. *Wilma Rudolph* (K–2). Series: First Biographies. 2005, Capstone LB $15.93 (0-7368-4234-9). 24pp. With its simple sentences and clear black-and-white photographs, this profile of the first African American woman to win three gold medals at a single Olympic Games gives basic, introductory information. (Rev: SLJ 2/06) [921]

TUBMAN, HARRIET

2722 Turner, Glenette Tilley. *An Apple for Harriet Tubman* (K–2). Illus. by Susan Ketter. 2006, Albert

Whitman $15.95 (0-8075-0395-9). 32pp. This picture book poignantly re-creates unhappy incidents from Harriet Tubman's childhood as a slave. (Rev: BL 8/06; SLJ 10/06) [921]

2723 Weatherford, Carole Boston. *Moses: When Harriet Tubman Led Her People to Freedom* (1–3). Illus. by Kadir Nelson. 2006, Hyperion $15.99 (0-7868-5175-9). 48pp. Harriet Tubman's first trip north and her determination to return south to rescue others are celebrated in this moving blend of free verse and beautiful art. (Rev: BL 8/06; SLJ 10/06*) [921]

WALKER, MADAM C. J.

2724 Nichols, Catherine. *Madame C. J. Walker* (K–2). Illus. Series: Scholastic News Nonfiction Readers: Biographies. 2005, Scholastic LB $18.00 (0-516-24941-X). 24pp. This brief biography chronicles the inspiring story of the pioneering African American hair-care entrepreneur; large type, simple text, and ample illustrations make this suitable for beginning readers. (Rev: BL 2/1/06; SLJ 4/06) [338.7]

WASHINGTON, BOOKER T.

2725 Braun, Eric. *Booker T. Washington: Great American Educator* (2–6). Illus. by Cynthia Martin. Series: Graphic Library, Graphic Biographies. 2005, Capstone LB $25.26 (0-7368-4630-1). 32pp. This graphic-novel biography profiles the life and career of the noted African American educator and author. (Rev: SLJ 3/06) [921]

YORK (c. 1775–1815)

2726 Pringle, Laurence. *American Slave, American Hero: York of the Lewis and Clark Expedition* (3–5). Illus. by Cornelius Wright. 2006, Boyds Mills $17.95 (1-59078-282-8). 32pp. This is a careful, well-illustrated picture-book biography of York, the slave who was part of the famous expedition, drawing largely on historical journals. (Rev: BL 11/1/06; SLJ 1/07) [917.8]

Hispanic Americans

CHAVEZ, CESAR

2727 Apte, Sunita. *Cesar Chavez: We Can Do It!* (3–4). Series: Defining Moments. 2005, Bearport LB $22.60 (1-59716-073-3). 32pp. An easy-to-read biography with plenty of photographs, this covers Chavez's childhood as well as his achievements. (Rev: SLJ 1/06) [921]

2728 Braun, Eric. *Cesar Chavez: Fighting for Farmworkers* (2–6). Illus. by Harry Roland, et al. Series:

Graphic Library, Graphic Biographies. 2005, Capstone LB $25.26 (0-7368-4631-X). 32pp. A graphic-novel biography that introduces the life of the Mexican American labor leader; includes highlighted quotations from primary sources. (Rev: SLJ 3/06) [921]

2729 Guzman, Lila, and Rick Guzman. *César Chávez: Fighting for Fairness* (3–4). Series: Famous Latinos. 2006, Enslow LB $22.60 (0-7660-2370-2). 32pp. A look at Chavez's early life and his peaceful fight for better conditions for migrant workers, with an attractive layout and many photographs. (Rev: SLJ 3/07) [921]

HUERTA, DOLORES

2730 Gillis, Jennifer Blizin. *Dolores Huerta* (3–6). Series: American Lives. 2005, Heinemann LB $26.79 (1-4034-6980-6). 32pp. Using large type and simple text, this volume describes the Mexican American labor leader's efforts to improve working conditions for farm workers. (Rev: SLJ 4/06) [921]

MORENO, LUISA

2731 Moore, Heidi. *Luisa Moreno* (3–6). Series: American Lives. 2005, Heinemann LB $26.79 (1-4034-6978-4). 32pp. Using large type and simple text, this volume describes the Guatemalan American social activist's fight to improve working conditions for factory workers, particularly those from Latin America. (Rev: SLJ 4/06) [921]

Historical Figures and Important Contemporary Americans

ARNOLD, BENEDICT

2732 Sonneborn, Liz. *Benedict Arnold: Hero and Traitor* (4–8). Series: Leaders of the American Revolution. 2005, Chelsea House LB $24.95 (0-7910-8617-8). 130pp. An even-handed introduction to Arnold's life, presented chronologically with occasional factboxes; suitable for report writers. (Rev: SLJ 1/06) [921]

BATES, MARTIN VAN BUREN

2733 Andreasen, Dan. *The Giant of Seville: A "Tall" Tale Based on a True Story* (PS–2). Illus. 2007, Abrams $15.95 (978-0-8109-0988-5). 32pp. As a retired circus performer, Martin Van Buren Bates, nearly 8 feet tall, wanted a quiet place to live, and the residents of Seville, Ohio, were determined to give him just that. (Rev: BL 2/1/07) [921]

BECKWOURTH, JAMES

2734 Gregson, Susan R. *James Beckwourth: Mountaineer, Scout, and Pioneer* (5–8). Series: Signature Lives. 2005, Compass Point LB $22.95 (0-7565-1000-7). 112pp. Beckwourth was one of the first African Americans to play a role in the exploration of the West. (Rev: SLJ 2/06) [921]

CHAPMAN, OSCAR

2735 Hopkinson, Deborah. *Sweet Land of Liberty* (3–7). 2007, Peachtree $16.95 (978-1-56145-395-5). 32pp. With bold illustrations, this volume traces the life of Oscar Chapman, a white government official who spent much of his life fighting injustice, most notably finding a public venue for singer Marian Anderson after she was denied the right to perform in Constitution Hall. (Rev: BL 4/15/07) [921]

CRANDALL, PRUDENCE

2736 Jurmain, Suzanne. *The Forbidden Schoolhouse: The True and Dramatic Story of Prudence Crandall and Her Students* (5–8). Illus. 2005, Houghton $18.00 (0-618-47302-5). 160pp. The inspiring story of Prudence Crandall, who in the 1830s risked ostracism — and worse — from the townspeople of Canterbury, Connecticut, when she opens her academy to young African American women. (Rev: BCCB 11/05; BL 10/1/05*; HB 11–12/05; HBG 4/06; LMC 8–9/05; SLJ 11/05) [370]

FRANKLIN, BENJAMIN

2737 Barretta, Gene. *Now and Ben: The Modern Inventions of Benjamin Franklin* (2–4). 2006, Holt $16.95 (0-8050-7917-3). 40pp. Franklin's many interests and inventions are the focus of this reader-friendly overview with appealing illustrations. (Rev: BL 3/1/06; SLJ 3/06) [609]

2738 Collard, Sneed B., III. *Benjamin Franklin: The Man Who Could Do Just about Anything* (3–5). Series: American Heroes. 2006, Benchmark LB $19.95 (978-0-7614-2161-0). 40pp. An excellent introductory biography of Franklin, covering his many talents and including attractive well-chosen illustrations and easy-to-read text. (Rev: SLJ 3/07) [921]

2739 Harness, Cheryl. *The Remarkable Benjamin Franklin* (2–5). 2005, National Geographic $17.95 (0-7922-7882-8). 48pp. An appealing profile that combines interesting text with striking illustrations full of details, quotations, and a timeline. (Rev: BCCB 4/06; BL 3/1/06*; HB 3–4/06; HBG 10/06; LMC 3/06; SLJ 11/05) [921]

GLENN, JOHN

2740 Hilliard, Richard. *Godspeed, John Glenn* (1–3). 2006, Boyds Mills $16.95 (1-59078-384-0). 32pp. This picture-book biography offers a brief overview of the astronaut's life but focuses primarily on his first space voyage in the *Friendship 7* capsule. (Rev: BL 10/1/06; SLJ 10/06) [921]

2741 Mitchell, Don. *Liftoff: A Photobiography of John Glenn* (4–6). 2006, National Geographic $17.95 (0-7922-5899-1). 64pp. This photo-filled biography offers a brief overview of the former astronaut's life and many accomplishments. (Rev: BL 8/06) [629.45]

GREENE, NATHANAEL

2742 Mierka, Gregg A. *Nathanael Greene: The General Who Saved the Revolution* (5–8). Illus. Series: Forgotten Heroes of the American Revolution. 2006, OTTN LB $23.95 (1-59556-012-2). 88pp. Employing primary and previously unpublished sources, Mierka's lively text examines Greene's pivotal role as quartermaster general and southern commander in Washington's Revolutionary army. (Rev: BL 1/1–15/07) [973.3]

HAYSLIP, LE LY

2743 Englar, Mary. *Le Ly Hayslip* (5–8). Series: Asian-American Biographies. 2005, Raintree LB $32.86 (1-4109-1055-5). 64pp. An interesting profile of the Vietnamese-born woman who started the East Meets West Foundation. (Rev: SLJ 3/06) [921]

HOOVER, J. EDGAR

2744 Cunningham, Kevin. *J. Edgar Hoover: Controversial FBI Director* (5–8). Series: Signature Lives. 2005, Compass Point LB $22.95 (0-7565-0997-1). 112pp. This introduction to Hoover's career provides limited personal details, concentrating instead on his political ambitions and tendency to ignore ethical standards. (Rev: SLJ 1/06) [921]

HOUSTON, SAM

2745 Harkins, Susan, and William H. Harkins. *Sam Houston* (2–4). Series: A Robbie Reader: What's So Great About? 2006, Mitchell Lane LB $16.95 (1-58415-482-9). 32pp. A life of the Virginia native who led the fight for Texas's independence and was elected its first president after it became a republic. (Rev: SLJ 1/07) [921]

JONES, JOHN PAUL

2746 Cooper, Michael L. *Hero of the High Seas: John Paul Jones* (4–7). 2006, National Geographic $21.95 (0-7922-5547-X). 128pp. This biography focuses on the Scottish immigrant's naval heroics during the American Revolution and includes a detailed timeline and a useful listing of "Words and Expressions from the Days of Sailing Ships." (Rev: BL 6/1–15/06; SLJ 9/06) [973.3]

KENNEDY, ROBERT F.

2747 Koestler-Grack, Rachel A. *The Assassination of Robert F. Kennedy* (5–8). Series: American Moments. 2005, ABDO LB $25.65 (1-59197-931-5). 48pp. Kennedy's assassination is placed in historical context, with a brief biography and discussion of the aftermath of this tragedy. (Rev: SLJ 11/05) [921]

KEY, FRANCIS SCOTT

2748 Kjelle, Marylou Morano. *Francis Scott Key* (1–4). Series: A Robbie Reader, What's So Great About? 2006, Mitchell Lane LB $16.95 (1-58415-474-8). 32pp. This brief biography covers the life of the man who wrote "The Star-Spangled Banner." (Rev: SLJ 11/06)

MACARTHUR, DOUGLAS

2749 Haugen, Brenda. *Douglas MacArthur: America's General* (5–8). Series: Signature Lives. 2005, Compass Point LB $22.95 (0-7565-0994-7). 112pp. This introduction to MacArthur's career provides limited personal details but concentrates instead on his leadership abilities and military achievements. (Rev: SLJ 1/06) [921]

OBAMA, BARACK

2750 Brill, Marlene Targ. *Barack Obama: Working to Make a Difference* (5–8). Illus. Series: Gateway Biography. 2006, Lerner LB $23.93 (0-8225-3417-7). 48pp. Obama, the U.S. senator from Illinois, is profiled with details of his family life, education, and entrance to politics. (Rev: BL 3/15/06; SLJ 8/06) [328.73]

OMIDYAR, PIERRE

2751 Viegas, Jennifer. *Pierre Omidyar: The Founder of eBay* (5–8). Illus. Series: Internet Career Biographies. 2006, Rosen LB $31.95 (1-4042-0715-5). 112pp. A look at the successful founder of eBay and his hopes for the future. (Rev: BL 10/15/06) [921]

PATTON, GEORGE S., JR.

2752 Sutcliffe, Jane. *George S. Patton Jr.* (2–5). Illus. Series: History Maker Bios. 2005, Lerner LB $25.26 (0-8225-2436-8); paper $6.95 (0-8225-5461-5). 48pp. The life and times of the general, with plenty of information for report writers; includes photographs, drawings, and Web sites. (Rev: SLJ 8/05) [921]

POWELL, COLIN

2753 Shichtman, Sandra H. *Colin Powell: "Have a Vision. Be Demanding."* (5–8). Series: African-American Biography Library. 2005, Enslow LB $31.93 (0-7660-2464-4). 128pp. Sandra H. Shichtman profiles former Secretary of State Colin Powell in this title from the African-American Biography Library series. (Rev: SLJ 11/05) [921]

REVERE, PAUL

2754 Tieck, Sarah. *Paul Revere* (K–3). Series: First Biographies. 2006, ABDO LB $15.95 (978-1-59679-787-1). 32pp. A beginner's profile of Paul Revere and his contributions to American history, with lots of illustrations, a large typeface, and highlighted words that appear in the glossary. (Rev: SLJ 3/07) [921]

TIENDA, MARTA

2755 O'Connell, Diane. *People Person: The Story of Sociologist Marta Tienda* (5–8). Series: Women's Adventures in Science. 2005, Watts LB $31.00 (0-531-16781-X). 108pp. An informative and accessible profile of sociologist Marta Tienda and her work to create opportunities for people around the world. (Rev: SLJ 12/05) [921]

Native Americans

CRAZY HORSE (SIOUX CHIEF)

2756 Haugen, Brenda. *Crazy Horse: Sioux Warrior* (5–8). Series: Signature Lives. 2005, Compass Point LB $22.95 (0-7565-0999-8). 112pp. Crazy Horse's life and efforts to save his native lands and way of life are documented here. (Rev: SLJ 2/06) [921]

GERONIMO

2757 Feinstein, Stephen. *Read About Geronimo* (2–4). Series: I Like Biographies! 2006, Enslow LB $21.26 (0-7660-2598-5). 24pp. This brief, introductory biography of Geronimo offers an overview of Apache life and the achievements of one of its greatest chiefs. (Rev: SLJ 4/06) [921]

2758 Haugen, Brenda. *Geronimo: Apache Warrior* (5–8). Series: Signature Lives. 2005, Compass Point LB $22.95 (0-7565-1002-3). 112pp. Geronimo's unsuccessful efforts to secure freedom for his people are documented in this attractive book. (Rev: SLJ 2/06) [921]

HAYES, IRA

2759 Nelson, S. D. *Quiet Hero* (3–5). 2006, Lee & Low $16.95 (1-58430-263-1). 32pp. Traces the short life of Ira Hayes, a shy Native American who was one of the marines shown raising the flag at Iwo Jima but, despite his acclaim as a hero, slid into depression on his return home. (Rev: BL 9/15/06; SLJ 9/06) [921]

SACAGAWEA

2760 Collard, Sneed B., III. *Sacagawea: Brave Shoshone Girl* (2–4). Illus. Series: American Heroes. 2006, Marshall Cavendish LB $19.95 (978-0-7614-2166-5). 48pp. Archival images add to this life of the Shoshone Indian, which looks at her early life as well as her experiences on the Lewis and Clark expedition. (Rev: BL 1/1–15/07; SLJ 3/07) [921]

Presidents

BUSH, GEORGE W.

2761 Jones, Veda Boyd. *George W. Bush* (5–8). Illus. Series: Modern World Leaders. 2006, Chelsea House $30.00 (0-7910-9217-8). 128pp. This biography traces Bush's life and political career from his 1946 birth in New Haven, Connecticut, through the first five years of his presidency. (Rev: BL 10/15/06) [973.9]

2762 Marquez, Heron. *George W. Bush* (5–8). Illus. Series: Presidential Leaders. 2006, Lerner LB $29.27 (0-8225-1507-5). 112pp. A balanced profile that examines Bush's childhood and adolescence as well as his accomplishments and the controversies surrounding some of his decisions. (Rev: BL 10/15/06) [921]

GRANT, ULYSSES S.

2763 Sapp, Richard. *Ulysses S. Grant and the Road to Appomattox* (5–8). Series: In the Footsteps of American Heroes. 2006, World Almanac LB $32.67 (0-8368-6431-X). 64pp. This life of Grant includes information on historical sites in sidebar features. (Rev: SLJ 9/06) [921]

KENNEDY, JOHN F.

2764 Jones, Veda Boyd. *John F. Kennedy* (1–2). Series: Rookie Biographies. 2006, Children's Pr. LB $19.50 (0-516-25038-8); paper $4.95 (0-516-29797-X). 32pp. For beginning readers, this is a simple introduction to the life of the president. (Rev: SLJ 9/06) [921]

LINCOLN, ABRAHAM

2765 *Abraham Lincoln: Defender of the Union* (4–6). Series: The Civil War. 2005, Cobblestone

$17.95 (0-8126-7902-4). 47pp. This solid profile with excellent illustrations covers Lincoln's childhood, courtship of Mary Todd, family life, political career, and presidency. (Rev: HBG 10/06; SLJ 3/06) [921]

2766 Collard, Sneed B., III. *Abraham Lincoln: A Courageous Leader* (3–5). Series: American Heroes. 2006, Benchmark LB $19.95 (978-0-7614-2162-7). 40pp. A basic biography of the sixteenth president, featuring interesting facts about his life and career presented in large typeface with large illustrations. (Rev: SLJ 3/07) [921]

2767 Olson, Kay Melchisedech. *The Assassination of Abraham Lincoln* (3–6). Illus. by Otha Zachariah Edward Lohse. Series: Graphic Library/Graphic History. 2005, Capstone LB $22.60 (0-7368-3831-7). 32pp. This graphic "novel" — factual, but embellished — about the fateful event will appeal to reluctant readers. (Rev: SLJ 7/05) [921]

ROOSEVELT, FRANKLIN D.

2768 Haugen, Brenda. *Franklin Delano Roosevelt: The New Deal President* (4–8). Series: Signature Lives. 2006, Compass Point LB $30.60 (0-7565-1586-6). 112pp. Slim but fact-filled, this is a useful biography for report writers, with excerpts from speeches and writings and full discussion of key events in Roosevelt's life. (Rev: SLJ 9/06) [921]

2769 St. George, Judith. *Make Your Mark, Franklin Roosevelt* (2–5). Illus. by Britt Spencer. Series: Turning Point. 2007, Philomel $16.99 (978-0-399-24175-8). Focuses on the president's childhood and his decision as a teenager to move beyond his life of privilege and devote himself to public service. (Rev: BL 11/15/06; SLJ 2/07*) [921]

ROOSEVELT, THEODORE

2770 Keating, Frank. *Theodore* (2–6). Illus. by Mike Wimmer. 2006, Simon & Schuster $16.95 (0-689-86532-5). This attractive and compelling biography of Theodore Roosevelt examines all aspects of his life and emphasizes his loves of nature, reading, and hard work. (Rev: SLJ 3/06*) [921]

TYLER, JOHN

2771 Venezia, Mike. *John Tyler* (3–5). Illus. by author. Series: Getting to Know the U.S. Presidents. 2005, Children's Pr. LB $26.00 (0-516-22615-0). 32pp. A lighthearted introduction to the 10th president, with plenty of visual information. (Rev: SLJ 7/05) [921]

WASHINGTON, GEORGE

2772 Adler, David A. *President George Washington* (1–3). Illus. by John Wallner. Series: Holiday House

Reader. 2005, Holiday $16.95 (0-8234-1604-6). 32pp. For beginning readers, this picture-book biography that gives a brief overview of Washington's youth and adult accomplishments uses short sentences, large typeface, and lots of white space. (Rev: BL 9/15/05; SLJ 11/05) [921]

2773 Jurmain, Suzanne. *George Did It* (2–4). Illus. by Larry Day. 2005, Dutton $16.99 (0-525-47560-5). 40pp. George Washington's reluctance to take on the responsibilities of the presidency is depicted in lively text and cartoon drawings. (Rev: BL 12/15/05*; SLJ 12/05*) [921]

2774 McNeese, Tim. *George Washington: America's Leader in War and Peace* (4–8). Series: Leaders of the American Revolution. 2005, Chelsea House LB $24.95 (0-7910-8619-4). 140pp. An even-handed introduction to Washington's life and contributions, presented chronologically with occasional factboxes; suitable for report writers. (Rev: SLJ 1/06) [921]

First Ladies and Other Women

ANTHONY, SUSAN B.

2775 Hopkinson, Deborah. *Susan B. Anthony: Fighter for Women's Rights* (2–4). Illus. by Amy Bates. Series: Ready to Read: Stories of America. 2005, Simon & Schuster $11.89 (0-689-86910-X); paper $3.99 (0-689-86909-6). 32pp. This brief biography focuses on Anthony's lifelong fight for women's rights. (Rev: BL 2/1/06; SLJ 5/06) [305.42]

BARTON, CLARA

2776 Dubowski, Cathy East. *Clara Barton: I Want to Help!* (3–5). Illus. Series: Defining Moments. 2005, Bearport LB $16.95 (1-59716-075-X). 32pp. This inspiring biography of Clara Barton tells how she overcame her shyness to nurse the wounded on bloody Civil War battlefields and later established the American Red Cross. (Rev: BL 10/15/05; SLJ 2/06) [921]

MORGAN, JULIA

2777 Mannis, Celeste Davidson. *Julia Morgan Built a Castle* (2–4). Illus. by Miles Hyman. 2006, Viking $17.99 (0-670-05964-1). 40pp. This intriguing large-format biography covers the life of Julia Morgan, who grew up in the late 19th century, achieved many "firsts" for women in the field, and designed many impressive buildings — including William Randolph Hearst's huge castle at San Simeon. (Rev: BL 11/15/06; SLJ 11/06) [921]

MORRIS, ESTHER

2778 White, Linda Arms. *I Could Do That! Esther Morris Gets Women the Vote* (2–4). Illus. by Nancy Carpenter. 2005, Farrar $16.00 (0-374-33527-3). 40pp. The story of Esther Morris, the little-known suffragist who led a successful campaign to win the vote for women in the Wyoming Territory. (Rev: BL 9/15/05*; SLJ 9/05) [324.6]

O'CONNOR, SANDRA DAY

2779 O'Connor, Sandra Day. *Chico: A True Story from the Childhood of the First Woman Supreme Court Justice* (1–3). Illus. by Dan Andreasen. 2005, Dutton $16.99 (0-525-47452-8). 32pp. Former Supreme Court justice O'Connor gives a good sense of her youth in Arizona in this story about coming across a rattlesnake when riding on her horse Chico as a 6-year-old. (Rev: BL 10/1/05; SLJ 9/05) [921]

OTERO, KATHERINE STINSON

2780 Petrick, Neila Skinner. *Katherine Stinson Otero: High Flyer* (K–3). Illus. by Daggi Wallace. 2006, Pelican $15.95 (1-58980-368-X). The story of one of the first American women pilots, with information about her world travels and plenty of illustrations. (Rev: SLJ 6/06) [921]

PEARY, MARIE AHNIGHITO

2781 Kirkpatrick, Katherine. *The Snow Baby: The Arctic Childhood of Robert E. Peary's Daring Daughter* (5–8). Illus. 2007, Holiday $16.95 (978-0-8234-1973-9). 48pp. This engaging account of a child growing up partly among the Inuit and partly in her mother's nice home in the United States is based on the autobiography, published in 1934, of Marie Ahnighito Peary, daughter of explorer Robert E. Peary, who was born north of the Arctic Circle in 1893. (Rev: BL 4/15/07) [921]

RANKIN, JEANNETTE

2782 Marx, Trish. *Jeannette Rankin: First Lady of Congress* (3–5). Illus. by Dan Andreasen. 2006, Simon & Schuster $18.95 (0-689-86290-3). 48pp. This biography uses clear and simple text to chronicle the life and times of the first woman elected to the U.S. House of Representatives. (Rev: BL 1/1–15/06; SLJ 2/06) [921]

ROOSEVELT, ELEANOR

2783 Jacobson, Ryan. *Eleanor Roosevelt: First Lady of the World* (2–6). Illus. by Gordon Purcell and Barbara Schulz. Series: Graphic Library, Graphic Biographies. 2005, Capstone LB $25.26 (0-7368-4969-6). 32pp. This graphic-novel biography introduces Roosevelt's life and discusses her active support of her husband's domestic programs and her increased involvement in foreign affairs after her husband's death. (Rev: SLJ 3/06) [921]

2784 Lassieur, Allison. *Eleanor Roosevelt: Activist for Social Change* (5–8). Series: Great Life Stories. 2006, Watts LB $30.50 (978-0-531-13871-7). 111pp. This biography of Eleanor Roosevelt focuses on the first lady's personal life and on her social activism while in the White House and later as an envoy to the United Nations. (Rev: SLJ 2/07) [921]

2785 MacLeod, Elizabeth. *Eleanor Roosevelt: An Inspiring Life* (4–6). 2006, Kids Can $14.95 (1-55337-778-8); paper $6.95 (1-55337-811-3). 32pp. Traces the first lady's life from her difficult childhood to the humanitarian work that she pursued after the death of her husband, with many quotations and period photographs. (Rev: SLJ 11/06) [921]

2786 Somervill, Barbara A. *Eleanor Roosevelt: First Lady of the World* (5–8). Illus. Series: Signature Lives: Modern America. 2005, Compass Point $22.95 (0-7565-0992-0). 112pp. An appealing biography that traces the First Lady's life and focuses on her tireless efforts to make life better for America's disadvantaged minorities. (Rev: BL 10/15/05) [973.917]

STANTON, ELIZABETH CADY

2787 Miller, Connie Colwell. *Elizabeth Cady Stanton: Women's Rights Pioneer* (2–6). Illus. by Cynthia Martin. Series: Graphic Library, Graphic Biographies. 2005, Capstone LB $25.26 (0-7368-

4971-8). 32pp. This graphic-novel biography covers Stanton's role in the women's rights movement and provides links to related online resources. (Rev: SLJ 3/06) [921]

SUZUKI, HIROMI

2788 Barasch, Lynne. *Hiromi's Hands* (K–3). Illus. 2007, Lee & Low $17.95 (978-1-58430-275-9). 32pp. This picture-book biography of Japanese American sushi chef Hiromi Suzuki begins with the immigration of her father — also a successful sushi chef — to the United States from Japan. (Rev: BL 3/15/07) [921]

WHITMAN, NARCISSA

2789 Harness, Cheryl. *The Tragic Tale of Narcissa Whitman and a Faithful History of the Oregon Trail* (4–7). Illus. 2006, National Geographic $16.95 (0-7922-5920-3). 144pp. A biography of Narcissa Whitman, the first woman to cross the Rockies on the perilous Oregon Trail in order to bring her Christian beliefs to the Indians of that area. (Rev: BL 12/1/06) [917.804]

WONG, LI KENG

2790 Wong, Li Keng. *Good Fortune: My Journey to Gold Mountain* (4–7). 2006, Peachtree $14.95 (1-56145-367-6). 144pp. Wong, who migrated to the United States from China with her mother and sister in 1933, writes about the challenges of adjusting to a new culture. (Rev: BL 3/1/06; SLJ 7/06) [979.4]

Scientists, Inventors, Naturalists, and Business Figures

Collective

2791 Kang, Zhu. *Science and Scientists* (3–5). Illus. by Hong Tao and Feng Congying. Series: True Stories from Ancient China. 2005, Long River $9.95 (1-59265-038-4). 48pp. Profiles the lives and accomplishments of four ancient Chinese scientists — Zhang Heng, Zu Chongzhi, Yi Xing, and Xu Xiake. (Rev: BL 12/1/05) [509.22]

2792 Kimmel, Elizabeth Cody. *Dinosaur Bone War: Cope and Marsh's Fossil Feud* (4–7). Illus. 2006, Random $11.99 (0-375-91349-1); paper $5.99 (0-375-81349-7). 128pp. The story of American fossil hunters Edward Cope and Othniel Charles Marsh and the bitter rivalry that led to many dinosaur fossil discoveries and spurred the development of paleontology as a science. (Rev: BL 12/1/06) [560.92]

Individual

ARCHIMEDES

2793 Gow, Mary. *Archimedes: Mathematical Genius of the Ancient World* (5–8). Illus. Series: Great Minds of Science. 2005, Enslow LB $26.60 (0-7660-2502-0). 128pp. Archimedes' mathematical discoveries are explained and placed in social, scientific, and cultural context. (Rev: SLJ 12/05) [921]

BELL, ALEXANDER GRAHAM

2794 Williams, Brian. *Bell and the Science of the Telephone* (4–6). Illus. by David Antram. Series: The Explosion Zone. 2006, Barron's $12.99 (0-7641-5972-0). 32pp. This biography focuses on Bell's invention of the telephone and its impact but also touches on the related topics of Morse code,

BROWN, BARNUM

2795 Sheldon, David. *Barnum Brown: Dinosaur Hunter* (2–4). Illus. by author. 2006, Walker $16.95 (0-8027-9602-8). 32pp. A compelling picture-book biography of dinosaur hunter Barnum Brown, who was fascinated by fossils from a young age and discovered a Tyrannosaurus rex in the early 20th century. (Rev: BL 12/1/06; SLJ 11/06) [560.92]

CRUM, GEORGE

2796 Taylor, Gaylia. *George Crum and the Saratoga Chip* (2–4). Illus. by Frank Morrison. 2006, Lee & Low $16.95 (1-58430-255-0). 32pp. This attractive picture book recounts how George Crum, a chef of mixed African American and Native American ancestry, invented the potato chip to please a demanding customer and eventually opened his own restaurant. (Rev: BL 4/1/06; SLJ 5/06) [921]

CURIE, MARIE

2797 Birch, Beverley. *Marie Curie, Spanish and English* (5–8). Series: Giants of Science Bilingual. 2005, Gale LB $21.96 (1-4103-0505-8). 64pp. English and Spanish versions of this life of Curie are presented side by side, and the timeline, glossary, and index are also bilingual. (Rev: SLJ 2/06) [921]

2798 Graham, Ian. *Curie and the Science of Radioactivity* (4–6). Illus. by David Antram. Series: The Explosion Zone. 2006, Barron's $12.99 (0-7641-5973-9). 32pp. This biography of Marie Curie covers the Polish-born scientist's life and career and explains concepts related to her work, including half-life, transmutation, and the measurement of radiation; suitable for report writers despite cartoon illustrations. (Rev: SLJ 11/06) [921]

2799 McCormick, Lisa Wade. *Marie Curie* (1–2). Series: Rookie Biographies. 2006, Children's Pr. LB $19.50 (0-516-25040-X); paper $4.95 (0-516-21445-4). 32pp. For beginning readers, this is a simple overview of the scientist's life with emphasis on her discoveries. (Rev: SLJ 9/06) [921]

DARWIN, CHARLES

2800 Greenberger, Robert. *Darwin and the Theory of Evolution* (5–8). Series: Primary Sources of Revolutionary Scientific Discoveries and Theories. 2005, Rosen LB $29.25 (1-4042-0306-0). 64pp. Profiles English naturalist Charles Darwin and the events that led up to his groundbreaking theory of evolution; useful for brief reports. (Rev: SLJ 11/05) [921]

EDISON, THOMAS ALVA

2801 Carlson, Laurie. *Thomas Edison for Kids: His Life and Ideas: 21 Activities* (4–7). Illus. 2006, Chicago Review paper $14.95 (1-55652-584-2). 160pp. Activities allow readers to try some of the inventor's experiments; the biography section covers Edison's personal life as well as his achievements and introduces some of his contemporaries. (Rev: BL 2/15/06; SLJ 6/06) [621.3]

2802 Dooling, Michael. *Young Thomas Edison* (1–3). Illus. 2005, Holiday $16.95 (0-8234-1868-5). 40pp. This engaging biography focuses on the inventor's youth, his hearing loss, his homeschooling, and his early experiments. (Rev: BL 1/1–15/06; SLJ 2/06*) [921]

EINSTEIN, ALBERT

2803 Lakin, Patricia. *Albert Einstein: Genius of the Twentieth Century* (2–4). Illus. by Alan Daniel. Series: Ready-to-Read: Stories of Famous Americans. 2005, Simon & Schuster LB $11.89 (0-689-87035-3); paper $3.99 (0-689-87034-5). 48pp. This effective easy-to-read biography describes Einstein's intelligence and key accomplishments. (Rev: BL 12/1/05) [921]

2804 Lassieur, Allison. *Albert Einstein: Genius of the Twentieth Century* (5–8). Series: Great Life Stories. 2005, Watts LB $29.50 (0-531-12401-0). 127pp. In addition to placing Einstein's life (including his childhood) and contributions in historical and social context, Lassieur explains his theories and their application. (Rev: SLJ 9/05) [921]

ERICSSON, JOHN

2805 Wooldridge, Connie Nordhielm. *Thank You Very Much, Captain Ericsson* (1–5). Illus. by

Andrew Glass. 2005, Holiday House $16.95 (0-8234-1626-7). The struggles of the Civil-War era inventor are presented in lighthearted text with funny cartoons. (Rev: SLJ 8/05) [921]

FULTON, ROBERT

2806 Whiting, Jim. *Robert Fulton* (2–4). Series: A Robbie Reader: What's So Great About? 2006, Mitchell Lane LB $16.95 (1-58415-478-0). 32pp. With large text and lots of white space, this introductory biography looks at the life and career of the man responsible for developing the first commercially successful steam-powered vessel. (Rev: SLJ 1/07) [921]

GALILEO

2807 Hilliam, Rachel. *Galileo Galilei: Father of Modern Science* (5–8). Series: Rulers, Scholars, and Artists of the Renaissance. 2005, Rosen LB $31.95 (1-4042-0314-1). 112pp. Ford places Galileo's life and accomplishments in the context of culture and politics of the time. (Rev: SLJ 10/05) [921]

2808 Lewis, J. Patrick. *Galileo's Universe* (3–5). Illus. by Tom Curry. 2005, Creative Editions $17.95 (1-56846-183-6). 18pp. This unusual pop-up biography recounts the life of Galileo in rhyming verse. (Rev: BL 12/1/05) [921]

2809 Panchyk, Richard. *Galileo for Kids: His Life and Ideas* (5–9). Illus. 2005, Chicago Review paper $16.95 (1-55652-566-4). 166pp. A clearly written and well-illustrated overview of Galileo's life and scientific achievements, with excerpts from Galileo's writings and suggested activities. (Rev: SLJ 9/05) [921]

2810 Steele, Philip. *Galileo: The Genius Who Faced the Inquisition* (3–6). Series: National Geographic World History Biographies. 2005, National Geographic $17.95 (0-7922-3656-4). 64pp. The scientist's place in history is clearly set out in this well-designed, informative book. (Rev: SLJ 6/06) [921]

GOODALL, JANE

2811 Kittinger, Jo S. *Jane Goodall* (1–2). Series: Scholastic News Nonfiction Readers. 2005, Children's Pr. LB $18.00 (0-516-24940-1). 24pp. This simple, photo-filled biography for beginning readers spotlights Goodall's breakthrough work with chimpanzees. (Rev: SLJ 4/06) [921]

HOWARD, LUKE

2812 Hannah, Julie, and Joan Holub. *The Man Who Named the Clouds* (3–5). Illus. by Paige Billin-Frye. 2006, Albert Whitman $15.95 (0-8075-4974-6). 40pp. This fascinating book intertwines a profile of

Luke Howard, the man who classified clouds into seven types, with a contemporary boy's weather journal. (Rev: BL 8/06; SLJ 10/06) [921]

JACKSON, SHIRLEY ANN

2813 O'Connell, Diane. *Strong Force: The Story of Physicist Shirley Ann Jackson* (5–8). Series: Women's Adventures in Science. 2005, Watts LB $31.00 (0-531-16784-4). 110pp. The life and scientific career of Jackson, physicist and former chairman of the U.S. Nuclear Regulatory Commission. (Rev: SLJ 12/05) [921]

KNIGHT, MARGARET E.

2814 McCully, Emily Arnold. *Marvelous Mattie: How Margaret E. Knight Became an Inventor* (K–3). Illus. 2006, Farrar $16.00 (0-374-34810-3). 32pp. The life of the 19th-century inventor of a machine that made paper grocery bags, among other products, and fought a court battle to get a patent. (Rev: BL 2/15/06; SLJ 2/06) [921]

MENDEL, GREGOR

2815 Bardoe, Cheryl. *Gregor Mendel: The Friar Who Grew Peas* (2–4). Illus. by Joe A. Smith. 2006, Abrams $18.95 (0-8109-5475-3). 32pp. A biography of the father of genetics, with child-friendly explanations of the science and accompanied by beautiful watercolors. (Rev: BL 7/06) [921]

MUIR, JOHN

2816 Lasky, Kathryn. *John Muir: America's First Environmentalist* (4–7). Illus. by Stan Fellows. 2006, Candlewick $16.99 (0-76361-957-4). 32pp. Quotations from Muir's diary and double-page landscape watercolors add to the narrative about the pioneering environmentalist in this attractive picture-book biography. (Rev: BL 2/1/06; SLJ 4/06) [333.7]

NEWTON, SIR ISAAC

2817 Krull, Kathleen. *Isaac Newton* (5–8). Illus. by Boris Kulikov. Series: Giants of Science. 2006, Viking $15.99 (0-670-05921-8). 128pp. Newton's childhood and adult personality are highlighted in this readable biography that gives good explanations

of his scientific theories. (Rev: BL 4/1/06; SLJ 3/06*; VOYA 6/06) [530]

OPPENHEIMER, J. ROBERT

2818 Allman, Toney. *J. Robert Oppenheimer: Father of the Atomic Bomb* (5–9). Series: Giants of Science. 2005, Gale $24.95 (1-56711-889-5). 64pp. Controversial physicist Oppenheimer, who played a key role in the development of the atomic bomb, is profiled in readable text with lots of details for report writers. (Rev: SLJ 7/05) [921]

RINGLING BROTHERS

2819 Apps, Jerry. *Tents, Tigers, and the Ringling Brothers* (3–7). Illus. 2006, Wisconsin Historical Soc. paper $12.95 (978-0-87020-374-9). The true story of how the seven Ringling Brothers followed their dreams and began their own circus, describing their day-to-day struggles to keep the business successful. (Rev: BL 2/15/07) [920]

VEDDER, AMY

2820 Ebersole, Rene. *Gorilla Mountain: The Story of Wildlife Biologist Amy Vedder* (5–8). Series: Women's Adventures in Science. 2005, Watts LB $31.00 (0-531-16779-8). 118pp. An informative and accessible account of Vedder's efforts to protect the endangered mountain gorillas of Rwanda. (Rev: SLJ 12/05)

WHITNEY, ELI

2821 Gibson, Karen Bush. *The Life and Times of Eli Whitney* (5–8). Illus. Series: Profiles in American History. 2006, Mitchell Lane LB $19.95 (1-58415-434-9). 48pp. An interesting profile of the cotton gin inventor, with period reproductions and relevant sidebar features. (Rev: BL 10/15/06) [609.2]

WRIGHT, WILBUR AND ORVILLE

2822 Tieck, Sarah. *Wright Brothers* (K–3). Series: First Biographies. 2006, ABDO LB $15.95 (978-1-59679-790-1). 32pp. A beginner's profile of Wilbur and Orville Wright and their contributions to the development of the airplane, with lots of illustrations, a large typeface, and highlighted words that appear in the glossary. (Rev: SLJ 3/07) [921]

Sports Figures

Collective

2823 Hotchkiss, Ron. *The Matchless Six: The Story of Canada's First Women's Olympic Team* (5–8). Illus. 2006, Tundra $16.95 (0-88776-738-9). 200pp. Profiles the individual athletes and achievements of Canada's groundbreaking women's Olympic team of 1928. (Rev: BL 3/15/06; SLJ 6/06) [796.48]

2824 Lipsyte, Robert. *Heroes of Baseball: The Men Who Made It America's Favorite Game* (4–7). Illus. 2006, Simon & Schuster $19.95 (0-689-86741-7). 96pp. As well as introducing key players of the game, this volume presents a concise history of the sport itself. (Rev: BL 2/15/06; SLJ 4/06) [796.357]

2825 Piven, Hanoch. *What Athletes Are Made Of* (2–4). 2006, Simon & Schuster $16.95 (1-4169-1002-6). 40pp. Each of the well-known athletes in this visually interesting, offbeat book has an unusual feature to show what he or she is "made of." (Rev: BL 7/06; SLJ 8/06) [920]

2826 Rappoport, Ken. *Profiles in Sports Courage* (4–7). 2006, Peachtree $15.95 (1-56145-368-4). 160pp. Twelve stories of bravery on and off the playing field (or court, ring, or track) by men and women from all types of sport and from all around the world. (Rev: BL 7/06; SLJ 6/06) [796.092]

2827 Shea, Therese. *Soccer Stars* (3–5). Series: Greatest Sports Heroes. 2006, Children's Pr. $24.00 (0-531-12588-2). 48pp. Profiles some of today's best-known soccer players, including Freddy Adu, David Beckham, and Kristine Lilly. (Rev: BL 9/1/06) [920]

2828 Woods, Bob. *Racer Girls* (2–5). Series: Girls Rock! 2006, The Child's World LB $24.21 (1-59296-742-6). 32pp. Profiles female racing car drivers around the world in large text and full-color photographs; suitable for browsing by beginning readers. (Rev: SLJ 4/07) [920]

Automobile Racing

LABONTE, TERRY AND BOBBY

2829 Hubbard-Brown, Janet. *The Labonte Brothers* (4–8). Series: Race Car Legends: Collector's Edition. 2005, Chelsea House LB $25.00 (0-7910-8767-0). 72pp. The famous brothers Terry and Bobby Labonte and their racing rivalry and successes are the focus of this readable, photo-filled volume. (Rev: SLJ 5/06) [921]

UNSER FAMILY

2830 Bentley, Karen. *The Unsers* (4–8). Series: Race Car Legends: Collector's Edition. 2005, Chelsea House LB $25.00 (0-7910-8764-6). 72pp. The famous Unser automobile racing family is the focus of this book that describes their rivalries with the Andretti family and their victories at important races including the Indianapolis 500. (Rev: SLJ 5/06) [921]

Baseball

CAMPANELLA, ROY

2831 Adler, David A. *Campy: The Story of Roy Campanella* (2–4). Illus. by Gordon C. James. 2007, Viking (978-0-670-06041-2). African American baseball player joined the Brooklyn Dodgers only a year after Jackie Robinson and was a major star until a 1958 accident left him paralyzed. (Rev: BL 2/1/07; SLJ 4/07) [921]

GREENBERG, HANK

2832 McDonough, Yona Zeldis. *Hammerin' Hank: The Life of Hank Greenberg* (K–2). Illus. by Malcah Zeldis. 2006, Walker $16.95 (0-8027-8997-8). 32pp. This profile of the first Jewish American baseball star discusses his parents' disapproval of his choice of career, the prejudice he faced, and the difficult decisions he had to make. (Rev: BL 3/1/06; SLJ 4/06*) [921]

JETER, DEREK

2833 Robinson, Tom. *Derek Jeter: Captain On and Off the Field* (5–8). Series: Sports Stars with Heart. 2006, Enslow LB $23.95 (0-7660-2819-4). 128pp. This biography focuses primarily on Jeter's career in baseball and his work with the philanthropic Turn 2 Foundation. (Rev: BL 9/1/06) [921]

PAIGE, SATCHEL

2834 Adler, David A. *Satchel Paige: Don't Look Back* (K–3). Illus. by Terry Widener. Series: Paige, Satchel. 2007, Harcourt $16.00 (0-15-205585-1). 32pp. This picture-book biography gives a the great pitcher's early life and successful career in both the Negro leagues and the majors. (Rev: BL 1/1–15/07) [921]

ROBINSON, JACKIE

2835 Ford, Carin T. *Jackie Robinson: Hero of Baseball* (2–4). Illus. Series: Heroes of American History. 2006, Enslow LB $16.95 (0-7660-2600-0). 32pp. A brief, readable account of Robinson's life and accomplishments, with information about segregation in general. (Rev: BL 2/1/06; SLJ 8/06) [921]

2836 Wukovits, John F. *Jackie Robinson and the Integration of Baseball* (5–8). Series: The Lucent Library of Black History. 2006, Gale LB $28.70 (978-1-59018-913-9). 104pp. The social background to Robinson's achievements is well laid out in this biography suitable for report writers. (Rev: SLJ 3/07) [921]

Boxing

LOUIS, JOE

2837 Adler, David A. *Joe Louis: America's Fighter* (2–6). Illus. by Terry Widener. 2005, Harcourt $16.00 (0-15-216489-4). 32pp. This picture-book biography looks at the obstacles the boxer had to overcome to become a world champion. (Rev: BCCB 12/05; BL 9/1/05; HB 1–2/06; HBG 4/06; LMC 3/06) [921]

Football

BARBER, RONDE AND TIKI

2838 Barber, Tiki, and Ronde Barber. *Game Day* (1–3). Illus. by Barry Root. 2005, Simon & Schuster $16.95 (1-4169-0093-4). 32pp. The NFL's Barber twins tell a simple story about their football-playing youth and the rivalry between them. (Rev: BL 9/1/05; SLJ 1/06) [921]

2839 Barber, Tiki, and Ronde Barber. *Teammates* (1–3). Illus. by Barry Root. 2006, Simon & Schuster $16.95 (1-4169-2489-2). 32pp. Downcast after their football team loses a game, twin brothers Tiki and Ronde begin a morning practice routine designed to improve Tiki's ball-handling abilities; a large-format picture book illustrated with watercolor-and-gouache paintings. (Rev: BL 9/1/06; SLJ 11/06) [921]

Tennis

ASHE, ARTHUR

2840 Mantell, Paul. *Arthur Ashe: Young Tennis Champion* (3–5). Illus. by Meryl Henderson. Series: Childhood of Famous Americans. 2006, Simon & Schuster paper $5.99 (0-689-87346-8). 224pp. Ashe's childhood encounters with prejudice and his success on the tennis court are recounted in this fictionalized biography that is faithful to real events. (Rev: BL 2/1/06) [921]

WILLIAMS, VENUS

2841 Sandler, Michael. *Tennis: Victory for Venus Williams* (3–5). Series: Upsets and Comebacks. 2006, Bearport LB $23.96 (1-59716-170-5). 32pp. Venus Williams's determination to keep winning despite physical and emotional challenges is underlined here. (Rev: SLJ 7/06) [796.352]

Track and Field

THORPE, JIM

2842 Brown, Don. *Bright Path: Young Jim Thorpe* (K–3). Illus. by author. 2006, Roaring Brook $17.95 (1-59643-041-9). The importance of athletics in Thorpe's unhappy childhood is emphasized in this nicely illustrated biography. (Rev: SLJ 11/06) [921]

2843 Bruchac, Joseph. *Jim Thorpe: Original All-American* (5–8). 2006, Dial $16.99 (0-8037-3118-3). 208pp. Using the first person, this biography chronicles the Native American's youth, his amazing sporting abilities, and his quiet determination to overcome barriers. (Rev: BL 6/1–15/06; SLJ 8/06) [921]

Miscellaneous Sports

ADU, FREDDY

2844 Murcia, Rebecca Thatcher. *Freddy Adu: Young Soccer Superstar* (3–5). Illus. Series: A Robbie Reader. 2005, Mitchell Lane $16.95 (1-58415-385-7). 32pp. A brief, photo-filled biography of the young Ghanaian-born soccer phenomenon. (Rev: BL 10/15/05; SLJ 10/05) [921]

HAMILTON, BETHANY

2845 Sandler, Michael. *Bethany Hamilton: Follow Your Dreams!* (3–6). Series: Defining Moments, Overcoming Challenges. 2006, Bearport LB $23.96 (1-59716-270-1). 32pp. Surfer Bethany Hamilton lost her left arm in a shark attack when she was only 13; she was back on her surfboard only weeks after the attack and has since worked to raise funds for victims of disasters. (Rev: SLJ 1/07) [921]

MURPHY, ISAAC

2846 Trollinger, Patsi B. *Perfect Timing: How Issac Murphy Became One of the World's Greatest Jockeys* (1–3). Illus. by Jerome Lagarrigue. 2006, Viking $15.99 (0-670-06083-6). 32pp. This attractive picture-book biography describes how Isaac Murphy, the Kentucky-born grandson of slaves, became one of horse racing's most illustrious jockeys, riding to victory in three Kentucky Derbys. (Rev: BL 9/1/06; SLJ 12/06) [798.40092]

WHITE, SHAUN

2847 Doeden, Matt. *Shaun White* (2–4). Series: Amazing Athletes. 2006, Lerner LB $23.93 (0-8225-6840-3). 32pp. At the age of 19, snowboarder White won a gold medal at the 2006 Olympics. (Rev: SLJ 1/07) [921]

WICKENHEISER, HAYLEY

2848 Etue, Elizabeth. *Hayley Wickenheiser: Born to Play* (4–7). Illus. 2005, Kids Can paper $6.95 (1-55337-791-5). 40pp. The story of Canadian-born Wickenheiser, a member of Canada's gold medal-winning women's ice hockey team at the Salt Lake City Olympics, who went on to become the first woman to play professional hockey. (Rev: BL 9/1/05) [921]

World Figures

Collective

2849 Chin-Lee, Cynthia. *Akira to Zoltan: Twenty-Six Men Who Changed the World* (3–5). Illus. by Megan Halsey. 2006, Charlesbridge $15.95 (1-57091-579-2). 32pp. A companion to *Amelia to Zora: Twenty-Six Women Who Changed the World* (2005), this volume spotlights the accomplishments of 26 men who have made significant contributions in diverse walks of life, including the arts, sciences, politics, and sports. (Rev: BL 6/1–15/06; SLJ 7/06) [920.7109]

2850 Fleischman, John. *Black and White Airmen: Their True History* (5–8). Illus. 2007, Houghton $20.00 (978-0-618-56297-8). 160pp. At a reunion decades later, white bomber pilot Herb Heilbrun and Tuskegee Airman John Leahr discover how much of World War II they shared although separated by segregation. (Rev: BL 2/1/07) [920]

2851 Haskins, Jim. *African Heroes* (5–8). Series: Black Stars. 2005, Wiley $24.95 (0-471-46672-7). 163pp. Profiles 27 important Africans, both contemporary and from the past, in entries of varying length. (Rev: SLJ 7/05) [920]

2852 Sanderson, Ruth. *More Saints: Lives and Illuminations* (4–7). Illus. 2007, Eerdmans $20.00 (978-0-8028-5272-4). 32pp. A sequel to *Saints: Lives and Illuminations* (2003), this volume adds profiles of 36 saints, this time of the second millennium. (Rev: BL 2/1/07) [270]

2853 Stewart, Gail B. *The Renaissance* (4–6). Series: People at the Center Of. 2006, Gale LB $23.70 (1-56711-922-0). 48pp. Profiles some of the great minds of the Renaissance and their contributions to art, science, literature, education, and architecture. (Rev: SLJ 3/07) [920]

2854 Wales, Dirk. *Twice a Hero: Polish American Heroes of the American Revolution* (3–5). Illus. by Lynn Ihsen Peterson. 2007, Great Plains $18.95 (978-0-963245-94-6). 32pp. Profiles two Polish-born heroes — Thaddeus Kosciuszko and Casimir Pulaski — who helped Americans to defeat the British during the Revolutionary War; an accompanying DVD expands the briefer information on Pulaski. (Rev: BL 4/15/07) [920]

2855 Zalben, Jane Breskin. *Paths to Peace: People Who Changed the World* (4–7). Illus. 2006, Dutton $18.99 (0-525-47734-9). 48pp. Zalben profiles 16 individuals who have devoted much of their lives to the goal of making peace a reality. (Rev: BL 1/1–15/06; SLJ 2/06) [920]

Individual

ALEXANDER THE GREAT

2856 Adams, Simon. *Alexander: The Boy Soldier Who Conquered the World* (5–7). Series: National Geographic World History Biographies. 2005, National Geographic LB $27.90 (0-7922-3661-0). 64pp. An attractive, well-illustrated account of Alexander's life and accomplishments, with references to his less-appealing characteristics. (Rev: HBG 4/06; SLJ 9/05) [921]

2857 McGowen, Tom. *Alexander the Great: Conqueror of the Ancient World* (5–8). Series: Rulers of the Ancient World. 2006, Enslow LB $20.95 (0-7660-2560-8). 160pp. Excellent for report writers, this biography covers Alexander the Great's life and distinguishes between fact and legend. (Rev: BL 6/1–15/06; SLJ 6/06) [921]

2858 Saunders, Nicholas. *The Life of Alexander the Great* (5–8). Illus. Series: Stories from History.

2006, School Specialty $14.95 (0-7696-4713-8); paper $6.95 (0-7696-4694-8). 48pp. Full-color illustrations and graphic-novel format make this engaging biography — which covers the bond between Alexander and his horse as well as his relationship with Hephaestion — attractive to reluctant readers. (Rev: SLJ 1/07) [921]

2859 Shecter, Vicky Alvear. *Alexander the Great Rocks the World* (5–8). Illus. by Terry Naughton. 2006, Darby Creek $18.95 (1-58196-045-X). 128pp. Shecter employs an irreverent, kid-appealing tone to accurately present Alexander's amazing travels; cartoons, historical depictions, detailed notes, and resources round out the volume. (Rev: BL 1/1–15/07; SLJ 12/06) [921]

BAKER, ALIA MUHAMMAD

2860 Stamaty, Mark Alan. *Alia's Mission: Saving the Books of Iraq* (4–7). Illus. by author. 2004, Knopf LB $14.99 (0-375-93217-8). 32pp. In graphic novel format, this is the inspiring story of Iraqi librarian Alia Muhammad Baker, who hid thousands of books in advance of the 2003 invasion of her country. (Rev: BL 2/1/05*; SLJ 3/05) [020]

BUDDHA

2861 Gedney, Mona. *The Life and Times of Buddha* (5–7). Series: Biography from Ancient Civilizations: Legends, Folklore, and Stories of Ancient Worlds. 2005, Mitchell Lane LB $19.95 (1-58415-342-3). 48pp. Gedney recounts what is known of the life of Siddartha Gautama, whose search for a better way of living led to the founding of Buddhism. (Rev: SLJ 9/05) [921]

2862 Stewart, Whitney. *Becoming Buddha: The Story of Siddhartha* (3–5). Illus. by Sally Rippin. 2005, Lothian $16.95 (0-89346-946-7). 32pp. A picture-book biography of Buddha that chronicles Prince Siddhartha's lifelong search for enlightenment. (Rev: BL 10/1/05; SLJ 11/05) [921]

CAEDMON

2863 Ashby, Ruth. *Caedmon's Song* (1–3). Illus. by Bill Slavin. 2006, Eerdmans $16.00 (0-8028-5241-6). This picture-book biography introduces young readers to Caedmon, the 7th-century English cowherd who is said to be that country's first poet. (Rev: HBG 10/06; SLJ 3/06) [921]

CAESAR, JULIUS

2864 Saunders, Nicholas. *The Life of Julius Caesar* (5–8). Illus. Series: Stories from History. 2006, School Specialty $14.95 (0-7696-4717-0); paper $6.95 (0-7696-4697-2). 48pp. Full-color illustrations and graphic-novel format make this engaging

biography attractive to reluctant readers. (Rev: SLJ 1/07) [921]

CHURCHILL, WINSTON

2865 Haugen, Brenda. *Winston Churchill: British Soldier, Writer, Statesman* (4–8). 2006, Compass Point LB $30.60 (0-7565-1582-3). 112pp. Slim but fact-filled, this is a useful biography for report writers, with excerpts from speeches and writings and full discussion of key events in Churchill's life. (Rev: SLJ 9/06) [921]

CYR, LOUIS

2866 Debon, Nicolas. *The Strongest Man in the World: Louis Cyr* (2–4). Illus. 2007, Groundwood $17.95 (978-0-88899-731-9). 36pp. The exploits of circus strongman Cyr, a Canadian who amazed audiences in America and Europe at the end of the 19th century, are shown in this visual biography. (Rev: BL 4/1/07) [921]

ELIZABETH I, QUEEN OF ENGLAND

2867 Adams, Simon. *Elizabeth I: The Outcast Who Became England's Queen* (3–6). Series: National Geographic World History Biographies. 2005, National Geographic $17.95 (0-7922-3649-1). 64pp. The queen's life and accomplishments are placed in historical context in this well-designed, informative book. (Rev: HBG 10/06; SLJ 6/06) [921]

2868 Brassey, Richard. *Elizabeth I* (3–5). Series: Brilliant Brits. 2006, Orion paper $8.99 (1-84255-233-3). 24pp. The queen up-close and personal, with lots of illustrations in comic-book style and an emphasis on the quirks and the drama of the royal family and their times. (Rev: BL 7/06) [921]

FRANK, ANNE

2869 Hermann, Spring. *Anne Frank: Hope in the Shadows of the Holocaust* (5–7). Series: Holocaust Heroes and Nazi Criminals. 2005, Enslow LB $27.93 (0-7660-2531-4). 160pp. The story of Anne Frank before, during, and after the two years she and her family hid from the Nazis. (Rev: SLJ 11/05) [921]

HALILBEGOVICH, NADJA

2870 Halilbegovich, Nadja. *My Childhood Under Fire: A Sarajevo Diary* (4–7). 2006, Kids Can $14.95 (1-55337-797-4). 120pp. As a 12-year-old, Halilbegovich kept a diary that reveals the frightening details of her life during the Balkans war. (Rev: BL 5/15/06; SLJ 6/06) [949.703]

HANNIBAL

2871 Warrick, Karen Clemens. *Hannibal: Great General of the Ancient World* (5–8). Series: Rulers of the Ancient World. 2006, Enslow LB $27.93 (0-7660-2564-0). 160pp. The story of Hannibal's life and successes against the Romans are placed in historical context, with details of important battles as well as insight into his character. (Rev: SLJ 6/06) [921]

HATSHEPSUT

2872 Galford, Ellen. *Hatshepsut: The Princess Who Grew Up to Be King* (4–6). Illus. Series: World History Biographies. 2005, National Geographic $17.95 (0-7922-3645-9). 64pp. A life of Hatshepsut, who ruled Egypt about 3,500 years ago, with well-chosen illustrations, interesting sidebars, and clear distinctions between fact and surmise. (Rev: BL 7/05; SLJ 9/05) [921]

HILLARY, SIR EDMUND

2873 Elish, Dan. *Edmund Hillary: First to the Top* (5–9). Series: Great Explorations. 2006, Benchmark LB $22.95 (0-7614-2224-2). 80pp. This biography focuses on the New Zealand mountain climber's 1953 conquest of Mount Everest and includes coverage of Sherpa Tenzing Norgay. (Rev: SLJ 1/07) [921]

HYPATIA

2874 Love, D. Anne. *Of Numbers and Stars: The Story of Hypatia* (1–3). Illus. by Pam Paparone. 2006, Holiday $16.95 (0-8234-1621-6). 32pp. This picture-book biography of Hypatia profiles the life of the female scholar and philosopher whose father's devotion opened up to her worlds that were forbidden to most women. (Rev: BL 4/15/06; SLJ 5/06) [510]

JESUS CHRIST

2875 Demi. *Jesus* (3–5). Illus. 2005, Simon & Schuster $19.95 (0-689-86905-3). 48pp. Striking illustrations illustrate this life of Jesus, told chronologically in the tone of the King James version of the Bible. (Rev: BL 10/1/05; SLJ 10/05) [921]

LAMBKE, BRYAN

2876 Lambke, Bryan, and Tom Lambke. *I Just Am: A Story of Down Syndrome Awareness and Tolerance* (4–10). 2006, Five Star $14.99 (1-58985-020-3). 86pp. In this compelling photoessay, a young adult with Down syndrome — with some help from his father — explains what it's like to live with this disability. (Rev: SLJ 10/06) [921]

MACHIAVELLI, NICCOLÒ

2877 Ford, Nick. *Niccolò Machiavelli: Florentine Statesman, Playwright, and Poet* (5–8). Series: Rulers, Scholars, and Artists of the Renaissance. 2005, Rosen LB $31.95 (1-4042-0316-8). 112pp. Ford places Machiavelli's life and accomplishments in the context of culture and politics of the time. (Rev: SLJ 10/05) [921]

MANDELA, NELSON

2878 Kramer, Ann. *Mandela: The Rebel Who Led His Nation to Freedom* (4–6). Series: National Geographic World History Biographies. 2005, National Geographic $17.95 (0-7922-3658-0). 64pp. Mandela's life and accomplishments are placed in the context of the changing political climate in South Africa. (Rev: SLJ 10/05) [921]

MEDICI, LORENZO DE

2879 Hancock, Lee. *Lorenzo De' Medici: Florence's Great Leader and Patron of the Arts* (5–8). Series: Rulers, Scholars, and Artists of the Renaissance. 2005, Rosen LB $31.95 (1-4042-0315-X). 112pp. Ford places de Medici's life and accomplishments in the context of culture and politics of the time. (Rev: SLJ 10/05) [921]

MENCHU, RIGOBERTA

2880 Menchú, Rigoberta, and Dante Liano. *The Girl from Chimel* (4–7). Trans. by David Unger. Illus. by Domi. 2005, Groundwood $16.95 (0-88899-666-7). 56pp. Rigoberta Menchu, winner of the 1992 Nobel Peace Prize and Maya activist, tells about growing up in the Guatemalan Indian village of Chimel. (Rev: BL 11/1/05; SLJ 2/06) [868]

MOHAPATRA, JYOTIRMAYEE

2881 Woog, Adam. *Jyotirmayee Mohapatra: Advocate for India's Young Women* (4–8). Illus. Series: Young Heroes. 2006, Gale LB $23.70 (978-0-7377-3611-3). 48pp. From a village in rural India, Mohapatra became worried at a young age about the challenges facing girls and young women; she went on to found the network of Meena Clubs for which she received the prestigious Youth Action Network award. (Rev: BL 1/1–15/07; SLJ 4/07) [921]

NIGHTINGALE, FLORENCE

2882 Tieck, Sarah. *Florence Nightingale* (K–3). 2006, ABDO LB $15.95 (978-1-59679-786-4). 32pp. A brief biography that introduces the life and work of the famous nurse in clear text and many photograhs and reproductions. (Rev: SLJ 3/07) [921]

187

SCHLIEMANN, HEINRICH

2883 Schlitz, Laura Amy. *The Hero Schliemann: The Dreamer Who Dug for Troy* (4–6). Illus. by Robert Byrd. 2006, Candlewick $17.99 (0-7636-2283-4). 72pp. This frank biography of Heinrich Schliemann reveals the flaws in the man who excavated Troy. (Rev: SLJ 9/06) [921]

SOCRATES

2884 Dell, Pamela. *Socrates: Ancient Greek in Search of Truth* (5–8). Illus. Series: Signature Lives. 2006, Compass Point LB $23.95 (0-7565-1874-1). 112pp. A solid profile of the Greek philosopher that underlines his importance and provides insight into life in ancient Athens. (Rev: BL 10/15/06) [183]

2885 Usher, M. D. *Wise Guy: The Life and Philosophy of Socrates* (2–4). Illus. by William Bramhall. 2005, Farrar $16.00 (0-374-31249-4). 40pp. This is a useful but not altogether successful effort to combine a life of Socrates, including his childhood, and a discussion of his philosophical beliefs. (Rev: BL 1/1–15/06; SLJ 1/06) [921]

SU, DONGPO

2886 Demi. *Su Dongpo: Chinese Genius* (2–4). Illus. 2006, Lee & Low $24.00 (1-58430-256-9). 56pp. This picture-book biography chronicles the life and accomplishments of Su Dongpo (also known as Su Shi), a Chinese poet and statesman in the 11th century. (Rev: BL 11/1/06; SLJ 11/06) [921]

TENZING NORGAY

2887 Burleigh, Robert. *Tiger of the Snows: Tenzing Norgay: The Boy Whose Dream Was Everest* (4–6). Illus. by Ed Young. 2006, Simon & Schuster $16.95 (0-689-83042-4). 40pp. This picture-book biography of Tenzing Norgay uses beautiful illustrations and poetry to tell the story of the Sherpa guide who conquered Mount Everest in 1953 with Sir Edmund Hillary. (Rev: BL 6/1–15/06; SLJ 6/06) [921]

TUTANKHAMEN, KING

2888 Hawass, Zahi. *Tutankhamun: The Mystery of the Boy King* (4–7). Illus. 2005, National Geographic $17.95 (0-7922-8354-6). 64pp. The director of excavations at key Egyptian archaeological sites offers a fascinating account of the life, death, and burial of King Tut and of new revelations about his fate. (Rev: BL 11/1/05; SLJ 10/05*) [932]

WALLENBERG, RAOUL

2889 McArthur, Debra. *Raoul Wallenberg: Rescuing Thousands from the Nazis' Grasp* (5–7). Series: Holocaust Heroes and Nazi Criminals. 2005, Enslow LB $27.93 (0-7660-2530-6). 160pp. A well-documented profile of the courageous Swedish diplomat who saved thousands of Hungarian Jews and disappeared after the end of the war. (Rev: SLJ 11/05) [921]

WEISSBERGER, ELA

2890 Rubin, Susan G., and Ela Weissberger. *The Cat with the Yellow Star: Coming of Age in Terezin* (3–6). 2006, Holiday House $16.95 (0-8234-1831-6). 40pp. A survivor of the Terezin death camp recalls her time there as a child, especially playing the role of a cat in the opera Brundibar; photographs and other features help young children to understand what happened at the camp. (Rev: SLJ 6/06*) [940.53]

WILLIAMS, J. W.

2891 Barbour, Karen. *Mr. Williams* (K–3). Illus. 2005, Holt $16.95 (0-8050-6773-6). 32pp. An African American farmer's matter-of-fact recollections of his childhood in Louisiana in the 1930s and 1940s are enhanced by the compelling illustrations. (Rev: BL 9/1/05; SLJ 8/05*) [973]

ZHENG HE

2892 Zhang, Hao Yu, and Song Nan Zhang. *The Great Voyages of Zheng He* (4–6). Illus. by Song Nan Zhang. 2005, Pan Asian $16.95 (1-57227-088-8). 32pp. The voyages of discovery of Zheng He, a Chinese explorer in the early 1400s, are described in this large-format, richly illustrated volume. (Rev: BL 10/15/05; SLJ 11/05) [910.92]

The Arts and Language

Art and Architecture

General and Miscellaneous

2893 Agee, Jon, et al. *Why Did the Chicken Cross the Road?* (1–4). Illus. 2006, Dial $16.99 (0-8037-3094-2). Why did the chicken cross the road? Fourteen artists — including Chris Raschka, Mo Willems, and Jerry Pinkney — answer the question. (Rev: BCCB 11/06; BL 10/1/06; HBG 4/07; LMC 4/07; SLJ 10/06*) [741.5]

2894 Bingham, Jane. *Science and Technology* (4–7). 2006, Raintree LB $32.86 (1-4109-2241-3). 56pp. A brief but interesting exploration of the ways in which artists have documented the progress of science and technology over the years. Also use *Landscape and the Environment* and *Society and Class* (both 2006). (Rev: SLJ 1/07)

2895 Bingham, Jane. *War and Conflict* (3–5). Illus. Series: Through Artists' Eyes. 2006, Raintree LB $23.00 (978-1-4109-2236-6). 56pp. This title examines works of art — fine art but also cartoons, posters, films, stories, plays, and poems — that explore themes of war and conflict. (Rev: BL 8/06; SLJ 1/07) [700]

2896 Desnoëttes, Caroline. *Look Closer: Art Masterpieces Through the Ages* (3–6). 2006, Walker $18.95 (0-8027-9614-1). Readers' attention to the diverse masterpieces is focused through the innovative use of flaps that ask questions, offer information, and pinpoint areas of interest. (Rev: SLJ 12/06) [759]

2897 D'Harcourt, Claire. *Masterpieces Up Close: Western Painting from the 14th to 20th Centuries* (4–8). Trans. from French by Shoshanna Kirk. Series: Up Close. 2006, Chronicle $22.95 (0-8118-5403-5). 63pp. An oversize volume that challenges readers to analyze major works of Western art. (Rev: SLJ 7/06) [759]

2898 Domeniconi, David. *M Is for Masterpiece: An Art Alphabet* (4–6). Illus. by Will Bullas. 2006, Sleeping Bear $17.95 (1-58536-276-X). 32pp. An A-to-Z look at the world of art, covering everything from famous artists and artwork to different art styles and the various tools needed. (Rev: BL 12/1/06; SLJ 11/06) [700]

2899 Gonyea, Mark. *A Book About Design: Complicated Doesn't Make It Good* (1–5). Illus. by author. 2005, Holt $18.95 (0-8050-7575-5). This introduction to graphic design tackles ratios, color contrast, white space and other tricky concepts, with plenty of illustrations to help young artists see what good design looks like. (Rev: SLJ 7/05) [745.4]

2900 Lach, William. *Can You Hear It?* (K–3). Illus. 2007, Abrams $18.95 (978-0-8109-5721-3). 32pp. A handsome picture book in which reproductions of artistic masterpieces are paired with classical music selections on the accompanying CD; author Lach suggests connections and focal points and provides information on the artists, composers, and musical instruments. (Rev: BL 3/15/07) [780]

2901 Micklethwait, Lucy. *Children: A First Art Book* (PS–2). Illus. Series: First Art Book. 2006, Frances Lincoln $14.95 (1-84507-116-6). 24pp. This beautiful introduction showcases diverse works of art that depict children in everyday activities, such as washing, learning to write, and playing music. (Rev: BL 11/1/06; SLJ 12/06)

2902 Nilsen, Anna. *Art Auction Mystery* (5–8). Illus. 2005, Kingfisher $16.95 (0-7534-5842-X). 48pp. Wannabe art sleuths are challenged to find forgeries hidden in a selection of world-famous paintings. (Rev: BL 11/1/05; SLJ 1/06; VOYA 12/05) [759]

2903 Raczka, Bob. *Here's Looking at Me: How Artists See Themselves* (3–5). 2006, Lerner LB $23.90 (0-7613-3404-1). 32pp. Self-portraits of important artists throughout the ages, with an emphasis on form and technique. (Rev: BL 5/1/06; SLJ 6/06) [760]

2904 Raczka, Bob. *Unlikely Pairs: Fun with Famous Works of Art* (4–10). 2005, Millbrook LB $23.93 (0-7613-2936-6); paper $9.95 (0-7613-2378-3). 32pp. Raczka pairs famous works from different eras and styles (Rodin's The Thinker appears to be considering a move on Klee's chessboard, for example); a closing catalog offers factual information. (Rev: SLJ 12/05) [750]

2905 Raimondo, Joyce. *Express Yourself!* (3–5). Illus. Series: Art Explorers. 2005, Watson-Guptill $12.95 (0-8230-2506-3). 48pp. Introduces readers to the work of six expressionist painters — Edvard Munch, Vincent van Gogh, Ernest Ludwig Kirchner, Vasily Kandinsky, Willem de Kooning, and Jackson Pollack — and examines a representative work and outlines projects that further illuminate each artist's style. (Rev: BL 11/1/05; SLJ 2/06) [372.5]

2906 Ruggi, Gilda Williams. *The Art Book for Children* (2–4). Illus. 2005, Phaidon $19.95 (0-7148-4511-6). 72pp. Art critic Ruggi introduces young readers to classic and contemporary works of art and encourages critical thinking and creating connections to children's own experiences. (Rev: BL 11/1/05) [701]

2907 Schulte, Jessica. *Can You Find It Outside?* (2–4). Illus. 2005, Abrams $10.95 (0-8109-5795-7). 32pp. Rhyming text provides clues to help readers find details in these paintings from the collections of New York's Metropolitan Museum of Art. (Rev: BL 11/1/05; SLJ 12/05) [759]

2908 Shofner, Shawndra. *Sydney Opera House* (3–6). Series: Modern Wonders of the World. 2006, Creative Editions LB $18.95 (1-58341-442-8). 32pp. The story of the construction and current uses of the eye-catching Opera House on Sydney's harbor, completed in 1973. (Rev: BL 10/15/06) [725]

2909 Sousa, Jean. *Faces, Places, and Inner Spaces* (5–8). Illus. 2006, Abrams $18.95 (0-8109-5966-6). 48pp. The director of interpretive exhibitions and family programs at the Art Institute of Chicago introduces a variety of works — portraits, landscapes, and abstract pieces — and asks questions that stimulate analysis. (Rev: BL 5/15/06; SLJ 7/06) [701]

2910 Swain, Sally. *Once Upon a Picture* (1–5). Illus. by author. 2005, Allen & Unwin $16.95 (1-74114-001-3). Four world-famous paintings are used as the departure point for storytelling and additional paintings. (Rev: SLJ 2/06) [759]

2911 Van Gogh, Vincent. *Vincent's Colors: Words and Pictures by Vincent van Gogh* (1–3). Ed. by William Lach. 2005, Chronicle $14.95 (0-8118-5099-4). 48pp. An excellent introduction to the Dutch artist's works, this attractive volume couples key paintings with excerpts from letters Vincent wrote to his brother Theo. (Rev: BL 11/1/05*; HBG 4/06; SLJ 11/05) [759.9]

2912 Vogel, Jennifer. *A Library Story: Building a New Central Library* (4–7). 2006, Lerner $25.26 (0-8225-5916-1). 64pp. The construction of the new central library in Minneapolis is the topic of this lively, well-illustrated book that looks at the reasons for the building, architectural and engineering concerns, and artistic choices that were made. (Rev: BL 8/06; SLJ 9/06) [727]

2913 Wallace, Nancy Elizabeth, and Linda K. Friedlaender. *Look! Look! Look!* (K–3). 2006, Marshall Cavendish $16.95 (0-7614-5282-6). 40pp. Three mice are so inspired by a beautiful postcard that they learn to make their own pictures; followed by instructions on making a self-portrait postcard. (Rev: BL 5/1/06; SLJ 3/06)

The Ancient World

2914 Mann, Elizabeth. *The Parthenon: The Height of Greek Civilization* (4–7). Illus. by Yuan Lee. 2006, Mikaya $22.95 (1-931414-15-7). 48pp. The engineering feats involved in the construction of the Parthenon are placed in historical and cultural context; includes a foldout spread, a useful map, and many illustrations. (Rev: BL 12/1/06; SLJ 3/07) [938.5]

United States

2915 Curlee, Lynn. *Skyscraper* (4–7). Illus. 2007, Simon & Schuster $17.99 (0-689-84489-1). 48pp. Accompanied by striking acrylic paintings, Curlee's detailed narrative explores the architectural history and engineering of skyscrapers. (Rev: BL 1/1–15/07) [720]

2916 Leach, Deba Foxley. *Grant Wood: The Artist in the Hayloft* (2–4). Illus. by Grant Wood. Series: Adventures in Art. 2005, Prestel $14.95 (3-7913-3401-8). 30pp. Large, color reproductions of Wood's works are accompanied by brief text that will engage readers' attention plus biographical information. (Rev: BL 11/1/05) [745.13]

Communication

Language and Languages

2917 Evans, Lezlie. *Can You Greet the Whole Wide World? 12 Common Phrases in 12 Different Languages* (K–3). Illus. by Denis Roche. 2006, Houghton $16.00 (0-618-56327-X). 32pp. A new school year gives a little kitten a chance to greet others in 12 languages, including Arabic, Hindi, Japanese, and Zulu. (Rev: BL 5/1/06; SLJ 6/06) [395.4]

2918 Park, Linda Sue, and Julia Durango. *Yum! Yuck! A Foldout Book of People Sounds* (PS–3). Illus. by Sue Ramá. 2005, Charlesbridge $9.95 (1-57091-659-4). 36pp. The different noises that people of different cultures make to express themselves are paired with illustrations of children from around the world. (Rev: SLJ 8/05) [418]

2919 Prap, Lila. *Animals Speak* (PS–2). Illus. 2006, North-South $15.95 (0-7358-2058-9). 40pp. More than 40 languages are included in this multilingual guide to the pronunciation of animal sounds in countries around the world. (Rev: BL 3/1/06; SLJ 5/06)

Reading, Speaking, and Writing

Books, Printing, Libraries, and Schools

2920 Forget, Thomas. *The Creation of Captain America* (4–6). Illus. Series: Action Heroes. 2006, Rosen LB $29.25 (1-4042-0766-X). 48pp. A look at Captain America, one of Marvel's most famous superheroes and an American icon, and how he was created. (Rev: SLJ 3/07) [741.5]

2921 Hayward, Linda. *I Am a Book* (1–3). Illus. by Carol Nicklaus. Series: Silly Millies. 2005, Lerner LB $18.60 (0-7613-2905-6); paper $4.99 (0-7613-

1826-7). 32pp. In easy-to-understand text with whimsical illustrations, a book explains how it was made. (Rev: BL 1/1–15/06; SLJ 10/05) [002]

2922 Ruurs, Margriet. *My Librarian Is a Camel: How Books are Brought to Children Around the World* (3–5). Illus. 2005, Boyds Mills $16.95 (1-59078-093-0). 32pp. Boats, camels, bicycles, wheelbarrows — this is a look at the unusual means librarians employ to get books to readers in remote areas of the world. (Rev: BL 7/05; SLJ 8/05) [027.4]

2923 Sawa, Maureen. *The Library Book: The Story of Libraries from Camels to Computers* (3–5). Illus. by Bill Slavin. 2006, Tundra $18.95 (0-88776-698-6). 72pp. This appealing study of libraries and their widespread impact traces their history from the ancient Library of Alexandria to electronic texts available from digital archives. (Rev: SLJ 12/06) [027]

2924 Shea, Kitty. *Out and About at the Public Library* (1–3). Illus. by Zachary Trover. 2005, Picture Window LB $23.93 (1-4048-1150-8). 24pp. This attractive title takes readers on a field trip to a public library, where they learn about everything from checking out books to using the computer catalog and consulting the reference department. (Rev: SLJ 2/06) [027.4]

2925 Somervill, Barbara A. *The History of the Library* (3–6). Series: Our Changing World: The Timeline Library. 2006, The Child's World LB $27.07 (1-59296-438-9). 32pp. An exploration of how books have been made and stored from ancient times to today, with a peek at future developments. (Rev: SLJ 7/06) [027.009]

2926 Teitelbaum, Michael. *Making Comic Books* (2–5). Illus. by Howard Bender and David Tanguay. Series: Boys Rock! 2006, The Child's World LB $24.21 (1-59296-733-7). 32pp. Follows a comic book's creation from script through storyboard through illustration and lettering; a good choice for beginning and reluctant readers (girls as well as boys). (Rev: SLJ 2/07) [741.5]

Signs and Symbols

2927 Ault, Kelly. *Let's Sign! Every Baby's Guide to Communicating with Grownups* (PS). Illus. by Leo Landry. 2005, Houghton $17.00 (0-618-50774-4). 77pp. Simple stories about mealtime, playtime, and bedtime are accompanied by attractive illustrations and depictions of signs. (Rev: SLJ 12/05) [419]

2928 Petelinsek, Kathleen, and E. Russell Primm. *At School / En la escuela* (K–2). Illus. by Kathleen Petelinsek. Series: Talking Hands. 2006, The Child's World LB $21.36 (1-59296-450-8). 24pp. Students demonstrate simple school-related words using American Sign Language; the text is in both English and Spanish. (Rev: SLJ 6/06) [419]

2929 Searcy, John. *Signs in Our World: Spot the Signs All Around You!* (PS–2). Illus. 2006, DK $15.99 (0-7566-1834-7); paper $5.99 (0-7566-1827-4). 32pp. A colorful introduction to a wide variety of signs — some wordless — found across America and in some foreign countries. (Rev: BL 4/15/06) [302.2]

2930 Warner, Penny. *Signing Fun: American Sign Language Vocabulary, Phrases, Games and Activities* (4–8). Illus. by Paula Gray. 2006, Gallaudet Univ. paper $19.95 (1-56368-292-3). 218pp. This fun-filled introduction to American Sign Language introduces the basic vocabulary of ASL and offers a wide selection of related games and puzzles. (Rev: SLJ 12/06) [419]

Words and Grammar

2931 Agee, Jon. *Smart Feller Fart Smeller* (2–4). Illus. 2006, Hyperion $14.95 (0-7868-3692-X). 64pp. Black-and-white cartoons illustrate this celebration of spoonerisms, such as the one about the smart student who "burned a lunch." (Rev: BCCB 6/06; BL 3/15/06; HB 5–6/06; HBG 10/06; LMC 11–12/06; SLJ 5/06) [793.734]

2932 Alda, Arlene. *Did You Say Pears?* (K–3). Illus. 2006, Tundra $16.95 (0-88776-739-7). 32pp. Fun with homonyms and homophones is provided in minimal text and eye-catching photographs. (Rev: BL 3/1/06; HBG 10/06; LMC 10/06; SLJ 6/06) [428.1]

2933 Cleary, Brian P. *A Lime, a Mime, a Pool of Slime: More About Nouns* (2–4). Illus. by Brian Gable. Series: Words Are CATegorical. 2006, Lerner $15.95 (1-57505-937-1). 32pp. Cartoon drawings and appealing rhymes introduce nouns of all kinds. (Rev: BL 1/1–15/07; SLJ 11/06) [428.1]

2934 Cleary, Brian P. *How Much Can a Bare Bear Bear? What Are Homonyms and Homophones?* (2–5). Illus. by Brian Gable. Series: Words Are CATegorical. 2005, Millbrook LB $15.95 (1-57505-824-3). Rhyming wordplay introduces readers to homonyms and homophones. (Rev: SLJ 11/05)

2935 Cleary, Brian P. *Rhyme and PUNishment: Adventures in Wordplay* (2–5). Illus. by J. P. Sandy. 2006, Millbrook LB $15.95 (1-57505-849-9). 48pp. Puns — some of them quite sophisticated — are delivered inside brief poems accompanied by cartoonish illustrations. (Rev: SLJ 6/06) [811]

2936 Cleary, Brian P. *Stop and Go, Yes and No: What Is an Antonym?* (K–3). Illus. by Brian Gable. Series: Words Are CATegorical. 2006, Millbrook LB $15.95 (1-57505-860-X). Simple and not-so-simple antonyms — from "front and back" to "excite and soothe" — are accompanied by amusing drawings; Cleary also explains the use of prefixes such as "un" and "im." (Rev: SLJ 6/06) [428.1]

2937 Dahl, Michael. *If You Were a Noun* (1–3). Illus. by Sara Gray. Series: Word Fun. 2006, Picture Window LB $23.95 (1-4048-1355-1). 24pp. An attractive and accessible introduction to nouns and their roles in speech. Also use *f You Were a Verb* and *If You Were an Adverb* (2006). (Rev: SLJ 9/06) [428.1]

2938 Dahl, Michael. *If You Were an Adjective* (1–3). Illus. by Sara Gray. Series: If You Were. 2006, Picture Window LB $17.95 (1-4048-1356-X). 24pp. A picture-book format is used to introduce young readers to adjectives and the role they play in English grammar and sentence structure. (Rev: BL 4/1/06; SLJ 9/06) [428.1]

2939 *Flip-a-Word: Pig Wig* (K–2). Illus. by Yukiko Kido. 2006, Blue Apple $12.95 (1-59354-175-9); paper $5.95 (1-59354-178-3). Bright, colorful pictures introduce three-letter words containing the letter combinations of "at," "ig," and "ug." Also use *Flip-a-Word: Snake Cake* (2006). (Rev: SLJ 11/06)

2940 Guy, Ginger Foglesong. *My School / Mi escuela* (PS–1). Illus. by Vivi Escriva. 2006, HarperCollins $12.99 (0-06-079101-2). 24pp. An attractive introduction to school vocabulary in English and Spanish. (Rev: BL 8/06; SLJ 6/06) [372.21]

2941 Hambleton, Laura, and Sedat Turhan. *Monkey Business: Fun with Idioms* (K–3). Illus. by Herve Tullet. Series: Milet Wordwise. 2007, Milet paper $5.99 (978-1-840594-99-7). 28pp. Illustrations provide literal interpretations of such idioms as "monkey business," "I'll give you a hand," and "barking up the wrong tree." (Rev: BL 4/15/07) [440]

2942 Heinrichs, Ann. *Similes and Metaphors* (3–6). Series: The Magic of Language. 2005, The Child's World LB $27.07 (1-59296-434-6). 32pp. Advice on using similes and metaphors to brighten sentences is accompanied by attractive graphics and photographs. Also use *Spelling Rules* and *Synonyms and Antonyms* (both 2005). (Rev: SLJ 12/05) [808]

2943 Pulver, Robin. *Nouns and Verbs Have a Field Day* (K–3). Illus. by Lynn Rowe Reed. 2006, Holiday $16.95 (0-8234-1982-7). 32pp. A companion to *Punctuation Takes a Vacation* (2003), this zany volume features a field day in which verbs and nouns refuse to cooperate with each other. (Rev: BL 4/1/06; SLJ 3/06)

2944 Rayevsky, Kim. *Antonyms, Synonyms and Homonyms* (1–3). Illus. by Robert Rayevsky. 2006, Holiday $16.95 (0-8234-1889-8). 32pp. Learn all about antonyms, synonyms, and homonyms with this funny book about an alien trying to make some sense out of life on Earth. (Rev: BL 12/1/06; SLJ 1/07) [428.1]

2945 Swanson, Diane. *A Crash of Rhinos, A Party of Jays* (K–2). Illus. by Mariko Ando Spencer. 2006, Annick $19.95 (1-55451-048-1); paper $8.95 (1-55451-047-3). 24pp. Introduces collective nouns for groups of animals, including the well-known (a pride of lions) and the obscure (a bouquet of pheasants), and provides interesting facts and eye-catching illustrations. (Rev: BL 1/1–15/07) [591]

2946 Truss, Lynne. *Eats, Shoots, and Leaves: Why, Commas Really Do Make a Difference* (2–4). Illus. by Bonnie Timmons. 2006, Putnam $15.99 (0-399-24491-3). 32pp. The scope of Truss's bestseller for adults is narrowed to the role of the comma in this effective picture book full of funny examples of its misuse — "Eat here and get gas," for example. (Rev: BL 9/1/06; SLJ 8/06) [428.2]

Writing and Speaking

2947 Farrell, Tish. *Write Your Own Fantasy Story* (4–8). Series: Write Your Own. 2006, Compass Point LB $30.60 (0-7565-1639-0). 64pp. Covering characters, viewpoint, plot, and speech, this is a helpful guide to writing fantasy literature. Also use *Write Your Own Mystery Story* and *Write Your Own Science Fiction Story* (both 2006). (Rev: SLJ 8/06) [808.3]

2948 Levine, Gail Carson. *Writing Magic: Creating Stories That Fly* (5–10). 2006, HarperCollins $16.99 (978-0-06-051961-2); paper $5.99 (978-0-06-051960-5). 167pp. Well-known author Levine provides upbeat, practical tips on such topics as finding story ideas, character and plot development, and investigating the possibility of publication. (Rev: BL 12/15/06; SLJ 2/07*) [808.3]

2949 Nobleman, Marc Tyler. *Extraordinary E-Mails, Letters, and Resumes* (5–8). Illus. by Kevin Pope. Series: F. W. Prep. 2005, Watts LB $30.50 (0-531-16759-3). 128pp. Advice for students who want to write effective e-mails, letters, and resumés, with an explanation of the importance of communicating clearly. (Rev: SLJ 1/06) [808]

2950 Otfinoski, Steven. *Extraordinary Short Story Writing* (5–8). Illus. by Kevin Pope. Series: F. W. Prep. 2005, Watts LB $30.50 (0-531-16760-7). 128pp. Tips and activities reinforce the information on writing different types of stories, choosing ideas, and using available resources effectively; a sample short story offers step-by-step guidance. (Rev: SLJ 2/06) [808]

2951 Sullivan, George. *Journalists at Risk: Reporting America's Wars* (5–8). 2005, Twenty-First Century LB $26.60 (0-7613-2745-2). 128pp. A timely discussion of the role journalists play in covering wars and how that responsibility has evolved over the years. (Rev: BL 10/15/05; SLJ 12/05; VOYA 2/06) [070.4]

Music

General

2952 Barnes, Deb. *Inside a Rock Band* (2–4). Series: Girls Rock! 2006, Child's World $16.95 (1-59296-745-0). 32pp. An inside look at what it's like to be in a professional band. (Rev: BL 11/15/06; SLJ 4/07) [781.66]

2953 Bertholf, Bret. *The Long Gone Lonesome History of Country Music* (5–8). Illus. 2007, Little, Brown $18.99 (978-0-316-52393-6). 64pp. A chatty survey of country music, discussing its roots and early instruments, tracing the evolution to today's sounds, and introducing some of its greatest performers. (Rev: BL 4/1/07) [781.642]

2954 Bryan, Ashley. *Let It Shine: Three Favorite Spirituals* (PS–5). Illus. by author. 2007, Simon & Schuster $16.99 (0-689-84732-7). This large-format, beautifully illustrated volume showcases three familiar spirituals: "This Little Light of Mine," "He's Got the Whole World in His Hands," and "When the Saints Go Marching In." (Rev: BL 11/15/06; SLJ 1/07*)

2955 Corr, Christopher. *Whole World* (PS). Illus. 2007, Barefoot Bks. $16.99 (978-1-846860-43-0). 32pp. This illustrated version of the classic spiritual (with a sing-along CD) shows children around the world enjoying nature and makes a clear plea for environmental protection. (Rev: BL 4/15/07) [782.42]

2956 Handyside, Christopher. *Country* (5–9). Series: A History of American Music. 2006, Heinemann LB $31.43 (1-4034-8151-2). 48pp. This history of country music traces the genre from its hillbilly roots to the present and introduces some of its most influential figures, including the Carter family,

Johnny Cash, Loretta Lynn, and John Denver. (Rev: SLJ 9/06) [781.642]

2957 Hannah, Johnny. *Hot Jazz Special* (4–6). Illus. 2005, Candlewick $16.99 (0-7636-2308-3). 40pp. This brightly illustrated volume with a fold-out poster celebrates the contributions of jazz players including Louis Armstrong, Duke Ellington, Billie Holliday, Jelly Roll Morton, and Django Reinhardt. (Rev: BL 7/05; SLJ 3/05)

2958 Joel, Billy. *New York State of Mind* (PS–2). Illus. by Izak. 2005, Scholastic $16.99 (0-439-55382-2). 32pp. Using Billy Joel's song as the framework, Izak portrays the essence of New York City through a dog's Christmas visit. (Rev: BL 11/15/05) [782.42164]

2959 Moore, Mary-Alice. *The Wheels on the School Bus* (K–2). Illus. by Laura Huliska-Beith. 2006, HarperCollins $15.99 (0-06-059427-6). 32pp. In this adaptation of the popular song, the action is focused on a bus full of students — and also commuting teachers — as it makes its way to school. (Rev: BL 8/06; SLJ 8/06) [782.42]

2960 Nelson, Kadir. *He's Got the Whole World in His Hands* (PS–3). Illus. 2005, Dial $16.99 (0-8037-2850-6). 32pp. An African American boy savors life with his family and the wonders of the world around him in this picture-book interpretation of the popular spiritual. (Rev: BL 10/1/05*; HBG 4/06; SLJ 9/05)

2961 Olson-Brown, Ellen. *Hush Little Digger* (PS–K). Illus. by Lee White. 2006, Tricycle $12.95 (1-58246-160-0). 28pp. This twist on the popular lullaby "Hush Little Baby" features a father promising his son increasingly large pieces of equipment. (Rev: BL 4/1/06; SLJ 6/06) [782.42]

2962 Pinkney, Gloria Jean. *Music from Our Lord's Holy Heaven* (2–4). Illus. by Jerry Pinkney and others. 2005, HarperCollins $17.99 (0-06-000768-0). 48pp. Children's author Pinkney pairs the lyrics of African American spirituals with relevant psalms in this beautifully illustrated picture book that comes bundled with an audio CD. (Rev: BL 10/1/05; SLJ 12/05) [264]

Ballads and Folk Songs

2963 Boynton, Sandra. *Dog Train* (PS–2). Illus. by author. 2005, Workman $17.95 (0-7611-3966-4). 64pp. A collection of songs with a distinct rock 'n' roll, this book provides spreads for songs that are included on the accompanying CD. (Rev: SLJ 3/06) [782.4]

2964 Emmett, Jonathan. *She'll Be Coming 'Round the Mountain* (PS–K). Illus. 2007, Simon & Schuster $16.99 (978-1-4169-3652-7). 32pp. A lively cowgirl dressed in pink pajamas and a huge green hat stars in this rollicking expanded version of the classic song. (Rev: BL 4/1/07; SLJ 3/07) [782.42]

2965 Handyside, Christopher. *Folk* (5–9). 2006, Heinemann LB $31.43 (1-4034-8150-4). 48pp. This attractive volume traces the evolution of American folk music from its post-Civil War roots to its influence on the contemporary music scene and introduces some of its most influential figures, including Leadbelly, Woody Guthrie, Joan Baez, and Bob Dylan. (Rev: SLJ 9/06) [781.62]

2966 Penner, Fred. *The Cat Came Back* (PS–2). Illus. by Renee Reichert. 2005, Roaring Brook $15.95 (1-59643-030-3). 32pp. Excellent artwork elevates the humor of the traditional song about a man determined to rid himself of a pesky cat. (Rev: BL 11/1/05; SLJ 10/05) [782.4]

2967 Pinkney, Brian. *Hush, Little Baby* (PS). Illus. 2006, Greenwillow $15.99 (0-06-055993-4). 32pp. Mama has gone off for the day and it is up to Papa and older brother to look after the little girl; set in an African American family in the early 1900s. (Rev: BL 2/1/06; SLJ 3/06) [782.42125]

2968 Yolen, Jane. *Apple for the Teacher: Thirty Songs for Singing While You Work* (4–7). Illus. 2005, Abrams $24.95 (0-8109-4825-7). 160pp. This collection of work songs, compiled by Yolen and featuring music arrangements by her son Adam Stemple, celebrates 30 diverse occupations from astronaut to weaver. (Rev: BL 10/1/05; SLJ 10/05) [782.42]

Holidays

2969 Brebeuf, Jean de. *The Huron Carol* (PS–2). Trans. by Jesse Edgar Middleton. Illus. by Ian Wallace. 2006, Groundwood $16.95 (0-88899-711-6). 32pp. Wallace illustrates in watercolor the 17th-century Christmas carol that sets the Nativity in Huron culture. (Rev: BL 10/15/06; SLJ 10/06) [782.28]

2970 Conahan, Carolyn. *The Twelve Days of Christmas Dogs* (K–3). Illus. 2005, Dutton $15.99 (0-525-47486-2). 32pp. A rambunctious parody involving a lot of dogs and one intrusive cat. (Rev: BL 10/15/05; SLJ 10/05)

2971 Katz, Alan. *Where Did They Hide My Presents? Silly Dilly Christmas Songs* (2–5). Illus. by David Catrow. 2005, Simon & Schuster $15.95 (0-689-86214-8). New lyrics for familiar songs celebrate the silly side of Christmas. (Rev: SLJ 10/05) [782.42]

2972 Neale, John M. *Good King Wenceslas* (PS–2). Illus. by Tim Ladwig. 2005, Eerdmans $16.00 (0-8028-5209-2). 32pp. The words of the familiar Christmas carol and oversize double-spread, expressive artwork combine to celebrate the story of King Wenceslas, a 10th-century Bohemian monarch. (Rev: BL 10/15/05; SLJ 10/05) [782.28]

2973 Thuswaldner, Werner, and Patricia Crampton. *Silent Night, Holy Night* (K–3). Illus. by Robert Ingpen. 2005, Penguin $16.99 (0-698-40032-1). 40pp. Gorgeous illustrations are the highlight of this history of one of the world's best-known Christmas carols. (Rev: BL 10/15/05; SLJ 10/05) [782.28]

Musical Instruments

2974 Aylmore, Angela. *Banging* (PS–K). Illus. Series: Making Music. 2005, Raintree LB $20.64 (1-4109-1604-9). 24pp. Children show how to use a variety of instruments including drums and Indonesian gongs in this brightly illustrated volume; companion volumes are *Blowing*, *Plucking*, and *Shaking* (all 2005). (Rev: SLJ 1/06) [786.819]

2975 Barber, Nicola. *Should I Play the Flute?* (3–5). Illus. Series: Learning Musical Instruments. 2006, Heinemann LB $28.21 (978-1-4034-8187-0). 32pp. Chapter answer such questions as "How does a flute make its sound?", "What types of music can you play on a flute?", and "How would I learn to play the flute?" Also use *Should I Play the Piano?* (2006). (Rev: SLJ 2/07) [788.3]

2976 Crask, Tom. *Should I Play the Drums?* (3–5). Illus. Series: Learning Musical Instruments. 2006,

Heinemann LB $28.21 (978-1-4034-8186-3). 32pp. Answering the title question, this well-organized and attractive volume gives the history of the drums, discusses how their sound is produced, and names famous drum players and drum recordings. Also use *Should I Play the Guitar?* and *Should I Play the Violin?* (both 2006). (Rev: SLJ 2/07) [786.9]

Singing Games and Songs

2977 Katz, Alan. *Are You Quite Polite?* (K–3). Illus. by David Catrow. 2006, Simon & Schuster $15.95 (0-689-86970-3). 32pp. Silly verses set to familiar tunes focus on poor behavior (lateness, bad table manners, nose-picking, and so forth), enhanced by suitably lively cartoon art. (Rev: BL 11/15/06; SLJ 10/06) [782.42]

2978 Rueda, Claudia. *Let's Play in the Forest While the Wolf Is Not Around* (PS). Illus. 2006, Scholastic $16.99 (0-439-82323-4). 32pp. The animals of the forest come out to play unaware that the wolf is in fact getting dressed and is hungry — all shown in facing pages — but it turns out that he's just hungry for pancakes; this song is based on a traditional one and the music is appended. (Rev: BL 11/15/06; SLJ 10/06) [782.42]

Performing Arts

Circuses, Fairs, and Parades

2979 Schubert, Leda. *Ballet of the Elephants* (K–3). Illus. by Robert Andrew Parker. 2006, Roaring Brook $17.95 (1-59643-075-3). 32pp. The fascinating story of the collaboration of circus owner John Ringling North, choreographer George Balanchine, and composer Igor Stravinsky to create a ballet featuring 50 elephants with ballerinas on their backs; vivid illustrations accompany the text and the author's note at the end includes a few black-and-white photographs of the performance. (Rev: BL 4/1/06; SLJ 4/06) [796.8]

Dance

2980 Castle, Kate. *My First Ballet Book* (K–3). 2006, Kingfisher $9.95 (0-7534-6026-2). 48pp. The fundamentals of ballet — from basic positions to arabesques, jumps, and pas de deux — are shown in color photographs of ethnically diverse children, accompanied by concise text. (Rev: SLJ 12/06) [792.8]

2981 Dillman, Lisa. *Ballet* (4–7). Illus. Series: Get Going! Hobbies. 2005, Heinemann LB $19.45 (1-4034-6115-5). 32pp. A photo-filled introduction to ballet, with historical information plus basic positions and steps and exercises to help would-be dancers get in shape; also use *Tap Dancing* (2005). (Rev: BL 11/1/05; SLJ 3/06) [792.8]

2982 Keeler, Patricia, and Julio Leitao. *Drumbeat in Our Feet* (3–5). Illus. by Patricia Keeler. 2006, Lee & Low $16.95 (1-58430-264-X). 32pp. Information on — and illustrations of — traditional African dances are paired with pictures of young Americans learning these dances at a studio in Harlem. (Rev: BL 11/1/06; SLJ 12/06) [793.3]

2983 Schorer, Suki, and School of American Ballet. *Put Your Best Foot Forward: A Young Dancer's Guide to Life* (4–8). Photos by Chris Carroll. Illus. by Donna Ingemanson. 2005, Workman $9.95 (0-7611-3795-5). 96pp. Practical tips are combined with artistic advice in this helpful guide for young ballet dancers, written by a former principal dancer. (Rev: SLJ 3/06) [792.8]

Motion Pictures, Radio, and Television

2984 Baker, Frank W. *Coming Distractions: Questioning Movies* (3–6). Illus. Series: Fact Finders: Media Literacy. 2007, Capstone LB $16.95 (978-0-7368-6766-5). 32pp. Readers are encouraged to analyze the images and messages they see projected on the big screen and to be aware of stereotypes and deliberate product placements; the dynamic format adds interest. (Rev: BL 4/1/07) [300]

2985 Horn, Geoffrey M. *Movie Animation* (4–6). Series: Making Movies. 2007, Gareth Stevens LB $23.93 (0-8368-6837-4). 32pp. This book provides a brief overview of the production of animated movies and gives snapshots of key figures including

Walt Disney and Jayao Miyazaki. (Rev: SLJ 1/07) [791.43]

2986 McCarthy, Meghan. *Aliens are Coming! The True Account of the 1938 War of the Worlds Radio Broadcast* (1–3). Illus. 2006, Knopf $16.95 (0-375-83518-0). 40pp. With varied artwork, this effective picture book presents the 1938 radio broadcast of *War of the Worlds* and the panic that followed in a way that will keep contemporary readers on the edge of their seats. (Rev: BL 2/1/06; SLJ 4/06*) [791.44]

Theater and Play Production

2987 Jacobs, Paul Dubois, and Jennifer Swender. *Putting on a Play: Drama Activities for Kids* (3–4). Illus. by Debra Spina Dixon. 2005, Gibbs Smith paper $9.95 (1-58685-767-3). 64pp. An excellent introduction to staging a play — as a writer, designer, actor, or any support person — with ideas for story lines and discussion of improvising scenery from everyday materials. (Rev: SLJ 4/06) [792.02]

History and Geography

History and Geography in General

Miscellaneous

2988 Defries, Cheryl L. *Seven Natural Wonders of the United States and Canada* (4–7). Illus. Series: Seven Wonders of the World. 2005, Enslow LB $25.26 (0-7660-5291-5). 48pp. This tour of seven of North America's natural wonders, including the Grand Canyon, Everglades, and Niagara Falls, is extended by constantly updated links to Web sites. (Rev: SLJ 11/05) [557]

2989 Graham, Amy. *Seven Wonders of the Natural World* (4–7). Illus. Series: Seven Wonders of the World. 2005, Enslow LB $25.26 (0-7660-5290-7). 48pp. A tour of seven of the world's natural wonders, including Mount Everest, the Great Barrier Reef, and the Grand Canyon; the text is extended by constantly updated links to Web sites. (Rev: SLJ 11/05)

2990 Lendroth, Susan. *Why Explore?* (K–3). Illus. by Enrique S. Moreiro. 2005, Tricycle $15.95 (1-58246-150-3). An interesting overview of human exploration of all kinds over the centuries. (Rev: SLJ 1/06)

2991 Phillips, Dee, et al. *People of the World* (4–7). Illus. Series: Just the Facts. 2006, School Specialty paper $9.95 (0-7696-4257-8). 64pp. Statistics and fast facts on the countries and peoples of the world are presented on double-page spreads. (Rev: BL 4/1/06) [305.8]

2992 Reynolds, Jan. *Celebrate! Connections Among Cultures* (3–5). Illus. 2006, Lee & Low $16.95 (1-58430-253-4). 32pp. Sharing photographs from her travels, the author introduces readers to diverse cultures around the world and their traditions, including the Tuareg of the Sahara, Tibetans, and the Yanomami of the Amazon rain forest. (Rev: BL 3/15/06; SLJ 8/06) [394.26]

2993 Wojtanik, Andrew. *Afghanistan to Zimbabwe: Country Facts That Helped Me Win the National Geographic Bee* (5–12). 2005, National Geographic LB $28.90 (0-7922-7442-3); paper $12.95 (0-7922-7981-6). 384pp. Facts and figures about the world's 192 independent countries are organized into three categories: Physical, Political, and Environmental/Economic. (Rev: SLJ 10/05; VOYA 8/05) [910]

Maps and Globes

2994 Baber, Maxwell. *Map Basics* (4–6). Illus. Series: Map Readers. 2006, Heinemann LB $18.95 (1-4034-6794-3). 32pp. This easy-to-understand introduction to mapping offers a brief history of cartography and examines such topics as projections, scale, keys, specialized maps, and the future of cartography; projects and a glossary round out the volume. (Rev: BL 10/15/06) [912]

Paleontology and Dinosaurs

2995 Ashby, Ruth. *Pteranodon: The Life Story of a Pterosaur* (1–3). Illus. by Phil Wilson. 2005, Abrams $14.95 (0-8109-5778-7). With simple text and striking images, the author presents what life might have been like for an ancient flying dinosaur. (Rev: SLJ 7/05) [567.918]

2996 Barker, Robert T. *Dactyls! Dragons of the Air* (3–4). Illus. by Luis V. Key. Series: Step into Reading. 2005, Random LB $11.99 (0-375-93013-2); paper $3.99 (0-375-83013-8). 48pp. In conversational, easy-to-understand language, Barker discusses the pterodactyl and its characteristics and conveys the excitement he finds in paleontology. (Rev: SLJ 2/06) [567.918]

2997 Bradley, Timothy J. *Paleo Sharks: Survival of the Strangest* (4–7). Illus. 2007, Chronicle $15.95 (978-0-8118-4878-7). 47pp. Well-arranged double-page spreads introduce sharks of prehistoric times and examine how they compare to their modern descendants. (Rev: BL 4/1/07) [567]

2998 Brown, Charlotte Lewis. *After the Dinosaurs: Mammoths and Fossil Mammals* (K–3). Illus. by Phil Wilson. Series: An I Can Read Book. 2006, HarperCollins $15.99 (978-0-06-053053-2). 32pp. Double-page spreads introduces some of the mammals — including woolly mammoths and saber-toothed tigers — that followed the dinosaurs; suitable for beginning readers, this solid volume includes a pronunciation guide. (Rev: SLJ 2/07) [569]

2999 Brown, Charlotte Lewis. *The Day the Dinosaurs Died* (1–3). Illus. by Phil Wilson. Series: I Can Read! 2006, HarperCollins $15.99 (0-06-000528-9). The author imagines what it would have been like when an asteroid hit the earth 65 million years ago, triggering the demise of the dinosaurs; suitable for beginning readers. (Rev: SLJ 6/06) [567.9]

3000 Dahl, Michael. *Double Bones: The Adventure of Diplodocus* (K–3). Illus. by Garry Nichols. Series: Dinosaur World. 2005, Picture Window $22.60 (1-4048-0940-6). 24pp. Facts about the diplodocus appear alongside a simple story about its life in this review of what we know about the dinosaur. Also use *Long Arm: The Adventure of Brachiosaurus* and *Monster Fish: The Adventure of the Ichthyosaurs* (both 2005). (Rev: SLJ 8/05) [567.913]

3001 Dixon, Dougal. *Tyrannosaurus and Other Dinosaurs of North America* (2–4). Illus. by Steve Weston. Series: Dinosaur Find. 2007, Picture Window LB $17.95 (978-1-4048-2265-8). 24pp. Double-page spreads introduce the prehistoric reptiles that roamed North America with eye-catching art, brief text, and a box that looks at similar contemporary animals. (Rev: BL 3/15/07) [567.9097]

3002 Gibbons, Gail. *Dinosaur Discoveries* (1–3). Illus. 2005, Holiday $16.95 (0-8234-1971-1). 32pp. Gibbons reviews dinosaur history in light of new discoveries and tells about paleontologists' ongoing efforts to learn more about these prehistoric creatures. (Rev: BL 10/1/05; SLJ 2/06) [597.9]

3003 Goldish, Meish. *The Fossil Feud: Marsh and Cope's Bone Wars* (3–5). Series: Fossil Hunters. 2006, Bearport LB $17.97 (1-59716-256-6). 32pp. The story of the dramatic 19th-century clash between American paleontologists Othniel Marsh and Edward Cope. (Rev: BL 10/15/06; SLJ 1/07) [560.92]

3004 Hort, Lenny. *Did Dinosaurs Eat Pizza? Mysteries Science Hasn't Solved* (PS–3). Illus. by John O'Brien. 2006, Holt $15.95 (0-8050-6757-4). 32pp. A lighthearted look at science's ongoing quest to learn more about what life was like for the dinosaurs. (Rev: BL 4/1/06; SLJ 3/06) [567.9]

3005 Jenkins, Steve. *Prehistoric Actual Size* (1–3). Illus. 2005, Houghton $16.00 (0-618-53578-0). 32pp. Dramatic cut-paper artwork offers actual-size representations of anatomical features from such prehistoric creatures as the eight-foot-tall "terror bird" and the Gigantosaurus. (Rev: BCCB 10/05; BL 10/15/05*; HB 1–2/06; HBG 4/06; LMC 8–9/06; SLJ 12/05) [560]

3006 Johnson, Jinny. *Dino Wars* (3–5). Illus. 2005, Abrams $17.95 (0-8109-5798-1). 144pp. Dinosaurs are rated by assets including strength, armor, speed, agility, and scariness in this informative guide with a wrestling TV show feel. (Rev: BL 12/15/05; SLJ 2/06) [567.9]

3007 Kudlinski, Kathleen V. *Boy, Were We Wrong About Dinosaurs!* (K–3). Illus. by S. D. Schindler. 2005, Dutton $15.99 (0-525-46978-8). 32pp. Scientists' misconceptions about dinosaurs and other prehistoric creatures are highlighted in interesting, thought-provoking text and realistic illustrations. (Rev: BCCB 1/06; BL 12/1/05*; HB 11–12/05; HBG 4/06; SLJ 12/05) [567.9]

3008 Landau, Elaine. *Pterosaurs* (2–4). Illus. Series: True Book Dinosaurs. 2006, Scholastic LB $25.00 (0-531-16829-8). 48pp. Colorful clear illustrations add to the appeal of this fact-packed survey of pterosaurs, fossils, and dinosaur extinction. (Rev: BL 1/1–15/07) [567.918]

3009 Lessem, Don. *The Fastest Dinosaurs* (2–4). Illus. by John Bindon. Series: Meet the Dinosaurs. 2005, Lerner LB $23.93 (0-8225-1422-2); paper $6.95 (0-8225-2620-4). 32pp. Which dinosaurs were fastest? And how did scientists find out? Conversational text tackles these questions. Also use *The Smartest Dinosaurs* and *Flying Giants of Dinosaur Time* (both 2005). (Rev: SLJ 7/05) [567.9]

3010 Lessem, Don. *Sea Giants of Dinosaur Time* (2–3). Illus. by John Bindon. Series: Meet the Dinosaurs. 2005, Lerner LB $23.95 (0-8225-1425-7); paper $7.95 (0-8225-2623-9). 32pp. The fascinating creatures that filled the prehistoric seas are the focus of this book, complete with illustrations. (Rev: SLJ 9/05) [567.9]

3011 Lunis, Natalie. *A T. Rex Named Sue: Sue Hendrickson's Huge Discovery* (3–6). Illus. Series: Fossil Hunters. 2006, Bearport LB $23.96 (1-59716-259-0). 32pp. In 1990 Sue Hendrickson discovered a Tyrannosaurus rex skeleton in South Dakota; this is a simply written account of the discovery and the lengthy legal battle to determine custody of the dinosaur remains. (Rev: SLJ 1/07) [567.912]

3012 McMullan, Kate. *Dinosaur Hunters* (2–4). Illus. by John R. Jones. Series: Step into Reading. 2005, Random LB $11.99 (0-375-92450-7); paper $3.99 (0-375-82450-2). 48pp. A new edition of the easy reader on how fossils are found and studied, with updated text and illustrations. (Rev: BL 9/1/05) [560]

3013 Malam, John. *Dinosaur* (5–8). Illus. 2006, DK $15.99 (978-0-7566-1412-6). 70pp. Tyrannosaurus rex is the star of this attractive, DK-style book that covers the dinosaur's anatomy, life cycle, and hunting techniques plus archaeological findings and the

science that has allowed to reconstruct what we know today. (Rev: SLJ 4/07) [567.9]

3014 Padma, T. V. *The Albertosaurus Mystery: Philip Currie's Hunt in the Badlands* (3–6). Illus. Series: Fossil Hunters. 2006, Bearport LB $23.96 (1-59716-254-X). 32pp. Describes paleontologist Philip Currie's search for a site containing the remains of multiple dinosaurs. (Rev: SLJ 1/07) [567.912]

3015 Sabuda, Robert, and Matthew Reinhart. *Encyclopedia Prehistorica: Dinosaurs* (K–4). Illus. by authors. 2005, Candlewick $26.99 (0-7636-2228-1). Beautifully engineered fold-outs introduce a variety of dinosaurs. (Rev: SLJ 9/05)

3016 Sabuda, Robert, and Matthew Reinhart. *Sharks and Other Sea Monsters* (1–3). Series: Encyclopedia Prehistorica. 2006, Candlewick $27.99 (0-7636-2229-X). 12pp. Elaborate pop-ups highlight facts about sharks, megalodons, and other prehistoric sea predators. (Rev: BL 6/1–15/06; SLJ 7/06) [566.22]

3017 Schomp, Virginia. *Ceratosaurus: And Other Horned Meat-Eaters* (3–4). Illus. Series: Prehistoric World. 2005, Benchmark LB $17.95 (0-7614-2009-6). 32pp. Vivid illustrations and conversational text introduce the Ceratosaurus and related prehistoric horned animals. Also use *Therizinosaurus* and *Plateosaurus* (both 2005). (Rev: SLJ 3/06)

3018 Schomp, Virginia. *Iguanodon: And Other Spiky-Thumbed Plant-Eaters* (2–4). Illus. Series: Prehistoric World. 2005, Marshall Cavendish LB $17.95 (0-7614-2005-3). 32pp. Accessible text and eye-catching images make this an appealing introduction to this prehistoric animal's appearance, diet, habitat, and behavior. (Rev: BL 3/1/06) [567.912]

3019 Skrepnick, Michael W. *Sinosauropteryx: Mysterious Feathered Dinosaur* (3–4). Illus. by author. Series: I Like Dinosaurs! 2005, Enslow LB $21.26 (0-7660-2623-X). 24pp. Introduces the Sinosauropteryx, a small, feathered, poultry-size dinosaur whose fossilized remains were found in China in the mid-1990s. (Rev: SLJ 2/06) [567.912]

3020 Walker, Sally M. *Fossils* (2–4). Illus. Series: Early Bird Earth Science. 2006, Lerner LB $25.26 (0-8225-5945-5). 48pp. Walker explains how fossils are formed, where they're mostly likely to be found, and what can be learned by studying them. (Rev: SLJ 1/07) [560]

3021 Wheeler, Lisa. *Mammoths on the Move* (K–2). Illus. by Kurt Cyrus. 2006, Harcourt $16.00 (0-15-204700-X). 32pp. A woolly mammoth migration is the subject of this rhyming book with large illustrations. (Rev: BL 5/1/06; SLJ 6/06) [569]

3022 Zoehfeld, Kathleen W. *Dinosaur Tracks* (2–4). Illus. by Lucia Washburn. Series: Let's-Read-and-Find-Out Science. 2007, HarperCollins $15.99 (0-06-029024-2). 40pp. A look at how dinosaur tracks are discovered and what they can tell us about the animals that made them. (Rev: BL 12/1/06) [567.9]

Anthropology and Prehistoric Life

3023 Goldenberg, Linda. *Little People and a Lost World: An Anthropological Mystery* (5–8). Illus. 2006, Twenty-First Century LB $29.27 (0-8225-5983-8). 112pp. In 2003, a team of archaeologists and anthropologists discovered the skeleton of what's believed to be a small human being who lived more than 12,000 years ago on Flores Island in Indonesia; this book looks at the controversy over the discovery and the insights it has given into early human life. (Rev: BL 12/1/06; SLJ 4/07) [569.909598]

Archaeology

3024 Dean, Arlan. *Terra-Cotta Soldiers: Army of Stone* (4–7). Illus. Series: High Interest Books: Digging Up the Past. 2005, Children's Pr. LB $23.00 (0-516-25124-4); paper $6.95 (0-516-25093-0). 40pp. For reluctant readers, this is a useful introduction to one of the world's most extraordinary archaeological finds: the 8,000 terracotta warriors of China. (Rev: BL 10/15/05; SLJ 2/06) [931]

3025 Shuter, Jane. *Ancient China* (4–6). Illus. Series: Excavating the Past. 2005, Heinemann LB $31.43 (1-4034-5995-9). 48pp. The work of archaeologists is clearly shown in this well-illustrated exploration of the early history of China. (Rev: SLJ 2/06) [931]

World History

General

3026 Andryszewski, Tricia. *Walking the Earth: The History of Human Migration* (5–9). 2006, Twenty-First Century LB $27.93 (0-7613-3458-0). 80pp. A thorough introduction to the movements of human population across more than 150,000 years, with many illustrations, maps, and charts. (Rev: HBG 4/07; LMC 3/07; SLJ 1/07; VOYA 12/06) [304.8]

3027 Burgan, Michael. *The Spanish Conquest of America: Prehistory to 1775* (5–8). Series: Latino-American History. 2006, Chelsea House LB $35.00 (978-0-8160-6440-3). 106pp. A thorough and clear account of Spain's influence on the Americas, with discussion of individual explorers as well as the impact on native peoples and the conflicts with other colonial powers. (Rev: BL 3/15/07) [979]

3028 Connolly, Sean. *Gender Equality* (5–8). Series: Campaigns for Change. 2005, Smart Apple Media LB $29.95 (1-58340-515-1). 48pp. An exploration of women's status and struggles to improve it throughout history; also use *The Right to Vote* (2005). (Rev: SLJ 5/06) [305.42]

3029 Deary, Terry. *The Wicked History of the World: History with the Nasty Bits Left In!* (4–7). Illus. by Martin Brown. 2006, Scholastic $10.99 (0-439-87786-5). 93pp. This pun-filled survey of world history, with its emphasis on the shadier side, will attract reluctant readers with sections on "Beastly Barbarians," "Rotten Rules," and "Vicious Villains." (Rev: SLJ 12/06) [909]

3030 Hansen, Dianne. *Agriculture* (3–5). Series: Yesterday and Today. 2005, Gale LB $22.45 (1-56711-827-5). 32pp. A broad overview of the history of agriculture, from the dawn of man through today, with photographs, illustrations and a timelines; suitable for browsing. (Rev: SLJ 7/05)

3031 Harper, Charise Mericle. *Flush! The Scoop on Poop Throughout the Ages* (2–4). Illus. 2007, Little, Brown $15.99 (0-316-01064-2). 32pp. Combining rhyming verse, sidebar facts, and bright illustrations, this paean to poop disposal will fascinate kids drawn to its mix of gross-out humor and arcane historical information. (Rev: BL 1/1–15/07; SLJ 9/06) [392.3]

3032 Kurlansky, Mark. *The Story of Salt* (4–6). Illus. by S. D. Schindler. 2006, Putnam $16.99 (0-399-23998-7). 48pp. History, science, politics, and technology come together in this story of the sought-after element, adapted from the adult version. (Rev: BL 7/06; SLJ 10/06*) [553.6]

3033 Lassieur, Allison. *The History of Pirates: From Privateers to Outlaws* (2–4). Illus. Series: Edge Books: Real World of Pirates. 2006, Capstone LB $17.95 (0-7368-6423-7). 32pp. Ideal for beginning readers, this attractive title offers a brief history of pirates with eye-catching illustrations. (Rev: BL 10/15/06) [910.4]

3034 Lauber, Patricia. *What You Never Knew About Beds, Bedrooms, and Pajamas* (2–5). Illus. by John Manders. Series: Around the House History. 2006, Simon & Schuster $16.95 (978-0-689-85211-4). A light history of sleeping customs from the Stone Age to today, with comical commentary in cartoons; suitable for browsing. (Rev: SLJ 2/07)

3035 Love, Ann, and Jane Drake. *Sweet!* (3–5). Illus. by Claudia Dávila. 2007, Tundra $19.95 (978-0-88776-752-4). 64pp. This is an appealing survey of candy from ancient history to today, with a running timeline, cartoon illustrations, and many funny and appropriate anecdotes; more suited to browsing than reports. (Rev: BL 2/1/07) [641.8]

3036 Mara, Wil. *The Seven Continents* (K–2). Series: Rookie Read-About Geography. 2005, Children's Pr. LB $19.50 (0-516-22748-3). 31pp. A broad geographical overview of the continents, with a picture glossary to aid new readers. (Rev: SLJ 7/05)

3037 Markle, Sandra. *Outside and Inside Mummies* (4–6). Illus. Series: Outside and Inside. 2005, Walker $17.95 (0-8027-8966-8). 40pp. This photo-filled title provides an overview of what cutting-edge medical imaging technology reveals about mummies and mummification practices. (Rev: BL 9/15/05; SLJ 8/05) [393]

3038 Markle, Sandra. *Rescues!* (4–7). Illus. 2006, Lerner LB $25.26 (0-8225-3413-4). 88pp. Markle covers rescue efforts in 11 recent disasters (2004 to 2005), giving details of technology used and providing accounts by victims, rescuers, and eyewitnesses. (Rev: BL 4/1/06*; HBG 10/06; LMC 11–12/06; SLJ 8/06; VOYA 6/06) [363.34]

3039 O'Brien, Patrick. *Mutiny on the Bounty* (4–7). Illus. 2007, Walker $17.95 (0-8027-9587-0). 40pp. Clear, balanced narrative and vivid illustrations tell both sides of the story of the famous mutiny and its aftermath. (Rev: BL 1/1–15/07) [910.4]

3040 Parks, Peggy J. *Clothing* (3–5). Series: Yesterday and Today. 2005, Gale LB $22.45 (1-56711-828-3). 32pp. A broad overview of the history of apparel, from the dawn of man through today, with photographs, illustrations and a timelines; suitable for browsing. Also use *Entertainment* (2005). (Rev: SLJ 7/05)

3041 Shapiro, Stephen. *Battle Stations! Fortifications Through the Ages* (5–8). Illus. 2005, Annick LB $19.95 (1-55037-889-9); paper $7.95 (1-55037-888-0). 32pp. A tall, slim, and very visual overview of fortifications around the world and throughout history. (Rev: BL 9/15/05) [355.7]

3042 Tanaka, Shelley. *Mummies: The Newest, Coolest and Creepiest from Around the World* (4–7). Illus. 2005, Abrams $16.95 (0-8109-5797-3). 48pp. Mummies from across history and around the world are on display in the colorful — and often graphic — pages of this fascinating book. (Rev: BL 12/1/05*; HBG 4/06; LMC 4–5/06; SLJ 12/05*) [393]

Ancient History

General and Miscellaneous

3043 Anderson, Jameson. *History and Activities of Ancient China* (3–6). Illus. Series: Hands-on Ancient History. 2006, Heinemann LB $28.21 (978-1-4034-7922-8). 32pp. Social life, arts and culture, games, and holidays and celebrations are covered in this attractive and accessible volume that includes a recipe and two crafts. (Rev: HBG 4/07; SLJ 4/07) [931]

3044 Ball, Jacqueline, and Richard H. Levey. *Ancient China: Archaeology Unlocks the Secrets of China's Past* (5–8). Illus. Series: National Geographic Investigates. 2006, National Geographic $17.95 (978-0-7922-7783-5). 64pp. After an introduction to China and its history, this volume looks at individual archaeological finds and at the lives revealed; vivid illustrations and good descriptions of archaeological techniques add to the value. (Rev: BL 10/15/06) [931]

3045 Barr, Gary E. *History and Activities of the Islamic Empire* (3–6). Illus. Series: Hands-on Ancient History. 2006, Heinemann LB $28.21 (978-1-4034-7926-6). 32pp. Social life, arts and culture, games, and holidays and celebrations are covered in this attractive and accessible volume that includes a recipe and three crafts. (Rev: SLJ 4/07) [909]

3046 Barr, Gary E. *History and Activities of the West African Kingdoms* (3–6). Illus. Series: Hands-on Ancient History. 2006, Heinemann LB $28.21 (978-1-4034-7925-9). 32pp. Social life, arts and culture, games, and holidays and celebrations are covered in this attractive and accessible volume that includes a recipe, two crafts, and an activity (a game of Mancala). (Rev: SLJ 4/07) [966]

3047 Barter, James. *The Ancient Persians* (5–8). Series: Lost Civilizations. 2005, Gale LB $28.70 (1-59018-621-4). 112pp. The lost civilization of the ancient Persians, with information about the society's people, customs, monetary system, and military, with maps and illustrations. (Rev: SLJ 6/06) [935]

3048 Bingham, Jane. *The Ancient World*, vol. 1 (5–8). Illus. Series: A History of Fashion and Costume. 2005, Facts on File $35.00 (0-8160-5944-6). 64pp. A broad overview of the clothing and personal adornment worn during ancient times, with many visual aids. (Rev: SLJ 5/06) [391]

3049 Calvert, Patricia. *The Ancient Celts* (5–8). Series: People of the Ancient World. 2005, Watts LB $29.50 (0-531-12359-6); paper $9.95 (0-531-16845-X). 112pp. Introduces readers to the arts, religious beliefs, and society of the ancient Celts, with discussion of individual occupations and of the discoveries by archaeologists and anthropologists. (Rev: SLJ 9/05) [973]

3050 Glaser, Jason, and Don Roley. *Ninja* (3–6). Series: Edge Books: Warriors of History. 2006, Capstone LB $23.93 (0-7368-6432-6). 32pp. A colorfully introduction to Japan's ninja warriors, their history, weapons, and way of life. (Rev: SLJ 1/07) [355.5]

3051 Gruber, Beth. *Ancient Inca: Archaeology Unlocks the Secrets of Inca's Past* (3–7). Series: National Geographic $17.95 (978-0-7922-7827-6). 64pp. This well-illustrated title examines how archaeologists gain knowledge about the ancient Inca civilization of pre-Columbian America, including information on pottery, textiles, and mummies. (Rev: SLJ 2/07) [985]

3052 Landau, Elaine. *Exploring the World of the Vikings with Elaine Landau* (3–6). Illus. Series: Exploring Ancient Civilizations with Elaine Landau. 2005, Enslow LB $23.93 (0-7660-2340-0). 48pp. Readers explore the time of the Vikings along with the author and her dog Max, learning about many aspects of early Norse life and culture, including housing, food, apparel, religion, occupations, and relations with the outside world. (Rev: SLJ 12/05) [948.022]

3053 Leavitt, Caroline. *Samurai* (3–5). Illus. Series: Edge Books: Warriors of History. 2006, Capstone LB $17.95 (0-7368-6433-4). 32pp. A solid exploration of the history and traditions associated with Japan's samurai warriors, with a wealth of illustrations. (Rev: BL 10/15/06; SLJ 1/07) [952]

3054 Lourie, Peter. *Hidden World of the Aztec* (5–8). Illus. 2006, Boyds Mills $17.95 (1-59078-069-8). 45pp. This lavishly illustrated title uses modern archaeological projects to introduce the history and culture of the ancient Aztec civilization. (Rev: BL 10/15/06; SLJ 10/06) [972]

3055 MacDonald, Fiona. *How to Be a Samurai Warrior* (2–5). Illus. by John James. Series: How to Be. 2005, National Geographic $14.95 (0-7922-3618-1). 32pp. A glimpse of what life was like for samurai warriors, touching on such fundamentals as clothing, weapons, job requirements, family life, and pay. (Rev: SLJ 12/05) [952.02]

3056 Morley, Jacqueline. *You Wouldn't Want to Work on the Great Wall of China! Defenses You'd Rather Not Build* (3–6). Illus. by David Antram. Series: You Wouldn't Want To. 2006, Watts LB $27.50 (0-531-12424-X); paper $9.95 (0-531-12449-5). 32pp. An unflinching look at what life was like for the workers who built the Great Wall of China, with cartoon illustrations that lighten the grimness. (Rev: SLJ 9/06) [951]

3057 Perl, Lila. *The Ancient Maya* (5–8). Series: People of the Ancient World. 2005, Watts LB $29.50 (0-531-12381-2); paper $9.95 (0-531-16848-4). 112pp. Introduces readers to the arts, religious beliefs, and society of the Maya, with discussion of individual occupations and of the discoveries by archaeologists and anthropologists. (Rev: SLJ 9/05) [973]

3058 Reece, Katherine. *West African Kingdoms: Empires of Gold and Trade* (3–5). Illus. Series: Ancient Civilizations. 2005, Rourke LB $20.95 (1-5951-5508-2). 48pp. This striking photoessay introduces the culture, geography, people, language, religion, and wildlife of three ancient West African

kingdoms — Ghana, Mali, and Songhai. (Rev: BL 3/15/06; SLJ 4/06) [966]

3059 Richardson, Hazel. *Life in Ancient Africa* (4–7). Illus. Series: Peoples of the Ancient World. 2005, Crabtree LB $23.92 (0-7787-2043-8); paper $8.95 (0-7787-2073-X). 32pp. Introduces the early civilizations of Africa, examining their arts, spiritual beliefs, government, language, and technology; color photographs, sidebars, and timelines add information and appeal. (Rev: SLJ 11/05) [973]

3060 Richardson, Hazel. *Life in Ancient Japan* (4–7). Illus. Series: Peoples of the Ancient World. 2005, Crabtree LB $23.92 (0-7787-2041-1); paper $8.95 (0-7787-2071-3). 32pp. Introduces ancient Japan's arts, spiritual beliefs, government, language, and technology; color photographs, sidebars, and timelines add information and appeal. (Rev: SLJ 11/05) [952]

3061 Richardson, Hazel. *Life in the Ancient Indus River Valley* (4–7). Illus. Series: Peoples of the Ancient World. 2005, Crabtree LB $23.92 (0-7787-2040-3); paper $8.95 (0-7787-2070-5). 32pp. Introduces life in the earliest urban civilization on the Indian subcontinent, examining the arts, spiritual beliefs, government, language, and technology; color photographs, sidebars, and timelines add information and appeal. (Rev: SLJ 11/05) [973]

3062 Richardson, Hazel. *Life of the Ancient Celts* (4–7). Illus. Series: Peoples of the Ancient World. 2005, Crabtree LB $23.92 (0-7787-2045-4); paper $8.95 (0-7787-2075-6). 32pp. Introduces the early Celtic civilization, examining arts, spiritual beliefs, government, language, and technology; color photographs, sidebars, and timelines add information and appeal. (Rev: SLJ 11/05) [973]

3063 Shuter, Jane. *Life in a Viking Town* (2–4). Illus. Series: Picture the Past. 2005, Heinemann LB $25.64 (1-4034-6440-5). 32pp. This colorful title gives young readers a sampling of what life was like in a Viking town, covering such topics as dwellings, jobs, food, apparel, and leisure activities. (Rev: SLJ 11/05)

3064 Shuter, Jane. *Life on a Viking Ship* (2–4). Illus. Series: Picture the Past. 2005, Heinemann LB $25.64 (1-4034-6441-3). 32pp. This attractive title gives young readers an overview of what life was like on a Viking ship. (Rev: SLJ 11/05)

3065 Silate, Jennifer. *The Inca Ruins of Machu Picchu* (4–6). Illus. Series: Wonders of the World. 2005, Gale LB $23.70 (0-7377-3068-4). 48pp. This is a useful, easy-to-read introduction to the current knowledge about the Incas and the construction of Machu Picchu, with details of contemporary cable-car access and attempts to preserve the site. (Rev: SLJ 7/06) [985]

3066 Sonneborn, Liz. *The Ancient Kushites* (5–8). Series: People of the Ancient World. 2005, Watts

LB $29.50 (0-531-12380-4); paper $9.95 (0-531-16847-6). 112pp. Explores the arts, religious beliefs, and culture of Africa's ancient Kushites, who were also known as Nubians. (Rev: SLJ 9/05) [973]

Egypt and Mesopotamia

3067 Adams, Simon. *Ancient Egypt* (4–6). Illus. Series: Kingfisher Voyages. 2006, Kingfisher $15.95 (978-0-7534-6027-6). 54pp. Viewed from the perspective of an Egyptologist named Dr. Kent Weeks, this is a tour of important sites of ancient Egypt, with discussion of the embalming and engineering practices of the time and the modern technologies that have uncovered the answers to some mysteries. (Rev: SLJ 2/07)

3068 Burgan, Michael. *The Curse of King Tut's Tomb* (3–6). Illus. by Barbara Schulz. Series: Graphic Library/Graphic History. 2004, Capstone LB $22.60 (0-7368-3833-3). 32pp. A graphic "novel" — factual, but embellished — about the discovery of Tut's tomb and the legendary curse associated with it; will appeal to reluctant readers. (Rev: SLJ 7/05) [973]

3069 Chrisp, Peter. *Pyramid* (4–8). Illus. Series: DK Experience. 2006, DK $15.99 (0-7566-1410-4). 67pp. Full-color illustrations, 3-D diagrams, and CT scans make this survey of the construction and importance of the Great Pyramid of Giza informative and attractive. (Rev: SLJ 11/06) [932]

3070 Cline, Eric H., and Jill Rubalcaba. *The Ancient Egyptian World* (5–10). Series: The World in Ancient Times. 2005, Oxford LB $32.95 (0-19-517391-0). 190pp. An overview of ancient Egyptian history and culture, with chronologically arranged chapters covering religion, medicine, clothing, arts, and so forth and introducing key figures such as Hatshepsut, Tutankhamen, and Cleopatra. (Rev: SLJ 1/06) [932]

3071 Filer, Joyce. *Pyramids* (3–8). Illus. 2006, Oxford Univ. $16.95 (0-19-530521-3). 48pp. A detailed introduction to the pyramids of ancient Egypt and their design, their builders, their construction, and their contents; there is also information on pyramids outside Egypt. (Rev: SLJ 7/06) [932]

3072 Hibbert, Clare. *Ancient Egypt* (3–6). Illus. by Adam Hook. Series: Rich and Poor in. 2005, Smart Apple Media LB $27.10 (1-58340-720-0). 32pp. Compares the everyday lives of the rich and the poor in ancient Egypt. (Rev: SLJ 5/06) [932.01]

3073 Hynson, Colin. *The Building of the Great Pyramid* (5–8). Illus. Series: Stories from History. 2006, School Specialty $14.95 (978-0-7696-4708-1); paper $6.95 (0-7696-4692-1). 48pp. Full-color illustrations and graphic-novel format make this sur-

vey of the ancient engineering feat attractive to reluctant readers. (Rev: SLJ 1/07)

3074 Kaplan, Sarah Pitt. *The Great Pyramid at Giza: Tomb of Wonders* (5–8). Series: Digging Up the Past. 2005, Children's Pr. LB $23.00 (0-516-25131-7); paper $6.95 (0-516-25095-7). 48pp. A richly illustrated survey of the important pyramid and the reasons for its creation; suitable for reluctant readers. (Rev: SLJ 2/06) [932]

3075 Manning, Mick, and Brita Granström. *Fly on the Wall: Pharaoh's Egypt* (2–4). Illus. by authors. 2006, Frances Lincoln $15.95 (1-84507-100-X). 37pp. Ancient Egypt's way of life — its history, culture, and mythology in particular — is shown in an appealing scrapbook format full of facts and following several characters as they go about their business. (Rev: SLJ 4/06) [932]

3076 Rubalcaba, Jill. *Ancient Egypt: Archaeology Unlocks the Secrets of Egypt's Past* (3–7). 2006, National Geographic $17.95 (978-0-7922-7784-2). 64pp. This well-illustrated overview of what archaeologists have uncovered about life in ancient Egypt highlights two related events: the 1922 discovery of King Tutankhamen's tomb and the 2005 CT scan of the boy king's mummy. (Rev: SLJ 2/07) [932]

Greece

3077 Ackroyd, Peter. *Ancient Greece* (5–8). Series: Voyages Through Time. 2005, DK $19.99 (0-7566-1368-X). 144pp. A handsome introduction to the history and culture of ancient Greece, with photographs and illustrations. (Rev: BL 10/1/05; SLJ 2/06) [938.21]

3078 Broida, Marian. *Projects About Ancient Greece* (4–6). Illus. Series: Hands-on Ancient History. 2006, Benchmark LB $20.95 (978-0-7614-2259-4). 48pp. Ten projects — including Minoan bull-dancer paintings, Mycenaean writing, and black-figure pottery — are accompanied by fictionalized scenarios that add context. (Rev: SLJ 4/07) [938]

3079 McGee, Marni. *Ancient Greece: Archaeology Unlocks the Secrets of Greece's Past* (3–7). Series: National Geographic Investigates. 2006, National Geographic $17.95 (978-0-7922-7826-9). 64pp. This well-illustrated title looks at archaeologists' efforts over the years to uncover — on land and under the sea — information about life in ancient Greece. (Rev: SLJ 2/07)

3080 Shuter, Jane. *Life in a Greek Temple* (2–4). Illus. Series: Picture the Past. 2005, Heinemann LB $17.95 (1-4034-6442-1). 32pp. A basic, attractive overview of Greek temples and their construction as well as the religious beliefs and practices of the ancient Greeks. (Rev: BL 9/15/05) [292.3]

3081 Shuter, Jane. *Life in a Greek Trading Port* (2–4). Illus. Series: Picture the Past. 2005, Heinemann LB $25.64 (1-4034-6444-8). 32pp. This title explores various aspects of everyday life in an ancient Greek port city, including housing, cuisine, clothing, occupations, and leisure pursuits. (Rev: SLJ 11/05)

Rome

3082 Dargie, Richard. *Rich and Poor in Ancient Rome* (3–6). Illus. by Adam Hook. 2005, Smart Apple Media LB $27.10 (1-58340-722-7). 32pp. The everyday lives of the rich and the poor in ancient Rome are compared. (Rev: SLJ 5/06) [937]

3083 Deem, James M. *Bodies from the Ash: Life and Death in Ancient Pompeii* (5–8). Illus. 2005, Houghton $16.00 (0-618-47308-4). 48pp. This photoessay full of vivid illustrations outlines what archaeologists have uncovered about the destruction of Pompeii when Mount Vesuvius erupted nearly 2,000 years ago. (Rev: BL 11/1/05; SLJ 12/05*) [937]

3084 Landau, Elaine. *Exploring Ancient Rome with Elaine Landau* (3–5). Illus. Series: Exploring Ancient Civilizations. 2005, Enslow LB $17.95 (0-7660-2337-0). 48pp. The author and her dog Max give readers a tour of ancient Rome's society, trade, engineering, architecture, religion, and food and clothing. (Rev: BL 9/1/05; SLJ 12/05) [937]

3085 MacDonald, Fiona. *How to Be a Roman Soldier* (2–5). Illus. by Nicholas Hewetson. Series: How to Be. 2005, National Geographic $14.95 (0-7922-3616-5). 32pp. Soldiers' training, weapons, compensation, recreation, and home and family life are all covered in a reader-friendly, well-illustrated format. (Rev: SLJ 12/05) [355]

3086 Martin, Michael. *Gladiators* (3–6). Series: Edge Books: Warriors of History. 2006, Capstone LB $23.93 (0-7368-6429-6). 32pp. This colorful introduction to gladiators examines the history of this class of professional warriors in ancient Rome, their weapons, and their way of life. (Rev: SLJ 1/07) [796.8]

3087 Osborne, Mary Pope. *Pompeii: Lost and Found* (2–4). Illus. by Bonnie Christensen. 2006, Knopf $16.95 (0-375-82889-3). 40pp. In addition to describing the eruption of Vesuvius in 79 A.D., Osborne discusses its excavation and how archaeological discoveries allow us to imagine daily life in the city at that time. (Rev: BL 12/1/05; SLJ 1/06) [937]

3088 Osborne, Mary Pope, and Natalie Pope Boyce. *Ancient Rome and Pompeii: A Nonfiction Companion to Vacation Under the Volcano* (2–4). Illus. by Sal Murdocca. 2006, Random $4.99 (0-375-83220-3). 128pp. This nonfiction companion to *Vacation Under the Volcano* provides a fascinating introduc-

tion to the history and culture of ancient Rome and Pompeii. (Rev: BL 6/1–15/06) [937]

3089 Parker, Vic. *Pompeii AD 79: A City Buried by a Volcanic Eruption* (4–7). Series: When Disaster Struck. 2006, Raintree LB $32.86 (1-4109-2276-6). 56pp. Parker looks at Pompeii both before and after its destruction by the eruption of Mount Vesuvius, discussing the nature (and likelihood) of volcanic eruptions and what archaeologists have learned from their excavations. (Rev: SLJ 1/07) [937.7]

3090 Stewart, David. *You Wouldn't Want to Be a Roman Soldier! Barbarians You'd Rather Not Meet* (3–6). Illus. by David Antram. Series: You Wouldn't Want To. 2006, Watts LB $27.50 (0-531-12423-1); paper $9.95 (0-531-12448-7). 32pp. This book banishes romantic notions about the lives of Roman soldiers, but the cartoon illustrations lighten the portrayal of harsh conditions and deadly challenges. (Rev: SLJ 9/06) [937]

Middle Ages

3091 Adkins, Jan. *What If You Met a Knight?* (3–5). Illus. 2006, Roaring Brook $16.95 (1-59643-148-2). 32pp. Presents a realistic view of the life of knights in the Middle Ages and of their daily responsibilities and challenges. (Rev: BL 8/06; HBG 4/07; LMC 2/07; SLJ 9/06; VOYA 2/07) [940.1088]

3092 Currie, Stephen. *Miracles, Saints, and Superstition: The Medieval Mind* (5–9). 2006, Gale LB $28.70 (1-59018-861-6). 104pp. Describes the Middle Ages and the role of Christianity at that time. (Rev: SLJ 3/07*) [940.1]

3093 Gravett, Christopher. *Real Knights: Over 20 True Stories of Battle and Adventure* (4–6). Illus. by John James. 2005, Enchanted Lion $15.95 (1-59270-034-9). 48pp. This collection of tales about real-life knights in action includes the exploits of Richard the Lionheart, El Cid, Braveheart, and some others who are less well known. (Rev: SLJ 8/06) [940.1]

3094 MacDonald, Fiona. *How to Be a Medieval Knight* (2–5). Illus. by Mark Bergin. Series: How to Be. 2005, National Geographic $14.95 (0-7922-3619-X). 32pp. Knights' training, equipment, weapons, compensation, tournaments, and peacetime occupations and family life are all covered in a reader-friendly, well-illustrated format. (Rev: SLJ 12/05) [940.1]

3095 MacDonald, Fiona. *Knights, Castles, and Warfare in the Middle Ages* (5–8). Series: World Almanac Library of the Middle Ages. 2005, World Almanac LB $30.00 (0-8368-5895-6). 48pp. Describes the role of knights, the equipment they used, and their lives and homes. Also use *The*

Plague and Medicine in the Middle Ages (2005). (Rev: SLJ 1/06) [940.1]

3096 Martin, Michael. *Knights* (3–6). 2006, Capstone LB $23.93 (0-7368-6431-8). 32pp. This colorful overview of knights examines the history, weapons, and way of life of these medieval warriors. (Rev: SLJ 1/07) [940.1]

3097 Olmon, Kyle. *Sabuda and Reinhart Present Castle: Medieval Days and Knights* (3–5). Illus. by Tracy Sabin. 2006, Scholastic $19.99 (0-439-54324-X). 6pp. An intriguing look at medieval times and castles featuring three-dimensional pop-up images of everything from the castle itself to drawbridges and catapults. (Rev: BL 11/15/06; SLJ 12/06) [940.1]

3098 Padrino, Mercedes. *Cities and Towns in the Middle Ages* (5–8). Series: World Almanac Library of the Middle Ages. 2005, World Almanac LB $30.00 (0-8368-5893-X). 48pp. A look at medieval urban living — social structure, government structure, employment, education, religion, food and clothing, and so forth. Also use *Feudalism and Village Life in the Middle Ages* (2005). (Rev: SLJ 1/06) [940.1]

3099 Senker, Cath. *The Black Death 1347–1350: The Plague Spreads Across Europe* (4–7). Series: When Disaster Struck. 2006, Raintree LB $32.86 (1-4109-2278-2). 56pp. Documents the widespread devastation caused by the plague that spread across Europe in the mid-14th century causing an estimated 20 million deaths and discusses current medical understanding and practices. (Rev: SLJ 1/07) [614.5732]

3100 Steele, Philip. *The Medieval World*, vol. 2 (5–8). Illus. Series: A History of Fashion and Costume. 2005, Facts on File $35.00 (0-8160-5945-4). 64pp. A broad overview of the clothing and personal adornment worn during this time period, with many visual aids. (Rev: SLJ 5/06) [391]

3101 Steer, Dugald A. *Knight: A Noble Guide for Young Squires* (2–6). Illus. by Milivoj Ceran and Neil Chapman,. 2006, Candlewick $17.99 (978-0-7636-3062-1). This fact-filled guide to the ways of knighthood is written as though it were a letter of guidance from an imprisoned knight to his son; the delicate flaps and playing pieces for a game called "Squire Fight" will restrict this book's circulation. (Rev: SLJ 2/07) [940.1]

World War I

3102 Myers, Walter Dean, and Bill Miles. *The Harlem Hellfighters: When Pride Met Courage* (5–8). Illus. 2006, HarperCollins LB $17.89 (0-06-001137-8). 160pp. A tribute to the World War I

heroism of the 369th Infantry Regiment, which was made up entirely of African Americans. (Rev: BL 2/1/06; SLJ 4/06) [940.4]

World War II

3103 Fitzgerald, Brian. *Under Fire in World War II* (4–6). Series: On the Front Line. 2005, Raintree LB $29.93 (1-4109-1468-2). 48pp. This is an accessible overview of the key events of World War II, with first-person accounts, photographs, fact boxes, and a timeline. (Rev: SLJ 12/05) [940.54]

3104 Hama, Larry, and Anthony Williams. *The Battle of Iwo Jima: Guerrilla Warfare in the Pacific* (5–8). Illus. Series: Graphic Battles of World War II. 2007, Rosen LB $21.95 (1-4042-0781-3). 48pp. After background text to provide context, this graphic-novel account of the battle of Iwo Jima takes readers behind the lines on both sides of the bloody conflict. (Rev: BL 4/1/07) [940.54]

3105 Kacer, Kathy. *Hiding Edith: A Holocaust Remembrance Book for Young Readers* (4–7). Illus. 2006, Second Story $10.95 (1-897187-06-8). 120pp. Focusing on a young Jewish girl named Edith Schwalb, this is the story of a French couple who hid 100 Jewish refugee children during World War II with the help of their town. (Rev: BL 12/1/06; SLJ 12/06) [940.53]

3106 Nicholson, Dorinda Makanaonalani. *Remember World War II: Kids Who Survived Tell Their Stories* (5–8). Illus. Series: Remember. 2005, National Geographic LB $27.90 (0-7922-7191-2). 64pp. First-person accounts of World War II are given historical context plus illustrations, maps, and so forth; Madeleine Albright contributes an effective introduction. (Rev: BL 7/05; SLJ 8/05) [940.53]

3107 Nobleman, Marc Tyler. *The Sinking of the USS Indianapolis* (4–7). Series: We the People. 2006, Compass Point LB $25.26 (0-7565-2031-2). 48pp. The story of the sinking of the *USS Indianapolis*, two weeks before the end of World War II, is told in straightforward text, with photographs and useful "Did You Know?" features. (Rev: SLJ 1/07)

3108 Steele, D. Kelly. *Would You Salute? One Child's Story of the Holocaust* (3–4). Illus. by Becky Hyatt Rickenbaker. 2006, Hidden Path $22.95 (0-9711534-2-6). 48pp. Margot, whose mother is Christian and whose father is Jewish, faces difficult choices in Nazi Germany. (Rev: BL 7/06) [940.53]

3109 Whiteman, Dorit Bader. *Lonek's Journey: The True Story of a Boy's Escape to Freedom* (5–8). Illus. 2005, Star Bright $15.95 (1-59572-021-9). 144pp. In this gripping true story that starts in 1939, a young Jew named Lonek survives the Nazis' arrival in Poland, a slave labor camp in Siberia, and the long, perilous journey to Palestine. (Rev: BL 11/15/05*; HBG 4/06; LMC 4–5/06; SLJ 1/06) [940.53]

3110 Whiting, Jim. *The Story of the Holocaust* (5–7). Series: Monumental Milestones: Great Events of Modern Times. 2006, Mitchell Lane LB $19.95 (1-58415-400-4). 48pp. Although slim, this volume conveys a lot of information about the roots and atrocities of the Holocaust. (Rev: SLJ 5/06) [940.53]

Modern History

3111 Burgan, Michael. *The Berlin Airlift* (4–7). Series: We the People. 2006, Compass Point LB $25.26 (0-7565-2024-X). 48pp. The story of the Berlin Airlift is told in straightforward text, with photographs and useful "Did You Know?" features. (Rev: SLJ 1/07) [943]

3112 Gallagher, Jim. *Causes of the Iraq War* (5–8). Illus. Series: Road to War. 2005, OTTN LB $22.95 (1-59556-009-4). 72pp. Explores the case put forward for the recent Iraq War, along with the views of those who oppose the conflict with good illustrations and appended material. (Rev: BL 10/15/05) [956.7044]

3113 Santella, Andrew. *The Korean War* (4–7). Series: We the People. 2006, Compass Point LB $25.26 (0-7565-2027-4). 48pp. A brief overview of the roots and progress of the conflict between the two parts of a divided nation. (Rev: SLJ 1/07) [951.904]

Geographical Regions

Africa

General

3114 Bowden, Rob. *Africa* (5–8). Series: Continents of the World. 2006, World Almanac LB $32.67 (0-8368-5910-3). 64pp. Factboxes and "In Focus" articles add to this overview of the history, geography, people, culture, and so forth of the continent of Africa. (Rev: SLJ 2/06)

3115 Croze, Harvey. *Africa for Kids: Exploring a Vibrant Continent* (4–7). Illus. 2006, Chicago Review paper $17.95 (1-55652-598-2). 176pp. Africa's diversity is highlighted in this accessible volume that covers history, nature, key individuals, and contemporary problems such as poverty, war, AIDS, and the environment; there are 19 activities. (Rev: BL 8/06) [916.22]

Central and Eastern Africa

3116 Nicolotti, Muriel. *Kuntai: A Masai Child* (K–3). Series: Children of the World. 2005, Gale LB $21.20 (1-4103-0290-3). 24pp. Using many photographs, this volume introduces the lifestyle and customs of the Masai, a nomadic people living in East Africa; suitable for browsers rather than report writers. (Rev: SLJ 10/05) [967.62]

3117 Shoveller, Herb. *Ryan and Jimmy: And the Well in Africa That Brought Them Together* (3–6). Illus. 2006, Kids Can $16.95 (1-55337-967-5). 55pp. In this inspiring story of one boy's efforts to make a difference in the world, readers learn about Ryan Hreljac, a Canadian boy who raised money to build a well in Africa and worked to rescue Akana Jimmy, the young Ugandan friend abducted by rebels. (Rev: SLJ 11/06) [361.7]

3118 Tanguay, Bridget. *Kenya* (4–7). Illus. Series: Countries of the World. 2006, National Geographic $19.95 (978-0-7922-7628-9). 64pp. An overview of Kenya with information on the country's history, land, people, government, economy and present issues; excellent color photographs and maps are included. (Rev: SLJ 3/07) [967.6]

Northern Africa

3119 Bodden, Valerie. *Suez Canal* (3–6). Series: Modern Wonders of the World. 2006, Creative Education LB $27.10 (1-58341-441-X). 32pp. An interesting overview of the canal's history, construction, and impact on both world commerce and politics. (Rev: SLJ 12/06) [386]

3120 Giraud, Hervé. *Leila: A Tuareg Child* (K–3). Photos by Jean-Charles Rey. 2005, Gale LB $21.20 (1-4103-0545-7). 24pp. Using many photographs, this volume introduces the rootless, nomadic lifestyle of a young Berber girl. (Rev: SLJ 10/05) [966.0049]

3121 Hintz, Martin. *Algeria* (5–8). Illus. 2006, Children's Pr. LB $36.00 (0-516-24855-3). 144pp. An updated version of a 1993 book on the country, with more information on the current political situation, a section on music, and a chapter following an Algerian boy through a typical day. (Rev: SLJ 7/06) [965]

Southern Africa

3122 *To Everything There Is a Season* (2–4). Illus. by Jude Daly. 2006, Eerdmans $16.00 (0-8028-5286-6). 32pp. The familiar words from Ecclesiastes are used as the framework for a portrait of life in rural South Africa. (Rev: BL 4/15/06; SLJ 3/06) [223]

Asia

General

3123 Bowden, Rob. *Asia* (5–8). Series: Continents of the World. 2006, World Almanac LB $32.67 (0-8368-5911-1). 64pp. Factboxes and "In Focus" articles add to this overview of the history, geography, people, culture, and so forth of the continent of Asia. (Rev: SLJ 2/06) [915]

China

3124 Crane, Carol. *D Is for Dancing Dragon* (1–4). Illus. by Zong-Zhou Wang. 2006, Sleeping Bear $17.95 (1-58536-273-5). An A to Z journey through China's history and culture, describing various Chinese inventions, the Great Wall, the Chinese New Year, pandas, and so forth. (Rev: SLJ 3/07) [951]

3125 Pilon, Pascal, and Elizabeth Thomas. *We Live in China* (4–7). Illus. Series: Kids Around the World. 2006, Abrams $15.95 (0-8109-5735-3). 48pp. Four children from different areas of China introduce their region and everyday life; the lack of an index and photo captions limit the book's usefulness for reports, but it will nevertheless serve as an attractive introduction. (Rev: BL 10/15/06)

3126 Qing, Zheng. *China* (4–7). Illus. by Tim Hutchinson. Series: Find Out About. 2007, Barron's $12.99 (978-0-7641-5952-7). 64pp. This well-organized, attractively illustrated guide looks at China's history and contemporary life, and introduces basic phrases in Mandarin. (Rev: BL 4/1/07) [951]

3127 So, Sungwan. *Shanyi Goes to China* (PS–2). Series: Children Return to Their Roots. 2006, Frances Lincoln $15.95 (1-84507-470-X). 32pp. A little girl named Shanyi visits China with her family, visiting relatives and learning about everything from food and famous sites to calligraphy and religious customs. (Rev: BL 10/15/06; SLJ 12/06) [951.06]

3128 Wang, Xiaohong. *One Year in Beijing* (1–4). Illus. by Grace Lin. 2006, China Sprout $16.95 (0-9747302-5-4). 32pp. Eight-year-old Ling Ling conducts readers on a tour of popular attractions in Beijing, explaining Chinese customs and traditions as she goes; the end matter adds more facts. (Rev: BL 10/15/06; SLJ 3/07)

India

3129 Castelain, Céline, and Aurélien Liutkus. *Asha: A Child of the Himalayas* (K–3). Series: Children of the World. 2005, Gale LB $21.20 (1-4103-0286-5). 24pp. Full-color photographs introduce young readers to Asha, who lives in India's mountainous state

of Himachal Pradesh; suitable for browsers rather than report writers. (Rev: SLJ 10/05) [954.5203]

3130 Godard, Philippe. *We Live in India* (3–6). Illus. by Sophie Duffet. Series: Kids Around the World. 2006, Abrams $15.95 (978-0-8109-5736-7). 47pp. Three Indian children from different backgrounds — one Tamil, one Bengali, and one an "untouchable" Hindi — are featured in an overview suitable for browsers. (Rev: SLJ 2/07) [954.052]

3131 Parker, Victoria. *India* (1–3). Illus. Series: We're From. 2005, Heinemann LB $16.95 (1-4034-5785-9). 32pp. Using three children from very different backgrounds as examples, Parker explores the cultural and economic diversity of life in India. (Rev: BL 8/05) [954.05]

Japan

3132 Nishimura, Shigeo. *An Illustrated History of Japan* (4–7). Illus. 2005, Tuttle $19.95 (0-8048-3670-1). 64pp. Key events in Japanese history come alive in the striking tableaux of Shigeo Nishimura. (Rev: BL 10/15/05) [952]

Other Asian Lands

3133 Alberti, Theresa. *Vietnam ABCs* (2–4). Illus. by Alex Blanks. Series: Country ABCs. 2007, Picture Window LB $18.95 (978-1-4048-2251-1). 32pp. This alphabet-book introduction to Vietnam offers basic information about the Southeast Asian country and its troubled history. (Rev: BL 3/15/07) [959.7]

3134 Ali, Sharifah Enayat. *Afghanistan*. 2nd ed. (5–9). Illus. Series: Cultures of the World. 2006, Benchmark LB $27.95 (978-0-7614-2064-4). 144pp. A revised and updated edition of the guide to Afghanistan and its history, geography, culture, and government including maps and color photographs. (Rev: SLJ 3/07) [958.1]

3135 Giraud, Hervé. *Basha: A Hmong Child* (K–3). Photos by Jean-Charles Rey. Series: Children of the World. 2005, Gale LB $21.20 (1-4103-0547-3). 24pp. Using many photographs, this volume introduces the lifestyle and customs of the Hmong people who live in northern Vietnam; suitable for browsers rather than report writers. Also use *Kradji: A Child of Cambodia* (2005). (Rev: SLJ 10/05) [305.8959]

Australia and the Pacific Islands

3136 Darian-Smith, Kate. *Australia, Antarctica, and the Pacific* (5–8). Series: Continents of the World. 2006, World Almanac LB $32.67 (0-8368-5912-X).

64pp. Factboxes and "In Focus" articles add to this overview of the history, geography, people, culture, and so forth of the continents of Australia, Antarctica, and island of the Pacific. (Rev: SLJ 2/06)

3137 Fox, Mary Virginia. *Australia* (1–3). Series: Continents. 2006, Heinemann LB $25.36 (1-57572-449-9). 32pp. For beginning report writers, this is a survey of Australia's geography, flora, fauna, weather, and history. (Rev: SLJ 1/07) [994]

Europe

General and Miscellaneous

3138 Flint, David. *Europe* (5–8). Series: Continents of the World. 2006, World Almanac LB $32.67 (0-8368-5913-8). 64pp. Factboxes and "In Focus" articles add to this overview of the history, geography, people, culture, and so forth of the continent of Europe. (Rev: SLJ 2/06) [940]

Great Britain and Ireland

3139 Elgin, Kathy. *Elizabethan England*, vol. 3 (5–8). Illus. Series: A History of Fashion and Costume. 2005, Facts on File $35.00 (0-8160-5946-2). 64pp. A broad overview of the clothing and personal adornment worn during this time period, with many visual aids. (Rev: SLJ 5/06) [391]

3140 Hynson, Colin. *Elizabeth I and the Spanish Armada* (5–8). Illus. Series: Stories from History. 2006, School Specialty $14.95 (0-7696-4703-0); paper $6.95 (0-7696-4629-8). 48pp. A graphic-novel presentation of the confrontation between England's Queen Elizabeth I and the Spanish empire, climaxing in the defeat of the Spanish Armada by the English; full-color depictions of battles, fast facts, and maps aid comprehension. (Rev: BL 10/15/06; SLJ 1/07) [942.05]

3141 Petrini, Catherine M. *Stonehenge* (4–6). Illus. Series: Wonders of the World. 2005, Gale LB $23.70 (0-7377-3073-0). 48pp. A slim and attractive overview of the mysterious stone monuments of Stonehenge. (Rev: SLJ 12/05) [936.2]

Russia and the Former Soviet States

3142 Aizpuriete, Amanda. *Latvia* (5–8). Trans. by Katarina Hartgers. Photos by Jan Willem Bultje. Series: Looking at Europe. 2006, Oliver $22.95 (1-881508-37-4). 48pp. This colorful volume with excellent photographs introduces readers to Latvia's geography, history, people, culture, economy, and lifestyle. (Rev: LMC 4/07; SLJ 1/07) [947.96]

3143 Bultje, Jan Willem. *Lithuania* (5–8). Trans. by Wilma Hoving. Photos by author. Series: Looking

at Europe. 2006, Oliver $22.95 (1-881508-43-9). 48pp. This colorful volume with excellent photographs introduces readers to Lithuania's geography, history, people, culture, economy, and lifestyle. (Rev: SLJ 1/07) [947.93]

3144 Kollár, Daniel. *Slovakia* (4–7). Series: Looking at Europe. 2006, Oliver $22.95 (1-881508-49-8). 48pp. This photo-filled introduction to Slovakia explores its geography, history, people, culture, cuisine, economy, transportation, tourism, and natural resources. (Rev: SLJ 12/06) [943.73]

3145 Veceric, Danica. *Slovenia* (4–7). Series: Looking at Europe. 2006, Oliver $22.95 (1-881508-74-9). 48pp. A tour of Slovenia, examining the country's geography, history, people, culture, cuisine, economy, transportation, tourism, and natural resources. (Rev: SLJ 12/06) [949.73]

The Middle East

General

3146 Steele, Philip. *Middle East* (4–7). Series: Kingfisher Knowledge. 2006, Kingfisher LB $12.95 (0-7534-5984-1). 64pp. Traces the history of the region — extending from Eastern Mediterranean countries into Iraq, Iran, and Afghanistan — as well as its geography, peoples, cultures, religions, economies, and politics. (Rev: SLJ 12/06) [956]

Israel

3147 Bowden, Rob. *Jerusalem* (3–6). Series: Great Cities of the World. 2005, World Almanac LB $22.50 (0-8368-5051-3). 48pp. With color photographs and informative sidebars, this volume introduces the geography, history, culture, religion, work, and recreation of Jerusalem. (Rev: SLJ 11/05)

Other Middle Eastern Lands

3148 Augustin, Byron, and Jake Kubena. *Iraq* (5–8). Illus. Series: Enchantment of the World. 2006, Children's Pr. LB $36.00 (0-516-24852-9). 144pp. An updated version of a 1998 book on the country, with additional information on ethnic groups, the environment, and continuing violence. (Rev: SLJ 7/06) [956.7]

3149 Barber, Nicola. *Istanbul* (3–6). Series: Great Cities of the World. 2005, World Almanac LB $22.50 (0-8368-5050-5). 48pp. With color photographs and informative sidebars, this volume introduces the geography, history, culture, religion, work, and recreation of the Turkish city of Istanbul. (Rev: SLJ 11/05)

3150 Boueri, Marijean, and Jill Boutros. *Lebanon A to Z: A Middle Eastern Mosaic* (4–8). Illus. by Tatiana Sabbagh. 2006, Publishing Works $25.00 (0-9744803-4-7). 77pp. Eleven-year-old Kareem takes readers on a tour through the country's present and past, with an emphasis on cultural traditions and Lebanon's people. (Rev: SLJ 7/06) [956.92]

3151 Graham, Amy. *Iran in the News: Past, Present, and Future* (5–8). Illus. Series: Middle East Nations in the News. 2006, Enslow LB $24.95 (1-59845-022-0). 128pp. History, culture, people, and current political issues are all covered in this readable overview of Iran that includes links to Web sites that extend the text. (Rev: BL 4/1/06; SLJ 5/06) [955]

3152 Haskins, Jim, and Kathleen Benson. *Count Your Way Through Iran* (2–4). Illus. by Farida Zaman. Series: Count Your Way. 2006, Lerner LB $19.93 (1-57505-881-2). 24pp. Aspects of Iranian life from 1 to 10 are accompanied by a map and various other key facts. (Rev: BL 8/06) [955]

3153 Van Der Gaag, Nikki, and Felicity Arbuthnot. *Baghdad* (3–6). Series: Great Cities of the World. 2005, World Almanac LB $22.50 (0-8368-5049-1). 48pp. With color photographs and informative sidebars, this volume introduces the geography, history, culture, religion, work, and recreation of Baghdad. (Rev: SLJ 11/05)

North and South America (Excluding the United States)

North and South America

3154 Fox, Mary Virginia. *North America* (1–3). Series: Continents. 2006, Heinemann LB $25.36 (1-58810-001-4). 32pp. For beginning report writers, this is a survey of North America's geography, flora, fauna, weather, and history. (Rev: SLJ 1/07) [970]

Canada

3155 Bowers, Viven. *Crazy About Canada! Amazing Things Kids Want to Know* (4–6). Illus. by Dianne Eastman. Series: Canadian Geographic Kids. 2006, Maple Tree $28.95 (1-897066-47-3); paper $18.95 (1-897066-48-1). 96pp. Cartoon figures Vivien and Morton ask questions about various aspects of Canada (geography, history, wildlife, and so forth) in this attractive fact-filled volume. (Rev: BL 4/1/06; SLJ 8/06) [971]

Mexico

3156 Clare, John D. *Aztec Life* (5–8). Illus. 2006, Saddleback paper $8.95 (1-59905-050-1). 32pp. Covers the lifestyle, culture, and traditions of the Aztecs, with quotations from poems and sayings. (Rev: SLJ 9/06) [972]

3157 Krebs, Laurie. *Off We Go to Mexico! An Adventure in the Sun* (PS–K). Illus. by Christopher Corr. 2006, Barefoot Bks. $16.99 (1-905236-40-9). 32pp. Readers journey to Mexico, visit some ancient sites and natural wonders, have typical tourist fun, and learn Spanish vocabulary and about Mexican culture. (Rev: BL 3/1/06; SLJ 4/06) [972]

3158 MacDonald, Fiona. *How to Be an Aztec Warrior* (2–5). Illus. by David Antram and Mark Bergin. Series: How to Be. 2005, National Geographic $14.95 (0-7922-3617-3). 32pp. This attractive title gives readers a look at what life was like for Aztec warriors, touching on such topics as uniforms, weapons, rank, and traditions. (Rev: SLJ 12/05) [972]

Puerto Rico and Other Caribbean Islands

3159 Matthews, John. *Pirates* (3–6). 2006, Simon & Schuster $19.95 (1-4169-2734-4). 32pp. The foldouts, flaps, treasure maps, and other features of this fact-packed interactive book will keep browsers and researchers happy. (Rev: BL 7/06) [364.164]

Polar Regions

3160 Bledsoe, Lucy Jane. *How to Survive in Antarctica* (5–8). 2006, Holiday $16.95 (0-8234-1890-1). 102pp. An account of the author's trips to Antarctica, filled with interesting facts about the frigid land — from wildlife notes to survival tips — plus photographs by the author. (Rev: BCCB 10/06; BL 7/06; HBG 4/07; SLJ 8/06; VOYA 8/06) [919.8]

3161 Goodman, Susan E. *Life on the Ice* (3–5). Photos by Michael J. Doolittle. 2006, Millbrook LB $22.60 (0-7613-2775-4). 32pp. This brief introduction to the world's polar regions explores their geographical remoteness, weather extremes, and the scientific research projects conducted there. (Rev: BL 3/15/06; SLJ 8/06) [910]

United States

General History and Geography

3162 Armstrong, Jennifer. *The American Story: 100 True Tales from American History* (4–7). Illus. by

Roger Roth. 2006, Knopf $34.95 (0-375-81256-3). 368pp. The 100 stories in this large-format collection bring American history to life and include such diverse events as Paul Revere's midnight ride, the first flight of the Wright brothers, the eruption of Mount St. Helens, and the Supreme Court decision resolving the disputed 2000 presidential election. (Rev: BCCB 10/06; BL 8/06; HBG 4/07; SLJ 8/06*) [973]

3163 Backer, Miles. *Travels with Charlie: Way Out West* (1–3). Illus. by Chuck Nitzberg. 2006, Blue Apple $15.95 (1-59354-134-1). Charlie the dog visits interesting and quirky sites in the western United States; maps of the states he visits, as well as a U.S. map, will help readers as they follow Charlie on his travels. (Rev: SLJ 6/06) [978]

3164 Buckley, Susan, and Elspeth Leacock. *Journeys for Freedom: A New Look at America's Story* (4–7). Illus. by Rodica Prato. 2006, Houghton $17.00 (0-618-22323-1). 48pp. Twenty stories of personal struggles for freedom — ranging from the early 17th century to the late 20th century — feature quotations from primary sources. (Rev: BL 11/15/06; SLJ 1/07) [973]

3165 Buckley, Susan, and Elspeth Leacock. *Kids Make History: A New Look at America's Story* (4–8). Illus. by Randy Jones. 2006, Houghton $17.00 (0-618-22329-0). 48pp. Twenty stories of young people who experienced milestone events in American history — from Pocahontas in 1607 to a high school senior on 9/11 — are told in text, quotations, fictionalized dialogue, and illustrations. (Rev: SLJ 1/07) [973.09]

3166 Cheney, Lynne. *Our 50 States: A Family Adventure Across America* (4–6). Illus. by Robin Preiss Glasser. 2006, Simon & Schuster $17.95 (0-689-86717-4). 74pp. Follow a family as they travel all over the United States, visiting interesting destinations and learning historical, geographical, and cultural facts. (Rev: BL 11/15/06; SLJ 1/07) [973]

3167 Floca, Brian. *Lightship* (PS–2). Illus. 2007, Simon & Schuster $16.99 (978-1-4169-2436-4). 48pp. This is a detailed and attractive account of the role of lightships — which were used where lighthouses were not suitable; the last one in the United States was retired in 1983. (Rev: BL 2/1/07) [387.2]

3168 Heinz, Brian J. *Nathan of Yesteryear and Michael of Today* (4–6). Illus. by Joanne Friar. 2006, Lerner LB $22.60 (0-7613-2893-9). 32pp. This thought-provoking picture book for older students contrasts the daily life of a 12-year-old boy living today and that of his great-great-grandfather, who lived in the 1880s. (Rev: BL 10/15/06) [303.4]

3169 Hicks, Terry Allan. *The Bald Eagle* (3–5). Series: Symbols of America. 2006, Benchmark LB $19.95 (0-7614-2133-5). 40pp. Information on the bald eagle and its selection as the national bird of the United States are accompanied by archival and contemporary images. Also use *Uncle Sam* (2006). (Rev: SLJ 12/06) [929.9]

3170 Jordan, Anne Devereaux, and Virginia Schomp. *Slavery and Resistance* (5–8). Illus. 2006, Marshall Cavendish LB $23.95 (978-0-7614-2178-8). 70pp. A well-illustrated, well-organized history of slavery in America from the first colony in Jamestown up until the Civil War. (Rev: BL 2/1/07) [306.3]

3171 Masoff, Joy. *We Are All Americans: Understanding Diversity* (4–7). 2006, Five Ponds $26.50 (0-9727156-2-2). 63pp. This celebration of immigration to America — full of photographs, maps, and diagrams — looks at the reasons for migration, the problems involved, and the contributions made by immigrants in all aspects of American life, including music, sports, games, celebrations, literature, food, and art. (Rev: SLJ 1/07) [304.8]

3172 Neubecker, Robert. *Wow! America!* (PS–K). Illus. 2006, Hyperion $16.99 (0-7868-3816-7). 48pp. In this rollicking sequel to *Wow! City!* (2004), Izzy and Jo visit some of America's most famous sights. (Rev: BL 4/15/06; SLJ 6/06) [973]

3173 Yorinks, Adrienne. *Quilt of States: Piecing Together America* (5–8). Illus. 2005, National Geographic LB $29.90 (0-7922-7286-2). 128pp. With contributions from librarians from all 50 states, this beautifully illustrated volume offers a brief story of each state's accession to the Union, along with other pertinent facts and figures. (Rev: BL 10/1/05; SLJ 12/05) [973]

Historical Periods

NATIVE AMERICANS

3174 Aloian, Molly, and Bobbie Kalman. *Nations of the Southeast* (3–5). Illus. Series: Native Nations of North America. 2006, Crabtree $23.92 (0-7787-0385-1); paper $8.95 (0-7787-0477-7). 32pp. An interesting overview of the Native American tribes of the American Southeast, examining their culture, language, customs, and contemporary status. (Rev: SLJ 11/06) [975.004]

3175 Bial, Raymond. *The Delaware* (5–9). Series: Lifeways. 2005, Benchmark LB $23.95 (0-7614-1904-7). 127pp. The history, culture, traditions, and present-day life of the Native American tribe, with photographs and other visuals. (Rev: SLJ 6/06) [974.004]

3176 Bial, Raymond. *The Menominee* (5–9). Series: Lifeways. 2005, Benchmark LB $23.95 (0-7614-1903-9). 127pp. The history, culture, traditions and present-day life of the Native American tribe, with photographs and other visuals. (Rev: SLJ 6/06) [977.4004]

3177 Englar, Mary. *The Cherokee and Their History* (3–5). Series: We the People. 2005, Compass Point

LB $23.93 (0-7565-1273-5). 48pp. Suitable for report writers, this history starts with an account of the Trail of Tears and then covers traditions, achievements, life today, and so forth. Also use *The Sioux and Their History* (2006). (Rev: SLJ 9/06) [973]

3178 Englar, Mary. *The Great Plains Indians: Daily Life in the 1700s* (2–4). Series: Native American Life. 2005, Capstone LB $21.26 (0-7368-4315-9). 24pp. A brief, attractive introduction to the tribes of the Great Plains, covering their social structure, homes, food, clothing, and traditions. (Rev: SLJ 12/05) [978.004]

3179 Gibson, Karen Bush. *The Great Basin Indians: Daily Life in the 1700s* (2–4). Series: Native American Life. 2005, Capstone LB $21.26 (0-7368-4318-3). 24pp. A brief, attractive introduction to the tribes of the Great Basin region, covering their social structure, homes, food, clothing, and traditions. (Rev: SLJ 12/05) [979.004]

3180 Lassieur, Allison. *The Navajo: A Proud People* (3–5). Series: American Indians. 2005, Enslow LB $23.93 (0-7660-2453-9). 48pp. The history of the Navajo (properly called Diné, the book notes), with information about their accomplishments and their lives today. (Rev: SLJ 5/06) [979.1004]

3181 Monroe, Judy. *The Northwest Indians: Daily Life in the 1700s* (2–4). Series: Native American Life. 2005, Capstone LB $21.26 (0-7368-4316-7). 24pp. A brief, attractive introduction to the tribes of the Pacific Northwest, covering their social structure, homes, food, clothing, and traditions. (Rev: SLJ 12/05) [977.004]

3182 Patent, Dorothy Hinshaw. *The Buffalo and the Indians: A Shared Destiny* (4–8). Illus. by William Muñoz. 2006, Clarion $18.00 (0-618-48570-8). 85pp. This beautifully illustrated title explores the unique bonds — both spiritual and economic — between Native Americans and the American bison. (Rev: BL 6/1/06*; HBG 4/07; LMC 2/07; SLJ 8/06*) [978.004]

3183 Quigley, Mary. *Mesa Verde* (4–6). Illus. Series: Excavating the Past. 2005, Heinemann LB $31.43 (1-4034-5997-5). 48pp. The work of archaeologists is clearly shown in this well-illustrated exploration of the Mesa Verde site and the people who created it. (Rev: SLJ 2/06) [978.8]

3184 Smithyman, Kathryn, and Bobbie Kalman. *Native North American Foods and Recipes* (3–5). Illus. Series: Native Nations of North America. 2006, Crabtree LB $23.92 (0-7787-0383-5); paper $8.95 (0-7787-0475-0). 32pp. Maple sugar, wild rice, squash, and corn are just a few of the foods mentioned in this survey of the Native American diet and methods of food preparation and conservation. (Rev: SLJ 11/06) [641.59]

3185 Sonneborn, Liz. *The Apache* (3–5). Illus. 2005, Watts LB $24.50 (0-531-12295-6). 64pp. Explores the history and culture of the Apache people, with period and contemporary illustrations and a timeline. (Rev: BL 7/05) [979.004]

3186 Walker, Niki, and Bobbie Kalman. *Native North American Wisdom and Gifts* (3–5). Illus. Series: Native Nations of North America. 2006, Crabtree LB $23.92 (0-7787-0384-3); paper $8.95 (0-7787-0476-9). 32pp. Culture, hunting traditions, medicine and health, language, sports and games, are all covered in this survey of Native American beliefs and respect for the environment. (Rev: SLJ 11/06) [970.004]

DISCOVERY AND EXPLORATION

3187 Cook, Peter. *You Wouldn't Want to Sail on the Mayflower! A Trip That Took Entirely Too Long* (3–6). Illus. by Kevin Whelan. Series: You Wouldn't Want to . . . 2005, Watts LB $27.50 (0-531-12411-8); paper $9.95 (0-531-12391-X). 32pp. An engaging account of the grim realities and hardships of the Pilgrims' voyage, with cartoon art, a diagram of the ship's layout, and maps. (Rev: SLJ 3/06) [973.2]

3188 Eisenberg, Jana. *Lewis and Clark: Path to the Pacific* (4–6). Series: Trailblazers of the West. 2005, Children's Pr. LB $23.00 (0-516-25126-0); paper $6.95 (0-516-25096-5). 48pp. The hardships on this epic expedition, and the relations with Native Americans, are portrayed in short chapters suitable for reluctant readers. (Rev: SLJ 4/06) [917.804]

3189 King, David C. *Projects About the Spanish West* (3–5). Illus. Series: Hands-on History. 2005, Benchmark LB $18.95 (0-7614-1982-9). 47pp. The projects outlined in this book — including a yarn picture, a luminaria, an ojo de Dios (eye of God), and a piñata — are designed to help students understand the early Spanish exploration and colonization of the American West. (Rev: SLJ 4/06) [979.0046]

3190 Owens, L. L. *Pilgrims in America* (4–6). 2007, Rourke LB $29.93 (1-60044-122-X). 48pp. A well-illustrated overview of the Pilgrims who settled in Plymouth, explaining who they were and covering their trip to the New World, the first Thanksgiving, and relations with the native peoples. (Rev: SLJ 4/07) [974.4]

COLONIAL PERIOD

3191 Bauer, Brandy. *The Virginia Colony* (2–4). Series: Fact Finders: The American Colonies. 2005, Capstone LB $22.60 (0-7368-2684-X). 32pp. A very basic overview of the geography, history, religion, and everyday life of the Virginia colony, with large type and short paragraphs. (Rev: SLJ 12/05) [975.5]

3192 Cooper, Michael L. *Jamestown, 1607* (4–7). 2007, Holiday House $18.95 (978-0-8234-1948-7). 98pp. The story of the Jamestown colony is told in concise text with excellent illustrations, quotations from primary sources, and background context. (Rev: SLJ 4/07) [973.2]

3193 Deady, Kathleen W. *The Massachusetts Bay Colony* (2–4). Illus. Series: Fact Finders: American Colonies. 2005, Capstone LB $16.95 (0-7368-2676-9). 32pp. Researchers will find solid information on the colony, covering education, religion, work, trade, and community life. (Rev: BL 10/15/05) [974.4]

3194 Deady, Kathleen W. *The New Hampshire Colony* (2–4). Series: Fact Finders: The American Colonies. 2005, Capstone LB $22.60 (0-7368-2677-7). 32pp. A very basic overview of the geography, history, religion, and everyday life of the New Hampshire colony, with large type and short paragraphs. (Rev: SLJ 12/05) [974.2]

3195 Doherty, Craig A., and Katherine M. Doherty. *North Carolina* (5–9). Illus. Series: The Thirteen Colonies. 2005, Facts on File LB $35.00 (0-8160-5412-6). 116pp. Traces the history of North Carolina from the early settlers through 1787, with discussion of the Native American culture and with excerpts from primary documents, maps, and profiles of key individuals. (Rev: SLJ 8/05) [973]

3196 Doherty, Craig A., and Katherine M. Doherty. *Pennsylvania* (5–9). Illus. Series: The Thirteen Colonies. 2005, Facts on File LB $35.00 (0-8160-5413-4). 142pp. Traces the history of Pennsylvania from the early settlers through 1787, with discussion of the Native American culture, the Quakers, and with excerpts from primary documents, maps, and profiles of key individuals. (Rev: SLJ 8/05) [973]

3197 Doherty, Craig A., and Katherine M. Doherty. *Rhode Island* (5–9). Illus. Series: The Thirteen Colonies. 2005, Facts on File LB $35.00 (0-81605-415-0). 126pp. Traces the history of Rhode Island from the early settlers through 1787, with discussion of the Native American culture and with excerpts from primary documents, maps, and profiles of key individuals. (Rev: SLJ 8/05) [973]

3198 Dubois, Muriel L. *The Delaware Colony* (2–4). Series: Fact Finders: The American Colonies. 2005, Capstone LB $22.60 (0-7368-2673-4). 32pp. A very basic overview of the geography, history, religion, and everyday life of the Delaware colony, with large type and short paragraphs. (Rev: SLJ 12/05) [975.1]

3199 Dubois, Muriel L. *The New Jersey Colony* (2–4). Series: Fact Finders: The American Colonies. 2005, Capstone LB $22.60 (0-7368-2678-5). 32pp. A very basic overview of the geography, history, religion, and everyday life of the New Jersey

colony, with large type and short paragraphs. (Rev: SLJ 12/05) [974.9]

3200 Fradin, Dennis Brindell. *Jamestown, Virginia* (3–5). Illus. Series: Turning Points in U.S. History. 2006, Marshall Cavendish LB $20.95 (978-0-7614-2122-1). 47pp. This volume discusses Jamestown's founding, the dire conditions of its early settlers, and the critical aid provided by Native Americans as well as new arrivals to the settlement. (Rev: BL 1/1–15/07) [975.5]

3201 Haberle, Susan E. *The South Carolina Colony* (2–4). Series: Fact Finders: The American Colonies. 2005, Capstone LB $22.60 (0-7368-2683-1). 32pp. A very basic overview of the geography, history, religion, and everyday life of the South Carolina colony, with large type and short paragraphs. (Rev: SLJ 12/05) [975.7]

3202 Harkins, Susan, and William H. Harkins. *Jamestown: The First English Colony* (4–6). Series: Building America. 2006, Mitchell Lane LB $19.95 (1-58415-458-6). 48pp. A mixture of fact and educated conjecture, this well-organized overview of Jamestown underscores the difficulties faced by the settlers who established the first permanent English colony in America. (Rev: BL 10/15/06; SLJ 11/06) [975.5]

3203 Harness, Cheryl. *Our Colonial Year* (1–3). Illus. 2005, Simon & Schuster $16.95 (0-689-83479-9). 40pp. Double-page spreads with short, free-verse text follow everyday life in the 13 colonies through the 12 months of the year, plus a spread for New Year's Day. (Rev: BL 12/1/05; SLJ 12/05) [973.2]

3204 Hinman, Bonnie. *Pennsylvania: William Penn and the City of Brotherly Love* (4–7). Series: Building America. 2006, Mitchell Lane LB $19.95 (978-1-58415-463-1). 48pp. This history of colonial Pennsylvania explores the reasons why William Penn established the colony in the late 17th century. (Rev: SLJ 2/07) [974.8]

3205 Hossell, Karen. *Delaware 1638–1776* (5–8). Series: Voices from Colonial America. 2006, National Geographic $21.95 (0-7922-6408-8). 109pp. This well-illustrated title traces the history of Delaware from the 17th-century massacre of Dutch settlers by Native Americans to the eve of the American Revolution; maps and a timeline make this useful for research. (Rev: SLJ 1/07) [975.1]

3206 Lange, Karen. *1607: A New Look at Jamestown* (4–6). Illus. by Ira Block. 2007, National Geographic $17.95 (1-4263-0012-3). 48pp. In the light of new information discovered about Jamestown in the late 20th century, this book describes what we now understand about life in the colony. (Rev: BL 12/1/06; SLJ 1/07*) [973.21]

3207 Martin, Michael. *The Salem Witch Trials* (3–6). Illus. by Brian Bascle. Series: Graphic

221

Library/Graphic History. 2004, Capstone LB $22.60 (0-7368-3847-3). 32pp. This broad overview in graphic-novel format — factual but embellished — of this chapter of American history will appeal to reluctant readers. (Rev: SLJ 7/05) [973.2]

3208 Marx, Mandy R. *The Maryland Colony* (2–4). Series: Fact Finders: The American Colonies. 2005, Capstone LB $22.60 (0-7368-2675-0). 32pp. A very basic overview of the geography, history, religion, and everyday life of the Maryland colony, with large type and short paragraphs. (Rev: SLJ 12/05) [975.2]

3209 Schumacher, Tyler. *The Georgia Colony* (2–4). Series: Fact Finders: The American Colonies. 2005, Capstone LB $22.60 (0-7368-2674-2). 32pp. A very basic overview of the geography, history, religion, and everyday life of the Georgia colony, with large type and short paragraphs. (Rev: SLJ 12/05) [975.8]

3210 Worth, Richard. *Colonial America: Building Toward Independence* (5–8). Series: The American Saga. 2006, Enslow LB $23.95 (0-7660-2569-1). 128pp. Tracing the history of the original 13 colonies from the earliest English settlements through the ratification of the Constitution, this volume will be useful for report writers seeking information on politics, government, economy, and culture. (Rev: SLJ 12/06) [973.2]

3211 Yero, Judith Lloyd. *The Mayflower Compact* (4–7). Series: American Documents. 2006, National Geographic $15.95 (0-7922-5891-6). 40pp. Yero distinguishes fact from myth in this examination of the *Mayflower*'s voyage, the colony the Separatists create, and the document they drafted as their governing compact. (Rev: BL 9/15/06; SLJ 10/06) [974.4]

REVOLUTIONARY PERIOD

3212 Anderson, Dale. *The American Colonies Declare Independence* (5–8). Series: World Almanac Library of the American Revolution. 2005, World Almanac LB $30.00 (0-8368-5926-X). 48pp. Excerpts from primary sources bolster the informative, clearly written text, which is sprinkled with biographical sidebars. Also use *The Causes of the American Revolution, The Patriots Win the American Revolution,* and *Forming a New American Government* (all 2005). (Rev: SLJ 1/06) [973.3]

3213 Cook, Peter. *You Wouldn't Want to Be at the Boston Tea Party! Wharf Water Tea You'd Rather Not Drink* (3–6). Illus. by David Antram. Series: You Wouldn't Want To. 2006, Watts LB $27.50 (0-531-12422-3); paper $9.95 (0-531-12447-9). 32pp. A lively look at life in colonial Boston, with some unvarnished realities balanced by the lighthearted cartoon illustrations. (Rev: SLJ 9/06) [973.3]

3214 Deem, James M. *Primary Source Accounts of the Revolutionary War* (5–8). Illus. Series: America's Wars Through Primary Sources. 2006, Enslow LB $33.27 (1-59845-004-2). 128pp. Soldiers' journal entries, letters from home, personal recollections, songs and poetry, and newspaper articles are among the primary sources included in this general history of the war. (Rev: SLJ 4/07) [973.3]

3215 Fleming, Thomas. *Everybody's Revolution* (4–7). Illus. 2006, Scholastic $19.99 (0-439-63404-0). 96pp. A fascinating introduction to the diverse heroes and heroines of many nationalities who contributed to the success of the American Revolution. (Rev: BL 10/15/06; SLJ 11/06) [973.3]

3216 Fradin, Dennis Brindell. *The Declaration of Independence* (3–6). Series: Turning Points in U.S. History. 2006, Benchmark LB $20.95 (978-0-7614-2129-0). 45pp. Describes the events leading up to writing of the Declaration of Independence, its composition, and its impact on history. (Rev: SLJ 3/07) [973.3]

3217 Maestro, Betsy. *Liberty or Death: The American Revolution: 1763–1783* (3–5). Illus. by Giulio Maestro. Series: American Story. 2005, HarperCollins $15.99 (0-688-08802-3). 64pp. This attractive volume provides an easy-to-understand overview of the American Revolution and the events that led up to it. (Rev: BL 11/1/05; SLJ 9/05) [973.3]

3218 Miller, Brandon M. *Declaring Independence: Life During the American Revolution* (5–8). Series: People's History. 2005, Lerner LB $26.60 (0-8225-1275-0). 112pp. A thorough look at what life was like during the American Revolution, using primary sources. (Rev: SLJ 9/05; VOYA 6/05) [973.3]

3219 Minor, Wendell. *Yankee Doodle America: The Spirit of 1776 from A to Z* (2–5). Illus. 2006, Putnam $16.99 (0-399-24003-9). 48pp. An attractive and informative alphabetical tour of colonial America. (Rev: BL 4/15/06; SLJ 4/06) [973.3]

3220 Yero, Judith Lloyd. *The Declaration of Independence* (3–5). Series: American Documents. 2006, National Geographic $15.95 (0-7922-5397-3). 40pp. Discusses the events that led to this document and the important figures who signed it, with interesting sidebars. (Rev: SLJ 5/06) [973.3]

THE YOUNG NATION, 1789–1861

3221 Bozonelis, Helen Koutras. *Primary Source Accounts of the War of 1812* (5–8). Illus. Series: America's Wars Through Primary Sources. 2006, Enslow LB $33.27 (1-59845-006-9). 128pp. Soldiers' journal entries, letters from the homefront, personal recollections, songs and poetry, and newspaper articles are among the primary sources included in this general history of the war. (Rev: SLJ 4/07) [973.5]

3222 Coleman, Wim, and Pat Perrin. *The Amazing Erie Canal and How a Big Ditch Opened Up the West* (4–7). Illus. Series: Wild History of the American West. 2006, Enslow LB $24.95 (1-59845-017-4). 128pp. Why was the Erie Canal built? What was its impact on American commerce and history? This richly illustrated profile answers those questions and offers a general overview of canals; 30 Internet links are provided for further research. (Rev: BL 10/15/06) [386]

3223 Cosson, M. J. *Yankee Whalers* (4–6). Series: Events in American History. 2007, Rourke LB $29.93 (978-1-60044-140-0). 48pp. Life aboard whaling ships in the 1800s is a major focus of this volume. (Rev: BL 4/1/07; SLJ 4/07) [639.2]

3224 Fradin, Dennis Brindell. *The Alamo* (3–6). Series: Turning Points in U.S. History. 2006, Benchmark LB $20.95 (978-0-7614-2127-6). 45pp. A look at the famous battle, the events that led up to the fight for Texas's independence, the famous people involved, and its aftermath. (Rev: SLJ 3/07) [976.4]

3225 Martin, Michael. *Harriet Tubman and the Underground Railroad* (3–6). Illus. by Dave Hoover and Bill Anderson. Series: Graphic Library/Graphic History. 2004, Capstone LB $22.60 (0-7368-3829-5). 32pp. A graphic "novel" — factual, but embellished — about Tubman's role in the Underground Railroad; will appeal to reluctant readers. (Rev: SLJ 7/05) [973.7]

PIONEER LIFE AND WESTWARD EXPANSION

3226 Burnett, Linda. *Pioneers: Adventure in a New Land* (4–6). Series: Trailblazers of the West. 2005, Children's Pr. LB $23.00 (0-516-25127-9); paper $6.95 (0-516-25097-3). 48pp. The hard life of pioneers on the western frontier is portrayed in short chapters suitable for reluctant readers. (Rev: SLJ 4/06) [978.02]

3227 Coleman, Wim, and Pat Perrin. *What Made the Wild West Wild* (4–8). Illus. Series: The Wild History of the American West. 2006, Enslow LB $33.27 (1-59845-016-6). 128pp. The myths and legends of the Wild West are debunked in this expansive overview of media portrayals and reality. (Rev: SLJ 1/07) [978]

3228 Fine, Jil. *The Transcontinental Railroad: Tracks Across America* (4–6). Series: Trailblazers of the West. 2005, Children's Pr. LB $23.00 (0-516-25128-7); paper $6.95 (0-516-25098-1). 48pp. This attractive title chronicles the building of the transcontinental railroad, an important step in opening up the American West, and the hardships suffered by those involved; short, well-illustrated chapters are suitable for reluctant readers. (Rev: SLJ 4/06) [385]

3229 Klobuchar, Lisa. *The History and Activities of the Wagon Trail* (3–5). Series: Hands-on American History. 2006, Heinemann LB $19.75 (1-4034-6055-8). 32pp. An accessible and informative account of life on the westbound wagon trains is bolstered by illustrations and activities — a recipe, a toy, and a prairie schooner replica. (Rev: BL 9/1/06) [978]

3230 Landau, Elaine. *The Pony Express* (2–4). Illus. Series: Westward Expansion (True Book). 2006, Children's Pr. LB $17.50 (0-516-25873-7). 48pp. The colorful — but brief — history of the Pony Express, launched to move mail from St. Joseph, Missouri, to San Francisco in a scant ten days, is chronicled in readable text, drawings, and maps. (Rev: BL 4/1/06) [383]

3231 Landau, Elaine. *The Transcontinental Railroad* (5–8). Illus. Series: Watts Library: American West. 2005, Watts LB $25.50 (0-531-12326-X). 64pp. The story behind the building of the Transcontinental Railroad, with illustrations, maps, a timeline, and sidebar features. (Rev: SLJ 12/05)

3232 Schaffer, David. *The Louisiana Purchase: The Deal of the Century That Doubled the Nation* (5–8). Illus. Series: The Wild History of the American West. 2006, Enslow LB $33.27 (1-59845-018-2). 128pp. Tells the story behind America's negotiations to buy the vast Louisiana Territory for $15 million, or less than 3 cents an acre; includes a list of carefully selected Web sites that offer additional information. (Rev: SLJ 12/06) [973.4]

3233 Schlaepfer, Gloria G. *The Louisiana Purchase* (5–8). Illus. Series: Watts Library: American West. 2005, Watts LB $25.50 (0-531-12300-6). 64pp. The story behind the Louisiana Purchase and its role in America's westward expansion, with illustrations, maps, a timeline, and sidebar features. (Rev: SLJ 12/05)

3234 Sonneborn, Liz. *The Mormon Trail* (5–8). Illus. Series: Watts Library: American West. 2005, Watts LB $25.50 (0-531-12317-0). 64pp. The story behind the westward trek of thousands of Mormons during the middle of the 19th century, with illustrations, maps, a timeline, and sidebar features. (Rev: SLJ 12/05)

3235 Sonneborn, Liz. *Women of the American West* (4–7). Illus. Series: Watts Library: American West. 2005, Watts LB $25.50 (0-531-12318-9). 64pp. Excerpts from first-person accounts offer a glimpse into what life was like for the women who helped to open the American West. (Rev: BL 10/15/05) [978]

3236 Waldman, Stuart. *The Last River: John Wesley Powell and the Colorado River Exploring Expedition* (4–7). Illus. by Gregory Manchess. 2005, Mikaya $19.95 (1-931414-09-2). 48pp. This is the exciting story of the three-month exploration of the Colorado River led by the one-armed John Wesley

Powell in 1869; excerpts from journals and letters reveal details of the dangers faced. (Rev: BL 12/15/05; SLJ 2/06) [550.92]

THE CIVIL WAR

3237 Allen, Thomas B. *Harriet Tubman, Secret Agent: How Daring Slaves and Free Blacks Spied for the Union During the Civil War* (5–8). Illus. by Carla Bauer. 2006, National Geographic $16.95 (978-0-7922-7889-4). 191pp. The efforts of Tubman and other slaves to gather important information and pass it to the Union forces is the focus of this volume that includes examples of a code sometimes used. (Rev: BCCB 1/07; BL 12/1/06; HBG Sprin g07; LMC 4–5/07; SLJ 2/07*) [973.7]

3238 *Gettysburg: Bold Battle in the North* (4–6). Series: The Civil War. 2005, Cobblestone $17.95 (0-8126-7903-2). 47pp. A richly illustrated overview of this important battle. (Rev: SLJ 3/06) [973.7]

3239 High, Linda Oatman. *The Cemetery Keepers of Gettysburg* (3–5). Illus. by Laura Francesca Filippucci. 2007, Walker $16.95 (0-8027-8094-6). 32pp. The battle of Gettysburg is presented from the perspective of the oldest boy of a family of cemetery keepers trying to survive the Civil War while the father is off fighting. (Rev: BL 3/15/07) [973.7]

3240 McComb, Marianne. *The Emancipation Proclamation* (4–7). Illus. Series: American Documents. 2006, National Geographic LB $23.90 (0-7922-7936-0). 40pp. The background, nature, and impact of this important document are explained clearly, with photos and illustrations plus full texts of the Emancipation Proclamation, the Fugitive Slave Law of 1850, and Constitutional Amendments XIII through XV. (Rev: BL 2/1/06; SLJ 2/06; VOYA 8/06) [973.7]

3241 Rappaport, Doreen. *United No More! Stories of the Civil War* (4–6). Illus. by Rick Reeves. 2006, HarperCollins $15.99 (0-06-050599-0). 144pp. Seven stories of Civil War personalities and events give readers a feeling for the conflict. (Rev: BL 2/15/06; SLJ 2/06) [973.7]

3242 Walker, Sally M. *Shipwreck Search: Discovery of the H. L. Hunley* (2–4). Illus. by Elaine Verstraete. Series: On My Own Science. 2006, Lerner $23.93 (1-57505-878-2). 48pp. Chronicles the successful search for the wreckage of the *H. L. Hunley*, a Confederate submarine that was sunk in Charleston Harbor during the Civil War. (Rev: BL 6/1–15/06; SLJ 6/06) [973.7]

3243 Waryncia, Lou, and Sarah Elder Hale, eds. *Antietam: Day of Courage and Sacrifice* (4–6). Series: The Civil War. 2005, Cobblestone $17.95 (0-8126-7904-0). 48pp. Based on articles appearing in Cobblestone publications, this book consists of short chapters covering topics including the battle, the equipment used, the mascot dogs, and the role of Clara Barton. (Rev: BL 1/1–15/06) [973.7]

3244 *Young Heroes of the North and South* (4–6). Series: The Civil War. 2005, Cobblestone $17.95 (0-8126-7901-6). 47pp. A compelling look at the roles played by children on the home front and the battlefield, on both sides of the Civil War. (Rev: SLJ 3/06) [973.7]

RECONSTRUCTION TO THE KOREAN WAR, 1865–1950

3245 Burgan, Michael. *The Haymarket Square Tragedy* (4–6). Series: We the People. 2005, Compass Point LB $23.93 (0-7565-1265-4). 48pp. The story of the 1886 Haymarket Square riot in Chicago is placed in historical and social context, with period reproductions and photographs. (Rev: SLJ 2/06) [977.311]

3246 Freedman, Russell. *Children of the Great Depression* (5–8). Illus. 2005, Clarion $20.00 (0-618-44630-3). 128pp. The works of such notable photographers as Dorothea Lange and Walker Evans, moving quotations, and the accessible text of Freedman make this a memorable photoessay. (Rev: BCCB 12/05; BL 12/15/05*; HBG 4/05; LMC 3/06; SLJ 12/05*; VOYA 6/06) [305.23]

3247 Nobleman, Marc Tyler. *The Hindenburg* (4–6). Series: We the People. 2005, Compass Point LB $23.93 (0-7565-1266-2). 48pp. The story of the *Hindenburg*, the German dirigible that burst into flames as it was landing at Lakehurst, New Jersey, in 1937, is placed in historical context. (Rev: SLJ 2/06) [363.12]

3248 Rau, Dana Meachen. *The Harlem Renaissance* (4–6). Series: We the People. 2005, Compass Point LB $23.93 (0-7565-1264-6). 48pp. A look at the key characters and the artistic creations of the Harlem Renaissance, an African American cultural movement during the 1920s and early 1930s. (Rev: SLJ 2/06) [700]

3249 Santella, Andrew. *Roosevelt's Rough Riders* (4–6). Series: We the People. 2005, Compass Point LB $23.93 (0-7565-1268-9). 48pp. Profiles the men from diverse walks of life who volunteered to fight as part of Roosevelt's Rough Riders during the Spanish-American War. (Rev: SLJ 2/06) [973.8]

3250 Schwartz, Eric. *Crossing the Seas: Americans Form an Empire 1890–1899* (5–8). Series: How America Became America. 2005, Mason Crest LB $22.95 (1-59084-910-8). 91pp. Schwartz explores America's turn to imperialism in the final decade of the 19th century. Also use *Super Power: Americans Today* (2005). (Rev: SLJ 11/05) [973]

THE 1950S TO THE PRESENT

3251 Burgan, Michael. *Spying and the Cold War* (4–6). Series: On the Front Line. 2005, Raintree LB $29.93 (1-4109-1465-8). 48pp. This is an accessible overview of the Cold War, covering its roots and progress and looking in particular at the role of espionage; personal accounts add interest. (Rev: SLJ 12/05) [327.1209]

3252 Koestler-Grack, Rachel A. *The Kent State Tragedy* (4–7). Illus. Series: American Moments. 2005, ABDO LB $17.94 (1-59197-934-X). 48pp. A concise overview of the deadly 1970 clash between National Guard troops and war protesters on the campus of Ohio's Kent State University. (Rev: BL 9/1/05; SLJ 11/05) [378.771]

3253 Mason, Andrew. *The Vietnam War: A Primary Source History* (5–8). Illus. Series: In Their Own Words. 2005, Gareth Stevens LB $19.50 (0-8368-5981-2). 48pp. Primary sources — including letters, articles, speeches, and songs — deliver the views of combatants in Vietnam and people on the home front in this well-illustrated volume. (Rev: BL 10/15/05) [959.704]

Regions

MIDWEST

3254 Bial, Raymond. *Nauvoo: Mormon City on the Mississippi River* (4–7). Illus. 2006, Houghton $17.00 (0-618-39685-3). 48pp. This richly illustrated title profiles the Illinois city of Nauvoo and the important role it played in the history of the Church of Jesus Christ of Latter-day Saints. (Rev: BL 11/1/06; SLJ 12/06) [289.3]

3255 Bodden, Valerie. *Mount Rushmore* (3–6). Series: Modern Wonders of the World. 2006, Creative Education LB $27.10 (1-58341-440-1). 32pp. This is an interesting history of the memorial at Mount Rushmore, with good photographs and discussion of its contemporary importance. (Rev: SLJ 12/06) [978.3]

3256 Brill, Marlene Targ. *Illinois* (4–7). Illus. Series: Celebrate the States. 2005, Benchmark LB $25.95 (0-7614-1735-4). 144pp. A revised edition of this introduction to the state — including its history, culture, famous sites, and important individuals — with updated illustrations. (Rev: SLJ 5/06) [913.73]

3257 Dykstra, Mary. *Iowa* (2–4). Series: Portraits of the States. 2006, Gareth Stevens LB $23.33 (0-8368-4664-8). 32pp. Young report writers will find lots of useful information in this introduction to the state, with accessible text and graphic features that add interest. (Rev: SLJ 5/06) [977.7]

3258 Gedatus, Gus. *Minnesota* (2–4). Series: Portraits of the States. 2006, Gareth Stevens LB $23.33

(0-8368-4669-9). 32pp. Young report writers will find lots of useful information in this introduction to the state, with accessible text and graphic features that add interest. (Rev: SLJ 5/06) [977.6]

3259 Heinrichs, Ann. *Ohio* (3–5). Illus. by Matt Kania. Series: Welcome to the U.S.A. 2005, The Child's World LB $27.07 (1-59296-449-4). 40pp. Using an attractive scrapbook format featuring a family on vacation, this volume introduces the state's geography, history, people, major attractions, and state symbols. (Rev: SLJ 2/06) [977.1]

3260 Heinrichs, Ann. *South Dakota* (3–5). Illus. by Matt Kania. Series: Welcome to the U.S.A. 2005, The Child's World LB $27.07 (1-59296-483-4). 40pp. A basic introduction with maps, pertinent facts, discussion of the state's geography and history, plus popular destinations and cultural information. (Rev: SLJ 1/06) [979.2]

3261 Temple, Teri, and Bob Temple. *Welcome to Badlands National Park* (3–5). Series: Visitor Guides. 2006, The Child's World LB $27.07 (1-59296-693-4). 32pp. An attractively presented tour of the South Dakota park, with information on its geography, history, flora, fauna, and weather. (Rev: SLJ 2/07) [917.83]

3262 Thomas, William David. *Kansas* (2–4). Series: Portraits of the States. 2006, Gareth Stevens LB $17.50 (0-8368-4665-6). 32pp. History, geography, economy, and other research needs — including some interesting trivia — are covered in this concise volume. (Rev: BL 7/06) [978.1]

MOUNTAIN STATES

3263 Bauer, Marion Dane. *The Grand Canyon* (K–2). Illus. by John Wallace. Series: Ready-to-Read Wonders of America. 2006, Simon & Schuster LB $11.89 (0-689-86947-9); paper $3.99 (0-689-86946-0). 32pp. How the Grand Canyon was formed, and what it's like to visit it, in a format for beginning readers with cartoon-like illustrations. (Rev: SLJ 7/06) [917.91]

3264 Hall, M. C. *Glacier National Park* (K–4). Series: Symbols of Freedom: National Parks. 2005, Heinemann LB $24.21 (1-4034-6698-X). 32pp. Large color photographs and clear text introduce history, geography, flora, and fauna of this park; useful for basic research and reports. (Rev: SLJ 12/05) [978.6]

3265 Hall, M. C. *Grand Canyon National Park* (K–4). Series: Symbols of Freedom: National Parks. 2005, Heinemann LB $24.21 (1-4034-6699-8). 32pp. Large color photographs and clear text introduce the history, geography, flora, and fauna of this park; useful for basic research and reports. (Rev: SLJ 12/05) [979.1]

3266 Hall, M. C. *Rocky Mountain National Park* (K–4). Series: Symbols of Freedom: National Parks. 2005, Heinemann LB $24.21 (1-4034-6701-3). 32pp. Large color photographs and clear text introduce the history, geography, flora, and fauna of this park; useful for basic research and reports. (Rev: SLJ 12/05) [978.8]

3267 Hall, M. C. *Yellowstone National Park* (K–4). 2005, Heinemann LB $24.21 (1-4034-6702-1). 32pp. Large color photographs and clear text introduce the history, geography, flora, and fauna of this park; useful for basic research and reports. (Rev: SLJ 12/05) [978.7]

3268 Heinrichs, Ann. *Colorado* (3–5). Illus. by Matt Kania. Series: Welcome to the U.S.A. 2005, The Child's World LB $27.07 (1-59296-572-2). 40pp. A basic introduction with maps, pertinent facts, discussion of the state's geography and history, plus popular destinations and cultural information. (Rev: SLJ 1/06) [978.8]

3269 Heinrichs, Ann. *Utah* (3–5). Illus. by Matt Kania. Series: Welcome to the U.S.A. 2005, The Child's World LB $27.07 (1-59296-486-9). 40pp. A basic introduction with maps, pertinent facts, discussion of the state's geography and history, plus popular destinations and cultural information. (Rev: SLJ 1/06) [978.8]

3270 Higgins, Nadia. *Welcome to Glacier National Park* (3–5). Series: Visitor Guides. 2006, The Child's World LB $27.07 (1-59296-696-9). 32pp. An attractively presented tour of the Montana park, focusing on its geography, history, flora, fauna, and weather. (Rev: SLJ 2/07) [917.86]

3271 Lorbiecki, Marybeth. *Welcome to Grand Teton National Park* (3–5). Illus. Series: Visitor Guides. 2006, Child's World LB $18.95 (1-59296-698-5). 32pp. Despite confusing maps, this guide to the Wyoming park offers solid information for reports. (Rev: BL 10/15/06; SLJ 2/07) [917.87]

3272 Lynch, Wayne, and Aubrey Lang. *Rocky Mountains* (4–7). Illus. by Wayne Lynch. Series: Our Wild World. 2006, NorthWord $16.95 (1-55971-948-6); paper $8.95 (1-55971-949-4). 64pp. An appealing introduction to the geography, animals, and plants of the region, with full-color photographs and first-person anecdotes. (Rev: BL 10/15/06; SLJ 1/07*) [577.5]

3273 Trumbauer, Lisa. *Grand Canyon* (K–2). Series: Rookie Read-About Geography. 2005, Children's Pr. LB $19.50 (0-516-22747-5). 31pp. This simple easy-reader covers the basic facts about the geographic wonder. (Rev: SLJ 7/05) [979.1]

NORTHEAST

3274 Backer, Miles. *Travels with Charlie: Travelin' the Northeast* (1–4). Illus. by Chuck Nitzberg.

Series: A Search and Find Geography Book. 2006, Blue Apple $15.95 (978-1-59354-162-0). Charlie, a travel-loving mutt, takes readers on a light-hearted, seek-and-find hunt of the northeastern United States. (Rev: SLJ 2/07) [974]

3275 Bauer, Marion Dane. *Niagara Falls* (K–2). Illus. by John Wallace. Series: Ready-to-Read Wonders of America. 2006, Simon & Schuster LB $11.89 (0-689-86945-2); paper $3.99 (0-689-86944-4). 32pp. Basic information about the waterfall — geology and history, including daredevil feats — is presented in an attractive format suitable for beginning readers. (Rev: SLJ 6/06) [971.3]

3276 Burg, Ann K. *Times Square: A New York State Number Book* (2–5). Illus. by Maureen K. Brookfield. 2005, Sleeping Bear $16.95 (1-58536-195-X). Readers count to 100 while absorbing numerous facts — some little-known — about New York State. (Rev: SLJ 1/06) [974.7]

3277 Greene, Jacqueline Dembar. *The Triangle Shirtwaist Factory Fire* (3–5). Illus. Series: Code Red. 2007, Bearport LB $17.97 (1-59716-359-7). 32pp. This study of the tragic 1911 fire that killed 146 at a New York City clothing factory examines the disaster itself, the reasons for the heavy loss of life, and the lessons that were learned by city authorities. (Rev: BL 4/1/07) [974.7]

3278 Heinrichs, Ann. *Delaware* (3–5). Illus. by Matt Kania. Series: Welcome to the U.S.A. 2005, The Child's World LB $27.07 (1-59296-470-2). 40pp. Using an attractive scrapbook format featuring a family on vacation, this volume introduces the state's geography, history, people, major attractions, and state symbols. Also use *Maryland* (2005). (Rev: SLJ 2/06) [975.1]

3279 Hempstead, Anne. *The Statue of Liberty* (4–7). Series: Land of the Free. 2006, Heinemann LB $28.21 (1-4034-7004-9). 32pp. With many illustrations and interesting sidebars, this history of the Statue of Liberty details key events and examines its significance as an American symbol. (Rev: SLJ 10/06) [974.7]

3280 Hempstead, Anne. *The Supreme Court* (4–7). Series: Land of the Free. 2006, Heinemann LB $28.21 (1-4034-7001-4). 32pp. With many illustrations and interesting sidebars, this history of the U.S. Supreme Court details key events and examines its significance as an American symbol. Also use *The U.S. Capitol* and *The White House* (both 2006). (Rev: SLJ 10/06) [347]

3281 Hicks, Terry Allan. *The Capitol* (3–5). Series: Symbols of America. 2006, Benchmark LB $19.95 (0-7614-2132-7). 40pp. A look at the U.S. Capitol, its history, and the important role it plays as the home of America's legislative branch of government. (Rev: SLJ 12/06) [975.3]

3282 Hicks, Terry Allan. *Ellis Island* (3–5). Series: Symbols of America. 2006, Benchmark LB $19.95 (0-7614-2134-3). 40pp. An overview of the history of Ellis Island and its importance as a symbol of the United States. (Rev: SLJ 12/06) [4.6.8.4.3]

3283 Low, William. *Old Penn Station* (2–4). Illus. 2007, Holt $16.95 (978-0-8050-7925-8). 32pp. This photoessay celebrates the grandeur of the New York City landmark that was demolished in the 1960s. (Rev: BL 3/15/07) [385.3]

3284 Schaefer, Ted, and Lola M. Schaefer. *Independence Hall* (1–3). Series: Symbols of Freedom. 2005, Heinemann LB $24.21 (1-4034-6664-5). 32pp. Large color photographs and clear text introduce Philadelphia's Independence Hall and the important role it played in America's history; useful for basic research and reports. (Rev: SLJ 12/05) [974.811]

3285 Schaefer, Ted, and Lola M. Schaefer. *The Vietnam Veterans Memorial* (1–3). Series: Symbols of Freedom. 2005, Heinemann LB $24.21 (1-4034-6659-9). 32pp. Large color photographs and clear text introduce the Washington, D.C., memorial; useful for basic research and reports. (Rev: SLJ 12/05) [959.7043]

3286 Schomp, Virginia. *New York* (4–7). Illus. Series: Celebrate the States. 2005, Benchmark LB $25.95 (0-7614-1738-9). 144pp. A revised edition of this introduction to the Empire State — including its history, culture, famous sites, and distinguished New Yorkers — with updated illustrations. (Rev: SLJ 5/06) [917.47]

3287 Shea, Pegi Deitz. *Liberty Rising: The Story of the Statue of Liberty* (2–4). Illus. by Wade Zahares. 2005, Holt $17.95 (0-8050-7220-9). 44pp. Bold illustrations highlight the story of the creation of the statue; also includes a timeline and pronunciation guide. (Rev: BL 8/05; SLJ 10/05) [974.7]

3288 Smith, Marie, and Roland Smith. *N Is for Our Nation's Capital: A Washington, DC Alphabet* (K–4). Illus. by Barbara Leonard Gibson. 2005, Sleeping Bear $17.95 (1-58556-148-8). An inventive alphabet book that introduces historical information about the capital and the people who have worked there. (Rev: SLJ 8/05) [957.3]

PACIFIC STATES

3289 Aillaud, Cindy Lou. *Recess at 20 Below* (K–3). Illus. 2005, Alaska Northwest $15.95 (0-88240-604-3); paper $8.95 (0-88240-609-4). 32pp. Though the temperature outside can be nearly 20 degrees below zero (Fahrenheit), Alaskan schoolchildren still find a way to play outdoors. (Rev: BL 12/15/05; HB 1–2/06; HBG 4/06; SLJ 3/06) [371.2]

3290 Altman, Linda J. *California* (5–8). Series: Celebrate the States. 2005, Benchmark LB $25.95 (0-

7614-1737-0). 143pp. This revised edition updates facts and adds information on the government and economy plus new, full-color photographs. (Rev: SLJ 3/06) [979.4]

3291 Cosson, M. J. *Welcome to Redwood National and State Parks* (3–5). Series: Visitor Guides. 2006, The Child's World LB $27.07 (1-59296-701-9). 32pp. An attractively presented tour of three California parks, focusing on their geography, history, flora, fauna, and weather. (Rev: SLJ 2/07) [917.94]

3292 Dell, Pamela. *Welcome to Mount Rainier National Park* (3–5). Series: Visitor Guides. 2006, The Child's World LB $27.07 (1-59296-700-0). 32pp. An attractively presented tour of the Washington state park, focusing on its geography, history, flora, fauna, and weather. (Rev: SLJ 2/07) [979.7]

3293 Doak, Robin. *California 1542–1850* (5–8). Series: Voices from Colonial America. 2006, National Geographic $21.95 (0-7922-6391-X). 109pp. This well-illustrated title traces the history of California from its 1542 "discovery" by Juan Rodriguez Cabrillo to the frenzied Gold Rush years of the mid-19th century; maps and a timeline make this useful for research. (Rev: SLJ 1/07) [979.4]

3294 Fandel, Jennifer. *Golden Gate Bridge* (3–6). Series: Modern Wonders of the World. 2006, Creative Education LB $27.10 (1-58341-437-1). 32pp. This is an attractive overview of the history of the famous bridge, the engineering challenges involved in its construction, and its importance today as a span and a symbol. (Rev: SLJ 12/06) [624.2]

3295 Gill, Shelley. *Hawai'i* (5–8). Illus. by Scott Goto. 2006, Charlesbridge paper $6.95 (0-88106-297-9). 32pp. A boy and his father tour the state of Hawaii by kayak; as they pass each island the father tells his son a little about its history, geography, people, culture, and economy. (Rev: SLJ 8/06) [996.9]

3296 Hall, M. C. *Hawaii Volcanoes National Park* (K–4). Series: Symbols of Freedom: National Parks. 2005, Heinemann LB $24.21 (1-4034-6700-5). 32pp. Large color photographs and clear text introduce the history, geography, flora, and fauna of this park; useful for basic research and reports. (Rev: SLJ 12/05) [919.69]

3297 Hall, M. C. *Welcome to Denali National Park* (3–5). Series: Visitor Guides. 2006, The Child's World LB $27.07 (1-59296-695-0). 32pp. An attractively presented tour of the Alaskan park, focusing on its geography, history, flora, fauna, and weather. (Rev: SLJ 2/07) [979.8]

3298 Heinrichs, Ann. *Oregon* (3–5). Illus. by Matt Kania. Series: Welcome to the U.S.A. 2005, The Child's World LB $27.07 (1-59296-479-6). 40pp. Using an attractive scrapbook format featuring a family on vacation, this volume introduces the state's geography, history, people, major attractions, and state symbols. (Rev: SLJ 2/06) [979.5]

3299 Labella, Susan. *Washington* (K–2). Series: Rookie Read-About Geography. 2006, Scholastic LB $19.50 (0-516-24993-2); paper $5.95 (0-516-26455-9). 32pp. A slim, square volume on Washington state that will be a good start for young researchers. (Rev: BL 7/06) [917.97]

3300 Mannis, Celeste Davidson. *Snapshots: The Wonders of Monterey Bay* (K–4). Photos by author. 2006, Viking $16.99 (0-670-06062-3). All about the varied plants and animals of California's spectacular Monterey Bay, with plenty of eye-catching photographs and clearly presented information. (Rev: SLJ 6/06*)

3301 Miller, Debbie S. *Big Alaska: Journey Across America's Most Amazing State* (2–4). Illus. by Jon Van Zyle. 2006, Walker $17.95 (0-8027-8069-5). 40pp. Sixteen of Alaska's most breathtaking natural wonders are shown in this large-format, photo-filled book that uses a bald eagle's flight as a unifying element; facts, state symbols, and Internet sites are appended. (Rev: BL 3/1/06; SLJ 5/06) [917.98]

3302 Murphy, Claire Rudolf. *Children of Alcatraz: Growing Up on the Rock* (4–7). Illus. 2006, Walker $17.95 (0-8027-9577-3). 64pp. This is the story of the children who have grown up on Alcatraz Island over time — early Native American children, children of lighthouse keepers, children of prison authorities, and so forth — with archival photographs and a timeline. (Rev: BL 12/15/06; SLJ 11/06) [979.4]

3303 Stefoff, Rebecca. *Alaska* (4–6). Illus. Series: Celebrate the States. 2006, Benchmark LB $27.95 (0-7614-2153-X). 144pp. An updated edition that includes attractive photographs, maps, and graphs and covers Alaska's history, geography, government, economy, and natural and man-made landmarks; fun facts, famous people, and places to visit, plus a list of Web sites round out this useful volume. (Rev: SLJ 12/06) [979.8]

3304 Temple, Teri, and Bob Temple. *Welcome to Hawai'i Volcanoes National Park* (3–5). Series: Visitor Guides. 2006, The Child's World LB $27.07 (1-59296-699-3). 32pp. An attractively presented tour of the Hawaiian state park, with information on its geography, history, flora, fauna, and weather plus discussion of the legend of Pele, the goddess of fire. (Rev: SLJ 2/07) [996.9]

SOUTH

3305 Barrett, Tracy. *Virginia* (4–7). Illus. Series: Celebrate the States. 2005, Benchmark LB $25.95 (0-7614-1734-6). 142pp. A revised edition of this introduction to the state — including its history, culture, famous sites, and important Virginians — with updated illustrations. (Rev: SLJ 5/06) [975.5]

3306 Bjorklund, Ruth. *Louisiana* (3–5). Illus. Series: It's My State. 2006, Benchmark LB $18.95 (0-7614-1863-6). 80pp. Report writers will find all the facts they need on the history, geography, government, and economy of Louisiana — including information on the effects of Hurricane Katrina — plus a state-themed craft. (Rev: SLJ 6/06) [976.3]

3307 Bredeson, Carmen, and Mary Dodson Wade. *Texas* (5–8). Series: Celebrate the States. 2005, Benchmark LB $25.95 (0-7614-1736-2). 144pp. This revised edition updates facts and adds information on the government and economy plus new, full-color photographs. (Rev: SLJ 3/06) [976.4]

3308 Harkins, Susan, and William H. Harkins. *Georgia: The Debtors Colony* (4–7). Series: Building America. 2006, Mitchell Lane LB $19.95 (978-1-58415-465-5). 48pp. A look at Georgia's early history — including climate, early industry, and population — with information on James Oglethorpe, a key figure who aimed to provide a haven in America for debtors imprisoned in England. (Rev: SLJ 2/07) [975.8]

3309 Haywood, Karen Diane. *Georgia* (3–5). Illus. Series: It's My State! 2006, Benchmark LB $18.95 (0-7614-1862-8). 79pp. Report writers will find all the facts they need in this book that comes complete with a state-themed craft. (Rev: SLJ 6/06) [975.8]

3310 Heinrichs, Ann. *West Virginia* (3–5). Illus. by Matt Kania. 2005, The Child's World LB $27.07 (1-59296-490-7). 40pp. Using an attractive scrapbook format featuring a family on vacation, this volume introduces the state's geography, history, people, major attractions, and state symbols. (Rev: SLJ 2/06) [975.4]

3311 Higgins, Nadia. *Welcome to Everglades National Park* (3–5). 2006, The Child's World LB $27.07 (1-59296-702-7). 32pp. An attractively presented tour of the South Florida park, focusing on its geography, history, flora, fauna, and weather. (Rev: SLJ 2/07) [917.59]

3312 Pobst, Sandy. *Virginia, 1607–1776* (5–8). Illus. Series: Voices from Colonial America. 2005, National Geographic LB $32.90 (0-7922-6771-0). 112pp. A thorough political and social history of early Virginia, with excellent illustrations. (Rev: BL 10/15/05; SLJ 11/05) [975.5]

3313 Raven, Margot Theis. *Let Them Play* (2–5). Illus. by Chris Ellison. 2005, Sleeping Bear $16.95 (1-58536-260-3). In this fact-based tale from the mid-1950s, an African American Little League team from Charleston, South Carolina, is snubbed by the state's white teams and by officials of the Little League World Series. (Rev: SLJ 11/05)

3314 Schaefer, Ted, and Lola M. Schaefer. *Arlington National Cemetery* (1–3). Series: Symbols of Freedom. 2005, Heinemann LB $24.21 (1-4034-6665-3). 32pp. The burial site for many Americans who served their country is introduced in simple text and archival and contemporary photographs; includes a "Fact File" and a timeline. (Rev: SLJ 12/05) [975.5]

3315 Schaefer, Ted, and Lola M. Schaefer. *The Pentagon* (1–3). Series: Symbols of Freedom. 2005, Heinemann LB $24.21 (1-4034-6663-7). 32pp. Large color photographs and clear text introduce the Pentagon's role as the headquarters of the U.S. Defense Department, also covering the terrorist attack of 2001; useful for basic research and reports. (Rev: SLJ 12/05) [355.6]

SOUTHWEST

3316 Hicks, Terry Allan. *Nevada* (3–5). Illus. Series: It's My State! 2006, Benchmark LB $18.95 (0-7614-1860-1). 80pp. Report writers will find all the facts they need in this book that comes complete with a state-themed craft. (Rev: SLJ 6/06) [979.3]

Social Institutions and Issues

Business and Economics

Also use *Save, Spend, or Donate?* (2005). (Rev: SLJ 9/05) [332.4]

General

3317 Aaseng, Nathan. *Business Builders in Sweets and Treats* (5–8). Illus. Series: Business Builders. 2005, Oliver LB $24.95 (1-881508-84-6). 160pp. This attractive title examines food companies that succeed through satisfying America's sweet tooth. (Rev: BL 12/1/05; HBG 4/06) [338.7]

3318 Allman, Barbara. *Banking* (4–6). Illus. Series: How Economics Works. 2005, Lerner LB $25.26 (0-8225-2148-2). 48pp. An excellent overview of the banking system with cartoons and bright illustrations and sidebars; checking and savings accounts are among the topics covered and a glossary defines common banking terms. (Rev: BL 10/15/05) [332.1]

3319 Rau, Dana Meachen. *What Is a Bank?* (2–4). Illus. Series: Money and Banks. 2005, Weekly Reader LB $14.50 (0-8368-4873-X). 24pp. An inside (small-format) look at how a bank operates, covering checking and savings accounts, safe-deposit boxes, ATMs, and money lending. (Rev: BL 10/15/05) [332.1]

Consumerism

3320 Lewin, Ted. *How Much? Visiting Markets Around the World* (K–2). Illus. 2006, HarperCollins $15.99 (0-688-17552-X). 40pp. A large-format photographic tour of marketplaces on four continents, with text that enhances the images and offers the phrase "How much" in various languages. (Rev: BL 2/1/06; SLJ 1/06) [381]

3321 Loewen, Nancy. *Cash, Credit Cards, or Checks: A Book About Payment Methods* (3–5). Illus. by Brad Fitzpatrick. Series: Money Matters. 2005, Picture Window LB $22.60 (1-4048-0951-1). 24pp. Shopping for school necessities forms the backdrop for information on money and banking.

Money-Making Ideas and Budgeting

3322 Buckley, Annie. *Be a Better Babysitter* (5–6). Series: Girls Rock! 2006, The Child's World LB $24.21 (1-59296-740-X). 32pp. This introductory guide to baby-sitting explains the nature of the job, looks at its pros and cons and safety issues, and offers advice on doing a good job. (Rev: SLJ 2/07) [649]

3323 Holyoke, Nancy. *A Smart Girl's Guide to Money: How to Make It, Save It, and Spend It* (4–7). Illus. by Ali Douglass. Series: A Smart Girl's Guide. 2006, Pleasant paper $9.95 (1-59369-103-3). 94pp. Shopping and investing are only two of the topics covered in this user-friendly guide. (Rev: BL 5/15/06; SLJ 5/06) [332.024]

3324 Loewen, Nancy. *Lemons and Lemonade: A Book About Supply and Demand* (3–5). Illus. by Brian Jensen. Series: Money Matters. 2005, Picture Window LB $22.60 (1-4048-0956-2). 24pp. Karly learns about managing a small business — and about the principle of supply and demand — in this humorous entry in the series. (Rev: SLJ 9/05) [338.5]

3325 Rancic, Bill, and Karen Soenen. *Beyond the Lemonade Stand: Starting Small to Make It Big!* (3–5). 2005, Penguin $12.99 (1-59514-103-0). 159pp. This handbook offers solid advice for youthful entrepreneurs and includes the stories of young people who have launched business ventures of their own. (Rev: SLJ 2/06) [658.1]

3326 Willson, Sarah. *Pet Peeves* (1–3). Illus. by John Nez. Series: Social Studies Connects. 2005, Kane paper $4.99 (1-57565-149-1). 32pp. Children work together to become entrepreneurs in this story designed to support social studies. (Rev: SLJ 9/05)

Ecology and Environment

3327 Léger, Diane Carmel. *Who's in Maxine's Tree?* (1–4). Illus. by Darlene Gait. 2006, Orca $17.95 (1-55143-346-X). Maxine is thrilled to learn that her favorite tree will be protected from loggers because it is home to an endangered species of bird. (Rev: SLJ 6/06)

3328 Lorbiecki, Marybeth. *Planet Patrol* (3–5). Illus. by Nancy Meyers. 2005, Two-Can $15.95 (1-58728-514-2); paper $8.95 (1-58728-518-5). 48pp. This brightly illustrated title alerts readers to a wide range of environmental threats — pollution, overpopulation, climate change, deforestation, and species extinction — and what young people can do to help save the globe and reverse some of the damage. (Rev: BL 12/1/05; SLJ 12/05) [577]

3329 Nakaya, Andrea C., ed. *The Environment* (5–9). Series: Introducing Issues with Opposing Viewpoints. 2006, Gale LB $32.45 (0-7377-3459-0). 128pp. This thought-provoking study examines the delicate balance between the preservation of our natural environment and the need for energy to fuel economic growth. (Rev: SLJ 8/06)

3330 Parks, Peggy J. *Ecotourism* (5–8). Series: Our Environment. 2005, Gale LB $23.70 (0-7377-3048-X). 48pp. All about how ecologically sensitive areas can be protected while being explored, with explanations of the advantages and disadvantages of this type of travel. (Rev: SLJ 5/06) [338.4]

3331 Parry, Ann. *Greenpeace* (5–8). Illus. Series: Humanitarian Organizations. 2005, Chelsea House LB $20.95 (0-7910-8815-4). 32pp. Maps, timelines, factboxes, and color photographs add to this account of Greenpeace's history and mission. (Rev: SLJ 12/05)

3332 Rockwell, Anne. *Why Are the Ice Caps Melting? The Dangers of Global Warming* (2–4). Illus. by Paul Meisel. Series: Let's-Read-and-Find-Out Science. 2006, HarperCollins $15.99 (0-06-054669-7); paper $4.99 (0-06-054671-9). 33pp. The hot-button issue of global warming is discussed in easy-to-understand language, as are the greenhouse effect and the role of carbon dioxide emissions. (Rev: BL 12/15/06; SLJ 11/06) [363.738]

3333 Spilsbury, Louise, and Richard Spilsbury. *Water* (5–8). Series: Planet Under Pressure. 2006, Heinemann LB $31.43 (978-1-4034-8214-3). 48pp. Discusses the demand for water, its sources, and what's being done to conserve it. (Rev: SLJ 3/07)

3334 Strauss, Rochelle. *One Well: The Story of Water on Earth* (3–5). Illus. by Rosemary Woods. 2007, Kids Can $17.95 (978-1-55337-954-6). 32pp. The importance of water to life on earth and the connections between all uses of water are emphasized in this oversize picture book that also discusses water distribution and recycling and gives tips on conservation. (Rev: BL 2/15/07*) [553.7]

3335 Toft, Kim Michelle. *The World That We Want* (PS–3). Illus. by author. 2005, Charlesbridge paper $6.95 (1-58089-115-2). The interconnectedness of animals, plants, and their habitats is emphasized in this book with beautiful illustrations and an environmental message. (Rev: SLJ 9/05) [577]

3336 Walker, Jane. *Atmosphere in Danger* (4–6). 2005, Stargazer LB $27.10 (1-932799-12-5). Easy-to-understand language with helpful graphs, charts, and illustrations make this a useful introduction to the problems threatening the Earth's fragile atmosphere and the potential solutions. (Rev: SLJ 4/06) [363.739]

Cities

3337 Pancella, Peggy. *City* (K–2). Series: Neighborhood Walk. 2005, Heinemann LB $25.36 (1-4034-6215-1). 32pp. After a discussion of a neighborhood as part of a larger community, this book looks at various aspects of life in the city, including work, recreation, transportation, and shopping. Also use *Farm Community, Military Base, Small Town,* and *Suburb* (all 2005). (Rev: SLJ 2/06) [307.76]

Garbage and Waste Recycling

3338 Love, Ann, and Jane Drake. *Trash Action: A Fresh Look at Garbage* (3–6). Illus. by Mark Thurman. 2006, Tundra paper $14.95 (0-88776-721-4). 76pp. Examples of trash on Mount Everest and in space draw readers into this information-packed book that looks at the growing problems of garbage and waste disposal and outlines steps that can be taken to address the situation. (Rev: SLJ 8/06) [363.72]

Pollution

3339 Bellamy, Rufus. *Clean Air* (4–6). 2005, Smart Apple Media LB $27.10 (1-58340-594-1). This book takes a somewhat optimistic tack on the problem of global air pollution, citing numerous examples of programs that either have been put in place or are being considered. (Rev: SLJ 4/06) [363.739]

3340 Gifford, Clive. *Pollution* (4–7). Illus. Series: Planet Under Pressure. 2006, Heinemann LB $31.43 (1-4034-7742-6). 48pp. An overview of the various types of pollution, their sources and impact, and possible future remedies. (Rev: SLJ 6/06)

3341 Green, Jen. *Reducing Air Pollution* (4–6). 2005, Gareth Stevens LB $24.67 (0-8368-4428-9).

This easy-to-understand overview of air pollution looks at what's causing the problem, including such factors as acid rain, ozone depletion, and global warming, and examines ways in which the world can reduce its dependence on fossil fuels. (Rev: SLJ 4/06) [363.739]

3342 Ingram, W. Scott. *The Chernobyl Nuclear Disaster* (5–8). Series: Environmental Disasters. 2005, Facts on File $35.00 (0-8160-5755-9). 100pp. Ingram assesses the continuing environmental fallout from the 1986 Chernobyl nuclear disaster. (Rev: SLJ 11/05) [333.79]

3343 Leacock, Elspeth. *The Exxon Valdez Oil Spill* (5–8). Series: Environmental Disasters. 2005, Facts on File $35.00 (0-8160-5754-0). 100pp. A look at the environmental impact of the 1989 *Exxon Valdez* oil spill in Alaska's Prince William Sound. (Rev: SLJ 11/05) [363.7]

3344 Ostopowich, Melanie. *Water Pollution* (4–6). 2005, Weigl LB $24.45 (1-59036-307-8); paper $6.95 (1-59036-313-2). This overview of water pollution explores the water cycle and various causes of pollution and includes a few experiments to help readers better understand the concepts involved. (Rev: SLJ 4/06) [363.739]

Population

3345 Mason, Paul. *Population* (4–7). Series: Planet Under Pressure. 2006, Heinemann LB $31.43 (1-4034-7741-8). 48pp. The problems created by overpopulation are the focus of this book that also explores the underlying reasons and possible solutions. (Rev: SLJ 6/06)

3346 Mason, Paul. *Poverty* (4–7). Illus. Series: Planet Under Pressure. 2006, Heinemann LB $22.00 (1-4034-7743-4). 48pp. A clear presentation of how poverty affects people around the world, with charts, photographs, and profiles. (Rev: BL 4/1/06; SLJ 6/06) [362.5]

Government and Politics

United Nations and International Affairs

3347 Kramer, Ann. *Human Rights: Who Decides?* (5–8). Series: Behind the News. 2006, Heinemann LB $32.86 (978-1-4034-8832-9). 56pp. With photographs and examples of news stories, this volume offers various viewpoints on the information we receive on human rights and asks readers how they will make up their minds. (Rev: SLJ 4/07) [323]

3348 *Making It Home: Real Life Stories from Children Forced to Flee* (5–8). Illus. 2006, Dial $17.99 (0-8037-3083-7); paper $6.99 (0-14-240455-1). 144pp. The horrific impact of war on children is documented in these first-person accounts, with many photographs, from children who were displaced from their homes in Afghanistan, Bosnia, Burundi, Congo, Iraq, Kosovo, Liberia, and Sudan. (Rev: BL 12/1/05; SLJ 2/06) [305.23]

3349 Parry, Ann. *Red Cross* (4–6). Illus. Series: Humanitarian Organizations. 2005, Chelsea House LB $20.95 (0-7910-8814-6). 32pp. With many photographs, sidebars, and other features, this volume explores the history, mission, and core values of the Red Cross. (Rev: BL 10/15/05; SLJ 12/05) [361.77]

United States

Civil Rights

3350 Edwards, Pamela Duncan. *The Bus Ride That Changed History: The Story of Rosa Parks* (K–2). Illus. by Danny Shanahan. 2005, Houghton $16.00 (0-618-44911-6). 32pp. The story of Rosa Parks's bus ride is told in cumulative "This Is the House That Jack Built" fashion with cartoon illustrations featuring children's questions in dialogue balloons. (Rev: BL 9/1/05; SLJ 10/05) [323]

3351 Fitzgerald, Stephanie. *Struggling for Civil Rights* (4–6). Series: On the Front Line. 2005, Raintree LB $29.93 (1-4109-1467-4). 48pp. This is an accessible overview of the civil rights movement of the 1950s and 1960s, covering its roots and key events; personal profiles add interest. (Rev: SLJ 12/05) [323.1196]

3352 Freedman, Russell. *Freedom Walkers: The Story of the Montgomery Bus Boycott* (4–7). 2006, Holiday $18.95 (0-8234-2031-0). 114pp. First-person accounts enliven this history of the 381-day Montgomery Bus Boycott of the mid-1950s, which ended segregation on the buses. (Rev: BCCB 12/06; BL 9/15/06; HBG 4/07; LMC 3/07; SLJ 11/06*; VOYA 10/06) [323.1196]

3353 Price, Sean. *When Will I Get In?* (4–6). Series: American History Through Primary Sources. 2006, Raintree LB $19.75 (978-1-4109-2414-8); paper $7.99 (978-1-4109-2425-4). 32pp. An introduction for reluctant readers to the history of segregation and the important moments and people that were part of the fight for equal rights. (Rev: BL 2/1/07) [305.896]

3354 Rappaport, Doreen. *Nobody Gonna Turn Me 'Round* (4–7). Illus. by Shane Evans. 2006, Candlewick $19.99 (0-7636-1927-2). 64pp. This concluding volume of a trilogy documenting the black experience in America focuses on the stormy decade between the Montgomery bus boycott and the signing of the Voting Rights Act in August 1965, providing profiles of key figures. (Rev: BL 8/06; SLJ 10/06) [323.1196]

3355 Shore, Diane Z., and Jessica Alexander. *This Is the Dream* (2–4). Illus. by James Ransome. 2006, HarperCollins $15.99 (0-06-055519-X). 40pp. Mixing archival photographs, newspaper clippings, original paintings, and rhythmic verse, the creators of this book tell the story of the civil rights movement in an unusual and effective way. (Rev: BL 2/1/06*; SLJ 1/06) [811]

3356 Somervill, Barbara A. *Brown v. Board of Education: The Battle for Equal Education* (5–8). Series: Journey to Freedom. 2005, Child's World LB $28.50 (1-59296-229-7). 40pp. A brief overview of the landmark Supreme Court case that sounded a death knell for school segregation in America. (Rev: SLJ 8/05)

Constitution

3357 Allen, Kathy. *The U.S. Constitution* (PS–2). Illus. 2006, Capstone $19.93 (0-7368-9594-9). 32pp. This large-format picture book offers a child-friendly, very basic introduction to the U.S. Constitution. (Rev: BL 10/1/06) [342]

3358 Eck, Kristin. *Drafting the Constitution: Weighing the Evidence to Draw Sound Conclusions* (5–8). Illus. Series: Critical Thinking in American History. 2005, Rosen LB $18.95 (1-4042-0412-1). 48pp. This slim volume offers a review of the issues debated at the Constitutional Convention, plus study questions, a reading list, and a Web site with links to related online resources. (Rev: BL 10/15/05) [342.7302]

3359 Finkelman, Paul. *The Constitution* (4–8). Series: American Documents. 2006, National Geographic LB $23.90 (0-7922-7975-1). 48pp. An unusually attractive introduction to the Constitution, with reproductions, photographs, and profiles of key individuals. (Rev: SLJ 2/06; VOYA 8/06) [342.73]

Crime and Criminals

3360 Butterfield, Moira. *Pirates and Smugglers* (5–7). Series: Kingfisher Knowledge. 2005, Kingfisher paper $12.95 (0-7534-5864-0). 64pp. A broad historical survey of outlaws on the high seas, from early smugglers to today's dealers in drugs and exotic animals. (Rev: SLJ 12/05)

3361 Fridell, Ron. *Forensic Science* (4–7). Series: Cool Science. 2006, Lerner LB $25.25 (978-0-8225-5935-1). 48pp. The history of forensic science from 1910 to today is accompanied by information on the professionals involved (medical examiners, forensic entomologists) and the equipment used; effective photographs add to the appeal. (Rev: SLJ 4/07) [363.25]

3362 Fridell, Ron. *Spy Technology* (4–7). Series: Cool Science. 2006, Lerner LB $25.26 (978-0-8225-5934-4). 48pp. A review of the kinds of technology available in the past and today — including gadgets used by the CIA and KGB and spy satellites — is followed by accounts of dangerous missions

and discussion of future technologies. (Rev: SLJ 4/07) [623]

3363 Newcomb, Rain. *The Master Spy Handbook* (4–7). Illus. by Jason Chin. 2005, Lark $17.95 (1-57990-626-5). 96pp. This guide to the tricks of the trade for spies is presented in the form of a fictionalized first-person narrative by a kid detective. (Rev: BL 1/1–15/06) [327.12]

3364 Platt, Richard. *Forensics* (5–10). Illus. Series: Kingfisher Knowledge. 2005, Kingfisher paper $12.95 (0-7534-5862-4). 64pp. This introduction to the use of the forensic sciences in crime investigation is presented in short blocks of text that will make it appealing to reluctant readers. (Rev: SLJ 11/05) [363.2]

3365 Schroeder, Andreas. *Thieves!* (5–10). Series: True Stories from the Edge. 2005, Annick $18.95 (1-55037-933-X); paper $8.95 (1-55037-932-1). 164pp. Ten world-class crimes are described in compelling detail. (Rev: SLJ 3/06) [364]

3366 Townsend, John. *Breakouts and Blunders* (5–8). Series: True Crime. 2005, Raintree LB $31.43 (1-4109-1427-5). 48pp. Attempted and successful escapes through history are the subject of this book in the True Crime series, which features a scrapbook format with engaging photographs and graphics. Also use *Fakes and Forgeries* and *Kidnappers and Assassins* (both 2005). (Rev: SLJ 6/06) [365.641]

3367 Winchester, Elizabeth Siris. *The Right Bite: Dentists as Detectives* (4–8). Illus. Series: 24/7 Science Behind the Scenes: Forensic Files. 2007, Scholastic LB $25.00 (0-531-12062-7); paper $7.95 (0-531-18734-0). 64pp. Conversational text focuses on the work of forensic dentists and offers multiple (sometimes gruesome) examples of cases in which their findings identified victims and perpetrators; factual inserts add interest and a final section discusses the equipment used. (Rev: BL 4/1/07) [614]

Elections and Political Parties

3368 Giddens-White, Bryon. *National Elections and the Political Process* (4–6). Series: Our Government. 2005, Heinemann LB $28.21 (1-4034-6604-1). 32pp. This explanation of how elections in the United States work will be useful for report writers. (Rev: SLJ 5/06) [324.6097]

3369 Hamilton, John. *Running for Office* (3–5). Series: Government in Action! 2005, ABDO LB $15.95 (1-59197-822-X). 32pp. All about how one goes about being elected to public office, with discussion of the differences between the two major U.S. parties. (Rev: SLJ 7/05) [324.7]

Federal Government and Agencies

3370 Attebury, Nancy Garhan. *Out and About at the United States Mint* (1–3). Illus. by Zachary Trover. Series: Field Trips. 2005, Picture Window LB $23.93 (1-4048-1151-6). 24pp. Tour the U.S. Mint along with a group of children and learn about its operations and the money produced there. (Rev: SLJ 2/06) [737.4973]

3371 Giddens-White, Bryon. *The President and the Executive Branch* (4–6). Series: Our Government. 2005, Heinemann LB $28.21 (1-4034-6601-7). 32pp. This clear explanation of the executive power of the president of the United States will be useful for report writers. Also use *The Supreme Court and the Judicial Branch* (2005). (Rev: SLJ 5/06) [352.2309]

3372 Gorman, Jacqueline Laks. *Member of Congress* (2–4). Series: Our Government Leaders. 2005, Weekly Reader LB $19.33 (0-8368-4570-6). 24pp. Young researchers will find plenty of useful information on what a member of Congress does, how he or she is elected, and the responsibilities of the position. (Rev: SLJ 7/05) [328.73]

3373 Hamilton, John. *Becoming a Citizen* (3–5). Series: Government in Action! 2005, ABDO LB $15.95 (1-59197-642-1). 32pp. The steps to citizenship are well explained and accompanied by photographs of documents, sample questions, and the "Oath of Allegiance." (Rev: SLJ 7/05) [323.6]

3374 Hamilton, John. *How a Bill Becomes a Law* (3–5). Series: Government in Action! 2005, ABDO LB $15.95 (1-59197-646-4). 32pp. This look at the U.S. legislative system includes clear illustrations of the steps involved in a bill's passage. (Rev: SLJ 7/05) [328.73]

3375 Kennedy, Edward M. *My Senator and Me: A Dog's Eye View of Washington D.C* (2–4). Illus. by David Small. 2006, Scholastic $16.99 (0-439-65077-1). 56pp. Senator Kennedy's dog Splash narrates the events of a busy day on Capitol Hill. (Rev: BL 8/06; SLJ 8/06*) [328.73092]

3376 Teichmann, Iris. *Immigration and the Law* (5–8). Series: Understanding Immigration. 2006, Smart Apple Media LB $31.35 (978-1-58340-970-1). 44pp. Covers all aspects of immigration including the laws granting admission, visas, and how to gain citizenship. (Rev: SLJ 3/07)

State Government and Agencies

3377 Gorman, Jacqueline Laks. *Governor* (2–4). Series: Our Government Leaders. 2005, Weekly Reader LB $19.33 (0-8368-4567-6). 24pp. Young researchers will find plenty of useful information on what a governor is, how he or she is elected, and the responsibilties of the position. (Rev: SLJ 7/05) [352.23]

Municipal Government and Agencies

3378 Gorman, Jacqueline Laks. *Mayor* (2–4). Series: Our Government Leaders. 2005, Weekly Reader LB $19.33 (0-8368-4569-2). 24pp. The duties of this political office are clearly presented for young report-writers. (Rev: SLJ 7/05) [352.23]

Social Problems and Solutions

3379 Small, Mary. *Being a Good Citizen: A Book About Citizenship* (K–2). Illus. by Stacey Previn. Series: Way to Be! 2005, Picture Window LB $22.60 (1-4048-1050-1). 24pp. A slim overview of simple ways in which children can be good citizens and help improve their communities, such as picking up trash and planting flowers. (Rev: SLJ 12/05) [323.6]

Religion and Holidays

General and Miscellaneous

3380 Abrams, Judith Z. *The Secret World of Kabbalah* (5–9). Illus. 2006, Lerner paper $9.95 (1-58013-224-3). 80pp. This interesting introduction to Kabbalah defines this form of Jewish mysticism as "the journey to come as closely in touch with God as you can." (Rev: SLJ 12/06) [296.16]

3381 Barnes, Trevor. *Christianity* (5–8). Series: World Faiths. 2005, Kingfisher paper $6.95 (0-7534-5880-2). 40pp. This volume expands on the earlier *Kingfisher Book of Religions*, looking at the diversity of practices and rituals within the Christian church worldwide. (Rev: SLJ 10/05; VOYA 6/06) [202]

3382 Barnes, Trevor. *Islam* (5–8). Illus. Series: World Faiths. 2005, Kingfisher paper $6.95 (0-7534-5882-9). 40pp. Originally published in 1999 as part of *The Kingfisher Book of Religions: Festivals, Ceremonies, and Beliefs from Around the World*, this 40-page expanded volume provides a wide-ranging overview of Islam and its followers. (Rev: BL 10/1/05; SLJ 10/05; VOYA 6/06) [297]

3383 Brown, Tricia. *Salaam: A Muslim American Boy's Story* (K–3). Photos by Ken Cardwell. 2006, Holt $17.95 (0-8050-6538-5). A young Muslim American boy explains the basic tenets of his faith and the customs and rituals associated with it; full of photographs, this also includes a glossary. (Rev: SLJ 12/06) [073]

3384 Das, Rasamandala. *Hinduism* (4–6). Series: Religions of the World. 2005, World Almanac LB $30.00 (0-8368-5867-0). 48pp. A photo-filled introduction to Hinduism and its history, beliefs, rites, and holidays. (Rev: SLJ 1/06) [294.5]

3385 *A Faith like Mine* (3–5). Illus. 2005, DK $19.99 (0-7566-1177-6). 80pp. Children of different religious backgrounds describe the basics of their faith and what they like about their religion; includes background information on major and minor world religions. (Rev: BL 10/1/05; SLJ 11/05) [291]

3386 Ganeri, Anita. *Buddhism* (4–6). Series: Religions of the World. 2005, World Almanac LB $30.00 (0-8368-5865-4). 48pp. A photo-filled introduction to Buddhism and its history, beliefs, rites, and holidays. (Rev: SLJ 1/06) [294.3]

3387 Ganeri, Anita. *Buddhist Stories* (1–6). Illus. by Tracey Fennell. Series: Traditional Religious Tales. 2006, Picture Window LB $23.95 (1-4048-1311-X). 32pp. The stories in this appealing collection chronicle the life of the Buddha, focusing in particular on his lifelong search for enlightenment. (Rev: SLJ 4/06) [294.3]

3388 Ganeri, Anita. *Hindu Stories* (1–6). Illus. by Carole Gray. Series: Traditional Religious Tales. 2006, Picture Window LB $23.95 (1-4048-1309-8). 32pp. The seven stories in this collection are prime examples of classical Hindu mythology and include colorful tales about such deities and demons as Krishna the cowherd, Ganesh the elephant god, and Holika the demon princess. (Rev: SLJ 4/06) [294.5]

3389 Ganeri, Anita. *Sikh Stories* (1–6). Illus. by Rachael Phillips. Series: Traditional Religious Tales. 2006, Picture Window LB $23.95 (1-4048-1314-4). 32pp. This collection of stories documents incidents from the lives of Sikh spiritual leaders, emphasizing the moral lessons exemplified. (Rev: SLJ 4/06) [294.6]

3390 Jani, Mahendra, and Vandana Jani. *What You Will See Inside a Hindu Temple* (4–6). Illus. by Neirah Bhargava. Series: What You Will See Inside. 2005, SkyLight Paths $17.99 (1-59473-116-0). 32pp. Attractive double-page spreads look inside a typical Hindu temple and introduce the fundamental beliefs, rituals, and ceremonies of Hinduism. (Rev: BL 1/1–15/06; SLJ 2/06) [294.5]

3391 *Jesus Loves Me!* (K–2). Illus. by Tim Warnes. 2006, Simon & Schuster $12.95 (1-4169-0065-9). A happy family of bears living in a forest celebrate the classic Christian children's song; the music is appended. (Rev: SLJ 3/06) [242]

3392 Keene, Michael. *Judaism* (5–8). Series: Religions of the World. 2005, World Almanac LB $30.00 (0-8368-5869-7). 48pp. A basic introduction to the beliefs and practices of Judaism around the world, with a chronology of important events. (Rev: SLJ 2/06) [296]

3393 Pandell, Karen. *Saint Francis Sings to Brother Sun: A Celebration of His Kinship with Nature* (4–7). Illus. by Bijou Le Tord. 2005, Candlewick $18.99 (0-7636-1563-3). 64pp. The story of Saint Francis of Assisi and his unique relationship with nature includes excerpts from the priest's own writings and is enhanced by mixed-media illustrations. (Rev: BL 12/1/05; SLJ 2/06) [271.302]

3394 Rotner, Shelley, and Sheila M. Kelly. *Many Ways: How Families Practice Their Beliefs and Religions* (K–2). Illus. by Shelley Rotner. 2005, Millbrook $16.95 (0-7613-2873-5). 32pp. A simple child-friendly introduction to the customs followed by believers of six religions: Buddhism, Christianity, Hinduism, Islam, Judaism, and Sikhism. (Rev: BL 10/1/05) [200]

3395 Self, David. *Christianity* (5–8). Series: Religions of the World. 2005, World Almanac LB $30.00 (0-8368-5866-2). 48pp. A basic introduction to the beliefs and practices of Christianity, with a chronology of important events. (Rev: SLJ 2/06)

3396 Thompson, Jan. *Islam* (5–8). Series: World Religions. 2005, Walrus paper $12.95 (1-55285-654-2). 58pp. Using a question-and-answer format, this attractive introduction explores the history and beliefs of Islam; a first-person account by a 15-year-old Muslim boy in London starts the book. (Rev: BL 10/15/05) [297]

3397 Wallace, Holly. *Islam: Budi's Story* (3–5). Illus. Series: This Is My Faith. 2007, Barron's $11.99 (0-7641-3475-2); paper $4.99 (0-7641-3475-2). 32pp. Budi, a young Indonesian Muslim, introduces his family and neighbors and describes the ways in which his religion affects his life. (Rev: BL 4/1/07) [297]

3398 Wilson, Karma. *I Will Rejoice: Celebrating Psalm 118* (PS–2). Illus. by Amy June Bates. 2007, Zondervan $14.99 (0-310-71117-7). 32pp. Based on the psalm that reads "This is the day that the Lord has made, and I will rejoice and be glad in it," this book urges children to find happiness and joy in the world around them. (Rev: BL 10/1/06)

3399 Zarin, Cynthia. *Saints Among the Animals* (5–8). Illus. by Leonid Gore. 2006, Atheneum $17.95 (0-689-85031-X). 96pp. An attractive collection of ten stories about saints interacting with animals; brief biographies of the saints are appended. (Rev: BL 12/1/06; SLJ 1/07) [270]

Bible Stories

3400 Demi. *Mary* (4–7). 2006, Simon & Schuster $19.95 (0-689-87692-0). 48pp. Traces the story of the mother of Jesus from the days preceding her birth through her ascension into heaven. (Rev: BL 10/1/06; SLJ 11/06) [232.91]

3401 Hodges, Margaret. *Moses* (3–5). Illus. by Barry Moser. 2006, Harcourt $16.00 (0-15-200946-9). 32pp. From his birth and placement in the bulrushes to his retrieval of the Ten Commandments, this handsome volume highlights Moses' achievements and the obstacles he faced. (Rev: BL 10/1/06; SLJ 12/06) [222.1]

3402 Shaw, Luci. *The Genesis of It All* (K–3). Illus. by Sr. Huai-Kuang Miao. 2006, Paraclete $17.95 (1-55725-480-X). 32pp. This child-friendly retelling of the creation story imagines what God was thinking as He gave form to the world and breathed life into man and beast; the beautiful art progresses from black and white to color, and the author emphasizes that the story is speculation not fact. (Rev: BL 10/1/06) [222]

Holidays and Holy Days

General and Miscellaneous

3403 Dean, Sheri. *Flag Day / Día de la bandera* (K–2). Trans. by Tatiana Acosta and Guillermo Gutiérrez. Series: Our Country's Holidays / Las fiestas de nuestra nación. 2006, Weekly Reader LB $19.33 (0-8368-6518-9). 24pp. In English and Spanish, this is an introduction to the history behind Flag Day, with a look at the customs associated with the celebration. Also use *The Fourth of July / Cuatro de Julio, Martin Luther King Jr. Day / Día de Martin Luther King Jr.,* and *Presidents' Day / Día de los presidentes* (all 2006). (Rev: SLJ 10/06) [394.263]

3404 Doering, Amanda. *Cinco de Mayo: Day of Mexican Pride* (1–3). Series: First Facts: Holidays and Culture. 2005, Capstone LB $15.93 (0-7368-5387-1). 24pp. A craft, a story, and photographs accompany a brief introduction to the holiday and an explanation of why it is important; suitable for beginning readers. Also use *Day of the Dead* (2005). (Rev: SLJ 5/06) [394.2]

3405 Gibbons, Gail. *Groundhog Day* (PS–2). Illus. 2007, Holiday $16.95 (978-0-8234-2003-2). 32pp. This examination of the February holiday is accompanied by Gibbons's usual clear illustrations and augmented with information about groundhogs. (Rev: BL 1/1–15/07) [394.261]

3406 Gilley, Jeremy. *Peace One Day: How September 21 Became World Peace Day* (4–6). Illus. by Karen Blessen. 2005, Putnam $16.99 (0-399-24330-5). 48pp. British filmmaker Gilley tells the story behind World Peace Day, an annual observance he worked diligently to establish. (Rev: BL 10/1/05; SLJ 9/05) [303.6]

3407 Heiligman, Deborah. *Celebrate Diwali* (1–3). Series: Holidays Around the World. 2006, National Geographic $15.95 (0-7922-5922-X). 32pp. A look at the customs associated with the celebration of the Hindu holiday, in India and in four other countries. (Rev: SLJ 1/07) [294.5]

3408 Heiligman, Deborah. *Celebrate Ramadan and Eid al-Fitr* (1–3). Series: Holidays Around the World. 2006, National Geographic $15.95 (0-7922-5926-2). 32pp. A look at these Islamic observances and their religious significance as well as the associated customs and rituals. (Rev: SLJ 1/07) [297.3]

3409 Heinrichs, Ann. *Chinese New Year* (K–3). Illus. by Benrei Huang. Series: Holidays, Festivals, and Celebrations. 2006, The Child's World LB $22.79 (1-59296-572-5). 32pp. Examines the history, customs, and symbols of this holiday and includes a recipe and a craft. Also use *Saint Patrick's Day* (2006). (Rev: SLJ 9/06) [394.261]

3410 Heinrichs, Ann. *Cinco de Mayo* (2–3). Illus. by Kathleen Petelinsek. Series: Holidays, Festivals, and Celebrations. 2006, The Child's World LB $22.79 (1-59296-573-3). 32pp. Information about the holiday and how it is celebrated, plus photographs of the festivities, Spanish words, and a craft to try; also use *Día de los Muertos* (2006). (Rev: SLJ 5/06) [394.2]

3411 Nelson, Vaunda Micheaux, and Drew Nelson. *Juneteenth* (2–4). Illus. by Mark Schroder. Series: On My Own Holidays. 2006, Lerner $23.93 (1-57505-876-6); paper $5.95 (0-8225-5974-9). 48pp. The story behind the Juneteenth holiday is told for beginning readers. (Rev: BL 2/1/06; SLJ 3/06) [394.263]

3412 Petelinsek, Kathleen, and E. Russell Primm. *Holidays and Celebrations / Días de fiesta y celebraciones* (K–2). Illus. by Nichole Day Diggins. Series: Talking Hands. 2006, The Child's World LB $21.36 (1-59296-453-2). 24pp. Students demonstrate simple holiday-related words using American Sign Language; the text is in both English and Spanish. (Rev: SLJ 6/06) [419]

3413 Reynolds, Betty. *Japanese Celebrations: Cherry Blossoms, Lanterns and Stars!* (3–5). Illus. 2006, Turtle $16.95 (0-8048-3658-2). 48pp. A chronological survey of Japanese holidays throughout the year, covering food, dress, decoration, symbols, and so forth. (Rev: BL 12/1/06; SLJ 12/06) [394.2]

3414 Roberts, Russell. *Holidays and Celebrations in Colonial America* (4–6). Illus. Series: Building America. 2006, Mitchell Lane LB $19.95 (1-58415-467-5). 48pp. This attractive title, which features a timeline, glossary, and calendar, briefly profiles the holidays celebrated during America's colonial period and examines how those that are still observed today have changed over the years. (Rev: BL 11/1/06) [394.26973]

3415 Sievert, Terri. *Ramadan: Islamic Holy Month* (K–2). Illus. Series: First Facts: Holidays and Culture. 2006, Capstone LB $11.95 (0-7368-5392-8). 24pp. This photo-filled title introduces young readers to the Islamic holiday, exploring its religious significance and traditions. (Rev: BL 4/1/06) [297.3]

3416 Trueit, Trudi. *Kwanzaa* (1–3). Series: Rookie Read-about Holidays. 2006, Children's Pr. LB $20.50 (0-531-12458-4); paper $5.95 (0-531-11839-8). 32pp. This colorful introduction to the holiday examines its history and customs and provides a holiday-related recipe and craft. (Rev: SLJ 10/06) [394.2]

Christmas

3417 Box, Su. *Behind the Scenes Christmas* (3–5). Illus. by Jo Blake. 2006, Abingdon $14.00 (0-687-49121-5). 29pp. Arranged in question-and-answer format and featuring excerpted Bible stories, this colorful book pieces together the events surrounding the birth of Jesus Christ. (Rev: SLJ 10/06)

3418 Lankford, Mary D. *Christmas USA* (3–5). Illus. by Karen Dugan. 2006, HarperCollins $15.99 (0-688-15012-8). 48pp. A regional look at the various Christmas customs in the United States, including instructions for various crafts, recipes, and a timeline of popular Christmas toys over the years. (Rev: BL 11/15/06; SLJ 10/06) [394.2663]

3419 Onyefulu, Ifeoma. *An African Christmas* (K–2). Illus. 2005, Frances Lincoln $15.95 (1-84507-387-8). 32pp. A young Nigerian boy Afam hopes to create his own mask and to dance in the traditional Mmo masquerade. (Rev: BL 11/1/05) [394.2]

Easter

3420 Joslin, Mary. *On That Easter Morning* (K–3). Illus. by Helen Cann. 2006, Good Bks. $16.00 (1-56148-517-9). The biblical account of Jesus's last days on Earth, leading to his crucifixion and resurrection, is retold and accompanied by beautiful art-work. (Rev: SLJ 5/06) [232.9]

Halloween

3421 Zocchi, Judy. *On Halloween Night / La noche de Halloween* (2–4). Illus. by Rebecca Wallis. 2005, Dingles LB $15.50 (1-891997-76-9). A cartoon-filled bilingual introduction to the history and rituals of Halloween. (Rev: SLJ 2/06) [745.5]

Jewish Holy Days and Celebrations

3422 Baum, Maxie. *I Have a Little Dreidel* (PS–K). Illus. by Julie Paschkis. 2006, Scholastic $9.99 (0-439-64997-8). 32pp. Illustrations full of interesting details enhance this retelling of the traditional Hanukkah song. (Rev: BL 9/15/06; HB 11–12/06; HBG 4/07; SLJ 10/06) [782.42]

3423 Ben-Zvi, Rebecca Tova. *Four Sides, Eight Nights: A New Spin on Hanukkah* (2–4). Illus. by Susanna Natti. 2005, Roaring Brook $16.95 (1-59643-059-1). 48pp. Dreidels — their composition and rules and technique of the game — are the focus of this Hanukkah book that also touches on holiday food and the stories of Judith and Hannah. (Rev: BL 11/1/05; SLJ 10/05) [296.4]

3424 Fishman, Cathy Goldberg. *On Sukkot and Simchat Torah* (K–3). Illus. by Melanie Hall. 2006, Lerner $17.95 (1-58013-165-4). 32pp. Follows a Jewish family preparing a sukkah for the Sukkot harvest festival, and enjoying the celebration that accompanies the completion of the Torah reading on Simchat Torah. (Rev: BL 10/1/06; SLJ 9/06) [296.4]

3425 Heiligman, Deborah. *Celebrate Hanukkah with Light, Latkes, and Dreidels* (1–3). Illus. Series: Holidays Around the World. 2006, National Geographic $15.95 (0-7922-5924-6). 32pp. A colorful introduction to the history and traditions of Hanukkah, with photographs from countries around the world; appended materials include prayers, a recipe for latkes, a bibliography, and a glossary. (Rev: BL 10/15/06) [296.35]

3426 Heiligman, Deborah. *Celebrate Passover* (3–5). Illus. Series: Holidays Around the World. 2007, National Geographic LB $23.90 (978-1-4263-0019-6); paper $15.95 (978-1-4263-0018-9). 32pp. Introduces to the Jewish holiday and its religious significance, customs, and rituals in communities around the world. (Rev: BL 3/15/07) [296.4]

3427 Kropf, Latifa Berry. *It's Purim Time!* (PS). Photos by Tod Cohen. 2005, Lerner LB $12.95 (1-58013-153-0). Preschool children enjoy a fun-filled

Purim, selecting costumes, making noisemakers, and having traditional snacks. (Rev: SLJ 8/05) [296.4]

3428 Kropf, Latifa Berry. *It's Shofar Time!* (1–3). Illus. by Tod Cohen. 2006, Kar-Ben $12.95 (1-58013-158-1). 24pp. Color photographs show children enjoying the traditions associated with the Jewish holiday of Rosh Hashanah. (Rev: BL 10/1/06) [296.4]

Thanksgiving

3429 Heinrichs, Ann. *Thanksgiving* (K–3). Illus. by Charles Jordan. Series: Holidays, Festivals, and Celebrations. 2006, The Child's World LB $22.79 (1-59296-582-2). 32pp. Examines the history, customs, and symbols of this holiday and includes a recipe and a craft. (Rev: SLJ 9/06) [394.2649]

Valentine's Day

3430 Gibbons, Gail. *Valentine's Day Is . . .* (PS–1). Illus. 2006, Holiday $16.95 (0-8234-1852-9). 32pp. In spreads introduced by the title phrase, Gibbons explores the origins and customs of Valentine's Day. (Rev: BL 2/1/06; SLJ 3/06) [394.2681]

3431 Trueit, Trudi. *Valentine's Day* (K–2). Illus. Series: Rookie Read-about Holidays. 2006, Scholastic LB $20.50 (0-531-12461-4). 32pp. Brief information and stock photographs introduce beginning readers to Valentine's Day. (Rev: BL 1/1–15/07) [394.2618]

Prayers

3432 Brooks, Jeremy. *A World of Prayers* (PS–1). Illus. by Elena Gomez. 2006, Eerdmans $16.00 (0-8028-5285-8). 32pp. A collection of more than 25 prayers from around the world, organized by category rather than religion. (Rev: BL 12/15/05; SLJ 2/06) [204]

3433 *A Children's Treasury of Prayers* (PS–1). Illus. by Linda Bleck. 2006, Sterling $12.95 (1-4027-2982-0). 32pp. This child-friendly collection of prayers offers examples from a number of religions, including Christianity, Hinduism, Islam, and Judaism. (Rev: BL 10/1/06) [204]

3434 Rock, Lois. *A Child's Book of Graces* (PS–2). Illus. by Alison Jay. 2006, Good Books $5.95 (1-56148-514-4). 28pp. Prayers for before (and after) meals from many sources, Christian and non-Christian. (Rev: BL 7/06) [242]

Social Groups

Ethnic Groups

3435 Goldstein, Margaret J. *Japanese in America* (4–7). Series: In America. 2006, Lerner LB $27.93 (0-8225-3952-7). 80pp. The author discusses the history of U.S.-Japan relations and the course of Japanese immigration to America from the 1800s to today, including the internments during World War II; profiles of famous Japanese Americans are appended. (Rev: SLJ 5/06) [973.0495]

3436 Kyuchukov, Hristo, and Ian Hancock. *A History of the Romani People* (3–5). Illus. 2005, Boyds Mills $19.95 (1-56397-962-4). 48pp. An introductory overview of the history, culture, and language of the Roma or Gypsy people. (Rev: BL 12/1/05; SLJ 11/05) [909]

3437 Nichols, Catherine. *African American Culture* (4–6). Series: Discovering the Arts. 2006, Advantage World LB $20.95 (1-59515-516-3). 48pp. A concise history of African American arts, introducing key figures and placing them in historical context. (Rev: BL 2/1/06) [704.03]

3438 Petrillo, Valerie. *A Kid's Guide to Asian American History: More than 90 Activities* (3–6). 2007, Chicago Review paper $14.95 (978-1-55652-634-3). 256pp. Crafts, games, and other activities introduce various aspects of Asian American cultures. (Rev: BL 4/15/07) [973.3]

3439 Weber, Valerie J. *I Come from Afghanistan* (2–4). Illus. Series: This Is My Story. 2006, Gareth Stevens LB $14.95 (978-0-8368-7233-0). 24pp. Afghan American Bahishta, age 9, introduces readers to her family, Muslim faith, and cultural heritage in this series entry. (Rev: BL 1/1–15/07) [973]

Terrorism

3440 Uschan, Michael V. *The Beslan School Siege and Separatist Terrorism* (5–8). Illus. Series: Terrorism in Today's World. 2005, World Almanac LB $22.50 (0-8368-6555-3). 48pp. The deadly 2004 attack on a Russian school by Chechen Muslim terrorists is only the first of several attacks described in this volume on independence movements that use violence. (Rev: BL 4/1/06) [947.5]

Personal Development

Behavior

General

3441 Becker, Helaine. *Like a Pro: 101 Simple Ways to Do Really Important Stuff* (4–6). Illus. by Claudia Dávila. Series: Planet Earth News. 2006, Maple Tree $21.95 (1-897066-53-8); paper $9.95 (1-897066-54-6). 160pp. From changing a bike tire to telling jokes to making friends, this friendly, practical guide offers instructions and advice. (Rev: SLJ 6/06) [646.7]

3442 Buckley, Annie. *Hero Girls* (2–5). Series: Girls Rock! 2006, The Child's World LB $24.21 (1-59296-744-2). 32pp. Profiles American girls whose courage or other attributes can be classed as heroic; suitable for browsing by beginning readers. (Rev: SLJ 4/07) [305.2]

3443 Canfield, Jack, et al. *Chicken Soup for the Girl's Soul: Real Stories by Real Girls About Real Stuff* (4–6). 2005, Health Communications paper $12.95 (0-7573-0313-7). 345pp. Real-life stories tackle a wide variety of topics, including dealing with peer pressure, parental divorce, surviving middle school, first loves, and friendship. (Rev: SLJ 2/06) [158.1]

3444 Edelman, Marian Wright. *I Can Make a Difference* (2–4). Illus. by Barry Moser. 2005, HarperCollins $20.89 (0-06-028052-9). 112pp. This oversize collection of poems, stories, songs, quotations, art, and folk tales, organized in 12 sections dealing with such topics as honesty, courage, and compassion, includes selections from a wide variety of sources that emphasize children's capacity to make a difference. (Rev: BL 11/1/05) [808.8]

3445 Finn, Carrie. *Kids Talk About Bravery* (K–2). Illus. by Amy Bailey Muehlenhardt. Series: Kids Talk Jr. 2006, Picture Window LB $23.93 (1-4048-2314-X). 32pp. A question-and-answer format and simple language are used to discuss children's fears and ways of tackling them. (Rev: SLJ 1/07) [179]

3446 Fitzhugh, Karla. *Body Image* (5–9). Series: Health Issues. 2004, Steck-Vaughn LB $32.79 (0-7398-6891-8). Body image and such related issues as cosmetic surgery, piercing, tattooing, eating disorders, and physical culture are examined in attractive text with informative charts and sidebars. (Rev: SLJ 11/05) [155.2]

3447 King, Bart. *The Big Book of Girl Stuff* (4–8). Illus. by Jennifer Kalis. 2006, Gibbs Smith paper $19.95 (1-58685-819-X). 320pp. A lighthearted, lightly organized guide to a great many topics of interest to growing girls, including why boys smell bad, etiquette, dieting, how to shop, and how to get a boy's attention. (Rev: SLJ 1/07) [646.7]

3448 Moore-Mallinos, Jennifer. *Do You Have a Secret?* (PS–3). Illus. by Marta Fàbrega. Series: Let's Talk About It! 2005, Barron's paper $6.95 (0-7641-3170-2). 31pp. Moore-Mallinos explains the difference between good secrets and bad ones, and gives advice on getting help from adults. (Rev: SLJ 10/05)

3449 Nikola-Lisa, W. *How We Are Smart* (4–7). Illus. by Sean Qualls. 2006, Lee & Low $16.95 (1-58430-254-2). 32pp. A picture book for older readers that looks at different kinds of intelligence, using double-page spreads about 12 famous people to illustrate these concepts. (Rev: BL 4/1/06; SLJ 6/06) [811]

3450 Rosenthal, Amy Krouse. *Cookies: Bite Size Life Lessons* (PS–1). Illus. by Jane Dyer. 2006, HarperCollins $12.99 (0-06-058081-X). 40pp. Baking cookies serves as the framework for defining words and concepts in this attractive and child-friendly book. (Rev: BCCB 9/06; BL 4/1/06*; HBG 10/06; SLJ 5/06) [179]

3451 Small, Mary. *Being Fair: A Book About Fairness* (K–2). Illus. by Stacey Previn. Series: Way to Be! 2005, Picture Window LB $22.60 (1-4048-1051-X). 24pp. A slim overview of simple ways in which children can be fair in their dealings with others. Also use *Being Responsible* and *Being Trustworthy* (2005). (Rev: SLJ 12/05) [179]

3452 Thomas, Pat. *I'm Telling the Truth: A First Look at Honesty* (K–3). Illus. by Lesley Harker. Series: A First Look At. 2006, Barron's paper $6.99 (0-7641-3214-8). 29pp. Introduces the concept of honesty, explains its importance in dealing with others, and offers suggestions about how to incorporate this character trait into everyday life. (Rev: SLJ 9/06) [179.9]

3453 Zimmerman, Bill. *100 Things Guys Need to Know* (5–9). 2005, Free Spirit paper $13.95 (1-57542-167-4). Effective graphic design will draw teenage boys into this self-help guide that touches on a wide variety of topics, including body image, dating, school, friendship, and family. (Rev: SLJ 11/05) [305.235]

Introduces the concept of politeness, examines its importance in dealing with others, and offers suggestions about how to behave politely. (Rev: SLJ 9/06) [179.9]

3460 Wheeler, Valerie. *Yes, Please! No, Thank You!* (PS–3). Illus. by Glin Dibley. 2005, Sterling $14.95 (1-4027-1746-6). Playful questions remind young readers to say "Yes, please" and "No, thank you" when responding to any sort of invitation. (Rev: SLJ 8/05) [395.1]

3461 Willems, Mo. *Time to Say "Please"!* (PS–3). Illus. by author. 2005, Hyperion $15.99 (0-7868-5293-3). Mice give children playful tips on correct behavior. (Rev: SLJ 8/05) [395.1]

3462 Zemke, Deborah. *Don't Feed the Babysitter to Your Boa Constrictor: 43 Ridiculous Rules Every Kid Should Know* (2–3). Series: I'm Going to Read! 2006, Sterling paper $3.95 (1-4027-3429-8). 24pp. A funny, easy-reader collection of nonsensical rules for children — including "Never eat anything that's still moving" and "Don't eat spaghetti through your nose." (Rev: BL 11/1/06; SLJ 12/06) [818]

Etiquette

3454 Goldberg, Whoopi. *Whoopi's Big Book of Manners* (K–3). Illus. by Olo. 2006, Hyperion $15.99 (0-7868-5295-X). A funny, chatty guide to proper etiquette. (Rev: SLJ 11/06) [395]

3455 Goode, Diane. *Mind Your Manners!* (K–2). Illus. 2005, Farrar $16.00 (0-374-34975-4). 32pp. The illustrations in this comical belie the text, drawn verbatim from an 1802 primer on manners and sporting such advice as "Gnaw not bones at the table." (Rev: BL 11/15/05; SLJ 11/05) [395.1]

3456 Hample, Stoo. *Book of Bad Manners* (3–5). Illus. by author. 2006, Candlewick $15.99 (0-7636-2933-2). Examples of bad behavior are paired with lively drawings of the evil deeds, bound to amuse young readers. (Rev: SLJ 9/06) [395.12]

3457 Holyoke, Nancy. *A Smart Girl's Guide to Manners* (4–7). Illus. by Cathi Mingus. 2005, Pleasant paper $9.95 (1-58485-983-0). 120pp. A nice mix of good manners that ranges from introductions to cell phone etiquette to how and when to write real thank-you notes. (Rev: BL 11/1/05; SLJ 1/06; VOYA 12/05) [395]

3458 Post, Peggy, and Cindy Post Senning. *Emily's Everyday Manners* (PS–2). Illus. by Steven Björkman. 2006, HarperCollins $16.99 (0-06-076174-1). 32pp. Emily and Ethan outline the basics of good behavior. (Rev: BL 10/15/06) [395.1]

3459 Thomas, Pat. *My Manners Matter: A First Look at Being Polite* (K–3). Illus. by Lesley Harker. 2006, Barron's paper $6.99 (0-7641-3212-1). 29pp.

Family Relationships

3463 Ancona, George. *Mis abuelos / My Grandparents* (K–2). Photos by author. Illus. Series: Somos Latinos. 2005, Children's Pr. LB $21.00 (0-516-25294-1). 32pp. In this photo-filled bilingual picture book, Latino American children talk about their relationships with their grandparents. Also in this series: *Mis juegos / My Games*, *Mi música / My Music*, *Mis comidas / My Foods*, *Mis fiestas / My Celebrations*, and *Mis quehaceres / My Chores*. (Rev: SLJ 2/06) [977.5]

3464 Kinkade, Sheila. *My Family* (PS–2). Illus. by Elaine Little. 2006, Charlesbridge $16.95 (1-57091-662-4); paper $6.95 (1-57091-691-8). 32pp. In double-page spreads, this full-color photoessay shows the diversity and similarities of families around the world. (Rev: BL 1/1–15/06; SLJ 2/06) [306.85]

3465 Kuklin, Susan. *Families* (3–5). Illus. 2006, Hyperion $15.99 (0-7868-0822-5). 40pp. Kuklin explores the diversity of families in America through interviews of children who have single, mixed-race, divorced, immigrant, gay, and lesbian parents; photographs are included on the double-page spreads. (Rev: BL 12/15/05; SLJ 1/06*) [306.85]

3466 MacMahon, Patricia, and Conor Clarke McCarthy. *Just Add One Chinese Sister* (PS–2). Illus. by Karen A. Jerome. 2005, Boyds Mills $16.95 (1-56397-989-6). This is an affecting and convincing chronicle of the adoption of a Chinese girl, conveyed through a scrapbook created by Claire and her American mother with contributions by her new big brother Conor. (Rev: BL 8/05; SLJ 2/05) [362.734]

3467 Moore-Mallinos, Jennifer. *When My Parents Forgot How to Be Friends* (PS–3). Illus. by Marta Fàbrega. Series: Let's Talk About It! 2005, Barron's paper $6.95 (0-7641-3172-9). 31pp. A girl talks about her unhappiness and uncertainty when her parents were preparing to separate; the situation improves when her dad moves out. (Rev: SLJ 10/05) [306.89]

3468 Sheldon, Annette. *Big Sister Now: A Story About Me and Our New Baby* (PS). Illus. by Karen Maizel. 2006, Magination $14.95 (1-59147-243-1); paper $8.95 (1-59147-244-X). 32pp. A little girl has some difficulty adjusting to the presence of her new baby brother; a note at the end gives parents advice on easing the transition. (Rev: BL 8/06; SLJ 2/07) [306.875]

Personal Problems and Relationships

3469 Finn, Carrie. *Kids Talk About Bullying* (K–2). Illus. by Amy Bailey Muehlenhardt. Series: Kids Talk Jr. 2006, Picture Window LB $23.93 (1-4048-2315-8). 32pp. A question-and-answer format and simple language are used to discuss bullying and ways of coping with it. (Rev: SLJ 1/07) [303.6]

3470 MacGregor, Cynthia. *Jigsaw Puzzle Family: The Stepkids' Guide to Fitting It Together* (5–8). Series: Rebuilding Books. 2005, Impact paper $12.95 (1-886230-63-3). 128pp. Offers reassuring, practical advice — with an emphasis on talking through problems and seeking solutions — for stepchildren who are having difficulty adjusting to life in a blended family. (Rev: BL 9/1/05; SLJ 10/05) [306.874]

3471 Medina, Sarah. *Sad* (PS–K). Illus. Series: Feelings. 2007, Heinemann LB $21.36 (978-1-4034-9293-7). 24pp. In the form of questions and answers, this small volume tackles the topic of sadness and offers reassuring advice. (Rev: BL 4/15/07) [152.4]

3472 Moroney, Trace. *When I'm Feeling Angry* (PS). Illus. 2006, School Specialty $9.95 (0-7696-4424-4). 18pp. A bunny describes what makes him mad and what it's like to feel angry; readers learn when it's OK to feel angry and when they need to control their behavior. Also use *When I'm Feeling Scared* (2006). (Rev: BL 3/1/06) [152.4]

3473 Nelson, Robin. *Working with Others* (K–3). Series: Pull Ahead Books. 2006, Lerner LB $22.60 (0-8225-3488-X). 32pp. Easy-to-understand advice about how to work well with others, covering such topics as conflict resolution, respect for others' opinions, patience, and discussing all sides of an issue. (Rev: SLJ 8/06) [303.69]

3474 Rashkin, Rachel. *Feeling Better: A Kid's Book About Therapy* (4–8). Illus. by Bonnie Adamson. 2005, Magination paper $8.95 (1-59147-238-5). 48pp. Presented in journal format, this volume uses 12-year-old Maya's experiences with a therapist to offer useful insights into the process and its value. (Rev: SLJ 11/05) [618.92]

Careers

General and Miscellaneous

3475 *Food* (5–9). Series: Discovering Careers for Your Future. 2005, Ferguson $21.95 (0-8160-5848-2). 92pp. Education and training, salaries, and outlook for the field are all covered here along with a description of the kinds of daily activities found in various positions. (Rev: SLJ 1/06)

3476 Lowenstein, Felicia. *What Does a Teacher Do?* (K–2). Illus. Series: What Does a Community Helper Do? 2006, Enslow LB $21.26 (0-7660-2321-4). 24pp. Outlines in easy-to-understand language the job requirements and everyday responsibilities of a teacher. (Rev: SLJ 4/06) [371.1]

3477 Minden, Cecelia. *Coaches* (1–2). Series: Neighborhood Helpers. 2006, The Child's World LB $22.79 (1-59296-561-X). 32pp. This attractive overview introduces young children to the role and responsibilities of a coach, plus the equipment and training needed. (Rev: SLJ 8/06) [796]

3478 *Publishing* (5–9). Series: Discovering Careers for Your Future. 2005, Ferguson LB $21.95 (0-8160-5845-8). 92pp. Education and training, salaries, and outlook for the field are all covered here along with a description of the kinds of daily activities found in various positions. (Rev: SLJ 1/06)

3479 Simon, Charnan. *Lewis the Librarian* (K–2). Illus. by Rebecca Thornburgh. Series: Magic Door to Learning. 2006, The Child's World LB $21.36 (1-59296-624-1). 24pp. An inviting basic introduction to the role of a librarian. (Rev: SLJ 2/07) [020.92]

3480 Sweeney, Alyse. *Welcome to the Library* (K–2). Series: Scholastic News Nonfiction Readers. 2006, Children's Pr. LB $19.00 (0-531-16841-7). 24pp. Basic information for beginning readers about libraries and the work of librarians, with seven highlighted words that are featured in bold in the text. (Rev: SLJ 1/07) [027]

3481 Sweeney, Alyse. *Who Works at the Zoo?* (K–2). Series: Scholastic News Nonfiction Readers. 2006, Children's Pr. LB $19.00 (0-531-16842-5). 24pp. Basic information for beginning readers, with seven highlighted words that are featured in bold in the text. (Rev: SLJ 1/07) [590.73]

Arts and Entertainment

3482 Nathan, Amy. *Meet the Musicians: From Prodigy (or Not) to Pro* (5–8). Illus. 2006, Holt $17.95 (0-8050-7743-X). 156pp. Profiles of members of the New York Philharmonic give readers a good understanding of the different roles of various instruments and the careers of professional musicians. (Rev: BL 3/15/06; SLJ 5/06; VOYA 6/06) [750.92]

3483 *Radio and Television* (5–9). Series: Discovering Careers for Your Future. 2005, Ferguson LB $21.95 (0-8160-5846-6). 92pp. Education and training, salaries, and outlook for the field are all covered here along with a description of the kinds of daily activities found in various positions. (Rev: SLJ 1/06)

Business

3484 *Advertising and Marketing* (5–9). Series: Discovering Careers for Your Future. 2005, Ferguson $21.95 (0-8160-5847-4). 92pp. Education and training, salaries, and outlook for the field are all covered here along with a description of the kinds of daily activities found in various positions. (Rev: SLJ 1/06)

Engineering, Technology, and Trades

3485 Boekhoff, P. M. *What Does a Construction Worker Do?* (K–2). Illus. Series: What Does a Community Helper Do? 2006, Enslow LB $21.26 (0-7660-2326-5). 24pp. Outlines in easy-to-understand language the job requirements and everyday responsibilities of a construction worker. (Rev: SLJ 4/06) [690]

Health and Medicine

3486 Aylmore, Angela. *We Work at the Hospital* (PS–K). Series: Where We Work. 2006, Raintree LB $21.36 (1-4109-2246-4). 24pp. A basic introduction to what doctors, nurses, and other health-care workers do, with color photographs and simple text. (Rev: SLJ 7/06) [362.1]

3487 Lowenstein, Felicia. *What Does a Doctor Do?* (1–3). Series: What Does a Community Helper Do? 2005, Enslow LB $21.26 (0-7660-2542-X). 24pp. This easy-reader chapter book looks at the important tasks that doctors perform to preserve the health of the communities in which they live and also examines career opportunities in the field of medicine. (Rev: SLJ 11/05)

3488 Miller, Heather. *What Does a Dentist Do?* (K–2). Illus. Series: What Does a Community Helper Do? 2006, Enslow LB $21.26 (0-7660-2323-0). 24pp. Outlines in easy-to-understand language the job requirements and everyday responsibilities of a dentist. (Rev: SLJ 4/06) [617.6]

3489 Minden, Cecilia. *Nurses* (1–2). Series: Neighborhood Helpers. 2006, The Child's World LB $22.79 (1-59296-566-0). 32pp. This attractive overview introduces young children to the role and responsibilities of a nurse, plus the equipment and training needed and the nature of the workplace. (Rev: SLJ 8/06) [610]

3490 Simon, Charnan. *My Mother Is a Doctor* (K–2). Illus. by Patrick Girouard. Series: Magic Door to Learning. 2006, The Child's World LB $21.36 (1-59296-620-9). 24pp. An inviting basic introduction to doctors and their work, taking young readers through a typical day in a doctor's office. (Rev: SLJ 2/07) [610.69]

Police and Fire Fighters

3491 Aylmore, Angela. *We Work at the Fire Station* (PS–K). Series: Where We Work. 2006, Raintree LB $21.36 (1-4109-2243-X). 24pp. A basic introduction to what fire fighters do, with color photographs and simple text. (Rev: SLJ 7/06) [628.9]

3492 Ghione, Yvette. *This Is Daniel Cook at the Fire Station* (K–3). 2006, Kids Can $12.95 (1-55453-075-X); paper $4.95 (1-55453-076-8). In this companion to the popular Canadian-produced TV show, the young host invites readers to join him on a tour of a fire station. (Rev: SLJ 11/06) [628.9]

3493 Pohl, Kathleen. *What Happens at a Firehouse?* (PS–2). Series: Where People Work. 2006, Gareth Stevens LB $19.93 (978-0-8368-6887-6). 24pp. This small-format book combines cartoons and clear photographs with facts about day-to-day activities inside a firehouse. (Rev: BL 1/1–15/07) [628.9]

3494 Simon, Charnan. *Firefighter Tom to the Rescue!* (K–2). Illus. by Joel Snyder. Series: Magic Door to Learning. 2006, The Child's World LB $21.36 (1-59296-621-7). 24pp. An inviting basic introduction to firefighters' role in the community and a typical day on the job. (Rev: SLJ 2/07) [628.9]

3495 Sweeney, Alyse. *A Very Busy Firehouse* (K–2). Series: Scholastic News Nonfiction Readers. 2006, Children's Pr. LB $19.00 (0-531-16840-9). 24pp. Basic information for beginning readers, with seven highlighted words that are featured in bold in the text. (Rev: SLJ 1/07) [628.9]

Transportation

3496 Trumbauer, Lisa. *What Does a Truck Driver Do?* (K–2). Illus. Series: What Does a Community Helper Do? 2006, Enslow LB $21.26 (0-7660-2324-9). 24pp. Outlines in easy-to-understand language the job requirements and everyday responsibilities of a truck driver. (Rev: SLJ 4/06) [388.324]

Veterinarians

3497 Aylmore, Angela. *We Work at the Vet's* (PS–K). Series: Where We Work. 2006, Raintree LB $21.36 (1-4109-2245-6). 24pp. A basic introduction to what veterinarians and their assistants do, with color photographs and simple text. (Rev: SLJ 7/06) [636.089]

3498 Jackson, Donna M. *ER Vets: Life in an Animal Emergency Room* (5–8). Illus. 2005, Houghton

$18.00 (0-618-43663-4). 96pp. With many photos, this is a behind-the-scenes look at life in a veterinary emergency clinic and the frustrations and joys to be found working there. (Rev: BL 11/1/05; SLJ 1/06*) [636.089]

3499 Minden, Cecelia. *Veterinarians* (1–2). Series: Neighborhood Helpers. 2006, The Child's World LB $22.79 (1-59296-571-7). 32pp. This attractive overview introduces young children to the role and responsibilities of a vet, plus the equipment and training needed. (Rev: SLJ 8/06) [636]

3500 Simon, Charnan. *The Best Vet in the World* (K–2). Illus. by Carol Schwartz. Series: Magic Door to Learning. 2006, The Child's World LB $21.36 (1-59296-628-4). 24pp. An inviting basic introduction to the veterinary profession. (Rev: SLJ 2/07) [636]

Health and the Human Body

Aging and Death

3501 Sanders, Pete, and Steve Myers. *When People Die* (3–6). Illus. by Mike Lacey. Series: Choices and Decisions. 2005, Stargazer LB $27.10 (1-09604-076-9). 32pp. This reassuring title covers with sensitivity the topics of death, grieving, and funerals, and also discusses euthanasia. (Rev: SLJ 4/06) [155.9]

Alcohol, Drugs, and Smoking

3502 Green, Carl R. *Nicotine and Tobacco* (4–8). Illus. Series: Drugs. 2005, Enslow LB $25.26 (0-7660-5283-4). 48pp. Fictional scenarios are combined with information on the addictive qualities of nicotine and the dangers of smoking and other forms of tobacco use; Web links extend the text. (Rev: SLJ 11/05) [362.2]

3503 Murphy, Patricia J. *Avoiding Drugs* (1–3). Series: Pull Ahead. 2005, Lerner LB $22.60 (0-8225-2867-3); paper $5.95 (0-8225-2779-9). 32pp. Alcohol, tobacco, and "non-medicinal" drugs are defined and discussed in clear text and photographs; a question-and-answer section offers practice in rejecting drug offers. (Rev: SLJ 3/06) [362.29]

Bionics and Transplants

3504 Jango-Cohen, Judith. *Bionics* (4–6). 2006, Lerner LB $26.60 (978-0-8225-5937-5). 48pp. Covers the topic of bionics and how mechanical parts can replace human parts and can help the senses. (Rev: SLJ 3/07) [617]

Disabilities, Physical and Mental

3505 Bardhan-Quallen, Sudipta. *Autism* (3–6). Series: Understanding Diseases and Disorders. 2005, Gale LB $23.70 (0-7377-2167-7). 48pp. A well-presented look at the symptoms, diagnosis, treatment, and research relating to autism. (Rev: SLJ 8/05) [616.8]

3506 Dwight, Laura. *Brothers and Sisters* (K–3). Photos by author. 2005, Star Bright $15.95 (1-887734-80-5). Stories of children's lives with disabilities are told by siblings of the impaired and in some cases by the impaired children themselves. (Rev: SLJ 11/05)

3507 Taylor, John F. *The Survival Guide for Kids with ADD or ADHD* (3–5). Illus. by Tad Herr. 2006, Free Spirit paper $13.95 (1-57542-195-X). 119pp. This child-friendly guide to coping with ADD/ADHD offers information and advice on such topics as making friends, success at school, medications, eating sensibly, and so forth. (Rev: SLJ 12/06) [618.92]

Disease and Illness

3508 Ali, Rasheda. *I'll Hold Your Hand So You Won't Fall: A Child's Guide to Parkinson's Disease* (2–4). Illus. 2005, Merit $19.95 (1-873413-13-0). 40pp. Rasheda Ali, daughter of Muhammad Ali, describes the disease that afflicts her father and its debilitating symptoms. (Rev: SLJ 10/05) [616.8]

3509 Bardhan-Quallen, Sudipta. *AIDS* (4–6). Illus. Series: Understanding Diseases and Disorders. 2005, Gale LB $18.96 (0-7377-2638-5). 48pp. This overview of HIV/AIDS examines the virus and its symptoms, diagnosis, and treatment; also covered are research and availability of medication in the Third World; full-color photographs and quotations from young patients add to the succinct text. (Rev: BL 7/05; SLJ 8/05) [616.97]

3510 Barnard, Bryn. *Outbreak! Plagues That Changed History* (5–8). Illus. by author. 2005, Crown LB $19.99 (0-375-92986-X). 48pp. Information on microbes and the study of microorganisms precedes details of specific epidemics. (Rev: SLJ 2/06) [614.4]

3511 Bjorklund, Ruth. *Food-Borne Illnesses* (4–7). Illus. Series: Health Alert. 2005, Marshall Cavendish LB $19.95 (0-7614-1917-9). 64pp. This is a wide-ranging exploration of illnesses that can be caused by contaminated food — including those resulting from bacteria, poor hygiene, poor handling, and terrorism — and the treatments and preventions available. (Rev: SLJ 6/06) [615.9]

3512 Casil, Amy Sterling. *Hantavirus* (4–6). Series: Epidemics. 2005, Rosen LB $26.50 (1-4042-0254-4). 64pp. Casil offers basic information, suitable for report writers, about the discovery of this virus; its carriers, symptoms, and prevention; outbreaks; and any dangers of its use in bioterrorism. (Rev: SLJ 10/05) [616.9]

3513 Glaser, Jason. *Chicken Pox* (1–3). Series: First Facts: Health Matters. 2005, Capstone LB $21.26 (0-7368-4288-8). 24pp. Basic information on the causes, symptoms, and treatment of chickenpox is presented in simple text. Also use *Flu* and *Pinkeye* (both 2005). (Rev: SLJ 12/05) [618.92]

3514 Gordon, Sherri Mabry. *Peanut Butter, Milk, and Other Deadly Threats: What You Should Know About Food Allergies* (5–9). Series: Issues in Focus Today. 2006, Enslow LB $31.93 (0-7660-2529-2). 112pp. This information-packed survey of food allergies identifies common culprit foods, explains the mechanics of allergic reactions, and also reports on medical research to find better treatments. (Rev: SLJ 11/06) [616.97]

3515 Hicks, Terry Allan. *Allergies* (4–8). Illus. Series: Health Alert. 2005, Benchmark LB $19.95 (0-7614-1918-7). 64pp. All about what allergies are, what brings them on, and how they are treated, with colorful sidebars and features that add to the text. (Rev: SLJ 5/06) [616.97]

3516 Hoffmann, Gretchen. *Mononucleosis* (4–8). Illus. Series: Health Alert. 2005, Benchmark LB $19.95 (0-7614-1915-2). 64pp. All about what "mono" is, its symptoms, and its treatment, with graphic features that add to the text. (Rev: SLJ 5/06) [616.9]

3517 London, Melissa. *The GF Kid: A Celiac Disease Survival Guide* (3–5). Illus. by Eric Glickman. 2005, Woodbine paper $14.95 (1-890627-69-0). Eleven-year-old Paris describes celiac disease and its symptoms and treatment, along with the measures she takes to avoid eating gluten. (Rev: SLJ 1/06) [616.3]

3518 Lynette, Rachel. *Leprosy* (5–8). Illus. Series: Understanding Diseases and Disorders. 2005, Gale LB $23.70 (0-7377-3172-9). 48pp. Straightforward text discusses the plight of leprosy patients around the world and through history; causes, treatments, and transmission are also discussed. (Rev: SLJ 6/06) [616.9]

3519 Margulies, Phillip. *Diphtheria* (4–6). Series: Epidemics. 2005, Rosen LB $26.50 (1-4042-0253-6). 64pp. Suitable for report writers, this book covers the nature of diphtheria, important outbreaks of the disease, treatment, and efforts to prevent future epidemics. (Rev: SLJ 10/05) [616.9]

3520 Niner, Holly L. *I Can't Stop! A Story About Tourette Syndrome* (1–3). Illus. by Meryl Treatner. 2005, Albert Whitman $15.95 (0-8075-3620-2). 32pp. Nathan learns to deal with his Tourette syndrome in this realistic story that is bolstered by factual information contributed by a doctor. (Rev: BL 11/15/05)

3521 Ramen, Fred. *SARS (Severe Acute Respiratory Syndrome)* (4–6). Series: Epidemics. 2005, Rosen LB $26.50 (1-4042-0258-7). 64pp. Offers basic information, suitable for report writers, about the various outbreaks of Severe Acute Respiratory Syndrome and the symptoms, treatment, and research efforts. (Rev: SLJ 10/05) [614.5]

3522 Silverstein, Alvin. *The Asthma Update* (5–8). 2006, Enslow LB $23.95 (0-7660-2482-2). 128pp. A thorough look at asthma, its symptoms, history, treatments, and the research being done in hopes of finding a cure. (Rev: BL 12/1/06) [616.2]

3523 Silverstein, Alvin, et al. *The Flu and Pneumonia Update* (5–8). Illus. Series: Disease Update. 2006, Enslow LB $23.95 (0-7660-2480-6). 104pp. Symptoms, treatment, history, and new research are all included in this discussion of flu and pneumonia. (Rev: BL 4/1/06; SLJ 9/06) [616.2]

3524 Watters, Debbie. *Where's Mom's Hair? A Family's Journey Through Cancer* (2–5). 2005, Second Story paper $10.95 (1-896764-94-0). 32pp. This photo-essay documents how family members lovingly supported a cancer-stricken mother as she underwent the rigors of chemotherapy. (Rev: BL 10/1/05; SLJ 7/05) [362.196]

Doctors and Medicine

3525 Woods, Michael, and Mary B. Woods. *The History of Medicine* (5–8). Series: Major Inventions Through History. 2005, Twenty-First Century LB $26.60 (0-8225-2336-0). 56pp. An attractive look at medical developments through time and their impact on our lives. (Rev: SLJ 1/06) [610]

Genetics

3526 Phelan, Glen. *Double Helix: The Quest to Uncover the Structure of DNA* (5–8). Series: Science Quest. 2006, National Geographic $17.95 (978-0-7922-5541-3). 59pp. From Mendel's early experiments with pea plants through Crick and Watson's race to solve the mystery of DNA, this is an accessible and informative history that also looks at the wide range of social and scientific areas influenced by the discovery. (Rev: SLJ 4/07) [572.8]

Hospitals

3527 Attebury, Nancy Garhan. *Out and About at the Hospital* (1–3). Illus. by Zachary Trover. Series: Field Trips. 2005, Picture Window LB $23.93 (1-4048-1148-6). 24pp. Takes readers on a tour of a typical hospital, explaining its purpose and the roles of people who work there. (Rev: SLJ 2/06) [362.11]

The Human Body

General

3528 Levine, Shar, and Leslie Johnstone. *First Science Experiments: The Amazing Human Body* (PS–2). Illus. by Steve Harpster. 2006, Sterling LB $14.95 (1-4027-2437-3). 48pp. Simple activities using handy materials help students answer a wide range of questions, from "Do people with big ears hear better than people with small ears?" to "How can I tell how fast my heart is beating?" and "Why does my tummy growl or grumble when I am hungry?" (Rev: SLJ 11/06) [612.0078]

3529 Myers, Jack. *On Top of Mount Everest: And Other Explorations of Science in Action* (4–6). Illus. by John Rice. 2005, Boyds Mills $17.95 (1-59078-252-6). 64pp. A collection of science-related articles that have appeared in the magazine *Highlights for Children*, most relating to interesting abilities of the human body. (Rev: SLJ 8/05)

3530 Taylor-Butler, Christine. *Tiny Life on Your Body* (2–3). Series: Rookie Read-About Science. 2005, Children's Pr. LB $19.50 (0-516-25299-2); paper $4.95 (0-516-25480-4). 32pp. For beginning readers, this is an introduction to the kinds of bacteria — good and bad — that can be found on the human body. (Rev: SLJ 4/06) [612]

3531 Walker, Richard. *Body* (4–7). Illus. 2005, DK $19.99 (0-7566-1371-X). 96pp. With a spiral binding, acetate overlays, and computer-generated 3-D images, this volume gives an in-depth view of the human body; there is an accompanying CD. (Rev: BL 12/1/05; SLJ 3/06) [611]

3532 Walker, Richard. *Human Body* (5–9). Illus. Series: DK/Google e.guides. 2005, DK $17.99 (0-7566-1009-5). 96pp. This highly illustrated guide introduces readers to the human body and provides a link to a Web site that serves as a gateway to additional resources. (Rev: SLJ 8/05) [612]

Circulatory System

3533 Romanek, Trudee. *Squirt! The Most Interesting Book You'll Ever Read About Blood* (4–7). Illus. by Rose Cowles. Series: Mysterious You. 2006, Kids Can $14.95 (1-55337-776-1); paper $7.95 (1-55337-777-X). 160pp. This fascinating book with an engaging format discusses the human circulatory system, with information about other animals and their blood, too. (Rev: BL 5/15/06; HBG 10/06) [612.1]

Digestive and Excretory Systems

3534 Goodman, Susan E. *Gee Whiz! It's All About Pee* (4–6). Illus. by Elwood H. Smith. 2006, Viking $15.99 (0-670-06064-X). 40pp. This companion to *The Truth About Poop* (2004) provides facts and trivia — often-unexpected and humorous — about pee, with cartoon illustrations. (Rev: BL 11/1/06; SLJ 11/06) [612.4]

Nervous System

3535 Funston, Sylvia, and Jay Ingram. *It's All in Your Head: A Guide to Your Brilliant Brain*. 2nd ed. (3–6). Illus. by Gary Clement. 2005, Maple Tree $16.95 (1-897066-43-0); paper $9.95 (1-897066-44-9). 64pp. Answering questions in conversational text, this book explores the makeup and workings of the human brain, touches on brain research, and includes experiments and puzzles. (Rev: SLJ 1/06) [612.8]

Respiratory System

3536 Simon, Seymour. *Lungs: Your Respiratory System* (3–6). Illus. 2007, Collins $16.99 (978-0-06-054654-0). 32pp. From simple breathing to coughing, hiccups, and other respiratory problems, this is a clear overview of the lungs and their importance to human life. (Rev: BL 12/1/06; SLJ 4/07) [612.2]

Senses

3537 Olien, Rebecca. *Hearing* (PS–1). Series: First Facts, The Senses. 2005, Capstone LB $21.26 (0-736-84301-9). 24pp. This slim introduction to hearing includes an experiment to help young readers understand how this sense works. Also use *Tasting* and *Touching* (both 2005). (Rev: SLJ 1/06) [612.8]

3538 Schuette, Sarah L. *Taking Care of My Ears* (PS–1). Illus. Series: Keeping Healthy. 2005, Capstone LB $14.95 (0-7368-4259-4). 24pp. An easy-to-understand explanation of the sense of hearing plus basic information about ear care. (Rev: BL 10/15/05) [613]

3539 Woodward, Kay. *Hearing* (1–4). Series: Our Senses. 2005, Gareth Stevens LB $22.00 (0-8368-4406-8). 24pp. A book on how the sense of hearing works in humans and animals, with simple text, eye-catching illustrations, and related activities. Also use *Touch, Taste, Smell,* and *Sight* (all 2005). (Rev: SLJ 7/05) [612.8]

Skin and Hair

3540 Degezelle, Terri. *Taking Care of My Hair* (PS–2). Series: Keeping Healthy. 2005, Capstone LB $19.93 (0-7368-4261-6). 24pp. Easy-to-understand advice about hair care, in an oversize format with large color photographs. Also use *Taking Care of My Skin* (2005). (Rev: SLJ 12/05) [646.7]

3541 Glaser, Jason. *Head Lice* (1–3). Series: First Facts: Health Matters. 2005, Capstone LB $21.26 (0-7368-4291-8). 24pp. In simple text, this basic title looks at the causes, symptoms, and treatment of head lice. (Rev: SLJ 12/05) [616.5]

Teeth

3542 Degezelle, Terri. *Taking Care of My Teeth* (PS–2). Series: Keeping Healthy. 2005, Capstone LB $19.93 (0-7368-4264-0). 24pp. Easy-to-understand advice about dental care, in an oversize format with large color photographs. Also use *Taking Care of My Skin* (2005). (Rev: SLJ 12/05) [617.6]

Hygiene, Physical Fitness, and Nutrition

3543 Chryssicas, Mary Kaye. *I Love Yoga* (3–5). Photos by Angela Coppola. 2005, DK $12.99 (0-7566-1400-7). 48pp. Follows six children as they learn the basic techniques and positions of hatha yoga. (Rev: BL 11/15/05; SLJ 5/06) [613.7]

3544 Cole, Babette. *The Sprog Owner's Manual (or How Kids Work)* (K–3). 2006, Trafalgar Square paper $9.99 (0-09-944765-7). 32pp. Tips on health and grooming issues for kids ("sprogs" is a British term), presented with lots of humor. (Rev: BL 5/1/06) [823.914]

3545 Dalgleish, Sharon. *Exercise and Rest* (3–5). Illus. Series: Healthy Choices. 2007, Black Rabbit LB $18.95 (978-1-58340-755-4). 32pp. Square, colorful pages looks at the importance of both exercise and rest, recommending 30 minutes of exercise three or four times a week. (Rev: BL 4/1/07) [613.7]

3546 Ehrlich, Fred. *Does an Elephant Take a Bath?* (PS–K). Illus. by Emily Bolam. Series: Early Experiences. 2005, Blue Apple LB $13.50 (1-59354-111-2); paper $5.95 (1-59354-123-5). 32pp. Illustrations of animals in bathtubs are followed by views of the animals using their natural methods of hygiene in this book that also shows how humans keep clean; a small, square book. (Rev: BL 10/15/05) [617.6]

3547 Koellhoffer, Tara, ed. *Food and Nutrition* (4–6). Series: Science News for Kids. 2006, Chelsea House $30.00 (0-7910-9121-X). 110pp. A wide-ranging collection of articles on food and nutrition that originally appeared on the Science News for Kids Web site. (Rev: BL 6/1–15/06) [613.2]

3548 Miller, Edward. *The Monster Health Book: A Guide to Eating Healthy, Being Active and Feeling Great for Monsters and Kids!* (2–4). Illus. by author. 2006, Holiday $16.95 (0-8234-1956-8). 40pp. Basic health and nutrition facts and advice are presented in an enticing but brief format that may require amplification by adults. (Rev: BL 5/15/06; SLJ 6/06) [613.7]

3549 Mitchell, Melanie. *Eating Well* (K–3). Illus. Series: Pull Ahead Books. 2006, Lerner LB $22.60 (0-8225-2449-X). 32pp. An informative guide to the food pyramid and the fundamentals of healthy eating. (Rev: SLJ 8/06) [613.2]

3550 Nelson, Robin. *Staying Clean* (PS–1). Illus. Series: Pull-Ahead Books: Health. 2005, Lerner LB $22.60 (0-8225-2368-7); paper $5.95 (0-8225-2773-1). 32pp. Hand washing, brushing teeth, and avoiding head lice are among the topics addressed in simple text with full-color photographs. (Rev: BL 1/1–15/06) [613]

3551 Schuh, Mari C. *Being Active* (PS–2). Series: Healthy Eating with MyPyramid. 2006, Capstone LB $19.93 (0-7368-5368-5). 24pp. This simple, bright volume focuses on activities that promote physical fitness, including bicycling, swimming, baseball, volleyball, taking care of pets, and playing with friends. Also use *Drinking Water* (2006). (Rev: SLJ 8/06) [613.7]

3552 Schuh, Mari C. *Healthy Snacks* (PS–2). Illus. by author. Series: Healthy Eating with MyPyramid. 2006, Scholastic LB $19.93 (0-7368-5369-3). 24pp. A companion to the new USDA food pyramid, explaining which snacks are best to eat in simple language and photographs. (Rev: BL 5/15/06; SLJ 8/06) [641.5]

3553 Whitford, Rebecca. *Little Yoga: A Toddler's First Book of Yoga* (PS). Illus. by Martina Selway. 2005, Holt $9.95 (0-8050-7879-7). 28pp. Nine simple yoga exercises for children are shown in eye-catching spreads. (Rev: BL 10/1/05; SLJ 11/05) [613.7]

Safety and Accidents

3554 Llewellyn, Claire. *Around Town* (PS–2). Illus. by Mike Gordon. Series: Watch Out! 2006, Barron's paper $5.99 (0-7641-3326-8). 32pp. Readers learn about some of the dangers they might face in an urban setting, such as dogs, getting lost, and construction sites. Also use *At Home, Near Water,* and *On the Road* (2006). (Rev: SLJ 10/06)

3555 Pendziwol, Jean E. *Once Upon a Dragon: Stranger Safety Tips for Kids (and Dragons)* (PS–2). Illus. by Martine Gourbault. 2006, Kids Can $14.95 (1-55337-722-2); paper $6.95 (1-55337-969-1). 32pp. This companion to *No Dragons for Tea: Fire Safety for Kids (and Dragons)* uses fairy-tale characters as stand-ins for strangers, easing the scariness of this difficult topic. (Rev: BL 5/15/06; SLJ 6/06)

Sex Education and Reproduction

Sex Education and Puberty

3556 Harris, Robie H. *It's Not the Stork! A Book About Girls, Boys, Babies, Bodies, Families, and Friends* (K–3). Illus. by Michael Emberley. 2006, Candlewick $16.99 (0-7636-0047-4). 64pp. A frank, sensitive, and inevitably controversial discussion of gender differences, human anatomy, sexuality, and reproduction. (Rev: BCCB 10/06; BL 6/1–15/06; HBG 4/07; LMC 1/07; SLJ 9/06*) [613.9]

3557 Movsessian, Shushann. *Puberty Girl* (4–7). Illus. 2005, Allen & Unwin paper $15.95 (1-74114-104-4). 128pp. A frank and friendly guide covering such topics as body changes, conflict resolution, and personal boundaries, as well as the changes that puberty brings in the opposite sex. (Rev: BL 10/15/05; SLJ 10/05; VOYA 10/05) [612.6]

3558 Pfeifer, Kate Gruenwald. *Boy's Guide to Becoming a Teen* (4–7). Ed. by Amy B. Middleman. 2006, Jossey-Bass paper $12.95 (0-7879-8343-8). 128pp. A guide to handling the physical, emotional, and social changes that accompany puberty in boys. (Rev: BL 5/15/06) [613]

3559 Pfeifer, Kate Gruenwald. *Girl's Guide to Becoming a Teen* (4–7). Ed. by Amy B. Middleman. 2006, Jossey-Bass paper $12.95 (0-7879-8344-6). 128pp. A guide to handling the physical, emotional, and social changes that accompany puberty in girls. (Rev: BL 5/15/06) [613]

3560 Price, Geoff. *Puberty Boy* (5–8). 2006, Allen & Unwin paper $15.95 (1-74114-563-5). 128pp. A frank and friendly guide with an Australian accent that covers the important physical and emotional changes that accompany puberty. (Rev: BL 7/06; SLJ 9/06; VOYA 8/06) [612]

Physical and Applied Sciences

General Science

Miscellaneous

3561 Arnold, Nick. *The Stunning Science of Everything: Science with the Squishy Bits Left In!* (4–8). Illus. by Tony De Saulles. 2006, Scholastic $10.99 (0-439-87777-6). 96pp. This lighthearted look at science, brightly illustrated with cartoons, examines such diverse topics as the Big Bang theory, atoms, insects, humans, dinosaurs, and the universe. (Rev: HBG 4/07; LMC 3/07; SLJ 2/07; VOYA 2/07) [500]

3562 Boring, Mel, and Leslie Dendy. *Guinea Pig Scientists: Bold Self-Experimenters in Science and Medicine* (5–9). Illus. by C. B. Mordan. 2005, Holt $19.95 (0-8050-7316-7). 224pp. Scientists who served as their own guinea pigs — demonstrating their passion for science and often their foolhardiness — are the topic of this appealing volume. (Rev: BL 7/05*; SLJ 7/05*; VOYA 6/05) [616]

3563 Cole, Joanna. *The Magic School Bus and the Science Fair Expedition* (2–4). Illus. by Bruce Degen. Series: Magic School Bus. 2006, Scholastic $15.99 (0-590-10824-7). 32pp. Ms. Frizzle and her students travel on the bus to a nearby museum in search of inspiration for the upcoming science fair. (Rev: BL 9/15/06) [507.8]

3564 Dotlich, Rebecca Kai. *What Is Science?* (PS–2). Illus. by Sachiko Yoshikawa. 2006, Holt $16.95 (0-8050-7394-9). 32pp. A trio of children and their dog get a simple, poetic tour of the world of science. (Rev: BL 9/15/06; SLJ 11/06) [500]

3565 Fridell, Ron. *Genetic Engineering* (4–6). Illus. Series: Cool Science. 2005, Lerner LB $25.26 (0-8225-2633-6). 48pp. With many interesting examples and an attractive layout, this introduction explores how this cutting-edge branch of science is paving the way for new species of plant and animal

life and also helping to deal with human health problems. (Rev: SLJ 12/05) [660.6]

3566 Raab, Brigitte. *Where Does Pepper Come From? And Other Fun Facts* (K–3). Trans. from German by J. Alison James. Illus. by Manuela Olten. 2006, North-South $15.95 (0-7358-2070-8). A humorous and lively question-and-answer format provides answers to a wide variety of science questions. (Rev: SLJ 10/06)

3567 *Science Detectives: How Scientists Solved Six Real-Life Mysteries* (3–5). Illus. by Rose Cowles. 2006, Kids Can $15.95 (1-55337-994-2); paper $8.95 (1-55337-995-0). 48pp. An interesting selection of mysteries that were eventually solved through scientific means — including a typhoid outbreak in New York and a plunge in the number of vultures in central Asia. (Rev: BL 10/15/06) [501]

Experiments and Projects

3568 Bardhan-Quallen, Sudipta. *Championship Science Fair Projects: 100 Sure-to-Win Experiments* (5–9). Illus. 2005, Sterling $19.95 (1-4027-1138-7). 208pp. Clearly defined science projects (more than 100 at varying levels of difficulty) are accompanied by lists of materials, illustrations, and extension activities. (Rev: BL 8/05; SLJ 9/05; VOYA 8/05) [507]

3569 Buttitta, Hope. *It's Not Magic, It's Science! 50 Science Tricks that Mystify, Dazzle and Astound!* (4–6). Illus. by Tom LaBaff and Orrin Lundgren. 2005, Sterling $14.95 (1-57990-622-2). 80pp. Each "magic track" in this book demonstrates a scientific principle, making it a fun exploration of basic concepts. (Rev: SLJ 9/05) [793.8]

3570 Calhoun, Yael. *Plant and Animal Science Fair Projects Using Beetles, Weeds, Seeds, and More* (5–8). Illus. Series: Biology! Best Science Projects. 2005, Enslow LB $26.60 (0-7660-2368-0). 128pp. Great ideas for biology-based science fair projects, with plenty of information for performing and presenting each activity correctly plus helpful charts and graphs. (Rev: SLJ 7/06) [570]

3571 Fox, Tom. *Snowball Launchers, Giant-Pumpkin Growers, and Other Cool Contraptions* (5–8). Illus. by Joel Holland. 2006, Sterling paper $9.95 (978-0-8069-5515-5). 127pp. A collection of 20 creative projects with clear instructions and explanations of scientific principles. (Rev: BL 1/1–15/07; SLJ 3/07)

3572 Harris, Elizabeth Snoke. *First Place Science Fair Projects for Inquisitive Kids* (4–7). Illus. 2005, Sterling LB $19.95 (1-57990-493-9). 127pp. Project ideas in biology, chemistry, and physics mostly involve everyday materials and are presented in accessible text with an eight-week schedule and clear photographs. (Rev: SLJ 3/06) [507]

3573 Lemke, Donald B., and Thomas K. Adamson. *Lessons in Science Safety with Max Axiom, Super Scientist* (5–8). Illus. by Tod Smith. Series: Graphic Science. 2006, Capstone LB $18.95 (978-0-7368-6834-1). 32pp. This graphic-novel approach to teaching safe science procedures features an appealing adult. (Rev: BL 3/15/07) [507.8]

3574 Levine, Shar. *Sports Science* (3–5). Illus. by Leslie Johnstone. 2006, Sterling $19.95 (1-4027-1520-X). 80pp. A collection of 26 science experiments, each with a sports connection, that illustrate such scientific principles as gravity, aerodynamics, and buoyancy. (Rev: BL 12/1/06; SLJ 12/06) [507.8]

3575 Levine, Shar, and Leslie Johnstone. *Backyard Science* (3–5). Illus. 2005, Sterling $19.95 (1-4027-1519-6). 80pp. Biology, chemistry, even physics — the backyard provides lots of fodder for science experiments and projects. (Rev: BL 9/1/05; SLJ 11/05) [507]

3576 Murphy, Pat. *Exploratopia* (4–7). Illus. 2006, Little, Brown $29.99 (0-316-61281-2). 384pp. From San Francisco's Exploratorium, this is an interesting selection of facts, activities, and hands-on experiments that encourage students to learn about and explore the world around them. (Rev: BL 12/1/06; SLJ 1/07) [507.8]

3577 Newcomb, Rain, and Bobby Mercer. *Crash It! Smash It! Launch It!* (5–8). Illus. by Rain Newcomb. 2006, Sterling $14.95 (1-57990-795-4). 80pp. More than 40 experiments provide great entertainment as well as scientific knowledge. (Rev: BL 11/1/06; SLJ 12/06) [507.8]

3578 Rhatigan, Joe, and Veronika Alice Gunter. *Cool Chemistry Concoctions: 50 Formulas that Fizz, Foam, Splatter and Ooze* (3–6). Illus. by Tom LaBaff. 2005, Sterling $14.95 (1-57990-620-6). 80pp. Making slime and shrinking apples are just two of the experiments in this lively and well-organized collection of projects that use readily available materials. (Rev: SLJ 8/05) [540]

Astronomy

General

3579 Fleisher, Paul. *The Big Bang* (5–8). Illus. Series: Great Ideas in Science. 2005, Twenty-First Century LB $27.93 (0-8225-2133-4). 80pp. Students with a real interest in science will benefit most from this overview of theories about the creation of the universe, from creation myths onward. (Rev: BL 12/1/05; SLJ 12/05) [523.1]

3580 Gibbons, Gail. *Galaxies, Galaxies!* (2–3). Illus. by author. 2006, Holiday House $16.95 (0-8234-2002-7). 32pp. In addition to describing five forms of galaxies, Gibbons discusses telescopes and the study of astronomy. (Rev: SLJ 12/06) [523.1]

3581 Jefferis, David. *Black Holes and Other Bizarre Space Objects* (5–8). Illus. Series: Science Frontiers. 2006, Crabtree LB $25.26 (0-7787-2856-0); paper $8.95 (0-7787-2870-6). 32pp. Double-page spreads with color photographs and informative sidebars explore the life of stars, black holes, gamma-ray bursts, space telescopes, and so forth. (Rev: BL 4/1/06) [523.8]

3582 Kuhn, Betsy. *The Race for Space* (5–8). Series: People's History. 2006, Twenty-First Century LB $29.27 (978-0-8225-5984-9). 112pp. This fascinating overview of the race for space focuses on the heated rivalry between the United States and the Soviet Union for supremacy in outer space. (Rev: SLJ 2/07) [629.45]

3583 Rau, Dana Meachen. *Black Holes* (3–5). Illus. Series: Our Solar System. 2005, Compass Point $22.60 (0-7565-0849-5). 32pp. Good coverage of a tricky topic, describing black holes' nature and formation, with photographs and illustrations adding to the appeal. (Rev: SLJ 8/05) [523.8]

3584 *Scholastic Atlas of Space* (4–6). Illus. 2005, Scholastic $17.95 (0-439-67272-4). 80pp. All about the origins of the universe and the solar system,

with plenty of visual interest in the form of photographs, illustrations, diagrams, and charts. (Rev: SLJ 7/05) [520]

3585 Schorer, Lonnie Jones. *Kids to Space: A Space Traveler's Guide* (5–9). Illus. 2006, Apogee paper $29.95 (1-894959-42-6). 304pp. Organized in almost 100 categories, this volume includes thousands of questions about space posed by children and answered by experts including NASA engineers, former astronauts, and astronomy professors. (Rev: SLJ 12/06) [500.5]

Earth

3586 Nadeau, Isaac. *Learning About Earth's Cycles with Graphic Organizers* (3–6). 2005, Rosen LB $19.95 (1-4042-2807-1). This title uses a wide variety of graphic organizers, including concept webs, compare/contrast charts, Venn diagrams, graphs, timelines, and KWL charts, to introduce readers to Earth's natural cycles, including tidal ebb and flow; seasonal changes; and day and night. (Rev: SLJ 11/05)

3587 Taylor-Butler, Christine. *Earth* (1–2). Illus. Series: Scholastic News Nonfiction Readers. 2005, Children's Pr. LB $18.00 (0-516-24923-1). 24pp. This slim volume for beginning readers provides an overview of Earth's geological structure and its place in the solar system. (Rev: SLJ 12/05) [551.1]

Planets

3588 Chrismer, Melanie. *Neptune* (1–2). Illus. Series: Scholastic News Nonfiction Readers. 2005, Children's Pr. LB $18.00 (0-516-24922-3). 24pp.

This slim volume for beginning readers provides an overview of the planet, how it was identified, and its place in the solar system. (Rev: SLJ 12/05) [523.48]

3589 Feinstein, Stephen. *Saturn* (4–7). Illus. Series: Solar System. 2005, Enslow LB $25.26 (0-7660-5304-0). 48pp. Useful for reports, this clearly written title includes links to Web sites for further research. (Rev: SLJ 12/05) [523.46]

3590 Gibbons, Gail. *The Planets*. Rev. ed. (K–2). Illus. by author. 2005, Holiday House $16.95 (0-8234-1957-6). There are few changes in this revised edition of the popular introductory guide to the planets that was first published in 1993. (Rev: SLJ 11/05) [523.4]

3591 Leedy, Loreen, and Andrew Schuerger. *Messages from Mars* (2–4). 2006, Holiday $16.95 (0-8234-1954-1). 40pp. In 2106, six children take a trip to Mars, tour the planet, visit the sites of century-old landings, and send messages home reporting on their travels and discoveries. (Rev: BL 9/15/06; SLJ 10/06) [523.43]

3592 O'Connell, Kim A. *Mercury* (4–7). Illus. Series: Solar System. 2005, Enslow LB $25.26 (0-7660-5209-5). 48pp. A blend of easy-to-understand narrative, vivid color photographs, and links to related online resources introduce Mercury. Also use *Pluto* (2005). (Rev: SLJ 12/05) [523.4]

3593 Scherer, Glenn, and Marty Fletcher. *Neptune* (4–6). Illus. Series: The Solar System. 2005, Enslow LB $25.26 (0-7660-5211-7). 48pp. A useful overview of our knowledge about Neptune (including its recently discovered planetoid, Sedna), with 30 recommended Internet links. (Rev: SLJ 11/05)

3594 Scherer, Glenn, and Marty Fletcher. *Uranus* (4–6). Illus. Series: The Solar System. 2005, Enslow LB $25.26 (0-7660-5307-5). 48pp. A useful overview of our knowledge about Uranus, with 30 recommended Internet links. (Rev: SLJ 11/05) [523.4]

3595 Taylor-Butler, Christine. *Jupiter* (1–3). Illus. Series: Scholastic News Nonfiction Readers. 2005, Children's Pr. LB $18.00 (0-516-24924-X). 24pp. Facts about Jupiter are presented in simple, large text with lots of photographs and graphic images. Also use *Mercury* and *Saturn* (both 2005). (Rev: SLJ 1/06) [523.45]

Solar System

3596 Croswell, Ken. *Ten Worlds: Everything That Orbits the Sun* (4–6). 2006, Boyds Mills $19.95 (1-59078-423-5). 56pp. A large-format exploration of the solar system with striking images of the planets. (Rev: BL 8/06; SLJ 7/06) [523.4]

3597 Rau, Dana Meachen. *The Milky Way and Other Galaxies* (3–5). Illus. Series: Our Solar System. 2005, Compass Point $22.60 (0-7565-0853-3). 32pp. After a discussion of our own galaxy, Rau describes others including quasars, clusters, and superclusters; photographs and illustrations add to the appeal. (Rev: SLJ 8/05) [523.1]

Stars

3598 MacKall, Dandi Daley. *Seeing Stars* (PS–K). Illus. by Claudine Gevry. 2006, Simon & Schuster $9.99 (1-4169-0361-5). 16pp. An introduction to the constellations for very young children, with sparkling gold outlining stars that shine above people of many backgrounds. (Rev: BL 5/1/06) [520]

3599 Mitton, Jacqueline. *Zodiac* (2–4). Illus. by Christina Balit. 2005, Frances Lincoln $16.95 (1-84507-074-7). 44pp. This is an attractive introduction to the 12 constellations that make up the zodiac, also providing information on the fundamentals of astronomy and on the mythology surrounding these stars. (Rev: BL 11/15/05; SLJ 1/06) [133.5]

3600 Nicolson, Cynthia Pratt. *Discover the Stars* (1–3). Illus. by Bill Slavin. Series: Kids Can Read. 2006, Kids Can $14.95 (1-55337-898-9); paper $3.95 (1-55337-899-7). 32pp. Using a question-and-answer format, this easy reader introduces basic information about the stars, including constellations, galaxies, the typical life cycle of a star, and how we observe them. (Rev: BL 3/15/06; SLJ 8/06) [523.8]

3601 Sasaki, Chris. *Constellations: A Glow-in-the-Dark Guide to the Night Sky* (1–4). Illus. by Alan Flinn. 2006, Sterling $12.95 (1-4027-0385-6). 48pp. Introduces some of the best-known constellations, with the mythology behind them, and glow-in-the-dark outlines that will show when the lights are turned off. (Rev: SLJ 8/06) [523.8]

Sun and the Seasons

3602 Latta, Sara. *What Happens in Spring?* (PS–2). Illus. Series: I Like the Seasons! 2006, Enslow LB $21.26 (0-7660-2419-9). 24pp. Answers a parade of questions about spring ("What are the first signs . . ."), and provides an experiment and a glossary of seasonally related terms. Also use *What Happens in Winter?* (2006). (Rev: SLJ 12/06) [508.2]

3603 Lin, Grace, and Ranida T. McKneally. *Our Seasons* (1–3). Illus. by Grace Lin. 2006, Charlesbridge $15.95 (1-57091-360-9). 32pp. Questions and answers about the seasons, with paintings and haiku to accompany the factual information. (Rev: BL 7/06; SLJ 8/06) [508.2]

3604 Martin, Jr., Bill, and Michael Sampson. *I Love Our Earth* (PS–2). Illus. by Dan Lipow. 2006, Charlesbridge $14.95 (1-58089-106-3). 32pp. Impressive color photographs and minimal text celebrate the wonders of nature and the changing seasons. (Rev: BL 2/1/06; SLJ 2/06) [525]

3605 Pfeffer, Wendy. *We Gather Together: Celebrating the Harvest Season* (1–3). Illus. by Linda Bleck. 2006, Dutton $17.99 (0-525-47669-5). 40pp. This companion to *The Shortest Day: Celebrating the Winter Solstice* provides information on the autumnal equinox, ways in which humans and animals prepare for the winter during this season; facts on the harvest and its many celebrations around the world, plus experiments and activities. (Rev: BL 12/1/06; SLJ 11/06) [508.2]

Biological Sciences

General

3606 Early, Bobbi. *Tiny Life in a Puddle* (2–3). Series: Rookie Read-About Science. 2005, Children's Pr. LB $19.50 (0-516-25272-0); paper $4.95 (0-516-25475-8). 32pp. For beginning readers, this is an introduction to the kinds of bacteria — good and bad — that can be found in a small puddle of water. (Rev: SLJ 4/06) [579.176]

3607 Kelsey, Elin. *Strange New Species: Astonishing Discoveries of Life on Earth* (5–8). Illus. 2005, Maple Tree $24.95 (1-897066-31-7). 96pp. A large-format, well-illustrated introduction to plant and animal classification and to newly discovered species. (Rev: BL 10/15/05; SLJ 2/06) [578]

3608 Lindstrom, Karin. *Tiny Life on Plants* (2–3). Series: Rookie Read-About Science. 2005, Children's Pr. LB $19.50 (0-516-25297-6); paper $4.95 (0-516-25478-2). 32pp. For beginning readers, this is an introduction to the kinds of bacteria — good and bad — that thrive on the surface of plants. (Rev: SLJ 4/06) [577.852]

3609 MacAulay, Kelley, and Bobbie Kalman. *Backyard Habitats* (K–2). Illus. Series: Introducing Habitats. 2006, Crabtree LB $18.90 (0-7787-2957-5); paper $8.06 (0-7787-2985-0). 32pp. For beginning readers, this inviting volume introduces the diversity of animal and plant life that can be found in many backyards. (Rev: BL 10/15/06) [577.5]

3610 McNamara, Ken. *It's True: We Came from Slime* (4–6). Illus. by Andrew Plant. Series: It's True. 2006, Annick $19.95 (1-55037-953-4); paper $5.95 (1-55037-952-6). 96pp. Eye-catching artwork highlights this fascinating look at the origins of life on Earth — from primordial ooze through evolution across more than 3.5 billion years of history. (Rev: BL 4/1/06) [576.8]

3611 Manning, Mick, and Brita Granström. *Snap!* (PS–2). Illus. by authors. 2006, Frances Lincoln $14.95 (1-84507-408-4). A lighthearted look at the food chain in which one creature after another is gobbled up by a larger animal. (Rev: SLJ 11/06) [577.16]

3612 Singer, Marilyn. *What Stinks?* (4–6). 2006, Darby Creek $17.95 (1-58196-035-2). 64pp. The use of scent in the animal and plant kingdoms — to mark territory, to attract mates, and so forth — is presented in an entertaining format full of wordplay and illustrations. (Rev: BL 5/1/06) [591.5]

3613 Thomas, Keltie. *Nature Shockers* (4–6). Illus. by Greg Hall. Series: Planet Earth News. 2005, Maple Tree $16.95 (1-897066-29-5); paper $9.95 (1-897066-30-9). 64pp. Oddities of nature — including everything from a tree that's wrapped itself around a bicycle to the discovery of a strange-looking salamander — are reported in tabloid style. (Rev: BL 10/15/05; SLJ 1/06) [508]

3614 Trumbauer, Lisa. *Tiny Life in Your Home* (2–3). 2005, Children's Pr. LB $19.50 (0-516-25274-7); paper $4.95 (0-516-25477-4). 32pp. This fascinating title gives a close-up look at the diversity of microscopic life forms — mostly bacteria — that can be found in the average home. (Rev: SLJ 4/06) [579.1755]

3615 Wallace, Holly. *Classification* (4–7). Series: Life Processes. 2006, Heinemann LB $20.50 (1-4034-8845-2). 32pp. A clear and colorful introduction to the classification of plants and animals. (Rev: BL 10/15/06) [570.1]

Animal Life

General

3616 Aston, Dianna Hutts. *An Egg Is Quiet* (PS–2). Illus. by Sylvia Long. 2006, Chronicle $16.95 (0-8118-4428-5). 32pp. This exploration of eggs — from fish eggs to bird eggs — offers a blend of factual and poetic text plus detailed illustrations. (Rev: BL 4/15/06; SLJ 6/06) [591.4]

3617 Aston, Dianna Hutts. *Mama's Wild Child / Papa's Wild Child* (PS–2). Illus. by Nora Hilb. 2006, Charlesbridge $14.95 (1-57091-590-3). In this appealing "flip-me-over" book, a mother and father separately tell their child how various parents in the animal kingdom take care of their offspring. (Rev: SLJ 3/06) [591.56]

3618 Bloom, Steve. *Untamed: Animals Around the World* (4–7). Illus. by Emmanuelle Zicot. 2005, Abrams $18.95 (0-8109-5956-9). 75pp. Enthralling photographs of wild animals are accompanied by brief facts and an environmentalist message. (Rev: BL 12/1/05) [636]

3619 Ehrlich, Fred. *Does a Seal Smile?* (PS–2). Illus. by Emily Bolam. Series: Early Experiences. 2006, Blue Apple $13.50 (1-59354-168-6); paper $5.95 (1-59354-169-4). 32pp. An entertaining look at the different ways in which humans and animals communicate. (Rev: BL 8/06) [153.6]

3620 Ganeri, Anita. *Animals* (4–7). Series: Inside and Outside Guide. 2006, Heinemann LB $29.29 (1-4034-9084-8). 32pp. This attractive guide provides in-depth introductions to 12 animals, with double-page spreads focusing on each animal's identifying characteristics and behaviors. (Rev: BL 10/15/06) [571.3]

3621 Murawski, Darlyne A. *Animal Faces* (PS–2). Photos by author. 2005, Sterling LB $12.95 (1-4027-2295-8). A nature photographer offers close-up views of the faces of a wide variety of animals, introduced by brief poems. (Rev: SLJ 3/06) [590]

3622 Thornhill, Jan. *I Found a Dead Bird: The Kids' Guide to the Cycle of Life and Death* (3–6). Illus. 2006, Maple Tree $21.95 (1-897066-70-8); paper $9.95 (1-897066-71-6). 64pp. An attractive, thought-provoking approach to such sensitive topics as death and decomposition that covers scientific and social aspects. (Rev: SLJ 10/06)

3623 Tildes, Phyllis Limbacher. *Eye Guess: A Fold-out Guessing Game* (PS–2). Illus. 2005, Charlesbridge $9.95 (1-57091-650-0). 36pp. Each of eight foldouts shows close-ups of an animal's eye and part of the face; there are a few facts about each animal and a tantalizing glimpse of the next animal. (Rev: BL 9/1/05) [590]

3624 Ward, Jennifer. *Forest Bright, Forest Night* (K–3). Illus. by Jamichael Henterly. Series: Sharing Nature with Children. 2005, Dawn $16.95 (1-58469-066-6); paper $8.95 (1-58469-067-4). Diurnal animals go about daytime errands in the first part of this attractive book; readers flip it over to find these animals asleep and the nocturnal residents of the forest moving about. (Rev: SLJ 10/05) [591.5]

Amphibians and Reptiles

GENERAL AND MISCELLANEOUS

3625 Wilkes, Sarah. *Amphibians* (5–9). Series: World Almanac Library of the Animal Kingdom. 2006, World Almanac LB $30.00 (0-8368-6208-2). 48pp. This colorful guide identifies common species of amphibians and examines their physical characteristics, habitats, diets, behaviors, and life cycles. (Rev: SLJ 12/06) [597.5]

3626 Zabludoff, Marc. *The Reptile Class* (5–9). Illus. Series: Family Trees. 2005, Benchmark LB $29.92 (0-7614-1820-2). 95pp. Habits, habitats, and other aspects of this varied class of animals; an engaging book with plenty of facts for report-writers. (Rev: SLJ 6/06) [597.9]

ALLIGATORS AND CROCODILES

3627 Rockwell, Anne. *Who Lives in an Alligator Hole?* (K–3). Illus. by Lizzy Rockwell. Series: Let's-Read-and-Find-Out Science. 2006, HarperCollins $15.99 (978-0-06-028530-2); paper $4.99 (978-0-06-445200-7). 40pp. This informational picture book gives facts on the history and habitat of alligators; it also discusses threats to their existence, how their surroundings have changed, conservation efforts, and their key role in helping other species to survive. (Rev: BL 12/1/06; SLJ 11/06) [597.98]

3628 Snyder, Trish. *Alligator and Crocodile Rescue: Changing the Future for Endangered Wildlife* (4–8). Series: Firefly Animal Rescue. 2006, Firefly LB $19.95 (1-55297-920-2); paper $9.95 (1-55297-919-9). 64pp. Examines the work being done to protect alligators and crocodiles in their natural habitats and also looks at the physical characteristics, diets, behaviors, and life cycles of these reptiles. (Rev: SLJ 12/06) [597.98]

3629 Tourville, Amanda Doering. *A Crocodile Grows Up* (1–3). Illus. by Michael Denman and William J. Huiett. Series: Wild Animals. 2006, Picture Window LB $25.26 (978-1-4048-3157-5).

24pp. A crocodile's development from birth to full independence is described in brief text and realistic illustrations. (Rev: SLJ 4/07) [597.98]

FROGS AND TOADS

3630 Aloian, Molly, and Bobbie Kalman. *Endangered Frogs* (3–5). Illus. Series: Earth's Endangered Animals. 2006, Crabtree LB $25.20 (0-7787-1872-7). 32pp. Large text and clear color photographs focus on threatened frog species, presenting basic information about physical characteristics, diet, habitat, behavior, and discussing the specific threats they face. (Rev: SLJ 1/07) [597.8]

3631 Ganeri, Anita. *From Tadpole to Frog* (1–3). Illus. Series: How Living Things Grow. 2006, Heinemann LB $25.36 (1-4034-7859-7). 32pp. How a tadpole grows to be a frog, presented in an easy-to-read format. (Rev: SLJ 6/06) [597.8]

3632 Markle, Sandra. *Slippery, Slimy Baby Frogs* (3–5). 2006, Walker $16.95 (0-8027-8062-8). 32pp. This compelling photoessay pairs interesting facts about frogs and their development with beautiful photographs, including some great close-ups. (Rev: BL 5/1/06; SLJ 5/06) [597.8]

3633 Rau, Dana Meachen. *The Frog in the Pond* (PS–1). Series: Benchmark Rebus. 2006, Benchmark LB $15.95 (0-7614-2310-9). 24pp. With its child-friendly blend of rebuses and easy-to-understand text, this easy reader describes the physical characteristics, life cycle, and daily activities of frogs. (Rev: SLJ 12/06) [597.8]

3634 Spilsbury, Louise. *Frog* (K–2). Series: Life Cycles. 2005, Heinemann LB $20.64 (1-4034-6772-2). 24pp. Brief text consisting of questions and answers suitable for beginning readers and bold photographs focus on the life cycle of the frog. (Rev: SLJ 7/05) [597.8]

3635 Zollman, Pam. *A Tadpole Grows Up* (K–1). Series: Scholastic News Nonfiction Readers. 2005, Children's Pr. LB $18.00 (0-516-24947-9). 24pp. This photo-filled book introduces the life cycle of frogs and toads, focusing in particular on survival strategies of tadpoles. (Rev: SLJ 4/06) [597.8]

LIZARDS

3636 MacKen, JoAnn Early. *Gila Monsters / Monstruos de Gila* (2–4). Trans. by Tatiana Acosta and Guillermo Gutiérrez. Series: Animals That Live in the Desert / Animales del desierto. 2005, Weekly Reader LB $19.33 (0-8368-4841-1). 24pp. A beginning book with facts about gila monsters in both English and Spanish. (Rev: SLJ 6/06) [597.95]

3637 Maynard, Thane. *Komodo Dragons* (3–4). Series: New Naturebooks. 2006, The Child's World LB $27.07 (1-59296-642-X). 32pp. An introductory overview of this large lizard, with vivid color photographs. (Rev: SLJ 2/07) [597.95]

SNAKES

3638 MacKen, JoAnn Early. *Rattlesnakes / Serpientes de cascabel* (2–4). Trans. by Tatiana Acosta and Guillermo Gutiérrez. Series: Animals That Live in the Desert / Animales del desierto. 2005, Weekly Reader LB $19.33 (0-8368-4843-8). 24pp. A beginning book with facts about rattlesnakes in both English and Spanish. (Rev: SLJ 6/06) [597.96]

3639 Thomson, Sarah L. *Amazing Snakes!* (K–2). Illus. Series: I Can Read Book. 2006, HarperCollins $15.99 (0-06-054462-7). 32pp. This photo-filled beginning reader introduces young students to snakes, offering easy-to-understand basic information about the reptiles' physical characteristics and behavior. (Rev: BL 12/15/05; SLJ 7/06) [597.96]

TURTLES AND TORTOISES

3640 Chrustowski, Rick. *Turtle Crossing* (1–3). Illus. 2006, Holt $16.95 (0-8050-7498-8). 32pp. A painted turtle's life is portrayed in large-scale art and a simple narrative that offers a satisfying circular structure. (Rev: BL 3/1/06; SLJ 6/06) [597.92]

3641 Fletcher, Marty, and Glenn Scherer. *The Green Sea Turtle: Help Save This Endangered Species!* (5–7). Illus. Series: Saving Endangered Species. 2006, Enslow LB $33.27 (1-59845-033-6). 128pp. A well-illustrated look at the plight of the endangered green sea turtle, with an overview of its physical characteristics, diet, habitat, and behavior. (Rev: SLJ 9/06) [597.92]

3642 Hickman, Pamela. *Turtle Rescue: Changing the Future for Endangered Wildlife* (4–8). Series: Firefly Animal Rescue. 2006, Firefly $19.95 (1-55297-916-4); paper $9.95 (1-55297-915-6). 64pp. Hickman provides a detailed but accessible overview of the dangers facing turtles around the world and what is being done to protect them. (Rev: SLJ 6/06) [597.92]

3643 Lockwood, Sophie. *Sea Turtles* (4–7). Illus. Series: World of Reptiles. 2006, Child's World LB $20.95 (1-59296-550-4). 40pp. In addition to the kind of information needed for reports, Lockwood discusses conservation, how scientists track turtles, and the turtle's appearances in folklore and art. (Rev: BL 4/1/06) [597.92]

3644 Mason, Janeen. *Ocean Commotion: Sea Turtles* (3–5). Illus. 2006, Pelican $15.95 (1-58980-434-1). 32pp. Follow the journey of a female loggerhead sea turtle from the time she hatches on a Florida beach to the day she returns to mate and lay eggs of her own. (Rev: BL 12/1/06; SLJ 12/06) [597.92]

3645 Rathmell, Donna. *Carolina's Story: Sea Turtles Get Sick Too!* (2–4). Illus. 2005, Sylvan Dell $15.95 (0-9764943-0-2). 32pp. A sick loggerhead turtle's rehabilitation in South Carolina is documented in sensitive text and photographs. (Rev: BL 8/05; SLJ 11/05)

Animal Behavior and Anatomy

GENERAL

3646 Black, Sonia. *Animal Mysteries: A Chapter Book* (3–5). Series: True Tales. 2005, Children's Pr. LB $22.50 (0-516-25187-2). 48pp. This interesting book looks at examples of amazing animal behavior, such as the loggerhead turtle's ability to navigate by using the ocean's magnetic fields. (Rev: SLJ 1/06) [590]

3647 Bonnett-Rampersaud, Louise. *How Do You Sleep?* (PS). Illus. by Kristin Kest. 2005, Marshall Cavendish $14.95 (0-7614-5231-1). 32pp. A look at the sleeping habits of seven creatures, including human siblings, bears, and birds. (Rev: BL 10/1/05; SLJ 11/05) [573.8]

3648 Davies, Nicola. *Extreme Animals: The Toughest Creatures on Earth* (3–5). Illus. by Neal Layton. 2006, Candlewick $12.99 (0-7636-3067-5). 58pp. Reveals some of the world's most resilient creatures and how they've adapted to habitats that humans couldn't last minutes in. (Rev: BL 12/1/06; SLJ 12/06*) [590]

3649 Ehrlich, Fred. *You Can't Use Your Brain If You're a Jellyfish* (K–3). Illus. by Amanda Haley. 2005, Blue Apple $15.95 (1-59354-090-6). 44pp. A lighthearted but fact-packed look at the brains of a diverse range of creatures — from invertebrates to humans. (Rev: BL 12/1/05; SLJ 11/05) [612.8]

3650 Gilpin, Daniel. *Life-Size Killer Creatures* (3–6). Illus. 2006, Sterling $9.95 (1-4027-2701-1). 28pp. This oversized book with numerous eye-catching foldouts shows life-size illustrations of several predatory animals and offers basic facts on each. (Rev: BL 12/1/06; SLJ 12/1/06) [590]

3651 Hall, Kirsten. *Tracking Animals: A Chapter Book* (3–5). Series: True Tales. 2005, Children's Pr. LB $22.50 (0-516-25186-4). 48pp. An interesting exploration of scientists' ability to track animals and study their behavior using technology. (Rev: SLJ 1/06) [591.5]

3652 Jenkins, Steve, and Robin Page. *Move!* (PS–2). Illus. 2006, Houghton $16.00 (0-618-64637-X). 32pp. This engaging picture book shows diverse members of the animal kingdom in motion. (Rev: BL 3/15/06; SLJ 6/06*) [573.7]

3653 Karwoski, Gail Langer. *Water Beds: Sleeping in the Ocean* (PS–1). Illus. by Connie McLennan. 2005, Sylvan Dell $15.95 (0-9764943-1-0). 32pp. An educational and attractive bedtime book that conveys facts about the sleeping habits of water mammals. (Rev: SLJ 6/06) [599.5]

3654 Kudlinski, Kathleen V. *The Sunset Switch* (PS–2). Illus. by Lindy Burnett. 2005, NorthWord $15.95 (1-55971-916-8). Some animals settle in for the night while their nocturnal friends set off to hunt in this book that can double as a bedtime story and inspiration to learn more about animals. (Rev: SLJ 7/05) [591.5]

3655 Nunn, Daniel. *Ears* (PS–2). Series: Spot the Difference. 2006, Heinemann LB $20.71 (978-1-4034-8473-4). 24pp. Compares the ears of a cricket, chimpanzee, and bat, with color photographs illustrating the differences. (Rev: SLJ 2/07) [591.44]

3656 Nunn, Daniel. *Eyes* (PS–2). Series: Spot the Difference. 2006, Heinemann LB $20.71 (978-1-4034-8474-1). 24pp. Color photographs allow readers to compare the eyes of such animals ranging from moles to gorillas. (Rev: SLJ 2/07)

3657 Patkau, Karen. *Creatures Great and Small* (K–3). Illus. by author. 2006, Tundra LB $17.95 (0-88776-754-0). Large and small animals are juxtaposed on spreads that show relative sizes and give a good impression of the environments they inhabit. (Rev: SLJ 11/06) [591.4]

3658 Rylant, Cynthia. *The Journey: Stories of Migration* (2–4). Illus. by Lambert Davis. 2006, Scholastic $16.99 (0-590-30717-7). 48pp. Migrations of the desert locust, the blue whale, the American silver eel, the monarch butterfly, the caribou, and the Arctic tern are described in separate chapters in this large-format, well-illustrated book. (Rev: BL 12/1/05; SLJ 3/06) [591.56]

3659 Souza, D. M. *Look What Feet Can Do* (2–4). Illus. Series: Look What Animals Can Do. 2006, Lerner LB $25.26 (0-7613-9460-5). 48pp. An interesting look at all the ways in which animals — from slugs to ostriches — can use their feet. (Rev: BL 10/15/06) [573.9]

3660 Souza, D. M. *Look What Mouths Can Do* (2–4). Series: Look What Animals Can Do. 2006, Lerner LB $25.26 (0-7613-9462-1). 48pp. This photo-filled, chatty volume with large type shows the varied ways in which animals use their mouths. Also use *Look What Tails Can Do* and *Look What Whiskers Can Do* (both 2006). (Rev: SLJ 12/06) [573.9]

3661 Took, Atif. *Animal Encounters: A Chapter Book* (3–5). Series: True Tales. 2005, Children's Pr. LB $22.50 (0-516-25190-2). 48pp. This title examines encounters — friendly and dangerous — between humans and animals. (Rev: SLJ 1/06) [590]

DEFENSES

3662 Souza, D. M. *Packed with Poison! Deadly Animal Defenses* (1–3). Illus. by Jack Harris. Series: On

My Own Science. 2006, Millbrook LB $23.93 (1-57505-877-4). 48pp. For new readers, an introduction to several animals — spiders, scorpions, jellyfish, and so forth — that use poison as a defense. (Rev: SLJ 6/06) [591.65]

HIBERNATION

3663 Hickman, Pamela. *Animals Hibernating: How Animals Survive Extreme Conditions* (3–5). Illus. by Pat Stephens. Series: Animal Behavior. 2005, Kids Can $12.95 (1-55337-662-5); paper $5.95 (1-55337-663-3). 40pp. Hickman explains the reasons for hibernation and distinguishes between animals that go into true hibernation and those that merely retreat into deep sleep. (Rev: BL 11/1/05; SLJ 10/05) [591.56]

HOMES

3664 Jenkins, Steve, and Robin Page. *I See a Kookaburra! Discovering Animal Habitats Around the World* (K–3). Illus. by Steve Jenkins. 2005, Houghton $16.00 (0-618-50764-7). 32pp. A colorful and effective "I Spy" format is used to introduce the animals of six different wildlife habitats — tide pool, rain forest, grasslands, desert, pond, and forest. (Rev: BL 8/05; SLJ 5/05) [591.7]

REPRODUCTION

3665 Posada, Mia. *Guess What Is Growing Inside This Egg* (K–3). Illus. 2007, Millbrook $15.95 (978-0-8225-6192-7). 32pp. On the first spread of each pair, a close-up of an egg is accompanied by a rhyming clue; on the second spread, the answer is given as well as basic information about the animal in question. (Rev: BL 4/1/07) [591.4]

Animal Species

GENERAL AND MISCELLANEOUS

3666 Anderson, Jill. *Zebras* (PS–2). Series: Wild Ones. 2005, NorthWord $12.95 (1-55971-926-5); paper $6.95 (1-55971-927-3). With lots of photographs, many of them close-ups, this simple text introduces basic facts about zebras. (Rev: HBG 4/06; SLJ 1/06) [599.72]

3667 Arnold, Caroline. *A Zebra's World* (PS–2). Illus. by author. Series: Caroline Arnold's Animals. 2006, Picture Window LB $23.93 (1-4048-1324-1). 24pp. A baby zebra grows up and learns to fend for himself in this appealing fact-packed title. (Rev: LMC 11–12/06; SLJ 6/06) [599.72]

3668 Barbé-Julien, Colette. *Little Hippopotamuses* (1–3). Series: Born to Be Wild. 2005, Gareth Stevens LB $22.00 (0-8368-4736-9). 24pp. A close-up look at what life is like for baby hippopotamuses,

including their relationships with their parents; suitable for browsers. (Rev: SLJ 2/06) [599.63]

3669 Barnes, Julia. *Camels and Llamas at Work* (3–5). Series: Animals at Work. 2006, Gareth Stevens LB $23.33 (0-8368-6222-8). 32pp. Camels and llamas are not only used as pack animals; full-color photographs show them in various roles and the text discusses the animals' physical characteristics and relationship with humans. (Rev: SLJ 1/07) [636.2]

3670 Collard, Sneed B., III. *A Platypus, Probably* (K–3). Illus. by Andrew Plant. 2005, Charlesbridge $16.95 (1-57091-583-0); paper $6.95 (1-57091-584-9). 32pp. An accessible and attractive introduction to the platypus. (Rev: BL 9/15/05; SLJ 9/05) [599.2]

3671 Collard, Sneed B., III. *In the Rain Forest Canopy* (3–6). Series: Science Adventures. 2005, Benchmark LB $25.64 (0-7614-1954-3). 43pp. Readers meet a scientist who studies creatures that live high in the canopy of the rain forest. (Rev: SLJ 5/06) [578.734]

3672 Glaser, Linda. *Hello Squirrels! Scampering Through the Seasons* (K–2). Illus. by Gay W. Holland. 2006, Millbrook LB $22.60 (0-7613-2887-4). 32pp. An appealing look at the first year of a squirrel's life, narrated from the perspective of a young child and including realistic drawings. (Rev: BL 4/15/06) [599.36]

3673 Green, Jen, and David Burnie. *Mammal* (5–9). Illus. Series: DK/Google e.guides. 2005, DK $17.99 (0-7566-1139-3). 96pp. This highly illustrated guide introduces readers to the evolution and diversity of mammals and provides a link to a Web site that serves as a gateway to additional resources. (Rev: SLJ 8/05) [599]

3674 Guidoux, Valérie. *Little Zebras* (1–3). Series: Born to Be Wild. 2005, Gareth Stevens LB $22.00 (0-8368-4741-5). 24pp. This attractive title introduces the physical and behavioral characteristics of zebras and examines the role of zebra parents in feeding their young and protecting them from predators. (Rev: SLJ 2/06) [599.72]

3675 Hatkoff, Isabella, and Craig Hatkoff. *Owen and Mzee: The True Story of a Remarkable Friendship* (1–3). Illus. by Peter Greste. 2006, Scholastic $16.99 (0-439-82973-9). 32pp. A baby hippo and a giant tortoise form an unlikely bond following the hippo's rescue from the 2004 tsunami; photographs bring the unusual situation to life. (Rev: BL 5/15/06; SLJ 5/06*) [599.63]

3676 Jango-Cohen, Judith. *Hippopotamuses* (3–5). Illus. Series: Animals, Animals. 2006, Marshall Cavendish LB $19.95 (978-0-7614-2238-9). 47pp. This series entry combines full-color photographs and facts about hippos, including a chapter about interaction with humans. (Rev: BL 1/1–15/07) [599.63]

3677 Lang, Aubrey. *Baby Porcupine* (1–4). Photos by Wayne Lynch. Series: Nature Babies. 2006, Fitzhenry & Whiteside $13.95 (1-55041-560-3); paper $6.95 (1-55041-562-X). 36pp. Filled with photographs of a baby porcupine's growth until it's able to survive without its mother's protection and guidance. (Rev: SLJ 6/06) [599.35]

3678 MacKen, JoAnn Early. *Jackrabbits / Liebres americanas* (2–4). Trans. by Tatiana Acosta and Guillermo Gutiérrez. Series: Animals That Live in the Desert / Animales del desierto. 2005, Weekly Reader LB $19.33 (0-8368-4842-X). 24pp. A beginning book with facts about jackrabbits in both English and Spanish. (Rev: SLJ 6/06) [599.32]

3679 Markle, Sandra. *Musk Oxen* (K–4). Series: Animal Prey. 2007, Lerner LB $25.26 (978-0-8225-6064-7). 40pp. Eye-catching photographs and clear, readable text discuss musk oxen, their social structure, and how they deal with predators, mainly wolves that target the young or weak. (Rev: SLJ 4/07) [599.64]

3680 Marrin, Albert. *Saving the Buffalo* (5–7). 2006, Scholastic $18.99 (0-439-71854-6). 128pp. This well-written, well-illustrated history traces the fortunes of the American bison from the days when huge herds covered the plains to near extinction at the end of the 19th century and then to an amazing recovery over the past century or so. (Rev: SLJ 12/06*) [599.64]

3681 Mason, Adrienne. *Skunks* (2–4). Illus. by Nancy Gray Ogle. 2006, Kids Can LB $10.95 (1-55337-733-8); paper $6.95 (1-55337-734-6). 32pp. This picture-book introduction to skunks covers the often-maligned creature's physical characteristics, diet, habitat, behavior, and interaction with humans. (Rev: SLJ 9/06) [599.74]

3682 Merrick, Patrick. *Raccoons* (3–4). Series: New Naturebooks. 2006, The Child's World LB $27.07 (1-59296-647-0). 32pp. An introductory overview of this nocturnal mammal, with vivid color photographs. (Rev: SLJ 2/07) [599.76]

3683 Montgomery, Sy. *Quest for the Tree Kangaroo: An Expedition to the Cloud Forest of New Guinea* (5–8). Illus. by Nic Bishop. 2006, Houghton $18.00 (0-618-49641-6). 80pp. Join researchers on a challenging expedition to the cloud forests of Papua New Guinea to learn more about the rare Matschie's tree kangaroo. (Rev: BL 12/1/06; SLJ 12/06*) [599.2]

3684 Murray, Peter. *Rhinos* (4–7). Series: The World of Mammals. 2005, Child's World LB $29.93 (1-59296-502-4). 40pp. Arresting photographs and engaging text introduce the anatomy, behavior, habitat, and life cycle of the rhinoceros as well as the threats to the animal's survival in the wild. (Rev: SLJ 3/06) [599.72]

3685 Perry, Phyllis J. *Buffalo* (3–5). Illus. Series: Animals, Animals. 2005, Benchmark LB $17.95 (0-7614-1866-0). 48pp. Report writers will find plenty of clear photographs and maps plus well-organized information about the bison and its physical characteristics, diet, habitat, and behavior. (Rev: SLJ 2/06) [599.64]

3686 Pyers, Greg. *Why Am I a Mammal?* (3–5). Illus. Series: Classifying Animals. 2005, Raintree LB $27.50 (1-4109-2016-X); paper $7.85 (1-4109-2023-2). 32pp. Introduces readers to the process of scientific classification and then examines the unique characteristics of mammals. (Rev: SLJ 4/06) [599]

3687 Rau, Dana Meachen. *The Rabbit in the Garden* (PS–1). Series: Benchmark Rebus. 2006, Benchmark LB $15.95 (0-7614-2308-7). 24pp. This colorful easy reader, which features a blend of rebuses and easy-to-understand text, follows a typical day in the life of a rabbit and describes physical characteristics, habitat, diet, and behavior. (Rev: SLJ 12/06) [599.32]

3688 *Savanna Animals: Fun Facts and Stuff to Do* (PS–K). Illus. Series: Padded Animal Board Books. 2006, ME Media $7.95 (1-58925-798-7). 24pp. This richly illustrated board book introduces young readers to the animals of the African savanna, including elephants and chimpanzees. (Rev: BL 10/15/06) [591.74]

3689 Winter, Jeanette. *Mama: A True Story in Which a Baby Hippo Loses His Mama During a Tsunami, but Finds a New Home and a New Mama* (K–2). Illus. 2006, Harcourt $16.00 (0-15-205495-2). 32pp. In this affecting, well-illustrated picture book, a baby hippo is separated from his mother during a tsunami and later, at a wildlife preserve, adopts a giant tortoise as a surrogate parent. (Rev: BL 4/1/06; SLJ 5/06) [599.63]

APE FAMILY

3690 Kalman, Bobbie, and Hadley Dyer. *Endangered Chimpanzees* (3–5). Illus. Series: Earth's Endangered Animals. 2005, Crabtree LB $22.60 (0-7787-1859-X); paper $6.95 (0-7787-1905-7). 32pp. After giving a clear overview of the chimpanzee's physical characteristics, life cycle, and behavior, the authors discuss the reasons the animal is endangered and measures being taken to reduce the threat. (Rev: SLJ 12/05) [599.885]

3691 Lockwood, Sophie. *Baboons* (4–7). Series: The World of Mammals. 2005, Child's World LB $29.93 (1-59296-497-4). 40pp. Arresting photographs and engaging text introduce the anatomy, behavior, habitat, and life cycle of the baboon as well as the threats to the animal's survival in the wild. (Rev: SLJ 3/06) [599.8]

3692 Stefoff, Rebecca. *The Primate Order* (5–9). Illus. Series: Family Trees. 2005, Benchmark LB $29.92 (0-7614-1816-4). 92pp. Habits, habitats, and human-like aspects of this order of animals; an engaging book with plenty of facts for report-writers. (Rev: SLJ 6/06) [599.8]

BATS

3693 Simon, Seymour. *Amazing Bats* (1–3). Series: SeeMore Readers. 2005, Chronicle Bks. LB $14.50 (1-58717-261-5); paper $3.95 (1-58717-262-3). This photo-filled title provides beginning readers with an attractive overview of bats' physical characteristics, habitat, diet, and behavior. (Rev: SLJ 11/05)

3694 Vogel, Julia. *Bats* (2–4). Illus. Series: Our Wild World. 2007, NorthWord $10.95 (978-1-55971-968-1); paper $7.95 (978-1-55971-969-8). 48pp. This easy-to-understand and eye-catching guide to bats introduces a variety of different species, as well as general information about the flying mammals' physical characteristics, habitat, diet, predators, prey, and behavior. (Rev: BL 3/15/07) [599.4]

3695 Wheeler, Jill C. *Bumblebee Bats* (3–5). Illus. Series: Bats, Set II. 2005, ABDO LB $21.35 (1-59679-320-1). 24pp. Introduces the bumblebee bat, which is found in Thailand and is the world's smallest bat species. (Rev: SLJ 2/06) [599.4]

BEARS

3696 Davies, Nicola. *Ice Bear: In the Steps of the Polar Bear* (K–2). Illus. by Gary Blythe. 2005, Candlewick $16.99 (0-7636-2759-3). 32pp. Basic information about polar bears — and admiration for their survival — is delivered in a friendly narrative that also touches on what the Inuit have learned from these animals. (Rev: BL 12/1/05; SLJ 2/06) [599.796]

3697 Guidoux, Valérie. *Little Polar Bears* (1–3). Series: Born to Be Wild. 2005, Gareth Stevens LB $22.00 (0-8368-4739-3). 24pp. This colorful overview of polar bear cubs focuses on the role that their parents play in finding food for their offspring and protecting them from predators. (Rev: SLJ 2/06) [599.786]

3698 Hirschi, Ron. *Searching for Grizzlies* (3–5). Illus. 2005, Boyds Mills $15.95 (1-59078-014-0). 32pp. Beautiful photographs, factual text, and excerpts from notebooks make this a fascinating introduction to the grizzly bear, with enough information for report writers. (Rev: BL 9/1/05; SLJ 9/05) [599.784]

3699 Lang, Aubrey. *Baby Grizzly* (2–4). Photos by Wayne Lynch. Series: Nature Babies. 2006, Fitzhenry & Whiteside $13.95 (1-55041-577-8); paper $6.95 (1-55041-579-4). 36pp. This photo-filled title

follows the development of three grizzly cubs as they stay by their mother's side in the wilds of Alaska. (Rev: SLJ 11/06) [599.784]

3700 Lockwood, Sophie. *Polar Bears* (5–8). Illus. Series: World of Mammals. 2005, Child's World LB $20.95 (1-59296-501-6). 40pp. This slim but richly illustrated title looks at polar bears' physical characteristics, behavior, diet, relationship with the Inuit people, and the growing threats to their survival. (Rev: BL 10/15/05) [599.786]

3701 Ryder, Joanne. *A Pair of Polar Bears: Twin Cubs Find a Home at the San Diego Zoo* (K–2). Illus. 2006, Simon & Schuster $16.95 (0-689-85871-X). 32pp. This engaging photoessay chronicles the story of two orphaned polar bear cubs who find a home at the San Diego Zoo. (Rev: BL 2/1/06; SLJ 3/06) [599.786]

3702 Sartore, Joel. *Face to Face with Grizzlies* (2–5). Illus. Series: Face to Face with Animals. 2007, National Geographic $16.95 (1-4263-0050-6). 32pp. This close-up look at the grizzly bear describes the author/photographer's encounters with these huge animals and introduces readers to their physical characteristics, habitat, diet, behavior, and the threats to their survival. (Rev: BL 4/1/07) [599.784]

3703 Shea, Therese. *Bears* (PS–2). 2006, Rosen LB $19.95 (978-1-4042-3524-8). 24pp. An up-close look at various bears, with facts on their physical characteristics, the food they eat, their habitat, caring for their young, and their enemies. (Rev: SLJ 3/07) [599.78]

3704 Thomas, Keltie. *Bear Rescue: Changing the Future for Endangered Wildlife* (4–8). Series: Firefly Animal Rescue. 2006, Firefly LB $19.95 (1-55297-922-9); paper $9.95 (1-55297-921-0). 64pp. Focuses on work that's being done on behalf of threatened bear species, including Indian sloth bears, Chinese black bears, and polar bears. (Rev: SLJ 12/06) [599.78]

BIG CATS

3705 Hughes, Monica. *Tiger Cub* (K–2). Illus. Series: I Love Reading. 2006, Bearport LB $13.50 (1-59716-155-1). 24pp. Facts about tigers — their physical appearance, habitat, endangered status, and behavior — are given in concise answers to questions posed on colorful double-page spreads; a small-format book suitable for beginning readers. (Rev: BL 4/1/06) [599.756]

3706 MacKen, JoAnn Early. *Cougars / Puma* (2–4). Trans. by Tatiana Acosta and Guillermo Gutiérrez. Series: Animals That Live in the Mountains / Animales de las montañas. 2006, Weekly Reader LB $19.33 (0-8368-6448-4). 24pp. A beginning book with facts about cougars in both English and Spanish. (Rev: SLJ 6/06) [599.75]

3707 Patent, Dorothy Hinshaw. *Big Cats,* (2–4). Illus. by Kendahl Jan Jubb. 2005, Walker $16.95 (0-8027-8968-4). 32pp. An excellent overview — covering physical characteristics, diet, habitat, and behavior — of the world's big cat species, including the cheetah, cougar, jaguar, leopard, lion, and tiger. (Rev: BL 11/15/05; SLJ 12/05) [599.75]

3708 Spilsbury, Louise, and Richard Spilsbury. *Save the Bengal Tiger* (2–4). Series: Save Our Animals! 2006, Heinemann LB $25.36 (1-4034-7803-1). 32pp. Information about the threats to these tigers and the decline in their population is accompanied by information on their diet, habitat, and so forth, and on the ways in which readers can help. Also use *Save the Black Rhino, Save the Giant Panda, Save the Blue Whale,* and *Save the Florida Manatee* (all 2006). (Rev: SLJ 9/06) [599.75]

3709 Spilsbury, Louise, and Richard Spilsbury. *Watching Lions in Africa* (1–3). Series: Wild World. 2006, Heinemann LB $25.36 (1-4034-7222-X). 32pp. Provides details about lions' characteristics, diet, reproduction, predators, and so forth, with photographs, a world map, and a "Tracker's Guide." (Rev: SLJ 7/06) [599.757]

3710 Suen, Anastasia. *A Tiger Grows Up* (K–2). Illus. by Michael Denman and William J. Huiett. Series: Wild Animals. 2005, Picture Window LB $17.95 (1-4048-0987-2). 24pp. Minimal text paired with vivid paintings, in an oversize format, follow a Bengal tiger and her three cubs as they learn to fend for themselves. (Rev: BL 10/15/05) [599.756]

3711 Tourville, Amanda Doering. *A Jaguar Grows Up* (1–3). Illus. by Michael Denman and William J. Huiett. Series: Wild Animals. 2006, Picture Window LB $25.26 (978-1-4048-3159-9). 24pp. A jaguar's development from birth to full independence is described in brief text and realistic illustrations. (Rev: SLJ 4/07) [599.75]

COYOTES, FOXES, AND WOLVES

3712 Markle, Sandra. *Jackals* (2–5). Series: Animal Scavengers. 2005, Lerner LB $25.26 (0-8225-3197-5). 40pp. A well-written overview of jackals and their physical characteristics, diet, habitat, and behavior, with a focus on foraging for food. (Rev: SLJ 2/06) [599.77]

3713 Markle, Sandra. *Wolverines* (2–5). Series: Animal Scavengers. 2005, Lerner LB $25.26 (0-8225-3198-4). 40pp. A well-written overview of wolverines and their physical characteristics, diet, habitat, and behavior, with a focus on foraging for food. (Rev: SLJ 2/06) [599.76]

DEER FAMILY

3714 Estigarribia, Diana. *Moose* (3–5). Illus. Series: Animals, Animals. 2005, Benchmark LB $17.95 (0-

7614-1870-9). 48pp. Report writers will find plenty of clear photographs and maps plus well-organized information about the moose and its physical characteristics, diet, habitat, and behavior. (Rev: SLJ 2/06) [599.65]

3715 Heuer, Karsten. *Being Caribou: Five Months on Foot with a Caribou Herd* (3–6). Illus. 2007, Walker $17.95 (978-0-8027-9565-6). 48pp. Heuer tells the fascinating story of a five-month trip with a caribou herd whose Arctic birthing grounds are threatened by oil drilling. (Rev: BCCB 2/07; BL 4/15/07; HBG 10/07) [599.65]

ELEPHANTS

3716 Arnold, Katya. *Elephants Can Paint Too!* (1–3). Illus. 2005, Simon & Schuster $16.95 (0-689-86985-1). 40pp. Asian elephants' ability to paint is compared with the author's young human students in this affecting and informative picture book; the unemployed elephants' plight is explained, and additional facts are provided. (Rev: BCCB 11/05; BL 8/05; HBG 4/06; LMC 1/06; SLJ 9/05) [599.67]

3717 Barnes, Julia. *Elephants at Work* (3–5). Series: Animals at Work. 2006, Gareth Stevens LB $23.33 (0-8368-6224-4). 32pp. Full-color photographs show elephants being used in various roles and the text discusses the animal's physical characteristics, ability to learn commands, and relationship with humans. (Rev: SLJ 1/07) [636.9]

3718 Buckley, Carol. *Just for Elephants* (3–6). 2006, Tilbury House $16.95 (978-0-88448-283-3). This is the moving story of an aging circus elephant finding refuge after years of performing and then neglect in a zoo; the author's elephant sanctuary in Tennessee is the real star of this true story. (Rev: BL 12/06; SLJ 1/07) [639.97]

3719 Helfer, Ralph. *The World's Greatest Elephant* (1–3). Illus. by Ted Lewin. 2006, Philomel $16.99 (0-399-24190-6). 48pp. The amazing true story of the lifelong relationship between a boy and an elephant, who performed in circuses in Germany and the United States and had many adventures. (Rev: BCCB 4/06; BL 2/1/06*; HBG 10/06; SLJ 2/06) [791.3]

3720 Kalman, Bobbie. *Endangered Elephants* (3–5). Illus. Series: Earth's Endangered Animals. 2005, Crabtree LB $16.95 (0-7787-1860-3); paper $6.26 (0-7787-1906-5). 32pp. The dangers elephants face are highlighted in this photoessay that also covers physical characteristics, diet, behavior, habitat, and life cycle. (Rev: BL 9/15/05; SLJ 12/05) [599.67]

GIRAFFES

3721 Anderson, Jill. *Giraffes* (PS–K). Illus. Series: Wild Ones. 2005, North Word $12.95 (1-55971-928-1); paper $6.95 (1-55971-929-X). 24pp. This photo-filled title chronicles a day in the life of a giraffe and provides basic information about the animal's physical appearance, habitat, diet, and behavior. (Rev: BL 10/15/05; HBG 4/06; SLJ 1/06) [599.665]

3722 Tourville, Amanda Doering. *A Giraffe Grows Up* (1–3). Illus. by Michael Denman and William J. Huiett. Series: Wild Animals. 2006, Picture Window LB $25.26 (978-1-4048-3158-2). 24pp. A giraffe's development from birth to full independence is described in brief text and realistic illustrations. (Rev: SLJ 4/07) [599.638]

3723 Underwood, Deborah. *Watching Giraffes in Africa* (1–3). Series: Wild World. 2006, Heinemann LB $25.36 (1-4034-7230-0). 32pp. Provides details about giraffes' characteristics, diet, reproduction, predators, and so forth, with photographs, a world map, and a "Tracker's Guide." (Rev: SLJ 7/06) [599.638]

INVERTEBRATES

3724 Hartley, Karen, and others. *Centipede* (1–3). Illus. 2006, Heinemann LB $17.75 (1-4034-8295-0). 31pp. A simple question-and-answer format and eye-catching photographs introduce the life cycle of the centipede, as well as the invertebrate's physical characteristics, diet, habitat, and predators. (Rev: BL 9/15/06) [595.6]

MARSUPIALS

3725 Anderson, Jill. *Kangaroos* (PS–2). Series: Wild Ones. 2006, NorthWord $12.95 (1-55971-935-4); paper $6.95 (1-55971-936-2). This photo-filled title offers an excellent visual introduction to kangaroos and is appropriate for preschoolers and early elementary students. (Rev: HBG 10/06; SLJ 8/06)

3726 Markle, Sandra. *Tasmanian Devils* (2–5). Series: Animal Scavengers. 2005, Lerner LB $25.26 (0-8225-3199-9). 40pp. A well-written overview of the ill-tempered Tasmanian devil and its physical characteristics, diet, habitat, and behavior, with a focus on foraging for food. (Rev: SLJ 2/06) [599.2]

3727 Murray, Peter. *Kangaroos* (4–7). Series: The World of Mammals. 2005, Child's World LB $29.93 (1-59296-499-0). 40pp. Arresting photographs and engaging text introduce the anatomy, behavior, habitat, and life cycle of the kangaroo as well as the threats to the animal's survival in the wild. (Rev: SLJ 3/06) [599.2]

3728 Sill, Catherine. *About Marsupials: A Guide for Children* (K–2). Illus. by John Sill. 2006, Peachtree $15.95 (1-56145-358-7). 48pp. Kangaroos, wombats, and wallabies are only three of the marsupials covered in this useful, well-illustrated guide. (Rev: BL 2/15/06; SLJ 5/06) [599.2]

3729 Spilsbury, Louise, and Richard Spilsbury. *Watching Kangaroos in Australia* (1–3). Series: Wild World. 2006, Heinemann LB $25.36 (1-4034-7225-4). 32pp. Provides details about kangaroos' characteristics, diet, reproduction, predators, and so forth, with photographs, a world map, and a "Tracker's Guide." (Rev: SLJ 7/06) [599.2]

PANDAS

3730 Arnold, Caroline. *A Panda's World* (PS–2). Illus. by author. Series: Caroline Arnold's Animals. 2006, Picture Window LB $23.93 (1-4048-1322-5). 24pp. A baby panda grows up and learns to fend for himself in this appealing fact-packed title. (Rev: LMC 11–12/06; SLJ 6/06) [[599.789]

3731 Bredeson, Carmen. *Giant Pandas Up Close* (PS–3). Series: Zoom in on Animals. 2006, Enslow LB $21.26 (0-7660-2496-2). 24pp. Eye-catching full-color close-ups show key physical characteristics of the panda, and the text gives basic details on diet, habitat, life cycle, and so forth. (Rev: SLJ 11/06) [599.789]

3732 Crossingham, John, and Bobbie Kalman. *Endangered Pandas* (3–5). Illus. Series: Earth's Endangered Animals. 2005, Crabtree LB $22.60 (0-7787-1858-1); paper $6.95 (0-7787-1904-9). 32pp. After giving a clear overview of the giant panda's physical characteristics, life cycle, and behavior, the authors discuss the reasons the animal is endangered and measures being taken to reduce the threat. (Rev: SLJ 12/05) [599.789]

3733 Nagda, Ann Whitehead. *Panda Math: Learning About Subtraction from Hua Mei and Mei Sheng* (3–5). Illus. 2005, Holt $16.95 (0-8050-7644-1). 32pp. Using two giant panda siblings at the San Diego Zoo as the framework, this book teaches the fundamentals of subtraction as it considers topics including bamboo consumption, sleep habits, weight, and life expectancy. (Rev: BL 9/15/05; SLJ 9/05) [513.2]

RODENTS

3734 Jango-Cohen, Judith. *Porcupines* (3–5). Illus. Series: Animals, Animals. 2005, Benchmark LB $17.95 (0-7614-1868-7). 48pp. Report writers will find plenty of clear photographs and maps plus well-organized information about the porcupine and its physical characteristics, diet, habitat, and behavior. (Rev: SLJ 2/06) [599.35]

3735 Markle, Sandra. *Porcupines* (K–4). Series: Animal Prey. 2007, Lerner LB $25.26 (978-0-8225-6439-3). 40pp. Eye-catching photographs and clear, readable text discuss how porcupines, nocturnal rodents, repel predators with their sharp quills. (Rev: SLJ 4/07) [599.35]

3736 Marrin, Albert. *Oh, Rats! The Story of Rats and People* (3–5). Illus. by C. B. Mordan. 2006, Dutton $16.99 (0-525-47762-4). 48pp. All about rats and everything they do to both assist and annoy people, with red-accented illustrations. (Rev: BL 7/06; SLJ 8/06*) [599.35]

3737 Pascoe, Elaine. *Mice* (3–6). Illus. by Dwight Kuhn. Series: Nature Close-Up. 2005, Gale LB $18.96 (1-4103-0537-6). 48pp. The life cycle of mice, as well as their physical characteristics, different breeds, diet, and behavior, are examined in this book full of eye-catching photographs that also addresses the care of pet mice. (Rev: BL 2/1/06) [599.35]

SHEEP AND GOATS

3738 MacKen, JoAnn Early. *Bighorn Sheep / Carnero de Canadá* (2–4). Trans. by Tatiana Acosta and Guillermo Gutiérrez. Series: Animals That Live in the Mountains / Animales de las montañas. 2006, Weekly Reader LB $19.33 (0-8368-6446-8). 24pp. A beginning book with facts about bighorn sheep in both English and Spanish; also use *Mountain Goats / Cabra montés* (2006). (Rev: SLJ 6/06) [599.649]

Birds

GENERAL AND MISCELLANEOUS

3739 Bateman, Robert. *Bateman's Backyard Birds* (4–7). Illus. 2005, Barron's $14.99 (0-7641-5882-1). 48pp. Wildlife artist Bateman introduces readers to numerous North American species of birds and the joys of birding in this beautifully illustrated guide. (Rev: BL 10/15/05) [598]

3740 Guibert, Francoise de. *Sing, Nightingale, Sing!* (3–5). Illus. by Chiaki Miyamoto. 2006, Kane/Miller $13.95 (1-929132-98-0). 48pp. This brightly illustrated guide translated from French introduces 51 bird species, each with an illustration and a paragraph of text, and is accompanied by an audio CD of the birds' songs. (Rev: BL 4/1/06) [598]

3741 Kenyon, Linda. *Rainforest Bird Rescue: Changing the Future for Endangered Wildlife* (4–8). Series: Firefly Animal Rescue. 2006, Firefly LB $19.95 (1-55407-153-4); paper $9.95 (1-55407-152-6). 64pp. This book discusses the threats to the tropical bird species that live in the world's rain forests, habitat that is rapidly disappearing, and profiles the men and women who are crusading to save them. (Rev: SLJ 12/06) [598.1734]

3742 MacKen, JoAnn Early. *Roadrunners / Correcaminos* (2–4). Trans. by Tatiana Acosta and Guillermo Gutiérrez. Series: Animals That Live in the Desert / Animales del desierto. 2005, Weekly Reader LB $19.33 (0-8368-4844-6). 24pp. A beginning book with facts about roadrunners in both English and Spanish. (Rev: SLJ 6/06) [598.7]

3743 Markle, Sandra. *Vultures* (3–5). Illus. Series: Animal Scavenger. 2005, Lerner LB $25.26 (0-8225-3195-X). 40pp. Vultures' role as scavengers is the focus of this volume full of dramatic photographs that looks in particular at the vultures of the African savannah, the Gulf Coast of Florida, and the Peruvian jungle. (Rev: BL 12/1/05) [598.9]

3744 Maynard, Thane. *Ostriches* (3–4). Series: New Naturebooks. 2006, The Child's World LB $27.07 (1-59296-645-4). 32pp. An introductory overview of this huge bird, with vivid color photographs. (Rev: SLJ 2/07) [598.5]

3745 Pericoli, Matteo. *The True Story of Stellina* (K–3). Illus. 2006, Knopf $15.95 (0-375-83273-4). 40pp. In lyrical text and appealing art, Pericoli describes his wife's care for a baby finch she rescued from a busy New York City intersection. (Rev: BCCB 4/06; BL 2/1/06*; HBG 10/06; LMC 4–5/06; SLJ 4/06) [636.6]

3746 Pyers, Greg. *Why Am I a Bird?* (3–5). Illus. Series: Classifying Animals. 2005, Raintree LB $27.50 (1-4109-2014-3); paper $7.85 (1-4109-2021-6). 32pp. Introduces readers to the process of scientific classification and then examines the unique physical characteristics — such as feathers, wings, and hollow bones — of birds as a class. (Rev: SLJ 4/06) [598]

3747 Rau, Dana Meachen. *The Robin in the Tree* (PS–1). 2006, Benchmark LB $15.95 (0-7614-2304-4). 24pp. With its child-friendly blend of rebuses and easy-to-understand text, this easy reader follows a typical day in a robin's life, providing basic information about the bird's physical characteristics, habitat, diet, behavior, and life cycle. (Rev: SLJ 12/06) [598.8]

3748 Reynolds, Cynthia Furlong. *The Far-Flung Adventures of Homer the Hummer* (1–3). Illus. by Catherine McClung. 2005, Mitten $17.95 (1-58726-269-X). 32pp. In the spring a ruby-throated hummingbird called Homer leaves the jungles of Costa Rica on a long and dangerous journey north to the United States, where he meets a female called Ruby in an artist's garden. (Rev: BL 9/1/05; SLJ 12/05)

3749 Underwood, Deborah. *Colorful Peacocks* (2–3). Series: Pull Ahead Books. 2006, Lerner LB $22.60 (0-8225-5930-7). 32pp. This colorful introduction to peacocks examines the birds' physical characteristics, diet, behavior, and habitat, and looks at how peacock parents care for their young. (Rev: SLJ 9/06) [598.6]

3750 Willis, Nancy Carol. *Red Knot: A Shorebird's Incredible Journey* (2–4). 2006, Birdsong $15.95 (0-9662761-4-0); paper $6.95 (0-9662761-5-9). 32pp. Using the form of journal entries, this picture book follows the red knot shorebird on its incredible 20,000-mile annual migration. (Rev: BL 6/1–15/06; SLJ 7/06) [598.3]

DUCKS, GEESE, AND SWANS

3751 Spilsbury, Louise. *Duck* (K–2). Series: Life Cycles. 2005, Heinemann LB $20.64 (1-4034-6771-4). 24pp. Simple easy-reader questions and answers about ducks and how they grow are accompanied by color photographs. (Rev: SLJ 7/05) [598.4]

EAGLES, HAWKS, AND OTHER BIRDS OF PREY

3752 Colman, C. H. *The Bald Eagle's View of American History* (1–4). Illus. by Joanne Friar. 2006, Charlesbridge paper $5.95 (1-58089-301-5). 48pp. Postage-stamp depictions of the bald eagle illustrate this history of the bird, threats to its existence, and its importance as a symbol. (Rev: SLJ 1/07) [929.9]

3753 Evert, Laura, and Wayne Lynch. *Birds of Prey* (3–6). Illus. by Sherry Neidigh and John F. McGee. Series: Our Wild World. 2005, NorthWord $16.95 (1-55971-925-7). 191pp. An attractive, well-organized and easily accessible introduction to the four major subdivisions of raptors: eagles, falcons, owls, and vultures. (Rev: SLJ 11/05)

3754 Lynch, Wayne. *Falcons* (3–5). Photos by author. Illus. by Sherry Neidigh. Series: Our Wild World. 2005, NorthWord $10.95 (1-55971-911-7); paper $7.95 (1-55971-912-5). 47pp. With eye-catching photographs and readable text, this discusses the physical characteristics, life cycle, diet, habitat, and family life of the falcons of North America. Also use *Vultures* (2005). (Rev: SLJ 8/05) [598.9]

3755 MacKen, JoAnn Early. *Golden Eagles / Águila real* (2–4). Trans. by Tatiana Acosta and Guillermo Gutiérrez. Series: Animals That Live in the Mountains / Animales de las montañas. 2006, Weekly Reader LB $19.33 (0-8368-6450-6). 24pp. A beginning book with facts about golden eagles in both English and Spanish. (Rev: SLJ 6/06) [598.9]

OWLS

3756 Lynch, Wayne. *Owls* (3–5). Photos by author. Illus. by Sherry Neidigh. Series: Our Wild World. 2005, NorthWord $10.95 (1-55971-914-1); paper $7.95 (1-55971-915-X). 47pp. With eye-catching photographs and readable text, this discusses the physical characteristics, life cycle, diet, habitat, and family life of the owls of North America. (Rev: SLJ 8/05) [598.9]

PENGUINS

3757 Arnold, Caroline. *A Penguin's World* (PS–2). Illus. Series: Caroline Arnold's Animals. 2006, Picture Window LB $17.95 (1-4048-1323-3). 24pp. With an accessible blend of paper collage artwork and easy-to-understand text, this picture book introduces basic facts about Adelie penguins and their

family life. (Rev: BL 4/1/06; LMC 11–12/06; SLJ 6/06) [598.47]

3758 Barner, Bob. *Penguins, Penguins, Everywhere!* (PS–2). Illus. 2007, Chronicle $14.95 (978-0-8118-5664-5). 32pp. Basic information about penguins is couched in appealing rhyming text accompanied by bold illustrations. (Rev: BL 4/1/07) [598.47]

3759 Bredeson, Carmen. *Emperor Penguins Up Close* (PS–3). Series: Zoom in on Animals! 2006, Enslow LB $21.26 (0-7660-2497-0). 24pp. Eye-catching full-color close-ups show key physical characteristics of the penguins, and the text gives basic details on diet, habitat, life cycle, and so forth. (Rev: SLJ 11/06) [598.47]

3760 Jacquet, Luc. *March of the Penguins* (3–5). Illus. by Jerome Maison. 2005, National Geographic $30.00 (0-7922-6190-9). 160pp. A companion to the movie, this book also tells the story of emperor penguins' life cycle, and features many striking images; back matter includes a behind-the-scenes look at the making of the movie and additional information about the emperor penguins that were its stars. (Rev: BL 11/15/05) [598.47]

3761 Jonas, Anne. *Little Penguins* (1–3). Series: Born to Be Wild. 2005, Gareth Stevens LB $22.00 (0-8368-4738-5). 24pp. This colorful title introduces the physical and behavioral characteristics of penguins and examines how adult birds feed their offspring and protect them from predators. (Rev: SLJ 2/06) [598.4]

3762 Markle, Sandra. *A Mother's Journey* (K–3). Illus. by Alan Marks. 2005, Charlesbridge $15.95 (1-57091-621-7). 32pp. This handsome picture book chronicles the arduous journey of a female Emperor penguin from laying an egg through hunting for food for the newborn chick. (Rev: BL 9/1/05; SLJ 9/05) [598.47]

3763 Spilsbury, Louise, and Richard Spilsbury. *Watching Penguins in Antarctica* (1–3). Series: Wild World. 2006, Heinemann LB $25.36 (1-4034-7223-8). 32pp. Provides details about penguins' characteristics, diet, reproduction, predators, and so forth, with photographs, a world map, and a "Tracker's Guide." (Rev: SLJ 7/06) [598.47]

3764 Stefoff, Rebecca. *Penguins* (4–8). Illus. Series: AnimalWays. 2005, Benchmark LB $21.95 (0-7614-1743-5). 112pp. Beautiful photographs enrich this well-organized volume that provides basic information on the penguin's characteristics, habits, and habitat. (Rev: SLJ 5/06) [598.4]

Conservation of Endangered Species

3765 Collard, Sneed B., III. *In the Wild* (3–6). Series: Science Adventures. 2005, Benchmark LB $25.64 (0-7614-1955-1). 43pp. Readers meet scientists at Zoo Atlanta who work with endangered primates. (Rev: SLJ 5/06) [599.8]

3766 Jenkins, Steve. *Almost Gone: The World's Rarest Animals* (1–3). Illus. Series: Let's-Read-and-Find-Out Science. 2006, HarperCollins $16.99 (0-06-053598-9); paper $5.99 (0-06-053600-4). 40pp. Striking cut-paper collages and brief text introduce 21 animal species that are endangered. (Rev: BL 12/1/05; SLJ 2/06*) [574.529]

3767 McDaniel, Melissa. *Mysterious Nature: A Chapter Book* (3–6). Series: True Tales. 2005, Children's Pr. LB $22.50 (0-516-25183-4); paper $4.95 (0-516-25453-7). 48pp. Scientists discuss the causes of mysterious animal extinctions around the world; clear illustrations add to the easy-reading text. (Rev: SLJ 5/06) [591.68]

Insects and Arachnids

GENERAL AND MISCELLANEOUS

3768 Blobaum, Cindy. *Insectigations! 40 Hands-on Activities to Explore the Insect World* (3–6). Illus. by Gail Rattray. 2005, Chicago Review paper $12.95 (1-55652-568-0). 133pp. From collecting and drawing insects to raising mealworms, keeping a scientific journal, and gardening for butterflies, this useful volume offers both activities and facts. (Rev: SLJ 1/06) [595.7]

3769 Bulion, Leslie. *Hey There, Stink Bug!* (4–6). 2006, Charlesbridge $12.95 (1-58089-304-X). 48pp. Poems about bugs full of dramatic and often gross details are designed to fascinate the older elementary student. (Rev: BL 7/06; SLJ 7/06) [595.7]

3770 Burnie, David. *Bug Hunter* (4–6). Illus. Series: Nature Activities. 2005, DK paper $9.99 (0-7566-1030-3). 72pp. Bright, attractive double-page spreads explore the study of bugs (insects, spiders, and some worms) and provide activities. (Rev: BL 7/05) [595.7]

3771 Burnie, David. *Insect* (5–9). Illus. Series: DK/Google e.guides. 2005, DK $17.99 (0-7566-1010-9). 96pp. This highly illustrated guide introduces readers to the life cycle, behavior, diet, and habitat of insects and provides a link to a Web site that serves as a gateway to additional resources. (Rev: SLJ 8/05)

3772 Crowley, Ned. *Ugh! A Bug!* (K–2). Series: Silly Millies. 2005, Millbrook LB $18.60 (0-7613-3450-5); paper $4.99 (0-7613-2475-8). 32pp. This photo-filled title with rhyming text introduces young readers to 25 kinds of insects, provides some fascinating facts, and includes a "pictionary" index. (Rev: SLJ 11/05)

3773 Pyers, Greg. *Why Am I an Insect?* (3–5). Illus. Series: Classifying Animals. 2005, Raintree LB $27.50 (1-4109-2019-4); paper $7.85 (1-4109-2026-7). 32pp. Introduces readers to the process of scien-

tific classification and then examines the unique characteristics of insects. (Rev: SLJ 4/06) [595.7]

3774 Sayre, April Pulley. *Ant, Ant, Ant: An Insect Chant* (K–3). Illus. by Trip Park. 2005, NorthWord $15.95 (1-55971-922-2). With a rhyming chant as its narrative line, this colorful and humorous picture book introduces 60 American insects and highlights their unusual features; a companion to *Trout, Trout, Trout! A Fish Chant* (2004). (Rev: SLJ 12/05) [595.7]

3775 Smithyman, Kathryn, and Bobbie Kalman. *Insects in Danger* (3–5). Illus. Series: The World of Insects. 2006, Crabtree LB $25.20 (0-7787-2344-5). 32pp. This brightly illustrated volume considers the dangers facing certain insect species, including the pressure put on some insects by the migratory patterns of other animals. (Rev: SLJ 1/07) [595.7168]

3776 Tokuda, Yukihisa. *I'm a Pill Bug* (PS–2). Illus. by Kiyoshi Takahashi. Series: Nature: A Child's Eye View. 2006, Kane/Miller paper $7.95 (1-929132-95-6). 28pp. This attractive picture book provides a wealth of information about pill bugs, including what they eat, how they defend themselves, their reproductive habits, why they live near people, and why they shed their shells. (Rev: BL 4/1/06*) [595.372]

3777 Wilkes, Sarah. *Insects* (5–9). Series: World Almanac Library of the Animal Kingdom. 2006, World Almanac LB $30.00 (0-8368-6211-2). 48pp. A helpful introduction to members of the insect kingdom, this guide looks at physical characteristics that help to define this group as a whole, as well as specific species, habitats, diets, behaviors, and life cycles. (Rev: SLJ 12/06) [595.7]

3778 Zabludoff, Marc. *The Insect Class* (5–9). Illus. Series: Family Trees. 2005, Benchmark LB $29.92 (0-7614-1819-9). 95pp. Habits, habitats, and other aspects of this varied class of animals; an engaging book with plenty of facts for report-writers. (Rev: SLJ 6/06) [595.7]

BEES AND WASPS

3779 Starosta, Paul. *The Bee* (2–4). Illus. Series: Animal Close-Ups. 2005, Charlesbridge paper $6.95 (1-57091-629-2). 28pp. Plenty of close-up photographs accompany information about the life cycle of honeybees and the important role they play in nature. (Rev: BL 9/15/05) [575.79]

CATERPILLARS, BUTTERFLIES, AND MOTHS

3780 Kalman, Bobbie, and Robin Johnson. *Endangered Butterflies* (3–5). Illus. Series: Earth's Endangered Animals. 2006, Crabtree LB $25.20 (0-7787-1870-0). 32pp. Large text and clear color photographs focus on endangered butterfly species, presenting basic information about physical characteristics, diet, habitat, behavior, and discussing the specific threats they face. (Rev: SLJ 1/07) [595.78]

3781 Loewen, Nancy. *Flying Colors: Butterflies in Your Backyard* (PS–2). Illus. by Rick Peterson. Series: Backyard Bugs. 2005, Picture Window LB $22.60 (1-4048-1143-5). 24pp. Butterflies' importance as plant pollinators is emphasized in this large, horizontal volume that includes an activity and a craft project. (Rev: BL 12/1/05) [595.78]

3782 Rea, Ba. *Monarch! Come Play with Me* (K–2). Illus. by author. 2006, Bas Relief paper $10.95 (0-9657472-5-5). 32pp. A young girl's conversation with a monarch caterpillar that is concentrating on metamorphosis offers insights into the process. (Rev: SLJ 8/06) [595]

3783 Schlaepfer, Gloria G. *Butterflies* (4–8). Illus. Series: AnimalWays. 2005, Benchmark LB $21.95 (0-7614-1745-1). 112pp. Beautiful photographs of butterfly specimens enrich this well-organized volume that provides basic information on the butterfly's characteristics, habits, and habitat. (Rev: SLJ 5/06) [595.78]

3784 Spilsbury, Louise. *Butterfly* (K–2). Series: Life Cycles. 2005, Heinemann LB $20.64 (1-4034-6770-6). 24pp. Brief text and bold photographs suitable for beginning readers focus on the life cycle of the butterfly. (Rev: SLJ 7/05) [595.78]

3785 Stewart, Melissa. *A Place for Butterflies* (K–3). Illus. by Higgins Bond. 2006, Peachtree $16.95 (1-56145-357-9). 32pp. This richly illustrated book takes readers on a tour of butterfly habitats where human intervention has helped the insects to survive. (Rev: BL 3/15/06; SLJ 6/06) [595.7]

3786 Swinburne, Stephen R. *Wings of Light: The Migration of the Yellow Butterfly* (K–3). Illus. by Bruce Hiscock. 2006, Boyds Mills $15.95 (1-59078-082-5). 32pp. Traces the migration of the cloudless sulphur butterfly from its winter home in Mexico's Yucatan to its summer range in the northeastern United States. (Rev: BL 4/1/06; SLJ 5/06) [595.78]

SPIDERS AND SCORPIONS

3787 Allman, Toney. *From Spider Webs to Man-Made Silk* (4–7). Illus. Series: Imitating Nature. 2005, Gale LB $17.96 (0-7377-3124-9). 48pp. An introduction to scientists' attempts to replicate spider silk in the laboratory. (Rev: BL 10/15/05; LMC 3/06) [595.4]

3788 Dinaberg, Leslie. *Spider Life* (2–5). Series: Boys Rock! 2006, The Child's World LB $24.21 (1-59296-737-X). 32pp. A good choice for beginning and reluctant readers (girls as well as boys), this colorful volume looks at spiders' physical and behav-

ioral characteristics, habitat, diet, predators, and life cycle. (Rev: SLJ 2/07) [595.4]

3789 Ganeri, Anita. *From Egg to Spider* (1–3). Illus. Series: How Living Things Grow. 2006, Heinemann LB $25.36 (1-4034-7860-0). 32pp. The life cycle of the garden spider, presented in an easy-to-read format. (Rev: SLJ 6/06) [595.4]

3790 Gilpin, Daniel. *Centipedes, Millipedes, Scorpions and Spiders* (4–6). Illus. Series: Animal Kingdom Classification. 2005, Compass Point LB $19.95 (0-7565-1254-9). 48pp. Spiders and other members of the arachnid family, including mites, scorpions, and ticks, are introduced in informative spreads with eye-catching illustrations. (Rev: BL 11/1/05) [595.6]

3791 Morley, Christine. *Freaky Facts About Spiders* (2–4). Illus. Series: Freaky Facts About. 2007, Two-Can $13.95 (978-1-58728-596-7); paper $8.95 (978-1-58728-597-4). 32pp. A colorful introduction to spiders and their weirder characteristics, full of graphic elements that will appeal to reluctant readers. (Rev: BL 3/15/07) [595.4]

3792 Zabludoff, Marc. *Spiders* (4–8). Illus. Series: AnimalWays. 2005, Benchmark LB $21.95 (0-7614-1747-8). 112pp. Beautiful photographs enrich this well-organized volume that provides basic information on the insect's characteristics, habits, and habitat. (Rev: SLJ 5/06) [595.4]

3793 Zollman, Pam. *A Spiderling Grows Up* (K–1). Series: Scholastic News Nonfiction Readers. 2005, Children's Pr. LB $18.00 (0-516-24946-0). 24pp. Covers the life cycle of a spider, with a focus on spider eggs and young spiderlings and their survival tactics. (Rev: SLJ 4/06) [595.4]

Land Invertebrates

3794 Dixon, Norma. *Lowdown on Earthworms* (2–4). Illus. 2005, Fitzhenry & Whiteside $16.95 (1-55041-114-8). 32pp. This attractive title digs into the anatomy, behavior, and habitat of earthworms and describes worm-related projects. (Rev: BL 9/1/05) [592.64]

3795 Parker, Steve. *Nematodes, Leeches and Other Worms* (4–6). Illus. Series: Animals Kingdom Classification. 2006, Compass Point LB $26.60 (0-7565-1615-3). 48pp. Concise, well-written text, color photographs, diagrams, and charts cover the physical characteristics, habitat, diet, and behavior of worms. (Rev: SLJ 11/06) [592]

Marine and Freshwater Life

GENERAL AND MISCELLANEOUS

3796 Butterworth, Chris. *Sea Horse: The Shyest Horse in the Sea* (K–2). Illus. by John Lawrence.

2006, Candlewick $16.99 (0-7636-2989-8). 32pp. Lovely, detailed illustrations and appealing narrative combined with facts trace the life cycle of an endangered sea horse. (Rev: BCCB 10/06; BL 4/15/06*; HB 7–8/06; HBG 10/06; SLJ 6/06*) [597]

3797 Collard, Sneed B., III. *In the Deep Sea* (3–6). Illus. Series: Science Adventures. 2005, Benchmark LB $25.64 (0-7614-1952-7). 43pp. Readers meet a scientist who studies creatures of the deep sea that use bioluminescence. (Rev: SLJ 5/06) [572]

3798 Herriges, Ann. *Sea Horses* (K–3). Series: Blastoff! Readers: Oceans Alive! 2006, Children's Pr. LB $18.50 (978-1-60014-020-4). 24pp. Habitat, anatomy, and characteristics of sea horses are covered in large text accompanied by eye-catching photographs. Also use *Sea Stars* (2006). (Rev: SLJ 2/07) [597]

3799 Lindeen, Carol K. *Sea Horses* (K–3). Series: Under the Sea. 2004, Capstone LB $19.93 (0-7368-3662-4). 24pp. A simple, easy-to-read description of the sea horse, with bright photographs. (Rev: SLJ 7/05) [597]

3800 Parker, Steve. *Sponges, Jellyfish and Other Simple Animals* (4–6). Illus. Series: Animal Kingdom Classification. 2006, Compass Point LB $26.60 (0-7565-1614-5). 48pp. Concise, well-written text, color photographs, diagrams, and charts cover the physical characteristics, habitat, diet, and behavior of animals such as sea anemones, corals, sponges, and jellyfish. (Rev: SLJ 11/06) [592]

3801 Rhodes, Mary Jo, and David Hall. *Partners in the Sea* (2–4). Photos by David Hall. Series: Undersea Encounters. 2005, Children's Pr. LB $25.00 (0-516-24397-7). 48pp. This photo-filled title explores the symbiotic relationship between different forms of marine life. (Rev: BL 10/15/05) [591.77]

3802 Taylor-Butler, Christine. *A Home in the Coral Reef* (1–3). 2006, Children's Pr. LB $19.00 (978-0-516-25344-2). 24pp. This easy-to-understand introduction to the coral reef looks at the nature of the coral, its climate, flora, and the animals that call it home. (Rev: SLJ 2/07) [574.9]

3803 Zabludoff, Marc. *The Protoctist Kingdom* (5–9). Series: Family Trees. 2005, Benchmark LB $29.92 (0-7614-1818-0). 95pp. Habits, habitats, and other aspects of this newly classified kingdom of animals that includes algae; an engaging book with plenty of facts for report-writers. (Rev: SLJ 6/06) [579]

CORALS AND JELLYFISH

3804 Collard, Sneed B., III. *On the Coral Reefs* (4–7). Illus. Series: Science Adventures. 2005, Marshall Cavendish LB $17.95 (0-7614-1953-5). 48pp. In addition to a profile of a marine biologist who studies fish that eat parasites living on other fish,

Collard presents information on scientific research methods and on global warming and other environmental threats. (Rev: BL 2/1/06; SLJ 5/06) [577.7]

3805 Herriges, Ann. *Jellyfish* (K–3). Series: Blastoff! Readers: Oceans Alive! 2006, Children's Pr. LB $18.50 (978-1-60014-018-1). 24pp. Habitat, anatomy, and characteristics of the jellyfish are covered in large text accompanied by eye-catching photographs. (Rev: SLJ 2/07) [593.5]

3806 Rhodes, Mary Jo, and David Hall. *Life on a Coral Reef* (4–6). Photos by David Hall. Series: Undersea Encounters. 2006, Children's Pr. LB $27.00 (978-0-516-24395-5). 48pp. A look at life on a coral reef, with facts on life cycles, reproduction, and threats from pollution. (Rev: SLJ 3/07) [574]

DOLPHINS AND PORPOISES

3807 Thomson, Sarah L. *Amazing Dolphins!* (K–3). Series: I Can Read. 2006, HarperCollins $15.99 (0-06-054453-8). 32pp. For beginning readers, this introduces the world of dolphins, discussing their physical characteristics, communications, habitat, behavior, and how they care for their young. (Rev: BL 6/1–15/06; SLJ 7/06) [599.53]

FISH

3808 Einhorn, Kama. *My First Book About Fish* (PS–1). Illus. by Christopher Moroney. Series: Sesame Subjects. 2006, Random paper $7.99 (0-375-83513-X). Muppets Grover and Elmo, the latter accompanied by his pet goldfish, team up to introduce basic information about fish, including their physical characteristics, habitat, diet, and behavior. (Rev: SLJ 12/06) [597]

3809 Pyers, Greg. *Why Am I a Fish?* (3–5). Illus. Series: Classifying Animals. 2005, Raintree LB $27.50 (1-4109-2015-1); paper $7.85 (1-4109-2022-4). 32pp. Introduces readers to the process of scientific classification and then examines the unique physical characteristics — such as fins, gills, and a streamlined body — of fish as a class. (Rev: SLJ 4/06) [597]

3810 Stewart, Melissa. *How Do Fish Breathe Underwater?* (2–4). Series: Tell Me Why, Tell Me How. 2006, Marshall Cavendish LB $19.95 (0-7614-2109-2). 32pp. In brief chapters with easy-to-understand text and eye-catching full-color photos, the author discusses how fish breathe. (Rev: BL 10/15/06; SLJ 12/06) [573.2]

3811 Weber, Valerie J. *Anglerfish* (3–5). Series: Weird Wonders of the Deep. 2005, Gareth Stevens LB $22.00 (0-8368-4560-9). 24pp. A look at the unusual anglerfish and its ability to swallow prey much larger than itself. (Rev: SLJ 8/05) [597]

3812 Weber, Valerie J. *Coelacanth: The Living Fossil* (3–5). Series: Weird Wonders of the Deep. 2005,

Gareth Stevens LB $22.00 (0-8368-4561-7). 24pp. An introduction to a interesting fish that lived 400 million years ago and had no backbone — and still exists today. (Rev: SLJ 8/05) [597.3]

3813 Wilkes, Sarah. *Fish* (5–9). Series: World Almanac Library of the Animal Kingdom. 2006, World Almanac LB $30.00 (0-8368-6210-4). 48pp. This brightly illustrated guide to fish introduces specific species, physical characteristics, habitats, diets, behaviors, and life cycles. (Rev: SLJ 12/06) [597]

MOLLUSKS, SPONGES, AND STARFISH

3814 Gilpin, Daniel. *Snails, Shellfish and Other Mollusks* (4–6). Illus. Series: Animal Kingdom Classification. 2006, Compass Point LB $26.60 (0-7565-1613-7). 48pp. Concise, well-written text, color photographs, diagrams, and charts cover the physical characteristics, habitat, diet, and behavior of mollusks. (Rev: SLJ 11/06)

OCTOPUS

3815 Herriges, Ann. *Octopuses* (K–3). Series: Blastoff! Readers: Oceans Alive! 2006, Children's Pr. LB $18.50 (978-1-60014-019-8). 24pp. Habitat, anatomy, and characteristics of the octopus are covered in large text accompanied by eye-catching photographs. (Rev: SLJ 2/07) [594]

3816 Lindeen, Carol K. *Octopuses* (K–3). Series: Under the Sea. 2004, Capstone LB $19.93 (0-7368-3661-6). 24pp. A simple, easy-to-read description of the octopus, with bright photographs. (Rev: SLJ 7/05) [594]

3817 Markle, Sandra. *Octopuses* (3–5). Illus. Series: Animal Prey. 2007, Lerner $25.26 (978-0-8225-6063-0). 40pp. Stunning color photography highlights this well-written introduction to the octopus that covers its physical characteristics, habitat, diet, behavior, and life cycle. (Rev: BL 4/1/07) [594]

3818 Spirn, Michele Sobel. *Octopuses* (3–6). Series: Smart Animals. 2006, Bearport LB $23.96 (1-59716-250-7). 32pp. The octopus's intelligence and ability to solve problems are discussed here; a facts page gives details about physical characteristics and so forth and a diagram labels body parts. (Rev: SLJ 1/07) [594]

SEA MAMMALS

3819 Arnold, Caroline. *Super Swimmers* (2–4). Illus. by Patricia J. Wynne. 2007, Charlesbridge $16.95 (978-1-57091-588-8); paper $6.95 (978-1-57091-589-5). 32pp. A wide variety of marine mammals are introduced in this clear text with well-chosen illustrations. (Rev: BL 2/1/07) [599.5]

3820 Fetty, Margaret. *Sea Lions* (3–6). Series: Smart Animals. 2006, Bearport LB $23.96 (1-59716-274-

4). 32pp. Sea lions' intelligence is clearly shown in stories of their ability to communicate and their work for the U.S. Navy; a facts page gives details about physical characteristics and so forth. (Rev: SLJ 1/07) [599.79]

3821 Leon, Vicki. *A Raft of Sea Otters: The Playful Life of a Furry Survivor*. 2nd ed. (4–7). Illus. 2005, London Town paper $7.95 (0-9666490-4-4). 48pp. This accessible introduction to the sea otter and its physical characteristics, behavior, diet, habitat, life cycle, and conservation threats is a picture-book-size revision of an earlier edition and contains excellent photographs. (Rev: BL 7/05) [599.7695]

3822 Lindeen, Carol K. *Seals* (K–3). Series: Under the Sea. 2004, Capstone LB $19.93 (0-7368-3663-2). 24pp. A simple, easy-to-read description of the seal, with bright photographs. (Rev: SLJ 7/05) [599.79]

3823 Marsico, Katie. *A Manatee Calf Grows Up* (PS–2). Illus. Series: Scholastic News Nonfiction Readers: Life Cycles. 2007, Children's Pr. LB $19.00 (978-0-531-17479-1). 24pp. This photo-filled title traces the life cycle of a female manatee, introducing young readers to the marine mammal's physical and behavioral characteristics, habitat, and diet. (Rev: BL 3/15/07) [599.55]

3824 Swinburne, Stephen R. *Saving Manatees* (4–6). 2006, Boyds Mills $16.95 (1-59078-319-0). 40pp. This tour of Florida's manatee country includes discussions with biologists and park rangers and a class of fourth-graders swimming with manatees, as well as information on the mammal's physical appearance, diet, behavior, and habitat, plus the threats it faces. (Rev: BL 9/1/06; SLJ 11/06) [599.5]

3825 Tatham, Betty. *Baby Sea Otter* (PS–2). Illus. by Joan Paley. 2005, Holt $16.95 (0-8050-7504-6). 32pp. With some tender and some exciting moments, this book follows the life of a sea otter from birth through mating and caring for its own pups. (Rev: BL 11/1/05; SLJ 9/05) [599.769]

SHARKS

3826 Shea, Therese. *Sharks* (PS–2). Series: Big Bad Biters. 2006, Rosen LB $19.95 (978-1-4042-3519-1). 24pp. A look at the world of sharks and learn about their physical characteristics, habitat, what they eat, how they raise their young, and their enemies in the sea. (Rev: SLJ 3/07) [597.3]

3827 Thomson, Sarah L. *Amazing Sharks!* (K–2). Illus. Series: I Can Read. 2005, HarperCollins $15.99 (0-06-054458-9). 32pp. Short sentences and bright photographs make this overview of sharks and shark behavior suitable for beginning readers. (Rev: BL 10/1/05; SLJ 1/06) [597.3]

3828   Woods, Bob. *Shark Attack!* (2–5). Series: Boys Rock! 2006, The Child's World LB $24.21 (1-59296-734-5). 32pp. A non-alarmist overview of the danger posed by sharks, suitable for beginning and reluctant readers (girls as well as boys). (Rev: SLJ 2/07) [597.3]

3829   Zollman, Pam. *A Shark Pup Grows Up* (K–1). Series: Scholastic News Nonfiction Readers. 2005, Children's Pr. LB $18.00 (0-516-24945-2). 24pp. Covers the life cycle of a shark, with a focus on newborn pups and their survival tactics. (Rev: SLJ 4/06) [597.3]

WHALES

3830   Arnold, Caroline. *A Killer Whale's World* (PS–2). Illus. by author. Series: Caroline Arnold's Animals. 2006, Picture Window LB $23.93 (1-4048-1321-7). 24pp. A baby killer whale grows up and learns to fend for himself in this appealing fact-packed title. (Rev: LMC 11–12/06; SLJ 6/06) [599.53]

3831   Hoyt, Erich. *Whale Rescue: Changing the Future for Endangered Wildlife* (4–6). Illus. Series: Animal Rescue. 2005, Firefly $19.95 (1-55297-601-7); paper $9.95 (1-55297-600-9). 64pp. An interesting discussion of international efforts to conserve the world's whales, with coverage of the various species and their characteristics plus information on whale researchers. (Rev: BL 8/05; SLJ 12/05) [599.5]

Oceanography

CURRENTS, TIDES, AND WAVES

3832   Allen, Judy, et al. *Higher Ground* (5–8). Illus. 2006, Chrysalis paper $8.99 (1-84458-581-6). 156pp. First-person accounts of survivors and rescue workers mixed with fictional treatments based on fact portray the impact on children of the deadly Indian Ocean tsunami of December 2004. (Rev: BCCB 5/06; BL 2/1/06; SLJ 3/06) [363.349]

3833   Fine, Jil. *Tsunamis* (3–5). Illus. Series: Natural Disaster. 2006, Children's Pr. LB $24.00 (0-531-12444-4). 48pp. A photo-filled exploration of tsunamis and the geological events that can cause these massive tidal waves, focusing in particular on the deadly Indian Ocean tsunami of December 2004. (Rev: BL 11/1/06) [551.46]

3834   Hamilton, John. *Tsunamis* (3–4). Series: Nature's Fury. 2005, ABDO LB $24.21 (1-59679-333-3). 32pp. Well-chosen color photographs and clear text explore tsunamis, their causes and impact, and specific tidal waves of the past. (Rev: SLJ 3/06) [551.55]

3835   Karwoski, Gail Langer. *Tsunami: The True Story of an April Fools' Day Disaster* (4–7). Illus.

by John MacDonald. 2006, Darby Creek $17.95 (1-58196-044-1). 64pp. Karwoski tells the story of a devastating 1946 tsunami, and expands the coverage to other destructive waves and their causes, effects, and the measures being taken to alert residents to their arrival. (Rev: SLJ 1/07) [363.34]

3836   Morris, Ann, and Heidi Larson. *Tsunami: Helping Each Other* (2–4). 2005, Millbrook $15.95 (0-7613-9501-6). 48pp. Focusing on the experiences of two Thai brothers, 8-year-old Chaiya and 12-year-old Chaipreak, who lose their father to the tsunami, this is a more personal treatment than many of the books about tsunamis and includes many photographs of the disaster and the progress toward recovery. (Rev: BL 12/1/05; SLJ 7/06) [959.304]

3837   Morrison, Taylor. *Tsunami Warning* (4–6). Illus. 2007, Houghton $17.00 (978-0-618-73463-4). 32pp. Morrison discusses the tsunamis of 1946 and 1957 in this overview of warning systems and how they work. (Rev: BL 2/1/07) [551.47]

3838   Stewart, Gail B. *Catastrophe in Southern Asia: The Tsunami of 2004* (5–8). Series: Overview. 2005, Gale LB $28.70 (1-59018-831-4). 112pp. An information-packed review of the tsunami itself, the human costs of the disaster, and the reconstruction efforts. (Rev: SLJ 12/05)

3839   Torres, John A. *Disaster in the Indian Ocean: Tsunami 2004* (5–8). Illus. Series: Monumental Milestones: Great Events of Modern Times. 2005, Mitchell Lane LB $19.95 (1-58415-344-X). 48pp. This slim volume, uneven in its coverage, nonetheless offers a chilling overview of the devastating Indian Ocean tsunami of December 2004 and includes a number of eyewitness accounts. (Rev: BL 10/15/05; SLJ 12/05) [909]

SEASHORES AND TIDAL POOLS

3840   Kudlinski, Kathleen V. *The Seaside Switch* (K–2). Illus. by Lindy Burnett. 2007, NorthWord $16.95 (978-1-55971-964-3). 32pp. An appealing look at the changing of the tides and the seashore and the effects on the varied life there. (Rev: BL 3/15/07) [577.69]

UNDERWATER EXPLORATION

3841   Lindop, Laurie. *Venturing the Deep Sea* (4–8). Series: Science on the Edge. 2005, Twenty-First Century LB $27.93 (0-7613-2701-0). 80pp. A behind-the-scenes look at the technology employed by modern-day undersea explorers, with a clear explanation of the types of knowledge these researchers are seeking. (Rev: SLJ 8/06; VOYA 4/06) [551.46]

3842   Mallory, Kenneth. *Diving to a Deep-Sea Volcano* (4–7). Illus. 2006, Houghton $17.00 (0-618-

33205-7). 64pp. Take a dive with marine biologists as they explore deep-sea volcanoes and the creatures that live and thrive around them; scientific method, adventure, biography, and insight into a career are intertwined in this portrait of a marine biologist's work in an underwater habitat. (Rev: BL 12/1/06; SLJ 2/07) [551.2]

3843 Sandler, Michael. *Oceans: Surviving in the Deep Sea* (3–5). Illus. Series: X-treme Places. 2005, Bearport LB $22.60 (1-59716-087-3). 32pp. This overview of the deep ocean environment is given added punch by the first-person account of marine biologist Dr. Sylvia Earle, who has explored the ocean depths in submersibles and pressurized suits. (Rev: SLJ 1/06) [551.46]

Pets

GENERAL AND MISCELLANEOUS

3844 Barnes, Julia. *Pet Guinea Pigs* (2–5). 2006, Gareth Stevens LB $23.93 (978-0-8368-6779-4). 32pp. This handy guide full of advice on caring for a guinea pig also examines the qualities that make them desirable pets, looks at how they communicate, and explores the guinea pig's roots in the wild. Also use *Pet Rabbits* (2006). (Rev: SLJ 2/07) [636.9]

3845 Barnes, Julia. *Pet Parakeets* (2–5). 2006, Gareth Stevens LB $23.93 (0-8368-6780-7). 32pp. This handy guide full of advice on caring for a parakeet also examines the qualities that make them such popular pets, looks at how they communicate, and explores their roots in the wild. (Rev: SLJ 12/06) [636.6]

3846 Richardson, Adele. *Caring for Your Hamster* (K–3). Illus. Series: First Facts, Positively Pets. 2006, Capstone LB $21.26 (0-7368-6387-7). 24pp. Hamster selection, care and feeding, health, safety, relations in the wild, and behavior are all covered in this attractive, concise title that includes commentary by a cartoon hamster. (Rev: SLJ 12/06) [636]

3847 Richardson, Adele. *Caring for Your Hermit Crab* (K–3). Illus. Series: First Facts, Positively Pets. 2006, Capstone LB $21.26 (0-7368-6388-5). 24pp. Hermit crab selection, care and feeding, health, safety, and roots in the wild are all covered in this attractive, concise title that includes commentary by a cartoon crab. (Rev: SLJ 12/06) [639]

3848 Verdick, Elizabeth. *Tails Are Not for Pulling* (PS). Illus. by Marieka Heinlen. 2005, Free Spirit $7.95 (1-57542-180-1). Preschoolers will learn the right and wrong way to play with a pet from this simple board book. (Rev: SLJ 6/06) [636.088]

CATS

3849 Barnes, Julia. *Pet Cats* (3–5). Illus. Series: Pet Pals. 2006, Gareth Stevens $17.95 (0-8368-6776-9). 32pp. This guide to cats provides tips about care and feeding as well as exploring cat behavior, human-feline interaction, and the diversity of cat breeds. (Rev: BL 10/15/06; SLJ 2/07) [636.8]

3850 Bidner, Jenni. *Is My Cat a Tiger? How Your Pet Compares to Its Wild Cousins* (3–5). Illus. 2007, Sterling $9.95 (978-1-57990-815-7). 64pp. Clearly written and illustrated with crisp photos, this book examines cats' behavior in relationship to the larger cat family, presenting information about the body language and curious antics of these pets. (Rev: BL 1/1–15/07) [636.8]

3851 Roca, Núria. *Let's Take Care of Our New Cat* (K–3). Illus. by Rosa M. Curto. Series: Let's Take Care of. 2006, Barron's paper $6.99 (978-0-7641-3452-4). 35pp. An appealing introduction to the care and feeding of a cat, with watercolor illustrations. (Rev: SLJ 2/07) [636.8]

3852 Singer, Marilyn. *Cats to the Rescue* (4–7). Illus. by Jean Cassels. 2006, Holt $16.95 (0-8050-7433-3). 160pp. This collection of true cat stories focuses on feats ranging from catching tens of thousands of mice to detecting a gas leak. (Rev: BL 9/15/06; SLJ 11/06) [636.8]

DOGS

3853 Anderson, Bendix. *Security Dogs* (2–4). Illus. Series: Dog Heroes. 2005, Bearport LB $22.60 (1-59716-015-6). 32pp. Features dogs who work to keep people safe, with photographs and factoids emphasizing their helpfulness to humans. (Rev: SLJ 8/05) [363.2]

3854 Barnes, Julia. *Pet Dogs* (2–5). 2006, Gareth Stevens LB $23.93 (978-0-8368-6777-0). 32pp. This handy guide full of advice on caring for a dog also examines the qualities that make cats such popular pets, looks at how they communicate, and explores the dog's roots in the wild. (Rev: SLJ 2/07) [636.7]

3855 Bidner, Jenni. *Is My Dog a Wolf? How Your Dog Compares to Its Wild Cousin* (4–6). 2006, Sterling $9.95 (1-57990-732-6). 64pp. Using many vivid photographs, this is a fascinating look at the similarities — and differences — between domestic dogs and wild wolves. (Rev: BL 9/1/06; SLJ 10/06) [636.7]

3856 Calmenson, Stephanie. *May I Pet Your Dog? The How-to Guide for Kids Meeting Dogs (and Dogs Meeting Kids)* (PS–2). Illus. by Jan Ormerod. 2007, Clarion $9.95 (978-0-618-51034-4). 32pp. A dachshund named Harry patiently explains how to approach an unfamiliar dog. (Rev: SLJ 4/07)

3857 Collard, Sneed B., III. *Shep: Our Most Loyal Dog* (2–4). Illus. by Joanna Yardley. 2006, Sleeping Bear $16.95 (1-58536-259-X). This is the moving story of Shep, a sheepdog that watched its master's coffin being loaded onto a train in Montana and met every passenger train arriving at that station from that day until his death more than five years later. (Rev: SLJ 8/06) [636.737]

3858 Coren, Stanley. *Why Do Dogs Have Wet Noses?* (2–4). Illus. 2006, Kids Can $12.95 (1-55337-657-9). 64pp. The famous dog expert offers a wealth of doggy facts in an appealing format suited more to browsing than report writing. (Rev: BL 4/15/06; SLJ 5/06) [636.7]

3859 Guy, Ginger Foglesong. *Perros! Perros! / Dogs! Dogs! A Story in English and Spanish* (PS–K). Illus. by Sharon Glick. 2006, Greenwillow $15.99 (0-06-083574-5). 32pp. Dogs of all sizes and shapes are the focus of this simple bilingual book. (Rev: BL 9/1/06; SLJ 10/06) [468.1]

3860 Halls, Kelly Milner. *Wild Dogs: Past and Present* (4–7). Illus. 2005, Darby Creek $18.95 (1-58196-027-1). 64pp. A wide-ranging introduction to dogs and their history, with attractive design, many photographs, and lots of factboxes about dogs both wild and domestic. (Rev: BL 12/1/05; SLJ 11/05) [599.77]

3861 McDaniel, Melissa. *Disaster Search Dogs* (2–4). Illus. Series: Dog Heroes. 2005, Bearport LB $22.60 (1-59716-012-1). 32pp. Dogs that work to find people in trouble are the focus of this photo-filled volume. Also use *Guide Dogs* (2005). (Rev: SLJ 8/05) [363.2]

3862 O'Sullivan, Robyn. *More than Man's Best Friend: The Story of Working Dogs* (2–4). Illus. Series: National Geographic Science Chapters. 2006, National Geographic $17.90 (0-7922-5940-8). 40pp. Six chapters look at the different kinds of jobs performed by working dogs; photos and easy vocabulary make this suitable for young readers. (Rev: BL 10/15/06) [636.7]

3863 Roca, Núria. *Let's Take Care of Our New Dog* (K–3). Illus. by Rosa M. Curto. Series: Let's Take Care of . . . 2006, Barron's paper $6.99 (978-0-7641-3455-5). 35pp. An appealing introduction to the care and feeding of a dog, with watercolor illustrations. (Rev: SLJ 2/07) [636.7]

3864 Tagliaferro, Linda. *Therapy Dogs* (2–4). Illus. Series: Dog Heroes. 2005, Bearport LB $22.60 (1-59716-018-0). 32pp. Features dogs that work to help people with special needs, with photographs and factoids emphasizing their helpfulness to humans. (Rev: SLJ 8/05) [363.2]

3865 Williams, Chris. *One Incredible Dog! Kizzy* (1–5). Illus. by Judith Friedman. 2006, Keene LB $15.95 (978-0-9766805-5-0). This photoessay documents a day in the life of Kizzy, a therapy dog that offers a kind and interested ear to children and adults practicing reading and speaking. (Rev: SLJ 2/07) [636.7]

FISH

3866 Barnes, Julia. *Pet Goldfish* (2–5). Series: Pet Pals. 2006, Gareth Stevens LB $23.93 (0-8368-6778-5). 32pp. This handy guide full of advice on caring for goldfish also examines their history. (Rev: SLJ 12/06) [639.3]

3867 Richardson, Adele. *Caring for Your Fish* (K–3). Illus. Series: First Facts, Positively Pets. 2006, Capstone LB $21.26 (0-7368-6386-9). 24pp. Fish selection, care and feeding, health, and safety are all covered in this attractive, concise title that includes commentary by a cartoon fish. (Rev: SLJ 12/06) [639.34]

HORSES AND PONIES

3868 Barnes, Julia. *Horses at Work* (3–5). Series: Animals at Work. 2006, Gareth Stevens LB $23.33 (0-8368-6225-2). 32pp. Full-color photographs show horses working in many roles and the text discusses the animal's physical characteristics, ability to learn commands, and relationship with humans. (Rev: SLJ 1/07) [636.1]

3869 Crisp, Marty. *Everything Horse: What Kids Really Want to Know About Horses* (3–5). Series: Kids' FAQs. 2005, NorthWord $10.95 (1-55971-920-6); paper $7.95 (1-55971-921-4). 63pp. Answers to frequently asked questions about horses, with photographs and a diagram of a horse's body. (Rev: SLJ 9/05)

3870 Draper, Judith. *My First Horse and Pony Book* (2–4). Illus. 2005, Kingfisher $9.95 (0-7534-5878-0). 48pp. All about looking after and riding horses and ponies, with details of the animals' physical characteristics and discussion of Western and English riding, proper clothing, jumping, and so forth. (Rev: BL 7/05; SLJ 8/05) [636.1]

3871 Draper, Judith. *My First Horse and Pony Care Book* (2–4). Photos by Matthew Roberts. 2006, Kingfisher $9.95 (0-7534-5989-2). 48pp. Feeding, grooming, tack cleaning, and safety tips are all covered in this British import that focuses on English-style equipment. (Rev: SLJ 1/07) [636.1]

3872 Funny Cide Team. *A Horse Named Funny Cide* (2–4). Illus. by Barry Moser. 2006, Putnam $16.99 (0-399-24462-X). 32pp. This is a beautifully illustrated tribute to the little race horse that overcame a number of obstacles to win both the Kentucky Derby and Preakness in 2003. (Rev: BL 4/15/06; SLJ 5/06) [798.4]

3873 Hansen, Rosanna. *Panda: A Guide Horse for Ann* (3–5). Illus. by Neil Soderstrom. 2005, Boyds Mills $19.95 (1-59078-184-8). 48pp. This photoessay presents the heartwarming story of Panda, a miniature horse trained to be a guide for a blind woman. (Rev: BL 1/1–15/06; SLJ 10/05) [362.40483]

3874 McKerley, Jennifer. *Man o' War: Best Racehorse Ever* (1–3). Illus. by Terry Widener. Series: Step into Reading. 2005, Random LB $11.99 (0-375-93164-3); paper $3.99 (0-375-83164-9). 48pp. The exciting story of the famous, independent-minded racehorse who was the grandfather of Seabiscuit. (Rev: BL 11/1/05; SLJ 1/06) [798.4]

3875 Simon, Seymour. *Horses* (2–4). Illus. 2006, HarperCollins $15.99 (0-06-028944-9). 40pp. Basic facts about horses — their history, physical characteristics, breeds, and so forth — are accompanied by eye-catching photographs. (Rev: BL 12/1/05; SLJ 2/06) [636.1]

3876 Yerxa, Leo. *Ancient Thunder* (K–3). Illus. by author. 2006, Groundwood $18.95 (0-88899-746-9). This handsome book with a spare text and illustrations that appear to be painted shirts celebrates the wild horses that roamed the Great Plains and their contributions to the Native Americans living there. (Rev: SLJ 11/06) [599.665]

Zoos and Marine Aquariums

3877 Zoehfeld, Kathleen W. *Wild Lives: A History of the People and Animals of the Bronx Zoo* (4–7). Illus. 2006, Knopf LB $20.99 (0-375-90630-4). 96pp. The colorful history of the Bronx Zoo, which opened in 1899, is presented with many photographs and with discussion of changing trends in zookeeping. (Rev: BL 3/15/06; SLJ 6/06) [590.73747]

Botany

General and Miscellaneous

3878 Kudlinski, Kathleen V. *What Do Roots Do?* (K–3). Illus. by David Schuppert. 2005, NorthWord $15.95 (1-55971-896-X). This colorfully illustrated picture book explores in rhyming verse the role of roots in the lives of plants, flowers, and trees. (Rev: SLJ 12/05) [581.4]

Flowers

3879 Farndon, John. *Flowers* (2–5). Illus. Series: World of Plants. 2006, Gale LB $22.45 (1-4103-0423-X). 24pp. Diagrams and photographs supplement the clear text describing flowers and the role they play in the overall life of the plant. (Rev: SLJ 2/07)

Foods and Farming

GENERAL

3880 Jango-Cohen, Judith. *The History of Food* (5–8). Series: Major Inventions Through History. 2005, Twenty-First Century LB $26.60 (0-8225-2484-8). 56pp. Addresses inventions in the food industry such as canning, pasteurization, and genetically modified crops. (Rev: SLJ 2/06)

FARMS, RANCHES, AND FARM ANIMALS

3881 Ghione, Yvette. *This Is Daniel Cook at the Farm* (K–3). 2006, Kids Can $12.95 (1-55453-077-6); paper $4.95 (1-55453-078-4). In this companion to the popular Canadian-produced TV show, the young host invites readers to join him on a journey of discovery around a busy farmyard. (Rev: SLJ 11/06) [636]

3882 Pipe, Jim. *Farm Animals* (PS–1). Illus. Series: Read and Play. 2007, Stargazer LB $15.95 (978-1-59604-112-7). 32pp. Very basic facts about farm animals are presented with eye-catching photographs and a "Let's Play" section with easy games. (Rev: BL 4/15/07) [636]

3883 Sweeney, Alyse. *Let's Visit a Dairy Farm* (K–2). Series: Scholastic News Nonfiction Readers. 2006, Children's Pr. LB $19.00 (0-531-16843-3). 24pp. Basic information for beginning readers, with seven highlighted words that are featured in bold in the text. (Rev: SLJ 1/07) [069]

3884 Urbigkit, Cat. *A Young Shepherd* (1–3). Illus. 2006, Boyds Mills $15.95 (1-59078-364-6). 32pp. This photoessay documents a year in the life of a 12-year-old boy who tends his own sheep on a Wyoming ranch. (Rev: BL 2/15/06; SLJ 5/06) [636]

FOODS

3885 Cobb, Vicki. *Junk Food* (3–5). Illus. by Michael Gold. Series: Where's the Science Here? 2005, Millbrook LB $23.93 (0-7613-2773-8). 48pp. Candy, corn chips, and soda are among the popular products explored here; clear text and easy projects will grab attention. (Rev: BL 10/15/05; HBG 4/06; SLJ 2/06) [664]

3886 Eagen, Rachel. *The Biography of Bananas* (4–7). Illus. Series: How Did That Get Here? 2005, Crabtree LB $17.94 (0-7787-2483-2). 32pp. This richly illustrated title offers a wealth of information about the science and business of producing bananas. (Rev: BL 3/1/06) [634]

3887 Gibbons, Gail. *Ice Cream: The Full Scoop* (K–2). 2006, Holiday $16.95 (0-8234-2000-0). 32pp. A delicious history of ice cream from the days of Marco Polo to the present, with a tour of a contemporary factory. (Rev: BL 6/1–15/06; SLJ 8/06) [641.8]

3888 Morris, Neil. *Do You Know Where Your Food Comes From?* (4–7). Illus. 2006, Heinemann LB $23.00 (1-4034-8575-5). 56pp. In this informative book students learn all about the global food market, where and how their food is produced, and how to make good food choices. (Rev: BL 12/1/06) [363.8]

3889 Ridley, Sarah. *A Chocolate Bar* (3–5). Illus. Series: How It's Made. 2006, Gareth Stevens LB $23.33 (0-8368-6293-7). 32pp. This attractive volume traces the history of a chocolate bar from a cacao farm in Ghana to the factory in which the final product is made; suitable both for reports and browsing. (Rev: BL 4/1/06) [664]

3890 Rotner, Shelley, and Gary Goss. *Where Does Food Come From?* (PS–2). Illus. 2006, Millbrook LB $22.60 (0-7613-2935-8). 32pp. The origins of the foods we eat — and the many varieties available — are presented in simple, informative text and color photographs. (Rev: BL 3/1/06; SLJ 5/06) [664]

3891 Royston, Angela. *How Is Chocolate Made?* (2–4). Illus. Series: How Are Things Made? 2005, Heinemann LB $16.95 (1-4034-6641-6). 32pp. Follows the chocolate manufacturing process from the harvesting of cacao beans to the delivery of the finished product to a retailer's shelves. (Rev: BL 9/15/05) [641.3]

FRUITS

3892 Ganeri, Anita. *From Seed to Apple* (1–3). Illus. Series: How Living Things Grow. 2006, Heinemann LB $25.36 (1-4034-7862-7). 32pp. How a Red Delicious apple grows from a seed, presented in an easy-to-read format. (Rev: SLJ 6/06) [583]

3893 Robbins, Ken. *Pumpkins* (PS–2). 2006, Roaring Brook $14.95 (1-59643-184-9). 32pp. Full of dramatic color photographs, this celebration of the pumpkin traces its growing cycle and offers step-by-step instructions for carving a jack-o'-lantern. (Rev: BL 9/1/06; SLJ 8/06) [635]

Leaves and Trees

3894 Farndon, John. *Leaves* (2–5). Illus. 2006, Gale LB $22.45 (1-4103-0422-1). 24pp. Diagrams and photographs supplement the clear text describing leaves and the role they play in the overall life of the plant. (Rev: SLJ 2/07)

Plants

3895 Farndon, John. *Roots* (2–5). Illus. 2006, Gale LB $22.45 (1-4103-0421-3). 24pp. Diagrams and photographs supplement the clear text describing roots and the role they play in the overall life of the plant. Also use *Stems* (2006). (Rev: SLJ 2/07)

Seeds

3896 Aston, Dianna Hutts. *A Seed Is Sleepy* (PS–2). Illus. by Sylvia Long. 2007, Chronicle $16.95 (978-0-8118-5520-4). 32pp. Using poetic text and lush watercolors, this picture book explores the mysteries of seeds and how they are transformed into colorful plants and flowers of very varying sizes. (Rev: BL 3/15/07) [581.4]

3897 Farndon, John. *Seeds* (2–5). Illus. 2006, Gale LB $22.45 (1-4103-0419-1). 24pp. Diagrams and photographs supplement the clear text describing seeds and the role they play in the overall life of the plant. (Rev: SLJ 2/07)

Geology and Geography

Earth and Geology

3898 Calhoun, Yael. *Earth Science Fair Projects Using Rocks, Minerals, Magnets, Mud, and More* (5–8). Illus. Series: Earth Science! Best Science Projects. 2005, Enslow LB $19.95 (0-7660-2363-X). 128pp. More than 20 geology-related projects are introduced with clear instructions and interesting background information. (Rev: BL 11/1/05) [550]

3899 Gardner, Robert. *Super Science Projects About Earth's Soil and Water* (3–5). Illus. Series: Rockin' Earth Science Experiments. 2007, Enslow LB $17.95 (0-7660-2735-X). 48pp. The experiments and projects outlined here teach important lessons about soil and water, touching on such topics as the makeup of soil, evaporation, and pollution of aquifers; scientific principles are reinforced, and symbols flag projects especially suited to science fairs. (Rev: BL 4/1/07) [631.4078]

3900 Storad, Conrad J. *Earth's Crust* (2–4). Series: Early Bird Earth Science. 2006, Lerner $25.25 (0-8225-5944-7). 48pp. This attractive, readable overview of the earth's geological makeup examines the structure of the planet, changes in its crust, plate tectonics, and such features as mountains, volcanoes, and faults. (Rev: BL 9/1/06; SLJ 1/07) [851.1]

Earthquakes and Volcanoes

3901 Green, Emily K. *Volcanoes* (2–4). Series: Blastoff! Readers: Learning About the Earth. 2006, Children's Pr. LB $18.50 (0-531-17893-5). 24pp. A basic, photo-filled introduction to volcanoes, examining in double-page spreads with brief text their formation and what happens during an eruption. (Rev: BL 10/15/06) [551.21]

3902 Harper, Kristine C. *The Mount St. Helens Volcanic Eruptions* (5–8). Series: Environmental Disasters. 2005, Facts on File $35.00 (0-8160-5757-5). 100pp. The environment impact of Mount St. Helens' eruptions is examined in this title from the Environmental Disasters series. (Rev: SLJ 11/05)

3903 Woods, Michael, and Mary B. Woods. *Volcanoes* (4–6). Series: Disasters Up Close. 2006, Lerner LB $27.93 (0-8225-4715-5). 64pp. With charts, photographs, and quotes from survivors, this book clearly demonstrates the devastating power of volcanic eruptions, and provides information on the formation of volcanoes and the ways we measure their activity. (Rev: SLJ 1/07) [551.21]

3904 Worth, Richard. *The San Francisco Earthquake* (5–8). Illus. Series: Environmental Disasters. 2005, Facts on File $35.00 (0-8160-5756-7). 100pp. Worth examines how the San Francisco earthquake of 1906 affected the region's environment. (Rev: SLJ 11/05) [363.34]

Icebergs and Glaciers

3905 Harrison, David L. *Glaciers: Nature's Icy Caps* (1–3). Illus. by Cheryl Nathan. Series: Earthworks. 2006, Boyds Mills $15.95 (1-59078-372-7). 32pp. A solid introduction to glaciers, with digital illustrations and large maps. (Rev: BL 4/1/06; SLJ 8/06) [551.31]

Physical Geography

General and Miscellaneous

3906 Banting, Erinn. *Caves* (4–6). Illus. Series: Biomes. 2006, Weigl LB $26.00 (1-59036-436-8). 32pp. Five different types of caves are covered here, with information on physical characteristics, climate, plants and animals, the science and technology used by researchers, and related careers. (Rev: SLJ 12/06) [577.5]

3907 De Medeiros, Michael. *Chaparrals* (4–6). Illus. Series: Biomes. 2006, Weigl LB $26.00 (1-59036-438-4). 32pp. Along with the physical characteristics of a chapparal, this volume looks at climate, plants and animals, the science and technology used by researchers, and related careers. (Rev: SLJ 12/06) [577.38]

3908 Marsico, Katie. *A Home on the Tundra* (1–3). 2006, Children's Pr. LB $19.00 (978-0-516-25345-9). 24pp. This easy-to-understand introduction to the tundra as a natural habitat looks at the nature of the land itself, its climate, flora, and the animals that call it home. (Rev: SLJ 2/07) [577.5]

3909 Zollman, Pam. *Gulf of Mexico* (1–2). Series: Rookie Read-About Geography. 2006, Children's Pr. LB $19.50 (0-516-25035-3). 32pp. Geographical and geological facts about this body of water are presented in an airy format that will appeal to beginning readers. (Rev: SLJ 6/06) [911.6364]

Deserts

3910 Moss, Miriam. *This Is the Oasis* (K–2). Illus. by Adrienne Kennaway. 2005, Kane/Miller $14.95 (1-929132-76-X). Lush illustrations enhance this large-format introduction to the people, plants, and animals of a Saharan oasis. (Rev: SLJ 3/06) [574.5]

3911 Sandler, Michael. *Deserts: Surviving in the Sahara* (3–5). Illus. Series: X-treme Places. 2005, Bearport LB $22.60 (1-59716-085-7). 32pp. A compelling overview of deserts and the challenges to their human and animal inhabitants is given added punch by the inclusion of the story of René Caillié, who crossed the Sahara in 1828. (Rev: SLJ 1/06) [916.6]

3912 Sill, Cathryn. *Deserts* (1–4). Illus. by John Sill. Series: About Habitats. 2007, Peachtree $16.95 (978-1-56145-390-0). 48pp. The landscape, flora, and fauna of the desert are introduced in appealing illustrations and accessible text. (Rev: BL 4/1/07) [577.54]

Forests and Rain Forests

3913 Aspen-Baxter, Linda. *Rain Forests* (4–6). Illus. Series: Biomes. 2006, Weigl LB $26.00 (1-59036-446-5). 32pp. Both tropical and temperate rain forests are covered here, with information on physical characteristics, climate, plants and animals, the science and technology used by researchers, and related careers. (Rev: SLJ 12/06) [574.5]

3914 Godkin, Celia. *Fire!* (1–3). 2006, Fitzhenry & Whiteside $17.95 (1-55041-889-0). 40pp. Double-page spreads show the role fire plays in forest ecology, with a frightening blaze followed by returning animals and plants. (Rev: BL 8/06; SLJ 11/06) [577.24]

3915 Hurtig, Jennifer. *Deciduous Forests* (4–6). Illus. Series: Biomes. 2006, Weigl LB $26.00 (1-59036-440-6). 32pp. Along with the physical characteristics of deciduous forests, this volume looks at climate, plants and animals, the science and technology used by researchers, and related careers. (Rev: SLJ 12/06) [577.3]

3916 Morrison, Taylor. *Wildfire* (4–6). Illus. 2006, Houghton $17.00 (0-618-50900-3). 48pp. Explores the contradiction between the destruction caused by wildfires and their beneficial impact on forests; with descriptions of the roles of firefighters, scientists, and foresters. (Rev: BL 4/1/06; SLJ 5/06) [634.9]

3917 Sandler, Michael. *Rain Forests: Surviving in the Amazon* (3–5). Illus. Series: X-treme Places. 2005, Bearport LB $22.60 (1-59716-089-X). 32pp. This colorful overview of the world's rain forests includes the harrowing survival story of Yossi Ghinsberg, who became lost in the wilds of the Amazon basin. (Rev: SLJ 1/06) [578.734]

Mountains

3918 Gill, Shelley. *Up on Denali* (2–4). Illus. by Shannon Cartwright. 2006, Sasquatch $16.95 (1-57061-366-4); paper $10.95 (1-57061-365-6). 32pp. Explores the geology and plants and animals of Denali, North America's tallest mountain, in an appealing and humorous blend of fact and fiction. (Rev: BL 6/1–15/06) [551.43]

3919 Harrison, David L. *Mountains: The Tops of the World* (1–3). Illus. by Cheryl Nathan. 2005, Boyds Mills $15.95 (1-59078-326-3). 32pp. Explores the ways in which mountains were created and provides explanations for such puzzling phenomena as the discovery of a fish fossil on a mountaintop. (Rev: BL 11/1/05; SLJ 10/05) [551.43]

3920 Sandler, Michael. *Mountains: Surviving on Mt. Everest* (3–5). Series: X-treme Places. 2005, Bearport LB $22.60 (1-59716-086-5). 32pp. The first-person account of Temba Tsheri Sherpa, a Nepalese climber who lost fingers to frostbite during a successful assault on Mount Everest, gives added punch to this overview of mountain climbing. (Rev: SLJ 1/06) [796.52]

3921 Tocci, Salvatore. *Alpine Tundra: Life on the Tallest Mountain* (4–7). Series: Biomes and Habitats. 2005, Watts LB $24.50 (0-531-12365-0). 63pp. Introduces the climate, flora, and fauna found high above sea level on the world's highest mountains. Also use *Arctic Tundra: Life at the North Pole* (2005). (Rev: SLJ 7/05) [577.5]

Ponds, Rivers, and Lakes

3922 Bryan, Dale-Marie. *The Colorado River* (1–2). Series: Rookie Read-About Geography. 2006, Children's Pr. LB $19.50 (0-516-25033-7). 32pp. Beginning readers and report writers will get all the facts about this grand river in this well-designed book. (Rev: SLJ 6/06) [917.91]

3923 Castaldo, Nancy. *River Wild: An Activity Guide to North American Rivers* (4–7). Illus. 2006, Chicago Review $14.95 (1-55652-585-0). 150pp. From a general introduction to the water cycle and watersheds, this volume narrows in on specific rivers in North America and the flora and fauna found there, even offering profiles of riverkeepers. (Rev: BL 3/1/06; SLJ 6/06) [372.8991]

3924 Schulte, Mary. *Great Salt Lake* (1–2). Series: Rookie Read-About Geography. 2006, Children's Pr. LB $19.50 (0-516-25034-5). 32pp. Beginning readers and report writers will get all the facts about this unusual lake in this well-designed book. (Rev: SLJ 6/06) [979.2]

3925 Viera, Linda. *The Mighty Mississippi: The Life and Times of America's Greatest River* (3–5). Illus. by Higgins Bond. 2005, Walker $16.95 (0-8027-8943-9). 32pp. Viera explores the geology and history of America's mighty Mississippi River. (Rev: BL 10/1/05; SLJ 11/05) [917.7]

3926 Wechsler, Doug. *Frog Heaven: Ecology of a Vernal Pool* (3–6). 2006, Boyds Mills $17.95 (1-59078-253-4). 48pp. This is a vivid, richly illustrated, and thorough exploration of life in a vernal pool in Delaware over the period of a year. (Rev: BL 11/1/06*; HBG 4/07; LMC 3/08; SLJ 11/06) [577.63]

3927 Zollman, Pam. *Lake Tahoe* (1–2). Series: Rookie Read-About Geography. 2006, Children's Pr. LB $19.50 (0-516-25036-1). 32pp. Geographical and geological facts about this body of water are presented in an airy format that will appeal to beginning readers. (Rev: SLJ 6/06) [917.9438]

Prairies and Grasslands

3928 Lion, David C. *A Home on the Prairie* (1–3). Series: Scholastic News Nonfiction Readers. 2006, Children's Pr. LB $19.00 (978-0-516-25346-6). 24pp. This easy-to-understand introduction to the prairie as a natural habitat looks at the nature of the land itself, its climate, flora, and the animals that call it home. (Rev: SLJ 2/07) [574.5]

3929 Toupin, Laurie Peach. *Life in the Temperate Grasslands* (4–7). Series: Biomes and Habitats. 2005, Watts LB $24.50 (0-531-12385-5). 63pp. Introduces the climatic conditions, plants, and wildlife of the world's temperate grasslands. Also use *Savannas: Life in the Tropical Grasslands* (2005). (Rev: SLJ 7/05) [577.4]

Rocks, Minerals, and Soil

3930 Estigarribia, Diana. *Learning About Rocks, Weathering, and Erosion with Graphic Organizers* (3–6). Series: Graphic Organizers in Science. 2005, Rosen LB $19.95 (1-4042-2806-3). 24pp. This title uses a wide variety of graphic organizers, including concept webs, compare/contrast charts, Venn diagrams, graphs, timelines, and KWL charts, to illustrate geological concepts. (Rev: SLJ 11/05)

3931 Farndon, John. *Rock and Mineral* (5–9). Illus. Series: DK/Google e.guides. 2005, DK $17.99 (0-7566-1140-7). 96pp. This highly illustrated guide introduces readers to the basics of geology and provides a link to a Web site that serves as a gateway to additional resources. (Rev: SLJ 8/05) [552]

3932 Walker, Sally M. *Rocks* (2–4). Series: Early Bird Earth Science. 2006, Lerner LB $25.26 (0-8225-5947-1). 48pp. This attractive, readable overview of rocks and crystals examines the three families into which rocks are divided and also how they're formed. (Rev: BL 9/1/06; SLJ 1/07) [352]

Mathematics

General

3933 Barasch, Lynne. *Ask Albert Einstein* (3–5). Illus. 2005, Farrar $16.00 (0-374-30435-1). 40pp. In 1952 Princeton, 7-year-old April asks Albert Einstein to help her older sister with a math problem and he sends her a clue; based on a newspaper article at the time. (Rev: BL 9/1/05; SLJ 1/06) [530]

3934 Cleary, Brian P. *The Action of Subtraction* (K–4). Illus. by Brian Gable. Series: Math Is CATegorical. 2006, Millbrook LB $15.95 (1-7613-9461-3). 32pp. Cartoon-style illustrations and a rap-style rhyming text introduce subtraction with child-friendly examples. (Rev: SLJ 11/06) [513.2]

3935 Goldstone, Bruce. *Great Estimations* (2–4). 2006, Holt $16.95 (0-8050-7446-5). 32pp. Through eye-catching photographs of well-arranged items, readers learn progressively to recognize larger and larger quantities, from groupings of 10 to 100 to 1000, and then to estimate amounts. (Rev: BL 9/1/06; SLJ 11/06) [519.5]

3936 Leech, Bonnie Coulter. *Mesopotamia: Creating and Solving Word Problems* (4–8). Series: Math for the Real World. 2007, Rosen LB $23.95 (1-4042-3357-1). 32pp. Ancient number systems are among the mathematical concepts highlighted in this overview of the civilization of Mesopotamia that covers its people, buildings, writings, and calendars. (Rev: SLJ 2/07) [510]

3937 Leedy, Loreen. *It's Probably Penny* (1–3). Illus. 2007, Holt $16.95 (978-0-8050-7389-8). 32pp. Lisa uses her dog Penny to anchor her probability calculations — for example, Will Penny want to go for a walk? (Rev: BL 4/1/07) [519.2]

3938 Mattern, Joanne. *I Use Math at the Doctor's / Uso las matemáticas en el médico* (K–2). Trans. by Tatiana Acosta and Guillermo Gutiérrez. Photos by Gregg Andersen. Series: I Use Math / Uso las matemáticas. 2005, Weekly Reader LB $19.33 (0-8368-5999-5). 24pp. A bilingual visit to the doctor's office, where a child is weighed and measured, and his heartbeats are counted. Also use *I Use Math at the Store*, *I Use Math in the Kitchen*, and *I Use Math on a Trip* (all 2005). (Rev: SLJ 2/06) [618.92]

3939 Murphy, Stuart J. *Mall Mania* (K–2). Illus. by Renée Andriani. Series: MathStart. 2006, HarperCollins $15.99 (0-06-055776-1); paper $4.99 (0-06-055776-X). 40pp. Who will be the 100th person to enter Parkside Mall? Children counting the shoppers learn addition strategies. (Rev: BL 2/1/06) [513.2]

3940 Murphy, Stuart J. *Same Old Horse* (1–3). Illus. by Steven Björkman. Series: MathStart. 2005, HarperCollins $15.99 (0-06-055770-2); paper $4.99 (0-06-055771-0). 40pp. The story of a horse whose life has become boring and routine is used to explain how to predict the future based on the past. (Rev: BL 9/1/05; SLJ 3/06) [519.2]

3941 Neuschwander, Cindy. *Sir Cumference and the Isle of Immeter: A Math Adventure* (3–6). Illus. by Wayne Geehan. 2006, Charlesbridge paper $6.95 (1-57091-681-0). 32pp. Per pays a visit to her uncle and aunt — Sir Cumference and Lady Di of Ameter — and with her cousin Radius uses skills of establishing perimeter and area to solve a riddle about the Isle of Immeter. (Rev: SLJ 8/06) [516]

3942 Reisberg, Joanne A. *Zachary Zormer: Shape Transformer* (2–4). Illus. by David Hohn. Series: Math Adventures. 2006, Charlesbridge paper $6.95 (1-57091-876-7). 32pp. A forgetful but resourceful student comes up with some ingenious ways to measure area, perimeter, length, and width. (Rev: SLJ 8/06) [516]

3943 Ribke, Simone T. *Grouping at the Dog Show* (1–2). Series: Rookie Read-about Math. 2006, Children's Pr. LB $19.50 (0-516-24959-2). 32pp. For beginning readers, an introduction to the concept of grouping, using different attributes of different breeds of dogs. (Rev: SLJ 6/06) [511.3]

3944 Ribke, Simone T. *Pet Store Subtraction* (K–2). Series: Rookie Read-about Math. 2006, Children's Pr. LB $20.50 (0-516-29673-6). 32pp. A pet store employee uses subtraction skills to determine how many new animals and supplies she needs to order. (Rev: SLJ 12/06) [513.2]

3945 Roy, Jennifer, and Gregory Roy. *Graphing in the Desert* (2–4). Series: Math All Around. 2006, Benchmark LB $19.95 (0-7614-2262-5). 32pp. Introduces different types of graphs and uses them to convey information about the Sonoran Desert and its flora and fauna. (Rev: SLJ 12/06) [518]

3946 Roy, Jennifer, and Gregory Roy. *Multiplication on the Farm* (2–4). Illus. Series: Math All Around. 2006, Benchmark LB $19.95 (0-7614-2268-4). 32pp. This title focuses on multiplication and gives multiple examples of how it can be used to make important calculations on the farm. (Rev: SLJ 12/06) [513.2]

3947 Roy, Jennifer, and Gregory Roy. *Subtraction at School* (K–3). Series: Math All Around. 2005, Benchmark LB $25.64 (0-7614-2003-7). 32pp. Everyday situations are used to illustrate the principles of subtraction. Also use *Sorting at the Ocean* and *Patterns in Nature* (both 2005). (Rev: SLJ 3/06)

3948 Sargent, Brian. *Guess the Order* (1–2). Series: Rookie Read-about Math. 2006, Children's Pr. LB $19.50 (0-516-24963-0). 32pp. An introduction to the mathematical concept of placing things in order using pictures from a day at a carnival; for beginning readers. (Rev: SLJ 6/06) [513.2]

3949 Sargent, Brian. *Slumber Party Problem Solving* (1–2). Series: Rookie Read-about Math. 2006, Children's Pr. LB $19.50 (0-516-24962-2). 32pp. For beginning readers, this book has a girl using basic math to plan a slumber party. (Rev: SLJ 6/06) [513]

3950 Shea, Therese. *America's Electoral College: Choosing the President: Comparing and Analyzing Charts, Graphs, and Tables* (4–8). Series: Math for the Real World. 2007, Rosen LB $23.95 (1-4042-3358-X). 32pp. Results of various elections, including the controversial 2000 polls, are used to demonstrate fundamental mathematical principles. (Rev: SLJ 2/07) [324.6097]

3951 Shea, Therese. *The Great Barrier Reef: Using Graphs and Charts to Solve Word Problems* (4–8). Series: Math for the Real World. 2007, Rosen LB $23.95 (1-4042-3359-8). 32pp. Charts and graphs are used to show the number of species found on the

reef, the percentages of coral, the number of visitors, and so forth. (Rev: SLJ 2/07) [510]

3952 Shea, Therese. *The Transcontinental Railroad: Using Proportions to Solve Problems* (4–8). Series: Math for the Real World. 2007, Rosen LB $23.95 (1-4042-3361-X). 32pp. The cost of laying the track, number of rails laid in a period, and other interesting aspects of construction of the railroad are considered using ratios, proportions, and other mathematical techniques. (Rev: SLJ 2/07) [513.24]

3953 Stewart, Melissa. *Giraffe Graphs* (K–2). Series: Rookie Read-about Math. 2006, Children's Pr. LB $20.50 (0-516-23798-5). 32pp. Students on a class trip to the zoo use graphs and charts to keep track of the animals they've seen. (Rev: SLJ 12/06) [511]

3954 Sullivan, Navin. *Area, Distance, and Volume* (4–7). Illus. Series: Measure Up. 2006, Marshall Cavendish LB $20.95 (978-0-7614-2323-2). 44pp. Includes information on the history of measuring area, distance, and volume along with how to measure each and the devices used. (Rev: BL 2/15/07) [598.47]

3955 Wingard-Nelson, Rebecca. *Division Made Easy* (1–4). Illus. by Tom LaBaff. Series: Making Math Easy. 2005, Enslow LB $23.93 (0-7660-2511-X). 48pp. An easy-to-understand introduction to the fundamentals of division. Also use *Multiplication Made Easy* and *Word Problems Made Easy* (2005). (Rev: SLJ 1/06) [513.2]

Geometry

3956 Murphy, Stuart J. *Hamster Champs* (2–4). Illus. by Pedro Martin. Series: MathStart. 2005, HarperCollins $15.99 (0-06-055772-9). 40pp. This tale of three car-racing hamsters and their scheme to outwit a pesky cat provides a valuable lesson about angles. (Rev: BL 10/15/05; SLJ 3/06) [516]

3957 Roy, Jennifer, and Gregory Roy. *Shapes in Transportation* (2–4). Illus. Series: Math All Around. 2006, Benchmark LB $19.95 (0-7614-2265-X). 32pp. Using traffic signs, bridges, buildings, and other transport-related items, this volume introduces shapes of all kinds and discusses such topics as angles and dimensions. (Rev: SLJ 12/06) [516]

3958 Sargent, Brian. *Grandfather's Shape Story* (K–2). Series: Rookie Read-about Math. 2006, Children's Pr. LB $20.50 (0-516-29919-0). 32pp. A grandfather entertains his granddaughter with tangrams while telling her a story. (Rev: SLJ 12/06) [793.74]

Mathematical Puzzles

3959 Adler, David A. *You Can, Toucan, Math: Word Problem-Solving Fun* (1–3). Illus. by Edward Miller. 2006, Holiday $16.95 (0-8234-1919-3). 32pp. This collection of 20 bird-themed word problems — rhyming riddles posing math questions — covers the basics of addition, subtraction, multiplication, and division. (Rev: BL 8/06; HBG 4/07; SLJ 10/06) [511.3]

3960 Ball, Johnny. *Go Figure! A Totally Cool Book About Numbers* (4–7). Illus. 2005, DK $15.99 (0-7566-1374-4). 96pp. A fascinating volume for math-minded youngsters and adults, introducing number-related games and puzzles as well as more sophisticated mathematical disciplines, such as chaos theory, fractals, and topology. (Rev: BL 10/15/05; SLJ 1/06) [510]

3961 Fisher, Valorie. *How High Can a Dinosaur Count? And Other Math Mysteries* (1–3). Illus. 2006, Random $16.95 (0-375-83608-X). 40pp. Fifteen entertaining math mysteries are presented with interesting text and eye-catching illustrations. (Rev: BL 1/1–15/06; SLJ 2/06*) [513]

3962 Tang, Greg. *Math Potatoes: Mind-Stretching Brain Food* (3–5). Illus. by Harry Briggs. 2005, Scholastic $16.95 (0-439-44390-3). 40pp. Games involving humorous rhymes and appealing illustrations teach readers how to approach grouping numbers efficiently. (Rev: BL 7/05; SLJ 8/05) [793.74]

Statistics

3963 Leedy, Loreen. *The Great Graph Contest* (2–4). Illus. 2005, Holiday $16.95 (0-8234-1710-7). 32pp. Gonk the toad and Beezy the lizard compete in a graph contest in a lively tale displaying all kinds of graphs and methods of gathering data. (Rev: BL 8/05; SLJ 9/05*)

Time, Clocks, and Calendars

3964 Murphy, Stuart J. *Rodeo Time* (2–4). Illus. by David Wenzel. Series: MathStart. 2006, HarperCollins $15.99 (0-06-055778-8); paper $4.99 (0-06-055779-6). 40pp. While helping their uncle, a bull rider at the rodeo, Katie and Cameron learn some important lessons about time and schedules. (Rev: BL 3/1/06; SLJ 10/06) [529]

3965 Somervill, Barbara A. *The History of the Calendar* (3–6). Series: Our Changing World: The Timeline Library. 2006, The Child's World LB $27.07 (1-59296-436-2). 32pp. Two students and their teacher explore how different cultures have measured days, months, and years through the ages. (Rev: SLJ 7/06) [529]

Weights and Measures

3966 Chrismer, Melanie. *Math Tools* (1–2). Series: Rookie Read-about Math. 2006, Children's Pr. LB $19.50 (0-516-24961-4). 32pp. For beginning readers, an introduction to the tools used to measure distance, time, volume, and other quantities. (Rev: SLJ 6/06) [681]

3967 Roy, Jennifer, and Gregory Roy. *Measuring at Home* (2–4). Series: Math All Around. 2006, Benchmark LB $19.95 (0-7614-2263-3). 32pp. Everyday items such as a ruler, thermometer, and measuring cup are used to introduce the concepts of measuring area, weight, volume, and time. (Rev: SLJ 12/06) [516]

Meteorology

Air

3968 Kaner, Etta. *Who Likes the Wind?* (PS–2). Illus. by Marie Lafrance. Series: Exploring the Elements. 2006, Kids Can $14.95 (1-55337-839-3). 32pp. Children's questions about the wind are answered in attractive illustrations using foldout pages. (Rev: BL 4/1/06) [551.51]

3969 Vogt, Gregory L. *The Atmosphere: Planetary Heat Engine* (5–8). Illus. Series: Earth's Spheres. 2007, Lerner $29.27 (0-7613-2841-6). 80pp. Examines a wide array of topics, including the composition of our air, weather and climate, and the use of satellites and other tools to study the atmosphere. (Rev: BL 4/1/07) [551.5]

Storms

3970 Ceban, Bonnie J. *Tornadoes: Disaster and Survival* (4–7). Series: Deadly Disasters. 2005, Enslow LB $23.93 (0-7660-2383-4). 48pp. Explores the science behind tornadoes and offers advice about how to prepare for and survive such natural disasters. (Rev: SLJ 10/05) [551.5]

3971 Demarest, Chris. *Hurricane Hunters! Riders on the Storm* (2–4). Illus. 2006, Simon & Schuster $17.95 (0-689-86168-0). 40pp. Pastel paintings introduce the work of the pilots and planes that fly into hurricanes on weather reconnaissance missions. (Rev: BL 2/1/06; SLJ 6/06) [551.55]

3972 Gibson, Karen Bush. *The Fury of Hurricane Andrew, 1992* (3–5). Illus. Series: Robbie Reader: Natural Disasters. 2006, Mitchell Lane LB $16.95 (1-58415-416-0). 32pp. Explores the economic and social impact of the devastating 1992 hurricane,

with photographs, personal stories, and resources for further research. (Rev: BL 4/1/06; SLJ 5/06) [363.34]

3973 Harper, Kristine C. *Hurricane Andrew* (5–8). Series: Environmental Disasters. 2005, Facts on File $35.00 (0-8160-5759-1). 100pp. The impact of 1992's Hurricane Andrew on Florida's wetlands is seen as a warning about the need to be more prepared. (Rev: SLJ 11/05) [551.5]

3974 Langley, Andrew. *Hurricanes, Tsunamis, and Other Natural Disasters* (4–6). Series: Kingfisher Knowledge. 2006, Kingfisher $12.95 (0-7534-5975-2). 64pp. This well-illustrated volume examines a wide range of natural disasters and looks at the ways in which humans respond and what they are doing to better predict or prevent these disasters in the future. (Rev: BL 9/1/06; SLJ 10/06) [363.34]

3975 McGrath, Barbara Barbieri, comp. *The Storm: Students of Biloxi, Mississippi, Remember Hurricane Katrina* (3–8). Illus. 2006, Charlesbridge $18.95 (1-58089-172-1). 64pp. Artwork and writings show the impact of the storm on K–12 students in Biloxi; the book is divided into four sections: "Evacuation," "Storm," "Aftermath," and "Hope." (Rev: SLJ 12/06) [976.2]

3976 Miller, Mara. *Hurricane Katrina Strikes the Gulf Coast* (5–8). Series: Deadly Disasters. 2006, Enslow LB $17.95 (0-7660-2803-8). 48pp. The story of Hurricane Katrina and its disastrous impact on the Gulf Coast in 2005 is accompanied by personal stories plus information on other deadly storms. (Rev: BL 7/06; SLJ 9/06) [363.34]

3977 Torres, John A. *Hurricane Katrina and the Devastation of New Orleans* (4–7). Series: Monumental Milestones. 2006, Mitchell Lane $19.95 (1-58415-473-X). 48pp. An interview with a newlywed couple who lost everything in the storm draws readers into this account of the devastation. (Rev: BL 9/1/06) [976.3]

3978 Visser, Reona. *Story of a Storm: A Book About Hurricane Katrina* (K–3). 2006, Quail Ridge $15.95 (1-893062-86-4). 32pp. Thirty students at a Mississippi school contributed to the moving text and collage art describing the hurricane and its destruction. (Rev: BL 8/06) [976]

3979 Webster, Christine. *Storms* (2–4). Illus. 2006, Weigl $24.45 (1-59036-418-X). 24pp. An engaging and detailed introduction to storms, their meteorological origins, extreme phenomena such as hail and tornadoes, and the technologies that allow us to predict and track them. (Rev: BL 12/1/06) [551.55]

3980 Woods, Michael, and Mary B. Woods. *Hurricanes* (4–6). Series: Disasters Up Close. 2006, Lerner LB $27.93 (0-8225-4710-4). 64pp. With charts, photographs, and quotes from survivors, this book clearly demonstrates the power of hurricanes, and provides quick facts plus tips on preparing for a storm. (Rev: SLJ 1/07) [551.5]

3981 Woods, Michael, and Mary B. Woods. *Tornadoes* (5–8). Illus. Series: Disasters Up Close. 2006, Lerner $27.93 (0-8225-4714-7). 64pp. Eyewitness accounts add to this well-illustrated overview of tornadoes and the destruction they can cause. (Rev: BL 10/15/06) [551.55]

Water

3982 Morrison, Gordon. *A Drop of Water* (K–3). 2006, Houghton $16.00 (0-618-58557-5). 32pp. A gentle account of the water cycle, following the path of a drop of rainwater as it makes its way downhill past different settings, plants, and animals. (Rev: BL 8/06; SLJ 10/06) [508]

3983 Nadeau, Isaac. *Learning About the Water Cycle with Graphic Organizers* (3–6). Series: Graphic Organizers in Science. 2005, Rosen LB $19.95 (1-4042-2808-X). 24pp. This title uses a wide variety of graphic organizers, including concept webs, compare/contrast charts, Venn diagrams, graphs, timelines, and KWL charts, to introduce readers to the water cycle. (Rev: SLJ 11/05)

3984 Parker, Steve. *The Science of Water: Projects and Experiments with Water Science and Power* (4–7). Illus. Series: Tabletop Scientist. 2005, Heinemann LB $27.79 (1-4034-7282-3). 32pp. The 12 experiments and projects in this collection demonstrate the basic scientific properties of water. (Rev: SLJ 12/05)

3985 Royston, Angela. *Water: Let's Look at a Puddle* (K–3). Illus. Series: Read and Learn: Material Detectives. 2005, Heinemann LB $14.95 (1-4034-7676-4). 24pp. Examples from daily life — What

happens to a frozen puddle? What makes a puddle dry up? — make basic science concepts clear. (Rev: BL 12/1/05) [553.7]

3986 Swanson, Diane. *The Wonder in Water* (3–5). 2006, Annick $19.95 (1-55037-937-2); paper $8.95 (1-55037-936-4). 44pp. The many faces of water — from beads of human perspiration to raindrops to the world's largest oceans — are explored in conversational text with lots of interesting sidebars, photographs, and diagrams. (Rev: BL 1/1–15/06) [553.7]

3987 Wells, Robert E. *Did a Dinosaur Drink This Water?* (1–3). Illus. by author. 2006, Albert Whitman $15.95 (978-0-8075-8839-0); paper $6.95 (978-0-8075-8840-6). This cartoon-style introduction to the water cycle takes readers on a world tour to explore a wide variety of issues, including water's importance in sustaining the life of plants and animals; its three states; water use policies; conservation efforts; and water pollution. (Rev: BL 12/1/06; SLJ 2/07) [551.48]

Weather

3988 Banqueri, Eduardo. *Weather* (4–8). Illus. by Estudio Marcel Socías and Gabi Marfil. Series: Field Guides. 2006, Enchanted Lion $16.95 (1-59270-059-4). 33pp. This information-packed guide explores a broad array of weather-related topics, including seasonal change, climatic zones, the science of meteorology, clouds, winds, storms, and the atmosphere. (Rev: SLJ 1/07) [551.5]

3989 Carson, Mary Kay. *Weather Projects for Young Scientists* (4–7). 2007, Chicago Review paper $14.95 (1-55652-629-6). 160pp. A detailed look at weather basics is intertwined with more than 40 projects, many appropriate for science fairs, and a few career profiles. (Rev: BL 12/1/06) [551.5078]

3990 Estigarribia, Diana. *Learning About Weather with Graphic Organizers* (3–6). Series: Graphic Organizers in Science. 2005, Rosen LB $19.95 (1-4042-2803-9). 24pp. This title uses a wide variety of graphic organizers, including concept webs, compare/contrast charts, Venn diagrams, graphs, timelines, and KWL charts, to introduce topics such as global warming, the greenhouse effect, seasonal change, and weather forecasting. (Rev: SLJ 11/05)

3991 Kaner, Etta. *Who Likes the Snow?* (PS–2). Illus. by Marie Lafrance. Series: Exploring the Elements. 2006, Kids Can $14.95 (1-55337-842-3). This slim book uses questions and flaps to offer interesting information about snow. (Rev: SLJ 12/06) [551.51]

3992 Marsico, Katie. *Snowy Weather Days* (K–2). Series: Scholastic News Nonfiction Readers. 2006,

Children's Pr. LB $19.00 (0-531-16773-9). 24pp. Basic information for beginning readers, with seven highlighted words that are featured in bold in the text. Also use *Wild Weather Days* (2006). (Rev: SLJ 1/07) [551.57]

3993 Michaels, Pat. *W Is for Wind: A Weather Alphabet* (1–4). Illus. by Melanie Rose. 2005, Sleeping Bear $16.95 (1-58536-237-9). A rhyming alphabet book about the weather with useful information for young elementary students. (Rev: SLJ 7/05) [428.1]

3994 Rosenberg, Pam. *Sunny Weather Days* (K–2). Series: Scholastic News Nonfiction Readers. 2006, Children's Pr. LB $19.00 (0-531-16770-4). 24pp. This colorful picture book introduces young readers to the properties of the sun and introduces seven weather-related vocabulary words. (Rev: SLJ 1/07) [551.5]

3995 Rustad, Martha E. H. *Today Is Hot* (PS–3). 2005, Capstone LB $19.93 (0-7368-5343-X). 24pp. A very basic introduction to climate and weather, emphasizing aspects that affect a child's life. Also in this series: *Today Is Cold, Today Is Rainy,* and *Today Is Snowy* (all 2005). (Rev: SLJ 7/06) [551.5]

3996 Solway, Andrew. *A Pirate Adventure: Weather* (3–6). Illus. Series: Raintree Fusion. 2005, Raintree LB $28.21 (1-4109-1926-9). 32pp. An exciting voyage on an 18th-century ship serves as the backdrop for information about wind, weather, and weather forecasting. (Rev: SLJ 5/06) [551.6]

Physics

General

3997 Gardner, Robert. *Melting, Freezing, and Boiling Science Projects with Matter* (3–5). Series: Fantastic Physical Science Experiments. 2006, Enslow LB $17.95 (0-7660-2589-6). 48pp. Nine science projects that explore the properties of matter are introduced in double-page spreads, with discussion of the principles demonstrated. Also use *Sizzling Science Projects with Heat and Energy* (2006). (Rev: BL 9/15/06) [507]

3998 Hammond, Richard. *Can You Feel the Force?* (5–8). Illus. 2006, DK $15.99 (0-7566-2033-3). 96pp. Light, matter, friction, gravity, velocity — these and other basic physics principles are explained in a reader-friendly format that includes experiments, captions, sidebars, and other eye-catching elements. (Rev: SLJ 10/06) [530]

3999 Jerome, Kate Boehm. *Atomic Universe: The Quest to Discover Radioactivity* (5–8). Series: Science Quest. 2006, National Geographic $17.95 (978-0-7922-5543-7). 59pp. An attractive and informative history of radioactivity, profiling key figures and placing the discovery and subsequent developments in scientific and social context. (Rev: SLJ 4/07) [539.7]

4000 Mason, Adrienne. *Touch It! Materials, Matter and You* (K–2). Illus. by Claudia Dávila. Series: Primary Physical Science. 2005, Kids Can $12.95 (1-55337-760-5); paper $5.95 (1-55337-761-3). 32pp. This easy-to-understand approach to science introduces the various properties of matter and suggests simple activities and projects. (Rev: BL 10/15/05) [530]

4001 Stille, Darlene R. *Physical Change: Reshaping Matter* (5–8). Illus. Series: Exploring Science. 2005, Compass Point LB $18.95 (0-7565-1257-3). 48pp.

An attractive format with plenty of graphics adds to the appeal of this brief discussion of the states of matter. (Rev: SLJ 7/06) [530]

4002 Twist, Clint. *Light and Sound* (K–1). Illus. Series: Check It Out! 2005, Bearport LB $19.96 (1-59716-060-1). 24pp. Presents the basics of the science behind light and sound. (Rev: BL 10/15/05) [535]

Energy and Motion

General

4003 Bradley, Kimberly Brubaker. *Forces Make Things Move* (1–3). Illus. by Paul Meisel. Series: Let's-Read-and-Find-Out Science. 2005, HarperCollins $15.99 (0-06-028906-6); paper $4.99 (0-06-445214-X). 40pp. Using a toy car as an example, this is a basic exploration of the physics of motion and such related concepts as inertia, friction, and gravity. (Rev: BL 9/15/05) [531]

4004 Egendorf, Laura K., ed. *Energy Alternatives* (5–9). Series: Introducing Issues with Opposing Viewpoints. 2006, Gale LB $32.45 (0-7377-3458-2). 120pp. Presents basic information about alternatives to fossil fuel-driven energy, along with diverse views on the feasibility and practicality of these alternative energy sources. (Rev: SLJ 8/06) [333.79]

4005 Landau, Elaine. *The History of Energy* (5–8). Series: Major Inventions Through History. 2005, Twenty-First Century LB $26.60 (0-8225-3806-7). 56pp. An attractive look at developments through time in the use of various forms of energy (fire, wind, water, coal, steam, oil and gasoline, electricity, and so forth) and their application in transportation and other sectors. (Rev: SLJ 1/06)

4006 Stille, Darlene R. *Waves: Energy on the Move* (5–8). Illus. Series: Exploring Science. 2005, Compass Point LB $18.95 (0-7565-1259-X). 48pp. An attractive format with plenty of graphics adds to the appeal of this brief discussion of waves in water, light, air, and other media. (Rev: SLJ 7/06) [531]

4007 Woodford, Chris. *Energy* (4–7). Illus. Series: See for Yourself. 2007, DK $14.99 (978-0-7566-2561-0). 64pp. This introductory guide to energy provides an easy-to-understand definition, offers examples of both kinetic and potential energy, identifies major energy sources, explains the processes through which energy is released, and discusses the problems inherent in energy usage. (Rev: BL 4/1/07) [333.79]

Light and Color

4008 Gardner, Robert. *Dazzling Science Projects with Light and Color* (4–6). Illus. by Tom LaBaff. Series: Fantastic Physical Science Experiments. 2006, Enslow LB $23.93 (0-7660-2587-X). 48pp. Experiments involving readily available materials demonstrate the properties of light and color and how the two interact; advice on developing these into science fair projects follows. (Rev: SLJ 8/06) [535]

4009 Stille, Darlene R. *Manipulating Light: Reflection, Refraction, and Absorption* (5–8). Illus. Series: Exploring Science. 2005, Compass Point LB $18.95 (0-7565-1258-1). 48pp. An attractive format with plenty of graphics adds to the appeal of this brief discussion of the nature of light. (Rev: SLJ 7/06) [535]

Magnetism and Electricity

4010 Levine, Shar, and Leslie Johnstone. *Magnet Power!* (2–4). Illus. by Steve Harpster. Series: First Science Experiments. 2006, Sterling $14.95 (1-4027-2438-1). 48pp. Clearly explained experiments and activities demonstrate the properties of magnets. (Rev: BL 11/1/06) [538]

4011 Walker, Sally M. *Electricity* (3–5). Photos by Andy King. Illus. Series: Early Bird Energy. 2005, Lerner LB $25.26 (0-8225-2919-X). 48pp. After a basic explanation of how electricity works, this volume looks at static electricity, currents, circuits, and

so forth and suggests a number of activities that use materials including batteries, light bulbs, and aluminum foil. (Rev: BL 12/1/05) [537]

Optical Illusions

4012 Illusionworks. *Amazing Optical Illusions* (3–5). Illus. 2005, Firefly LB $16.95 (1-55297-961-X); paper $5.95 (1-55237-962-8). 32pp. Twenty-nine optical illusions challenge readers. (Rev: SLJ 8/05) [152]

Simple Machines

4013 Gardner, Robert. *Sensational Science Projects with Simple Machines* (4–6). Illus. by Tom LaBaff. Series: Fantastic Physical Science Experiments. 2006, Enslow LB $23.93 (0-7660-2585-3). 48pp. The experiments and projects in this volume are designed to help readers understand the workings of simple machines — such as inclined planes, levers, and pulleys — and to incorporate them in exciting science fair projects. (Rev: SLJ 8/06) [621.8]

4014 Solway, Andrew. *Castle Under Siege! Simple Machines* (3–5). Illus. 2005, Raintree LB $28.21 (1-4109-1918-8). 32pp. Covering the construction of a medieval castle and its forms of defense, this book also introduces simple machines — wedges, inclined planes, levers, and so forth. (Rev: SLJ 4/06) [621.8]

4015 Tieck, Sarah. *Inclined Planes* (2–4). Series: Buddy Books: Simple Machines. 2006, ABDO $14.95 (1-59679-818-1). 32pp. A concise explanation of inclined planes and their importance, with illustrations that aid comprehension. (Rev: BL 10/15/06) [621.8]

Sound

4016 Parker, Steve. *The Science of Sound: Projects and Experiments with Music and Sound Waves* (4–7). Illus. Series: Tabletop Scientist. 2005, Heinemann LB $27.79 (1-4034-7281-5). 32pp. The 12 experiments and projects in this collection demonstrate the basic scientific principles of sound waves. (Rev: SLJ 12/05)

Space Exploration

4017 Britton, Tamara L. *NASA* (3–5). Series: Symbols, Landmarks, and Monuments. 2005, ABDO LB $15.95 (1-59197-836-X). 32pp. American space exploration and the key role of the National Aeronautics and Space Administration are the focus of this informative book that includes photographs and graphics. (Rev: SLJ 9/05) [354.79]

4018 Carson, Mary Kay. *Exploring the Solar System* (5–8). 2006, Chicago Review paper $17.95 (1-55652-593-1). 176pp. A history of man's exploration of space, from "prehistory" forward to 2010, with activities, diagrams, a timeline, and other interesting features. (Rev: BL 5/1/06; SLJ 9/06) [523.2]

4019 Goldsmith, Mike. *Space* (4–7). Illus. Series: Kingfisher Voyages. 2005, Kingfisher $14.95 (0-7534-5910-8). 60pp. An appealing overview of space exploration, with concise text, good photographs, and a foreword and comments by astronaut Sally Ride. (Rev: BL 10/15/05) [629.45]

4020 Thimmesh, Catherine. *Team Moon: How 400,000 People Landed Apollo 11 on the Moon* (5–10). 2006, Houghton $19.95 (0-618-50757-4). 80pp. A breathless account of all the behind-the-scenes work that went into the Apollo space program, with plenty of photographs. (Rev: SLJ 6/06) [629.45]

Technology, Engineering, and Industry

General and Miscellaneous Industries and Inventions

4021 Cobb, Vicki. *Fireworks* (4–8). Photos by Michael Gold. Series: Where's the Science Here? 2005, Lerner LB $23.93 (0-7613-2771-1). 48pp. A well-illustrated, engaging text covers the history and science of pyrotechnics; experiments require adult supervision. Also recommended in this series are *Junk Food* and *Sneakers*(both 2005). (Rev: SLJ 2/06)

4022 Collicutt, Paul. *This Rocket* (PS–2). Illus. 2005, Farrar $16.00 (0-374-37484-8). 32pp. A colorful overview of rockets and spacecraft ranging from Fourth of July fireworks to the space shuttle. (Rev: BL 12/1/05; SLJ 9/05) [621.43]

4023 Koscielniak, Bruce. *Looking at Glass Through the Ages* (3–6). Illus. by author. 2006, Houghton $16.00 (0-618-50750-7). From the earliest faience of ancient Egypt to today's optical fiber, this is a fascinating review of glassmaking, covering everything from magnifying lenses to stained glass, lead crystal, and neon tubes. (Rev: SLJ 8/06) [666]

4024 Landau, Elaine. *The History of Everyday Life* (5–8). Series: Major Inventions Through History. 2005, Twenty-First Century LB $26.60 (0-8225-3808-3). 56pp. Fireplaces, washing machines, and microwave ovens are among the inventions discussed here that have improved our everyday lives. (Rev: SLJ 2/06)

4025 Romanek, Trudee. *Switched On, Flushed Down, Tossed Out: Investigating the Hidden Workings of Your Home* (3–5). Illus. by Stephen MacEachern. 2005, Annick LB $24.95 (1-55037-903-8); paper $12.95 (1-55037-902-X). 48pp. Casey, who has a vivid imagination, is curious about the workings of all kinds of household features — plumbing, electricity, thermostats, phones — and his funny theories are balanced by clear explanations of the real thing. (Rev: BL 7/05; SLJ 12/05) [643]

4026 Slavin, Bill. *Transformed: How Everyday Things Are Made* (4–7). Illus. 2005, Kids Can $24.95 (1-55337-179-8). 160pp. A behind-the-scenes look at the manufacturing process for a wide array of everyday products. (Rev: BL 10/15/05; SLJ 1/06) [670]

4027 Smith, Ryan A. *Trading Cards: From Start to Finish* (3–5). Illus. Series: Made in the U.S.A. 2005, Gale LB $17.96 (1-4103-0374-8). 48pp. A behind-the-scenes glimpse at how trading cards are manufactured and distributed. (Rev: BL 9/15/05) [976]

4028 Whiting, Jim. *James Watt and the Steam Engine* (5–8). Series: Uncharted, Unexplored, and Unexplained: Scientific Advancements of the 19th Century. 2006, Mitchell Lane LB $19.95 (1-58415-371-7). 48pp. Brief biographical information about Watt is accompanied by a more detailed discussion of his invention and its importance. (Rev: SLJ 5/06) [621]

4029 Williams, Marcia. *Hooray for Inventors!* (3–5). Illus. 2005, Candlewick $16.99 (0-7636-2760-7). 40pp. This attractive large-format book tells the stories behind some of the world's most notable inventions and their creators, pairing a light-hearted text full of asides and snippets of dialogue. (Rev: BL 12/1/05; SLJ 12/05) [609.2]

4030 Woods, Michael, and Mary B. Woods. *The History of Communication* (5–8). Series: Major Inventions Through History. 2005, Twenty-First Century LB $26.60 (0-8225-3807-3). 56pp. An attractive look at developments through time in methods of communication — the printing press, telephone, radio, television, and the Internet — and the impact on our lives. (Rev: SLJ 1/06) [302.2]

Aeronautics and Airplanes

4031 Ghione, Yvette. *This Is Daniel Cook on a Plane* (K–3). 2006, Kids Can $12.95 (1-55453-081-4); paper $4.95 (1-55453-082-2). In this companion to the popular Canadian-produced TV show, the young host takes readers on a flight in a small airplane, introducing them to the parts of the airplane, flying techniques, and safety procedures. (Rev: SLJ 11/06) [629.13]

4032 Hill, Lee Sullivan. *The Flyer Flew! The Invention of the Airplane* (2–4). Illus. by Craig Orback. Series: On My Own Science. 2006, Millbrook LB $23.93 (1-57505-758-1). 48pp. This easy-reader chapter book tells the story of the Wright brothers' invention, discusses their scientific approach, and explains terms such as pitch and air pressure. (Rev: SLJ 8/06) [629.13]

4033 Johnson, Rebecca L. *Satellites* (4–6). Illus. Series: Cool Science. 2005, Lerner LB $25.26 (0-8225-2908-4). 48pp. With many interesting examples and an attractive layout, this introduction explores the history and science of the artificial satellites that orbit the earth and gather all sorts of data. (Rev: SLJ 12/05) [629.46]

4034 Oxlade, Chris. *Airplanes: Uncovering Technology* (4–8). Illus. Series: Uncovering. 2006, Firefly $16.95 (1-55407-134-8). 52pp. A well-illustrated survey of developments in air travel, with four overlay pages and a look at future possibilities. (Rev: SLJ 2/07) [629.133]

4035 Priceman, Marjorie. *Hot Air: The (Mostly) True Story of the First Hot-Air Balloon Ride* (K–3). Illus. 2005, Simon & Schuster $16.95 (0-689-82642-7). 40pp. The Montgolfier brothers' first successful hot-air balloon flight is detailed with humor, great illustrations, and a little embellishment. (Rev: BL 7/05; SLJ 7/05) [629.133]

Building and Construction

General

4036 Britton, Tamara L. *The Empire State Building* (3–5). Series: Symbols, Landmarks, and Monuments. 2005, ABDO LB $15.95 (1-59197-834-3). 32pp. All about the famous New York landmark, with information on its history, construction, and importance. (Rev: SLJ 9/05)

4037 Britton, Tamara L. *The Golden Gate Bridge* (3–5). Series: Symbols, Landmarks, and Monuments. 2005, ABDO LB $15.95 (1-59197-835-1). 32pp. All about the famous California landmark, with information on its history, its construction, and its importance. (Rev: SLJ 9/05) [624]

4038 Caney, Steven. *Steven Caney's Ultimate Building Book* (4–8). Illus. by Lauren House. 2006, Running Pr. $29.95 (0-7624-0409-4). 596pp. Starting with a history of construction and the basic techniques involved, Caney looks at the ways design and technology intersect and suggests a wide range of kid-tested building projects. (Rev: SLJ 1/07*) [624]

4039 Dreyer, Francis. *Lighthouses* (4–7). Photos by Philip Plisson. 2005, Abrams $18.95 (0-8109-5958-5). 78pp. A fascinating and strikingly beautiful overview of lighthouses — of the past and present — and of the courage and loneliness of the men and women who tend them. (Rev: BL 1/1–15/06) [387.1]

4040 Gonzales, Doreen. *Seven Wonders of the Modern World* (4–7). Illus. Series: Seven Wonders of the World. 2005, Enslow LB $25.26 (0-7660-5292-3). 48pp. Profiles seven marvels of modern construction, including the Panama Canal, Toronto's CN Tower, and the Empire State Building in New York City; the text is extended by constantly updated links to Web sites. (Rev: SLJ 11/05)

4041 Hudson, Cheryl Willis. *Construction Zone* (K–3). Illus. by Richard Sobol. 2006, Candlewick $15.99 (0-7636-2684-8). 32pp. A fascinating behind-the-scenes glimpse of the construction of a building designed by noted architect Frank Gehry, featuring eye-catching photographs and definitions of specialized vocabulary. (Rev: BL 9/1/06; SLJ 6/06) [690]

4042 Leboutillier, Nate. *Eiffel Tower* (3–6). Series: Modern Wonders of the World. 2006, Creative Education LB $27.10 (1-58341-438-X). 32pp. Leboutillier tells the story of the construction of the tower — in the face of much protest and technical challenges — and documents its history, including many unusual feats, and its contemporary importance as a symbol. (Rev: SLJ 12/06) [725]

4043 Levy, Debbie. *The World Trade Center* (4–6). Illus. Series: Great Structures in History. 2005, Gale LB $18.96 (0-7377-2071-9). 48pp. Chronicles the six-year construction project — including design and excavation, their symbolism, and the eventual destruction of the towers. (Rev: BL 12/1/05) [720]

4044 Oxlade, Chris. *Skyscrapers: Uncovering Technology* (4–6). Series: Uncovering. 2006, Firefly $16.95 (1-55407-136-4). 52pp. This overview of the world's skyscrapers — past, present, and future — looks briefly at some of the most notable structures, as well as the design and technological challenges involved in building them, and offers several mylar overlays. (Rev: BL 10/15/06; SLJ 2/07) [720]

4045 Sullivan, George. *Built to Last: Building America's Amazing Bridges, Dams, Tunnels, and Skyscrapers* (5–8). Illus. 2005, Scholastic $18.99 (0-439-51737-0). 128pp. Seventeen marvels of American engineering — including the Erie Canal, Hoover Dam, Brooklyn Bridge, and Boston's "Big Dig" — are presented in chronological chapters with good illustrations and fact boxes that add historical and technological context. (Rev: BL 12/1/05; SLJ 3/06*; VOYA 8/06) [624]

Computers and Automation

4046 Bingham, Jane. *Internet Freedom: Where Is the Limit?* (5–8). Series: Behind the News. 2006, Heinemann LB $32.86 (978-1-4034-8833-6). 56pp. Short news stories highlight the problems involved in the freedom we find on the Internet and chapters discuss how to evaluate the stories behind the news and the pros and cons of Internet regulation. (Rev: SLJ 4/07)

4047 Domaine, Helena. *Robotics* (4–6). Illus. Series: Cool Science! 2005, Lerner LB $25.26 (0-8225-2112-1). 48pp. An attractive, colorful exploration of the history of robotics and the ways in which this technology is likely to affect life in the future. (Rev: BL 9/1/05; SLJ 12/05) [629.8]

4048 Jones, David. *Mighty Robots: Mechanical Marvels That Fascinate and Frighten* (5–8). Illus. 2006, Annick $24.95 (1-55037-929-1); paper $14.95 (1-55037-928-3). 126pp. Artificial intelligence, mobility, and various robot roles are discussed in this look at the past, present, and future of robots. (Rev: BL 2/1/06) [629.8]

4049 Lemke, Donald B. *Steve Jobs, Steve Wozniak, and the Personal Computer* (4–6). Illus. by Tod Smith. Series: Graphic Library: Inventions and Discovery. 2006, Capstone LB $18.95 (0-7368-6488-1). 32pp. A graphic-novel presentation of the story of Apple Computer, profiling its two young creators; the art has less value than the information presented but will attract some students to this history. (Rev: BL 10/15/06) [621.39092]

4050 Rooney, Anne. *Computers: Faster, Smaller, and Smarter* (5–9). Illus. Series: The Cutting Edge. 2005, Heinemann LB $32.86 (1-4034-7426-5). 56pp. Looks at the technology behind computers of the past, present, and future; a high-tech design completes the package. (Rev: SLJ 6/06) [004]

4051 Somervill, Barbara A. *The History of the Computer* (3–6). Series: Our Changing World: The Timeline Library. 2006, The Child's World LB $27.07 (1-59296-437-0). 32pp. An exploration of how simple calculating methods and machines became more complex through the ages. (Rev: SLJ 7/06) [004]

4052 Wolinsky, Art. *Internet Power Research Using the Big6 Approach*. Rev. ed. (3–8). Illus. Series: The Internet Library. 2005, Enslow LB $22.60 (0-7660-1563-7). 64pp. Shows readers how to apply the "Big6" method to research done on the Internet; a revision of a 2002 title. (Rev: SLJ 11/05) [025.04]

4053 Woodford, Chris. *Digital Technology* (4–7). Series: Science in Focus. 2006, Chelsea House LB $27.00 (0-7910-8861-8). 48pp. A clear introduction to the world of digital technology, covering topics including smart cards, computer-aided design, mobile phones, and so forth in easy-to-understand language. (Rev: BL 10/15/06) [621.381]

Electronics

4054 Oxlade, Chris. *Electronics: MP3s, TVs, and DVDs* (5–9). Illus. Series: The Cutting Edge. 2005, Heinemann LB $32.86 (1-4034-7427-3). 56pp. Looks at the technology behind popular electronic devices and at predictions about gadgets of the future; a high-tech design completes the package. (Rev: SLJ 6/06)

Machinery

4055 Peterson, Cris. *Fantastic Farm Machines* (1–3). Illus. by David R. Lundquist. 2006, Boyds Mills $17.95 (1-59078-271-2). 32pp. Peterson gives readers a personal tour of the high-tech equipment used on today's farms. (Rev: BL 2/15/06; SLJ 3/06) [631.3]

4056 Whitehouse, Patty. *Moving Machines* (K–2). Illus. 2006, Rourke LB $14.95 (1-60044-192-0). 24pp. This attractive title explores the wide range of machines used to move materials, ranging from simple pulleys, shovels, and wheelbarrows to cherry pickers and scissor lifts. (Rev: BL 10/15/06) [621.8]

Metals

4057 Ridley, Sarah. *A Metal Can* (2–4). Illus. Series: How It's Made. 2006, Gareth Stevens $17.95 (0-8368-6702-5). 32pp. This photo-filled title traces the life cycle of an aluminum soda can from the mining of the raw material — bauxite — to the recycling bin. (Rev: BL 10/15/06) [670]

Television, Motion Pictures, Radio, and Recording

4058 Somervill, Barbara A. *The History of the Motion Picture* (3–6). Series: Our Changing World: The Timeline Library. 2006, The Child's World LB $27.07 (1-59296-440-0). 32pp. From moving shadows to computer video clips, this book traces the evolution of moving images and looks forward into the future. (Rev: SLJ 7/06) [791.43]

4059 Spilsbury, Richard. *Cartoons and Animation* (4–7). Illus. Series: Art off the Wall. 2006, Heinemann LB $23.00 (1-4034-8287-X). 56pp. Surveys the history, techniques, and movie applications of cartooning and animation, and includes bold color illustrations of familiar characters and animators at work. (Rev: BL 1/1–15/07) [741.5]

Transportation

General

4060 *Go! The Whole World of Transportation* (5–10). Illus. 2006, DK $26.99 (978-0-7566-2224-4). 240pp. This wide-ranging, visually fascinating journey through the world of transportation touches on everything from buses and ferries to speedboats and fighter jets. (Rev: SLJ 2/07*) [388]

4061 Herbst, Judith. *The History of Transportation* (5–8). Series: Major Inventions Through History. 2005, Twenty-First Century LB $26.60 (0-8225-2496-1). 56pp. From the wheel to the airplane, technological innovations involving transport have had a profound impact on our lives as shown in this attractive, well-written volume. (Rev: SLJ 2/06) [973]

4062 *Let's Get to Work! / ¡Vamos a trabajar!* (PS–2). Illus. by Gaétan Evrard. 2005, Two-Can $6.95 (1-58728-512-6). This attractive bilingual board book introduces young readers to a variety of vehicles and their names in both English and Spanish; also use *Let's Go! / ¡Vamos a Viajar!* (2005). (Rev: SLJ 10/05)

4063 Prince, April Jones. *What Do Wheels Do All Day?* (PS–2). Illus. by Giles Laroche. 2006, Houghton $16.00 (0-618-56307-5). 32pp. This oversized picture book explores wheels of every size and description and the wide range of tasks they perform. (Rev: BL 4/15/06; SLJ 6/06) [621.8]

Automobiles and Trucks

4064 Hubbell, Patricia. *Cars: Rushing! Honking! Zooming!* (PS–2). Illus. by Megan Halsey. 2006, Marshall Cavendish $14.99 (0-7614-5296-6). 32pp. Rhyming text and intricate illustrations introduce everything from family cars to limousines and hot rods. (Rev: BL 11/1/06; SLJ 11/06)

4065 Newhouse, Maxwell. *Let's Go for a Ride* (K–4). Illus. by author. 2006, Tundra $16.95 (0-88776-748-6). From the earliest automobiles through the "glory days" of the 1950s, this friendly, first-person overview gives a good feeling of the joys of driving as they change over time. (Rev: SLJ 4/06) [629.222]

4066 Roberts, Cynthia. *Tow Trucks* (PS). Illus. Series: Machines at Work. 2007, Child's World LB $14.95 (1-59296-836-8). 24pp. With close-up photographs and dramatic photographs, this small book looks at the different tasks these vehicles can perform and the equipment they use to do the job. (Rev: BL 4/15/07) [629.225]

Railroads

4067 Crowther, Robert. *Trains: A Pop-Up Railroad Book* (2–4). Illus. by author. 2006, Candlewick $17.99 (0-7636-3082-9). Suitably linear pop-ups supply a lot of information about train history and engineering. (Rev: SLJ 10/06) [625]

4068 Weitzman, David. *A Subway for New York* (4–7). Illus. 2005, Farrar $17.00 (0-374-37284-5). 40pp. The story behind the early-20th-century construction of New York City's first subway is presented in picture-book format. (Rev: BL 12/1/05; SLJ 2/06) [625.4]

4069 Zimmermann, Karl. *All Aboard! Passenger Trains Around the World* (4–7). Illus. 2006, Boyds Mills $19.95 (1-59078-325-5). 48pp. Photo-filled double-page spreads show the excitement of travel by train and interweave history, geography, commerce, and technology. (Rev: BL 2/15/06; SLJ 6/06) [385]

Ships, Boats, and Lighthouses

4070 Zimmermann, Karl. *Steamboats: The Story of Lakers, Ferries, and Majestic Paddle-Wheelers* (4–7). Illus. 2007, Boyds Mills $19.95 (978-1-59078-434-1). 48pp. Carefully researched by an aficionado, this detailed examination of the history, purpose, and engineering of steamboats contains biographical information and excellent archival and modern illustrations. (Rev: BL 1/1–15/07) [623.82]

Weapons, Submarines, and the Armed Forces

4071 Bledsoe, Karen, and Glen Bledsoe. *Helicopters: High-Flying Heroes* (4–6). Series: Mighty Military Machines. 2006, Enslow LB $23.93 (0-7660-2663-9). 48pp. Describes how military helicopters are used in a variety of tasks that display their nimbleness and versatility. (Rev: SLJ 4/07) [358.4]

4072 Byers, Ann. *America's Star Wars Program* (5–7). Series: The Library of Weapons of Mass Destruction. 2005, Rosen LB $26.50 (1-4042-0287-0). 64pp. Photographs and text document the development of 20th-century missiles and America's controversial "Star Wars" strategy. (Rev: SLJ 11/05) [623]

4073 Egan, Tracie. *Weapons of Mass Destruction and North Korea* (5–7). Series: The Library of Weapons of Mass Destruction. 2005, Rosen LB $26.50 (1-4042-0296-X). 64pp. Explores what the West knows about North Korea's efforts to build stockpiles of biological, chemical, and — potentially — nuclear weapons. (Rev: SLJ 11/05) [623]

4074 Herbst, Judith. *The History of Weapons* (5–8). Series: Major Inventions Through History. 2005, Twenty-First Century LB $26.60 (0-8225-3805-9). 56pp. An attractive look at the evolution of weapons from rocks and sticks to today's weapons of mass destruction. (Rev: SLJ 1/06) [623.4]

4075 Zeinert, Karen, and Mary Miller. *The Brave Women of the Gulf Wars: Operation Desert Storm and Operation Iraqi Freedom* (5–8). Illus. Series: Women at War. 2005, Twenty-First Century LB $30.60 (0-7613-2705-3). 112pp. Highlights women's roles in the Persian Gulf military campaigns. (Rev: BL 10/1/05; SLJ 11/05) [956.7]

Recreation

Crafts

General and Miscellaneous

4076 Boonyadhistarn, Thiranut. *Fingernail Art: Dazzling Fingers and Terrific Toes* (4–8). Illus. Series: Snap Books: Crafts. 2006, Capstone LB $25.26 (978-0-7368-6474-9). 32pp. This colorful, well-thought-out guide offers interesting tips on decorating nail. (Rev: SLJ 2/07) [646.7]

4077 Boonyadhistarn, Thiranut. *Stamping Art: Imprint Your Designs* (4–8). Illus. Series: Snap Books: Crafts. 2006, Capstone LB $25.26 (978-0-7368-6477-0). 32pp. Simple, step-by-step instructions guide readers through a variety of stamping projects that use accessible materials. (Rev: SLJ 2/07) [761]

4078 Boston, Lisa. *Sing! Play! Create! Hands-On Learning for 3- to 7-Year-Olds* (PS–2). Illus. by Sarah Cole. Series: A Williamson Little Hands Book. 2006, Williamson $14.95 (0-8249-6781-X); paper $12.95 (0-8249-6780-1). 126pp. Crafts, poems, and songs are among the activities suggested here and centered around a pond, garden, zoo, and farm. (Rev: SLJ 8/06) [372.21]

4079 Broida, Marian. *Projects About Nineteenth-Century Chinese Immigrants* (3–5). Illus. Series: Hands-on History. 2005, Benchmark LB $18.95 (0-7614-1978-0). 48pp. Crafts — a miner's scale, an abacus, a fan — plus recipes and other projects are accompanied by historical and cultural information. (Rev: SLJ 5/06)

4080 Broida, Marian. *Projects About Nineteenth-Century European Immigrants* (3–5). Illus. Series: Hands-on History. 2005, Benchmark LB $18.95 (0-7614-1980-2). 47pp. Through the varied projects in this book, students will learn the details of the sometimes-difficult lives of 19th-century immigrants from Europe; cultural and historical notes precede the activities. (Rev: SLJ 5/06) [973.5085]

4081 Bull, Jane. *The Merry Christmas Activity Book: 50 Ways to Make Your Spirits Bright* (1–3). Illus. 2005, DK $12.99 (0-7566-1369-8). 48pp. This collection of Christmas-themed crafts and activities includes ornaments for the holiday tree, potpourri, candles, cookies, and candies. (Rev: SLJ 10/05) [745.594]

4082 Dickins, Rosie. *Art Treasury: Pictures, Paintings, and Projects* (4–7). 2007, Usborne LB $19.99 (978-0-7945-1452-5). 96pp. Each of the art projects in this exciting collection is inspired by an existing work of art. (Rev: BL 4/1/07) [709]

4083 Erlbach, Arlene, and Herbert Erlbach. *Mother's Day Crafts* (3–5). Illus. Series: Fun Holiday Crafts Kids Can Do! 2005, Enslow LB $22.60 (0-7660-2348-6). 32pp. Ten original gifts for Mom that students will enjoy making; photographs help them picture the finished product. (Rev: SLJ 8/05) [745.594]

4084 *Fun-to-Make Crafts for Halloween* (3–6). 2005, Boyds Mills $15.95 (1-59078-343-3); paper $7.95 (1-59078-368-9). 63pp. The crafts and projects here include edible treats, masks, decorations, gifts, and other goodies for Halloween and the entire harvest season. (Rev: SLJ 9/05)

4085 Hankin, Rosie. *Crafty Kids: Fun Projects for You and Your Toddler* (K–2). Illus. by author. 2006, Barron's paper $8.99 (0-7641-3542-2). 64pp. Adults and young children work together on the 28 simple projects here, many of them created from paper plates with a variety of adornments. (Rev: BL 1/1–15/07; SLJ 12/06) [745.5]

4086 Hosking, Wayne. *Asian Kites* (3–6). Illus. Series: Asian Arts and Crafts for Creative Kids. 2005, Tuttle $9.95 (0-8048-3545-4). 63pp. A thorough how-to guide to making 15 kites from China,

Japan, Korea, Malaysia, and Thailand, with historical and cultural background. (Rev: SLJ 9/05)

4087 Jovinelly, Joann, and Jason Netelkos. *The Crafts and Culture of a Medieval Monastery* (4–8). Illus. Series: Crafts of the Middle Ages. 2006, Rosen LB $29.25 (1-4042-0759-7). 48pp. Crafts and history are interwoven in this interesting that looks at the history of monasteries, life within them, and the work that took place in scriptoria, gardens, and hospitals; crafts include prayer beads and a plague mask. Also use *The Crafts and Culture of a Medieval Town* (2006). (Rev: SLJ 4/07) [271.0094]

4088 Lipsey, Jennifer. *I Love to Collage* (2–4). Illus. Series: My Favorite Art Book. 2006, Sterling $9.95 (1-57990-770-9). 48pp. Provides lots of practical, well-described ideas for making collages from materials ranging from leaves to candy wrappers to pasta. (Rev: BL 12/15/06; SLJ 12/06) [702]

4089 Luxbacher, Irene. *The Jumbo Book of Outdoor Art* (3–6). Photos by Ray Boudreau and Doug Hall. Illus. by author. 2006, Kids Can paper $16.95 (1-55337-680-3). 144pp. This large-format volume provides step-by-step instructions for nearly 60 outdoor art projects and activities. (Rev: SLJ 11/06) [704.9]

4090 Mitchell, Mari Rutz. *Creating Clever Castles and Cars (from Boxes and Other Stuff): Kids Ages 3–8 Make Their Own Pretend Play Spaces* (PS–3). Illus. by Michael Kline. 2006, Williamson $14.95 (0-8249-6783-6); paper $12.95 (0-8249-6782-8). 128pp. Directions for making pretend-play items such as a fairy house, a barn, a fire engine, and a pyramid; the crafts are of varying levels of difficulty and all include illustrations and a list of needed supplies. (Rev: SLJ 7/06) [745.5]

4091 Monaghan, Kimberly. *Organic Crafts: 75 Earth-Friendly Art Activities* (3–5). Illus. 2007, Chicago Review $14.95 (978-1-55652-640-4). 160pp. The crafts, games, and activities in this collection use natural, renewable materials such as leaves and twigs, pebbles and shells. (Rev: BL 4/1/07) [745.5]

4092 Murillo, Kathy Cano. *The Crafty Diva's Lifestyle Makeover: Awesome Ideas to Spice Up Your Life!* (5–12). Illus. by Carrie Wheeler. 2005, Watson-Guptill paper $12.95 (0-8230-1008-2). 144pp. The Crafty Diva is back with this collection of easy-to-follow instructions for 50 projects that cover everything from room makeovers to fashion accessories. (Rev: SLJ 9/05)

4093 Owen, Cheryl. *Gifts for Kids to Make* (2–4). 2006, Sterling $14.95 (0-600-61502-2). 128pp. More than 50 projects involve sewing, art, clay and dough, and other materials, some of which require adult supervision. (Rev: BL 1/1–15/07; SLJ 12/06) [745.5083]

4094 Robinson, Fay. *Father's Day Crafts* (3–5). Illus. 2005, Enslow LB $22.60 (0-7660-2343-5). 32pp. Ten original gifts for Dad that students will enjoy making. Photographs help them picture the finished product. (Rev: SLJ 8/05)

4095 Robinson, Fay. *Hispanic-American Crafts Kids Can Do!* (3–5). Series: Multicultural Crafts Kids Can Do! 2006, Enslow LB $16.95 (0-7660-2459-8). 32pp. Easy-to-follow instructions are provided for ten crafts that originated in various corners of Latin America. (Rev: BL 8/06) [745.5089]

4096 Ross, Kathy. *All-Girl Crafts* (2–4). Illus. by Elaine Garvin. Series: Girl Crafts. 2005, Lerner LB $25.26 (0-7613-2776-2); paper $7.95 (0-7613-2391-0). 48pp. Clear directions and lists of required items are a strong feature of this collection of 22 craft projects designed to appeal to elementary-school girls and including doll furniture, a change purse, fancy envelopes, and a pillow-doll pajama bag. (Rev: BL 12/15/05; SLJ 10/05) [745.5]

4097 Ross, Kathy. *All New Crafts for Kwanzaa* (K–3). Illus. by Sharon Lane Holm. 2006, Lerner LB $25.26 (0-7613-3401-7); paper $7.95 (0-8225-3435-5). 48pp. This new version of a 1994 title by the same authors includes additional projects related to the holiday. (Rev: BL 1/1–15/07; SLJ 10/06) [745.594]

4098 Ross, Kathy. *All New Crafts for Thanksgiving* (3–5). Illus. by Sharon Lane Holm. 2005, Millbrook LB $25.26 (0-7613-2922-6); paper $7.95 (0-7613-2398-5). 48pp. More than 20 Thanksgiving-themed craft ideas use readily available materials and vary in difficulty. (Rev: BL 10/1/05) [745.594]

4099 Ross, Kathy. *Community Workers* (K–2). Illus. by Jan Barger. Series: Crafts for Kids Who Are Learning About. 2005, Millbrook LB $25.26 (0-7613-2743-6). 48pp. Twenty crafts introduce children to the activities of various community workers, including firefighters, dentists, shopkeepers, and librarians. (Rev: SLJ 1/06) [745.5]

4100 Ross, Kathy. *The Scrapbooker's Idea Book* (3–5). Illus. by Nicole in den Bosch. Series: Girl Crafts. 2006, Millbrook LB $25.26 (0-7613-2777-0). 48pp. An excellent introduction to scrapbooking, with step-by-step instructions for 22 projects. (Rev: SLJ 9/06)

4101 Ross, Kathy. *Step-by-Step Crafts for Winter* (K–3). Illus. by Jennifer Emery. 2006, Boyds Mills $15.95 (1-59078-449-9); paper $6.95 (1-59078-358-1). 48pp. Step-by-step instructions for 20 winter-themed crafts using everyday materials include projects appropriate for Christmas, Kwanzaa, Hanukkah, Lincoln's Birthday, and Valentine's Day. (Rev: SLJ 12/06) [745]

4102 Van Vleet, Carmella. *Great Ancient Egypt Projects You Can Build Yourself* (4–6). Illus. 2006, Nomad paper $14.95 (0-9771294-5-4). 122pp. More than two dozen hands-on activities explore life in ancient Egypt — everything from hieroglyphs and papyrus to perfume and pyramids — and are supplemented by background information. (Rev: SLJ 2/07) [932]

4103 Wagner, Lisa. *Cool Melt and Pour Soap* (4–7). Photos by Kelly Doudna. Illus. Series: Cool Crafts. 2005, ABDO LB $15.95 (1-59197-741-X). 32pp. Coloring, fragrance, and packaging are all covered in this guide to projects using soap. (Rev: SLJ 7/05)

4104 Walsh, Danny, et al. *The Cardboard Box Book: 25 Things to Make and Do with Empty Boxes* (3–5). Photos by Martin Norris. Illus. by Josh Halloran. 2006, Watson-Guptill paper $12.95 (0-8230-0610-7). 112pp. The authors — a father and sons — offer a number of kid-tested ways to convert empty boxes to better use. (Rev: SLJ 2/07) [745.54]

Clay and Other Modeling Crafts

4105 Scheunemann, Pam. *Cool Clay Projects* (4–7). Photos by Anders Hanson. Illus. Series: Cool Crafts. 2005, ABDO LB $15.95 (1-59197-740-1). 32pp. Clear, step-by-step instructions for a number of clay projects are accompanied by full-color photos and tips about safety. (Rev: SLJ 7/05) [731.4]

Costume and Jewelry Making

4106 Boonyadhistarn, Thiranut. *Beading: Bracelets, Barrettes, and Beyond* (4–8). Illus. Series: Snap Books: Crafts. 2006, Capstone LB $25.26 (978-0-7368-6472-5). 32pp. Simple, step-by-step instructions guide readers through a variety of fashion accessories that use accessible materials. (Rev: SLJ 2/07) [745.58]

4107 Di Salle, Rachel, and Ellen Warwick. *Junk Drawer Jewelry* (4–7). Photos by Ray Boudreau. Illus. by Jane Kurisu. Series: Kids Can Do It. 2006, Kids Can $12.95 (1-55337-965-9); paper $6.95 (1-55337-966-7). 40pp. This innovative craft book offers step-by-step instructions for making jewelry using odds and ends found in the junk drawer at home. (Rev: SLJ 11/06) [745.5]

4108 Scheunemann, Pam. *Cool Beaded Jewelry* (4–7). Photos by Anders Hanson. Illus. Series: Cool Crafts. 2005, ABDO LB $15.95 (1-59197-739-8). 32pp. Step-by-step instructions and full-color photo-graphs guide the user through beaded jewelry projects. (Rev: SLJ 7/05) [745]

Drawing and Painting

4109 Artell, Mike. *Funny Cartooning for Kids* (3–6). Illus. by author. 2007, Sterling LB $17.95 (978-1-4027-2260-8). 128pp. This guide emphasizes the importance of humor in cartooning and explains the basics — exaggeration, simplification, anthropomorphism, and so forth. (Rev: SLJ 4/07) [741.5]

4110 Gray, Peter. *Heroes and Villains* (5–8). Series: Kid's Guide to Drawing. 2006, Rosen LB $18.95 (1-4042-3330-X). 32pp. Shows clearly how to draw manga heroes and villains and offers guidance on getting facial expressions just right. (Rev: BL 9/1/06; SLJ 9/06) [741.5]

4111 Hart, Christopher. *Manga Mania Chibi and Furry Characters: How to Draw the Adorable Mini-People and Cool Cat-Girls of Japanese Comics* (5–12). Illus. 2006, Watson-Guptill paper $19.95 (0-8230-2977-8). 144pp. Fans of these super-cute manga characters will appreciate the step-by-step directions in this informative book. (Rev: SLJ 5/06) [741.5]

4112 Hart, Christopher. *Xtreme Art: Draw Manga Monsters!* (1–4). Illus. by author. Series: Xtreme Art. 2005, Watson-Guptill paper $6.95 (0-8230-0372-8). 64pp. A simple guide to drawing in the manga style for children; also use *Draw Mini Manga!* (2005). (Rev: SLJ 9/05) [741.5]

4113 Lipsey, Jennifer. *I Love to Finger Paint!* (1–3). Series: My Very Favorite Art Book. 2006, Sterling $9.95 (1-57990-771-7). 48pp. This attractive guide to finger painting lists essential supplies, explores various techniques, and describes several projects. (Rev: BL 6/1–15/06) [751.4]

4114 Lipsey, Jennifer. *I Love to Paint!* (3–5). Illus. 2006, Lark $9.95 (1-57990-630-3). 48pp. Finger painting, watercolors, scratch art, and sponge painting are among the painting techniques introduced in this attractive and well-organized guide. (Rev: BL 2/15/06) [751.4]

4115 Peffer, Jessica. *DragonArt: How to Draw Fantastic Dragons and Fantasy Creatures* (5–12). Illus. by author. 2005, Impact paper $19.99 (1-58180-657-4). 127pp. Beautiful creatures from the author's imagination fill the pages of this well-written book and will inspire young artists to develop their own fantasy style. (Rev: SLJ 5/06) [743]

4116 Roche, Art. *Cartooning: The Only Cartooning Book You'll Ever Need to Be the Artist You've*

Always Wanted to Be (3–6). Illus. by author. Series: Art for Kids. 2005, Sterling $17.95 (1-57990-623-0). 111pp. An engaging guide to the basics of cartooning, encouraging young artists to seek their own style. (Rev: SLJ 7/05) [741.5]

4117 Wheeler, Annie. *Painting on a Canvas: Art Adventures for Kids* (5–8). Illus. by Debra Spina Dixon. 2006, Gibbs Smith $9.95 (1-58685-839-4). 63pp. These projects are designed to get children's creative juices flowing and to introduce them to some of the techniques used by such world-famous artists as Matisse, Michelangelo, and Picasso. (Rev: SLJ 11/06) [701]

4118 Zemke, Deborah. *Doodle a Zoodle* (3–5). 2006, Blue Apple $12.95 (1-59354-140-6). Gives step-by-step instructions for drawing 39 "zoodles" — animals, such as squirrels and jackrabbits, that have double letters in their names; brief information is provided on each animal. (Rev: SLJ 12/06) [743]

4119 Zemke, Deborah. *2 Is for Toucan: Oodles of Doodles from 0 to 42* (3–5). Illus. by author. 2005, Handprint $12.95 (1-59354-075-2). Step-by-step instructions show how to do creative doodles integrating art and numbers; a spiral binding allows the book to open flat. (Rev: SLJ 9/05) [741]

Paper Crafts

4120 Hufford, Deborah. *Greeting Card Making: Send Your Personal Message* (3–5). Illus. Series: Snap Books Crafts. 2005, Capstone LB $16.95 (0-7368-4385-X). 32pp. Clear directions will help readers create a variety of greeting cards, including pop-ups, collage cards, mosaic cards, and photo cards. (Rev: BL 12/15/05) [745.594]

4121 Lassus, Irene, and Marie-Anne Voituriez. *Papier Mâché* (2–5). Series: I Made It Myself! 2005, Gareth Stevens LB $22.00 (0-8368-5966-9). 24pp. Following an introduction to the properties of papier mâché and the ways to work with it, nine projects include beads, candy, and a crocodile. (Rev: SLJ 2/06) [745.54]

Sewing and Needle Crafts

4122 Blanchette, Peg, and Terri Thibault. *12 Easy Knitting Projects* (3–6). Illus. by Norma Jean Martin-Jourdenais. Series: Quick Starts for Kids! 2006, Williamson $12.95 (0-8249-6784-4); paper $8.95 (0-8249-6785-2). 63pp. Offering features for both beginners and more advanced knitters, this book provides basic information about knitting and step-by-step instructions for 12 projects of differing complexity, including a scarf, doggy turtleneck sweater, and a poncho. (Rev: SLJ 8/06) [746.4]

4123 Guy, Lucinda. *Kids Learn to Knit* (2–4). Illus. by Francois Hall. 2007, Trafalgar $14.95 (1-57076-335-6). 96pp. After basic instructions for beginners, this book includes six simple projects suitable for this age group, with clear instructions and advice on troubleshooting problems such as dropped stitches. (Rev: BL 12/15/06) [746.43]

4124 Okey, Shannon. *Knitgrrl: Learn to Knit with 15 Fun and Funky Projects* (5–8). Photos by Shannon Fagan. Illus. 2005, Watson-Guptill paper $9.95 (0-8230-2618-3). 96pp. Up-to-date designs are shown clearly and explained in detail. (Rev: BL 12/15/05*; SLJ 11/05; VOYA 12/05) [746.43]

4125 Okey, Shannon. *Knitgrrl 2: Learn to Knit with 16 All-New Patterns* (4–7). 2006, Watson-Guptill paper $9.99 (0-8230-2619-1). 96pp. This sequel to *Knitgrrl* (2005) offers step-by-step instructions for 16 new projects, including bracelets, a sports bottle holder, and a cardigan. (Rev: BL 6/1–15/06; SLJ 6/06) [746]

4126 Sadler, Judy Ann. *Quick Knits* (5–8). Illus. by Esperanca Melo. 2006, Kids Can $12.95 (1-55337-963-2); paper $6.95 (1-55337-964-0). 40pp. Clear instructions, appealing projects, and suggestions for personalizing these are features of this introduction to knitting. (Rev: BL 1/1–15/07; SLJ 12/06) [746.43]

4127 Warwick, Ellen. *Injeanuity* (5–8). Illus. by Bernice Lum. 2006, Kids Can $12.95 (1-55337-681-1). 80pp. Seventeen projects involving jeans and a sewing machine are shown with clear directions. (Rev: BL 6/1–15/06; SLJ 6/06) [746.9]

Hobbies

General and Miscellaneous

4128 Bull, Jane. *The Party Book* (3–5). Photos by Andy Crawford. 2005, DK $12.99 (0-7566-1028-1). 48pp. A guide to hosting five different types of parties that will appeal to both boys and girls, with instructions for crafts as well as advice on party etiquette. (Rev: SLJ 9/05) [793]

4129 Burnie, David. *Bird Watcher* (3–6). Illus. Series: Smithsonian Nature Activity Guides. 2005, DK paper $9.99 (0-7566-1029-X). 72pp. All sorts of fun and facts for children fascinated by birds, including experiments, crafts, and photographs. (Rev: SLJ 8/05) [598]

Cooking

4130 Brennan, Georgeanne. *Green Eggs and Ham Cookbook* (3–6). Photos by Frankie Frankeny. 2006, Random $16.95 (978-0-679-88440-8). 64pp. Diverse recipes requiring different levels of skill and varied ingredients (no green coloring) are featured here. (Rev: SLJ 2/07) [641.5]

4131 Dunnington, Rose. *The Greatest Cookies Ever: Dozens of Delicious, Chewy, Chunky, Fun and Foolproof Recipes* (4–8). Photos by Stewart O'Shields. 2005, Sterling $9.95 (1-57990-627-3). 96pp. More than 70 recipes are included in this spiral-bound guide to cookie making, with useful information about measuring, substitutions, types of mixers, and safety. (Rev: BL 1/1–15/06; SLJ 2/06) [641.8]

4132 Gold, Rozanne. *Kids Cook 1-2-3: Recipes for Young Chefs Using Only 3 Ingredients* (3–6). Illus. by Sara Pinto. 2006, Bloomsbury $17.95 (978-1-58234-735-6). 144pp. A beginner's cookbook offering 125 recipes that use only three ingredients for each meal of the day. (Rev: BL 12/1/06; SLJ 3/07)

4133 Ichord, Loretta Frances. *Double Cheeseburgers, Quiche, and Vegetarian Burritos: American Cooking from the 1920s through Today* (5–8). Illus. by Jan Davey Ellis. 2007, Lerner $25.26 (978-0-8225-5969-6). 64pp. This title traces American cuisine from 1920 to the present, with chapters highlighting such trends as TV dinners, fast food, and the rise of organic foods; recipes round out a volume useful for both reports and browsing. (Rev: BL 1/1–15/07) [394.1]

4134 Ichord, Loretta Frances. *Pasta, Fried Rice, and Matzoh Balls: Immigrant Cooking in America* (3–5). Illus. by Jan Davey Ellis. 2006, Millbrook LB $25.26 (0-7613-2913-7). 64pp. French, Italian, Jewish, Polish, Portuguese, Spanish, and Swedish immigrant recipes are included, as well as a few foreign phrases and customs. (Rev: SLJ 5/06) [394.1]

4135 Jacques, Brian. *The Redwall Cookbook* (3–7). Illus. by Christopher Denise. 2005, Philomel paper $24.99 (0-399-23791-7). 96pp. "Hare's Pawspring Vegetable Soup" and "Savoury Squirrel Bakes" are among the recipes grouped by season and introduced by a tale about preparations for a feast; the recipes themselves are quite complex. (Rev: SLJ 1/06)

4136 Katzen, Mollie. *Salad People and More Real Recipes* (PS–2). Illus. 2005, Ten Speed $17.95 (1-58246-141-4). 96pp. Healthy, kid-tested recipes for a range of tastes include instructions for children and for adults. (Rev: BL 11/15/05*; SLJ 11/05*) [641.5]

4137 Lagasse, Emeril. *Emeril's There's a Chef in My World!* (5–8). Illus. 2006, HarperCollins $22.99 (0-06-073926-6). 224pp. The famous chef adds to his successful series with a basic introduction to sandwiches, meals, snacks, and more from around the world, with sections on basic skills, safety, and equipment for beginners; cultural facts accompany each recipe. (Rev: BL 12/1/06) [641.59]

4138 Lewis, Sara. *Kids' Baking: 60 Delicious Recipes for Children to Make* (4–7). 2006, Sterling $12.95 (0-600-61561-4). 144pp. Well-illustrated recipes for cakes, cookies, and breads are suitable for children working with adult help. (Rev: BL 12/1/06) [641.8]

4139 Sheen, Barbara. *Foods of Greece* (4–6). Illus. Series: Taste of Culture. 2005, Gale LB $19.96 (0-7377-3033-1). 64pp. Eight recipes introduce the cuisine of Greece, with sidebars that add information plus a map, Web sites, and other features. (Rev: BL 1/1–15/06; SLJ 4/06) [394.1]

4140 Sheen, Barbara. *Foods of Italy* (4–8). Series: A Taste of Culture. 2005, Gale LB $24.95 (0-7377-3034-X). 64pp. Cultural and historical notes add to the simple, traditional recipes provided. Also use *Foods of Mexico* (2005). (Rev: SLJ 2/06) [641]

4141 Yolen, Jane, and Heidi E. Y. Stemple. *Fairy Tale Feasts: A Literary Cookbook for Young Read-*

ers and Eaters (K–3). Illus. by Philippe Beha. 2006, Interlink $24.95 (1-56656-643-6). 224pp. A tasty, oversized collection of 20 fairy tales accompanied by kid-friendly recipes, presented in four sections: breakfast, lunch, dinner, and desert. (Rev: BL 11/1/06; SLJ 11/06) [641.5]

Magic

4142 Keable, Ian. *The Big Book of Magic Fun* (5–9). Photos by Steve Tanner. Illus. 2005, Barron's paper $14.99 (0-7641-3222-9). 192pp. Step-by-step instructions, with photographs, are given for 40 tricks plus discussion of suitable props and a history of different kinds of magic and famous performers. (Rev: SLJ 3/06) [793.8]

4143 *Wizardology: The Book of the Secrets of Merlin* (5–8). Illus. 2005, Candlewick $19.99 (0-7636-2895-6). 32pp. This follow-up to *Dragonology* offers a variety of information for wannabe wizards. (Rev: BL 10/15/05)

Jokes, Puzzles, Riddles, Word Games

Jokes and Riddles

4144 Becker, Helaine. *Funny Business: Clowning Around, Practical Jokes, Cool Comedy, Cartooning, and More* (5–8). Illus. by Claudia Dávila. 2005, Maple Tree $21.95 (1-897066-40-6); paper $9.95 (1-897066-41-4). 160pp. Tips on body language, stand-up routines, clowning, and so forth are accompanied by discussion of various types of humor, a self-quiz, and recipes for delights including "Moose Droppings." (Rev: SLJ 1/06) [808.7]

4145 Calmenson, Stephanie. *Kindergarten Kids: Riddles, Rebuses, Wiggles, Giggles, and More!* (PS–K). Illus. by Melissa Sweet. 2005, Harper-Collins $15.99 (0-06-000713-3). 32pp. This well-illustrated collection of riddles and rhymes celebrates typical kindergarten activities. (Rev: BL 8/05; SLJ 8/05) [811]

4146 Fisher, Doris. *Happy Birthday to Whooo? A Baby Animal Riddle Book* (K–3). Illus. by Lisa Downey. 2006, Sylvan Dell $15.95 (0-9768823-1-0). Birth announcements give relevant details about new animal arrivals, and readers must turn the page to find out the animal in question. (Rev: SLJ 10/06)

4147 Hall, Katy, and Lisa Eisenberg. *Stinky Riddles* (1–4). Illus. by Renée Andriani. Series: Easy-to-Read. 2005, Dial $14.99 (0-8037-2928-6). 40pp. Skunks are the focus of the riddles and wordplay in this colorful book for beginning readers. (Rev: SLJ 12/05) [818]

4148 Leno, Jav. *How to Be the Funniest Kid in the Whole Wide World (or Just in Your Class)* (2–6). Illus. by S. B. Whitehead. 2005, Simon & Schuster $12.95 (1-4169-0631-2). 140pp. Jokes, tongue twisters, riddles, and wordplay are sprinkled with practical advice. (Rev: SLJ 1/06) [818]

4149 Morrison, Lillian. *Guess Again! Riddle Poems* (K–3). Illus. by Christy Hale. 2006, August House $16.95 (0-87483-730-8). 48pp. A collection of 23 rhyming riddles — some simple some challenging — with colorful illustrations. (Rev: BL 5/1/06; SLJ 6/06) [811]

Puzzles

4150 Dispezio, Michael A. *How Bright Is Your Brain? Amazing Games to Play with Your Mind* (3–5). Illus. by Catherine Leary. 2005, Sterling LB $14.95 (1-4027-0651-0). 80pp. A collection of games that test brainpower, with some information about the structure of the brain and how it works. (Rev: SLJ 7/05) [612.8]

4151 Kidslabel. *Spot 7 School* (K–4). 2006, Chronicle $12.95 (0-8118-5324-1). Readers are challenged to identify objects in photographs and at the same time to solve riddles that continue throughout the book. (Rev: SLJ 10/06)

4152 Phillips, Dee. *Find It at the Beach* (K–3). Series: Can You Find It? 2005, Gareth Stevens LB $22.00 (0-8368-6298-8). 24pp. This hunt for animals and objects found at the beach will prompt children to study the detailed photographs. Also use *Find It in a Rain Forest, Find It in the Desert,* and *Find It on the Farm* (all 2005). (Rev: SLJ 6/06) [578.7699]

4153 Philpot, Lorna, and Graham Philpot. *Find Anthony Ant* (PS–1). Illus. by Lorna Philpot. 2006, Sterling $12.95 (1-905417-10-1). 24pp. Children will enjoy hunting for Anthony on each spread of this detailed book featuring "The Ants Go Marching." (Rev: BL 5/15/06)

4154 Whybrow, Ian. *Faraway Farm* (PS–K). Illus. by Alex Ayliffe. 2006, Carolrhoda LB $15.95 (1-57505-938-X). Rhyming text encourages readers to locate specific animals and inanimate objects in the illustrations that chronicle a day in the life of Farmer Flat and his family. (Rev: SLJ 11/06)

4155 Wick, Walter. *Can You See What I See? Once Upon a Time* (PS–2). Illus. by author. 2006, Scholastic $13.99 (0-439-61777-4). 40pp. Twelve classic fairy tales are the setting for this new picture puzzle book; each spread comes with a list of items to find in each fairy tale scene. (Rev: BL 12/1/06; SLJ 2/07) [793.3]

4156 Wick, Walter. *Can You See What I See? Seymour Makes New Friends* (PS–K). Illus. Series: Seymour. 2006, Scholastic $8.99 (0-439-61780-4). 32pp. Readers must seek out specific objects on the spreads while Seymour makes a seesaw and two rabbits. (Rev: BL 2/1/06; SLJ 2/06) [793.73]

Mysteries, Monsters, Curiosities, and Trivia

4157 Blackwood, Gary. *Debatable Deaths* (4–8). Series: Unsolved History. 2005, Benchmark LB $20.95 (0-7614-1888-1). 72pp. Mysterious deaths discussed include those of Tutankhamen, Mozart, Sacagawea, and Meriwether Lewis. Also recommended in this series (both published in 2005) are *Legends or Lies?* (Atlantis, King Arthur, Robin Hood, and so forth) and *Perplexing People* (Anastasia and Billy the Kid, to name just two). (Rev: SLJ 3/06; VOYA 6/06)

4158 Blackwood, Gary. *Enigmatic Events* (5–8). Illus. Series: Unsolved History. 2005, Marshall Cavendish LB $20.95 (0-7614-1889-X). 80pp. Explores some of history's most enduring mysteries — the disappearance of the dinosaurs and of the *Mary Celeste*, to name only two. (Rev: BL 3/1/06; SLJ 3/06) [904]

4159 Burns, Jan. *Crop Circles* (4–6). Series: Wonders of the World. 2005, Gale LB $23.70 (0-7377-3063-3). 48pp. A slim overview of the history of crop circles over the past century, with discussion of the various theories about these strange phenomena. (Rev: SLJ 12/05) [001.94]

4160 Fecher, Sarah, and Clare Oliver. *Freaky Facts About Natural Disasters* (3–5). Illus. Series: Freaky Facts. 2006, Two-Can $13.95 (1-58728-539-8); paper $8.95 (1-58728-542-8). 32pp. Great for browsing, this is an overview of the impact of events ranging from extreme weather to earthquakes and volcanic eruptions. (Rev: BL 4/15/06) [363.34]

4161 Grace, N. B. *UFO Mysteries* (2–5). Series: Boys Rock! 2006, The Child's World LB $24.21 (1-59296-738-8). 32pp. A good choice for beginning and reluctant readers (girls as well as boys), this is a photo-filled exploration of the search for life outside our solar system and of the possibility that other life forms have visited earth. (Rev: SLJ 2/07) [001.942]

4162 Halls, Kelly Milner. *Tales of the Cryptids: Mysterious Creatures That May or May Not Exist* (4–7). Illus. by Rick Spears. 2006, Darby Creek $18.95 (1-58196-049-2). 72pp. A fun, close-up look at cryptozoology, the study of legendary animals (that may or may not be real) such as the Loch Ness Monster and Bigfoot. (Rev: BL 11/15/06; SLJ 12/06) [001.944]

4163 Krensky, Stephen. *Frankenstein* (4–7). Illus. Series: Monster Chronicles. 2006, Lerner LB $26.60 (978-0-8225-5923-8). 48pp. A survey of the folklore and fiction featuring Frankenstein's monster, including excerpts from the famous Mary Shelley novel. Also use *Vampires* and *Werewolves* (both 2006). (Rev: SLJ 2/07) [823]

4164 Messenger, Norman. *Imagine* (3–5). Illus. 2005, Candlewick $17.99 (0-7636-2757-7). 32pp. This inventively constructed book, with folds, wheels, and flaps, offers a variety of visual stimuli and puzzles. (Rev: BL 1/1–15/06) [793.73]

4165 Pascoe, Elaine. *Fooled You! Fakes and Hoaxes Through the Years* (4–6). Illus. by Laurie Keller. 2005, Holt $16.95 (0-8050-7528-3). 96pp. Pascoe tells the stories behind some of the world's most infamous hoaxes, including the Cardiff Giant, Bigfoot, crop circles, and Piltdown Man. (Rev: BL 9/15/05; SLJ 11/05) [001.9]

4166 *Pick Me Up* (4–8). Illus. 2006, DK $29.99 (0-7566-2159-3). 351pp. This attractive, child-friendly compilation of facts and figures offers information on a wide variety of topics, including nature, fashion, math, politics, popular culture, geography, music, movies, and technology. (Rev: SLJ 12/06) [900]

4167 Slade, Arthur. *Monsterology: Fabulous Lives of the Creepy, the Revolting, and the Undead* (5–8). Illus. by Derek Mah. 2005, Tundra paper $8.95 (0-88776-714-1). 95pp. Dracula, Medusa, Dr. Jekyll/

Mr. Hyde, and Sasquatch are among the characters profiled in this entertaining volume, each with a list of loves and hates, favorite saying, and fashion rating. (Rev: SLJ 2/06; VOYA 2/06)

4168 Spirn, Michele Sobel. *Mysterious People: A Chapter Book* (3–6). Series: True Tales. 2005, Children's Pr. LB $22.50 (0-516-25181-3); paper $4.95 (0-516-25454-5). 48pp. A compelling account of four people who met mysterious fates — Queen Nefertiti, Kaspar Hauser, Ishi, and a 5,000-year-old corpse called Otzi — and how they were discovered. (Rev: SLJ 5/06) [920]

4169 Szpirglas, Jeff. *They Did What?! Your Guide to Weird and Wacky Things People Do* (3–6). Illus. by Dave Whamond. 2005, Maple Tree $16.95 (1-897066-22-8); paper $9.95 (1-897066-23-6). 64pp. A fascinating look at weird human behavior and inventions (think pet rocks, hoaxes, air-guitar competitions, and so forth). (Rev: SLJ 3/06) [031.02]

Sports and Games

General and Miscellaneous

4170 Caldwell, Michaela. *The Girls' Yoga Book: Stretch Your Body, Open Your Mind, and Have Fun!* (4–6). Illus. by Claudia Dávila. 2005, Maple Tree $16.95 (1-897066-24-4); paper $9.95 (1-897066-25-2). 64pp. This book emphasizes the psychological benefits of yoga in a bright and vibrant format. (Rev: SLJ 5/06) [613.7]

4171 Connolly, Helen. *Field Hockey: Rules, Tips, Strategy, and Safety* (4–8). Series: Sports from Coast to Coast. 2005, Rosen LB $26.50 (1-4042-0182-3). 48pp. This title puts the spotlight on field hockey, including a brief history of the sport as well as a look at its rules, equipment, training, and so forth. (Rev: SLJ 10/05)

4172 Egan, Tracie. *Water Polo: Rules, Tips, Strategy, and Safety* (4–8). Series: Sports from Coast to Coast. 2005, Rosen LB $26.50 (1-4042-0186-6). 48pp. Introduces readers to the sport of water polo, along with its rules, training, and equipment. (Rev: SLJ 10/05)

4173 Giddens, Sandra, and Owen Giddens. *Volleyball: Rules, Tips, Strategy, and Safety* (4–8). Series: Sports from Coast to Coast. 2005, Rosen LB $26.50 (1-4042-0185-8). 48pp. Introduces the sport of volleyball — including its rules, equipment, and strategies. (Rev: SLJ 10/05) [796.32]

4174 Jones, Jen. *Cheer Tryouts: Making the Cut* (3–7). Illus. Series: Snap Books Cheerleading. 2005, Capstone LB $22.60 (0-7368-4361-2). 32pp. The focus here is on preparation — from good nutrition and regular stretching to practicing drills and a good attitude; part of a series that also includes *Cheer Squad: Building Spirit and Getting Along* (2005). (Rev: SLJ 1/06) [791.6]

4175 Kalman, Bobbie. *Extreme Wakeboarding* (3–10). Illus. Series: Extreme Sports: No Limits! 2006, Crabtree LB $25.20 (978-0-7787-1680-8); paper $6.95 (978-0-7787-1726-3). 32pp. The history wakeboarding is covered here, as well as the fundamental techniques, equipment, and safety considerations. (Rev: SLJ 2/07) [797.3]

4176 Kalman, Bobbie, and John Crossingham. *Extreme Skydiving* (3–10). Illus. Series: Extreme Sports: No Limits! 2006, Crabtree LB $25.20 (978-0-7787-1684-6); paper $6.95 (978-0-7787-1730-0). 32pp. This colorful introduction to skydiving chronicles the sport's long history, which can be traced back to the late 18th century, and describes its different disciplines and required equipment. (Rev: SLJ 2/07)

4177 Lindeen, Carol K. *Let's Downhill Ski!* (PS–1). Series: Sports and Activities. 2006, Capstone LB $19.93 (978-0-7368-6359-9). 24pp. A large-format, simply written introduction that covers basic techniques, equipment, and safety and includes color photographs. (Rev: SLJ 2/07) [796.9]

4178 Lourie, Peter. *First Dive to Shark Dive* (5–8). Illus. 2006, Boyds Mills $17.95 (1-59078-068-X). 48pp. This attractive, interesting photoessay documents a 12-year-old girl's introduction to scuba diving among sharks. (Rev: BL 2/15/06; SLJ 6/06) [797.2]

4179 MacAulay, Kelley, and Bobbie Kalman. *Extreme Skiing* (3–9). Illus. Series: Extreme Sports: No Limits! 2006, Crabtree LB $25.20 (978-0-7787-1682-2); paper $6.95 (978-0-7787-1728-7). 32pp. This slim, well-illustrated volume looks at freestyle skiing, offering a brief history of the sport and touching on such topics as skiing styles, equipment, and competition rules. (Rev: SLJ 2/07) [797.937]

4180 Ripoll, Oriol. *Play with Us: 100 Games from Around the World* (3–5). Illus. 2005, Chicago

Review paper $16.95 (1-55652-594-X). 128pp. Ball games, card games, checkers, hopscotch — these are only a few of the 100 games, both indoor and outdoor, included in this international collection that is indexed by continent. (Rev: BL 11/15/05; SLJ 1/06) [793]

4181 Rosen, Michael J. *Balls!* (4–7). 2006, Darby Creek $18.95 (1-58196-030-1). 72pp. Balls used in all sorts of sports and their history, choice of shape, and method of construction are the topic of light-hearted discussion. (Rev: BL 6/1–15/06) [796.3]

4182 Schindler, John E. *Hang Gliding and Parasailing* (2–5). Series: Extreme Sports: An Imagination Library Series. 2005, Gareth Stevens LB $22.00 (0-8368-4540-4); paper $5.95 (0-8368-4547-1). 24pp. An introduction to this "extreme" sport, with brief text and colorful photographs suitable for reluctant readers. (Rev: SLJ 9/05) [797.5]

4183 Schindler, John E. *Skydiving* (2–5). 2005, Gareth Stevens LB $22.00 (0-8368-4543-9); paper $5.95 (0-8368-4550-1). 24pp. A basic introduction to this "extreme" sport, with brief text and colorful photographs that will appeal to reluctant readers. (Rev: SLJ 9/05) [797.5]

4184 Schindler, John E. *Triathlons* (2–5). 2005, Gareth Stevens LB $22.00 (0-8368-4544-7); paper $5.95 (0-8368-4551-X). 24pp. A basic introduction to this "extreme" sport, with brief text and colorful photographs that will appeal to reluctant readers. (Rev: SLJ 9/05) [796.42]

4185 Szwast, Ursula. *Cheerleading* (3–6). Series: Get Going! Hobbies. 2005, Heinemann LB $27.79 (1-4034-6116-3). 32pp. This guide reviews basic moves and positions and discusses both competitive cheerleading and the history of cheerleading. (Rev: SLJ 3/06) [791.6]

4186 Wells, Don. *For the Love of Golf* (3–5). Illus. Series: For the Love of Sports. 2005, Weigl LB $24.45 (1-59036-296-9). 24pp. Colorful double-page spreads present the fundamentals of golf, as well as the history of the game and information on famous players. (Rev: BL 9/1/05) [796.352]

4187 Wurdinger, Scott, and Leslie Rapparlie. *Ice Climbing* (5–9). Series: Adventure Sports. 2006, Creative Education LB $31.35 (1-58341-393-6). 48pp. This well-designed guide to ice climbing familiarizes readers with the sport's history, equipment, competitions, and safety measures. (Rev: SLJ 12/06) [796.52]

4188 Wurdinger, Scott, and Leslie Rapparlie. *Rock Climbing* (5–9). Series: Adventure Sports. 2006, Creative Education LB $31.35 (1-58341-394-4). 48pp. Using many eye-catching photographs, this slim volume introduces to rock climbing and examines the sport's history, equipment, competitions, and safety measures. (Rev: SLJ 12/06) [796.5]

Automobile Racing

4189 Braun, Eric. *Hot Rods* (3–5). Illus. Series: Motor Mania. 2006, Lerner LB $26.60 (978-0-8225-3531-7). 48pp. A basic introduction to these customized cars and how they're raced as well as information on their history, how they're built, and what they look like. (Rev: BL 10/1/06; SLJ 3/07) [629.228]

4190 Buckley, James, Jr. *NASCAR* (5–8). Illus. Series: Eyewitness Books. 2005, DK LB $19.99 (0-7566-1193-8). 72pp. A visual pleasure for NASCAR fans, full of information about people, places, individual races, engineering advances, and so forth. (Rev: BL 9/1/05) [796.72]

4191 Caldwell, Dave. *Speed Show: How NASCAR Won the Heart of America* (5–8). 2006, Kingfisher $16.95 (0-7534-6011-4). 128pp. The history of NASCAR, the basics of stock car racing, its famous drivers, its fans, and so forth are all described in this very readable book by a *New York Times* sports writer. (Rev: BL 11/15/06) [796.720973]

4192 Doeden, Matt. *NASCAR's Wildest Wrecks* (3–6). Series: Edge Books/NASCAR Racing. 2004, Capstone LB $22.60 (0-7368-3775-2). 32pp. An overview of famous NASCAR crashes, complete with color photographs, and of the safety measures prompted by these accidents. (Rev: SLJ 7/05) [796.72]

4193 Doeden, Matt. *Stock Cars* (3–5). Illus. Series: Motor Mania. 2006, Lerner LB $26.60 (978-0-8225-3530-0). 48pp. Describes stock cars and their history, racing, and famous drivers. (Rev: SLJ 3/07) [796.72]

4194 Eagen, Rachel. *NASCAR* (4–7). Series: Auto-mania. 2006, Crabtree $18.90 (0-7787-3007-7). 32pp. An excellent, photo-filled overview of NASCAR's history, rules, safety measures, cars, and leading drivers. (Rev: BL 9/1/06) [796.720973]

4195 Herzog, Brad. *R Is for Race: A Stock Car Alphabet* (3–5). 2006, Sleeping Bear $16.95 (1-58536-272-7). 32pp. The variety of formats in this A to Z of auto racing will suit readers of different ages and needs. (Rev: BL 8/06) [796.72]

4196 Miller, Tim. *Vroom!* (4–6). 2006, Tundra paper $17.95 (0-88776-755-9). 64pp. A large-format introduction to the many different types of auto racing, featuring facts and history on each and plenty of action photographs. (Rev: BL 11/15/06) [796]

4197 Pearce, Al. *Famous Tracks* (4–8). Series: Race Car Legends: Collector's Edition. 2005, Chelsea House LB $25.00 (0-7910-8692-5). 77pp. Four well-known racetracks are the focus of this readable title full of photographs. (Rev: SLJ 5/06; VOYA 4/06) [796.72]

4198 Piehl, Janet. *Formula One Race Cars* (3–5). Illus. 2006, Lerner LB $26.60 (978-0-8225-5929-0). 48pp. Describes Formula One racing cars and their history and famous drivers. (Rev: SLJ 3/07)

4199 Schaefer, A. R. *Racing with the Pit Crew* (3–6). Series: Edge Books/NASCAR Racing. 2005, Capstone paper $7.95 (0-7368-5235-2). 32pp. A look at the work performed by the pit crew and the safety and other concerns they must monitor. Also use *The History of NASCAR* (2005). (Rev: SLJ 7/05) [796.72]

Baseball

4200 Buckley, James, Jr. *A Batboy's Day* (1–3). Illus. Series: DK Readers. 2005, DK $12.99 (0-7566-1206-3); paper $3.99 (0-7566-1207-1). 32pp. A batboy for the Anaheim Angels describes the responsibilities of his job in this engaging title for beginning readers. (Rev: BL 9/1/05; SLJ 12/05) [796.357]

4201 Buckley, James, Jr. *Let's Go to the Ballpark* (2–3). Series: DK Readers: MLB. 2005, DK $12.99 (0-7566-1208-X); paper $3.99 (0-7566-1209-8). 32pp. For beginning readers, this book follows a family's visit to a big-league ballpark. (Rev: SLJ 12/05) [796.357]

4202 Burke, Jim. *Take Me Out to the Ball Game* (2–4). Illus. 2006, Little, Brown $16.99 (0-316-75819-1). 32pp. Burke uses the classic song as the backdrop for the story of a famous 1908 game between the New York Giants and the Chicago Cubs. (Rev: BL 4/1/06; SLJ 4/06) [796.357]

4203 Cook, Sally, and James Charlton. *Hey Batta Batta Swing!* (3–5). Illus. by Ross MacDonald. 2007, Simon & Schuster $17.99 (1-4169-1207-X). 56pp. This buoyant history of baseball's early years provides fascinating facts about team names, players' numbers, equipment, and so forth; antique typography and colorful illustrations recalling early cartoons complement the lively text. (Rev: BL 1/1–15/07) [796.3]

4204 Sandler, Michael. *Baseball: The 2004 Boston Red Sox* (3–5). Illus. Series: Upsets and Comebacks. 2006, Bearport LB $17.97 (1-59716-165-9). 32pp. Full of photographs, this tells the story of Red Sox' triumphant 2004 season; with trivia, timeline, bibliography, glossary, and Web sites. (Rev: BL 4/1/06; SLJ 7/06) [796.357]

4205 Stewart, Mark, and Mike Kennedy. *Long Ball: The Legend and Lore of the Home Run* (3–5). Illus. 2006, Millbrook LB $22.60 (0-7613-2779-7). 64pp. Containing photographs and reproductions of baseball cards and magazine covers, this attractive book chronicles the history of the home run and profiles some of baseball's most notable long-ball hitters. (Rev: BL 4/1/06; SLJ 6/06; VOYA 6/06) [796.357]

4206 Thomas, Ron, and Joe Herran. *Getting into Baseball* (2–4). Illus. by Nives Porcellato and Andy Craig. Series: Getting into Sports. 2005, Chelsea House LB $20.95 (0-7910-8808-1). After a brief history of the game, this book covers rules, equipment, clothing, and competitions and provides color photographs, useful diagrams, and interesting trivia. (Rev: SLJ 12/05) [796.357]

4207 Uhlberg, Myron. *Dad, Jackie, and Me* (2–4). Illus. by Colin Bootman. 2005, Peachtree $16.95 (1-56145-329-3). 32pp. A young Brooklyn boy (the author) and his deaf father grow closer as they follow the baseball exploits of Jackie Robinson during his first year with the Dodgers. (Rev: BL 8/05; SLJ 5/05)

Basketball

4208 Stewart, Mark. *The Miami Heat* (3–5). Illus. Series: Team Spirit. 2006, Norwood House LB $18.95 (0-59953-009-0). 48pp. An attractive profile of professional basketball's Miami Heat, examining the team's brief history, its standout players, and performance in recent seasons. (Rev: BL 4/1/06) [796.323]

Bicycles

4209 Buckley, Annie. *Be a Better Biker* (5–6). Series: Girls Rock! 2006, The Child's World LB $24.21 (1-59296-741-8). 32pp. As well as advice on safety and maintenance, this volume (which is suitable for boys too) covers the history of bicycles and the various types available today. (Rev: SLJ 2/07) [796.6]

4210 Hinman, Bonnie. *Extreme Cycling with Dale Holmes* (2–4). Illus. Series: Robbie Reader: Extreme Sports. 2006, Mitchell Lane LB $16.95 (1-58415-487-X). 32pp. This high-interest volume combines information on extreme cycling with a biographical profile of British-born BMX bike racer Dale Holmes. (Rev: BL 10/15/06) [796.6]

4211 Schoenherr, Alicia, and Rusty Schoenherr. *Mountain Biking* (4–6). Series: Kids' Guides. 2005, The Child's World LB $24.21 (1-59296-209-2). 32pp. An introduction to mountain biking, describing its history and equipment and key athletes and competitions, with plenty of photographs and a glossary. (Rev: SLJ 7/05) [796.6]

4212 Wurdinger, Scott, and Leslie Rapparlie. *Mountain Biking* (5–9). Series: Adventure Sports. 2006,

Creative Education LB $31.35 (1-58341-396-0). 48pp. Using many eye-catching photographs, this slim volume introduces the popular sport's history, equipment, competitions, and safety measures. (Rev: SLJ 12/06) [796.6]

Camping and Backpacking

4213 Ghione, Yvette. *This Is Daniel Cook on a Hike* (K–3). 2006, Kids Can $12.95 (1-55453-079-2); paper $4.95 (1-55453-080-9). In this companion to the popular Canadian-produced TV show, the young host takes readers on a walk in the woods, introducing them to hiking equipment, safety precautions, and the animals and plants they encounter. (Rev: SLJ 11/06) [796.51]

4214 Mader, Jan. *Let's Go Camping!* (PS–1). Series: Sports and Activities. 2006, Capstone LB $19.93 (978-0-7368-6360-5). 24pp. A large-format, simply written introduction that covers basic techniques, equipment, and safety and includes color photographs. (Rev: SLJ 2/07) [796.54]

4215 Weber, Sandra. *Two in the Wilderness: Adventures of a Mother and Daughter in the Adirondack Mountains* (3–5). Photos by Carl E. Heilman. Illus. 2005, Boyds Mills $19.95 (1-59078-182-1). 48pp. This photoessay covers a 12-day journey the author took with her preteen daughter through New York's Adirondack Mountains, describing various physical and meteorological challenges as well as the geological and historical sights along the way; excerpts from daughter Marcy's journal add another perspective. (Rev: BL 7/05; SLJ 11/05) [508.747]

Fishing

4216 Arnosky, Jim. *Hook, Line, and Seeker: A Beginners Guide to Fishing, Boating, and Watching Water Wildlife* (4–6). Illus. 2005, Scholastic $14.95 (0-439-45584-7). 192pp. Outdoorsman (and illustrator) Arnosky draws on personal experience in this information-packed guide to boating, fishing, and wildlife watching. (Rev: BL 8/05; VOYA 4/06) [799.1]

Football

4217 Madden, John, and Bill Gutman. *John Madden's Heroes of Football: The Story of America's Game* (5–8). 2006, Dutton $18.99 (0-525-47698-9). 80pp. The former NFL coach and popular football commentator chronicles the history of professional football, looking at how the game has changed over the years and profiling some of its best-known players and coaches. (Rev: BL 9/1/06; SLJ 2/07) [796.332092]

4218 Mader, Jan. *Let's Play Football!* (PS–1). Series: Sports and Activities. 2006, Capstone LB $19.93 (978-0-7368-6361-2). 24pp. A large-format, simply written introduction that covers basic techniques, equipment, and safety and includes color photographs. (Rev: SLJ 2/07) [796.332]

4219 Woods, Bob. *NFC North* (4–6). Series: Inside the NFL. 2005, Child's World LB $18.95 (1-59296-513-X). 48pp. Introduces the four teams that make up the NFC North division of the National Football League, with discussion of their history and famous games and players. (Rev: BL 9/1/05) [796.332]

Gymnastics

4220 Bray-Moffatt, Naia. *I Love Gymnastics* (K–3). Photos by avid Handley. Illus. 2005, DK $12.99 (0-7566-1011-7). 48pp. Excellent photographs show a young girl's introduction to the world of gymnastics, showing both basic and advanced moves. (Rev: BL 9/1/05; SLJ 5/06) [796.44]

Ice Hockey

4221 McKinley, Michael, and Suzanne Levesque. *Ice Time: The Story of Hockey* (5–8). Illus. 2006, Tundra $18.95 (0-88776-762-1). 80pp. This history of ice hockey focuses mainly on the development and current status of the game in Canada, also covering international stars. (Rev: BL 12/1/06; SLJ 1/07) [796.962]

Ice Skating

4222 Lindeen, Carol K. *Let's Ice-Skate!* (K–2). Series: Sports and Activities. 2005, Capstone LB $19.93 (0-7368-5360-X). 24pp. An attractive introduction to the sport for beginning readers. (Rev: SLJ 6/06) [796.91]

Indoor Games

4223 Gunter, Veronika Alice. *The Ultimate Indoor Games Book: The 200 Best Boredom Busters Ever!* (3–5). Illus. by Clay Meyer. 2005, Sterling $19.95

(1-57990-625-7). 128pp. Provides lots of child-friendly activities, including ball games, brain teasers, and pen-and-paper games, all guaranteed to banish boredom on a cold or rainy day. (Rev: BL 11/1/05; SLJ 3/06) [793]

Sailing and Boating

4224 Bass, Scott. *Kayaking* (4–6). Series: Kids' Guides. 2005, The Child's World LB $24.21 (1-59296-208-4). 32pp. An introduction to kayaking, describing its history and equipment and key athletes and competitions, with plenty of photographs and a glossary. (Rev: SLJ 7/05) [797.12]

4225 Wurdinger, Scott, and Leslie Rapparlie. *Kayaking* (5–9). Series: Adventure Sports. 2006, Creative Education LB $31.35 (1-58341-397-9). 48pp. Using many eye-catching photographs, this slim volume introduces the sport's history, equipment, competitions, and safety measures. (Rev: SLJ 12/06) [797.122]

Self-Defense

4226 Ancona, George. *Capoeira: Game! Dance! Martial Art!* (2–4). Illus. 2007, Lee & Low $18.95 (978-1-58430-268-1). 32pp. Capoeira — a Brazilian blend of dance, martial art, and game — is shown in eye-catching photographs of students practicing in California. (Rev: BL 4/15/07) [793.3]

Skateboarding

4227 Hocking, Justin. *Awesome Obstacles: How to Build Your Own Skateboard Ramps and Ledges* (4–6). Illus. Series: Skateboarder's Guide to Skate Parks, Half-Pipes, Bowls, and Obstacles. 2005, Rosen LB $19.95 (1-4042-0337-0). 48pp. Along with advice on safety, this volume provides plans for the construction of six wooden ramps and boxes. (Rev: BL 9/1/05) [796.22]

4228 Spencer, Russ. *Skateboarding* (4–6). Series: Kids' Guides. 2005, The Child's World LB $24.21 (1-59296-210-6). 32pp. An introduction to skateboarding, describing its history and equipment and

key athletes and competitions, with plenty of photographs and a glossary. (Rev: SLJ 7/05) [796.2]

Snowboarding

4229 Degezelle, Terri. *Let's Snowboard!* (K–2). Series: Sports and Activities. 2005, Capstone LB $19.93 (0-7368-5366-9). 24pp. An attractive introduction to the sport for beginning readers, with emphasis on equipment and safety. (Rev: SLJ 6/06) [796.9]

4230 Woods, Bob. *Snowboarding* (4–6). Series: Kids' Guides. 2005, The Child's World LB $24.21 (1-59296-211-4). 32pp. An introduction to snowboarding, describing its history and equipment and key athletes and competitions, with plenty of photographs and a glossary. (Rev: SLJ 7/05) [796.9]

Soccer

4231 Buckley, James, Jr. *Soccer Superstars* (2–5). Series: Boys Rock! 2006, The Child's World LB $24.21 (1-59296-736-1). 32pp. A good choice for beginning and reluctant readers (girls as well as boys), this colorful book looks at the status of soccer and profiles some of the game's most popular players. (Rev: SLJ 2/07) [796.3]

4232 Buckley, James, Jr. *Soccer Superwomen* (1–3). Series: Girls Rock! 2006, The Child's World LB $24.21 (1-59296-750-7). 32pp. Introduces readers to some of the world's best female soccer players and looks at the overall popularity of soccer. (Rev: SLJ 2/07) [796.3]

4233 Saunders, Catherine. *Play Soccer* (3–6). Photos by Russell Sadur. 2006, DK LB $12.99 (0-7566-2032-5). 63pp. This is a practical book that will help soccer players improve their passing and control of the ball; photographs demonstrate techniques. (Rev: SLJ 7/06) [796.334]

4234 Thomas, Ron, and Joe Herran. *Getting into Soccer* (2–4). Illus. by Nives Porcellato and Andy Craig. Series: Getting into Sports. 2005, Chelsea House LB $20.95 (0-7910-8806-5). After a brief history of the game, this book covers rules, equipment, clothing, and competitions and provides color photographs, useful diagrams, and interesting trivia. (Rev: SLJ 12/05) [796.334]

Author and Illustrator Index

Authors and illustrators are arranged alphabetically by last name, followed by book titles — which are also arranged alphabetically — and the text entry number. Book titles may refer to those that appear as a main entry or as an internal entry mentioned in the annotation. Fiction titles are indicated by (F) following the entry number.

Aaseng, Nathan. *Business Builders in Sweets and Treats*, 3317
Abbott, Jason. *The Ravioli Kid*, 924(F)
Abbott, Tony. *Firegirl*, 1958(F)
Kringle, 1753(F)
Abdullah, Patricia. *Saving Daddy*, 722(F)
Abela, Deborah. *Mission*, 1584(F)
Abercrombie, Barbara. *The Show-and-Tell Lion*, 1256(F)
Abeya, Elisabet. *Hansel and Gretel / Hansel y Gretel*, 2374
Abolafia, Yossi. *It's Snowing! It's Snowing! Winter Poems*, 2601
Abrams, Judith Z. *The Secret World of Kabbalah*, 3380
Abramson, Beverley. *Off We Go!* 44(F)
Ackroyd, Peter. *Ancient Greece*, 3077
Ada, Alma Flor. *Tales Our Abuelitas Told*, 2416
Adams, Simon. *Alexander*, 2856
Ancient Egypt, 3067
Elizabeth I, 2867
Adams, Steve. *The Boy Who Grew Flowers*, 1951(F)
Adamson, Bonnie. *Feeling Better*, 3474
Adamson, Thomas K. *Lessons in Science Safety with Max Axiom, Super Scientist*, 3573
Addy, Sean. *Trains*, 1298(F)
Addy, Sharon Hart. *Lucky Jake*, 1037(F)
Adinolfi, JoAnn. *Alfie the Apostrophe*, 224(F)
Hippopotamus Stew, 2565
Leaping Lizards, 117
Adkins, Jan. *What If You Met a Knight?* 3091
Adler, David A. *Bones and the Dinosaur Mystery*, 1413(F)

Cam Jansen and the Secret Service Mystery, 1585(F)
Cam Jansen and the Valentine Baby Mystery, 1586(F)
Campy, 2831
Joe Louis, 2837
President George Washington, 2772
Satchel Paige, 2834
You Can, Toucan, Math, 3959
Young Cam Jansen and the Substitute Mystery, 1414(F)
Adler, Tzivia. *The Sefer Torah Parade*, 1397(F)
Agard, John. *Half-Caste and Other Poems*, 2509
Agee, Jon. *Smart Feller Fart Smeller*, 2931
Terrific, 609(F)
Why Did the Chicken Cross the Road? 2893
Ahlberg, Allan. *The Children Who Smelled a Rat*, 2238(F)
The Runaway Dinner, 882(F)
Ahmed, Said Salah. *The Lion's Share / Qayb Libaax*, 2426
Aillaud, Cindy Lou. *Recess at 20 Below*, 3289
Aizpuriete, Amanda. *Latvia*, 3142
Akaba, Suekichi. *Suho's White Horse*, 2429
Akib, Jamel. *Bringing Asha Home*, 788(F)
Robinson Crusoe, 1638(F)
Akimoto, Nami. *Ultra Cute. Vol. 1*, 1976(F)
Alarcón, Francisco X. *Poems to Dream Together / Poemas para soñar juntos*, 2510
Alberti, Theresa. *Vietnam ABCs*, 3133
Alberto, Daisy. *No Rules for Rex!* 621(F)
Alborough, Jez. *Hit the Ball Duck*, 319(F)

Hug, 126(F), 320(F)
Tall, 320(F)
Yes, 126(F)
Alcántara, Felipe Ugalde. *Little Crow to the Rescue / El cuervito al rescate*, 2424
Alda, Arlene. *Did You Say Pears?* 2932
Aldinolfi, JoAnn. *A Circle in the Sky*, 83(F)
Alexander, Jessica. *Look Both Ways*, 555(F)
This Is the Dream, 3355
Alexander, Lloyd. *Dream-of-Jade*, 2099(F)
Alexander, Martha. *The Little Green Witch*, 1392(F)
Ali, Rasheda. *I'll Hold Your Hand So You Won't Fall*, 3508
Ali, Sharifah Enayat. *Afghanistan*, 3134
Aliki. *A Play's the Thing*, 1257(F)
Allen, Jonathan. *I'm Not Cute!* 321(F)
Allen, Joy. *Lindy's Happy Ending*, 709(F)
Allen, Judy. *Higher Ground*, 3832
Allen, Kathy. *The U.S. Constitution*, 3357
Allen, Susan. *Written Anything Good Lately?* 1
Allen, Thomas B. *Harriet Tubman, Secret Agent*, 3237
Alley, R. W. *Ballerino Nate*, 339(F)
Being Teddy Roosevelt, 2311(F)
Dear Santa, 1337(F)
The Prince Has a Boo-Boo! 1487(F)
Tiger Can't Sleep, 138(F)
We're Off to Find the Witch's House, 1390(F)
Ziggy's Blue-Ribbon Day, 1286(F)
Allison, Jennifer. *Gilda Joyce*, 1587(F)
Allman, Barbara. *Banking*, 3318

Fischer, Scott M. *Secrets of Dripping Fang*, 1823(F)
Treachery and Betrayal at Jolly Days, 1619(F)
Fisher, Aileen. *Know What I Saw?* 99(F)
Fisher, Doris. *One Odd Day*, 920(F)
Happy Birthday to Whooo? 4146
Fisher, Jane Smith. *WJHC*, 1986(F)
Fisher, Leonard Everett. *Blackbeard's Last Fight*, 2147(F)
Dybbuk, 2468
Fisher, Valorie. *How High Can a Dinosaur Count? And Other Math Mysteries*, 3961
Fishman, Cathy Goldberg. *On Sukkot and Simchat Torah*, 3424
Fitzgerald, Brian. *Under Fire in World War II*, 3103
Fitzgerald, Dawn. *Getting in the Game*, 2359(F)
Soccer Chick Rules, 2297(F)
Vinnie and Abraham, 2644
Fitzgerald, Stephanie. *Struggling for Civil Rights*, 3351
Fitzhugh, Karla. *Body Image*, 3446
Fitzpatrick, Brad. *Cash, Credit Cards, or Checks*, 3321
Fitzpatrick, Marie-Louise. *I Am I*, 1119(F)
Silly Mommy, Silly Daddy, 764(F)
Flanagan, John. *The Burning Bridge*, 1814(F)
Fleischman, John. *Black and White Airmen*, 2850
Fleischman, Sid. *The White Elephant*, 2100(F)
Escape! 2658
Fleischner, Jennifer. *Nobody's Boy*, 2176(F)
Fleisher, Paul. *The Big Bang*, 3579
Fleming, Candace. *Muncha! Muncha! Muncha!* 921(F)
Sunny Boy! The Life and Times of a Tortoise, 613(F)
Tippy-Tippy-Tippy, Hide! 921(F)
Fleming, Charles. *Nicky Deuce*, 1745(F)
Nicky Deuce: Welcome to the Family, 1746(F)
Fleming, Denise. *The Cow Who Clucked*, 395(F)
The First Day of Winter, 1017(F)
Fleming, Thomas. *Everybody's Revolution*, 3215
Fletcher, Bob. *I Grew Up on a Farm*, 1075(F)
Fletcher, Marty. *The Green Sea Turtle*, 3641
Neptune, 3593
Uranus, 3594
Fletcher, Ralph. *Marshfield Dreams*, 2678
Moving Day, 2519
Fletcher, Rusty. *I'm Not Afraid of Halloween!* 1378(F)
Flinn, Alan. *Constellations*, 3601

Flint, David. *Europe*, 3138
Floca, Brian. *From Slave to Soldier*, 2177(F)
Lightship, 3167
Flood, Pansie Hart. *Sometimey Friend*, 1721(F)
Tiger Turcotte Takes on the Know-It-All, 2298(F)
Flook, Helen. *Something Slimy on Primrose Drive*, 1581(F)
Florczak, Robert. *Horses of Myth*, 2418
Florian, Douglas. *Autumnblings*, 2597
Comets, Stars, the Moon and Mars, 2596
Handsprings, 2597
Summersaults, 2597
Winter Eyes, 2597
Florie, Christine. *Lara Ladybug*, 1439(F)
Floyd, Madeleine. *Cold Paws, Warm Heart*, 228(F)
Foley, Greg. *Thank You Bear*, 396(F)
Fontes, Justine. *Black Meets White*, 74(F)
Ford, Bernette. *First Snow*, 1018(F)
No More Diapers for Ducky! 645(F)
Ford, Carin T. *Jackie Robinson*, 2835
Ford, Christine. *The Soldiers' Night Before Christmas*, 1340(F)
Ford, Nick. *Niccolò Machiavelli*, 2877
Fore, S. J. *Tiger Can't Sleep*, 138(F)
Foreman, George. *Let George Do It!* 1311(F)
Foreman, Michael. *Classic Fairy Tales*, 2391
Mia's Story, 1057(F)
The Wonderful Wizard of Oz, 1767(F)
Foreman, Michael, retel. *Classic Fairy Tales*, 2391
Forest, Heather, retel. *The Little Red Hen*, 2449
Forget, Thomas. *The Creation of Captain America*, 2920
Forman, Ruth. *Young Cornrows Callin Out the Moon*, 2557
Fortune, Eric. *Bunnicula Meets Edgar Allan Crow*, 2258(F)
Fowkes, Charlie. *Riddle of the Raptors*, 2322(F)
Fowler, Jim. *First Salmon*, 835(F)
Fowler, Richard. *Under the Bed!* 312(F)
Fowles, Shelley. *Climbing Rosa*, 229(F)
Fox, Christyan. *How Many Sharks in the Bath?* 104(F)
Tyson the Terrible, 397(F)
Fox, Diane. *Tyson the Terrible*, 397(F)
Fox, Helen. *Eager*, 1815(F)
Eager's Nephew, 1815(F)
Fox, Mary Virginia. *Australia*, 3137

North America, 3154
Fox, Mem. *A Particular Cow*, 922(F)
Fox, Tom. *Snowball Launchers, Giant-Pumpkin Growers, and Other Cool Contraptions*, 3571
Fradin, Dennis Brindell. *The Alamo*, 3224
The Declaration of Independence, 3216
The Founders, 2702
Jamestown, Virginia, 3200
Frampton, David. *The Song of Francis and the Animals*, 1086(F)
Frampton, Otis. *Oddly Normal*, 1987(F)
Francis, Guy. *Dance by the Light of the Moon*, 538(F)
Mrs. McBloom, Clean Up Your Room! 1269(F)
Shelly, 515(F)
Francis, Pauline. *Sam Stars at Shakespeare's Globe*, 1058(F)
Franco, Betsy. *Birdsongs*, 100(F)
Franson, Leanne. *Thumb on a Diamond*, 2367(F)
Franson, Scott E. *Un-Brella*, 230(F)
Fraser, Mary Ann. *I.Q. Goes to the Library*, 398(F)
I.Q., It's Time, 398(F)
Frazee, Marla. *Clementine*, 1969(F)
Santa Claus, 1336(F)
The Talented Clementine, 2271(F)
Walk On! A Guide for Babies of All Ages, 923(F)
Frazier, Craig. *Stanley Goes Fishing*, 231(F)
Frederick, Heather. *For Your Paws Only*, 1816(F)
Spy Mice, 1817(F)
Fredericks, Mariah. *In the Cards*, 2299(F)
Freedman, Claire. *Snuggle Up, Sleepy Ones*, 139(F)
Freedman, Michelle. *The Ravioli Kid*, 924(F)
Freedman, Russell. *Children of the Great Depression*, 3246
Freedom Walkers, 3352
Freeman, Don. *Earl the Squirrel*, 399(F)
Freeman, Kathryn. *Loon Chase*, 1168(F)
Freeman, Martha. *Mrs. Wow Never Wanted a Cow*, 1440(F)
Who Stole Halloween? 1612(F)
Freeman, Tor. *Sleepy Places*, 143(F)
Fremaux, Charlotte. *The Best Worst Brother*, 844(F)
French, Jackie. *Pete the Sheep-Sheep*, 925(F)
Rover, 2108(F)
French, Martin. *Sophisticated Ladies*, 2631
Stompin' at the Savoy, 2662
French, Vivian. *The Daddy Goose Treasury*, 176
Freymann, Saxton. *Fast Food*, 1297

Ghiuselev, Iassen. *The King of the Golden River*, 2410

Gibbons, Gail. *Dinosaur Discoveries*, 3002

Galaxies, Galaxies! 3580

Groundhog Day, 3405

Ice Cream, 3887

The Planets, 3590

Valentine's Day Is . . ., 3430

Gibfried, Diane. *Brother Juniper*, 1061(F)

Giblin, James Cross. *The Boy Who Saved Cleveland*, 2157(F)

Gibson, Barbara Leonard. *N Is for Our Nation's Capital*, 3288

Gibson, Karen Bush. *The Fury of Hurricane Andrew, 1992*, 3972

The Great Basin Indians, 3179

The Life and Times of Eli Whitney, 2821

Giddens, Owen. *Volleyball*, 4173

Giddens, Sandra. *Volleyball*, 4173

Giddens-White, Bryon. *National Elections and the Political Process*, 3368

The President and the Executive Branch, 3371

The Supreme Court and the Judicial Branch., 3371

Giff, Patricia Reilly. *Maggie's Door*, 2190(F)

Nory Ryan's Song, 2190(F)

Water Street, 2190(F)

Willow Run, 2209(F)

Giffard, Hannah. *Pablo Goes Hunting*, 410(F)

Gifford, Clive. *Pollution*, 3340

Giganti, Paul. *How Many Blue Birds Flew Away? A Counting Book with a Difference*, 103(F)

Gilbert, Yvonne. *The Ice Dragon*, 1864(F)

Pirateology, 2091(F)

Gilchrist, Jan Spivey. *The Friendly Four*, 866(F)

My America, 2520

When the Horses Ride By, 2521

Gill, Shelley. *Hawai'i*, 3295

Up on Denali, 3918

Gilley, Jeremy. *Peace One Day*, 3406

Gillham, Bill. *How Many Sharks in the Bath?* 104(F)

Gilliland, Judith Heide. *Strange Birds*, 1820(F)

Gillis, Jennifer Blizin. *Dolores Huerta*, 2730

John Philip Sousa, 2654

Scott Joplin, 2649

Gilman, Laura Anne. *Grail Quest*, 2109(F)

Gilmore, Rachna. *Grandpa's Clock*, 1120(F)

Gilpin, Daniel. *Centipedes, Millipedes, Scorpions and Spiders*, 3790

Life-Size Killer Creatures, 3650

Snails, Shellfish and Other Mollusks, 3814

Gilpin, Stephen. *The Hero Revealed*, 1774(F)

Pirate Mom, 1513(F)

Gilson, Jamie. *Gotcha!* 2301(F)

Gimbergsson, Sara. *The Rabbit Who Couldn't Find His Daddy*, 380(F)

Gingras, Charlotte. *Emily's Piano*, 2027(F)

Ginkel, Anne. *I've Got an Elephant*, 105(F)

Giraud, Hervé. *Basha*, 3135

Kradji, 3135

Leila, 3120

Girouard, Patrick. *My Mother Is a Doctor*, 3490

Givner, Joan. *Ellen Fremedon*, 1541(F)

Ellen Fremedon, Journalist, 1541(F)

Ellen Fremedon, Volunteer, 1614(F)

Glaser, Jason. *Chicken Pox*, 3513

Flu, 3513

Head Lice, 3541

Ninja, 3050

Pinkeye, 3513

Glaser, Linda. *Bridge to America*, 2110(F)

Hello Squirrels! Scampering Through the Seasons, 3672

Glass, Andrew. *Sketches from a Spy Tree*, 2040(F)

Thank You Very Much, Captain Ericsson, 2805

The Tortoise and the Hare Race Again, 334(F)

Glass, Beth Raisner. *Noises at Night*, 140(F)

Glasser, Robin Preiss. *Fancy Nancy*, 973(F)

Our 50 States, 3166

Glatshteyn, Yankev. *Emil and Karl*, 2111(F)

Gleeson, Libby. *Half a World Away*, 865(F)

Gleitzman, Morris. *Toad Away*, 2252(F)

Glick, Sharon. *Perros! Perros! / Dogs! Dogs!* 3859

Glickman, Eric. *The GF Kid*, 3517

Gliori, Debi. *Pure Dead Batty*, 1615(F)

Pure Dead Trouble, 1821(F)

Godard, Philippe. *We Live in India*, 3130

Godin, Celia. *Fire!* 3914

Wolf Island, 1020(F)

Godwin, Laura. *The Flower Girl*, 648(F)

The Ring Bearer, 648(F)

Goembel, Ponder. *Castaway Cats*, 590(F)

Gold, August. *Does God Hear My Prayer?* 768(F)

Gold, Maya. *Harriet the Spy, Double Agent*, 1616(F)

Gold, Michael. *Junk Food*, 3885

Gold, Rozanne. *Kids Cook 1-2-3*, 4132

Goldberg, Whoopi. *Whoopi's Big Book of Manners*, 3454

Goldenberg, Linda. *Little People and a Lost World*, 3023

Goldfinger, Jennifer P. *The King's Chorus*, 424(F)

Goldish, Meish. *The Fossil Feud*, 3003

Goldsmith, Mike. *Space*, 4019

Goldstein, Margaret J. *Japanese in America*, 3435

Goldstone, Bruce. *Great Estimations*, 3935

Gomez, Elena. *Mama's Saris*, 802(F)

A World of Prayers, 3432

Gomi, Taro. *My Friends / Mis amigos*, 649(F)

Spring Is Here / Llegó la primavera, 1021(F)

Gonyea, Mark. *A Book About Design*, 2899

Gonzales, Doreen. *Seven Wonders of the Modern World*, 4040

Gonzalez, Maya Christina. *Nana's Big Surprise / Nana, Que Sorpresa!* 822(F)

González, Ada Acosta. *Mayte and the Bogeyman / Mayte y el Cuco*, 650(F)

Goobie, Beth. *Something Girl*, 1723(F)

Goode, Diane. *Mind Your Manners!* 3455

The Most Perfect Spot, 769(F)

Goodell, Jon. *The Gold Miner's Daughter*, 940(F)

Merry Christmas, Merry Crow, 1318(F)

Goodman, Susan E. *Gee Whiz! It's All About Pee*, 3534

Life on the Ice, 3161

The Truth About Poop, 3534

Goodrich, Carter. *A Creature Was Stirring*, 1356(F)

Goossens, Philippe. *Back into Mommy's Tummy*, 831(F)

Sam Is Never Scared, 1139(F)

Gopnik, Adam. *The King in the Window*, 1822(F)

Goppel, Christine. *Anna Aphid*, 411(F)

Gorbachev, Valeri. *All for Pie, Pie for All*, 493(F)

Big Little Elephant, 412(F)

Heron and Turtle, 413(F)

Ms. Turtle the Babysitter, 1442(F)

Gordon, Amy. *The Gorillas of Gill Park*, 1617(F)

Return to Gill Park, 1617(F)

Gordon, Carl. *Do Princesses Really Kiss Frogs?* 755(F)

Hocking, Justin. *Awesome Obstacles*, 4227

Hockinson, Liz. *Marcello the Movie Mouse*, 434(F)

Hodges, Jared. *Peach Fuzz*, 2247(F)

Hodges, Margaret. *Dick Whittington and His Cat*, 2451
Moses, 3401

Hodgkins, Fran. *The Cat of Strawberry Hill*, 1185(F)

Hoena, B. A. *Matthew Henson*, 2621

Hofer, Ernst. *Clever Katarina*, 2412

Hofer, Nelly. *Clever Katarina*, 2412

Hoffman, Kimberly. *Tito, the Firefighter / Tito, el bombero*, 655(F)

Hoffmann, Gretchen. *Mononucleosis*, 3516

Hogan, Jamie. *Rickshaw Girl*, 1092(F)

Hogg, Gary. *Beautiful Buehla and the Zany Zoo Makeover*, 244(F)
Look What the Cat Dragged In! 938(F)

Hohn, David. *Zachary Zormer*, 3942

Holabird, Katharine. *Angelina at the Palace*, 435(F)

Holland, Carola. *Heave Ho!* 1189(F)

Holland, Gay W. *Hello Squirrels! Scampering Through the Seasons*, 3672

Holland, Joel. *Snowball Launchers, Giant-Pumpkin Growers, and Other Cool Contraptions*, 3571

Holland, Trish. *The Soldiers' Night Before Christmas*, 1340(F)

Hollander, Nicole. *I Love Messes!* 774(F)
I'm All Dressed! 775(F)

Hollyer, Belinda, sel. *She's All That!* 2523

Holm, Jennifer. *You Only Have Nine Lives*, 1622(F)

Holm, Jennifer L. *Babymouse: Beach Babe*, 1831(F)
Babymouse: Our Hero, 1993(F)
Babymouse: Queen of the World, 1994(F)
Babymouse: Rock Star, 1832(F)

Holm, Matthew. *Babymouse: Beach Babe*, 1831(F)
Babymouse: Our Hero, 1993(F)
Babymouse: Queen of the World, 1994(F)
Babymouse: Rock Star, 1832(F)

Holm, Sharon. *Twelve Plump Cookies*, 1422(F)

Holm, Sharon Lane. *All New Crafts for Kwanzaa*, 4097
All New Crafts for Thanksgiving, 4098

Holmes, Sara. *Letters from Rapunzel*, 2054(F)

Holmes, Victoria. *Heart of Fire*, 2135(F)

Holt, Kimberly Willis. *Part of Me*, 2347(F)

Waiting for Gregory, 778(F)

Holub, Joan. *The Man Who Named the Clouds*, 2812

Holyfield, John. *Bessie Smith and the Night Riders*, 1504(F)

Holyoke, Nancy. *A Smart Girl's Guide to Manners*, 3457
A Smart Girl's Guide to Money, 3323

Homel, David. *Travels with My Family*, 1722(F)

Hong, Chen Jiang. *The Magic Horse of Han Gan*, 2432

Hook, Adam. *Ancient Egypt*, 3072
Rich and Poor in Ancient Rome, 3082

Hooper, Meredith. *Celebrity Cat*, 939(F)

Hoover, Dave. *Harriet Tubman and the Underground Railroad*, 3225

Hopkins, Jackie Mims. *The Gold Miner's Daughter*, 940(F)

Hopkins, Lee Bennett, ed. *Behind the Museum Door*, 2524
Got Geography! 2525

Hopkins, Lee Bennett, sel. *Halloween Howls*, 2580

Hopkinson, Deborah. *From Slave to Soldier*, 2177(F)
Into the Firestorm, 2194(F)
Sky Boys, 2195(F)
Susan B. Anthony, 2775
Sweet Land of Liberty, 2735

Hopman, Philip. *Earth to Stella!* 160(F)

Hoppe, Paul. *Travis and Freddy's Adventures in Vegas*, 1628(F)

Hoppey, Tim. *Tito, the Firefighter / Tito, el bombero*, 655(F)

Horacek, Petr. *Butterfly Butterfly*, 1023(F)
Silly Suzy Goose, 436(F)

Horn, Geoffrey M. *Movie Animation*, 2985

Hornsey, Chris. *Why Do I Have to Eat off the Floor?* 1186(F)

Hornung, Phyllis. *Bubbe Isabella and the Sukkot Cake*, 1406(F)

Horowitz, Anthony. *Alex Rider*, 1623(F)
Evil Star, 1833(F)
Raven's Gate, 1834(F)
South by Southeast, 1624(F)

Horowitz, Dave. *Five Little Gefiltes*, 941(F)
The Ugly Pumpkin, 1387(F)

Horrocks, Anita. *Almost Eden*, 2055(F)

Horse, Harry. *Little Rabbit Runaway*, 437(F)

Hort, Lenny. *Did Dinosaurs Eat Pizza? Mysteries Science Hasn't Solved*, 3004

Horton, Joan. *Hippopotamus Stew*, 2565

Horvath, Polly. *The Vacation*, 2056(F)

Hoshino, Felicia. *Finding the Golden Ruler*, 1454(F)
Little Sap and Monsieur Rodin, 1078(F)
A Place Where Sunflowers Grow / Sabaku Ni Saita Himawari, 1073(F)

Hosking, Wayne. *Asian Kites*, 4086

Hossell, Karen. *Delaware 1638–1776*, 3205

Hostetter, Joyce Moyer. *Blue*, 2212(F)

Hotchkiss, Ron. *The Matchless Six*, 2823

Houghton, Gillian. *Mildred Taylor*, 2696

House, Lauren. *Steven Caney's Ultimate Building Book*, 4038

Howard, Arthur. *Mr. Putter and Tabby Make a Wish*, 1495(F)
Mr. Putter and Tabby Spin the Yarn, 1496(F)

Howard, Ellen. *The Log Cabin Christmas*, 2158(F)
The Log Cabin Church, 2158(F)
Log Cabin Quilt, 2158(F)
The Log Cabin Wedding, 2158(F)

Howard, Paul. *The Cat Who Wanted to Go Home*, 570(F)

Howarth, Daniel. *I Love You Always and Forever*, 388(F)

Howe, James. *Bunnicula Meets Edgar Allan Crow*, 2258(F)
Houndsley and Catina, 1456(F), 1457(F)
Houndsley and Catina and the Birthday Surprise, 1457(F)
Rabbit-cadabra! 438(F)

Hoyt, Ard. *Bobby the Bold*, 504(F)
Love the Baby, 472(F)
When the Cows Got Loose, 1006(F)

Hoyt, Erich. *Whale Rescue*, 3831

Hsu, Stacey W. *Old Mo*, 1458(F)

Hu, Ying-Hwa. *Jigsaw Pony*, 1681(F)

Huang, Benrei. *Chinese New Year*, 3409

Huang, Hsiao-yen. *Homes*, 2575

Hubbard, Crystal. *Catching the Moon*, 1066(F)

Hubbard-Brown, Janet. *The Labonte Brothers*, 2829

Hubbell, Patricia. *Cars*, 4064(F)
Trains, 1298(F)

Hudson, Cheryl Willis. *Construction Zone*, 4041

Huey, Debbie. *Bumperboy and the Loud, Loud Mountain*, 1995(F)

Hufford, Deborah. *Greeting Card Making*, 4120

Huggins, Peter. *Trosclair and the Alligator*, 614(F)

Huggins-Cooper, Lynn. *Alien Invaders / Invasores extraterrestres*, 1187(F)

Hughes, Carol. *Dirty Magic*, 1835(F)

Hughes, Monica. *Tiger Cub*, 3705

Riddell, Chris. *Fergus Crane*, 1923(F)

Freeglader, 1922(F)

Hugo Pepper, 1924(F)

Joust of Honor, 2015(F)

Ridley, Sarah. *A Chocolate Bar*, 3889

A Metal Can, 4057

Ries, Lori. *Aggie and Ben*, 1490(F)

Fix It, Sam, 830(F)

Riggs, Shannon. *Not in Room 204*, 1138(F)

Riglietti, Serena. *The Boy and the Spell*, 299(F)

Riley-Webb, Charlotte. *The Entrance Place of Wonders*, 2560

Ringgold, Faith. *Bronzeville Boys and Girls*, 2556

The Three Witches, 2487

Ripoll, Oriol. *Play with Us*, 4180

Rippin, Sally. *Becoming Buddha*, 2862

Rissler, Albrecht. *Hubert and the Apple Tree*, 1542(F)

Ritchie, Alison. *What Bear Likes Best!* 529(F)

Ritter, Adam. *Old Mo*, 1458(F)

Rivers, Ruth. *It's Not Worth Making a Tzimmes Over!* 986(F)

Robberecht, Thierry. *Back into Mommy's Tummy*, 831(F)

Sam Is Never Scared, 1139(F)

Robbins, Jacqui. *The New Girl . . . and Me*, 879(F)

Robbins, Ken. *Pumpkins*, 3893

Roberts, Bruce. *Aunt Olga's Christmas Postcards*, 1352(F)

Roberts, Cynthia. *Tow Trucks*, 4066

Roberts, David. *Don't Say That, Willy Nilly!* 981(F)

The Dumpster Diver, 716(F)

Little Red, 2408(F)

Mrs. Crump's Cat, 1238(F)

Roberts, Diane. *Puppet Pandemonium*, 1575(F)

Roberts, Ken. *Thumb on a Diamond*, 2367(F)

Roberts, Lynn. *Little Red*, 2408(F)

Roberts, Russell. *Holidays and Celebrations in Colonial America*, 3414

Roberts, Willo Davis. *The One Left Behind*, 1655(F)

Robertson, M. P. *The Dragon Snatcher*, 289(F)

The Egg, 289(F)

The Great Dragon Rescue, 289(F)

Hieronymus Betts and His Unusual Pets, 984(F)

Robinson, Fay. *Father's Day Crafts*, 4094

Faucet Fish, 985(F)

Hispanic-American Crafts Kids Can Do! 4095

Robinson, Sharon. *Safe at Home*, 1576(F)

Robinson, Tom. *Derek Jeter*, 2833

Robles, Anthony D. *Lakas and the Makibaka Hotel*, 1711(F)

Roca, François. *The Magic Shop*, 2354(F)

Twenty-One Elephants and Still Standing, 1095(F)

Roca, Núria. *Let's Take Care of Our New Cat*, 3851

Let's Take Care of Our New Dog, 3863

Rocco, John. *Wolf! Wolf!* 530(F)

Roche, Art. *Cartooning*, 4116

Roche, Denis. *A Truck Goes Rattley-Bumpa*, 1299(F)

Can You Greet the Whole Wide World? 2917

Rock, Lois. *A Child's Book of Graces*, 3434

Rockhill, Dennis. *Ocean Whisper / Susurro del oceano*, 162(F)

Rockwell, Anne. *Backyard Bear*, 1228(F)

Here Comes the Night, 163(F)

Who Lives in an Alligator Hole? 3627

Why Are the Ice Caps Melting? 3332

Rockwell, Lizzy. *Mary Clare Likes to Share*, 1459(F)

Who Lives in an Alligator Hole? 3627

Rodman, Mary Ann. *First Grade Stinks!* 1292(F)

Rodowsky, Colby. *Ben and the Sudden Too-Big Family*, 1743(F)

Rodriguez, Alex. *Out of the Ballpark*, 2368(F)

Rodriguez, Christina. *Mayte and the Bogeyman / Mayte y el Cuco*, 650(F)

Un día con mis tías / A Day with My Aunts, 1694(F)

Rodriguez, Pedro. *The Big Book of Horror*, 2341(F)

Rodríguez, Rachel Victoria. *Through Georgia's Eyes*, 2641

Roehe, Stephanie. *Double Birthday*, 1316(F)

Miko Goes on Vacation, 585(F)

Miko Wants a Dog, 586(F)

Rogasky, Barbara. *Dybbuk*, 2468

Rogé. *Taming Horrible Harry*, 902(F)

Rogers, Gregory. *Midsummer Knight*, 190(F)

Rogers, Jacqueline. *Princess for a Week*, 1676(F)

Turkeys Together, 1515(F)

Rogers, Jonathan. *The Secret of the Swamp King*, 1893(F)

Rogers, Sherry. *If You Were a Parrot*, 286(F)

Rohmann, Eric. *Clara and Asha*, 290(F)

Roitman, Tanya. *Circus Parade*, 721(F)

Roland, Harry. *Cesar Chavez*, 2728

Roley, Don. *Ninja*, 3050

Roman, Irena. *A Mother's Wish*, 852(F)

Romanek, Trudee. *Switched On, Flushed Down, Tossed Out*, 4025

Squirt! 3533

Romanenko, Vitaliy. *Way Too Much Challah Dough*, 1405(F)

Romanova, Yelena. *The Perfect Friend*, 1229(F)

Rooney, Anne. *Computers*, 4050

Rooney, Frances. *Extraordinary Women Explorers*, 2617

Roonie, Ronnie. *Bess and Tess*, 1419(F)

Roos, Maryn. *Who Do I Look Like?* 1499(F)

Root, Barry. *Banjo Granny*, 742(F)

Game Day, 2838

Teammates, 2839

Root, Kimberly Bulcken. *Clown Child*, 1076(F)

The Doll with the Yellow Star, 2116(F)

Root, Phyllis. *Looking for a Moose*, 1230(F)

Lucia and the Light, 291(F)

Ros, Roser. *Musicians of Bremen / Los musicos de Bremner*, 2409

Rose, Deborah Lee. *The Twelve Days of Winter*, 121(F)

Rose, Melanie. *W Is for Wind*, 3993

Rosen, Michael. *Dickens*, 2677

Totally Wonderful Miss Plumberry, 1293(F)

Rosen, Michael J. *Balls!* 4181

Rosenbaum, Andria Warmflash. *A Grandma Like Yours / A Grandpa Like Yours*, 832(F)

Rosenberg, Pam. *Sunny Weather Days*, 3994

Rosenbluth, Roz. *Getting to Know Ruben Plotnick*, 880(F)

Rosenthal, Amy Krouse. *Cookies*, 3450

One of Those Days, 694(F)

Rosenthal, Betsy R. *It's Not Worth Making a Tzimmes Over!* 986(F)

Ross, Graham. *Alphabetter*, 2(F)

Ross, Kathy. *All-Girl Crafts*, 4096

All New Crafts for Kwanzaa, 4097

All New Crafts for Thanksgiving, 4098

Community Workers, 4099

The Scrapbooker's Idea Book, 4100

Step-by-Step Crafts for Winter, 4101

Ross, Richard. *Arctic Airlift*, 2234(F)

Ross, Stewart. *Egypt in Spectacular Cross-Section*, 2096

Ross, Tony. *Badness for Beginners*, 1007(F)

Bravo, Max! 2053(F)

Dear Max, 1964(F)

Gorilla! Gorilla! 597(F)

Title Index

This index contains both main entry and internal titles cited in the entries. References are to entry numbers, not page numbers. Fiction titles are indicated by (F) following the entry number.

389

397

Subject/Grade Level Index

All entries are listed by subject and then according to grade level suitability (see the key at the foot of pages for grade level designations). Subjects are arranged alphabetically and subject heads may be subdivided into nonfiction (e.g., "Trucks") and fiction (e.g., "Trucks — Fiction"). References to entries are by entry number, not page number.

A

Abenaki Indians — Fiction
PI: 2142 IJ: 1730

Abraham (Bible) — Fiction
I: 2230

Accidents — Fiction
P: 1487

Activism — Fiction
IJ: 1568, 2068

Actors and actresses — Biography
PI: 2660, 2665

Actors and actresses — Fiction
PI: 1058 I: 2255 IJ: 1524, 2203

Addition (mathematics)
P: 103, 3939

Adirondack Mountains (N.Y.)
I: 4215

Adjectives
P: 2938

Adoption
P: 3466

Adoption — Fiction
P: 753, 788, 845, 857 PI: 1698
IJ: 1627

Adu, Freddy
I: 2844

Adventure stories — Fiction
See also Mystery stories; Survival stories
P: 609, 611–12, 614 I: 1567, 1584, 1596–97, 1619, 1651, 1671, 1924, 2155 IJ: 1602, 1605, 1608, 1611, 1618, 1620, 1628, 1638, 1645–47, 1654, 1656, 1658, 1663, 1667, 1670, 1672, 2052, 2082, 2240, 2278

Adventurers and explorers
P: 2990 IJ: 3236

Adventurers and explorers — Biography
PI: 2616, 2618 I: 2628, 2892
IJ: 2615, 2617, 2619, 2621–23, 2627

Adverbs
P: 2937

Advertising — Careers
IJ: 3484

Aeronautics — History
IJ: 4034

Aesop fables
P: 2460

Afghan Americans
PI: 3439

Afghanistan
IJ: 3134

Africa
See also specific countries and regions, e.g., Kenya
P: 3120 I: 3117 IJ: 3114–15

Africa — Biography
IJ: 2851

Africa — Dance
I: 2982

Africa — Fiction
P: 1050 PI: 2346 IJ: 1880

Africa — History
I: 3058 IJ: 3059

Africa — Peoples
IJ: 3059

African Americans
See also Civil rights; Civil War (U.S.); Kwanzaa; Slavery; and names of individuals, e.g., Robinson, Jackie
PI: 3313

African Americans — Armed Forces
IJ: 3102

African Americans — Arts
I: 3437

African Americans — Baseball
P: 2834

African Americans — Biography
P: 2707, 2709–10, 2715, 2721–24, 2846, 2891 PI: 2649, 2657, 2706, 2713, 2718, 2725, 2831, 2835, 2837
I: 2642, 2711, 2714, 2716–17, 2840, 2844 IJ: 2621–22, 2656, 2662, 2667, 2696, 2708, 2712, 2719–20, 2734, 2750, 2753, 2813, 2836

African Americans — Fiction
P: 212, 282, 305, 657, 690, 701, 726, 761, 771, 823, 839–40, 866–67, 876, 879, 931, 1040, 1059, 1066, 1069, 1085, 1098, 1123, 1178, 1204, 1295, 1467, 2160 PI: 1043, 1082, 1504, 1712, 1729, 2161 I: 1531, 1535, 1538, 1583, 1710, 1721, 1965, 2164, 2204, 2217, 2350, 2366 IJ: 1523, 1576–77, 1702, 2069, 2154, 2159, 2163, 2171, 2176, 2188, 2205

African Americans — Folklore
PI: 2487, 2489

African Americans — History
I: 3248, 3353 IJ: 2736, 3237, 3354

African Americans — Holidays
P: 3416

African Americans — Poetry
P: 2557–58, 2561 PI: 2556 I: 2560

African Americans — Songs
PI: 2962

Aging — Fiction
P: 756 PI: 1542

P = Primary; PI = Primary-Intermediate; I = Intermediate; IJ = Intermediate-Junior High

P = Primary; PI = Primary-Intermediate; I = Intermediate; IJ = Intermediate-Junior High

P = Primary; PI = Primary-Intermediate; I = Intermediate; IJ = Intermediate-Junior High

Bed wetting — Fiction
P: 358

Bedtime books
P: 88, 126–51, 153–70, 172–74, 178, 237, 295, 301, 321, 406, 592, 947, 1227, 3647, 3653 PI: 152, 171

Bee-keeping — Fiction
P: 1070

Beethoven, Ludwig van — Fiction
I: 2124

Beetles — Fiction
P: 1111

Beginning readers
See Books for beginning readers

Behavior
P: 71, 3445, 3448, 3450–52, 3473 PI: 3442, 3444

Behavior — Fiction
P: 299, 408, 621, 624, 630, 670–71, 703, 774–75, 872, 974, 1126, 1284, 1454, 1512 PI: 2058

Being different — Fiction
P: 458

Belize — Fiction
I: 1596

Bell, Alexander Graham
I: 2794

Berber (African people)
P: 3120

Berlin Airlift
IJ: 3111

Bible stories
P: 3402 I: 3401, 3417 IJ: 3400

Bible stories — Fiction
P: 1079

Bicycles
PI: 4210 I: 4209 IJ: 4212

Bicycles — Biography
PI: 4210

Bicycles — Fiction
P: 627 I: 1546

Big Bang theory
IJ: 3579

Big cats
See also individual species, e.g., Lions
P: 3711 PI: 3707

Bighorn sheep
PI: 3738

Biography
See also under specific occupations, e.g., Art; specific sports, e.g., Baseball; and cultural groups, e.g., African Americans

Biography — Collective
I: 2630, 2827, 2849 IJ: 2632, 2700, 2704, 2855

Biology
See Animals; Botany; Marine biology

Biomes
See also Deserts
P: 3912 I: 3906–7, 3913, 3915

Bionics
I: 3504

Biracial families — Fiction
P: 1141 IJ: 2029

Bird watching
I: 4129

Birdhouses — Fiction
P: 706

Birds
P: 3745, 3747 PI: 3750 I: 3740, 3746 IJ: 3739

Birds — Fiction
P: 451, 536, 1019, 1046, 1156, 1168 I: 1685

Birds — Pets
PI: 3845

Birds — Poetry
P: 2571

Birds — Songs
I: 3740

Birth — Fiction
P: 307

Birthday cakes — Fiction
P: 1314

Birthdays — Fiction
P: 248, 323, 326, 392, 465, 541, 546, 596, 838, 1052, 1180, 1310–13, 1316, 1447, 1457, 1460, 1491, 1495, 1508, 1510 PI: 1962

Bison
I: 3685 IJ: 3182, 3680

Bison — Fiction
P: 1148

Black Death
IJ: 3099

Black holes
I: 3583

Blind
I: 3873

Blind — Fiction
PI: 1131

Blizzard of 1888 — Fiction
I: 2167

Blizzards — Fiction
P: 1067

Board books
P: 125, 4062

Board books — Fiction
P: 1401

Boats and boating
See also Ships and boats

I: 4216

Boats and boating — Fiction
P: 1014

Body image
IJ: 3446

Bombs — Fiction
IJ: 2134

Bonaparte, Napoleon — Fiction
I: 2079

Book fairs — Fiction
P: 1289

Books and reading
P: 2921

Books and reading — Fiction
P: 223, 243, 1087, 1272

Books for beginning readers
P: 1262, 2724, 2921, 2939, 2998–99, 3036, 3154, 3263, 3273, 3275, 3404, 3431, 3462, 3480, 3495, 3530, 3587–88, 3595, 3606, 3608–9, 3614, 3619, 3631, 3633–34, 3662, 3687, 3705, 3747, 3749, 3751, 3784, 3789, 3799, 3805, 3807, 3816, 3822, 3827, 3874, 3883, 3892, 3909, 3922, 3924, 3927–28, 3943, 3948–49, 3966, 3992, 4147, 4200–1 PI: 3012, 3033, 3191, 3194, 3198–99, 3201, 3208–9, 3332, 3411, 3442, 3636, 3638, 3678, 3706, 3738, 3742, 3755

Books for beginning readers — Biography
P: 2655, 2673, 2691–92, 2710, 2715, 2764, 2772, 2799 PI: 2706, 2803, 2828

Books for beginning readers — Fiction
P: 322, 403, 426, 468, 498, 540, 724, 816, 917, 1215–16, 1235, 1413–15, 1417–29, 1431–42, 1444–45, 1447–52, 1454–55, 1457–64, 1466–74, 1477–87, 1489–503, 1505, 1507–16 PI: 1430, 1446, 1453, 1456, 1465, 1476, 1488, 1504, 2177

Books for beginning readers — Folklore
P: 2446, 2482, 2490

Books for beginning readers — Poetry
P: 2580

Books for reluctant readers
P: 4232 PI: 2926, 3788, 3828, 4161, 4182–84, 4231 IJ: 3024, 3074, 3364

Books for reluctant readers — Biography
IJ: 2858, 2864, 3073

Books for reluctant readers — Fiction
PI: 2243 I: 1659 IJ: 1723, 1870, 1943, 1953, 2038, 2052, 2140, 2335, 2349

P = Primary; PI = Primary-Intermediate; I = Intermediate; IJ = Intermediate-Junior High

P = Primary; PI = Primary-Intermediate; I = Intermediate; IJ = Intermediate-Junior High

P = Primary; PI = Primary-Intermediate; I = Intermediate; IJ = Intermediate-Junior High

P = Primary; PI = Primary-Intermediate; I = Intermediate; IJ = Intermediate-Junior High

P = Primary; PI = Primary-Intermediate; I = Intermediate; IJ = Intermediate-Junior High

Crime
See Crime and criminals; and specific crimes, e.g., Robbers and robbery

Crime and criminals
IJ: 3365–66

Crime and criminals — Fiction
P: 616 PI: 2112 IJ: 1533, 1577, 1644, 1675, 1745, 2127

Crocodiles
See Alligators and crocodiles

Crop circles
I: 4159

Crows — Fiction
P: 1240

Crows — Folklore
P: 2424

Crum, George
PI: 2796

Crutcher, Chris
IJ: 2670

Cryptozoology
IJ: 4162

Cuba — Fiction
IJ: 2022

Cuban Americans — Fiction
I: 2189

Curie, Marie
P: 2799 I: 2798 IJ: 2797

Curiosities
I: 4165, 4168–69 IJ: 4157

Cycles (nature)
I: 3586

Cycling
See Bicycles

Cyr, Louis
PI: 2866

D

Dahl, Roald
IJ: 2671

Dairy farms
P: 3883

Dakota Indians
See also Sioux Indians

Dakota Indians — Fiction
IJ: 2172

Dancers and dancing
I: 2982

Dancers and dancing — Biography
PI: 2661 IJ: 2662

Dancers and dancing — Fiction
P: 418, 538 PI: 1043, 1078

Dandelions — Fiction
P: 455

Danziger, Paula
IJ: 2672

Darwin, Charles
IJ: 2800

Dating (social) — Fiction
IJ: 1976

da Vinci, Leonardo
IJ: 2637

Davis, Miles
IJ: 2656

Day of the Dead
P: 3404, 3410

Deafness and the deaf
PI: 4207

Deafness and the deaf — Fiction
P: 1103, 1140 PI: 1704 I: 2077 IJ: 2219–20

Death
I: 3501

Death — Fiction
P: 200, 723, 841, 1137, 1164, 1260, 2296 PI: 783 I: 1693, 2031 IJ: 1576, 1580, 1716, 2025, 2030, 2043, 2073, 2216

Death — Poetry
PI: 2590

Declaration of Independence (U.S.)
I: 3216, 3220

Delano, Poli
I: 2685

Delaware (state)
I: 3278

Delaware (state) — History
PI: 3198 IJ: 3205

Delaware Indians
IJ: 3175

Dementia — Fiction
P: 880

Denali National Park (Alaska)
PI: 3918 I: 3297

Denmark — Biography
IJ: 2669

Denmark — Fiction
IJ: 2123

Dental care
P: 3542

Dental care — Fiction
P: 360

Dentists — Careers
P: 3488

Dentists — Fiction
P: 1467

dePaola, Tomie
P: 2673 PI: 2675–76 IJ: 2674

Depression, Great
IJ: 3246

Depression, Great — Fiction
P: 2192 I: 2189 IJ: 1841, 2199

Depression (mental) — Fiction
IJ: 2054

Deserts
P: 3910, 3912, 4152 PI: 3945 I: 3911

Devils — Fiction
PI: 238

Diaries
See also Journals
IJ: 2699, 2870

Diaries — Fiction
P: 908 PI: 1540, 1731–32 I: 1739, 1872, 2037, 2095, 2314 IJ: 1557, 1967, 2062, 2083

Dickens, Charles
IJ: 2677

Dinosaurs
See also Fossils; Paleontology; Prehistoric animals
P: 2995, 2999–3000, 3002, 3004, 3007 PI: 31, 2795, 2996, 3001, 3008–9, 3012, 3015, 3017–19, 3022 I: 3006, 3011, 3014 IJ: 3013

Dinosaurs — Fiction
P: 195, 233–34, 335, 373, 383, 397, 408, 476, 600, 714, 1152, 1364, 1385, 1403, 1423, 1474 PI: 976

Diphtheria
I: 3519

Disabilities
See also Physical disabilities
P: 3506

Disabilities — Fiction
P: 587

Disasters
IJ: 3038

Disease and illness
See also Doctors; Epidemics; Medicine; and specific diseases, e.g., Asthma
I: 3512, 3519 IJ: 3095, 3511

Disease and illness — Fiction
P: 588, 1461

Diversity — Fiction
P: 874

Division (mathematics)
P: 3955

Divorce
P: 3467

Divorce — Fiction
P: 740 PI: 1732 I: 1931, 2026, 2040 IJ: 1523, 1975, 2046

P = Primary; PI = Primary-Intermediate; I = Intermediate; IJ = Intermediate-Junior High

P = Primary; PI = Primary-Intermediate; I = Intermediate; IJ = Intermediate-Junior High

P = Primary; PI = Primary-Intermediate; I = Intermediate; IJ = Intermediate-Junior High

P = Primary; PI = Primary-Intermediate; I = Intermediate; IJ = Intermediate-Junior High

P = Primary; PI = Primary-Intermediate; I = Intermediate; IJ = Intermediate-Junior High

P = Primary; PI = Primary-Intermediate; I = Intermediate; IJ = Intermediate-Junior High

P = Primary; PI = Primary-Intermediate; I = Intermediate; IJ = Intermediate-Junior High

Immigration (U.S.) — Fiction
P: 1109, 1121, 1145, 1261 **PI:** 1113
I: 1560, 2081, 2110 **IJ:** 1696,
1700–1, 1705, 1708, 2183

Immigration (U.S.) — History
I: 3282, 4079

Immigration (U.S.) — Poetry
PI: 2559

Impersonation — Fiction
IJ: 2135

Impressionism (art)
IJ: 2539

Incas
I: 3051, 3065

Inclined planes (physics)
PI: 4015

Indentured servants — Fiction
IJ: 2148, 2150

Independence Day
P: 3403

Independence Day (Mexico)
See Cinco de Mayo

**Independence Hall
(Philadelphia, PA)**
P: 3284

India
P: 3131 **I:** 3130

India — Biography
IJ: 2881

India — Fiction
P: 1046, 1108 **I:** 1662, 1777, 2102

India — Folklore
P: 2434

India — History
IJ: 3061

**Indian (Asian) Americans —
Fiction**
P: 788, 802 **I:** 1693

Indians of North America
See Native Americans and specific
Indian tribes, e.g., Navajo Indians

Indonesia
IJ: 3839

Indonesia — Folklore
PI: 2439

Influenza
IJ: 3523

Insects
See also names of specific insects,
e.g., Butterflies; Pill bugs
P: 3772, 3774 **I:** 3773, 3775
IJ: 3771, 3777–78

**Insects — Experiments and
projects**
I: 3768, 3770

Insects — Fiction
P: 1023, 1187 **IJ:** 1601

Insects — Poetry
I: 3769

Intelligence
IJ: 3449

Interactive books
P: 72, 626, 682, 3623 **I:** 4164

Interactive books — Fiction
P: 60

Internet
IJ: 4046, 4052

Internet — Biography
IJ: 2751

Inuit — Fiction
P: 1249

Inventions
See Inventors and inventions; and
specific inventions, e.g.,
Telephones

Inventors and inventions
See also specific inventions, e.g.,
Telephones
I: 4029 **IJ:** 3880, 4024, 4061

**Inventors and inventions —
Biography**
P: 2802, 2814, 2822 **PI:** 2737, 2739,
2805–6 **I:** 2738, 2794 **IJ:** 2801,
2821

**Inventors and inventions —
Fiction**
P: 821 **I:** 2281

Invertebrates
I: 3795, 3800

Iowa
PI: 3257

Iowa — Fiction
I: 1850

Iran
PI: 3152 **IJ:** 3151

Iraq
See also Baghdad; Gulf War
(1991); Operation Iraqi Freedom
IJ: 3148

Iraq — Biography
IJ: 2860

Ireland — Fiction
P: 1109, 2392, 2453 **PI:** 253
I: 2081, 2129, 2235 **IJ:** 1528, 2332

Irish Americans — Fiction
P: 1098 **PI:** 1113 **IJ:** 2178, 2190

Islam
See also Muslims; Muslim
Americans; Ramadan
P: 3383 **PI:** 2473 **I:** 3397 **IJ:** 3382,
3396

Islam — Holidays
P: 3408

Islamic Empire
I: 3045

Islands — Fiction
P: 590, 1033

Istanbul
I: 3149

Italian Americans — Fiction
I: 1746, 2033 **IJ:** 1717, 2200

Italian Canadians — Fiction
I: 2085

Italy — Biography
IJ: 2807, 2877, 2879

Italy — Cookbooks
IJ: 4140

Italy — Fiction
IJ: 2119

Italy — Folklore
P: 2457

Italy — History
See also Pompeii, Italy; Rome —
History
PI: 3087 **IJ:** 3089

Iwo Jima, Battle of
IJ: 3104

**Iwo Jima, Battle of —
Biography**
I: 2759

J

Jackals
PI: 3712

Jackrabbits
PI: 3678

Jackson, Shirley Ann
IJ: 2813

Jaguars
P: 3711

Jamaican Americans — Fiction
P: 1145

Jamaican Americans — Poetry
PI: 2559

Jamestown Colony
I: 3200, 3202, 3206 **IJ:** 3192

Japan — Fiction
P: 1060, 2103

Japan — History
PI: 3055 **I:** 3053 **IJ:** 3060, 3132

Japan — Poetry
P: 2577

Japanese Americans
IJ: 3435

**Japanese Americans —
Biography**
P: 2788

Japanese Americans — Fiction
P: 1073 **IJ:** 2213

P = Primary; PI = Primary-Intermediate; I = Intermediate; IJ = Intermediate-Junior High

P = Primary; PI = Primary-Intermediate; I = Intermediate; IJ = Intermediate-Junior High

P = Primary; PI = Primary-Intermediate; I = Intermediate; IJ = Intermediate-Junior High

P = Primary; PI = Primary-Intermediate; I = Intermediate; IJ = Intermediate-Junior High

N

P = Primary; PI = Primary-Intermediate; I = Intermediate; IJ = Intermediate-Junior High

P = Primary; PI = Primary-Intermediate; I = Intermediate; IJ = Intermediate-Junior High

P = Primary; PI = Primary-Intermediate; I = Intermediate; IJ = Intermediate-Junior High

Peary, Marie Ahnighito
IJ: 2781

Peas — Fiction
P: 911

Pegasus (Greek mythology)
P: 2506

Pei, I. M.
I: 2643

Pelicans — Fiction
P: 1191

Pen pals — Fiction
P: 211, 448, 877

Penguins
P: 3757–58, 3761–63 I: 3760
IJ: 3764

Penguins — Fiction
P: 101, 871

Penn, William
IJ: 3204

Pennsylvania — History
IJ: 3196, 3204

Pennsylvania Station (NY)
PI: 3283

Pentagon (Washington, DC)
P: 3315

Perception — Fiction
P: 663

Persia
See also Iran

Persia — History
PI: 2088 IJ: 3047

Persian Gulf War
See Gulf War (1991)

Personal guidance
I: 3441 IJ: 3470

Personal guidance — Boys
IJ: 3453

Personal guidance — Girls
I: 3443 IJ: 3447, 3457

Personal problems
See also specific topics such as
   Bullies and bullying; Child abuse;
   Death; Divorce; Moving

Personal problems — Fiction
P: 1127, 1143 PI: 2060 I: 2053,
   2061, 2063 IJ: 1528, 1545, 1570,
   2051, 2054, 2064, 2073

Personal relationships
P: 3473

Pets
See also individual species, e.g.,
   Dogs
P: 3846–48, 3851, 3856, 3859, 3863,
   3867, 3876 PI: 3844–45, 3853–54,
   3857–58, 3861–62, 3864–66,
   3870–72, 3875 I: 3849–50, 3855,
   3868–69, 3873 IJ: 3852, 3860

Pets — Fiction
P: 586, 910, 1037, 1171, 1252,
   1270–71, 1418, 1440 PI: 1687
I: 1678

Philadelphia — Poetry
P: 2557

Philosophy — Biography
P: 2874 PI: 2885 IJ: 2884

Philosophy — Fiction
P: 644

Photography — Biography
I: 2642

Physical disabilites
See also Blind; Cerebral palsy;
   Deafness and the deaf; Obesity

**Physical disabilities —
Biography**
PI: 2665 I: 2845

Physical disabilities — Fiction
I: 2072 IJ: 1958

Physical fitness
P: 3551

Physical handicaps
See Physical disabilities

Physics
P: 4002 IJ: 3998, 4006

Physics — Biography
PI: 2803 IJ: 2804, 2813, 2818

**Physics — Experiments and
projects**
I: 3997

Pianos
I: 2975

Pianos — Fiction
I: 2027

Picnics — Fiction
P: 641

Picture puzzles
P: 47, 73, 682, 4152, 4154–56
PI: 2907, 4151

Pigeons — Fiction
P: 594, 1225 I: 1688

Pilgrims (U.S.)
I: 3187, 3190 IJ: 3211

Pill bugs
P: 3776

Pioneer life (U.S.)
See Frontier life (U.S.)

Pirates
PI: 3033 I: 3159 IJ: 3360

Pirates — Fiction
P: 142, 195, 251, 362, 464, 615, 798,
   958, 962, 1513 PI: 2147 I: 2326
IJ: 1656, 1667, 2091

Pirates — Poetry
I: 2530

Pizza — Fiction
P: 713, 1044

Plagues — History
IJ: 3099

Planets
See also Solar system; and specific
   planets, e.g., Mars (planet)
P: 3590

Planets — Fiction
P: 269

Planning — Fiction
P: 711

Plants
P: 3609 PI: 3879, 3894–95, 3897
I: 3612 IJ: 3607

Plants — Classification
IJ: 3615

Plants — Fiction
P: 972

Platypuses
P: 3670

Play
P: 44, 758, 2515, 4078

Play — Fiction
P: 335, 412, 625, 646, 652, 676, 750,
   856, 1455

Plays
PI: 2612, 2987 I: 2614 IJ: 2611

Plays — Anthologies
PI: 2612

Plays — Fiction
P: 953 PI: 1257 I: 2289

Plays — Shakespeare
IJ: 2613

Plumbing
PI: 3031

Pluto (planet)
IJ: 3592

Plymouth Colony
IJ: 3211

Pneumonia
IJ: 3523

Poe, Edgar Allan
IJ: 2688

Poetry
See also Haiku; Nursery rhymes; as
   subdivision of other subjects, e.g.,
   Babies — Poetry; and as
   subdivision of countries or ethnic
   groups, e.g., African Americans
   — Poetry
P: 602, 758, 2512, 2515–16, 2518,
   2520, 2524, 2527, 2533, 2535, 2537,
   2541, 2543, 2546, 2550, 2557–58,
   2561, 2565, 2568–69, 2571, 2573,
   2575, 2580, 2582–85, 2594,
   2597–602, 2604, 2606–8, 4078
PI: 2521, 2538, 2556, 2559, 2564,
   2570, 2581, 2588, 2603, 2609

P = Primary; PI = Primary-Intermediate; I = Intermediate; IJ = Intermediate-Junior High

P = Primary; PI = Primary-Intermediate; I = Intermediate; IJ = Intermediate-Junior High

P = Primary; PI = Primary-Intermediate; I = Intermediate; IJ = Intermediate-Junior High

S

P = Primary; PI = Primary-Intermediate; I = Intermediate; IJ = Intermediate-Junior High

436

Science
See also specific branches of
science, e.g., Physics
P: 3564 **PI:** 3563

Science — Biography
P: 2799 **I:** 2791, 2798, 2808
IJ: 2637, 2797, 2809, 2817, 4028

Science — Experiments and projects
See also under specific branches of
science, e.g., Chemistry —
Experiments and projects
I: 3569, 3574–75, 3899 **IJ:** 2801,
3568, 3570–73, 3576–77

Science — Fiction
P: 1025, 1028 **PI:** 1559

Science — General
P: 3566 **IJ:** 3561

Science — Methodology
I: 3567

Science — Projects
See Science — Experiments and
projects

Science — Research
IJ: 3562

Science fairs
I: 4008, 4013 **IJ:** 3568, 3898

Science fairs — Fiction
P: 995, 1482 **PI:** 2321 **I:** 2295

Science fiction
P: 211, 532, 1443 **I:** 1792, 2322–25,
2331, 2334 **IJ:** 1760, 1815, 2327–30,
2332–33, 2335–38, 2947

Scorpions
I: 3790

Scotland — Fiction
IJ: 1821

Scrapbooks
I: 4100

Scrapbooks — Fiction
P: 1045 **I:** 1710

Scuba diving
IJ: 4178

Sculpture
P: 32

Sculpture — Biography
PI: 2644

Sea horses
P: 3796, 3798–99

Sea lions
I: 3820

Sea monsters — Fiction
P: 315

Sea otters
P: 3825 **IJ:** 3821

Sea stars
P: 3798

Sea stories — Fiction
IJ: 1643, 1645, 2126

Sea turtles
PI: 3645 **IJ:** 3641, 3643

Sea turtles — Fiction
P: 1192

Seafaring — Fiction
IJ: 2082, 2128

Seals
P: 3822

Seashells — Fiction
P: 1050

Seashores
See also Beaches
P: 3840

Seashores — Fiction
P: 1030, 1032, 1036

Seasons
See also specific seasons, e.g.,
Autumn
P: 3602–4

Seasons — Fiction
P: 708, 1021

Seattle (WA)
P: 623

Secrets
P: 3448

Secrets — Fiction
P: 1047 **I:** 2283 **IJ:** 2134

Seeds
P: 3896 **PI:** 3897

Segregation (U.S.) — Fiction
P: 1040

Self-confidence — Fiction
P: 575, 1136 **I:** 2313 **IJ:** 2042

Self-esteem — Fiction
P: 330, 426, 554, 1123 **IJ:** 1938

Self-image — Fiction
P: 357, 620, 644, 1122 **PI:** 1566
IJ: 1547

Self-image — Poetry
P: 2547

Selfishness — Fiction
P: 495

Selkirk, Alexander
IJ: 2627

Seminole Indians — Fiction
IJ: 2163

Senate (U.S.)
IJ: 2750

Sendak, Maurice
P: 2691

Senegal — Fiction
P: 1121

Senses
See also specific senses, e.g., Taste

P: 67, 78

Senses — Fiction
P: 1030

September 11, 2001 — Fiction
IJ: 2300

Seuss, Dr.
P: 2692

Sewing
See also Needlecrafts
IJ: 4127

Sex education
P: 3556

Sex roles — Fiction
P: 625

Sexual abuse — Fiction
P: 1138

Shakespeare, William
IJ: 2693

Shakespeare, William — Fiction
PI: 1058

Shakespeare, William — Plays
I: 2614

Shapes
P: 3958 **PI:** 3942, 3957

Shapes — Experiments and projects
See Concept books — Sizes and
shapes

Sharing — Fiction
P: 58, 431, 457, 460, 493, 1220,
1372, 1422 **PI:** 1736

Sharks
P: 3016, 3826–27, 3829 **PI:** 3828
IJ: 2997, 4178

Sheep — Fiction
P: 925, 1244

Sheepdogs — Fiction
P: 925 **I:** 1683

Shelley, Mary Wollstonecraft
IJ: 4163

Shepherds
P: 3884

Sherlock Holmes — Fiction
IJ: 1665

Ships and boats
See also specific ships, e.g.,
Mayflower (ship)
IJ: 4070

Ships and boats — History
PI: 3064 **IJ:** 3039

Shipwrecks — Fiction
IJ: 1638

Shoemakers — Fiction
P: 200

Shoes — Fiction
P: 200, 685, 997, 1052, 1104

P = Primary; PI = Primary-Intermediate; I = Intermediate; IJ = Intermediate-Junior High

P = Primary; PI = Primary-Intermediate; I = Intermediate; IJ = Intermediate-Junior High

Solar system
See also Astronomy; Planets; Space exploration; Stars; Sun; and individual planets, e.g., Mars (planet)
P: 3588, 3590 I: 3596–97

Soldiers
See also Samurai

Soldiers — History
PI: 3055, 3085, 3158 I: 3053, 3090

Solitude — Fiction
I: 1518

Somali language — Fiction
P: 2426

Somalia — Folklore
P: 2426

Songhay Empire (Africa)
I: 3058

Songs
See also Christmas — Songs and carols; Folk songs; Hymns; and as subdivision of other subjects, e.g., Baseball — Songs
P: 758, 2515, 2955, 2958–60, 2963–64, 2977–78, 3422, 4078, 4153
PI: 2954, 2962

Songs — Collections
IJ: 2968

Songs — Fiction
P: 969

Sound
P: 4002

Sound — Experiments and projects
IJ: 4016

Sounds — Fiction
P: 1498

Sousa, John Philip
P: 2654

South (U.S.)
See also specific states, e.g., Florida
I: 3174

South (U.S.) — Fiction
P: 1040 PI: 1712 IJ: 2188, 2219

South (U.S.) — Folklore
P: 2484–85, 2491 I: 2492

South Africa
PI: 3122

South Africa — Biography
I: 2878

South Africa — Fiction
P: 1052

South Carolina — History
PI: 3201

South Dakota
I: 3260–61

Southwest (U.S.)
See also specific states, e.g., New Mexico

Southwest (U.S.) — Fiction
P: 970 PI: 976

Soviet Union
See also individual states, e.g., Russia

Space exploration
See also National Aeronautics and Space Administration (U.S.); Space travel; Spacecraft; and individual missions, as Apollo (space mission)
IJ: 3582, 3585, 4018–20

Space exploration — Fiction
I: 2214 IJ: 2216

Space travel
IJ: 3582, 3585, 4019

Space travel — Fiction
P: 211, 1084, 1301 I: 1535, 2326
IJ: 1929, 2000

Spacecraft
P: 4022 IJ: 3582

Spain — Fiction
P: 727

Spain — History
IJ: 3140

Spanish-American War
I: 3249

Spanish language
P: 66, 89, 2389, 2928, 2940, 3157, 3412, 3463, 3859, 3938, 4062
PI: 3636, 3638, 3678, 3706, 3738, 3742, 3755 IJ: 2797

Spanish language — Alphabet books
P: 15, 27

Spanish language — Biography
P: 2683

Spanish language — Counting books
P: 123

Spanish language — Fiction
P: 162, 637, 641, 643, 649, 655, 673, 749, 772, 804, 822, 870, 878, 1021, 1062, 1105, 1115, 1187, 1214, 1345, 1393, 2374 PI: 171, 650, 710, 1694, 1819, 2360 I: 1695

Spanish language — Folklore
P: 2379, 2424 I: 2459, 2476

Spanish language — Holidays
P: 3403 PI: 3421

Spanish language — Poetry
I: 2510 IJ: 2511

Special Olympics — Fiction
P: 668

Speech — Fiction
P: 1144

Spelling
I: 2942

Spelling — Fiction
I: 1538 IJ: 2308

Spiders
P: 3789, 3793 PI: 3788, 3791
I: 3790 IJ: 3792

Spiders — Experiments and projects
I: 3770

Spies and spying
I: 3251 IJ: 3362–63

Spies and spying — Fiction
P: 653, 929 I: 1584, 1674, 1816–17
IJ: 1623

Sponges
I: 3800

Spoonerisms
PI: 2931

Sports
See also Extreme sports; Games; and specific sports, e.g., Baseball
I: 3574

Sports — Biography
See also under specific sports, e.g., Baseball — Biography
P: 2842 PI: 2825 IJ: 2826, 2843

Sports — Careers
P: 3477

Sports — Fiction
P: 527 I: 2320

Sports — History
IJ: 4181

Sports — Poetry
PI: 2609

Sports — Short stories
IJ: 2353

Sports — Women
IJ: 2823

Spring
P: 3602

Spring — Poetry
P: 2597

Spying
See Spies and spying

Squirrels
P: 3672

Squirrels — Fiction
P: 1160

Stamps
P: 3752

Stanton, Elizabeth Cady
PI: 2787

Star-Spangled Banner
P: 2748

Stars
P: 3580, 3600

P = Primary; PI = Primary-Intermediate; I = Intermediate; IJ = Intermediate-Junior High

P = Primary; PI = Primary-Intermediate; I = Intermediate; IJ = Intermediate-Junior High

P = Primary; PI = Primary-Intermediate; I = Intermediate; IJ = Intermediate-Junior High

P = Primary; PI = Primary-Intermediate; I = Intermediate; IJ = Intermediate-Junior High

P = Primary; PI = Primary-Intermediate; I = Intermediate; IJ = Intermediate-Junior High

Westerns — Fiction
P: 924

Wetlands
IJ: 3973

Whales
P: 3830 PI: 3708 I: 3831

Whales — Fiction
P: 282 I: 1936

Whaling — Fiction
IJ: 1643

Whaling — History
I: 3223

Wheels
P: 4063

Wheels — Fiction
P: 688 IJ: 2266

White, E. B.
IJ: 2698

White, Shaun
PI: 2847

White House (Washington, DC)
IJ: 3280

White House (Washington, DC) — Fiction
P: 545

Whitman, Narcissa
IJ: 2789

Whitney, Eli
IJ: 2821

Wickenheiser, Hayley
IJ: 2848

Wild West shows — Biography
PI: 2663–64

Wilder, Laura Ingalls
IJ: 2699

Wildlife conservation
I: 3831

Wildlife conservation — Biography
IJ: 2820

Wildlife conservation — Fiction
I: 2097

Williams, Venus
I: 2841

Williamsburg (VA) — Fiction
I: 2152

Winds
P: 3968

Winds — Fiction
P: 2463

Winfrey, Oprah
IJ: 2667

Winter
P: 3602

Winter — Crafts
P: 4101

Winter — Fiction
P: 121, 291, 1017, 1029, 1031, 1035, 1166

Winter — Poetry
P: 2599, 2601 PI: 2603

Winter sports
See Ice climbing; Ice hockey; Ice skating; Skis and skiing; Snowboarding

Wishes — Fiction
P: 288, 665

Witchcraft trials — Salem
I: 3207

Witchcraft trials — Salem — Fiction
IJ: 2145

Witches — Fiction
P: 246, 268, 273, 892, 1377, 1383, 1390–91 I: 1784, 1796, 1934 IJ: 1935, 1987

Wolverines
PI: 3713

Wolves
I: 3855

Wolves — Fiction
P: 281, 1020, 1219 PI: 935

Wolves — Folklore
P: 2457

Women — Biography
P: 2641, 2655, 2683, 2707, 2709–10, 2721–22, 2780, 2788, 2799, 2811, 2814, 2874, 2882 PI: 2620, 2625–26, 2644, 2663–64, 2718, 2760, 2775, 2777, 2787, 2828 I: 2639, 2711, 2717, 2730–31, 2776, 2782, 2798, 2841, 2845, 2867–68, 2872 IJ: 2615, 2617, 2624, 2629, 2631, 2667, 2672, 2687, 2690, 2695–96, 2699, 2703, 2708, 2719–20, 2743, 2755, 2781, 2784, 2789, 2797, 2813, 2820, 2848, 2881

Women — Explorers
IJ: 2615, 2617

Women — Fiction
P: 1066

Women — Sports
IJ: 2823

Women's rights — History
IJ: 3028

Women's rights — Biography
PI: 2775, 2778, 2787 I: 2782

Women's suffrage
IJ: 3028

Women's suffrage — Fiction
I: 2196

Wong, Li Keng
IJ: 2790

Wood, Grant
PI: 2916

Woolly mammoths
P: 3021

Words
See also specific parts of speech, e.g., Adjectives
P: 2932, 2939, 2941 PI: 2934

Words — Fiction
P: 730, 1265, 1295 PI: 992 IJ: 2263

Work
P: 3463

Work — Fiction
P: 726, 744, 1060

Working dogs
PI: 3853, 3861–62, 3864–65

World history
PI: 3034 I: 3032 IJ: 3026, 3029

World Peace Day
I: 3406

World Trade Center
See also September 11, 2001
I: 4043

World War I
IJ: 3102

World War I — Fiction
PI: 1351 IJ: 1666, 2084, 2118

World War II
See also Iwo Jima, Battle of; and specific topics, e.g., Holocaust
PI: 3108 IJ: 3106

World War II — Biography
PI: 2675, 2752 I: 2759 IJ: 2650, 2749, 2850

World War II — Fiction
P: 1069, 1073, 1339 PI: 2115, 2221 I: 2122, 2208–9, 2218 IJ: 2111, 2119–20, 2123, 2134, 2140, 2210, 2212–13, 2215, 2222–23

World War II — History
I: 3103 IJ: 3104, 3107

Worms
I: 3795

Worms — Fiction
P: 1155

Wozniak, Stephen
I: 4049

P = Primary; PI = Primary-Intermediate; I = Intermediate; IJ = Intermediate-Junior High

Wrestling — Fiction
PI: 2360 IJ: 2038

Wright, Wilbur and Orville
P: 2822 PI: 4032

Writers
See Authors

Writing
P: 1 IJ: 2950

Writing — Fiction
P: 502 PI: 1964, 2287, 2307
I: 2294 IJ: 1536, 2057

Writing — Handbooks
IJ: 2947–48

Writing — Skills
IJ: 2949

Wyoming
P: 3884

Y

Yellowstone National Park
PI: 3267

Yoga
P: 3553 I: 2554, 3543, 4170

Yoga — Fiction
P: 1282

York (c. 1775–1815)
I: 2726

Z

Zebras
P: 3666–67, 3674

Zheng He
I: 2892

Zombies — Fiction
I: 1619

Zoos
P: 3701 IJ: 3877

Zoos — Careers
P: 3481

Zoos — Fiction
P: 244, 598, 883, 898, 971, 1177
I: 1813

P = Primary; PI = Primary-Intermediate; I = Intermediate; IJ = Intermediate-Junior High

About the Authors

CATHERINE BARR is the coauthor of other volumes in the Best Books series (*Best Books for Middle School and Junior High Readers* and *Best Books for High School Readers*) and of *Popular Series Fiction for K–6 Readers, Popular Series Fiction for Middle School and Teen Readers*, and *High/Low Handbook: Best Books and Web Sites for Reluctant Teen Readers, 4th Edition.*

JOHN T. GILLESPIE, renowned authority in children's literature, is the author of more than 30 books on collection development. In addition to the previous editions of *Best Books for Children*, other volumes in this series are *Best Books for Middle School and Junior High Readers* and *Best Books for High School Readers*. He is also the author of the Middleplots, Juniorplots, Teenplots, and Seniorplots Book Talk Guides as well as *The Newbery Companion: Booktalk and Related Materials for Newbery Medal and Honor Books* and *The Children's and Young Adult Literature Handbook: A Research and Reference Guide.*